Paradigm

Cost Accounting

First Edition Revised

ROBERT L. DANSBY, PH.D.
Columbus Technical Institute
Columbus, Georgia

MICHAEL D. LAWRENCE, MBA, CPA, CMA
Portland Community College
Portland, Oregon

Contributing Editors:
GREGORY K. LOWRY, MBA, CPA
Southern State Community College
Wilmington, Ohio

RODGER R. TRIGG, PH.D., CMA, CPA, CIA
Columbus College
Columbus, Georgia

WILLIAM H. WALLACE, MS, CPA
The National Technical Institute for the Deaf at
Rochester Institute of Technology
Rochester, New York

EMCParadigm

Previously published as *Cost Accounting*, 1995 by South-Western College Publishing.

Library of Congress Cataloging-in-Publication Data

Dansby, Robert L.
   Paradigm cost accounting : principles and applications / Robert L.
Dansby, Michael D. Lawrence ; contributing editors Gregory K. Lowry,
Roger R. Trigg, William H. Wallace. -- 1st ed. , rev.
      p. cm .
   Rev. ed . of : Cost accounting / Robert L. Dansby, Michael D.
Lawrence ; contributing editors Gregory K. Lowry, Roger R. Trigg.
c 1995.
   Includes index.
   ISBN 0-7638-0075-9
   1. Cost accounting.   I. Lawrence, Michael.
II. Dansby, Robert L.   Cost accounting.   III. Title.
HF5686.C8D2324   1997
657'.42--dc21   97-25595
                                                           CIP

© 1998 by Paradigm Publishing Inc.
      Published by **EMC**Paradigm
      875 Montreal Way
      St. Paul, MN 55102
      (800) 535-6865
      E-mail publish@emcp.com

Printed in the United States of America

10 9 8 7 6 5 4 3 2 1

Brief Contents

Contents

iv

2 Job-Order Costing 23

3 Purchasing and Storing Materials 43

4 Issuing Materials to Production 65

11 Equivalent Production—Weighted Average Costing of Work in Process 263

12 FIFO Costing of Work in Process 299

13 Units Lost or Increased in Production 335

14 Accounting for Joint Products and By-Products 369

Preface

NEED FOR COST ACCOUNTING

Cost accounting systems provide very important information to accountants and other business managers in a wide variety of organizations. This book presents the essential concepts of cost accounting that apply to both manufacturing and nonmanufacturing organizations. Managers and world-class competitive organizations must have accurate, timely, and relevant measures of the cost of all critical business activities, especially production. Conventional cost measurement and reporting systems do not always provide the required quality and type of information. The new, highly-automated production environments and just-in-time (JIT) environments demand new types of timely cost information. Consequently, many new cost procedures have developed in the last few years. This book covers both conventional cost systems and the new systems.

SPECIAL FEATURES OF THE BOOK

This book has certain unique features that will make cost accounting easier to learn and to remember.

- Superior Readability—writing style focuses on interesting, accurate, and easy-to-read text to enhance clarity and understanding

- Integrated Learning Objectives—each chapter begins with learning objectives—each learning objective is indicated in the text where first discussed—all end-of-chapter exercises and problems are identified by learning objectives
- Glossary—a glossary at the end of each chapter defines each key term
- Case for Critical Thinking—each chapter includes a short case that presents a thought-provoking issue related to the chapter and that requires reasoning rather than mere calculations
- Self-Study Quizzes—each chapter includes short self-check tests located at critical points within the text to help check understanding of key points and procedures—answers can be found at the end of the chapter
- Self-Study Problems—each chapter includes a self-check problem to check understanding of major topics and to use as a review before working end-of-chapter assignments—the solution follows the problem
- New Manufacturing Environment—JIT introduced in Chapter 3; Activity-Based Costing (ABC) introduced in Appendix 7A; conventional cost flows contrasted with JIT cost flows through journal entries in Appendix 8A
- Comprehensive Summary—each chapter includes a thorough summary of the terminology and procedures discussed in the chapter
- Electronic Spreadsheet Templates—spreadsheet templates are available for many end-of-chapter problems throughout the text
- Icons Identify Helpful Features—

Electronic Spreadsheet Template

Note

Self-Study Quiz

Self-Study Problem

Case For Critical Thinking

PURPOSE OF BOOK

This book, which is written and designed for students in postsecondary cost accounting courses, will:

1. Provide a practical knowledge of cost accounting systems and procedures
2. Present the essential concepts of cost accounting that apply to both manufacturing and nonmanufacturing organizations
3. Illustrate both conventional cost systems and new systems
4. Provide a basis for job entry or further study

INSTRUCTIONAL SYSTEM

We, the authors, have created an instructional system that includes learning objectives, highly-readable text, practical assignments, comprehensive projects, self-study quizzes and problems, and instructor's aids.

FOR THE STUDENT

- Study Guide and Working Papers bound in a single volume, with perforated pages for easy removal
- Practice Set designed for use with the textbook covers job-order costing
- Electronic Spreadsheet Templates for many text problems

FOR THE INSTRUCTOR

- Instructor's Manual contains solutions to all questions for review, exercises, A and B problems, and case for critical thinking; includes a test bank of objective questions and problems for each chapter, accompanied by solutions
- Electronic Test Bank provides true and false, multiple choice, and short answer problems for each chapter

ACKNOWLEDGMENTS

We would like to express our sincere thanks to our many academic colleagues who offered many excellent suggestions and recommendations for the first edition of this book and its supplements. We could never have undertaken such a daunting task without their expert assistance. We greatly appreciate the time, experience, and expertise provided by all our reviewers.

Kay Anderson
St. Cloud Technical College

Roy G. Androli
Brainerd Staples Technical College

Cheryl A. Bartlett
Albuquerque Technical-Vocational Institute

Sherrie Dusch
Barnes Business College

Lawrence J. Eaton
Gateway Technical College

Roger G. Hehman
Raymond Walters College

Fred R. Jex
Macomb Community College

Sharon Johnson
Kansas City Kansas Community College

Verna Mae Johnson
Brown Mackie College

William P. Logan
Middle Georgia Technical Institute

Gregory K. Lowry
Southern State Community College

Don Lucy
Ursuline College

Charles Mitchell
Central Carolina Community College

LaVonda Ramey
Schoolcraft College

Alice B. Sineath
*Forsyth Technical Community
College*

Betty Vergon-Slabaugh
Indiana Technical College

Scott Wallace
Blue Mountain Community College

Carole A. Weber
Alexandria Technical College

Dale Westfall
Midland College

We would also like to thank our very good friends at **EMC**Paradigm for their professionalism, hard work, and unflagging devotion to this project. Because of their commitment, we offer our sincere appreciation to the Paradigm staff: Mel Hecker, Vice President and Publisher; Christine Hurney, Developmental Editor; Jack Lamborn, National Sales Manager; Jan Johnson, Instructional Designer; Sharon Bouchard, Marketing Manager; and a special thanks to Rosemary Fruehling, President, for her energy, enthusiasm, and support.

Finally, we would like to thank three friends and professional colleagues who contributed much to the book. Gregory Lowry of Southern State Community College offered many helpful suggestions for many parts of the book. Dr. Rodger Trigg, professor of accounting at Columbus College, made a valuable contribution to the process costing chapters. William Wallace of The National Technical Institute for the Deaf at R.I.T. developed the electronic spreadsheet templates and wrote the electronic test bank for the revised first edition.

DEDICATION

This book is dedicated to our families for their love, support, and dedication during this project. To our wives and children, we owe you much.

Wives: Barbara O'Malley Dansby
            Raynette Lawrence
Children: Robert (Champ) Dansby
            Allison Dansby
            Ryan Lawrence
            Nicole Lawrence
            Kevin Lawrence

Bob Dansby

Michael Lawrence

Part I

Job-Order Costing

Chapter 1
Basic Cost Concepts

After studying Chapter 1, you should be able to:

1. Define cost accounting.
2. Differentiate between cost accounting and financial accounting.
3. Identify the elements of manufacturing costs.
4. Differentiate between prime costs and conversion costs.
5. Calculate cost of goods manufactured.
6. Prepare financial statements for a manufacturing firm.
7. Differentiate between job-order and process costing systems.

LEARNING OBJECTIVE 1
Acost is a use of a firm's resources, such as the payment of cash, the promise to pay cash, or the expiration of the value of an asset. Costs are necessary for a business to survive, because only by incurring costs can a business purchase inventory, acquire assets, pay operating expenses, and increase sales. Excessive costs, however, can cause a business to fail. Consequently, a firm's accounting system must provide accurate and up-to-date information needed to control costs and plan for the future. **Cost accounting** deals with the planning, measurement, and control of costs.

COST ACCOUNTING DIFFERENTIATED FROM FINANCIAL ACCOUNTING

LEARNING OBJECTIVE 2
Financial accounting, guided by **generally accepted accounting principles** (**GAAP**), primarily concerns recording, classifying, interpreting, and reporting accounting data. The end result of financial accounting is the preparation of financial statements that will be distributed to users "outside" the firm, such as stockholders, creditors, and taxing authorities.

Cost accounting differs in many ways from financial (or general) accounting. Cost accounting primarily concerns the accumulation of accounting information for users "inside" the firm, such as managers, supervisors, and officers, who rely on cost accounting to provide accurate and timely information needed to help run the business and control costs.

Traditionally, cost accounting has focused on manufacturing costs, due to the complexity of the manufacturing process and the need for accurate and ongoing cost data for pricing products and making other pertinent decisions. However, nonmanufacturing firms also use cost accounting techniques in an effort to control costs better.

"Cost control" have become the watchwords of the 1990's as many U.S. companies have been forced to cut costs in order to stay competitive with foreign products. Automobiles from Japan, heavy machinery from Germany, computers from Korea, and clothing from Taiwan are a few of the many imported products that spell intense competition for U.S. businesses. In 1991 and 1992, Chrysler Corporation cut 18,000 jobs in an effort to remain profitable. During the same period, General Motors closed plants and cut 40,000 jobs while trying to recover from a $1.75 billion loss in 1991. Similar stories can be told for many other U.S. companies, including Apple Computer, Sears, IBM, Ford, Digital Computers, and Delta Airlines.

MANUFACTURING ACTIVITY

Manufacturing is the process of transforming raw materials into finished products through the use of labor and other factory costs (such as rent, utilities, and repairs). The United States still leads the world in the production of goods. With only 5% of the world's population, the 322,000 factories in the U.S. produce over 22% of the world's goods. These firms employ about 20,000,000 people and have total annual payroll costs in excess of $400 billion.

ELEMENTS OF MANUFACTURING COSTS

All manufacturing costs (or *production costs*) are classified into three basic elements: direct materials, direct labor, and factory overhead.

Direct Materials

Direct materials, also called *raw materials*, become a significant part of the product being manufactured and can be conveniently identified with the finished product. Examples include cloth used in the manufacture of clothes, lumber used in the production of furniture, steel used in the manufacture of automobiles, and leather used in the production of shoes. Direct materials also include finished parts or components that are assembled to form a product. Examples include circuit boards and frames used in the manufacture of computers.

Let us stress that not all materials used in the manufacturing process are classified as direct materials. Many types of materials and factory supplies have insignificant costs or cannot be readily identified with any particular product. Examples of these materials include lubricants used on machinery, cleaning rags, glue, thread, nails, tacks, and rivets. Their costs are classified as **indirect materials** and are included in factory overhead (we will discuss factory overhead shortly).

Direct Labor

Direct labor includes the wages of all employees who work directly on the products being manufactured. For example, the wages of a sewing machine operator in a shirt factory are direct labor costs. Other examples of direct labor include the earnings of welders, machine operators, and assembly line workers.

In the preceding section we learned that not all materials are classified as direct materials. Likewise, not all factory labor is classified as direct labor. The earnings of employees who work in the manufacturing process, but not directly on the products being manufactured, are classified as **indirect labor** and are included in factory overhead. Examples of indirect labor include the earnings of janitors, inspectors, department heads, factory office workers, and the maintenance crew. Also, payroll related costs—such as payroll taxes, sick pay, vacation pay, insurance, retirement plans, and other fringe benefits—are usually included in factory overhead.

Factory Overhead

Factory overhead—also called *factory burden, manufacturing overhead,* and *factory expenses*—consists of all manufacturing costs not classified as direct materials or direct labor. Common examples of factory overhead include:

- Indirect materials
- Indirect labor
- Utilities
- Repairs and maintenance of factory machinery and equipment
- Depreciation of factory machinery, equipment, and building
- Taxes on factory building
- Insurance expense on factory machinery, equipment, and building
- Rent of factory building or machinery
- Payroll taxes applicable to factory wages

At one time, factory overhead was considered the least significant of the three elements of manufacturing costs. As plants have become more automated, however, factory overhead costs have increased as a percentage of total manufacturing costs. For example, advances in computer technology led many U.S. factories to install **computer-aided design** (CAD) and **computer-aided manufacturing** (CAM) systems. In CAD systems, computers efficiently design and test new products and modify existing ones. In CAM systems, computers develop and control the production process. With this type of equipment came increased costs of maintenance, insurance, depreciation, and utilities.

Summary of Manufacturing Costs

LEARNING OBJECTIVE 4 Cost accounting terminology often combines two of the three cost elements. The sum of direct materials and direct labor is called **prime costs**. Prime costs plus factory overhead equals total manufacturing costs. The sum of direct labor and factory overhead is called **conversion costs**, because direct labor and factory overhead are necessary to "convert" the direct materials into finished products. Figure 1–1 summarizes these relationships.

FIGURE 1–1
Summary of Manufacturing Costs

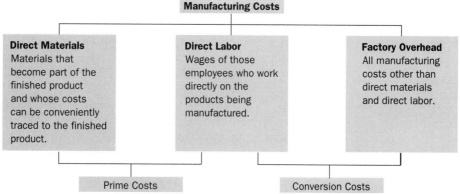

Manufacturing Costs		
Direct Materials Materials that become part of the finished product and whose costs can be conveniently traced to the finished product.	**Direct Labor** Wages of those employees who work directly on the products being manufactured.	**Factory Overhead** All manufacturing costs other than direct materials and direct labor.
Prime Costs	Conversion Costs	

INVENTORIES OF A MANUFACTURER

A merchandising business has one inventory, Merchandise Inventory. In contrast, a manufacturing business has three inventories: (1) Raw Materials Inventory, (2) Work in Process Inventory, and (3) Finished Goods Inventory. Each of these inventories will be discussed in detail as we move through the book. For the moment, let's look at what each inventory includes.

Raw Materials Inventory

The **Raw Materials Inventory** account shows the cost of raw materials on hand and intended for use in the manufacturing process. Coca-Cola's raw materials include flavorings, food color, sugar, and aspartame. Raw materials are often called *stores* and are kept in bins, vats, or other storage areas.

We should note that raw materials for one company are often the finished product for another company. For example, wheat flour is a finished product to the miller. To a bakery, however, wheat flour is a raw material.

Work In Process Inventory

The **Work in Process Inventory** account shows the cost of the goods in the manufacturing process, but not completed at the end of the accounting period. The Work in Process Inventory for Nike would include all costs incurred to date for shoes in various stages of production. The Work in Process Inventory account is sometimes called *Goods In Process Inventory*.

Finished Goods Inventory

The **Finished Goods Inventory** account shows the cost of goods completed and ready for sale. This account corresponds to the Merchandise Inventory account of a merchandising firm in that both accounts show the value of completed, but unsold, goods on hand at the end of an accounting period.

FINANCIAL STATEMENTS OF A MANUFACTURER

In previous accounting courses, you learned that business firms prepare financial statements at the end of an accounting period. These statements show the financial condition of the firm and the amount of the firm's net profit (or net loss) during the period.

The financial statements of a manufacturing firm differ somewhat from a merchandising firm. A merchandising firm buys its inventory, which is already finished and requires very little, if anything, to be done before it can be resold to customers. For example, Neal's Sporting Goods Store buys completed exercise equipment manufactured by TurboFlex Corporation. Neal's, in turn, marks up the equipment and resells it to the public.

The income statements of the two firms differ in the cost of goods sold section. Figure 1–2 compares the merchandiser's cost of goods sold (Neal's Sporting Goods Store) with the manufacturer's cost of goods sold (TurboFlex Corporation).

FIGURE 1–2
Cost of Goods Sold

Merchandising Firm	**Manufacturing Firm**
Beginning merchandise inventory	Beginning finished goods inventory
+ **Net purchases of merchandise**	+ **Cost of goods manufactured**
= Cost of goods available for sale	= Cost of goods available for sale
– Ending merchandise inventory	– Ending finished goods inventory
= Cost of goods sold	= Cost of goods sold

As we can see, the manufacturer's "cost of goods manufactured" compares to the merchandiser's "net purchases of merchandise." However, the calculation of the cost of goods manufactured is a rather lengthy process. Consequently, this calculation is usually not presented on the face of the income statement. Instead, accountants prepare a separate *statement of cost of goods manufactured* or *manufacturing statement*. Let's look at an outline of the manufacturing statement (small amounts are used to simplify the illustration):

Beginning work in process inventory		$10
Plus manufacturing costs:		
Direct materials	$12	
Direct labor	10	
Factory overhead	8	
Total manufacturing costs		30
Total goods in production		$40
Less ending work in process inventory		9
Cost of goods manufactured		$31

LEARNING OBJECTIVE 5   The "cost of goods manufactured" represents the total cost of all units completed during the period. Since some of the units completed in the current period were actually started in the previous period, the computation must begin with the beginning work in process inventory. To this figure, we add all manufacturing costs incurred in the current period. We then subtract the ending work in process inventory to get the cost of goods manufactured during the period. To illustrate, Figure 1–3 shows the statement of cost of goods manufactured prepared by TurboFlex Corporation for the year ending December 31, 19X5.

FIGURE 1–3
Statement of Cost of Goods Manufactured

TurboFlex Corporation Statement of Cost of Goods Manufactured For Year Ended December 31, 19X5			
Work in process inventory, Jan. 1			$ 67 0 0 0 00
Raw materials:			
Raw materials inventory, Jan. 1		$ 76 0 0 0 00	
Raw materials purchases		262 50 0 00	
Cost of materials available for use		$338 50 0 00	
Less raw materials inventory, Dec. 31		50 0 0 0 00	
Cost of raw materials used		$288 50 0 00	
Direct labor		280 0 0 0 00	
Factory overhead:			
Indirect labor	$65 0 0 0 00		
Indirect materials and supplies	48 60 0 00		
Depr. expense—factory equipment	40 0 0 0 00		
Depr. expense—factory building	30 0 0 0 00		
Utilities	28 90 0 00		
Payroll taxes—factory wages	24 40 0 00		
Insurance	12 0 0 0 00		
Repairs and maintenance	11 80 0 00		
Property taxes—factory building	10 0 0 0 00		
Miscellaneous factory expenses	8 0 0 0 00		
Total factory overhead		278 70 0 00	
Total manufacturing costs			847 20 0 00
Total goods in production			$914 20 0 00
Less work in process inventory, Dec. 31			64 0 0 0 00
Cost of goods manufactured			$850 20 0 00

Raw Materials (handwritten annotation with brace)

Factory Overhead. (handwritten annotation with brace)

The Income Statement

Let's now look at Figure 1–4, which shows TurboFlex's income statement for the year ended December 31, 19X5. As we can see, the cost of goods manufactured ($850,200) is necessary to calculate the cost of goods sold. Other amounts presented on the income statement were obtained by analyzing the appropriate general ledger accounts.

FIGURE 1–4
Income Statement for a Manufacturing Firm

TurboFlex Corporation **Income Statement** **For Year Ended December 31, 19X5**		
Sales	$1 862 00 0 00	
Less sales returns and allowances	12 00 0 00	
Net sales		$1 850 00 0 00
Cost of goods sold:		
Finished goods inventory, Jan. 1	$ 112 00 0 00	
Add cost of goods manufactured	850 20 0 00	
Goods available for sale	962 20 0 00	
Less finished goods inventory, Dec. 31	87 00 0 00	
Cost of goods sold		875 20 0 00
Gross profit		$ 974 80 0 00
Operating expenses:		
Selling expenses	$ 293 00 0 00	
General expenses	257 00 0 00	
Total operating expenses		550 00 0 00
Net income from operations		$ 424 80 0 00
Other expenses:		
Interest expense		23 20 0 00
Net income before income taxes		$ 401 60 0 00
Provision for income taxes		138 00 0 00
Net income after income taxes		$ 263 60 0 00

The Balance Sheet

LEARNING OBJECTIVE 6   The *only difference* between the balance sheet of a manufacturing firm and that of a merchandising firm is in the inventory accounts. A merchandiser, as you recall, has the one Merchandise Inventory account. Whereas, the manufacturer has three inventory accounts: Raw Materials Inventory, Work in

Process Inventory, and Finished Goods Inventory. To illustrate, Figure 1–5 shows the current asset section of TurboFlex Corporation's December 31, 19X5 balance sheet.

FIGURE 1–5
*Current Asset
Section of a
Manufacturer's
Balance Sheet*

TurboFlex Corporation Balance Sheet December 31, 19X5		
Current assets:		
Cash		$ 35 60 0 00
Accounts receivable		122 00 0 00
Inventories:		
Raw materials	$50 00 0 00	
Work in process	64 00 0 00	
Finished goods	87 00 0 00	201 00 0 00
Prepaid expenses		12 00 0 00
Total current assets		$370 60 0 00

SELF-STUDY QUIZ 1–2 The following cost data relate to Taylor Products Company for the year ending June 30, 19X2:

Direct materials	$55,600
Direct labor	72,400
Factory overhead.	36,500
Work in process inventory, July 1, 19X1	38,200
Work in process inventory, June 30, 19X2	34,800

1. Calculate the manufacturing costs for the year.
2. Calculate the cost of goods manufactured for the year.
Answers at end of chapter.

TYPES OF COST ACCOUNTING SYSTEMS

LEARNING OBJECTIVE 7   As we have discussed, an important objective of cost accounting is to provide information necessary for management to make decisions, to control costs, and to plan for the future. An equally important objective is to determine the unit cost of each product produced. This is accomplished by **accumulating** total production costs for a period of time (usually a month) and then dividing this total by the total number of units produced during the same period.

To achieve these objectives, two basic types of cost accounting systems have been developed, the job-order costing system and the process costing system. Both systems accumulate cost data and allocate production costs to goods manufactured. The choice of systems depends on the nature of the manufacturer's operations.

Job-Order Costing System

Big Projects

The **job-order costing system** is designed to accumulate cost data for firms that manufacture goods (1) as individual units or (2) in specific batches of varying quantities and types. This system is used primarily by firms that produce custom-made goods for a specific customer; that is, each product is made to order. Industries using job-order costing systems include those that manufacture aircraft, ships, locomotives, heavy machinery, books and magazines, and custom-built homes.

The essential feature of job-order costing is the allocation of production costs to a specific job. The job may consist of a single unit, such as the construction of an apartment building, or a batch of units, such as the manufacture of 100 rocking chairs.

Since this system focuses on the individual "job," the manufacturer accumulates costs (direct materials, direct labor, and factory overhead) by the job. Each job in production has a *job cost sheet*. The job cost sheet, discussed in detail in a later chapter, accumulates total costs relating to that individual job.

Process Costing System

General Mfg

The **process costing system** is designed to accumulate cost data for firms that mass produce large numbers of identical goods in a continuous sequence of steps, called *processes*. Industries of this type include those that manufacture food, cosmetics, chemicals, automobiles, tires, glass, petroleum, and tooth paste. Such firms are usually organized into departments, and each department has a specific function. For example, a firm that produces peanut butter could have one department for hulling and cleaning, one department for cooking, one department for grinding, and one department for packaging. Here, costs are accumulated by the individual department, rather than by the individual job as in the case of job-order costing. At the end of the accounting period, total manufacturing cost equals the sum of all costs accumulated in the individual departments. Unit cost is then calculated by dividing total manufacturing cost by the number of units produced.

Dual Costing System

Some manufacturers use both a job-order and a process costing system. This situation often occurs when a firm continuously produces small parts used as raw materials in products custom built to customer specifications. The process costing system would be used for small raw materials items continuously produced. The job-order costing system would be used for goods built to customer specifications. Let us stress, however, that in today's world of specialization, most manufacturers do not manufacture even a part of their raw materials. Instead, they purchase all raw materials from other manufacturing firms.

SELF-STUDY QUIZ 1–3 For each of the following products, state whether it would most likely be manufactured using a job-order costing system (joc) or a process costing system (pc):

a.   Breakfast cereal
b.   Mayonnaise
c.   Cement
d.   Yacht
e.   Soft drinks
f.   Passenger plane
Answers at end of chapter.

NOTE Both manufacturing and nonmanufacturing firms use cost accounting techniques to aid in controlling costs and in increasing profits. However, cost accounting is used more extensively in manufacturing firms because a manufacturer's operations are more complex than most other types of organizations. The reason that manufacturing firms are more complex is because their activities are broader, being involved in the production of goods as well as marketing and administration.

SELF-STUDY PROBLEM

Iowa Products Company accumulated the following data for 19X4.

	Jan. 1, 19X4	Dec. 31, 19X4
Inventories:		
Finished goods	$52,000	$ 54,500
Work in process	29,600	27,800
Raw materials	14,200	15,000
Direct labor		95,000
Raw materials purchases		138,900
Indirect labor		15,300
Indirect materials and supplies		10,800
Factory utilities		18,600
Depreciation expense—factory		14,000
Factory rent		18,000
Payroll taxes—factory wages		8,100

	Jan. 1, 19X4	Dec. 31, 19X4
Repairs and maintenance		$ 6,000
Insurance expense—factory		6,800
Miscellaneous factory expenses		5,200
Sales		710,000
Sales discounts		12,000
Selling expenses		95,600
General expenses		75,300
Interest expense		7,000

Required:

1. Prepare a statement of cost of goods manufactured.
2. Prepare an income statement (assume an income tax rate of 25%).

SOLUTION TO SELF-STUDY PROBLEM

1.

Iowa Products Company
Statement of Cost of Goods Manufactured
For Year Ended December 31, 19X4

Work in process inventory, Jan. 1			$ 29 600 00
Raw materials:			
Raw materials inventory, Jan. 1		$ 142 000 00	
Raw materials purchases		138 900 00	
Cost of materials available for use		$153 100 00	
Less raw materials inventory, Dec. 31		15 000 00	
Cost of raw materials used		$138 100 00	
Direct labor		95 000 00	
Factory overhead:			
Indirect labor	$15 300 00		
Indirect materials and supplies	10 800 00		
Factory utilities	18 600 00		
Depreciation expense—factory	14 000 00		
Factory rent	18 000 00		
Payroll taxes—factory wages	8 100 00		
Repairs and maintenance	6 000 00		
Insurance Expense—Factory	6 800 00		
Miscellaneous factory expenses	5 200 00		
Total factory overhead		102 800 00	
Total manufacturing costs			335 900 00
Total goods in production			$365 500 00
Less work in process inventory, Dec. 31			27 800 00
Cost of goods manufactured			$337 700 00

2.

Iowa Products Company Income Statement For Year Ended December 31, 19X4		
Sales	$710 00 0 00	
Less sales discounts	12 00 0 00	
Net sales		$698 00 0 00
Cost of goods sold:		
Finished goods inventory, Jan. 1	$ 52 00 0 00	
Add cost of goods manufactured	337 70 0 00	
Goods available for sale	$389 70 0 00	
Less finished goods inventory, Dec. 31	54 50 0 00	
Cost of goods sold		335 20 0 00
Gross profit		$362 80 0 00
Operating expenses:		
Selling expenses	95 60 0 00	
General expenses	$ 75 30 0 00	
Total operating expenses		170 90 0 00
Net income from operations		$191 90 0 00
Other expenses:		
Interest expense		7 00 0 00
Net income before income taxes		$184 90 0 00
Provision for income taxes		46 22 5 00
Net income after income taxes		$138 67 5 00

SUMMARY

A business survives and grows by incurring costs. For example, in order to make sales to customers, a sporting goods store must first purchase its merchandise. The purchase of merchandise is a cost. So is the buying of cash registers, the rental of a carpet cleaning machine, the payment of the utility bill, the cost of placing a newspaper ad, and the payment of employee salaries. These and other costs are necessary to stay in business. However, excessive costs can cause an otherwise successful business to fail. Consequently, the accounting system must be designed to provide accurate and up-to-date information that can be used to control costs and plan for the future.

Cost accounting is the branch of accounting that deals with the planning, measurement, and control of costs. While all types of businesses (service, merchandising, and manufacturing) must have accurate and reliable cost information, the traditional focus of cost accounting has been on manufacturing costs and activities. This is due to the complexity of the manufacturing process and the need for ongoing cost data that is necessary for decision making, product pricing, and planning for the future.

Manufacturing is the transforming of raw materials into finished products by incurring factory costs. All factory costs are classified as direct materials, direct labor, and factory overhead. **Direct materials,** also called raw materials, become an integral part of the finished product and can be conveniently traced to the finished product. Materials that do not become an integral part of the finished product, or that can only be traced to the finished product at great cost, are classified as **indirect materials** (which is a part of factory overhead). **Direct labor** is the wages of employees who work directly on the products being manufactured. The earnings of factory employees who do not work directly on the products being manufactured are classified as **indirect labor** and are included in factory overhead. **Factory overhead** consists of all factory costs except for direct materials and direct labor, such as indirect materials, indirect labor, rent, taxes, and utilities.

Financial statements for a manufacturing firm differ somewhat from the financial statements of a merchandising business. A manufacturer first prepares a statement of cost of goods manufactured in order to determine the total cost of goods produced during the period. The manufacturer's cost of goods manufactured is equivalent to the merchandiser's net purchases of merchandise. The manufacturer's Finished Goods Inventory account is equivalent to the merchandiser's Merchandise Inventory account.

There are two basic types of costing systems: the job-order costing system and the process costing system. The **job-order costing system** is used primarily by firms that tailor-make goods for specific customers. **The process costing system** is used by firms that mass produce large quantities of identical units, such as cases of Coca-Cola, boxes of Fruit & Fibre cereal, grosses of Bic Pens, and hundreds of Uniroyal tires.

KEY TERMS

Cost Accounting. The branch of accounting that deals primarily with accumulating detailed cost data needed by management to control current operations and plan for the future.

Conversion Costs. The sum of direct labor costs and factory overhead costs necessary to convert direct materials into a finished product.

Direct Labor. The cost of those employees who work directly on the product being manufactured.

Direct Materials. The cost of those raw materials that become a significant part of the product being manufactured and can be conveniently identified with the finished product.

Factory Overhead. All manufacturing costs not classified as direct materials or direct labor; these costs include indirect materials, indirect labor, factory utilities, factory rent, depreciation of factory equipment, and many others.

Finished Goods Inventory Account. An asset account that shows the cost of goods completed and awaiting sale to customers.

Indirect Labor. The wages and salaries of employees who work in the manufacturing process, but not directly on the products being manufactured; examples include inspectors, department heads, materials handlers, and the maintenance crew.

Indirect Materials. Materials and factory supplies that are necessary for the manufacturing process but whose costs are insignificant or cannot be readily identified with any particular product; examples include lubricants, cleaning rags, glue, thread, nails, and cleaning compounds.

Job-order Costing System. A costing system designed to accumulate cost data for firms that manufacture goods as individual units or in specific batches of varying quantities and types.

Prime Costs. The sum of direct materials cost and direct labor cost.

Process Costing System. A costing system designed to accumulate cost data for firms that mass produce large numbers of identical goods in a continuous sequence of steps.

Raw Materials Inventory Account. An asset account used to record the purchases of raw materials and show the cost of raw materials on hand and intended for use in the manufacturing process.

Work In Process Inventory Account. An asset account that shows the cost of goods in the manufacturing process, but not completed at the end of the accounting period.

QUESTIONS FOR REVIEW

1. How does cost accounting data assist management in the running of a business?
2. Define cost accounting.
3. How does cost accounting differ from general accounting?
4. Do nonmanufacturing businesses use cost accounting? Explain.
5. Identify and explain the elements of manufacturing costs.
6. How do prime costs differ from conversion costs?
7. List five examples of factory overhead.
8. Identify three alternate terms for factory overhead.
9. List and explain the inventories of a manufacturing firm.
10. How does the computation of cost of goods sold for a manufacturer differ from that of a merchandiser?
11. How does a manufacturer calculate cost of goods sold?
12. For each of the inventory items listed below, identify whether the item will appear on (a) the statement of cost of goods manufactured, (b) the income statement, or (c) the balance sheet.
    a. Beginning Raw Materials Inventory
    b. Ending Work in Process Inventory
    c. Ending Finished Goods Inventory
    d. Beginning Finished Goods Inventory
13. In what way does the balance sheet of a manufacturer differ from that of a merchandiser?
14. Differentiate between a job-order costing system and a process costing system?

EXERCISES

1–1. Learning Objective 3. Classifying Manufacturing Costs.
Classify the following as direct materials (dm), direct labor (dl), or factory overhead (fo).

a. Fiberglass used by a boat maker. DM
b. Rent paid for factory building. FO
c. Depreciation of factory equipment. FO
d. Wages of assembly line workers. DL
e. Lubricating oils used on machinery. FO
f. Electricity used in factory. FO
g. Steel used in an automobile assembly plant. DM
h. Earnings of factory supervisors. ~~DL~~ FO
i. Vacation pay of factory employees. ~~DL~~ FO

1–2. Learning Objective 4. Calculating Prime Costs and Conversion Costs.
Solar Products Company incurred the following costs during the year:

Direct materials	$89,600
Direct labor	98,400
Factory overhead	65,200

Calculate (a) prime costs for the year and (b) conversion costs for the year.

1–3. Learning Objective 5. Calculating Manufacturing Costs and Cost of Goods Manufactured.
Cost data for Butler Manufacturing Company are given for the year ended June 30, 19X2.

Direct materials	$60,400
Direct labor	72,000
Factory overhead	33,700
Work in process inventory, July 1, 19X1	26,000
Work in process inventory, June 30, 19X2	25,100

Calculate (a) manufacturing costs for the year and (b) costs of goods manufactured for the year.

1–4. Learning Objective 5. Calculating Cost of Raw Materials Used.
From the following data, calculate the cost of raw materials used during March.

Raw materials inventory, March 1	$24,000
Raw materials purchases during March	60,000
Raw materials inventory, March 31	22,800

1–5. Learning Objective 6. Calculating Cost of Goods Sold and Gross Profit.
The following data relate to Americus Manufacturing Company for August.

Finished goods inventory, August 1	$ 68,400
Finished goods inventory, August 31	65,200
Cost of goods manufactured	93,800
Sales (net)	167,000

Calculate (a) cost of goods sold and (b) gross profit.

1–6. Learning Objectives 5 & 6. Calculating Cost of Goods Manufactured, Cost of Goods Sold, and Gross Profit.
Sterling Toy Company released the following data for the year:

Raw materials inventory, January 1	$ 122,500
Raw materials inventory, December 31	112,300

Raw materials purchases	$ 545,600
Work in process inventory, January 1	101,600
Work in process inventory, December 31	92,000
Finished goods inventory, January 1	78,100
Finished goods inventory, December 31	65,000
Direct labor	346,700
Factory overhead	233,000
Sales (net)	1,600,000

Calculate (a) cost of goods manufactured, (b) cost of goods sold, and (c) gross profit.

GROUP A PROBLEMS

1–1A. Learning Objectives 5 & 6. Preparing a Statement of Cost of Goods Manufactured.

The following data pertain to Birmingham Steel Company for the year ended June 30, 19X7:

Raw materials inventory, July 1, 19X6	$ 64,000
Raw materials inventory, June 30, 19X7	55,000
Work in process inventory, July 1, 19X6	36,000
Work in process inventory, June 30, 19X7.	33,700
Finished goods inventory, July 1, 19X6	72,000
Finished goods inventory, June 30, 19X7	70,000
Materials purchases.	212,500
Direct labor.	121,300
Indirect labor.	15,400
Factory utilities.	25,500
Depreciation—factory machinery.	16,200
Depreciation—factory building.	9,500
Payroll taxes—factory.	9,200
Repairs and maintenance.	7,800
Indirect materials and factory supplies.	6,500
Insurance—factory.	5,600
Selling expenses	76,900
General expenses.	61,000
Sales (net).	1,690,000

Required:
Prepare a statement of cost of goods manufactured.

1–2A. Learning Objective 6. Preparing an Income Statement.

Required:
Using the data in Problem 1–1A, prepare an income statement (assume an income tax rate of 34%).

1–3A. Learning Objectives 5 & 6. Preparing a Statement of Cost of Goods Manufactured and an Income Statement.

The following data relate to California Technical Products Company for the year ended December 31, 19X1:

Inventories	Beginning	Ending
Finished goods . . . . \.	$90,000	$102,000
Work in process	70,000	77,000
Raw materials	88,000	92,000

Revenue and Costs		
Sales (net)		$980,000
Raw materials purchases		112,000
Direct labor		125,000
Factory overhead		109,800
Selling expenses		114,700
General expenses		102,400
Interest expense		12,900

Required:

1. Prepare a statement of cost of goods manufactured.
2. Prepare an income statement (assume an income tax rate of 34%). 34%

1–4A. Learning Objectives 5 & 6. Preparing a Statement of Cost of Goods Manufactured and an Income Statement.

Alabama Products Company manufactures computer chips and other computer components. The following data pertain to the firm:

	Jan. 1, 19X6	Dec. 31, 19X6
Inventories:		
Finished goods	$47,600	$ 53,200
Work in process	28,600	26,200
Raw materials	12,800	13,400
Direct labor		94,000
Raw materials purchases		145,600
Indirect labor		12,560
Indirect materials and supplies		10,400
Factory utilities		15,900
Depreciation expense—factory		12,000
Factory rent		18,000
Payroll taxes—factory wages		7,800
Repairs and maintenance		7,300
Insurance expense—factory		6,700
Miscellaneous factory expenses		5,800
Sales		690,000
Sales discounts		12,000
Selling expenses		84,000
General expenses		70,000
Interest expense		6,000

Required:

1. Prepare a statement of cost of goods manufactured.
2. Prepare an income statement (assume an income tax rate of 34%).

GROUP B PROBLEMS

1–1B. Learning Objectives 5 & 6. Preparing a Statement of Cost of Goods Manufactured.

The following data pertain to Iowa Machine Company for the year ended June 30, 19X5:

Raw materials inventory, July 1, 19X4	$ 62,000
Raw materials inventory, June 30, 19X5	58,000
Work in process inventory, July 1, 19X4	38,000
Work in process inventory, June 30, 19X5	35,700
Finished goods inventory, July 1, 19X4	64,000
Finished goods inventory, June 30, 19X5	62,000
Materials purchases	225,000
Direct labor	126,000
Indirect labor	18,200
Factory utilities	16,700
Depreciation—factory machinery	14,000
Depreciation—factory building	10,900
Payroll taxes—factory wages	9,300
Repairs and maintenance	6,800
Indirect materials and factory supplies	6,200
Insurance—factory	5,900
Selling expenses	80,000
General expenses	69,000
Sales (net)	1,575,000

Required:
Prepare a statement of cost of goods manufactured.

1–2B. Learning Objective 6. Preparing an Income Statement.

Required:
Using the data in Problem 1–1B, prepare an income statement (assume an income tax rate of 34%).

1–3B. Learning Objectives 5 & 6. Preparing a Statement of Cost of Goods Manufactured and an Income Statement.

The following data relate to Central Illinois Manufacturers for the year ended December 31, 19X9:

Inventories	Beginning	Ending
Finished goods	$92,000	$104,000
Work in process	74,000	79,000
Raw materials	86,000	90,000

Revenue and Costs	
Sales (net)	$998,000
Raw materials purchases	116,000
Direct labor	126,700
Factory overhead	112,300
Selling expenses	117,000
General expenses	104,200
Interest expense	10,800

Required:

1. Prepare a statement of cost of goods manufactured.
2. Prepare an income statement (assume an income tax rate of 34%).

1–4B. Learning Objectives 5 & 6. Preparing a Statement of Cost of Goods Manufactured and an Income Statement.

Colorado Chemicals Company manufactures lawn fertilizers and other chemical products. The following data pertain to the firm:

	Jan. 1, 19X3	Dec. 31, 19X3
Inventories:		
Finished goods	$45,000	$ 52,000
Work in process	27,000	25,400
Raw materials	10,800	12,500
Direct labor		88,000
Raw materials purchases		142,000
Indirect labor		12,000
Indirect materials and supplies		9,800
Factory utilities		15,200
Depreciation expense—factory		10,000
Factory rent		16,500
Payroll taxes—factory wages		7,400
Repairs and maintenance		6,800
Insurance expense—factory		6,200
Miscellaneous factory expenses		5,400
Sales		625,000
Sales discounts		9,000
Selling expenses		82,000
General expenses		68,000
Interest expense		6,800

Required:

1. Prepare a statement of cost of goods manufactured.
2. Prepare an income statement (assume an income tax rate of 34%).

CASE FOR CRITICAL THINKING

After attending a seminar on cost control, William Sanford understands the difference between job-order costing systems and process costing systems. However, he is confused about how a firm could use a dual costing system, since the type of product costed using a job-order costing system is usually quite different from the type of product costed using a process costing system. Explain how a dual costing system works and identify some businesses that could benefit from such a system.

ANSWERS TO SELF-STUDY QUIZ 1–1

a. fo
b. fo
c. fo
d. dm
e. dl

ANSWERS TO SELF-STUDY QUIZ 1–2

1. $ 55,600
        72,400
        36,500
     $164,500

2. Work in Process Inventory, July 1, 19X1 . . . . $ 38,200
       Direct materials $55,600
       Direct labor   72,400
       Factory overhead   36,500
     Total manufacturing costs   164,500
     Total cost goods in production $202,700
     Work in Process Inventory, June 30, 19X2   34,800
     Cost of goods manufactured $167,900

ANSWERS TO SELF-STUDY QUIZ 1–3

a. pc
b. pc
c. pc
d. joc
e. pc
f. joc

Chapter 2
Job-Order Costing

LEARNING OBJECTIVES

After studying Chapter 2, you should be able to:

1. Identify the types of businesses that use job-order costing.
2. Identify the document used to accumulate and control costs in a job-order costing system.
3. Prepare journal entries to record the flow of direct materials cost, direct labor cost, and factory overhead cost in a job-order costing system.
4. Explain why factory overhead is applied (estimated) to production.
5. Prepare journal entries to record the completion and sale of finished goods.

n Chapter 1, we learned about three categories of manufacturing costs: direct materials, direct labor, and factory overhead. We also learned about two principal types of costing systems: the job-order costing system and the process costing system.

In this chapter, we will study job-order costing and we will continue our study of job-order costing through Chapter 8. In Chapter 10, we will start our study of process costing systems.

JOB-ORDER COSTING—AN OVERVIEW

LEARNING OBJECTIVE 1   As we have learned, a **job-order costing system** is used in situations where many *different* products, or batches of products, are produced each period. Examples of industries that typically use job-order costing include shipbuilding, special-order printing, custom home building, and furniture manufacturing.

Job-order costing is also used in many service businesses, such as repair shops, CPA firms, advertising agencies, and law firms. For example, a CPA firm uses job-order costing to determine the amount to bill each client. Likewise, an advertising agency uses job-order costing to determine the total amount to charge a client for an advertising campaign.

To illustrate the design and operation of a job-order costing system, we will continue with our illustration of TurboFlex Corporation (from Chapter 1). TurboFlex, a small fitness equipment company, manufactures the TurboFlex II, a total-body workout machine. Most of TurboFlex's production results from orders from specific customers, such as retail department stores and sporting goods stores. However, the company does manufacture a few units for stock; that is, it manufactures a few units to maintain on hand as a minimum level of inventory.

TurboFlex is organized into three major divisions: Administration, Production, and Marketing. The Production Division is divided into five departments: Shaping, Assembling, Finishing, Maintenance, and General Factory Services.

Producing Departments

A **producing department** (also called *processing department*) is any part of the factory where work is performed and where materials, labor, and overhead are added to the product. TurboFlex has three producing departments: Shaping, Assembling, and Finishing.

Shaping Department. The Shaping Department measures, cuts, and trims rough lumber to form the bench, which is the main part of the TurboFlex II.

Assembling Department. The Assembling Department uses nails, bolts, screws, and glue to attach prefabricated parts (purchased from other suppliers) to the bench. The Assembling Department adds heavy duty legs to the bench, as well as the weight stack, cables, and pulleys. Most of the construction of the units occurs in this department.

Finishing Department. The Finishing Department paints all metal parts that are not prepainted, pads the bench, and covers the bench with high quality vinyl. The completed units move from the Finishing Department to the warehouse, where they will remain until shipment.

Service Departments

Service departments do not directly work on the goods in production. Rather, they provide services that assist or facilitate the work of the producing departments. TurboFlex has two service departments: Maintenance and General Factory Services.

Maintenance Department. The Maintenance Department is responsible for the maintenance and repair of the buildings, grounds, machinery, and equipment. It is also responsible for the janitorial service and the heating and lighting of the factory.

General Factory Services Department. This department is responsible for purchasing, receiving, and storing raw materials and factory supplies. It is also responsible for issuing raw materials and supplies to production, as well as timekeeping and payroll.

Chart of Accounts

As stated, TurboFlex Corporation uses the job-order costing system because it is a small manufacturer that produces most of its products for the special order of specific customers. In many cases, TurboFlex slightly modifies the design of its product and places on it the private name of the customer for whom it is made.

Figure 2–1 shows TurboFlex's chart of accounts. Most of the accounts will be familiar to you because of your previous accounting courses. However, you should pay particularly close attention to the manufacturing accounts*:

FIGURE 2–1
Chart of Accounts

TurboFlex Corporation
Chart of Accounts

Assets
111	Cash
112	Accounts Receivable
112.1	Allowance for Doubtful Accounts
121	Raw Materials Inventory*
122	Work in Process Inventory*
123	Finished Goods Inventory*
124	Prepaid Insurance
125	Supplies
130	Land
131	Buildings
131.1	Accumulated Depreciation—Buildings
132	Machinery
132.1	Accumulated Depreciation—Machinery
133	Furniture and Fixtures
133.1	Accumulated Depreciation—Furniture and Fixtures
134	Small Tools
134.1	Accumulated Depreciation—Small Tools
140	Patents

Liabilities
211	Accounts Payable
212	Salaries and Wages Payable
213	FICA Taxes Payable
214	FUTA Taxes Payable
215	SUTA Taxes Payable
216	Employees Income Tax Payable
217	Health Insurance Payable
218	Property Taxes Payable
219	Income Taxes Payable

Stockholders' Equity
311	Common Stock
312	Retained Earnings
320	Income Summary

Sales and Cost of Goods Sold
411	Sales
411.1	Sales Returns and Allowances
411.2	Sales Discounts
415	Cost of Goods Sold

Factory Overhead
510	Factory Payroll Clearing*
511	Factory Overhead Control*
512	Factory Overhead—Shaping Department*
513	Factory Overhead—Assembling Department*
514	Factory Overhead—Finishing Department*
515	Factory Overhead—Maintenance Department*
516	Factory Overhead—General Factory Services Department*
517	Under- or Overapplied Factory Overhead*

Operating Expenses
611	Selling Expense Control
612	General Expense Control

Other Expenses
711	Interest Expense

Job Cost Sheet

LEARNING OBJECTIVE 2

A Separate Cost Center

Remember that a job-order costing system considers each job to be a separate cost center. Thus, the manufacturing costs related to each job are kept separate from the costs of other jobs in production. To do this, each job is assigned a **job cost sheet,** which is a specially designed form on which charges for direct materials, direct labor, and factory overhead are accumulated as work progresses on the job. You are familiar with a job cost sheet if you have ever left your car with an auto service for repair. A work order (a form of job cost sheet) is prepared showing the needed parts (materials), the required labor, and sales taxes on the parts used (overhead). The total of the work order is the total cost of the job to the customer. This is how it works in a manufacturing situation. The job cost sheet accumulates cost as work progresses on the job. When the job is completed, the job cost sheet is totaled to get the total cost to produce the job.

The actual design of the job cost sheet is tailored to the needs of the individual business. Figure 2–2 illustrates a common form. Notice that the job cost sheet provides a separate section for each element of production cost: materials, direct labor and factory overhead.

FIGURE 2–2
Job Cost Sheet

Flow of Costs

LEARNING OBJECTIVE 3

A transfer of costs must be made within the costing system that parallels the physical movement of goods through the production process. In other words, the cost flow must match the work flow. In this section, we will examine the cost flow of TurboFlex and show how it matches the work flow. Let's start by looking at the opening balances of the following cost accounts:

Raw Materials Inventory	Work in Process Inventory	Finished Goods Inventory
Bal. 50,000	Bal. 64,000	Bal. 87,000

Purchasing Materials. Merchandise Inventory and Purchases are accounts commonly used in merchandising concerns. The Merchandise Inventory account shows the value of the most recent inventory, and the Purchases account is used to record the cost of merchandise bought for resale to customers. In a manufacturing business, all purchases of raw materials and factory supplies are typically recorded in a single controlling account entitled **Raw Materials Inventory**. To illustrate, during January, TurboFlex purchased $32,400 in materials for use in production. In practice, purchases of materials would be recorded daily. However, to simplify, the January purchases are recorded in Summary Entry (A).

(A)

1	Jan.	31	Raw Materials Inventory	32 40 0 00	**1**
2			Accounts Payable	32 40 0 00	**2**
3			Purchased materials.		**3**

After posting this entry, the Raw Materials Inventory account looks like this:

Raw Materials Inventory

Bal.	50,000	
(A)	32,400	

Issuing Materials to Production. During the month, TurboFlex issued materials costing $38,600 to production, as follows:

Direct materials	$37,200
Indirect materials	1,400
Total	$38,600

Summary Entry (B) shows the recording.

(B)

1	Jan.	31	Work in Process Inventory	37 20 0 00		**1**
2			Factory Overhead Control	1 40 0 00		**2**
3			Raw Materials Inventory		38 60 0 00	**3**
4			Issued materials to production.			**4**

Notice that the direct materials cost is recorded in the Work in Process Inventory account. The cost of these materials must also be recorded on the separate job cost sheets to which they relate. The cost of indirect materials (like all indirect costs) is recorded in the Factory Overhead Control account. The accounts affected by entry (B) now look like this:

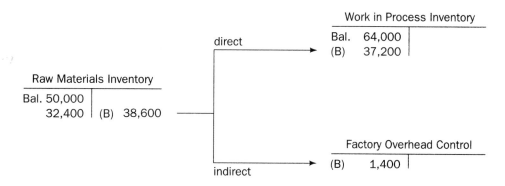

Factory Wages Earned. During the month, factory employees earned salaries and wages totaling $49,628. Summary Entry (C) shows the recording.

(C)

1	Jan.	31	Factory Payroll Clearing	4962800	**1**
2			Salaries & Wages Payable		4962800	**2**
3			Incurred salaries and wages.			**3**

After posting this entry, the Factory Payroll Clearing account looks like this:

Factory Payroll Clearing	
(C) 49,628	

Think of the Factory Payroll Clearing account as a "holding account." By this, we mean that the amount of the payroll will not permanently remain in the Factory Payroll Clearing account. The payroll is recorded there to give the accounting department time to analyze and determine what part was earned by direct labor employees and what part was earned by indirect labor employees. Once this determination has been made, the labor costs will be allocated to production.

Charging Labor to Production. To allocate the payroll to production, the accounting department must determine who earned the $49,628. Some of the workers are **direct labor**—those who worked directly on the products being manufactured. Others are **indirect labor**—those who did not work directly on the products—such as janitors, supervisors, and inspectors.

An analysis of the payroll records indicates that the labor costs should be allocated as follows:

Direct labor	$35,648
Indirect labor	13,980
Total	$49,628

Summary Entry (D) shows the required transfer of labor costs to production.

(D)

	Jan.					
1	31	Work in Process Inventory	35 64 8 00			**1**
2		Factory Overhead Control	13 98 0 00			**2**
3		Factory Payroll Clearing		49 62 8 00		**3**
4		Allocated labor costs to production.				**4**

Notice that the direct labor cost is recorded in the Work in Process Inventory account. At the same time, it is also recorded on the job cost sheet to which it relates. Indirect labor cost is a part of the factory overhead of a firm. It is therefore recorded in the Factory Overhead Control account. The effect of entry (D) on the various accounts looks like this:

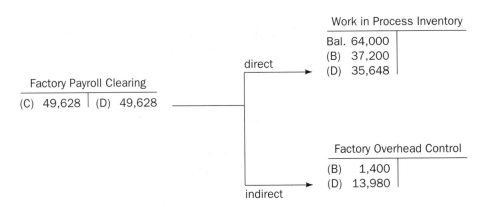

Factory Overhead Costs. As we have learned, all costs of operating the factory other than direct materials and direct labor are classified as factory overhead. As these costs are incurred, they are recorded in the Factory Overhead Control account. In addition to the indirect materials and indirect labor that we have already recorded, TurboFlex incurred the following indirect factory costs during January:

Utilities	$2,760
Repairs	3,200
Miscellaneous factory costs	2,200
Total	$8,160

Summary Entry (E) shows the recording of these costs:

(E)

1	Jan.	31	Factory Overhead Control	8 1 6 0 00	1
2			Accounts Payable	8 1 6 0 00	2
3			Incurred factory overhead costs.		3

In addition to these costs, assume that TurboFlex recognized payroll taxes of \$3,800, expired insurance of \$1,000, and accrued property taxes of \$810. Summary Entry (F) shows the recording:

(F)

1	Jan.	31	Factory Overhead Control	5 6 1 0 00	1
2			Payroll Taxes Payable*	3 8 0 0 00	2
3			Prepaid Insurance	1 0 0 0 00	3
4			Property Taxes Payable	8 1 0 00	4
5			Recognized factory overhead costs.		5

Finally, TurboFlex recognized \$2,750 depreciation on factory equipment and \$1,000 depreciation on the factory building, recorded in Summary Entry (G):

(G)

1	Jan.	31	Factory Overhead Control	3 7 5 0 00	1
2			Accum. Depr.—Equipment	2 7 5 0 00	2
3			Accum. Depr.—Building	1 0 0 0 00	3
4			Recognized depreciation.		4

The Factory Overhead Control account now looks like this:

Factory Overhead Control

(B)	1,400
(D)	13,980
(E)	8,160
(F)	5,610
(G)	3,750

*The liability for payroll taxes is often recorded in separate accounts that show the specific types of tax. Here, we recorded the liability in a single account to simplify the illustration. The entry is discussed further in Chapter 5.

LEARNING OBJECTIVE 4   **Applying Factory Overhead to Production.** Notice from the entries made so far that the amount of factory overhead has had no effect on the Work in Process Inventory account. Each time factory overhead costs were incurred, we recorded them in the Factory Overhead Control account. However, the Work in Process Inventory account must include all production costs (factory overhead as well as direct materials and direct labor).

How can we record the amount of overhead costs in the Work in Process Inventory account? The answer to this question is simple. We make an estimate of overhead applicable to each job. We estimate because it is impossible to determine the exact amount of overhead incurred by a particular job. How the estimate is determined is discussed in a later chapter. For the moment, let's look at the entry needed to apply overhead to the jobs in production. TurboFlex's cost accountant estimated that \$31,831.28 is a reasonable amount of overhead to charge to production during January:

(H)

1	Jan.	31	Work in Process Inventory		31 8 31 28		1
2			Factory Overhead Control			31 8 31 28	2
3			Applied overhead to production.				3

The effect of this entry (H) on the accounts involved follows:

Work in Process Inventory			Factory Overhead Control			
Bal.	64,000.00		(B)	1,400	(H)	31,831.28
(B)	37,200.00		(D)	13,980		
(D)	35,648.00		(E)	8,160		
(H)	31,831.28		(F)	5,610		
			(G)	3,750		

Notice that the amount of applied overhead is debited to the Work in Process Inventory account and credited to the Factory Overhead Control account. The debit to Work in Process Inventory has the effect of assigning overhead to the jobs in production. The credit to the Factory Overhead Control account is simply a convenient way of showing both the actual and applied overhead in this account (remember, the actual overhead costs are debited to the Factory Overhead Control account as incurred on a day-to-day basis). We can summarize the function of the Factory Overhead Control account as follows:

Factory Overhead Control	
Actual overhead for the period.	Overhead applied (estimated) to production.

Since the credit to Factory Overhead Control is an estimate, there will usually be a small balance left in the account at the end of the period. A debit balance means that actual overhead for the period exceeded the applied (underapplied overhead). A credit balance means that the applied overhead exceeded the actual (overapplied overhead). How to handle any overapplied or underapplied overhead is discussed in a later chapter.

NOTE You may be wondering why the applied (estimated) overhead is charged to production (and entered on the job cost sheets) when actual overhead costs are incurred every day. To address this, we simply need to remember that factory overhead costs are the indirect costs of production—such as utilities, rent, and repairs. As such, it is impossible to trace directly most factory overhead costs to a particular job. Consequently, the only acceptable way to assign factory overhead costs to production is through an estimate.

SELF-STUDY QUIZ 2–1 Delta Manufacturing Company incurred the following costs during June. Record these summary transactions in general journal form.

  a. Purchased materials on credit, $45,000.
  b. Issued materials to production as follows: direct, $37,800; indirect, $3,500.
  c. Recorded factory payroll for the month, $36,400.
  d. Charged labor to production as follows: direct, $34,000; indirect, $2,400.
  e. Recorded various factory overhead costs, $21,600 (make a credit to Various Accounts).
  f. Applied factory overhead to production, $22,500.
Answers at end of chapter.

Cost of Goods Manufactured

LEARNING OBJECTIVE 5 When a job is completed, the finished product is transferred from the producing departments to the warehouse, which completes the work flow. To complete the cost flow, an entry is needed to transfer the cost of the finished job to the Finished Goods Inventory account. To illustrate this entry, assume that during January, TurboFlex completed and transferred jobs costing $143,325 to the warehouse. Summary Entry (I) shows the transfer of finished jobs.

(I)

1	Jan.	31	Finished Goods Inventory	143 32 5 00		1
2			Work in Process Inventory		143 32 5 00	2
3			Transferred jobs of finished goods.			3

The ledger accounts now appear as follows:

Work in Process Inventory					Finished Goods Inventory		
Bal.	64,000.00				Bal.	87,000	
(B)	37,200.00	(I)	143,325 →		(I)	143,325	
(D)	35,648.00						
(E)	31,831.28						

Sale of Finished Goods

During the month, TurboFlex sold units costing $138,600 to various customers. These units are removed from the warehouse and shipped to the customers. Summary Entry (J) records the cost flow.

(J)

1	Jan.	31	Cost of Goods Sold		138 600 00		1
2			Finished Goods Inventory			138 600 00	2
3			Sold finished goods.				3

The accounts affected by entry (J) appear as follows:

Finished Goods Inventory					Cost of Goods Sold		
Bal.	87,000				(J)	138,600	
(I)	143,325	(J)	138,600 →				

This entry transfers the Cost of Units Sold to the Cost of Goods Sold account. Another entry is needed to record the selling price of the goods. This entry, discussed in detail later, involves a debit to either Cash or Accounts Receivable, and a credit to Sales.

SELF-STUDY QUIZ 2–2 During June, Delta Manufacturing Company (SELF-STUDY QUIZ 2–1) also completed the following transactions. Record these summary transactions in general journal form.

g. Transferred goods costing $94,200 to finished goods.
h. Sold goods costing $97,000.
Answers at end of chapter.

MATCHING COST FLOW WITH WORK FLOW

Earlier we mentioned that the flow of costs in the cost accounting system should match the flow of work in the factory. This was demonstrated as we recorded the January transactions of TurboFlex Corporation. To summarize, look at Figure 2–3, which shows all of TurboFlex's production accounts for the month.

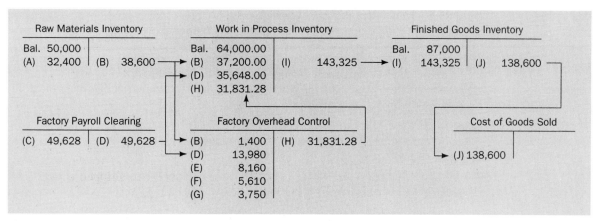

Raw Materials Inventory		Work in Process Inventory		Finished Goods Inventory	
Bal. 50,000		Bal. 64,000.00		Bal. 87,000	
(A) 32,400	(B) 38,600 →	(B) 37,200.00	(I) 143,325 →	(I) 143,325	(J) 138,600 →
		(D) 35,648.00			
		(H) 31,831.28			

Factory Payroll Clearing		Factory Overhead Control		Cost of Goods Sold	
(C) 49,628	(D) 49,628 →	(B) 1,400	(H) 31,831.28 →		
		(D) 13,980		→ (J) 138,600	
		(E) 8,160			
		(F) 5,610			
		(G) 3,750			

FIGURE 2–3
Production Accounts

By observing these accounts, we can see that entries (B), (D), and (H) appear as credits representing the flow of costs out of Raw Materials Inventory, Factory Payroll Clearing, and Factory Overhead Control into Work in Process Inventory. Entry (I) represents the flow of finished goods from Work in Process Inventory to Finished Goods. Entry (J) represents the flow of goods sold from Finished Goods Inventory to Cost of Goods Sold.

NOTE Job-order costing systems are used by organizations whose products or services can be readily identified by individual units or batches of units. Each unit, or batch of units, represents a "job" which receives inputs of direct materials, direct labor, and factory overhead. Manufacturing firms that commonly use job-order costing include aircraft, furniture, construction, and ship building. Examples of nonmanufacturing firms that use job-order costing include law firms, auto repair shops, printing shops, hospitals, and movie studios.

SELF-STUDY PROBLEM

Sterling Products Company uses a job-order costing system. The company incurred the following manufacturing costs during March:

a. Purchased materials on credit, $58,800.
b. Issued materials to production as follows: direct, $51,000; indirect, $11,300.
c. Incurred factory wages, $59,400.
d. Allocated factory wages to production as follows: direct, $45,000; indirect, $14,900.
e. Incurred factory overhead costs on account, $2,500.

f. Recognized other factory overhead costs as follows: depreciation of equipment, $4,000; depreciation of building, $5,000; expired insurance, $600; accrued property taxes, $1,800.
g. Applied factory overhead to production, $32,500.
h. Completed jobs costing $125,500.
i. Sold finished goods costing $118,900 to various customers; billed customers for $161,704 (make two entries).

Required:
Record these summary transactions in general journal form.

SOLUTION TO SELF-STUDY PROBLEM

General Journal

	Date		Account Title	P.R.	Debit	Credit	
1	Mar. 31	a.	Raw Materials Inventory		58 8 0 0 00		1
2			Accounts Payable			58 8 0 0 00	2
3		b.	Work in Process Inventory		51 0 0 0 00		3
4			Factory Overhead Control		11 3 0 0 00		4
5			Raw Materials Inventory			62 3 0 0 00	5
6		c.	Factory Payroll Clearing		59 4 0 0 00		6
7			Salaries and Wages Payable			59 4 0 0 00	7
8		d.	Work in Process Inventory		45 0 0 0 00		8
9			Factory Overhead Control		14 9 0 0 00		9
10			Factory Payroll Clearing			59 9 0 0 00	10
11		e.	Factory Overhead Control		2 5 0 0 00		11
12			Accounts Payable			2 5 0 0 00	12
13		f.	Factory Overhead Control		11 4 0 0 00		13
14			Accum. Depr.—Equipment			4 0 0 0 00	14
15			Accum. Depr.—Building			5 0 0 0 00	15
16			Prepaid Insurance			6 0 0 00	16
17			Property Taxes Payable			1 8 0 0 00	17
18		g.	Work in Process Inventory		32 5 0 0 00		18
19			Factory Overhead Control			32 5 0 0 00	19
20		h.	Finished Goods Inventory		125 5 0 0 00		20
21			Work in Process Inventory			125 5 0 0 00	21
22		i.	Cost of Goods Sold		118 9 0 0 00		22
23			Finished Goods Inventory			118 9 0 0 00	23
24			Accounts Receivable		161 7 0 4 00		24
25			Sales			161 7 0 4 00	25

SUMMARY

A **job-order costing system** is used by those businesses that produce many different products or distinct batches of products. Job-order costing is also used by service businesses that write up "work orders" for specific jobs—such as auto repair, CPA work, and appliance repair.

Factories are typically organized into major divisions, such as administration, production, and marketing. The production division is further divided into (1) producing (or processing) departments and (2) service departments. A **producing department** is any area of the factory where materials, labor, and overhead are added to the product. A **service department** is a department that provides a service that aids the producing departments. For example, the maintenance department cleans the factory and maintains the machinery, which allows the producing departments to perform their function.

The focal point of the job-order costing system is the **job cost sheet,** which is a form used to accumulate the direct materials, direct labor, and factory overhead applied to a particular job. A job cost sheet is tailored to the individual needs of the business using it.

When materials are purchased, their cost is debited to the Raw Materials Inventory account. No distinction is made between direct and indirect materials until materials are issued to production. The cost of direct materials issued to production is debited to the Work in Process Inventory account. The cost of indirect materials issued to production is debited to the Factory Overhead Control.

Factory salaries and wages are recorded in the Factory Payroll Clearing account to give the accounting department time to analyze the payroll to determine what part of the payroll is direct labor and what part is indirect labor. All direct labor charges are then debited to Work in Process Inventory, and all indirect labor charges are debited to Factory Overhead Control.

Factory Overhead costs are incurred on a day-to-day basis. These costs are debited to the Factory Overhead Control account. However, it is not the actual factory overhead costs that are entered in the Work in Process Inventory account and on the job cost sheet, because it is impossible to determine the exact amount of overhead to charge to a particular job. Instead, an estimate is made of the appropriate amount of overhead to charge to each job. The estimate is recorded by debiting Work in Process Inventory and crediting Factory Overhead Control.

When jobs are completed, their cost is transferred from the Work in Process account to the Finished Goods Inventory account. When the goods are sold, their cost is transferred from Finished Goods Inventory account to the Cost of Goods Sold account.

KEY TERMS

Applying Factory Overhead. The process of estimating factory overhead for costing purposes (rather than using actual factory overhead). Factory overhead is estimated because it is impossible to determine exactly how much indirect costs (such as utilities, rent, repairs, etc.) to charge to a particular job.

Job Cost Sheet. A specially designed form that accumulates the direct materials, direct labor, and factory overhead applied to a particular job.

Producing Department. Any area of the factory in which materials, labor, and overhead are added to the product.

Service Department. A department that performs services that make it possible for the producing departments to complete the jobs.

QUESTIONS FOR REVIEW

1. Explain how some nonmanufacturing firms use job-order costing.
2. Differentiate between a producing department and a service department.
3. What is a job cost sheet and what purpose does it serve?
4. What account is used to record the purchase of materials?
5. What is the purpose of the Factory Payroll Clearing account?
6. Identify the account debited for each of the following transactions:
   a. direct materials issued to production.
   b. indirect materials issued to production.
   c. direct labor charged to production.
   d. indirect labor charged to production.
   e. factory overhead applied to production.
   f. cost of completed jobs.
   g. cost of jobs sold.
7. Why is estimated factory overhead charged to production?
8. What does a debit balance in Factory Overhead Control at the end of an accounting period represent? What does a credit balance represent?
9. To what account is the cost of completed jobs transferred?
10. What is meant by "matching cost flow with work flow?"

NOTE Unless told otherwise in Exercises and Problems, record transactions in general journal form.

EXERCISES

2–1. Learning Objective 3. Recording Materials Purchase.
During August, National Products Company purchased materials costing $76,400. Record the purchase.

2–2. Learning Objective 3. Recording the Issue of Materials to Production.
During August, National Products Company (Exercise 1) issued materials to production as follows: direct materials, $62,500; indirect materials, $12,800. Record this issuance.

2–3. Learning Objective 3. Recording the Monthly Payroll.
The August factory payroll for National Products Company totaled $82,000. Record the payroll.

2–4. Learning Objective 4. Charging Labor Costs to Production.

The accountant for National Products Company determined that the August payroll (Exercise 3) should be allocated as follows: direct labor, $70,000; indirect labor, $12,000. Record the allocation.

2–5. Learning Objectives 3 & 4. Recording Factory Overhead Costs.

In addition to indirect materials and indirect labor, National Products Company incurred the following factory overhead costs during August: depreciation of factory equipment, $6,800; depreciation of factory building, $5,000; expired insurance, $800; factory utilities, $4,200 (credit Cash). Record these costs.

2–6. Learning Objective 4. Applying Overhead to Production.

The accountant for National Products Company determined that $38,000 is a reasonable amount of factory overhead to charge to production for August. Record this transaction.

2–7. Learning Objective 5. Recording Finished Goods.

National Products Company completed jobs costing $152,000 during August. Record the cost of the finished jobs.

2–8. Learning Objective 5. Recording Cost of Products Sold.

During August, National Products sold goods costing $148,000 on credit to various customers. These customers were billed for $190,600. Record these transactions (make two separate entries).

GROUP A PROBLEMS

2–1A. Learning Objectives 3, 4, 5. Recording Factory Costs.

Butler Manufacturing Company uses a job-order costing system and incurred the following manufacturing costs during April:

a. Purchased materials on credit, $62,000.
b. Issued materials to production as follows: direct materials, $54,000; indirect materials, $9,100.
c. Incurred factory wages, $57,000.
d. Allocated factory labor to production as follows: direct labor, $45,000; indirect labor, $12,000.
e. Incurred factory overhead costs on account, $3,600.
f. Recognized other factory overhead costs as follows: depreciation of factory equipment, $8,000; depreciation of building, $6,000; expired insurance, $720; accrued property taxes, $940.
g. Applied factory overhead to production, $42,000.
h. Completed jobs costing, $198,200.
i. Sold finished goods costing $174,000 to various customers; billed customers for $225,000 (make two entries).

Required:
Record these transactions.

2–2A. Learning Objectives 3, 4, 5. Recording Factory Costs.

Bilt-Rite Corporation is a furniture manufacturer. The firm's total cost for July follows.

a. Materials purchased, $88,900.
b. Materials issued to production: direct materials, $78,600; indirect materials, $12,450.

c. Factory wages earned, $108,700.
d. Factory wages allocated to production: direct labor, $98,200; indirect labor, $10,500.
e. Factory overhead costs incurred on account, $34,230.
f. Estimated overhead applied to jobs in progress, $55,300.
g. Cost of finished goods transferred to warehouse, $242,000.
h. Cost of finished goods sold to various customers, $238,900.
i. Selling price of goods sold to customers, $334,780.

Required:

1. Open the following general ledger accounts and enter the beginning balances: Raw Materials Inventory, $37,300; Work in Process Inventory, $46,500; Finished Goods Inventory, $29,068.
2. Record the July transactions.
3. Post the journal entries to the general ledger.

2–3A. Learning Objectives 3 & 5. Preparing a Statement of Cost of Goods Manufactured.
Required:
Using your solution to Problem 2–2A, prepare a statement of cost of goods manufactured.

2–4A. Learning Objective 3. Analyzing the Work in Process Inventory Account.
The Work in Process Inventory account for Tyler Company for May follows:

Work in Process Inventory

May 1 Bal.	64,800	May 31	299,790
31 Materials	99,600		
31 Labor	97,300		
31 Overhead	72,000		

Required:
Answer the following questions:

1. What are the manufacturing costs for the month?
2. What is the amount of applied factory overhead?
3. What is the cost of goods manufactured during the month?
4. What is the amount of goods in process at the end of the month?

GROUP B PROBLEMS

2–1B. Learning Objectives 3, 4, 5. Recording Factory Costs.
Mantabe Company uses a job-order costing system and incurred the following manufacturing costs during June:

a. Purchased materials on credit, $60,000.
b. Issued materials to production as follows: direct materials, $52,000; indirect materials, $7,300.
c. Incurred factory wages, $55,000.
d. Allocated factory labor to production as follows: direct labor, $43,000, indirect labor, $12,000.

e. Incurred factory overhead costs on account, $2,800.
f. Recognized other factory overhead costs as follows: depreciation of factory equip-
    ment, $7,400; depreciation of building, $5,500; expired insurance, $690; accrued
    property taxes, $820.
g. Applied factory overhead to production, $40,600.
h. Completed jobs costing $195,100.
i. Sold finished goods costing $172,000 to various customers; billed customers for
    $221,000 (make two entries).

Required:
Record these transactions.

2–2B. Learning Objectives 3, 4, 5. Recording Factory Costs.

Windsor Builders manufactures office furniture. The firm's total costs for October follow:

a. Materials purchased, $90,000.
b. Materials issued to production: direct materials, $80,200; indirect materials, $12,900.
c. Factory wages incurred, $112,000.
d. Factory wages allocated to production: direct labor, $97,000; indirect labor, $15,000.
e. Factory overhead costs incurred on account, $36,598.
f. Estimated overhead applied to jobs in progress, $56,700.
g. Cost of finished goods transferred to warehouse, $245,000.
h. Cost of finished goods sold to various customers, $241,000.
i. Selling price of goods sold to customers, $338,000.

Required:

1. Open the following general ledger accounts and enter the beginning balances: Raw
    Materials Inventory, $39,000; Work in Process Inventory, $47,200; Finished Goods
    Inventory, $31,400.
2. Record the July transactions.
3. Post the journal entries to the general ledger.

2–3B. Learning Objectives 3 & 5. Preparing a Statement of Cost of Goods Manufactured.

Required:
Using your solution to Problem 2–2B, prepare a statement of cost of goods manufactured.

2–4B. Learning Objective 3. Analyzing the Work in Process Inventory Account.

The Work in Process Inventory account for World Products Company for June follows:

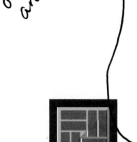

Work in Process Inventory

June 1 Balance	62,400	June 30	292,600
30 Materials	95,360		
30 Labor	96,700		
30 Overhead	73,500		

Required:
Answer the following questions:

1. What are the total manufacturing costs for the month?
2. What is the amount of applied factory overhead?
3. What is the cost of goods manufactured during the month?
4. What is the amount of goods in process at the end of the month?

CASE FOR CRITICAL THINKING

Traci Michaels is the office manager for a small law firm. In addition to Traci, the firm employs five lawyers, three legal assistants, and three secretaries. The firm does not charge clients based on the amount of time and materials devoted to the case. Instead, the firm makes a standard charge based on the nature of the case. For example, drafting a will costs a client $125, regardless of the amount of time devoted to the case.

After taking a cost accounting course in the evening, Traci believes that her firm's billing practice is outdated and inaccurate. She wonders if a job-order costing system may be appropriate. Explain how a law firm could benefit from a job-order costing system.

ANSWERS TO SELF-STUDY QUIZ 2–1

	Date		Account Title	P.R.	Debit	Credit	
			General Journal				
1		a.	Raw Materials Inventory		45 00 0 00		1
2			Accounts Payable			45 00 0 00	2
3		b.	Work in Process Inventory		37 80 0 00		3
4			Factory Overhead Control		3 50 0 00		4
5			Raw Materials Inventory			41 30 0 00	5
6		c.	Factory Payroll Clearing		36 40 0 00		6
7			Salaries and Wages Payable			36 40 0 00	7
8		d.	Work in Process Inventory		34 00 0 00		8
9			Factory Overhead Control		2 40 0 00		9
10			Factory Payroll Clearing			36 40 0 00	10
11		e.	Factory Overhead Control		21 60 0 00		11
12			Various Accounts			21 60 0 00	12
13		f.	Work in Process Inventory		22 50 0 00		13
14			Factory Overhead Control			22 50 0 00	14

ANSWERS TO SELF-STUDY QUIZ 2–2

	Date		Account Title	P.R.	Debit	Credit	
			General Journal				
1		g.	Finished Goods Inventory		94 20 0 00		1
2			Work in Process Inventory			94 20 0 00	2
3		h.	Cost of Goods Sold		97 00 0 00		3
4			Finished Goods Inventory			97 00 0 00	4

Chapter 3
Purchasing and Storing Materials

LEARNING OBJECTIVES

After studying Chapter 3, you should be able to:

1. Describe the need for material controls.
2. Describe forms and procedures related to the purchase and storage of materials.
3. Record the purchase of materials.
4. Record the return of materials.
5. Calculate the economic order quantity.

In Chapter 2, we began our study of job-order costing by overviewing the job-order costing cycle. Starting with this chapter, we will look very closely at the individual cost elements (materials, labor, and factory overhead) and how they relate to job-order costing.

NEED FOR MATERIALS CONTROL

LEARNING OBJECTIVE 1

In many factories, the cost of raw materials is the single largest element of production costs. Consequently, rigid internal controls are needed not only to safeguard materials from theft, but also to minimize waste and misuse from such factors as maintaining excessive inventory levels, improper documentation, spoilage, deterioration, and obsolescence. While specific internal control procedures are designed to meet a company's individual needs, the following controls should be included:

1. Materials of the desired quality must be maintained in proper quantities to keep production moving on schedule.
2. Materials must be purchased only when a need exists.
3. Materials must be purchased at the most favorable prices.
4. Materials must be physically protected from theft, waste, and misuse.
5. Funds that could be more efficiently invested elsewhere must not be tied up in excessive inventory levels.
6. Costs of handling and storing materials must be kept to a minimum.
7. Issues of materials from the storeroom to production must be properly authorized and accounted for.
8. All materials, at all times, must be the responsibility of someone.

MATERIALS PURCHASING PROCEDURES

LEARNING OBJECTIVE 2

The procedures for purchasing and receiving materials varies from business to business. Most firms have a **purchasing agent** who is responsible for all materials purchases. The purchasing agent has the responsibility of buying materials in the correct quantities, at the proper times, and from the most economical source of supply.

TurboFlex Corporation has a purchasing agent who is in charge of the Purchasing Department. The purchasing agent and staff maintain a file of various suppliers, negotiates purchase prices, prepares and mails purchase orders, and oversees the receipt of orders. In smaller organizations, one person may be responsible for all purchases. Regardless of the size of the business, however, the purchasing process starts with a purchase requisition, which we will discuss next.

Purchase Requisition

A **purchase requisition** is a form used to notify the purchasing agent that additional materials are needed. Purchase requisitions are an important part of the materials control process because materials can only be ordered in response to a properly prepared requisition. Further, the requisition serves as the purchasing agent's authority to buy materials.

Purchase requisitions can originate in several ways. At TurboFlex Corporation, the storeroom keeper, who is in charge of the materials after they have been received, completes a purchase requisition whenever the quantity of a standard material reaches a predetermined reorder point. For example, the established reorder point of Material B-10 (U-shaped metal legs for the weight bench) is 300. When the quantity of this material drops to around 300 units, the storeroom keeper prepares a purchase requisition and issues it to the purchasing agent.

Another way purchase requisitions are generated at TurboFlex is when production managers need materials that are not part of the standard materials maintained in the storeroom, or when standard materials are needed in unusually large quantities. These situations happen when special orders are received, or if an unusually large order is received from a customer.

To illustrate when and how a purchase requisition is generated, let's assume that as a result of jobs in progress during December 19X5, the quantity of Material B-10 dropped below the 300 unit reorder point. Accordingly, the storeroom keeper completed the purchase requisition shown in Figure 3–1. The purchase requisition is prepared in duplicate. The first copy is sent to the purchasing agent; the second copy is retained in the storeroom files. Some companies, for various reasons, prepare three or more copies of the purchase requisition.

Purchase Order

After receiving a purchase requisition, the purchasing department prepares a purchase order, which is sent to the chosen supplier. The **purchase order,** illustrated in Figure 3–2, is a form that describes the materials needed and identifies necessary details about the purchase—such as the price, terms of payment, delivery date, and method of shipment. The purchase order is prenumbered and prepared with several copies. The exact number of copies varies from company to company.

TurboFlex prepares a four-copy purchase order. The original goes to the supplier. The purchasing department retains one copy, one copy goes to the storeroom, another copy goes to the accounting department (for recording), and the fourth copy is sent to the receiving department (so the receiving clerk will know when the materials should arrive). For verification, the copy sent to the storeroom is compared with the purchase requisition on which the order is based. The storeroom clerk then files the purchase order in an *unfilled orders file.*

| Purchase Requisition | | No. 618 |

TurboFlex Corporation
6000 Industrial Blvd.
Glendale, AZ 85302

DATE _Jan. 2, 19X6_   DATE WANTED _Jan. 2, 19X6_

VENDOR _____   SHIP TO _____

QUANTITY	MATERIAL NO.	DESCRIPTION	PURPOSE
500	B-10	U-shaped bench legs	Current job

FOR:

Job ___101___   Acct. ___121___

FIGURE 3–1
Purchase Requisition

PURCHASE ORDER

TO:	Bessemer Company 612 Bealwood Blvd. Lincoln, Nebraska 68588	SHIP TO:	TurboFlex Corporation 6000 Industrial Blvd. Glendale, AZ 85302

DATE REQUIRED	JOB	TERMS	DATE	PURCHASE ORDER
1–2–X6	101		1–2–X6	10012

QUANTITY	DESCRIPTION	UNIT COST	TOTAL
500	U–shaped bench legs, Stock #2445	$10.00	$5,000.00

PURCHASE ORDER MUST APPEAR ON ALL INVOICE, SHIPPING MEMOS, BILLS OF LADING AND PACKAGES.

By _____

FIGURE 3–2
Purchase Order

At TurboFlex, all purchase orders are prenumbered. At the end of each month, the cost accountant, using copies sent to the accounting department, verifies that all orders have either been mailed to suppliers, or remain on hand waiting to be mailed. This is an internal control feature that helps ensure that purchase orders are used only for authorized purposes.

Receiving Report

As we mentioned above, a copy of the purchase order is sent to the receiving clerk to give notice that an order is forthcoming. This allows the receiving clerk time to plan work and allot space for the incoming materials.

The receiving clerk's copy of the purchase order is a **blind copy,** which means that it does not show the quantities ordered. This way, the receiving clerk will have to make an independent count of the quantities received, because the copy does not show how many units were ordered.

After counting and inspecting incoming materials, the receiving clerk prepares a **receiving report,** which shows the quantities and condition of materials received. Copies of the receiving report are distributed to the following:

1. *Accounting department.* This copy notifies the accounting department that materials ordered have been received.
2. *Storeroom keeper.* This copy is checked against the quantities actually delivered to the storeroom to ensure that all materials that come to the receiving department are put into the storeroom.
3. *Purchasing department.* The purchasing agent's copy of the receiving report is compared with the supplier's invoice and the purchase order to determine that the materials actually received are the ones that were ordered and billed.

The receiving report is illustrated in Figure 3–3.

Debit/Credit Memorandum

In the preceding section, we mentioned that TurboFlex's purchasing agent compares the receiving report with the supplier's invoice and the purchase order. This control feature helps ensure that:

- Materials received are those that were ordered.
- Materials are received in good condition.
- Unit prices, terms of payment, freight charges, and other details agree with the original purchase order.
- All computations are correct.

If all documents agree (the receiving report, invoice, and purchase order), a copy of each document is stapled together and sent to the accounting department which approves the invoice for payment.

TurboFlex Corporation

RECEIVING REPORT

DATE 1-2-X6	P.O. NO. OR RETURNED GOODS	VIA	FREIGHT BILL NO.	PREPAID	COLLECT

RECEIVED FROM *Bessemer Company*

ADDRESS *612 Bealwood Blvd. Lincoln, Nebraska 68588*

QUANTITY	ITEM NO.	DESCRIPTION	REMARKS—CONDITION—ETC.
1 *500*	*B-10*	*U-shaped bench legs*	*Good condition*
2			
3			
4			
5			
6			
7			
8			
9			
10			
11			
12			

NO. PACKAGES	WEIGHT	RECEIVED BY *CD*	CHECKED BY *RD*	DELIVERED TO

REMARKS: CONDITIONS, ETC.

FIGURE 3–3
Receiving Report

On occasion, materials will be received that do not match those ordered. When this happens, the cause of the difference is determined and the supplier is notified. Copies of all correspondence between TurboFlex and the supplier are placed in the file relating to the particular purchase.

If a quantity larger than that ordered is received, one of two courses of action may be taken. If the excess materials can be used, a credit memorandum is prepared in order to notify the supplier of the amount of the increase in the invoice. If the materials cannot be used, or materials are received that do not meet specifications, a debit memorandum is prepared to inform the supplier that the materials are being returned. TurboFlex uses a combined **debit/credit memorandum,** as illustrated in Figure 3–4. In this case, it is a debit memorandum for materials received that did not meet the specifications stated on the purchase order.

If, on the other hand, the quantity received is less than the quantity ordered, likewise two courses of action may be taken. If the materials received

---

TURBOFLEX CORPORATION

Debit/Credit Memorandum

TO: Fullmark Leather Products Company
911 East Industrial Blvd.
Chicago, IL 60612

DATE: _1–8–X6_

Invoice No. _18_

We have (Debited) Credited your account for:

Quantity	Description	Unit Price	Amount
5 rolls	Vinyl covering	$80.00/roll	$400.00

Explanation   _Did not meet specifications_

By _____, Purchasing Agent

FIGURE 3–4
*Debit/Credit
Memorandum*

can be used, they are retained and a debit memorandum is prepared to notify the supplier of the shortage. (If the materials are backordered, and TurboFlex has the time in its production schedule to wait for the short materials to be delivered, no debit memorandum is prepared). If the materials received cannot be used, a debit memorandum is prepared and the materials are returned to the supplier.

Summary of Steps in the Purchasing Process

Now that we have discussed the procedures used by TurboFlex to purchase and receive materials, let's take a moment to summarize these steps.

- A request for a purchase must be made by an authorized person by preparing a purchase requisition that is submitted to the purchasing agent.
- A purchase order is prepared by the purchasing agent after receipt of a properly prepared purchase requisition.
- All materials received are carefully checked to ensure that they are in good condition and correspond to those ordered.
- A receiving report is prepared to verify that materials received are those that were ordered and prices charged agree with the purchase order.
- Approval for payment is made only after the above steps have been completed.

SELF-STUDY QUIZ 3–1 Identify the document that would be prepared for each of the following situations:

a. Materials are needed.
b. Materials are received and placed in the storeroom.
c. Raw materials are returned to the supplier due to damage during shipment.
d. Materials are ordered.
e. Excess materials received in a shipment are returned.

Answers at end of chapter.

ACCOUNTING FOR MATERIALS

Literally tons of materials are used by many manufacturers on a daily basis. Consequently, a company's inventory records, to be of maximum use, must show (1) the number of units of each kind of materials on hand and (2) the cost of these materials. This is best achieved by maintaining a subsidiary ledger for materials and a related controlling account in the general ledger.

As we learned in Chapter 2, all purchases of materials are recorded by debiting the Raw Materials Inventory account, which is a general ledger account (the corresponding credit is either to the Cash account or to the Accounts Payable account). The Raw Materials Inventory account is a controlling account supported by a subsidiary ledger called the **materials ledger** (or the *stores ledger*), which contains an individual account for each item of material carried in stock. On a regular basis, usually once a month, the balance of the controlling account is compared with the total of the individual accounts in the materials ledger. Any significant difference between the two is investigated.

LEARNING OBJECTIVE 3

Each materials ledger card shows the quantity of that material on hand and its cost. In order to keep this information current, it is necessary to post to the materials ledger each time materials are purchased or issued. To illustrate this, let's look again at the summary entry we made in Chapter 2 to record TurboFlex's purchases of materials during January:

Purchase
→ Post to
MAT Ledger

1	Jan.	31	Raw Materials Inventory	32 40 0 00		1
2			Accounts Payable		32 40 0 00	2
3			Purchased materials.			3

The individual breakdown of these purchases follows:

Date of Purchase	Material	Description	Quantity	Unit Price	Total Cost
Jan. 2	B-10	U-shaped bench legs	500	$10.00	$ 5,000
5	B-12	Vinyl covering	30 rolls	80.00	2,400
9	D-2	Weight plates	10,000 lbs.	0.82	8,200
15	C-10	#14 pulleys	250	8.00	2,000
17	A-10	Tacks and nails	40 cases	12.00	480
18	C-12	#5 pulleys	250	4.00	1,000
21	B-12	#14 pulleys	250	8.00	2,000
25	A-10	Tubular bench legs	400	10.60	4,240
29	A-12	Lubricants	100 cans	3.00	300
30	D-8	Reset vinyl covering	300 rolls	10.00	3,000
30	B-20	#2 metal tubing	800 ft.	0.50	400
31	B-18	Triple metal cable	4,000 ft.	0.845	3,380
Total					$32,400

As we stated, a separate materials ledger account is maintained for each item of material. When materials are received, the storeroom clerk records the receipt on the appropriate materials ledger card. For example, Figure 3–5 shows the materials ledger card for Material B-10 (U-shaped bench legs) after the purchase of January 2. Notice that the card shows receipts, issues, and the balance on hand. The number of the purchase invoice is entered in the *Reference* column.

MATERIALS LEDGER CARD

Material _U-shaped bench legs_   Reorder Point _____ _300_ _____

Number _____ _B-10_ _____   Reorder Quantity _____ _500_ _____

DATE	REFERENCE	RECEIVED			ISSUED			BALANCE		
		UNITS	PRICE	AMOUNT	UNITS	PRICE	AMOUNT	UNITS	PRICE	AMOUNT
_19x6_										
Jan. 1	_Bal._							295	10 00	2950 00
_2_	_P.O. 10012_	500	10 00	500 00				795	10 00	795 00

FIGURE 3–5
Materials Ledger Card

Recording Returns

LEARNING OBJECTIVE 4   Earlier we stated that TurboFlex prepares a debit memorandum when materials are returned to the supplier. When this happens, an entry is made debiting the Accounts Payable account and crediting the Raw Materials Inventory account. As an example, let's look again at the debit memorandum illustrated in Figure 3–4. TurboFlex made the following entry to record this return.

1	Jan.	8	Accounts Payable		400 00		1
2			Raw Materials Inventory			400 00	2
3			(Material B–12)				3
4			Returned materials to supplier.				4

This entry will be posted to the general ledger accounts involved at the end of the month. To keep the materials ledger current, however, posting is made to the individual materials ledger card immediately, as illustrated in Figure 3–6.

Recording Payment for Materials

TurboFlex purchases the majority of its materials on 30-days credit. Most of these purchases carry credit terms of 2/10,n/30. When an invoice is paid in time to take advantage of a discount, the amount of the discount is credited to

MATERIALS LEDGER CARD

Material __Vinyl covering__   Reorder Point __20 rolls__

Number __B-12__   Reorder Quantity __30 rolls__

DATE	REFERENCE	RECEIVED			ISSUED			BALANCE		
		UNITS	PRICE	AMOUNT	UNITS	PRICE	AMOUNT	UNITS	PRICE	AMOUNT
19x6 Jan. 1								21	80 00	1 68 0 00
5	P.O. 11022	30	80 00	2 40 0 00				51	80 00	4 08 0 00
8	D.M. 18	(5)	80 00	(40 0 00)				46	80 00	3 68 0 00

FIGURE 3–6
Materials Ledger Card

the Purchases Discounts account. For example, on January 2, TurboFlex made payment for an $8,000 purchase of December 23 that carried terms of 2/10,n/30. The following entry records the payment and the discount.

1	Jan.	2	Accounts Payable	8 0 0 0 00		1
2			Purchases Discounts		1 6 0 00	2
3			Cash		7 8 4 0 00	3
4			Paid on account, 2/10, n/30.			4

You are familiar with the Purchases Discounts account from your study of general accounting. It was used to record discounts received for the early payment of merchandise bought on account. Here, the Purchases Discounts account serves the same purpose, except that it shows discounts received on materials.

SELF-STUDY QUIZ 3–2 Melwood Company engaged in the following selected transactions for October. Record these transactions in general journal form.

Oct. 5   Purchased $5,000 of Material 245 from Lakewood Company; terms, 2/10,n/30.
    8   Prepared a debit memorandum for the return of $1,000 of Material 245 that did not meet specifications.
   15   Issued a check for the balance owed to Lakewood Company.
Answers at end of chapter.

SPECIAL PURCHASING PROCEDURES

We have discussed the normal procedures TurboFlex follows when purchasing and storing materials. In this section, we will look at three additional topics: the bill of materials, the economic order quantity, and just-in-time inventory systems.

Bill of Materials

We stated earlier that TurboFlex has established a reorder point for each material item. TurboFlex has also established a reorder quantity for each item. This is done to maintain a level of inventory sufficient to keep production moving on schedule. There are times, however, when several jobs requiring the same materials are started about the same time. To avoid a materials shortage, the production manager may prepare a **bill of materials**, which is a form that lists all the raw materials and component parts necessary for a typical job. The bill of materials can be thought of as a "master requisition." This record, illustrated in Figure 3–7, allows the storeroom clerk to check inventory levels to make sure that sufficient materials are available, or will be delivered, to keep production moving.

TURBOFLEX CORPORATION
Bill of Materials

Date _____1–15–X6_____

Job __122__

To Be Started __1–18–X6__

Will require the following materials:

Material No.	Quantity	Description	Issued cost: Per unit	Total
B-10	300	U-shaped bench legs	10 00	3000 00

Date Received _____   Received By _____

FIGURE 3–7
Bill of Materials

Economic Order Quantity (EOQ)

LEARNING OBJECTIVE 5   In recent years, wholesale purchasing clubs have developed that allow us to save money when buying most consumer items—including groceries, electronics, clothes, and appliances. There is a catch to purchasing clubs, however: you must purchase in large quantities. For example, you may pay $1.99 per pound for hamburger meat in a supermarket. In a wholesale club, you may only pay $1.49 per pound; but you will have to buy a much larger quantity to get the lower price. Let's say that you bought 25 pounds of hamburger meat in order to get the best price per pound. By doing so, you saved $0.50 a pound ($1.99 –$1.49). Not a bad deal? Perhaps not. But consider that now you have to store your purchase. It must be broken down into smaller quantities, each of which must be wrapped, and stored in your freezer. So, the larger purchase saved you money on the purchase price, but it increases your cost to carry (store) the item.

Manufacturers and merchandisers are faced with the same problem. If purchases are made in large quantities, the cost of carrying the inventory is high because of the sizable investment in the purchase and the necessity of storing a large inventory. On the other hand, if purchases are made in small quantities, the result will be frequent orders with correspondingly higher costs.

In order to address this problem, a special formula called the **economic order quantity (EOQ)** was developed. The EOQ is the ideal amount of inventory to be ordered at one time for purposes of minimizing annual inventory costs. It is calculated as follows:

$$EOQ = \sqrt{\frac{2 \times \text{annual requirements} \times \text{cost of an order}}{\text{carrying cost per unit of inventory}}}$$

To illustrate how to apply this formula, assume that TurboFlex determined the following related to Material B-10 (U-shaped bench legs):

Number of units required annually	10,000
Cost of placing an order	$10.00
Annual carrying cost per unit of inventory	$ 0.80

The EOQ is 500 units, calculated as follows:

$$EOQ = \sqrt{\frac{2 \times 10,000 \times \$10.00}{\$0.80}}$$

$$= \sqrt{\frac{\$200,000}{\$0.80}}$$

$$= \sqrt{\$250,000}$$

$$= 500 \text{ units}$$

SELF-STUDY QUIZ 3–3 Leading Edge Products Company has determined that the cost to place an order for metal couplings is $5 and the annual carrying cost is $2 per unit. Calculate the EOQ if 8,000 units are needed annually.
Answers at end of chapter.

NOTE Order costs and carrying costs move in opposite directions, that is, order costs decrease when order size increases, while carrying costs increase with increases in order size. The *economic order quantity* is the order size which minimizes total order and carrying costs over the accounting period.

Just-In-Time Inventory Systems

In the previous section, we stated that TurboFlex maintains a minimum level of materials inventory. This is done to act as a buffer so that production can keep moving on schedule even if suppliers are late with deliveries. However, it is costly to carry inventories and many managers believe that having excessive inventory levels encourages inefficiency. As a result, **just-in-time (JIT) inventory systems** are coming into use.

Under a JIT inventory system, a company strives to purchase only enough inventory to meet daily needs. In other words, raw materials would be received *just in time* to go into production and goods are completed *just in time* to be shipped to customers. Thus, under ideal conditions, a company would have no goods still in process at the end of a day and no raw materials left over to store. All goods completed during the day would be shipped immediately to customers so that finished goods would not have to be stored in the warehouse. The focus of the system is on careful planning to increase efficiency and reduce (or eliminate) inventory levels and thereby reduce costs.

While few companies have been able to fully implement a JIT system, many companies are experiencing much success with the system. JIT systems are likely to grow in popularity as factories become more automated and as managers become more experienced with the actual working of a JIT system.

SELF-STUDY PROBLEM

The following selected transactions were completed by West Corporation during October:

Oct. 5   Prepared purchase Requisition 315 (by the storeroom clerk) requesting an order for 500 units of Material B-35. The supplier is Carroll Company and the unit cost is $3.15.

   6   Prepared Purchase Order 10-15 in response to Purchase Requisition 315. Terms of payment, 2/10,n/30.

   10   Received materials from Carroll Company and prepared Receiving Report 644.

   12   Issued Debit Memorandum 112 to Carroll Company for the return of 25 units of Material B-35 that were damaged during shipment.

   16   Made payment to Carroll Company for the purchase of October 6.

Required:
Record these transactions in general journal form.

SOLUTION TO SELF-STUDY PROBLEM

No transaction in GJ on Requisition. Only on P.O.

Rec'd at Clocks

1	Oct.	5	No Entry			1
2		6	Raw Materials Inventory	1 5 7 5 00		2
3			Accounts Payable		1 5 7 5 00	3
4		10	No Entry			4
5		12	Accounts Payable	7 8 75		5
6			Raw Materials Inventory		7 8 75	6
7		16	Accounts Payable	1 4 9 6 25		7
8			Cash		1 4 6 6 32	8
9			Purchases Discounts		2 9 93	9

SUMMARY

In most factories, the cost of materials is a significant part of production costs. As a result, internal controls are needed to safeguard materials from theft, minimize waste, and avoid excessive inventory levels.

One way to reduce materials cost is to order only materials actually needed to keep production moving on schedule. The purchasing process starts with a **purchase requisition** which is a form used to notify the purchasing department that certain materials are needed. The purchasing agent responds to a purchase requisition by preparing a **purchase order** which is sent to a supplier. When goods are received from a supplier, a **receiving report** is prepared to verify that all materials have been received and that prices charged agree with the purchase order.

For various reasons, it is sometimes necessary to return materials to a supplier. When this happens, a **debit memorandum** is prepared to notify the supplier of the return. A **credit memorandum** is prepared to notify the supplier of the amount of the increase in quantity in the invoice.

For control, a company's inventory records must show the quantity of each kind of materials on hand and the cost of these materials. To do this, most manufacturers maintain a **materials ledger** which contains a materials ledger card for each item of materials. The materials ledger is summarized (controlled) by the Raw Materials Inventory account in the general ledger.

It is costly to carry excessive inventory levels. However, a company must have enough raw materials on hand to keep production moving on schedule. Consequently, the production manager may prepare a **bill of materials,** which lists all the raw materials needed for a typical job. This allows the storeroom clerk to look at the jobs in process and check inventory levels to make sure that enough is on hand or will be ordered.

Two other ways to reduce inventory costs are the **economic order quantity (EOQ)** and **just-in-time (JIT) inventory systems.** EOQ is the ideal amount of inventory to be ordered at one time for purposes of minimizing annual inventory costs. JIT systems are designed to minimize storage costs and improve efficiency by purchasing just enough materials to meet current production needs, and finishing just enough goods to be timely shipped to customers.

KEY TERMS

Bill of Materials. A form that lists all the raw materials and parts necessary for a typical job or production run.

Debit/Credit Memorandum. A document used to notify a supplier that a price adjustment needs to be made on the invoice price of materials or supplies received.

Economic Order Quantity (EOQ). The ideal amount of inventory to be ordered at one time for purposes of minimizing annual inventory costs.

Just-In-Time (JIT) Inventory System. An inventory system designed to reduce storage costs and improve efficiency by ordering just enough raw materials to meet daily production needs and finishing just enough goods to be shipped to customers at the end of the day.

Materials Ledger. A subsidiary ledger containing a materials ledger card for each item of material used by a firm; it is controlled by the Raw Materials Inventory account in the general ledger.

Purchasing Agent. An individual responsible for the purchasing function of a firm; the purchasing agent is not only responsible for determining that an order is needed but is entrusted with finding the best source of supply at the most favorable prices.

Purchase Order. A form sent to a supplier (vendor) requesting the delivery of materials or supplies.

Purchase Requisition. A form prepared by a department head, manager, or storeroom clerk to inform the purchasing agent that certain materials or supplies are needed.

Receiving Report. A form that shows the quantities and condition of materials received and placed in the storeroom.

QUESTIONS FOR REVIEW

1. Why are special controls needed for materials?
2. List four internal control features for materials.
3. Differentiate between a purchase requisition and a purchase order.
4. Who prepares a receiving report and what purpose does it serve?
5. What is meant by a blind copy of the purchase order?
6. What type of information does a materials ledger card provide?
7. How often should materials ledger cards be updated? Why?
8. What is a bill of materials?
9. What is meant by the economic order quantity?
10. How are just-in-time (JIT) inventory systems being used to improve efficiency and reduce costs?

NOTE Unless told otherwise in Exercises and Problems, record transactions in general journal form.

EXERCISES

3–1. Learning Objective 2. Calculating the Ending Balance of a Materials Ledger Card.

Based on the following information, calculate the ending balance of Material 144 (aluminum couplings):

	Units	Price per Unit
Beginning balance	225	$ 9.50
Received	300	9.50
Issued	400	9.50
Received	300	9.75

3–2. Learning Objective 3. Recording the Purchase and Payment of Raw Materials.

On January 12, TechCo Corporation purchased materials costing $38,000 with terms of 3/10,n/30. Payment for the materials was made on January 22. Record both transactions.

3–3. Learning Objective 4. Determining the Amount To Be Paid a Supplier.

On June 2, Grant Company purchased materials costing $15,250 from York Enterprises. Terms of the purchase were 3/15,2/20,n/45. On June 5, Grant returned $200 worth of materials because of damage during shipment. Payment was then made on June 22. What is the amount of payment?

3–4. Learning Objectives 3, 4. Recording Transactions Relating to Materials.

Rodriguez Company incurred the following transactions during May. Record these transactions.

May 1   Purchased materials costing $12,000 from Turner Company; terms, 2/10,n/30.
    4   Returned defective materials to Turner Company, $500.
    9   Purchased materials costing $16,000 from DEC Products Company; terms, 3/10,n/30.
  11   Made payment to Turner Company for the purchase of May 1.
  19   Made payment to DEC Products Company for the purchase of May 9.

3–5. Learning Objective 5. Calculating the Economic Order Quantity.

Zeal Supply Company estimates that 100,000 units of Material H will be used during the year. The material has a cost of $5 per unit and it is estimated that it will cost $18 to place each order. The annual carrying cost is $0.10 per unit. Using the EOQ formula, calculate the most economical order quantity.

GROUP A PROBLEMS

3–1A. Learning Objectives 2, 3, 4. Preparing Forms Related to Purchasing and Receiving Materials.

Marshall Company, 211 Bradley Industrial Park, Atlanta, GA 30304, completed the following transactions during April:

April 5   In response to Purchase Requisition 212 from the storeroom clerk, the purchasing agent placed Purchase Order 718 for the following:

Material	Quantity	Description	Price	Purpose
644	300	#2 table legs	$2.00	Storeroom
618	500	#12 table legs	8.00	Storeroom
B-45	2,500	#18 metal inserts	0.09	Storeroom

8   Received all materials listed on Purchase order 718. Prepared receiving report 218.

12   Prepared Debit Memorandum 18 for ten damaged table legs (Material 618).

15   Paid for the purchase of April 5; terms, 2/10,n/30.

Required:

1. Using the blank forms in the Study Guide/Working Papers, prepare the form needed on each date.
2. Record these transactions. — *general journal*

3–2A. Learning Objective 2. Maintaining a Materials Ledger Card.

The following transactions relate to Material J-15.

Jan. 1   Balance on hand, 200 units with a cost of $2.00 each.
3   Purchased 500 units at $2.00 each.
8   Issued 300 units to production.
12   Issued 175 units to production.
18   Issued 50 units to production.
25   Purchased 500 units with a cost of $2.00 each.
31   Issued 275 units to production.

Required:

Post the above transactions to the materials ledger card supplied in the Study Guide/Working Papers.

3–3A. Learning Objectives 2, 3, 4. Recording Materials Transactions.

Baker Manufacturing Company completed the following transactions during July:

July 1   Purchase Requisition 111 for 3,800 units of Material K-15 is prepared by the storeroom clerk. The material has a unit cost of $2.12 and is to be ordered from Michaels Corporation; terms, 2/10,n/30.

2   Purchase Order 10018 is prepared in response to Purchase Requisition 111.

6   All materials listed on Purchase Order 10018 are received and placed in the storeroom.

8   Debit Memorandum 12 is prepared for the return of 12 damaged items of Material K-15.

11   Payment is made for the purchase of July 2.

Required:
Record these transactions.

3–4A. Learning Objective 5. Computing the Economic Order Quantity (EOQ).

Bradley Company has determined the following related to materials purchases:

Material	Annual Requirements	Cost of an Order	Carrying Cost
A	5,000	$12	$0.75
B	12,000	12	0.80
C	10,000	10	0.80

Required:
Compute the EOQ for each material.

GROUP B PROBLEMS

3–1B. Learning Objectives 2, 3, 4. Preparing Forms Related to Purchasing and Receiving Materials.

Bradley Company, 114 East Industrial Drive, Philadelphia, PA 19136, completed the following transactions during June, 19X1:

June 6 In response to Purchase Requisition 312 from the storeroom clerk, the purchasing agent placed Purchase Order 918 for the following:

Material	Quantity	Description	Price	Purpose
485	600	#18 table legs	$3.00	Storeroom
501	500	#28 table braces	4.50	Storeroom
H-10	3,000	#1 wood inserts	0.12	Storeroom

9   Received all materials listed on Purchase Order 918. Prepared Receiving Report 205.

14   Prepared Debit Memorandum 16 for 12 table legs (Material 485) that were damaged.

16   Paid for the purchase of June 6; terms, 2/10,n/30.

Required:

1. Using the blank forms in the Study Guide/Working Papers, prepare the form needed on each date.
2. Record these transactions.

3–2B. Learning Objective 2. Maintaining a Materials Ledger Card.

The following transactions relate to Material S-15.

Mar. 1 Balance on hand, 300 units with a cost of $2.50 each.

4   Purchased 600 units at $2.50 each.

9   Issued 400 units to production.
14 Issued 200 units to production.
19 Issued 75 units to production.
26 Purchased 600 units with a cost of $2.50 each.
30 Issued 300 units to production.

Required:
Post the above transactions to the materials ledger card supplied in the Study Guide/Working Papers.

3–3B. Learning Objectives 2, 3, 4. Recording Materials Transactions.

Spencer Corporation completed the following transactions during May:

May 1   Purchase Requisition 101 for 4,000 units of Material H-5 is prepared by the storeroom clerk. The material has a unit cost of $2.15 and is to be ordered from Daniels Corporation; terms, 2/10,n/30.
3   Purchase Order 13225 is prepared in response to Purchase Requisition 101.
7   All materials listed on Purchase Order 13225 are received and placed in the storeroom.
9   Debit Memorandum 18 is prepared for the return of 15 damaged items of Material H-5.
12 Payment is made for the purchase of May 3.

Required:
Record these transactions.

3–4B. Learning Objective 5. Computing the Economic Order Quantity (EOQ).

Paterson Company has determined the following related to materials purchases:

Material	Annual Requirements	Cost of an Order	Carrying Cost
A-4	10,000	$10	$0.80
A-9	25,000	10	0.50
B-6	20,000	9	1.00

Required:
Compute the EOQ for each material.

CASE FOR CRITICAL THINKING

Barrow Manufacturing Company is a small manufacturer of athletic uniforms. Since the company is small and most of its products are seasonal, the production manager does not see the need for close observation of materials inventory levels. Instead, he orders in large quantities and stores unused materials until the next season. Write a paragraph explaining why this system may not be cost effective.

ANSWERS TO SELF-STUDY QUIZ 3–1

a. Materials requisition
b. Receiving report
c. Debit/credit memorandum
d. Purchase order
e. Debit/credit memorandum

ANSWERS TO SELF-STUDY QUIZ 3–2

1	Oct.	5	Raw Materials Inventory	5 0 0 0 00		1
2			Accounts Payable		5 0 0 0 00	2
3						3
4		8	Accounts Payable	1 0 0 0 00		4
5			Raw Materials Inventory		1 0 0 0 00	5
6						6
7		15	Accounts Payable	4 0 0 0 00		7
8			Purchases Discounts		8 0 00	8
9			Cash		3 9 2 0 00	9

ANSWERS TO SELF-STUDY QUIZ 3–3

$$EOQ = \sqrt{\frac{2 \times 8{,}000 \times \$5}{\$2}}$$

$$= \sqrt{\frac{\$80{,}000}{\$2}}$$

$$= \sqrt{\$40{,}000}$$

$$= 200 \text{ units}$$

Chapter 4
Issuing Materials to Production

LEARNING OBJECTIVES

After studying Chapter 4, you should be able to:

1. Define and describe the materials requisition.
2. Record the issuance of materials to production and record the return of materials to the storeroom.
3. Determine the cost materials issued to production using the following methods: FIFO, LIFO, moving average.

In Chapter 3, we learned how a firm purchases and stores materials. In this chapter, we will continue our study of materials by examining how materials are issued to production and how a cost is assigned to those materials.

ISSUING MATERIALS TO PRODUCTION

In Chapter 3, we stressed the need for proper accounting controls during the purchase and storage of materials. There should likewise be proper controls when materials are issued to production. At TurboFlex Corporation, materials are carefully monitored to ensure that they are only used for authorized purposes. No material can be issued from the storeroom unless it is supported by a properly prepared materials requisition, which is discussed in detail next.

Materials Requisition

LEARNING OBJECTIVE 1

The **materials requisition** is a control device prepared by factory personnel who are authorized to withdraw materials from the storeroom. At TurboFlex, a department head or a job supervisor prepares the materials requisition in triplicate. The department head or supervisor keeps one copy of the requisition; the other two copies are forwarded to the storeroom keeper. The requisition for the withdrawal of 50 U-shaped bench legs (Material B-10) is illustrated in Figure 4–1. Notice that the requisition shows the quantity, material num-

(handwritten note in margin:) from the Store Room

TURBOFLEX CORPORATION

Materials Requisition

Date _January 4, 19X6_   No. _701_

To: Bill French

QUANTITY	MATERIAL NO.	DESCRIPTION	UNIT PRICE		AMOUNT	
50	B-10	U-shaped bench legs	10	00	500	00

Approved by _J.D._   Issued by _R.S._

Received by _H.T._   Charge to (Job) / Depart. _118_

FIGURE 4–1
Materials Requisition

ber, material description, unit price, total amount, and the number of the job to which the materials will be charged.

The materials requisition authorizes the storeroom keeper to issue materials from the storeroom. Upon receipt of a properly prepared requisition, the storeroom keeper issues the materials, makes the necessary notations on the requisition, enters the unit price, and calculates and enters the total amount. The storeroom keeper keeps the second copy of the requisition and sends the third copy to the accounting department for recording. (Remember, the first copy is kept by the individual who prepared it.)

Materials Ledger

As we discussed in Chapter 3, a materials ledger card is maintained for each type of material on hand. Each materials ledger card is a perpetual inventory record showing quantities and prices of materials received, issued, and on hand. The materials ledger cards form a subsidiary ledger summarized by the Raw Materials Inventory account located in the general ledger.

After Materials Requisition 701 was filled, the storeroom keeper updates the materials ledger card (for Material B-10) by making an entry in the Issued column, computing a new balance, and entering the new balance in the Balance column. The materials ledger card, Figure 4–2, now looks like this:

MATERIALS LEDGER CARD

Material ___U-shaped bench legs___   Reorder Point _____300_____

Number _____B –10_____   Reorder Quantity _____500_____

DATE	REFERENCE	RECEIVED			ISSUED			BALANCE		
		UNITS	PRICE	AMOUNT	UNITS	PRICE	AMOUNT	UNITS	PRICE	AMOUNT
19x6 Jan. 1	Bal.							295	10 00	2950 00
2	P.O. 112	500	10 00	5000 00				795	10 00	7950 00
4	M.R. 701				50	10 00	500 00	745	10 00	7450 00

FIGURE 4–2
Materials Ledger Card

Job Cost Sheet

As materials are physically moved from the storeroom to the production floor, entries must be made in the accounting system to match this flow. Thus, the cost clerk's next step is to post the information from the materials requisition to the Materials section of the proper job cost sheet. The job cost sheet, Figure 4–3, shows that Materials Requisition 701 was charged to Job 118 on January 4.

JOB COST SHEET																							

Customer __Sports World__   Job # __118__
Job Description __On file__   Date Started __1–2–X6__
Quantity __100__   Date Completed _____

| MATERIALS | | | DIRECT LABOR | | | | | | | | FACTORY OVERHEAD APPLIED | | | | | | | | | | | |
DATE	REQ. NO.	AMOUNT	DATE	REF.	SHAPING HRS.	SHAPING AMOUNT	ASSEMBLING HRS.	ASSEMBLING AMOUNT	FINISHING HRS.	FINISHING AMOUNT	DATE	REF.	SHAPING HRS.	SHAPING RATE	SHAPING AMOUNT	ASSEMBLING HRS.	ASSEMBLING RATE	ASSEMBLING AMOUNT	FINISHING HRS.	FINISHING RATE	FINISHING AMOUNT
1–4	701	500 00																			

FIGURE 4–3
Job Cost Sheet (through January 4)

Factory Overhead Analysis Sheet

As we have already learned, the cost of indirect materials cannot be charged to a specific job. Instead, indirect materials are charged to the department in which they were incurred. Each department maintains a **factory overhead analysis sheet** with individual columns for the various overhead classifications. When indirect materials are requisitioned, their cost is posted from the requisition to the Indirect Materials section of the overhead analysis sheet. To illustrate this, let's assume that Materials Requisition 708 was prepared on January 5 for $125 worth of cleaning compound to be used in the Assembling Department. The factory overhead analysis sheet, Figure 4–4, shows how this cost is charged to the Assembling Department.

FACTORY OVERHEAD ANALYSIS SHEET												

Department __Assembling__   Month __January__ 19 __X6__

DATE	REF.	TOTAL	01 INDIRECT MATERIALS	02 INDIRECT LABOR	03 PAYROLL TAXES	04 DEPREC.	05 REPAIRS & MAINT.	06 INSURANCE	07 UTILITIES	08 TAXES	09 OTHER OVERHEAD ITEM	AMOUNT
Jan. 5	M.R. 708	125 00	125 00									

FIGURE 4–4
Factory Overhead Analysis Sheet

The individual factory overhead analysis sheets form a subsidiary ledger for factory overhead costs. After all posting for a month is complete, the totals of the overhead analysis sheets should equal the Factory Overhead Control account in the general ledger.

Materials Requisition Journal

LEARNING OBJECTIVE 2   From our discussion thus far, we can conclude that when materials are requisitioned, it is necessary to post to the materials ledger cards, the job cost sheets, and the factory overhead analysis sheets. It is also necessary to post the cost of materials requisitioned to the proper general ledger cost accounts. This task is greatly facilitated by the use of a special journal called the **materials requisition journal.** This journal, illustrated in Figure 4–5, summarizes the total materials requisitioned in a month and identifies the job, or department, to which the material was charged. At month-end, the totals of the columns are posted directly to the ledger accounts identified in the heading of the column.

FIGURE 4–5
Materials Requisition Journal

MATERIALS REQUISITION JOURNAL
for Month of _____ January _____ 19 _X6_   Page __3__

DATE		REQ. NO.	✔	JOB/DEPT.	WORK IN PROCESS DR. 122	FAC. OVR. CONTROL DR. 511	RAW MATERIALS CR. 121
Jan.	4	701	✔	118	50000		50000
	5	708	✔	Assemb.		12500	12500
	31	Totals	✔		3720000	140000	3860000
					(✔)	(✔)	(✔)

NOTE Remember, the cost of direct materials requisitioned is debited to the Work in Process Inventory account; the cost of indirect materials requisitioned is debited to the Factory Overhead Control account.

RETURN OF MATERIALS TO THE STOREROOM

Materials issued to production are sometimes returned to the storeroom. This may happen when too much materials are requisitioned or when the wrong materials are issued from the storeroom. Regardless of the reason, however, any return of materials to the storeroom should be accompanied by a **returned materials report.** At TurboFlex, the return materials report is prepared by the department head or job supervisor who returns the materials. A copy of the report is sent to the storeroom keeper who uses it to adjust the materials ledger card. To illustrate, let's look at Figure 4–6, which shows a report for the return of five U-shaped bench legs that had been requisitioned for Job 118.

RETURNED MATERIALS REPORT

No. *12*

Date *Jan. 5. 19X6*   Department *Assembling*

CREDIT   ACCT. *122*
         JOB   *118*
         DEPT. _____

QUANTITY	MATERIAL NO.	DESCRIPTION	UNIT PRICE	AMOUNT
5	B-10	U-shaped bench legs	10 00	50 00

REASON FOR RETURN *Over requisitioned*   AUTHORIZED BY *J.D.*

FIGURE 4–6
*Returned
Materials Report*

After the storeroom keeper checks and verifies the return, the materials ledger card is adjusted. The preferred procedure is to record the return in parentheses in the Issued section. The number of units returned is then added back and a new balance is calculated. Figure 4–7 illustrates the procedure for Material B-10.

A copy of the returned materials report is also forwarded to the cost clerk who uses it to make two entries, as follows.

1. If the returned materials are indirect, an entry is made in parentheses in the Indirect Materials column of the factory overhead analysis sheet. If, on the other hand, the returned materials are direct, an entry is made in parentheses in the Materials section of the appropriate job cost sheet, as illustrated in Figure 4–8.

MATERIALS LEDGER CARD

Material __U-shaped bench legs__   Reorder Point _____300_____

Number __B –10__   Reorder Quantity _____500_____

DATE		REFERENCE	RECEIVED			ISSUED			BALANCE		
			UNITS	PRICE	AMOUNT	UNITS	PRICE	AMOUNT	UNITS	PRICE	AMOUNT
19x6 Jan.	1	Bal.							295	10 00	2 9 50 00
	2	P.O. 112	500	10 00	5 000 00				795	10 00	7 9 50 00
	4	M.R. 701				50	10 00	5 00 00	745	10 00	7 4 50 00
	5	R.M. 12				(5)	10 00	(50 00)	750	10 00	7 5 00 00

FIGURE 4–7
Materials Ledger Card

JOB COST SHEET

Customer __Sports World__   **Job #** _____118_____
Job Description __On file__   **Date Started** __1–2–X6__
Quantity __100__   **Date Completed** _____

	MATERIALS			DIRECT LABOR								FACTORY OVERHEAD APPLIED									
DATE	REQ. NO.	AMOUNT	DATE	REF.	SHAPING HRS.	SHAPING AMOUNT	ASSEMBLING HRS.	ASSEMBLING AMOUNT	FINISHING HRS.	FINISHING AMOUNT	DATE	REF.	SHAPING HRS.	SHAPING RATE	SHAPING AMOUNT	ASSEMBLING HRS.	ASSEMBLING RATE	ASSEMBLING AMOUNT	FINISHING HRS.	FINISHING RATE	FINISHING AMOUNT
1–4	701	50000																			
1–5	RM12	(5000)																			

FIGURE 4–8
*Job Cost Sheet
(through January 5)*

2. A general journal entry is also made so that controlling accounts will reflect the return. Since this return involved direct materials, the proper entry follows.

1	Jan.	5	Raw Materials Inventory	50 00		1
2			Work in Process Inventory		50 00	2
3			Returned materials to storeroom.			3

The journal entry to record indirect materials returned to the storeroom involves a debit to the Raw Materials Inventory account and a credit to the Factory Overhead Control account. To illustrate this entry, let's assume that Returned Materials Report 13 was prepared when the Shaping Department returned two boxes of sandpaper to the storeroom. The sandpaper, which had a cost of $15 per box, was not immediately needed in the Shaping Department. The entry to record the return of indirect materials to the storeroom follows.

1	Jan.	7	Raw Materials Inventory			30 00			1
2			Factory Overhead Control				30 00		2
3			Returned materials to storeroom.						3

If a company has numerous returns of materials to the storeroom, a special journal called the **returned materials journal** can be used to save journalizing and posting time. Had TurboFlex recorded the above returns in a returned materials journal, it would appear as illustrated in Figure 4–9.

FIGURE 4–9
*Returned
Materials Journal*

RETURNED MATERIALS JOURNAL
for Month of _____ January _____ 19 _X6_   Page __2__

DATE		REPORT NO.	✔	JOB/DEPT.	WORK IN PROCESS CR. 122	FACT. OVER. CR. 511	RAW MATERIALS DR. 121
19X6							
Jan.	5	R.M. 12	✓	118	50 00		50 00
	7	R.M.13	✓	Shaping		30 00	30 00
	31	Totals	✓		6 20 00	8 0 00	7 00 00
					(✓)	(✓)	(✓)

SELF STUDY QUIZ 4–1 Rucker Corporation incurred the following transactions during March. Record transactions in general journal form.

a. Materials purchased during the month totaled $200,000.
b. Direct materials requisitioned totaled $160,000.
c. Indirect materials requisitioned totaled $14,000.
d. Direct materials returned to the storeroom from production totaled $3,200.
e. Total materials returned to vendors totaled $1,200.
f. Invoices paid during the month for materials purchases totaled $150,000 with terms of 2/10,n/30.
Answers at end of chapter.

DETERMINING THE COST OF MATERIALS ISSUED TO PRODUCTION

LEARNING OBJECTIVE 3   A very important part of materials accounting is determining the cost of materials issued to production. This can be a simple process. For example, looking back at Materials Requisition 701 (Figure 4–1) we see that 50 units of Material B-10 were requisitioned to production on January 4. When the materials ledger card for Material B-10 was pulled (Figure 4–2), it showed a beginning balance of 295 units with a cost of $10 per unit. Further, the materials purchased on January 2 had a unit cost of $10. Thus, as of January 2, the entire balance of the account (795 units) had a unit cost of $10. As a result, it was easy to assign a cost to the 50 units that were requisitioned on January 4: 50 units × $10 cost per unit = $500 raw materials charged to production.

In this example, we are able to identify the units issued to production (50 units) with their actual cost ($10 per unit). This situation does not occur often, however. In reality, most materials on hand include items purchased on different dates and at different prices. Further, like items are usually comingled in the storeroom (in order to save space). As a result, it may be difficult (or impossible) to identify an issue of materials with the actual invoice price of the materials. Consequently, another method must be used to assign a cost to materials issued to production. There are several acceptable methods available to determine the cost of materials issued to production. The more common of these methods are:

1. First-in, first-out (FIFO).
2. Last-in, first-out (LIFO).
3. Moving average.

Each of these methods assumes a **flow of costs.** That is, materials are assumed to flow in a certain way and unit costs are assigned to the materials based on this assumed flow. We should strongly stress that an assumed cost flow is a costing technique; it does not have to match the actual flow of materials through the production process.

In the following examples, we assume the use of a perpetual inventory system whereby the materials ledger card is updated each time materials are received, issued, or returned. The alternative to a perpetual inventory system is the *periodic inventory system* whereby inventory is counted and costed at the end of an accounting period. Most manufacturers operate on a perpetual system.

First-in, First-out Method (FIFO)

The **first-in, first-out (FIFO)** method assumes that materials are issued in the order in which they were acquired; that is, the earliest materials purchased are assumed to be the first materials used. The materials remaining on hand are therefore assumed to be the latest ones acquired. To illustrate how to apply the FIFO method, let us consider the following transactions related to Material B-18 (Leg support braces):

Jan. 1   Balance on hand is 1,000 units with a cost of $3.00 per unit; total cost, $3,000.

   7   Purchased 1,000 units at $3.20 each (P.O. 121); total cost, $3,200.

   12   Issued 1,200 units to production on Materials Requisition 109.

20 Purchased 1,000 units at $3.30 each (P.O. 145); total cost, $3,300.

26 Issued 900 units to production on Material Requisition 126.

29 Prepared Returned Materials Report 18 for the return of 50 units to the storeroom. These units were issued to production on January 12 (Materials Requisition 109).

Figure 4–10, Materials Ledger Card, shows these transactions relating to Material B-18 assuming a FIFO cost flow:

**MATERIALS LEDGER CARD
(FIFO)**

Material ___Leg support and braces___   Reorder Point _____1,000_____

Number _____B –18_____   Reorder Quantity _____1,000_____

DATE	REFERENCE	RECEIVED			ISSUED			BALANCE		
		UNITS	PRICE	AMOUNT	UNITS	PRICE	AMOUNT	UNITS	PRICE	AMOUNT
19X6										
Jan. 1	Bal.							1,000	3 00	3 0 0 0 00
7	P.O. 121	1,000	3 20	3 2 0 0 00				1,000 / 1,000	3 00 } / 3 20 }	6 2 0 0 00
12	R–109				1,000 / 200	3 00 / 3 20	3 6 4 0 00	800	3 20	2 5 6 0 00
20	P.O. 145	1,000	3 30	3 3 0 0 00				800 / 1,000	3 20 } / 3 30 }	5 8 6 0 00
26	R–126				800 / 100	3 20 / 3 30	2 8 9 0 00	900	3 30	2 9 7 0 00
29	R.M. 18				(50)	3 20	(1 6 0 00)	50 / 900	3 20 } / 3 30 }	3 1 3 0 00

FIGURE 4–10
Materials Ledger Card (FIFO Cost Flow)

1. The issue of 1,200 units on January 12 includes the beginning balance of the account plus 200 of the units acquired on January 7. The 1,000 beginning balance was costed out first because these units were the "first in"; thus, they are assumed to be the "first out." The additional 200 units were from the January 7 balance.

2. The issue on January 26 includes the remaining 800 units from the January 7 purchase plus 100 units from the January 20 purchase. The 800 units were costed out first because they were the oldest costs in inventory as of this date.

3. The 50 excess units returned to the storeroom on January 29 are priced at $3.20 because they relate to the issue of January 12 and are assumed to be part of the 200 batch. Since the assumed cost flow is FIFO, all 1,000 units at $3.00 are assumed used (since they were the first ones in). The job will now be correctly charged for 1,000 units at $3.00 and 150 units at $3.20—the amount that would have been charged had there not been an over requisition.

Major arguments in favor of the FIFO method are that it is easy to use and it usually parallels the actual movement of goods. Also, since the latest costs are assigned to the ending inventory, the balance sheet shows recent costs.

A major argument against FIFO is that, since the ending inventory is priced at the most recent costs, the earlier costs are assigned to cost of goods sold. As a result, the oldest costs are presented on the income statement to be matched against current revenue. In periods of rapidly rising prices, this can *understate* cost of goods sold and, thereby, *overstate* net income.

Last-in, First-out Method (LIFO)

As the name implies, the **last-in, first-out (LIFO)** method assumes that the latest materials received are assumed to be the first materials used. As a result, materials issued are costed at the most recent prices, and inventories on hand are costed at the earliest prices. In most industries, LIFO does not match the physical flow of materials. However, remember that the cost flow method chosen by a company does not have to match its actual flow of materials.

To illustrate the LIFO method, Figure 4–11, let's look again at the January transactions relating to Material B-18. This time, however, we will assume the LIFO cost flow.

MATERIALS LEDGER CARD
(LIFO)

Material __Leg support and braces__   Reorder Point __1,000__

Number __B –18__   Reorder Quantity __1,000__

DATE	REFERENCE	RECEIVED			ISSUED			BALANCE		
		UNITS	PRICE	AMOUNT	UNITS	PRICE	AMOUNT	UNITS	PRICE	AMOUNT
19X6 Jan. 1	Bal.							1,000	3 00	3 0 0 0 00
7	P.O. 121	1,000	3 20	3 2 0 0 00				1,000 1,000	3 00 } 3 20 ∫	6 2 0 0 00
12	R–109				1,000 200	3 20 3 00	3 8 0 0 00	800	3 00	2 4 0 0 00
20	P.O. 145	1,000	3 30	3 3 0 0 00				800 1,000	3 00 } 3 30 ∫	5 7 0 0 00
26	R–126				900	3 30	2 9 7 0 00	800 100	3 00 } 3 30 ∫	2 7 3 0 00
29	R.M. 18				(50)	3 00	(1 5 0 00)	50 800 100	3 00 3 00 3 30	2 8 8 0 00

FIGURE 4–11
Materials Ledger Card (LIFO Cost Flow)

1. The issue on January 12 includes the entire purchase of January 7 plus 200 units from the January 1 balance. The 1,000 units from the January 12 purchase are costed out first because they were the "last ones in"; thus, under LIFO, they are assumed to be the "first ones out."
2. The issue on January 26 includes only the purchase of January 20. The January 20 purchase (1,000 units) were the last in. Thus, the January 26 issue of 900 units was costed at the latest cost ($3.30).
3. The 50 excess units returned to the storeroom on January 29 are priced at $3.00 because they relate to the issue of January 12 and are assumed to be part of the 200 batch. Since the assumed cost flow is LIFO, all 1,000 units at $3.20 are assumed used (since they were the last in). The job will now be correctly charged for 1,000 units at $3.20 and 150 units at $3.00—the amount that would have been charged had there not been an over requisition.

The major argument in favor of LIFO is that, since the earliest costs are assigned to inventory, the latest costs are assigned to cost of goods sold. As a result, current costs are presented on the income statement and thus matched against current revenue.

LIFO tends to be popular in periods of consistently rising prices because the earlier, lower costs assigned to inventory causes a higher cost of goods sold and, thus, a lower profit figure. And, of course, a lower profit figure means lower income taxes.

The major argument against LIFO is that, since the earliest costs are assigned to inventory, the inventory figures presented on the balance sheet do not reflect the real value of the inventory. Opponents also point out that in periods of rapidly rising prices, LIFO can dramatically understate reported net income.

Moving Average Method

The **moving average** method is based on the assumption that like materials are mixed in the storeroom and it would be difficult, or impossible, to identify the materials as being from a particular purchase. Under this method, an average unit price must be calculated every time a new batch of materials is received. This average price is then used to cost all materials issued to production— until another batch is purchased. Again using our example of Material B-18, we can illustrate the moving average method, Figure 4–12.

1. Each of the 1,200 units issued on January 12 is assigned a cost of $3.10, which is an average cost determined as follows:

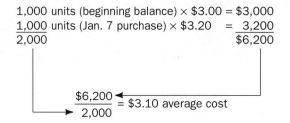

MATERIALS LEDGER CARD
(Moving Average)

Material ___Leg support and braces___   Reorder Point _____1,000_____

Number _____B–18_____   Reorder Quantity _____1,000_____

DATE		REFERENCE	RECEIVED			ISSUED			BALANCE		
			UNITS	PRICE	AMOUNT	UNITS	PRICE	AMOUNT	UNITS	PRICE	AMOUNT
19X6											
Jan.	1	Bal.							1,000	3 00	3 0 0 0 00
	7	P.O. 121	1,000	3 20	3 2 0 0 00				2,000	3 10	6 2 0 0 00
	12	R–109				1,200	3 10	3 7 2 0 00	800	3 10	2 4 8 0 00
	20	P.O. 145	1,000	3 30	3 3 0 0 00				1,800	3 21	5 7 8 0 00
	26	R–126				900	3 21	2 8 8 9 00	900	3 21	2 8 9 1 00
	29	R.M. 18				(50)	3 10	(1 5 5 00)	950	3 20	3 0 4 6 00*

*Adjusted for rounding difference, $6.00.

FIGURE 4–12
Materials Ledger Card (Moving Average Method)

2. Each of the 900 units issued on January 26 is assigned a cost of $3.21, which is an average cost calculated after the purchase on January 20 as follows:

$$\begin{array}{ll} 800 \text{ units} \times \$3.10 = \$2,480 \\ \underline{1,000} \text{ units} \times \$3.30 = \underline{\ 3,300} \\ 1,800 \qquad\qquad\quad \$5,780 \end{array}$$

$$\frac{\$5,780}{1,800} = \$3.21 \text{ average cost}$$

3. The 50 units returned to the storeroom on January 29 are assigned a unit cost of $3.10 because they are part of the January 12 issue (that were priced at $3.10). The job will not be correctly charged for 1,150 units at $3.10—the amount that would have been charged had there not been a return.

The major advantage of the moving average method is that it minimizes the effect of price fluctuations in periods in which prices are rapidly changing.

Its major disadvantage is the amount of time required to calculate a new average price each time new units are received (or a return is made to the storeroom). As manufacturing operations have become computerized, however, this disadvantage is being overcome.

NOTE 1. FIFO and LIFO may also be used with a periodic inventory system where the inventory is counted at the end of an accounting period and a cost is assigned to the goods that remain. The moving average method, however, would be replaced by the *weighted average* (or *month-end average*) method in which an average cost of an item is calculated and then multiplied by the number of units that remain.

2. In our examples in this chapter, we have applied the FIFO, LIFO and moving average methods to raw materials inventory. These methods can also be used for work in process inventory and finished goods inventory.

SELF STUDY QUIZ 4–2 The following information relates to Material 1129 (Folding leg sections):

May 1 Balance on hand, 500 units at $5.00 each.
    2 Issued 200 units to production.
    5 Received 250 units at $5.25 each.
    8 Issued 125 units to production.
  12 Issued 110 units to production.
  21 Received 250 units at $5.50 each.
  25 Issued 300 units to production.

Assuming the company maintains perpetual inventory records, calculate the cost of materials used and the cost of the May 31 inventory under each of the following methods: (a) FIFO, (b) LIFO, and (c) moving average.
Answers at end of chapter.

SELF-STUDY PROBLEM

Jackson Manufacturing Company uses a perpetual inventory system. The following information relates to one of its raw materials (bearings) for June 19X1:

June 1 Balance on hand, 500 units with a cost of $2.00 each.
    3 Issued 125 units (Materials Requisition 819).

    5   Received 250 units at $2.25 each (Purchase Order 612).
    7   Issued 125 units (Materials Requisition 851).
    9   Issued 265 units (Materials Requisition 860).
   12   Returned 10 units to the storeroom that were issued on the 9th (Returned Materials Report 18).
   15   Received 250 units at $2.50 each (Purchase Order 740).
   27   Issued 300 units (Materials Requisition 876).

Required:

1. Prepare materials ledgers cards to determine the cost of materials used and the cost of the June 30 inventory under each of the following methods: (a) FIFO, (b) LIFO, and (c) moving average.
2. Assuming the use of FIFO, record transactions in general journal form.

SOLUTION TO SELF-STUDY PROBLEM

1.

MATERIALS LEDGER CARD
(FIFO Cost Method)

DATE	REFERENCE	RECEIVED			ISSUED			BALANCE		
		UNITS	PRICE	AMOUNT	UNITS	PRICE	AMOUNT	UNITS	PRICE	AMOUNT
19X1 June 1	Bal.							500	2 00	1000 00
3	M.R. 819				125	2 00	250 00	375	2 00	750 00
5	P.O. 612	250	2 25	562 50				375 / 250	2 00 / 2 25	1312 50
7	M.R. 851				125	2 00	250 00	250 / 250	2 00 / 2 25	1062 00
9	M.R. 860				250 / 15	2 00 / 2 25	533 75	235	2 25	528 75
12	R.M. 18				(10)	2 25	(22 50)	10 / 235	2 25 / 2 25	551 25
15	P.O.740	250	2 50	625 00				10 / 235 / 250	2 25 / 2 25 / 2 50	1176 25
27	M.R. 876				10 / 235 / 55	2 25 / 2 25 / 2 50	688 75	195	2 50	487 50

MATERIALS LEDGER CARD
(LIFO Cost Method)

DATE		REFERENCE	RECEIVED			ISSUED			BALANCE		
			UNITS	PRICE	AMOUNT	UNITS	PRICE	AMOUNT	UNITS	PRICE	AMOUNT
19X1 June	1	Bal.							500	2 00	1000 00
	3	M.R. 819				125	2 00	250 00	375	2 00	750 00
	5	P.O. 612	250	2 25	562 50				375 250	2 00 2 25	1312 50
	7	M.R. 851				125	2 25	281 25	375 125	2 00 2 25	1031 25
	9	M.R. 860				125 140	2 25 2 00	561 25	235	2 00	470 00
	12	R.M. 18				(10)	2 00	(20 00)	235 10	2 00 2 00	490 00
	15	P.O.740	250	2 50	625 00				235 10 250	2 00 2 00 2 50	1115 00
	27	M.R. 876				250 10 40	2 50 2 00 2 00	725 00	195	2 00	390 00

MATERIALS LEDGER CARD
(Moving Average Cost Method)

DATE		REFERENCE	RECEIVED			ISSUED			BALANCE		
			UNITS	PRICE	AMOUNT	UNITS	PRICE	AMOUNT	UNITS	PRICE	AMOUNT
19X1 June	1	Bal.							500	2 00	1000 00
	3	M.R. 819				125	2 00	250 00	375	2 00	750 00
	5	P.O. 612	250	2 25	562 50				625	2 10	1312 50
	7	M.R. 851				125	2 10	262 50	500	2 10	1050 00
	9	M.R. 860				265	2 10	556 50	235	2 10	493 50
	12	R.M. 18				(10)	2 10	21 00	245	2 10	514 50
	15	P.O.740	250	2 50	625 00				495	2 30	1139 50*
	27	M.R. 876				300	2 30	690 00	195	2 30	449 50*

*Adjusted for rounding difference, $1.00

2.

1	June	3	Work in Process Inventory	2 5 0 00			1
2			Raw Materials Inventory		2 5 0 00		2
3		5	Raw Materials Inventory	5 6 2 50			3
4			Accounts Payable		5 6 2 50		4
5		7	Work in Process Inventory	2 5 0 00			5
6			Raw Materials Inventory		2 5 0 00		6
7		9	Work in Process Inventory	5 3 3 75			7
8			Raw Materials Inventory		5 3 3 75		8
9		12	Raw Materials Inventory	2 2 50			9
10			Work in Process Inventory		2 2 50		10
11		15	Raw Materials Inventory	6 2 5 00			11
12			Accounts Payable		6 2 5 00		12
13		27	Work in Process Inventory	6 8 8 75			13
14			Raw Materials Inventory		6 8 8 75		14

SUMMARY

Companies use definite control procedures when purchasing and storing materials. Likewise, definite controls are used when materials are taken from the storeroom and issued to production. One such control procedure limits the storeroom area to only a few authorized individuals. Another control feature requires that materials can only be withdrawn from the storeroom as a result of a properly prepared **materials requisition.** A department head or a job supervisor usually prepares the materials requisition, which is submitted to the storeroom keeper. The storeroom keeper fills the requisition, makes the necessary calculations and notations, and sends a copy to the accounting department for recording.

Each time materials are issued to production, it is necessary to update the materials ledger cards. This is done by making an entry in the Issued column of the materials ledger card, calculating a new balance, and entering the new balance in the Balance column. It is also necessary to post materials used to the proper job cost sheet (direct materials) or to the **factory overhead analysis sheet** (indirect materials).

In addition to posting the cost of materials used to the various subsidiary records, it is also necessary to post to the general ledger. To facilitate this, many companies use a special journal called the **materials requisition journal.** This journal summarizes the total materials requisitioned in a month and identifies the job, or department, to which the materials were charged. Month-end postings of column totals updates the controlling accounts located in the general ledger.

There are times when materials issued to production will be returned to the storeroom. This usually happens when too much materials are requisitioned, or when the wrong materials are removed from the storeroom. Any return of materials to the storeroom should be accompanied by a **returned materials report.** Subsidiary records must be updated to show that materials have been returned. Journal entries are also made so that general ledger controlling accounts will also show the return.

A very important part of materials accounting is determining the cost of materials issued to production. Since it is very difficult to identify materials in the storeroom with specific purchases, most companies assign a cost to materials based on an assumed **flow of costs.** The three most common cost flow methods are the **first-in, first-out (FIFO) inventory method,** the **last-in, first-out (LIFO) inventory method,** and the **moving average method.** These methods can be used with a perpetual inventory system or a periodic inventory system (except that in a periodic inventory system, the moving average method becomes the weighted average method).

Since no single inventory method is best suited to all manufacturing situations, the method chosen by a company should be the one that most accurately reflects its net income (or more advantageously states its reported net income). In periods of rising prices, LIFO tends to be popular because it results in a lower reported net income (or higher net losses) and, accordingly, lower income taxes.

SELF-STUDY TERMS

Factory Overhead Analysis Sheet. A departmentalized overhead sheet with columns for the various overhead classifications. The overhead analysis sheets form a subsidiary ledger that is summarized by the Factory Overhead Control account.

First-In, First-Out (FIFO) Inventory Method. A method of assigning a cost to materials (and ending inventory) based on the assumption that the earliest goods in are the first goods to be used (or the first goods sold if the inventory is of finished goods or merchandise).

Last-In, First-Out (LIFO) Inventory Method. A method of assigning a cost to materials (and ending inventory) based on the assumption that the latest goods in are the first goods to be used (or sold if the inventory is finished goods or merchandise).

Materials Requisition. A control device prepared by an authorized person when materials are withdrawn from the storeroom.

Materials Requisition Journal. A special journal used to record the issuances of materials to production.

Moving Average Inventory Method. A method of assigning a cost to materials (and ending inventory) based on the assumption that like units are mixed in the storeroom and that it would be difficult, or impossible, to identify an issue with a particular purchase. Instead, an average cost for materials is calculated and this average is used to assign a cost to materials until a new purchase is made (or when a return is made to the storeroom).

Returned Materials Journal. A special journal used to record the cost of materials returned from production to the storeroom.

Returned Materials Report. A report prepared when materials are returned from production to the storeroom; it shows the quantity returned, the price, and reason for the return.

QUESTIONS FOR REVIEW

1. What is a materials requisition and what purpose does it serve?
2. What is the major advantage of using a perpetual inventory system for materials?
3. How often are materials ledger cards updated?

4. What is the subsidiary ledger for materials?
5. What purpose is served by the factory overhead analysis sheet?
6. Describe the accounting treatment needed when (a) direct materials are returned to the storeroom; (b) indirect materials are returned to the storeroom.
7. Under which method of inventory costing are the materials on hand considered to be the last ones purchased?
8. Under which method of inventory costing are the materials on hand considered to be the first ones purchased?
9. When using the moving average method, when must a new unit cost be calculated?
10. What is the major argument in favor of the FIFO inventory method?
11. What is the major argument against the LIFO inventory method?
12. Explain the following statement: "Actual materials flow does not have to match cost flow."
13. The LIFO inventory method tends to be popular in periods of consistently rising prices. Why?
14. Explain how job-order costing is used by many service organizations.

NOTE Unless told otherwise in Exercises and Problems, record transactions in general journal form.

EXERCISES

4–1. Learning Objective 2. Recording Materials Transactions.
Record the following materials transactions.

a.   Purchased materials on account, $225,000.
b.   Requisitioned direct materials, $180,000.
c.   Requisitioned indirect materials, $12,000.
d.   Returned direct materials to the storeroom, $1,800.
e.   Returned indirect materials to the storeroom, $200.
f.   Paid for materials purchased on account, $200,000 less 2% discount.

4–2. Learning Objective 3. FIFO Costing.
Using FIFO and perpetual inventory costing, determine the cost of materials used and the cost of the April 30 inventory from the following information:

April 1   Balance on hand, 1,000 units with a cost of $8.00 each.
　　3   Issued 250 units.
　　4   Received 500 units at $8.50 each.
　　7   Issued 145 units.
　　11   Issued 115 units.
　　12   Returned 10 units to the storeroom (issued on the 11th).
　　15   Received 500 units at $9.00 each.
　　20   Returned 200 units to vendor from April 15 purchase.
　　27   Issued 590 units.

4–3. Learning Objective 3. Using LIFO Costing.

Using LIFO and perpetual inventory costing, determine the cost of materials used and the cost of the April 30 inventory from the information presented in Exercise 4–2.

4–4. Learning Objective 3. Moving Average Costing.

Using the moving average method, determine the cost of materials used and the cost of the April 30 inventory from the information presented in Exercise 4–2 (round unit prices to the nearest cent).

4–5. Learning Objectives 3. Computing the Cost of Materials.

Beechum Company made the following materials purchases and issues during March:

Beginning inventory:	March 1,	500 units at $1.25 each
Receipts:	March 5,	300 units at 1.30 each
	10,	400 units at 1.40 each
	25,	400 units at 1.45 each
Issues:	March 8,	580
	21,	200
	30,	125

Compute the cost of materials issued and the cost assigned to the ending inventory using a perpetual inventory system and (a) FIFO costing, (b) LIFO costing, and (c) moving average costing (round to nearest cent).

4–6. Learning Objective 3. Computing the Ending Inventory Balance and Cost Using FIFO, LIFO, and Moving Average.

Using the following information for Material 1195, 14" table leg sections, compute the number of units in ending inventory and their cost using (a) FIFO, (b) LIFO, and (c) moving average.

Beginning balance	500 units at $6.00 each
Purchase order 212	700 units at 6.25 each
Materials requisition 324	250
Materials requisition 341	318
Materials requisition 352	410
Purchase order 411	700 units at $6.50
Materials requisition 390	320
Materials requisition 401	175
Returned materials report 18 (from Materials requisition 390)	25

4–7. Learning Objective 3. Computing the Cost of Raw Materials Used.

The Ely Greer Company manufacturers toy airplanes. Selected accounts from Ely's general ledger on May 31 follow. Compute the cost of raw materials used during May.

Work in Process Inventory, May 1	$126,000
Work in Process Inventory, May 31	122,900
Raw Materials Inventory, May 1	28,200
Raw materials purchases during May	212,000
Raw Materials Inventory, May 31	27,900
Direct labor during May	180,000
Factory overhead applied to jobs during May	90,000

Finished goods inventory, May 1	$85,400
Finished goods inventory, May 31	92,800

4–8. Learning Objective 3. Computing the Cost of Goods Manufactured.

Using the information for Ely Greer Company (Exercise 4–7), compute the company's cost of goods manufactured during May.

4–9. Learning Objective 3. Computing the Cost of Goods Sold.

Using the information for Ely Greer Company (Exercise 4–7), compute the company's cost of goods sold during May.

GROUP A PROBLEMS

4–1A. Learning Objectives 2 & 3. Recording Materials Transactions.

Taylor-King Company incurred the following transactions during January:

a. Purchased materials, $190,000; terms, 2/30,n/90.
b. Issued direct materials to production, $38,900.
c. Issued indirect materials to production, $12,500.
d. Returned direct materials to the storeroom, $580.
e. Returned indirect materials to the storeroom, $235.
f. Purchased materials, $220,000; terms, 2/30,n/90.
g. Returned materials purchased in Transaction (f.) to the supplier receiving credit, $5,000.
h. Paid for the purchase in Transaction (a.), less discount.
i. Paid for the purchase in Transaction (f.), less discount.

Required:
Record these transactions dated January 31.

4–2A. Learning Objectives 2 & 3. Maintaining Materials Ledger Cards.

Charleston Equipment Company uses a perpetual inventory system for materials. The following information relates to Material 114-K during August.

August 1   Beginning balance, 2,000 units at $10.00 each.
    4   Issued 800 units (Materials Requisition 814).
  10   Received 1,200 units at $11.00 each (Purchase Order 519).
  12   Issued 1,700 units (Materials Requisition 912).
  21   Received 1,200 units at $11.50 each (Purchase Order 649).
  30   Issued 500 units (Materials Requisition 1080).

Required:
Enter the beginning balance and complete a materials ledger card for Material 114-K assuming the use of (a) FIFO, (b) LIFO, and (c) moving average.

4–3A. Learning Objective 2. Recording Materials Transactions.

Spector Products Company uses a job-order cost system. A partial list of their accounts, with balances as of October 1 follows:

Cash	$45,000
Raw Materials Inventory	34,600

Work in Process Inventory	$29,000
Accounts Payable	22,000
Factory Overhead	18,000

Spector completed the following transactions during the month:

a. Materials purchases, $38,000.
b. Direct materials requisitioned during the month, $42,000.
c. Indirect materials requisitioned during the month, $6,400.
d. Direct materials returned to storeroom during the month, $810.
e. Materials returned to vendors during the month, $760.
f. Invoices paid during the month, $36,000 less 2%.

Required:

1. Record these transactions.
2. Open T accounts, enter the beginning balance, post, and balance each T account.

4–4A. Learning Objective 3. Journalizing Materials Requisitions.

Delmar Corporation incurred the following materials transactions during June:

			Materials Requisitions	
Date	Req. No.	Use/Job	Direct Materials	Indirect Materials
1	212	Material X, Job 12	$32,000	
4	213	Material Y, Job 13	24,000	
8	214	Material X, Job 12	8,000	
9	215	Material Y, Job 13	18,000	
12	216	Factory supplies		$1,200
19	217	Material Z, Job 12	6,000	
21	218	Material Z, Job 13	4,800	
23	219	Factory supplies		670
25	220	Factory supplies		800
30	221	Material X, Job 14	36,700	

Required:
Prepare a summary entry, dated June 30, to record the cost of materials issued to production during the month.

4–5A. Learning Objective 3. Maintaining Materials Ledger Cards.

Records of Apex Company show the following purchases and issues of materials during December:

Dec. 1 Beginning balance, 3,000 units at $12.00 per unit.
    4 Issued 1,400 units; Materials Requisition 1112.
    6 Received 1,000 units at $12.50; Purchase Order 812.
    8 Issued 1,000 units; Materials Requisition 1119.
  14 Received 500 units at $13.25; Purchase Order 890.
  18 Issued 900 units; Materials Requisition 1123.
  20 Received 500 units at $13.40; Purchase Order 925.
  27 Issued 900 units.
  29 Received 1,200 units at $14.00; Purchase Order 939.

Required:

1. Prepare materials ledger cards using (a) FIFO costing, (b) LIFO costing, and (c) moving average costing.
2. Compute the cost of materials issued during December for each of the three methods.

GROUP B PROBLEMS

4–1B. Learning Objectives 2 & 3. Recording Materials Transactions.
Spencer Corporation incurred the following transactions during March:

a. Purchased materials, $225,000; terms, 2/45,n/90.
b. Issued direct materials to production, $42,000.
c. Issued indirect materials to production, $12,800.
d. Returned direct materials to the storeroom, $620.
e. Returned indirect materials to the storeroom, $316.
f. Purchased materials, $240,000; terms, 2/45,n/90.
g. Returned materials purchased in Transaction (f.) to the supplier receiving credit, $5,400.
h. Paid for the purchase in Transaction (a.), less discount.
i. Paid for the purchase in Transaction (f.), less discount.

Required:
Record these transactions dated March 31.

4–2B. Learning Objectives 2 & 3. Maintaining Materials Ledger Cards.
Chicago Equipment Company uses a perpetual inventory system for materials. The following information relates to Materials 112-G during July:

July 1   Beginning balance, 3,000 units at $12.00 each.
     5   Issued 1,800 units (Materials Requisition 312).
    10   Received 2,500 units at $12.50 each (Purchase Order 425).
    14   Issued 2,000 units (Materials Requisition 490).
    22   Received 2,500 units at $12.75 each (Purchase Order 511).
    29   Issued 1,500 units (Materials Requisition 499).

Required:
Enter the beginning balance and complete a materials ledger card for Material 112-G assuming the use of (a) FIFO, (b) LIFO, and (c) moving average.

4–3B. Learning Objective 2. Recording Materials Transactions.
Slusher Manufacturing Company uses a job-order costing system. A partial list of its accounts, with balances as of June 1, is shown below:

Cash	$60,000
Raw Materials Inventory	38,200
Work in Process Inventory	31,000
Accounts Payable	18,000
Factory Overhead Control	22,400

The following transactions were completed during the month:

a. Materials purchased on account, $40,000.
b. Direct materials requisitioned during the month, $45,600.
c. Indirect materials requisitioned during the month, $6,000.
d. Direct materials returned to storeroom during the month, $912.
e. Materials returned to vendors during the month, $800.
f. Invoices paid during the month, $45,000 less 2%.

Required:

1. Record these transactions.
2. Open T accounts, post, and balance each T account.

4–4B. Learning Objective 3. Journalizing Materials Requisitions.

Summitt Corporation incurred the following materials transactions during May:

Date	Req. No.	Use/Job	Materials Requisitions Direct Materials	Indirect Materials
1	112	Material A, Job 10	$28,000	
5	113	Material B, Job 11	22,000	
8	114	Material A, Job 10	10,000	
9	115	Material B, Job 11	12,000	
11	116	Factory supplies		$1,050
18	117	Material C, Job 10	6,000	
21	118	Material C, Job 11	4,200	
24	119	Factory supplies		982
27	120	Factory supplies		810
31	121	Material A, Job 12	32,500	

Required:

Prepare a summary entry, dated May 31, to record the cost of materials issued to production during the month.

4–5B. Learning Objective 3. Maintaining Materials Ledger Cards.

Records of CTI Corporation show the following purchases and issues of materials during October:

Oct. 1 Beginning balance, 2,000 units at $14.00 per unit.
    4 Issued 700 units; Materials Requisition 101.
    5 Received 500 units at $14.30; Purchase Order 218.
    8 Issued 500 units; Materials Requisition 121.
   14 Received 250 units at $14.40; Purchase Order 225.
   19 Issued 300 units; Materials Requisition 140.
   20 Received 250 units at $14.45; Purchase Order 235.
   28 Issued 450 units; Materials Requisition 152.
   31 Received 600 units at $14.50; Purchase Order 246.

Required:

1. Prepare materials ledger cards using (a) FIFO costing, (b) LIFO costing, and (c) moving average costing.
2. Calculate the cost of materials issued during October for each of the three methods.

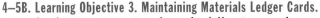

CASE FOR CRITICAL THINKING

Best-Bilt Products Company manufactures custom wood furniture. Since the company uses only one main material (wood), there is no assigned storeroom keeper. Instead, job supervisors remove necessary materials as needed and immediately make entries to update the subsidiary materials ledger. When the subsidiary computer records show that materials are near the reorder point, a purchase order is prepared. Are proper controls being followed? Explain. If not, suggest ways to improve the system.

ANSWERS TO SELF-STUDY QUIZ 4–1

1	Mar	31	Raw Materials Inventory	200 00 0 00	
2			Accounts Payable		200 0 0 0 00
3		31	Work in Process Inventory	160 00 0 00	
4			Raw Materials Inventory		160 0 0 0 00
5		31	Factory Overhead Control	14 00 0 00	
6			Raw Materials Inventory		14 0 0 0 00
7		31	Raw Materials Inventory	3 20 0 00	
8			Work in Process Inventory		3 2 0 0 00
9		31	Accounts Payable	1 20 0 00	
10			Raw Materials Inventory		1 2 0 0 00
11		31	Accounts Payable	150 00 0 00	
12			Purchases Discounts		3 0 0 0 00
13			Cash		147 0 0 0 00

ANSWERS TO SELF-STUDY QUIZ 4–2

(a) FIFO method.

May 2	Issued from the May 1 balance:	200 × $5.00 = $1,000.00
8	Issued from the May 1 balance:	125 × $5.00 = 625.00
12	Issued from the May 1 balance:	110 × $5.00 = 550.00
25	Issued 65 from the May 1 balance:	65 × $5.00 = 325.00
	Issued 235 from May 5 purchase:	235 × $5.25 = 1,233.70
Total issued to production		$3,733.70

Balance on hand:

Date of Purchase	Units on Hand	Unit Cost	Total Cost
May 5	15 (250 – 235)	$5.25	$ 78.75
21	250	5.50	1,375.00
Balance on hand			$1,453.75

(b) LIFO method.

May 2	Issued from the May 1 balance:	$200 \times \$5.00 = \$1,000.00$
8	Issued from the May 5 purchase:	$125 \times \$5.25 =$ 656.25
12	Issued from the May 5 purchase:	$110 \times \$5.25 =$ 577.50
25	Issued 250 from the May 21 purchase:	$250 \times \$5.50 =$ 1,375.00
	Issued 15 from May 5 purchase:	$15 \times \$5.25 =$ 78.75
	Issued 35 from May 1 balance:	$35 \times \$5.00 =$ 175.00

Total issued to production $3,862.50

Balance on hand:

Date of Purchase	Units on Hand	Unit Cost	Total Cost
Balance, May 1	265	$5.00	$1,325.00

(c) Moving average method.

May 2	Issued from the May 1 balance:	$200 \times \$5.00 = \$1,000.00$
8	Issued at an average cost of $5.11:	$125 \times \$5.11 =$ 638.75

$$300 \times \$5.00 = \$1,500.00$$
$$\underline{250} \times \$5.25 = \underline{\;1,312.50\;}$$
$$550 \qquad\qquad \$2,812.50$$

$$\$2,812.50 \div 550 = \$5.11$$

12	Issued at an average cost of $5.11:	$110 \times \$5.11 =$ 562.10
25	Issued at an average cost of $5.28:	$300 \times \$5.28 =$ 1,584.00

$$315 \times \$5.11 = \$1,609.65$$
$$\underline{250} \times \$5.50 = \underline{\;1,375.00\;}$$
$$565 \qquad\qquad \$2,984.65$$

$$\$2,984.65 \div 565 = \$5.28$$

Total issued to production $3,784.85

Balance on hand: 265 units (565 − 300) × $5.28 = $1,399.20

Chapter 5
Accounting for Labor

LEARNING OBJECTIVES

After studying Chapter 5, you should be able to:

1. Differentiate between direct and indirect labor costs.
2. Differentiate between clock cards and time tickets.
3. Compute gross earnings, payroll deductions, and net pay.
4. Prepare a payroll register.
5. Record the payroll.
6. Record the distribution of labor costs to production.
7. Compute and record the employer's payroll taxes.

In Chapters 3 and 4, we studied accounting procedures for materials which, in most companies, comprise a significant part of the cost of the finished product. In this chapter, we will discuss labor costs, which is also a significant cost for a manufacturing as well as a nonmanufacturing firm. In many companies, the cost of labor alone is fifty to sixty percent of all operating costs. Due to the significant amount of this expense, it is important to develop effective internal controls for all phases of the payroll process.

PAYROLL ACCOUNTING

Payroll accounting involves determining how much employees have earned during a period, and how these costs should be distributed. A law firm, for example, accumulates labor costs for each case that the firm is working on. These "billable labor hours," along with other costs such as supplies and transportation, comprise the total amount that the firm charges the client. A manufacturing firm assigns labor costs to production jobs (in a job-order costing system) or to departments (in a process costing system).

LEARNING OBJECTIVE 1

How a labor cost is assigned to production depends on whether it is classified as direct labor or indirect labor. As we learned in Chapter 1, *direct labor* represents the cost of those employees who work directly on the products being produced. By contrast, *indirect labor* consists of labor costs not directly related to the production process, or too remote or insignificant to justify the time involved in charging them to individual jobs in production during the accounting period. Examples of indirect labor costs include the salaries and wages of janitors, factory clerks, factory accountants and assistants, supervisors, and timekeepers.

The cost of direct labor is debited to the Work in Process Inventory account and recorded on the proper job cost sheet. Indirect labor costs are debited to the Factory Overhead Control account and recorded on the proper factory overhead analysis sheet. This is illustrated later. For the moment, our task is to examine how labor cost records are maintained.

LABOR COST RECORDS

At TurboFlex Corporation, maintaining labor records is the responsibility of the Timekeeping and Payroll Departments. The **Timekeeping Department** has two functions: (1) it keeps up with the total number of hours each employee works during the day and (2) it determines how the labor hours were spent so that labor costs can be charged to the proper jobs. The **Payroll Department** calculates each employee's gross earnings, payroll deductions, net amount, and issues a check for the net amount.

Timekeeping

The first step in labor costing is to accumulate a record of the time each employee actually spent working in the factory. This process is called **timekeeping.** Timekeeping provides records that are used by the Payroll Department to calculate an employee's gross earnings. From gross earnings, the proper payroll deductions are subtracted to calculate net pay. Timekeeping records are also used to determine the employer's payroll taxes.

LEARNING OBJECTIVE 2   The Timekeeping Department at TurboFlex maintains two labor records: *clock cards* and *time tickets.*

CLOCK CARDS

A **clock card** (also called a *time card*) is maintained for hourly rate employees who punch a time clock. Each card provides space for the name and number of the employee and is used to record the total amount of time the employee spends in the factory. When completed, the clock card shows the time an employee started and stopped work each day, or each work shift, during the payroll period. Figure 5–1 illustrates Sylvia Alvarado's clock card for the week ending January 6.

FIGURE 5–1
Clock Card

Employee	Alvarado, Sylvia	Dept.	Assembling
Clock No.	301	Week	Jan. 2 – 6, 19X6
Shift	1	Rate	$10

Day	Regular				Overtime		Hours	
	In	Out	In	Out	In	Out	Reg.	O.T.
Mon.	8:32	12:01	1:01	5:30			8	
Tues.	8:30	12:05	1:00	5:31			8	
Wed.	8:20	12:00	12:30	5:00			8	
Thurs.	8:30	12:00	1:00	5:30	5:30	7:30	8	2
Fri.	8:30	12:30	1:30	5:30	6:30	8:30	8	2
Sat.								
Sun.								
						Total	40	4

TurboFlex has set up each entrance to the factory as a *clock card* station with a time clock and a rack of time cards for the employees assigned to that station. Cards are placed in the rack according to the employee number, which is printed on the clock card. At the end of each day, the timekeeper collects the cards and calculates and enters the total time the employee worked that day.

TIME TICKETS

The clock card shows the total number of hours an employee works during the day. However, the clock card does not show the jobs on which the employee worked, or the specific function performed by the employee. Since labor costs must be charged to the jobs in progress, some type of record must be maintained to show how many hours an employee worked on a specific job. This is accomplished by the time ticket.

The **time ticket,** sometimes called a *job ticket,* shows the employee's name and number, the starting and stopping time on each job, the time spent on each job, the rate of pay, and the total earnings. In effect, time tickets constitute an hour-by-hour summary of the activities completed by the employee during the course of the day. Figure 5–2 illustrates a time ticket.

FIGURE 5–2
Time Ticket

Employee	Day, Samuel	Type of work	Covering
Shift	1	Units completed	3
Job	118	Date	Jan. 3, 19X6

Time Started	Time Stopped	Hours Worked	Rate	Amount
7:30	10:30	3	$10	$30

Approved by ___*B.T.*___

At TurboFlex, the job supervisor prepares time tickets and employees sign them. Each morning, after all employees have clocked in, the timekeeper collects the previous day's time tickets from the job supervisors. The timekeeper then compares the total time reported on each time ticket with the total hours of each employee's clock card. The total time worked, as shown on the employee's clock card, should correspond with the time reported on the time tickets. If there is a difference, it is investigated immediately. If the clock card shows more hours than the time tickets, it is reported as **idle time.**

Some idle time is bound to occur even in a well-managed plant, because it is impossible to convert all direct labor hours into productive time. Employees cannot move from job to job without losing some time in between. Additionally, there are other common causes of idle time, such as machine breakdowns, minor accidents, power failures, and materials shortages.

While idle time is considered an unavoidable cost of production, it must be kept within acceptable limits. Without proper controls, idle time can become excessive and thus increase the cost of finished goods. Generally, the cost of idle time *is not* absorbed as a direct labor cost, even though direct labor employees are involved. Instead, idle time is recorded as factory overhead. Managers believe that idle time should be spread over all jobs in production during the period, not just the jobs that happened to be in production when the idle time occurred.

After the clock cards and the time tickets have been compared, the clock cards are returned to the racks and the time tickets are sent on to the Payroll Department. The employee's pay rate is entered on each time ticket and the amount of direct labor to charge each job is calculated. The time tickets are then sent to the Accounting Department and used as source documents to post the cost of direct labor to individual jobs.

Time tickets are used only for direct labor employees. Since indirect labor is not traceable to a particular job, these costs are allocated to overhead using predetermined overhead rates.

DAILY TIME REPORT

In a large manufacturing firm, the use of individual time tickets could result in many time tickets to keep up with—because a new time ticket must be filled out for each job an employee works on during the day. To overcome this problem, some firms use a **daily time report** on which the employee lists all the jobs worked on during the day. After approval by the supervisor, the report is sent to the Payroll Department where the employee's earnings are calculated.

PAYROLL PROCEDURES

Before discussing how TurboFlex processes payroll information, let's review the functions of the Timekeeping Department:

1. Collects clock cards daily, calculates and enters the hours worked by each employee, and returns cards to the racks.
2. Collects time tickets daily and compares the hours shown on the clock cards with those reported on the time tickets.
3. Investigates discrepancies between clock cards and time tickets.
4. Forwards time tickets to the Payroll Department.

The Payroll Department uses the information provided by Timekeeping to complete the payroll process, which involves preparing a weekly payroll register and posting information from the payroll register to each employee's individual earnings record.

Payroll Register

LEARNING OBJECTIVES 3, 4 The **payroll register** is a summary of the gross earnings, payroll deductions, and net pay for all employees for a specific payroll period. The design of the payroll register depends on the number of employees and the method of processing payroll data. TurboFlex transfers the number of hours worked each day by hourly rate employees to the weekly payroll register. At the end of the week, regular earnings, overtime earnings, and total earnings are calculated and entered on the payroll register. The payroll register is then completed by calculating the appropriate deductions, entering the deductions in the proper columns, and calculating the net pay of each employee. This is illustrated in Figure 5–3.

Add Rate

(Left side)

PAYROLL REGISTER FOR PAY PERIOD ENDING Jan. 6, 19X6

Dept.	Name	Status	Tot. Hrs.	Regular Earnings	Overtime Premium	Total Earnings
A	Alvarado, Sylvia	M–2	44	440 00	20 00	460 00
S	Bailey, Bruce	S–1	42	420 00	10 00	430 00
F	Day, Samuel	M–1	40	480 00	—	480 00
M	Franks, Alicia	S–1	40	320 00	—	320 00
GF	Hamer, Grady	M–3	41	369 00	4 50	373 50
	Totals			9 520 00	45 50	9 975 00

(Right side)

FICA OASDI	FICA HIP	Federal Income Tax	State Income Tax	Medical Insurance	Savings Bonds	Union Dues	Total	Ck #	Net Amount	DIRECT LABOR	INDIRECT LABOR
28 52	6 67	39 00	21 60	28 00	25 00	—	148 79	141	311 21	440 00	20 00
26 66	6 24	52 00	23 65	28 00	—	5 00	141 55	142	288 45	420 00	10 00
29 76	6 96	49 00	23 04	28 00	25 00	5 00	166 76	143	313 24	480 00	—
19 84	4 64	35 00	18 56	28 00	—	—	106 04	144	213 96		320 00
23 16	5 42	19 00	14 94	28 00	—	5 00	95 52	145	277 98		373 50
61 845	14 464	154 612	70 823	33 600	20 000	4 500	359 844		637 656	831 300	166 200

FIGURE 5–3
Payroll Register

Overtime Premium

Employees who receive an hourly wage are generally covered by the Fair Labor Standards Act, which establishes standards for minimum wages and overtime pay. **Overtime pay** means that an employee who works more than 40 hours in a week must be paid *at least* 1½ the regular wage rate for all hours worked in excess of 40. Thus, overtime pay is often referred to as *time and a half*. Some companies pay double or triple time for work on Saturdays, Sundays, and holidays. Manufacturing firms, and some nonmanufacturing firms, usually pay overtime if an employee works more than eight hours in a day, even if total hours for the week do not exceed 40.

As we can see from the payroll register in Figure 5–3, gross earnings are divided into two parts: *regular earnings* and *overtime premium*. Regular earnings are calculated by multiplying the *total hours* worked by the *regular* pay rate. The overtime premium is calculated by multiplying the *overtime hours* (hours over 40) by the *overtime premium rate*. The overtime premium rate is determined by multiplying the regular hourly rate by 50% (one-half time). As an example, Sylvia Alvarado worked 44 hours during the week ending January 6. Her gross earnings are calculated as follows:

Regular earnings (44 hours × $10)	$440.00
Overtime premium [4 hours × $5 ($10 × .50)]	20.00
Gross earnings	$460.00

The total factory wages for all hours at the regular rate are recorded as a direct labor cost in the Work in Process Inventory account. However, the overtime premium is not recorded as a direct labor cost. It is, instead, recorded as factory overhead and thus spread over all jobs in production during the period. This may seem strange since all overtime is spent working on specific jobs. So, why not charge a specific job for the overtime spent on that job? The reason is that production is usually scheduled on a random basis—companies produce when they have orders from customers, and sometimes the orders cannot be filled by working the usual eight-hour day. Since production is randomly scheduled, it would not be logical to charge overtime premiums to a particular job, or jobs, simply because it happened to be in production when overtime was needed.

SELF-STUDY QUIZ 5–1 Randall Ward worked 45 hours last week at a rate of $8.00 an hour. Calculate his regular earnings and overtime premium if his employer paid 1½ times his regular rate for hours over 40.
Answers at end of chapter.

Payroll Deductions

The amount actually paid to employees (net pay) rarely equals the amount of gross earnings because employers must withhold amounts from employees' earnings. The federal government requires employers to withhold *social security taxes* and *federal income taxes*. Most state governments (and a few local governments) also require withholding for state or local income taxes. In some cases, taxes may also be withheld to provide funds for unemployment benefits or disability income; however, the employer usually pays these taxes on behalf of the employee.

In addition to the required deductions mentioned above, employers often agree to make withholdings for the benefit of employees—such as amounts for insurance premiums, charities, savings bonds, pension plans, work uniforms, union dues, and various other purposes. In order for an employer to make deductions of this type, there must be a written agreement between the employer and employee.

TurboFlex withholds amounts for social security, federal and state income taxes, medical insurance, savings bonds, and union dues.

SOCIAL SECURITY

Most workers in the Unites States are covered by the **Federal Insurance Contributions Act (FICA)**, commonly known as social security. FICA taxes are used to finance (1) the federal *Old-Age, Survivors, and Disability Insurance program* (OASDI) and (2) *the Hospital Insurance Plan* (HIP), or *Medicare*. The FICA tax is a matching tax; thus, both the employee and the employer contribute equal amounts.

Under the Social Security Act, as amended, separate tax rates are used to calculate OASDI and HIP. At the time of this writing, the OASDI rate is 6.2% of the first $60,200 earned by an employee during the year. Should an employee exceed this taxable base, no additional OASDI taxes will be withheld for the remainder of the year. The HIP rate is 1.45% of all earnings (no annual limit). Looking at the payroll register in Figure 5–3, we see that no employee has reached or exceeded the OASDI taxable base for the first payroll of the year. Therefore, both OASDI and HIP are withheld from the pay of all employees. This means that Sylvia Alvarado will pay $28.52 ($460 × 6.2%) in OASDI taxes and $6.67 ($460 × 1.45%) in HIP taxes.

SELF-STUDY QUIZ 5–2 For the pay period ending February 5, O'Malley Company had a total payroll of $680,000. No employee reached or exceeded the OASDI taxable base. Calculate the total FICA tax to be withheld.
Answers at end of chapter.

FEDERAL INCOME TAXES

Unless specifically exempted, all income (legal and illegal) earned by an individual is subject to the federal personal income tax. This tax, which is usually found by referring to government-issued tables, is based on an employee's gross earnings, marital status, and the number of withholding allowances (or exemptions) claimed. As we can see from the payroll register in Figure 5–3, Sylvia Alvarado's status is M-2, which means that she is married and claiming two withholding allowances. Based on Sylvia's filing status (and her earnings of $460) the payroll clerk used tax tables supplied by the Internal Revenue Service to determine a federal income tax deduction of $39.

STATE INCOME TAXES

TurboFlex is located in Arizona, one of the many states that levy a state income tax. Arizona, like the federal government, provides tax tables that can be used to determine income taxes. Sylvia's state income tax deduction is $21.60.

MEDICAL INSURANCE, SAVINGS BONDS, AND UNION DUES

TurboFlex has a contract with a private insurance company to provide medical insurance for all full-time employees. The weekly cost of the coverage is $28 for all participating employees. TurboFlex also participates in the payroll deduction plan for U.S. savings bonds. Each employee has informed the Payroll Department in writing how much to deduct each pay period to go toward the purchase of savings bonds. Sylvia has $25 each week withheld. Additionally, some employees have requested that union dues be withheld each pay period.

Semi-monthly Salaried Employees

The majority of TurboFlex's employees are paid weekly and their earnings are thus recorded in the weekly payroll register. However, a few salaried employees are paid semi-monthly on the fifteenth and last day of the month. Salaried employees include inspectors, factory supervisors, managers, factory office personnel, and the head of the Maintenance Department. A separate payroll register is prepared for these employees—because their payroll period is different and they do not work directly in the production process. The payroll register prepared for salaried employees is similar to the one prepared for hourly wage employees. All earnings of salaried employees are recorded as indirect labor.

Employee's Earnings Record

Employers must maintain a record of earnings and deductions for each employee. Consequently, a separate **employee's earnings record** is maintained for each employee. The information for this record is taken from the weekly payroll registers. The employee's earnings record is summarized at the end of each quarter and at the end of the year. The year-end totals are used to prepare the employee's Form W-2 (Wage and Tax Statement), which is required by federal and state law. Sylvia Alvarado's individual earnings record for 19X5 is shown in Figure 5–4.

NAME OF EMPLOYEE	Alvarado, Sylvia			SOCIAL SECURITY NUMBER	420–38–6372	

ADDRESS 212 Ashwood Ct.

CITY OR TOWN Glendale, AZ 85302

DATE OF BIRTH	MARRIED ☒ OR SINGLE ☐	NUMBER OF EXEMPTIONS	PHONE NO.	CLOCK NO.
3-18-63		2		301

POSITION	RATE	DATE	DATE STARTED	DATE TERMINATED
Cutter	$10.00/HR	1-2-X5	5-7-X2	

REMARKS

REASON

FOURTH QUARTER 19X5

WEEK	HOURS WORKED REG.	HOURS WORKED OVER-TIME	TOTAL EARNINGS	FICA TAX	FEDERAL TAX	STATE TAX	MEDICAL INSUR-ANCE	SAVINGS BONDS	UNION DUES	NET PAY	GROSS EARNINGS YEAR TO DATE
40	40	—	360 00	27 54	24 00	21 24	15 00	10 00	5 00	257 22	14,235 00
41	40	2	387 00	29 61	27 00	22 83	15 00	10 00	5 00	277 56	14,622 00
Quarter Totals			4,940 00	377 91	361 40	249 00	195 00	130 00	65 00	3,561 69	23,400 00
Yearly Totals			23,400 00	1,743 00	1,812 00	1,092 00	1,456 00	560 00	260 00	16,477 00	23,400 00

FIGURE 5–4
Employee's Earnings Record

RECORDING THE PAYROLL

LEARNING OBJECTIVE 5

The payroll register is used as a source document to record the weekly payroll. Using the payroll register in Figure 5–3, the following journal entry (A) records TurboFlex's payroll for the week ending January 6.

(A)

1	Jan.	6	Factory Payroll Clearing	9 9 7 5 00		1
2			FICA Taxes Payable—OASDI		6 1 8 45	2
3			FICA Taxes Payable—HIP		1 4 4 64	3
4			Federal Income Taxes Payable		1 5 4 6 12	4
5			State Income Taxes Payable		7 0 8 23	5
6			Medical Insurance Payable		3 3 6 00	6
7			Savings Bonds Payable		2 0 0 00	7
8			Union Dues Payable		4 5 00	8
9			Salaries and Wages Payable		6 3 7 6 56	9
10			Recorded weekly factory payroll.			10

Notice that the total earnings for the period is debited to the Factory Payroll Clearing account. You will remember from Chapter 2 that Factory Payroll Clearing is a holding account in which the payroll is recorded in order to give the Accounting Department time to analyze the payroll to determine what part is direct labor and what part is indirect labor. Also notice that each amount withheld is credited to an appropriate liability account. After paying these amounts to the appropriate agencies, the related liability account will be debited, and the Cash account will be credited.

SELF-STUDY QUIZ 5–3 Using the data shown below, prepare the general journal entry to record the factory payroll of Carbondale Manufacturers for the week ending August 15:

Total gross earnings	$98,200.00
FICA-OASDI withheld	7,512.30
FICA-HIP withheld	1,423.90
Federal income taxes withheld	26,490.00
State income taxes withheld	8,245.60
Group insurance withheld	3,600.00

Answer at end of chapter.

PAYING THE PAYROLL

TurboFlex maintains a special checking account just for the payroll. At the end of each pay period, a check for the net amount of the payroll is written on the company's regular checking account. This check is then deposited in the special checking account. When all checks have been cashed by the employees, the payroll account will have a zero balance. This practice makes it easier to reconcile both the regular checking account and the payroll account.

The checks issued to employees on January 6 will, of course, equal the net amount of the payroll for the period. The following entry is made to record the payment:

(B)

1	Jan.	6	Salaries and Wages Payable		6 3 7 6 56		1
2			Cash			6 3 7 6 56	2
3			Paid Jan. 6 payroll.				3

SELF-STUDY QUIZ 5–4 Using the payroll data from Self-Study Quiz 5–3, record the payment of the payroll.
Answers at end of chapter.

TIME TICKET ANALYSIS

Each week an analysis of the time tickets must be made so that the direct labor costs recorded on the time tickets can be posted to the proper job cost sheets. The **time ticket analysis (TTA)** shows the direct labor costs incurred on each job by each department and the total number of direct labor hours that each department worked on a particular job. The amount of indirect labor for the payroll period is also recorded on the TTA to show the total labor cost for the payroll period. Figure 5–5 illustrates the TTA for the week ending January 6. Notice that the total labor cost equals the total of the total earnings column of the payroll register for the period (Figure 5–3).

TIME TICKET ANALYSIS FOR PAY PERIOD ENDING   Jan. 6, 19X6

Direct Labor:	Shaping Department		Assembling Department		Finishing Department		Mainten. Dept.	Gen. Fac. Dept.	Total	Total Labor Cost
	Hours	Amount	Hours	Amount	Hours	Amount	Amount	Amount	Amount	Amount
Job 115	–0–	–0–	–0–	–0–	125	92500	—	—	92500	
116	–0–	–0–	30	21500	112	79500	—	—	101000	
117	180	133200	195	138743	38	27057	—	—	299000	
118	50	61200	180	162000	–0–	–0–	—	—	223200	
119	90	81600	–0–	–0–	–0–	–0–	—	—	81600	
120	–0–	–0–	35	34000	–0–	–0–	—	—	34000	
	320	276000	440	356243	275	199057			831300	
Indirect Labor:		20200		19500		10500	47000	69000	166200	
										997500

FIGURE 5–5
*Time Ticket
Analysis*

The TTA is used as a source document to update the job cost sheets and the *factory overhead analysis sheets.* To illustrate, the job cost sheet for Job 118 and the factory overhead analysis sheet for the Assembling Department, Figures 5–6 and 5–7, appear as follows after posting the information on the TTA for the Janaury 6 payroll.

JOB COST SHEET

Customer ___Sports World___   Job # ___118___
Job Description ___On file___   Date Started ___1–2–X6___
Quantity ___18___   Date Completed _____

| MATERIALS | | | DIRECT LABOR | | | | | | | | FACTORY OVERHEAD APPLIED | | | | | | | | | | | |
| | | | | | SHAPING | | ASSEMBLING | | FINISHING | | | | SHAPING | | | ASSEMBLING | | | FINISHING | | |
DATE	REQ. NO.	AMOUNT	DATE	REF.	HRS.	AMOUNT	HRS.	AMOUNT	HRS.	AMOUNT	DATE	REF.	HRS.	RATE	AMOUNT	HRS.	RATE	AMOUNT	HRS.	RATE	AMOUNT
1–4	701	500 00	1–6	TTA	50	6 12 00	180	16 20 00	—												
1–5	RM 12	(50 00)																			

FIGURE 5–6
Job Cost Sheet

FACTORY OVERHEAD ANALYSIS SHEET

Department ___Assembling___   Month ___January___ 19 _X6_

| DATE | REF. | TOTAL | 01 INDIRECT MATERIALS | 02 INDIRECT LABOR | 03 PAYROLL TAXES | 04 DEPREC. | 05 REPAIRS & MAINT. | 06 INSURANCE | 07 UTILITIES | 08 TAXES | 09 OTHER OVERHEAD | |
											ITEM	AMOUNT
Jan. 5	M.R. 708	125 00	125 00									
6	TTA			195 00								

FIGURE 5–7
Factory Overhead Analysis Sheet— Assembling Department

Analysis of Semi-monthly Factory Payroll

The semi-monthly payroll must also be analyzed so that the earnings of salaried employees can be posted to the appropriate factory overhead analysis sheet. The earnings of salaried employees are classified as indirect labor since they do not work directly in the production process. With the exception of the head of the Maintenance Department, all salaried employees work in the General Factory Services Department. TurboFlex's analysis of semi-monthly payroll for the period ended January 15, 19X6 follows:

TurboFlex Corporation
Analysis of Semimonthly Factory Payroll
For Pay Period Ending January 15, 19X6

Department	Indirect Labor
Maintenance	$ 810.00
General Factory Services	1,850.00
Total	$2,660.00

These indirect labor costs must now be posted to the factory overhead analysis sheets for the Maintenance Department and the General Factory Services Department, Figures 5–8 and 5–9.

FACTORY OVERHEAD ANALYSIS SHEET

Department __Maintenance__   Month _____January_____   19 _X6_

DATE	REF.	TOTAL	01 INDIRECT MATERIALS	02 INDIRECT LABOR	03 PAYROLL TAXES	04 DEPREC.	05 REPAIRS & MAINT.	06 INSURANCE	07 UTILITIES	08 TAXES	09 OTHER OVERHEAD ITEM	AMOUNT
Jan. 6	TTA	47000		47000								
15	SP	81000		81000								

FIGURE 5–8
Factory Overhead
Analysis Sheet—
Maintenance
Department

FACTORY OVERHEAD ANALYSIS SHEET

Department __General Factory Services__   Month _____January_____   19 _X6_

DATE	REF.	TOTAL	01 INDIRECT MATERIALS	02 INDIRECT LABOR	03 PAYROLL TAXES	04 DEPREC.	05 REPAIRS & MAINT.	06 INSURANCE	07 UTILITIES	08 TAXES	09 OTHER OVERHEAD ITEM	AMOUNT
Jan. 6	TTA	69000		69000								
15	SP	185000		185000								

FIGURE 5–9
Factory Overhead
Analysis Sheet—
General Factory
Services Department

Notice that the factory overhead analysis sheets for these departments show indirect labor costs from both the weekly payrolls (TTA) and the semi-monthly payrolls (SP). This is because some employees in these departments are paid an hourly wage while others are paid a semi-monthly salary.

CHARGING LABOR COSTS TO PRODUCTION

LEARNING OBJECTIVE 6

In the preceding section, we mentioned that direct labor costs are posted to the job cost sheets throughout the month, and indirect labor costs are posted to the factory overhead analysis sheets throughout the month. At month-end, total labor costs must also be posted to the general ledger. To do this, a summary of all factory wages earned during the month is prepared. This summary consists of the total of the weekly time analyses and the total of the semi-monthly payroll analyses. The *summary of factory earnings* is then used as a source document to charge labor costs to production. For example, Figure 5–10 shows TurboFlex's January, 19X6 summary of factory earnings.

SUMMARY OF FACTORY EARNINGS FOR MONTH OF ___ Jan. 19X6 ___

PAYROLL PERIOD	SHAPING DEPARTMENT DIRECT LABOR	INDIRECT LABOR	ASSEMBLING DEPARTMENT DIRECT LABOR	INDIRECT LABOR	FINISHING DEPARTMENT DIRECT LABOR	INDIRECT LABOR	MAINTEN.	GENERAL FACTORY	TOTAL
January 2–6	2760 00	202 00	3562 43	195 00	1990 57	105 00	470 00	690 00	9975 00
9–13	2945 00	218 00	2672 20	175 00	2147 80	126 00	525 00	850 00	9659 00
Semi-monthly 1–15	—0—	—0—	—0—	—0—	—0—	—0—	810 00	1850 00	2660 00
16–20	3242 00	224 00	2815 00	201 00	2415 00	130 00	515 00	825 00	10367 00
23–27	2710 00	190 00	2725 00	192 00	2018 00	117 00	522 50	830 00	9304 50
Semi-monthly 16–31	—0—	—0—	—0—	—0—	—0—	—0—	826 00	1948 00	2774 00
30–31	1210 00	58 00	1540 00	90 00	895 00	61 50	422 00	612 00	4888 50
Totals	12867 00	892 00	13314 63	853 00	9466 37	539 50	4090 50	7605 00	49628 00
Summary:									
Direct Labor	35648 00								
Indirect Labor	13980 00								
Total	49628 00								

FIGURE 5–10
Summary of Factory Earnings

The summary of factory earnings for January shows total direct labor costs of $35,648 and total indirect labor costs of $13,980. The following general journal entry (C) charges these amounts to production.

(C)

1	Jan.	31	Work in Process Inventory		35648 00		1
2			Factory Overhead Control		13980 00		2
3			Factory Payroll Clearing			49628 00	3
4			Charged labor to production.				4

After posting this entry, the Factory Payroll Clearing account appears as follows:

ACCOUNT Factory Payroll Clearing   **ACCOUNT NO.** 510

DATE		ITEM	P.R.	DEBIT	CREDIT	BALANCE DEBIT	BALANCE CREDIT
19X6 Jan.	6		WP	9975 00		9975 00	
	13		WP	9659 00		19634 00	
	15		SP	2660 00		22294 00	
	20		WP	10367 00		32661 00	
	27		WP	9304 50		41965 50	
	31		SP	2774 00		44739 50	
	31		J-8		49628 00		4888 50

The debits to Factory Payroll Clearing represents the gross amounts of wages paid during the month ($44,739.50); the credit represents the amount of labor charged to production during the month ($49,628).

At first glance, it would seem that the two amounts should be the same, that is, the amount factory employees were paid during the month should be the same as the amount of labor that was charged to production. However, the two amounts are not the same and the result is a $4,888.50 credit balance in the account.

This balance represents the amount of factory wages earned, and charged to production, but unpaid on January 31. This happened because the last weekly payroll period ended on Friday, January 27—two working days before the end of the month. During these two days (Monday, January 30 and Tuesday, January 31), employees were working and filling out time tickets. However, the wages earned will not be recorded on the payroll register until the next regular payday, which is on Friday, February 3. Consequently, wages for these two days have been earned, and recorded on the time tickets, but not yet paid.

TurboFlex reports the balance of the Factory Payroll Clearing account on the January 31 balance sheet as *Salaries and Wages Payable,* a current liability. When recording the February 3 payroll, the total amount of the payroll ($10,275) is debited to the Factory Payroll Clearing account, which then appears as follows:

ACCOUNT Factory Payroll Clearing					ACCOUNT NO. 510		
DATE	ITEM	P.R.	DEBIT	CREDIT	BALANCE		
					DEBIT	CREDIT	
19X6 Feb. 1	Balance	✔				4 888 50	
3		WP	10 275 00		5 386 50		

The balance of Factory Overhead Clearing is now $5,386.50, which represents wages earned on February 1, 2, and 3. This amount, along with other labor costs incurred during February, will be charged to production at the end of February.

NOTE Some accountants prefer not to report the balance of Factory Overhead Clearing as a current liability on the balance sheet. Instead, an adjusting entry is made debiting Factory Overhead Clearing and crediting Salaries and Wages Payable. The balance of Salaries and Wages Payable would then be debited when the next regular payroll is recorded.

SELF-STUDY QUIZ 5–5 Make a general journal entry for Thompson Company to distribute the following wages earned during October: direct labor, $156,700; indirect labor, $25,400.
Answers at end of chapter.

EMPLOYER'S PAYROLL TAXES

LEARNING OBJECTIVE 7   All employers must pay certain taxes to federal and state authorities on behalf of employees. The three payroll taxes imposed on employers are FICA (both OASDI and HIP), Federal Unemployment Tax (FUTA), and State Unemployment Tax (SUTA).

FICA Tax

FICA is a matching tax paid by both the employee and the employers. Thus, the FICA tax paid by the employer is the same as that paid by the employees. Accordingly, TurboFlex's FICA tax from the Janaury 6, 19X6 payroll is:

OASDI	$618.45
HIP	144.64
Total	$763.09

FUTA Tax

The **Federal Unemployment Tax Act (FUTA)** requires employers to pay taxes to provide benefits for unemployed workers. Unlike FICA, the FUTA tax is paid only by the employers; it cannot be withheld from the earnings of employees. The current FUTA rate is 6.2% of the first $7,000 of wages paid to each employee during the calendar year. However, a credit of up to 5.4% may be taken by the employer for timely contributions to state unemployment funds. And since all states have unemployment funds, this leaves an effective FUTA rate of only 0.8% (6.2% – 5.4%).

To calculate TurboFlex's FUTA tax for the payroll of January 6, refer back to the payroll register in Figure 5–3. Look at the total of the Total Earnings column in the Earnings section. This total, $9,975, is the amount of earnings this pay period subject to FUTA. (All earnings this pay period are subject to FUTA because this is the first payroll of the year and no employee has reached or exceeded $7,000.) We thus multiply this amount by the effective FUTA rate of .8% (.008):

$9,975 × .008 = $79.80

SUTA Tax

All states, and the District of Columbia, have passed unemployment compensation laws that, along with FUTA, provide benefits to qualified unemployed workers. State unemployment taxes are usually referred to as SUTA (**State Unemployment Tax Act**).

The taxable base for SUTA taxes varies from state to state. For our purposes, we will assume that the taxable base for SUTA is the first $7,000 of earnings by each employee in a calendar year. The SUTA rate also varies from state to state. Most states have a *merit-rating system* that provides a lower rate as an incentive for employers to stabilize employment. Under this system, employers who have had few layoffs can pay considerably less than the maximum rate. For TurboFlex Corporation, we will assume a SUTA rate of 2.7% (.027). Thus, TurboFlex calculated SUTA tax for the January 6 payroll as follows:

$9,975 × .027 = $269.33

Recording Employer's Payroll Taxes

Since payroll taxes must be paid on both direct labor and indirect labor employees, it would seem logical to charge the payroll taxes to these categories of labor cost. This, however, is usually not practical due to the time and expense such an allocation would require. Consequently, payroll taxes on all factory employees are usually recorded as factory overhead. Accordingly, TurboFlex made the following journal entry (D) to record payroll taxes related to the January 6 payroll.

(D)

1	Jan.	5	Factory Overhead Control	1 1 1 2 22		1
2			FICA Taxes Payable—OASDI		6 1 8 45	2
3			FICA Taxes Payable—HIP		1 4 4 64	3
4			FUTA Taxes Payable		7 9 80	4
5			SUTA Taxes Payable		2 6 9 33	5
6			Incurred employer payroll taxes.			6

SELF-STUDY QUIZ 5–6 Using the following data, calculate and record the employer's payroll taxes for Jaurez Company for March. (All earnings are subject to the various rates.)

Gross earnings $235,600
Taxable wages for FICA—OASDI $204,300
Taxable wages for FICA—HIP   235,600
FICA—OASDI rate 6.2%
FICA—HIP rate 1.45%
FUTA rate 0.8%
SUTA rate 2.7%

Answers at end of chapter.

FRINGE BENEFIT COSTS

The term *labor cost* no longer refers to just wages paid to employees. In recent years, there has been a tremendous growth in the amount of expenditures made by the employer on behalf of employees. These **fringe benefits costs** increase the employer's overall labor costs and include the costs of insurance programs, sick pay, retirement plans, supplemental unemployment insurance benefits, vacation and holiday pay, wellness programs, and day-care services.

Classifying fringe benefit costs is not as straightforward as overtime premiums and idle time. (Remember, accountants normally agree that these costs should be classified as factory overhead and thus spread over all jobs in production during the period.) Many firms make no attempt to trace fringe benefit costs to specific jobs; instead, they treat all such costs as indirect labor and record them as factory overhead. Other firms treat the part of fringe benefit costs that relate to direct labor as additional direct labor cost. In theory, this approach is superior because fringe benefits provided to direct labor employees clearly added to the cost of their services.

DIRECT LABOR AND AUTOMATION

Earlier in the chapter, we mentioned that the cost of labor is significant in most firms. This is a historical fact, especially in countries such as the United States and Germany. However, we should mention that, due to automation, major shifts are taking place in the structure of labor in some industries. Direct labor has decreased in importance in companies where workers have been replaced with robots and other automated equipment. In a few highly automated plants, direct labor has even disappeared as a separate element of production cost. For the rest of this book, we will continue to recognize direct labor as a separate and distinct cost of production—because the majority of companies worldwide are still very dependent on the input of direct labor employees.

SELF-STUDY PROBLEM

The following factory payroll data relate to Bay County Products Company for March:

EARNINGS:

Regular earnings	$245,000
Overtime premium	45,000
Gross earnings	$290,000

TAXABLE EARNINGS:

FICA—OASDI	$278,000
FICA—HIP	290,000
FUTA	25,000
SUTA	25,000

TAX RATES:

Federal income tax rate (assumed)	15%
FICA—OASDI rate	6.2%
FICA—HIP rate	1.45%
FUTA	0.8%
SUTA	3%

LABOR ALLOCATION:

Direct labor	$270,000
Indirect labor	30,000

OPTIONAL DEDUCTIONS:

U.S. Savings Bonds	$12,400
Medical Insurance	9,250
Union Dues	3,600

Required:

Prepare general journal entries dated March 31 to record the following:

1. Payroll.
2. Payment of the payroll.
3. Distribution of the payroll to production.
4. Employer's payroll taxes.

SOLUTION TO SELF-STUDY PROBLEM

1.

1	Mar.	31	Factory Payroll Clearing	290 000 00		1
2			FICA Taxes Payable—OASDI		17 236 00	2
3			FICA Taxes Payable—HIP		4 205 00	3
4			Federal Income Tax Payable		43 500 00	4
5			U.S. Savings Bonds Payable		12 400 00	5
6			Medical Insurance Payable		9 250 00	6
7			Union Dues Payable		3 600 00	7
8			Salaries and Wages Payable		199 809 00	8
9			Incurred payroll for March.			9

2.

	31	Salaries and Wages Payable	199 8 0 9 00		1
2		Cash		199 8 0 9 00	2
3		Paid payroll.			3

3.

1	31	Work in Process Inventory	270 0 0 0 00		1
2		Factory Overhead Control	30 0 0 0 00		2
3		Factory Payroll Clearing		300 0 0 0 00	3
4		Distributed labor to production.			4

4.

1	31	Factory Overhead Control	22 3 9 1 00		1
2		FICA Taxes Payable—OASDI		17 2 3 6 00	2
3		FICA Taxes Payable—HIP		4 2 0 5 00	3
4		FUTA Taxes Payable		2 0 0 00	4
5		SUTA Taxes Payable		7 5 0 00	5
6		Incurred employer payroll taxes.			6

SUMMARY

In manufacturing, the cost of labor, usually a significant cost of operating any business, is sometimes the single largest production cost. As a consequence, it is important to develop effective internal controls during all phases of the payroll process.

Payroll accounting involves more than just determining how much employees have earned during a period; these earnings must also be distributed to the operating units of a business. In a manufacturing firm, labor costs are assigned to production as direct labor and indirect labor. The cost of direct labor is debited to the Work in Process Inventory account and recorded on the proper job cost sheet. The cost of indirect labor is debited to the Factory Overhead Control account and recorded on the proper factory overhead analysis sheet.

The payroll process starts with maintaining good payroll records. This is usually done by the Timekeeping and Payroll Departments. The **Timekeeping Department** usually keeps up with the total number of hours employees work, and how these hours should be charged to production. The **Payroll Department** calculates each employee's gross earnings, payroll deductions, and net pay.

Timekeeping usually involves clock cards and time tickets. **Clock cards** are maintained for each employee who punches a time card. Clock cards show the total amount of time an employee is on the job (on the clock). **Time tickets** are routing devices that show the specific jobs on which an employee works during the day. Some firms use a **daily time report** to list all the jobs worked on by an employee. At regular intervals, the clock cards are compared with the time tickets. The amount of time shown on the clock cards should agree with the time recorded on the time tickets. Any discrepancies are recorded as **idle time.** Idle time can occur in any plant because employees cannot work on a specific job every minute they are on the clock. Only when idle time is excessive must corrective action must be taken. Idle time is usually recorded as factory overhead.

Indirect labor is not recorded on time tickets because indirect labor costs are not chargeable to a specific job. Instead, such costs are applied to production as overhead and thus spread over all jobs in production during the period.

Most companies prepare a **payroll register** which shows the gross earnings, deductions, net pay, and payroll distribution for all employees for a single payroll period. The payroll register is then used as a source document to record the payroll. Information from the payroll register is also posted to each **employee's earnings record,** which shows year-to-date payroll information about the employee.

Most employers are required to withhold taxes from the pay of employees for federal, state, and local taxing authorities. These required withholdings usually include federal income taxes, state income taxes, and social security taxes. In addition to the required withholdings, the employer and employees often agree to have other amounts withheld—such as amounts for medical insurance, savings bonds, and union dues. Additionally, employers are required to pay payroll taxes on behalf of employees. These taxes include social security (FICA), federal unemployment taxes (FUTA), and state unemployment taxes (SUTA).

At the end of each pay period, a **time ticket analysis (TTA)** is made of the time tickets to determine how labor cost should be charged to production. Direct labor is charged as work in process, while indirect labor is charged as factory overhead. Labor is usually charged to production in a summary entry at the end of the month. In addition to the earnings of indirect labor employees, other labor costs are usually recorded as factory overhead—such as overtime premiums, idle time, and fringe benefit costs.

KEY TERMS

Clock Card. A punch card used to record the total amount of time an employee spends in the factory; also called a *time card.*

Employee's Earnings Record. An individual form prepared for each employee showing the employee's earnings each pay period and cumulative earnings for each quarter and for the year.

Federal Insurance Contributions Act (FICA). Federal act requiring both employees and employers to pay social security taxes on the wages and salaries of employees.

Overtime Pay. The amount earned by employees at the regular hourly rate for hours worked in excess of the regularly scheduled time (usually 40 hours in a week).

Overtime Premium. An additional pay rate (usually one-half time) added to the employee's regular pay rate for hours worked in excess of the regularly scheduled time.

Payroll Department. A department responsible for maintaining payroll records and calculating each employee's gross earnings, payroll deductions, and net pay.

Payroll Register. A form used to record the earnings, deductions, net pay, and labor distribution for employees for a payroll period.

Timekeeping Department. The department responsible for determining how many hours employees work and the type of work performed by employees.

Time Ticket. A routing device that shows on which specific jobs an employee worked during the day.

Timekeeping. The accumulating of the time each employee actually spent working in the factory.

Idle Time. Occurs when the clock card shows more hours than the time tickets.

Daily Time Report. A form which lists all the jobs worked on during the day by the employee.

Time Ticket Analysis (TTA). A form that shows the direct labor costs incurred on each job by each department and the total number of direct labor hours that each department worked on a particular job.

Federal Unemployment Tax Act (FUTA). Requirement that employers pay taxes to provide benefits for unemployed workers.

State Unemployment Tax Act (SUTA). State unemployment compensation laws.

Fringe Benefits. Employees' benefits paid by the employer.

QUESTIONS FOR REVIEW

1. Differentiate between direct and indirect labor.
2. Define timekeeping.
3. What is the function of (a) the Timekeeping Department and (b) the Payroll Department?
4. How do clock cards differ from time tickets?
5. What is idle time and why does it occur?
6. Why is idle time usually accounted for as factory overhead?
7. What is a daily time report?
8. What function is served by the payroll register?
9. Differentiate between regular pay and overtime pay.
10. What is meant by overtime premium?
11. Why is overtime premium usually charged to factory overhead?
12. What withholdings must an employer take from the earnings of employees?
13. How does the payroll register differ from the employee's individual earnings record?

14. What account is debited to record the payroll?

15. What accounts are credited to record the payroll?

16. What account is debited when (a) direct labor costs are charged to production and (b) indirect labor costs are charged to production?

17. What is the source document for posting direct labor costs to the individual job cost sheets?

18. How do time ticket analyses differ from the summary of factory earnings?

19. Are accrued wages recorded on the time tickets? Explain.

20. Identify the payroll taxes imposed on employers.

21. To what account are payroll taxes imposed on the employer debited?

22. Are fringe benefit costs considered a part of direct labor? Explain.

23. How is automation changing labor as a component of production cost in some industries?

NOTE Unless told otherwise in Exercises and Problems, record transactions in general journal form.

EXERCISES

5–1. Learning Objective 3. Computing Gross Earnings.

During the last week, Gerri Hendrix worked 45 hours at a rate of $9.00 an hour. Compute her regular earnings, overtime premium, and gross earnings if she is paid time-and-a-half for all hours worked over 40 in a week.

5–2. Learning Objective 3. Computing FICA Taxes.

Using the FICA tax rates and the OASDI taxable base given in the chapter, compute the FICA taxes (OASDI and HIP) on the following employees.

Employee	Gross Earnings This Pay Period	Cumulative Earnings (Before This Period)
A	$495.00	$32,450.00
B	610.00	63,000.00
C	528.00	57,400.00
D	290.00	18,250.00

5–3. Learning Objective 3. Computing Payroll Deductions and Net Pay.

Assuming a federal income tax rate of 15%, a state income tax rate of 8%, and the FICA rates and taxable bases given in the chapter, compute the payroll deductions and net pay for each of the following employees for the pay period ending December 15:

Employee	Gross Earnings This Pay Period	Cumulative Earnings
John Able	$325.00	$16,900.00
Lisa Bennett	680.00	59,120.00
Charles Deen	450.00	38,900.00
Ashley Greene	425.50	42,356.70
Ben Henderson	630.00	64,200.00

5–4. Learning Objective 5. Recording the Payroll.
Using the information from Exercise 5–3, record the payroll.

5–5. Learning Objective 5. Recording Payroll Information.
Payroll data for Colorado Products, Inc. for the week ended March 18 follows. Record: (a) the weekly payroll and (b) payment of the payroll.

Total gross earnings	$125,600
FICA taxes—OASDI	6.2% of gross earnings
FICA taxes—HIP	1.45% of gross earnings
Employee federal income taxes	15% of gross earnings
Employee state income taxes	8% of gross earnings
Medical insurance deduction	$8,450
U.S. savings bonds deduction	$4,000

5–6. Learning Objective 6. Distributing Labor to Production.
Make a journal entry for Steelco, Inc. to distribute the following wages that were earned and recorded during August: direct labor, $78,900; indirect labor, $18,400.

5–7. Learning Objective 6. Analyzing the Balance of the Factory Payroll Clearing Account.
At the end of October, the Factory Payroll Clearing account of Bendell Company shows total debits of $198,600 and a credit of $201,000. Based on this information, answer the following questions:

a. What do the debits to the account represent?
b. What does the credit represent?
c. What is the balance of the account?
d. What does the balance represent?
e. What is the financial statement presentation of the balance?

5–8. Learning Objective 7. Recording Employer Payroll Taxes.
Scholar Publications incurred the following payroll taxes during April. Make a journal entry to record the payroll tax liability for the month.

FICA	$5,872.10
FUTA	798.49
SUTA	2,925.75

5–9. Learning Objective 7. Calculating Employer Payroll Taxes.
Based on the following data, compute the employer's payroll taxes for Star Products, Inc. for November.

Gross earnings	$95,600
Taxable OASDI earnings	88,900
Taxable HIP earnings	95,600

Taxable FUTA and SUTA earnings	$24,000
OASDI rate	6.2%
HIP rate	1.45%
FUTA rate	0.8%
SUTA rate	4.0%

GROUP A PROBLEMS

5–1A. Learning Objectives 1, 3, 5, 7. Computing and Recording Employee's Earnings and Taxes.

The weekly time ticket analysis of Jaurez Manufacturing Company showed the following data for the week ending March 8:

Employee	Classification	Hourly Rate	Hours Worked Regular	Hours Worked Overtime
Boyd, Jim	Direct labor	$12	40	6
Carter, Lisa	Direct labor	12	40	4
Franks, Kyle	Direct labor	10	40	–
Ian, Aimee	Direct labor	14	40	5
Robins, Charles	Indirect labor	8	40	–
Veal, David	Indirect labor	15	40	–

Required:

1. Compute the gross pay of each employee.
2. Compute the net pay of each employee using the FICA rates in the chapter, a federal income tax rate of 15%, and a state income tax rate of 8%.
3. Make journal entries to record: (a) the payroll; (b) payment of the payroll; (c) employer's payroll taxes assuming that no employee has reached or exceeded the maximum wage base for OASDI and unemployment taxes. The company's FUTA rate is 0.8% and SUTA rate is 3.1%.

5–2A. Learning Objective 4. Preparing a Payroll Register.

Cox Candy Company's payroll data for the pay period ending October 5 follows:

Employee	Classification	Hourly Pay Rate	Hours Worked	Total Earnings Up To This Week
Bullard, M.	Direct labor	$12.00	45	$33,600.00
Chafin, P.	Direct labor	10.90	42	29,958.60
Grey, L.	Indirect labor	7.50	40	24,700.00
Jinks, T.	Direct labor	14.00	48	46,000.00
Kelly, H.	Indirect labor	8.00	44	6,400.00
Lang, K.	Direct labor	12.00	40	4,590.00
Nash, B.	Direct labor	10.00	45	42,345.10
Reese, A.	Indirect labor	6.90	40	5,800.00
Sutton, K.	Direct labor	12.00	40	27,870.00
Veal, J.	Indirect labor	9.00	46	19,675.00
Wade, L.	Direct labor	10.50	41	34,500.00

Required:

Prepare a payroll register similar to the one illustrated in this chapter. Make the following withholdings:

Withholding	Rate/Amount
Federal income taxes	15%
State income taxes	7%
FICA—OASDI	6.2%
FICA—HIP	1.45%
Medical insurance	$25 per employee
Savings bonds	$15 per employee
Union dues	$6 per employee

5–3A. Learning Objectives 5, 7. Recording Payroll Information.
This problem is a continuation of Problem 5–2A.

Required:

Using your solution to Problem 5–2A, make journal entries to record: (a) the weekly payroll; (b) payment of the payroll; and (c) the employer's payroll taxes assuming a FUTA rate of 0.8% and a SUTA rate of 2.7%.

5–4A. Learning Objectives 5, 6, 7. Recording Labor Costs.
The following data relate to A-1 Products Company for the month ending May 31:

Credit balance of Factory Payroll Clearing on May 1	$ 9,820
Gross wages during May	78,600
FICA—OASDI withheld	4,873
FICA—HIP withheld	1,140
Federal income taxes withheld	11,790
State income taxes withheld	5,895
Medical insurance withheld	6,000

Required:

1. Open a Factory Payroll Clearing account and enter the beginning balance.
2. Make a journal entry to record the payroll.
3. Make a journal entry to record the employer's payroll taxes. The employer's FUTA rate is 0.8% and SUTA rate is 2.7%; wages subject to these rates are $35,400.
4. Make a journal entry to charge labor costs to production. The summary of factory earnings shows $63,670 for direct labor and $15,900 for indirect labor.
5. Post to the Factory Payroll Clearing account.
6. Answer the following questions about the Factory Payroll Clearing account:
   a.   What is the balance of the account?
   b.   What does this balance represent?
   c.   What is the financial statement presentation of this balance?

GROUP B PROBLEMS

5–1B. Learning Objectives 1, 3, 5, 7. Computing and Recording Employees' Earnings and Taxes.
The weekly time ticket analysis of Granger Company showed the following data for the week ending February 7:

Employee	Classification	Hourly Rate	Hours Worked Regular	Overtime
Allen, Bill	Direct labor	$10	40	8
Bilks, Lynn	Direct labor	12	40	2
Cortez, James	Direct labor	12	40	–
Davids, Lisa	Direct labor	11	40	6
Hall, Jerrod	Indirect labor	10	40	–
King, Lee	Indirect labor	9	40	–

Required:

1. Compute the gross pay of each employee.
2. Compute the net pay of each employee using the FICA rates in the chapter, a federal income tax rate of 15%, and a state income tax rate of 8%.
3. Make journal entries to record: (a) the payroll; (b) payment of the payroll; and (c) the employer's payroll taxes assuming that no employee has reached or exceeded the maximum wage base for FICA and unemployment taxes. The company's FUTA rate is 0.8% and its SUTA rate is 3.4%.

5–2B. Learning Objective 4. Preparing a Payroll Register.

Burton Products Company's payroll data for the pay period ending November 12 follows:

Employee	Classification	Hourly Pay Rate	Hours Worked	Total Earnings Up To This Week
Bell, H.	Direct labor	$14.00	44	$35,630.00
Carr, T.	Direct labor	12.00	45	36,790.00
Farah, B.	Direct labor	10.50	40	32,595.00
Goode, S.	Direct labor	11.25	45	29,610.12
Judd, N.	Indirect labor	10.00	40	18,450.00
Li, B.	Indirect labor	8.00	42	5,800.00
Mann, M.	Direct labor	10.25	40	3,560.00
Nash, R.	Direct labor	9.50	44	6,900.00
Potts, M.	Indirect labor	10.00	42	18,600.00
Roper, J.	Direct labor	12.90	40	29,800.00

Required:
Prepare a payroll register similar to the one illustrated in this chapter. Make the following withholdings:

Withholding	Rate/Amount
Federal income taxes	15%
State income taxes	8%
FICA—OASDI	6.2%
FICA—HIP	1.45%
Medical insurance	$29 per employee
Savings bonds	$20 per employee
Union dues	$6 per employee

5–3B. Learning Objectives 5, 7. Recording Payroll Information.
This problem is a continuation of Problem 5–2B.
Required:

Using your solution to Problem 5–2B, make journal entries to record: (a) the weekly payroll; (b) payment of the payroll; and (c) the employer's payroll taxes assuming a FUTA rate of 0.8% and a SUTA rate of 3.2%.

5–4B. Learning Objectives 5, 6, 7. Recording Labor Costs.

The following data relate to Hill Manufacturing Company for the month ending June 30:

Credit balance of Factory Payroll Clearing on June 1	$ 8,200
Gross wages during June	74,300
FICA—OASDI withheld	4,607
FICA—HIP withheld	1,077
Federal income taxes withheld	11,145
State income taxes withheld	5,235
Medical insurance withheld	5,500

Required:

1. Open a Factory Payroll Clearing account and enter the beginning balance.
2. Make a journal entry to record the payroll.
3. Make a journal entry to record the employer's payroll taxes. The employer's FUTA rate is 0.8% and SUTA rate is 2.7%; wages subject to these rates are $32,900.
4. Make a journal entry to charge labor costs to production. The summary of factory earnings shows $61,250 for direct labor and $14,100 for indirect labor.
5. Post to the Factory Payroll Clearing account.
6. Answer the following questions about the Factory Overhead Clearing account:
    a. What is the balance of the account?
    b. What does this balance represent?
    c. What is the financial statement presentation of this balance?

CASE FOR CRITICAL THINKING

Gina McDaniel just started work in the Cost Accounting Department at Prentice-Flowers Products Company. Gina is a little confused about why her company records overtime pay as factory overhead. After all, Gina reasons, the employees are still working on the job. So why shouldn't overtime be charged to Work in Process Inventory? Explain why most cost accountants believe that overtime should be recorded as indirect labor, rather than direct labor.

ANSWERS TO SELF-STUDY QUIZ 5–1

Regular earnings (45 hours × $8.00)	$360
Overtime premium {5 hours × $4 ($8 × .50)}	20
Gross earnings	$380

ANSWERS TO SELF-STUDY QUIZ 5–2

OASDI = $680,000 × 6.2% = $42,160
HIP = $680,000 × 1.45% =   9,860
Total FICA = $52,020

ANSWERS TO SELF-STUDY QUIZ 5–3

1	Aug	15	Factory Payroll Clearing	98 2 0 0 00		1
2			FICA Taxes Payable—OASDI		7 5 1 2 30	2
3			FICA Taxes Payable—HIP		1 4 2 3 90	3
4			Federal Income Taxes Payable		26 4 9 0 00	4
5			State Income Taxes Payable		8 2 4 5 60	5
6			Medical Insurance Payable		3 6 0 0 00	6
7			Salaries and Wages Payable		50 9 2 8 20	7

ANSWERS TO SELF-STUDY QUIZ 5–4

1	Aug	15	Salaries and Wages Payable	50 9 2 8 20		1
2			Cash		50 9 2 8 20	2

ANSWERS TO SELF-STUDY QUIZ 5–5

1			Work in Process Inventory	156 7 0 0 00		1
2			Factory Overhead Control	25 4 0 0 00		2
3			Factory Payroll Clearing		182 1 0 0 00	3

ANSWERS TO SELF-STUDY QUIZ 5–6

OASDI: $204,300 × 6.2% = $12,666.67
HIP: $235,600 × 1.45% =   3,416.20
FUTA: $235,600 × 0.8% =   1,884.80
SUTA: $235,600 × 2.7% =   6,361.20

1	Mar.	31	Factory Overhead Control	2432887		1
2			FICA Taxes Payable—OASDI		1266667	2
3			FICA Taxes Payable—HIP		341620	3
4			FUTA Taxes Payable		188480	4
5			SUTA Taxes Payable		636120	5

Chapter 6
Accounting for
Factory Overhead

After studying Chapter 6, you should be able to:

1. Identify factory overhead costs.
2. Discuss how factory overhead costs can be departmentalized.
3. Account for actual factory overhead.
4. Allocate overhead costs to jobs.
5. Distribute service department costs to production departments.

n the previous three chapters, we learned how direct materials and direct labor are charged to specific jobs in a job-order costing system. We also learned that indirect materials and indirect labor are charged to factory overhead. However, indirect labor and indirect materials are only two of the many factory costs classified as factory overhead. In this chapter, we will study how actual factory overhead costs are classified, recorded, and summarized. In Chapter 7, we will look at how factory overhead is applied to production.

CLASSIFYING FACTORY OVERHEAD COSTS

LEARNING OBJECTIVE 1

As discussed in Chapter 1, all costs incurred in the factory that cannot be identified with the finished product are called factory overhead. Factory overhead costs cannot be traced specifically to a unit of production, or can only be traced at great cost or inconvenience. Figure 6–1 shows a listing of common factory overhead costs.

ACCUMULATING ACTUAL FACTORY OVERHEAD COSTS

From the list of factory overhead costs shown in Figure 6–1, we can see that most of these items occur on a day-by-day basis throughout the accounting period. As a result, the cost accounting system must be designed to accumulate, classify, and summarize factory overhead costs as they are incurred.

To meet its particular needs, every firm will develop its own factory overhead accounts and methods of classifying them. In a small manufacturing firm with only one production department, a separate account could be maintained in the general ledger for each factory overhead cost. Thus, there would be a separate account for indirect materials, indirect labor, depreciation, factory utilities, and all other factory overhead costs.

However, this system quickly becomes cumbersome when the number of factory overhead accounts becomes sizeable. Instead, factory overhead costs are usually summarized in a single factory overhead control account that is kept in the general ledger. Details of the control account are then kept in a subsidiary factory overhead ledger. In this system, transactions are recorded in a general journal, or in special journals, at various times throughout the month. Frequent postings are made to the individual expense accounts in the factory overhead subsidiary ledger. Today, the factory overhead ledger is almost always maintained on the computer. Computer terminals placed strategically throughout the factory allow constant posting and updating of subsidiary records.

At month-end, posting is made to the Factory Overhead Control account in the general ledger. The Factory Overhead Control account is then proved by comparing its balance to the total of the account balances in the factory overhead subsidiary ledger.

FIGURE 6–1
*Common Factory
Overhead Costs*

Indirect Materials

Small tools
Lubricants
Factory supplies
Factory office supplies
Nuts, bolts, screws, etc.
Glue
Cleaning Compounds

Indirect Labor

Production supervisors and managers
Quality control
Factory office workers
Maintenance crew
Timekeepers
Receiving clerks
Storeroom supervisors
Storeroom clerks
Overtime premiums
Materials handling
Plant security
Idle time

Other Factory Overhead Costs

Workers' compensation insurance
Employee fringe benefits
Sick pay
Vacation pay
Payroll taxes
Property taxes
Factory rent
Repair and maintenance of factory equipment and machinery
Heat and light in the factory
Factory related insurance
Depreciation of factory building, equipment, and machinery
Spoilage
Factory telephone cost

DEPARTMENTALIZING FACTORY OVERHEAD

LEARNING OBJECTIVE 2   In a manufacturing firm with several departments, the accounting system is usually designed to accumulate costs by departments. For accounting purposes, dividing a firm into separate departments creates *cost centers* which provide more accurate costings of jobs and products and provides for more effective cost control.

Assigning factory overhead costs to departments is called **departmentalization**. There are two ways to achieve cost departmentalization: (1) maintaining a separate control account for each factory overhead cost and (2) maintaining one control account for all factory overhead costs.

Separate Control Account for Overhead Costs

Under this method, a separate control account is maintained in the general ledger for each factory overhead cost. A subsidiary ledger consisting of **expense-type factory overhead analysis sheets** is used to charge overhead costs to specific departments. The expense-type overhead anlysis sheet, illustrated in Figure 6–2, provides a separate amount column for each department, which makes it possible to distribute charges among departments as the expenses are recorded.

Indirect Labor   No. 602

Date	Explanation	Post. Ref.	Mainten- ance	General Factory	Shaping	Assembling	Finishing	Total
19X6 Jan. 6	Time ticket analysis	✓	470 00	690 00	202 00	195 00	105 00	1 662 00
13	Time ticket analysis	✓	525 00	850 00	218 00	175 00	126 00	1 894 00
15	Semi-monthly pay	✓	810 00	1850 00	—	—	—	2 660 00
20	Time ticket analysis	✓	515 00	825 00	224 00	201 00	130 00	1 895 00
27	Time ticket analysis	✓	522 50	830 00	190 00	192 00	117 00	1 851 50
31	Semi-monthly pay	✓	826 00	1948 00	—	—	—	2 774 00
31	Time ticket analysis	✓	422 00	612 00	58 00	90 00	61 50	1 243 50
31	Totals		4090 50	7605 00	892 00	853 00	539 50	13 980 00

FIGURE 6–2
Expense-Type Factory Overhead Analysis Sheet

Since each column represents a department, each analysis sheet replaces as many separate accounts as there are departments in the firm. In Figure 6–2, for example, indirect labor costs are charged to the various departments based on an analysis of the payroll.

One Control Account for All Factory Overhead Costs

Another way to achieve cost departmentalization is to use one general ledger control account for all factory overhead costs. A subsidiary ledger must then be set up to organize costs by departments. One way of doing this sets up a subsidiary ledger with accounts for each factory overhead cost (indirect materials, indirect labor, depreciation, etc.). This method, however, does not accumulate costs by individual departments. Thus, to charge overhead to the appropriate department, an analysis of the overhead costs for the period must be made. Such an analysis can be a lengthly process. To overcome this, TurboFlex uses factory overhead analysis sheets for each department. Each analysis sheet contains numbered columns for recording overhead items that occur often. An "other overhead" column is also used to record overhead costs that occur less frequently. Figure 6–3 shows the factory overhead analysis sheet for the Assembling Department for January.

FACTORY OVERHEAD ANALYSIS SHEET

Department __Assembling__ Month __January__ 19 __X6__

DATE	REF.	TOTAL	01 INDIRECT MATERIALS	02 INDIRECT LABOR	03 PAYROLL TAXES	04 DEPREC.	05 REPAIRS & MAINT.	06 INSURANCE	07 UTILITIES	08 TAXES	09 OTHER OVERHEAD ITEM	AMOUNT
Jan. 5	M.R. 708	12500	12500									
6	TTA	19500		19500								
13	TTA	17500		17500								
15	M.R. 727	19300	19300									
17	GJ10	32600					32600					
20	TTA	20100		20100								
25	GJ18	29200									Damaged Parts	29200
27	TTA	19200		19200								
30	M.R. 760	6965	6965									
31	TTA	9000		9000								
31	GJ12	14000								14000		
31	GJ14	11800						11800				
31	GJ14	21000				21000						
31	GJ16	83000							83000			
31	GJ18	1800									Permit	1800
Totals		317465	38765	85300		21000	32600	11800	83000	14000		31000

FIGURE 6–3
Factory Overhead Analysis Sheet

RECORDING FACTORY OVERHEAD COSTS

LEARNING OBJECTIVE 3   Actual factory overhead costs are always recorded by *debiting* the Factory Overhead Control account. The account credited can vary, however. If an outside party is involved, such as when factory rent or utilities are paid, the credit is to Cash or Accounts Payable. We saw in earlier chapters that Raw Materials Inventory is credited when indirect materials are issued to production, and Factory Payroll Clearing is credited when indirect labor is charged to production.

Factory overhead is also recorded by adjusting entries at the end of the accounting period. Most of the factory overhead recorded by adjusting entries involves fixed costs. A **fixed cost** does not vary in amount from month to month. For example, costs for items such as insurance, property taxes, and depreciation usually remain constant from month to month.

To facilitate recording fixed costs at the end of the accounting period, TurboFlex's cost accountant prepared the Schedule of Fixed Overhead Costs illustrated in Figure 6–4.

FIGURE 6–4
Schedule of Fixed Overhead Costs

Department	Property Taxes	Factory Insurance	Depreciation— Building	Depreciation— Equipment	Total
Shaping	$148	$ 142	–	$ 980	$1,270
Assembling	140	118	–	210	468
Finishing	174	140	–	450	764
Maintenance	190	200	$1,000	500	1,890
General Fact.	158	400	–	610	1,168
Totals	$810	$1,000	$1,000	$2,750	$5,560

Schedule of Fixed Overhead Costs
January, 19X6

This schedule allows us to quickly record TurboFlex's fixed overhead costs for January:

1	Jan.	31	Factory Overhead Control	731000		1
2			Property Taxes Payable		81000	2
3			Prepaid Insurance		100000	3
4			Accum. Depr.—Building		250000	4
5			Accum. Depr.—Machinery			5
6			and Equipment		300000	6
7			Charged fixed overhead costs.			7

These costs will be posted to the appropriate factory overhead analysis sheets, as well as to the Factory Overhead Control account in the general ledger.

SELF-STUDY QUIZ 6–1 From the following schedule, make a general journal entry to record Baker Company's fixed costs for March.

Schedule of Fixed Overhead Costs

Department	Insurance	Property Taxes	Depreciation—Building	Depreciation—Machinery	Total
Cutting	$112	$136	–	$1,020	$1,268
Forming	102	108	–	610	820
Finishing	175	150	–	525	850
Maintenance	180	162	$1,800	450	2,592
General Fact.	170	312	–	980	1,462
Totals	$739	$868	$1,800	$3,585	$6,992

Answers at end of chapter.

Summary of Factory Overhead

LEARNING OBJECTIVE 4

As we have seen, all factory overhead costs incurred during the month are recorded on factory overhead analysis sheets and in the Factory Overhead Control account in the general ledger. At the end of the month, the cost clerk prepares a summary showing the total amount of each type of cost incurred by each department. The total of this summary should equal the balance of the Factory Overhead Control account. Figure 6–5 illustrates TurboFlex's summary of factory overhead costs for January.

TurboFlex Corporation
Summary of Factory Overhead
January, 19X6

Cost	Shaping Dept.	Assembling Dept.	Finishing Dept.	Mainten. Dept.	Gen. Fact. Dept.	Total
Indirect Materials	2 1 2 00	3 8 7 65	4 0 8 35	2 8 5 00	1 0 7 00	1 4 0 0 00
Indirect Labor	8 9 2 00	8 5 3 00	5 3 9 50	4 0 9 0 50	7 6 0 5 00	1 3 9 8 0 00
Property Taxes	1 4 8 00	1 4 0 00	1 7 4 00	1 9 0 00	1 5 8 00	8 1 0 00
Factory Insurance	1 4 2 00	1 1 8 00	1 4 0 00	2 0 0 00	4 0 0 00	1 0 0 0 00
Depreciation	9 8 0 00	2 1 0 00	4 5 0 00	1 5 0 0 00	6 1 0 00	3 7 5 0 00
Utilities	1 8 2 0 00	8 3 0 00	4 3 8 00	2 8 4 0 00	6 3 2 00	6 5 6 0 00
Repair	1 6 0 0 00	3 2 6 00	9 5 00	6 5 8 00	5 2 1 00	3 2 0 0 00
Miscellaneous	4 1 8 00	3 1 0 00	2 1 2 00	6 4 5 00	6 1 5 00	2 2 0 0 00
Totals	6 2 1 2 00	3 1 7 4 65	2 4 5 6 85	1 0 4 0 8 50	1 0 6 4 8 00	3 2 9 0 0 00

FIGURE 6–5
Summary of Factory Overhead

DISTRIBUTING SERVICE DEPARTMENT COSTS

As discussed in Chapter 2, manufacturing operations are divided into departments called *producing departments* and *service departments*. A producing department engages in the actual manufacture of the product by physically changing the shape, form, or nature of materials in production, or by assembling parts into a finished product. Service departments do not work directly on the products in production. Instead, they provide a service that helps the producing departments and other service departments operate more efficiently. As a result, finished products receive an indirect benefit from the work performed by service departments.

Since the producing departments receive a benefit from the work performed by service departments, the total cost charged to each producing department must include a portion of the costs of operating the service departments, as well as the costs charged directly to that department. Thus, costs incurred by the service departments must be distributed to the producing departments.

The cost of operating each service department should be distributed in proportion to the services provided to the other departments. An analysis must thus be made to determine the relationship of each service department to the other departments. The distribution of service department costs is usually complicated because most service departments render a service to other service departments, as well as to the producing departments. To achieve an equitable distribution, the cost of operating a service department should be distributed to all departments that it serves—service as well as production.

The first consideration when distributing service department costs is determining how a particular service department divides its services among the other departments. Making a precise determination, however, is often a difficult task. For example, the Power Department may furnish power for the operation of all the factory's machinery, as well as lighting, heating, and cooling the factory. It would be very difficult to monitor the exact amount of power consumed in each department. Consequently, it would not be possible to make a direct charge from the Power Department to the other departments. Instead, the costs of operating the Power Department would be allocated on some equitable basis to the other departments.

Methods of Allocating Service Department Costs

In practice, there are various acceptable methods for allocating service department costs. In this section, we will discuss two common methods:

1. The direct method.
2. The step method.

DIRECT METHOD

The **direct method** makes no attempt to allocate the cost of a service department to other service departments. Instead, the cost of operating the service department is allocated <u>directly</u> to the producing departments. Assuming a firm with three service departments and two producing departments, we can illustrate the direct method as follows. (To simplify the illustration, we assumed that each producing department benefited equally from Service Department 1.)

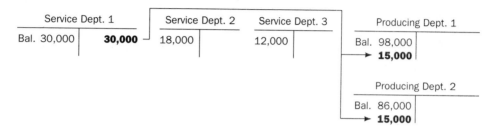

As we can see, the cost of Service Department 1 is allocated directly to the producing departments, while ignoring Service Departments 2 and 3. Service Department 2 would then be allocated to the producing departments, ignoring Service Department 3. Finally, Service Department 3 would be allocated to the producing departments. While this method offers the advantages of simplicity and ease of application, it has been criticized because it assumes that no service department benefits another service department. To overcome this problem, many companies use the step method.

STEP METHOD

The **step method,** also called the *sequential distribution method,* allocates service department costs to other service departments, as well as to producing departments. TurboFlex uses this method to distribute the costs of operating the Maintenance Department and the General Factory Services Department. The Maintenance Department costs are allocated among the General Factory Services, Shaping, Assembling, and Finishing Departments. The costs of the General Factory Services Department, which now include a portion of the Maintenance Department costs, are then allocated to the Shaping, Assembling, and Finishing Departments.

No attempt is made to allocate costs from the General Factory Services Department to the Maintenance Department, even though the Maintenance Department clearly benefits from the services of the General Factory Services Department. This is because the allocation and reallocation of costs between service departments could be repeated endlessly. Consequently, TurboFlex distributes first the cost of the service department that serves the greatest number of other departments. We can illustrate this situation as follows:

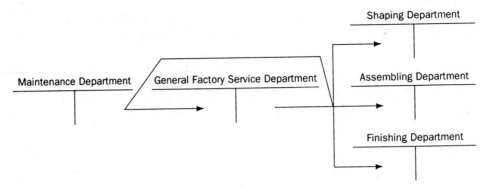

Basis for Allocation

The costs of the Maintenance Department are allocated first because it serves a greater number of departments than the General Factory Services Department. The Maintenance Department is responsible for the maintenance and repair of the buildings, grounds, machinery, and equipment, as well as providing janitorial service for the General Factory Services Department and the producing departments. The General Factory Services Department is responsible for raw materials, factory supplies, and payroll—activities that primarily benefit the producing departments.

   The basis chosen for allocating a service department's costs should express a relationship between the service provided by the department and some causal factor. TurboFlex uses square feet as a basis for allocating the costs of the Maintenance Department. This is a logical basis because the larger the square footage in a department, the more time is generally spent in that department by the Maintenance Department. The General Factory Services Department costs are allocated to the producing departments based on the total amount of direct labor costs charged to the producing department. This basis was chosen because there is a direct relationship between the labor costs in a department and the services provided by the General Factory Services Department.

Allocating Maintenance Department Costs. To allocate the Maintenance Department costs based on square feet, TurboFlex's cost accountant worked out the rate (percent) of each department's square feet to the total of the plant, as follows:

Department	Square Feet	Rate
General Factory Services	10,200	20%*
Shaping	15,300	30%
Assembling	13,770	27%
Finishing	11,730	23%
Totals	51,000	100%

$*\dfrac{10,200}{51,000} = .20 = 20\%$

We can now use these rates to allocate the Maintenance Department's January costs, totaling $10,408.50 (Figure 6–5), as follows:

Department	Maintenance Department Cost		Rate		Amount Allocated
General Factory	$10,408.50	×	.20	=	$ 2,081.70
Shaping	10,408.50	×	.30	=	3,122.55
Assembling	10,408.50	×	.27	=	2,810.30
Finishing	10,408.50	×	.23	=	2,393.95*
Total					$10,408.50

*Rounded down by $0.01

The General Factory Services Department will receive an allocation of $2,081.70 of the costs of the Maintenance Department. Likewise, the Shaping Department will receive an allocation of $3,122.55, the Assembling Department will receive an allocation of $2,810.30, and the Finishing Department will receive an allocation of $2,393.95. To record these allocations, journal entries are needed. These entries will be discussed shortly.

Allocating General Factory Services Department Costs. Using the Summary of Factory Earnings (Figure 5–10 in Chapter 5), TurboFlex's cost accountant calculated the rate of each department's direct labor cost to the total for the plant, as follows (rates were rounded correct to four places):

Department	Direct Labor Cost	Rate
Shaping	$12,867.00	36.0946%
Assembling	13,314.63	37.3503%
Finishing	9,466.37	26.5551%
Totals	$35,648.00	100.0000%

The General Factory Services Department costs now total $12,729.70 ($10,648 charged directly to the department as shown in Figure 6–5, and $2,081.70 allocated from the Maintenance Department), which is allocated as follows:

Department	General Factory Ser. Department Cost		Rate		Amount Allocated
Shaping	$12,729.70	×	.360946	=	$ 4,594.73
Assembling	12,729.70	×	.373503	=	4,754.58
Finishing	12,729.70	×	.265551	=	3,380.39*
Total					$12,729.70

*Rounded up by $0.01

The allocations of service department costs are often summarized on a work sheet, as Figure 6–6 illustrates.

	Mainten- ance	General Factory	Shaping	Assembling	Finishing	Total
TurboFlex Corporation **Work Sheet for Allocating Service Department Costs** **For Month Ended January 31, 19X6**						
Total from factory overhead analysis sheets.	10 40 8 50	10 64 8 00	6 21 2 00	3 17 4 65	2 45 6 85	32 90 0 00
Allocation of Maintenance Dept.	(10 40 8 50)	2 08 1 70	3 12 2 55	2 81 0 30	2 39 3 95	
Allocation of Gen. Fact. Dept.		(12 72 9 70)	4 59 4 73	4 75 4 58	3 38 0 39	
			13 92 9 28	10 73 9 53	8 23 1 19	32 90 0 00

FIGURE 6–6
Work Sheet for
Allocating Service
Department Costs

SELF-STUDY QUIZ 6–2 The Sterling Supply Corporation allocates the costs of its Building Services Department on the basis of floor space in the producing departments. Floor space is occupied as follows:

Mixing Department . . . . 3,000 square feet
Shaping Department . . . . 6,000 square feet
Finishing Department . . . . 3,000 square feet

The costs incurred by the Building Services Department during April totaled $92,000. Compute the amount of this cost that should be allocated to each producing department.
Answers at end of chapter.

RECORDING THE DISTRIBUTION OF OVERHEAD COSTS

The completed worksheet in Figure 6–6 is now used as the basis to record the distribution of overhead costs. Three journal entries are needed, as follows:

1. The balance of the Factory Overhead Control account is closed to departmental overhead accounts, as follows:

Page 10

1	Jan.	31	Factory Overhead—Maintenance Dept.	10 40 8 50		1
2			Factory Overhead—Gen. Fact. Dept.	10 64 8 00		2
3			Factory Overhead—Shaping Dept.	6 21 2 00		3
4			Factory Overhead—Assembling Dept.	3 17 4 65		4
5			Factory Overhead—Finishing Dept.	2 45 6 85		5
6			Factory Overhead Control		32 90 0 00	6
7			Closed factory overhead costs to			7
8			individual depts.			8

2. Overhead costs of the Maintenance Department are closed to the General Factory Services, Shaping, Assembling, and Finishing Departments, as follows:

9		31	Factory Overhead—Gen. Fact. Dept.	2 08 1 70		9
10			Factory Overhead—Shaping Dept.	3 12 2 55		10
11			Factory Overhead—Assembling Dept.	2 81 0 30		11
12			Factory Overhead—Finishing Dept.	2 39 3 95		12
13			Factory Overhead—Maintenance Dept.		10 40 8 50	13
14			Closed Maintenance Dept. costs to			14
15			other depts.			15

3. Overhead costs of the General Factory Services Department are closed to the producing departments, as follows:

16		31	Factory Overhead—Shaping Dept.	4 59 4 73		16
17			Factory Overhead—Assembling Dept.	4 75 4 58		17
18			Factory Overhead—Finishing Dept.	3 38 0 39		18
19			Factory Overhead—Gen. Fact. Dept.		12 72 9 70	19
20			Closed Gen. Fact. Dept. costs to			20
21			producing depts.			21

After these entries are posted, the ledger accounts affected appear as follows:

ACCOUNT Factory Overhead Control   **ACCOUNT NO.** 501

DATE		ITEM	P.R.	DEBIT	CREDIT	BALANCE DEBIT	BALANCE CREDIT
19X6 Jan.	31	Balance	✓			32 90 00 00	
	31	Closed to departmental accounts	GJ10		32 90 00 00		

ACCOUNT Factory Overhead—Maintenance Department   **ACCOUNT NO.** 502

DATE		ITEM	P.R.	DEBIT	CREDIT	BALANCE DEBIT	BALANCE CREDIT
19X6 Jan.	31		GJ10	10 40 8 50		10 40 8 50	
	31		GJ10		10 40 8 50		

ACCOUNT Factory Overhead—General Factory Department   **ACCOUNT NO.** 503

DATE		ITEM	P.R.	DEBIT	CREDIT	BALANCE DEBIT	BALANCE CREDIT
19X6 Jan.	31		GJ10	10 64 8 00		10 64 8 00	
	31		GJ10	2 08 1 70		12 72 9 70	
	31		GJ10		12 72 9 70		

ACCOUNT Factory Overhead—Shaping Department   **ACCOUNT NO.** 504

DATE		ITEM	P.R.	DEBIT	CREDIT	BALANCE DEBIT	BALANCE CREDIT
19X6 Jan.	31		GJ10	6 21 2 00		6 21 0 00	
	31		GJ10	3 12 2 55		9 33 4 55	
	31		GJ10	4 59 4 73		13 92 9 28	

ACCOUNT Factory Overhead—Assembling Department   **ACCOUNT NO.** 505

DATE		ITEM	P.R.	DEBIT	CREDIT	BALANCE DEBIT	BALANCE CREDIT
19X6 Jan.	31		GJ10	3 17 4 65		3 17 4 65	
	31		GJ10	2 81 0 30		5 98 4 95	
	31		GJ10	4 75 4 58		10 73 9 53	

ACCOUNT Factory Overhead—Finishing Department   **ACCOUNT NO.** 506

DATE		ITEM	P.R.	DEBIT	CREDIT	BALANCE DEBIT	BALANCE CREDIT
19X6 Jan.	31		GJ10	2 45 6 85		2 45 6 85	
	31		GJ10	2 39 3 95		4 85 0 80	
	31		GJ10	3 38 0 39		8 23 1 19	

SELF-STUDY QUIZ 6–3 Using the completed work sheet that follows, make general journal entries to close: (a) the balance of the Factory Overhead Control account to departmental overhead accounts, (b) overhead costs of the General Factory Department to the other departments, and (c) overhead costs of the Stores Department to the producing departments.
Answers at end of chapter.

Peak Products Company
Worksheet for Allocating Service Dept. Costs
For month ended Sept. 30 19X7

	General Factory	Stores	Cutting	Assembling	Finishing	Total
Total from factory overhead analysis sheets.	9 000 00	9 800 00	12 200 00	8 850 00	9 400 00	49 250 00
Allocation of Gen. Fact. Dept.	(9 000 00)	1 980 00	2 250 00	2 340 00	2 430 00	
Allocation of Stores Dept.		(11 780 00)	4 712 00	3 769 60	3 298 40	
			19 162 00	14 959 60	15 128 40	49 250 00

SELF-STUDY PROBLEM

The April data for allocating service department costs for the Thompson Company follows:

Department	Overhead Costs	Allocation of Maintenance Department	Allocation of General Factory Department
Maintenance	$ 9,200		
Gen. Factory	10,400	18%	
Grinding	10,800	30%	38%
Baking	8,600	28%	32%
Finishing	9,300	24%	30%
Totals	$48,300	100%	100%

Required:

1. Prepare a work sheet to allocate service department costs.
2. Prepare a general journal entry to close:
    a. the balance of the Factory Overhead Control account to departmental overhead accounts.
    b. overhead costs of the Maintenance Departments to the other departments.
    c. overhead costs of the General Factory Department to the producing departments.

SOLUTION TO SELF-STUDY PROBLEM

1.

Thompson Company
Worksheet for Allocating Service Deptartment Costs
For month ended April 30, 19X5

	Mainten-ance	General Factory	Grinding	Baking	Finishing	Total
Total from factory overhead analysis sheets.	920000	1040000	1080000	860000	930000	4830000
Allocation of Main Dept.	(920000)	165600	276000	257600	220800	
Allocation of Gen. Fact. Dept.		(1205600)	458128	385792	361680	
			1814128	1503392	1512480	4830000

2.

1	Apr.	30	Factory Overhead—Maintenance Dept.	9 20 0 00	**1**
2			Factory Overhead—Gen. Fact. Dept.	10 40 0 00	**2**
3			Factory Overhead—Grinding Dept.	10 80 0 00	**3**
4			Factory Overhead—Baking Dept.	8 60 0 00	**4**
5			Factory Overhead—Finishing Dept.	9 30 0 00	**5**
6			Factory Overhead Control	48 30 0 00	**6**
7			Closed factory overhead costs to		**7**
8			individual depts.		**8**

9		30	Factory Overhead—Gen. Fact. Dept.	1 65 6 00	**9**
10			Factory Overhead—Grinding Dept.	2 76 0 00	**10**
11			Factory Overhead—Baking Dept.	2 57 6 00	**11**
12			Factory Overhead—Finishing Dept.	2 20 8 00	**12**
13			Factory Overhead—Maintenance Dept.	9 20 0 00	**13**
14			Closed Maintenance Dept. costs to		**14**
15			other depts.		**15**

16		30	Factory Overhead—Grinding Dept.	4 58 1 28	**16**
17			Factory Overhead—Baking Dept.	3 85 7 92	**17**
18			Factory Overhead—Finishing Dept.	3 61 6 80	**18**
19			Factory Overhead—Gen. Fact. Dept.	12 05 6 00	**19**
20			Closed Gen. Fact. Dept. costs to		**20**
21			producing depts.		**21**

SUMMARY

All factory costs not classified as direct materials or direct labor are classified as factory overhead. This broad range of costs includes indirect labor, indirect materials, worker's compensation insurance, sick pay, vacation pay, payroll taxes, spoilage, factory rent, factory taxes, and factory utilities.

To meet its own particular needs, individual firms design cost accounting systems to accumulate, classify, and summarize factory overhead costs as incurred. Small firms could maintain a separate account in the general ledger for each factory overhead cost. This practice, however, is not practical if the number of overhead costs is sizable. Instead, individual factory overhead costs are usually maintained in a subsidiary ledger summarized by a single control account located in the general ledger.

When a firm has several departments, the accounting system is usually designed to accumulate costs by departments. Dividing a firm into departments is called **departmentalization.** There are two ways to achieve departmentalization: (1) maintaining a separate control account for each factory overhead cost and (2) maintaining one control account for all factory overhead costs. The first method involves maintaining a subsidiary ledger of **expense-type factory overhead analysis sheets** so that overhead can be charged to specific departments as it occurs. The second method involves the use of a single control account in the general ledger with a subsidiary ledger of overhead costs. The subsidiary ledger can be made up of individual overhead accounts (such as rent, utilities, depreciation, etc.) or departmental overhead analysis sheets.

Most factory overhead costs are recorded on a day-by-day basis. Some overhead, however, is not recorded until the end of an accounting period when adjusting entries are made. This usually involves **fixed costs,** which are costs that remain the same regardless of the level of production. Examples of fixed costs include depreciation, property taxes, and insurance.

Service departments do not actually work on the products in production but, instead, render a service to facilitate the work done by producing departments (and other service departments). Since producing departments are benefited by service departments, the costs incurred by a service department should be allocated to the producing departments. There are two common methods of allocating service department costs: the direct method and the indirect method. The **direct method** makes no attempt to allocate the cost of a service department to other service departments. Instead, the cost of operating the service department is allocated directly to the producing departments. The **step method** allocates the cost of a service department to other service departments as well as producing departments. Generally, the cost of the service department that serves the greatest number of other departments is allocated first. Work sheets are often prepared to aid in allocating service departments. The work sheets then are used as a basis to make journal entries to record the allocations.

KEY TERMS

Departmentalization. The process of assigning factory overhead costs to individual departments.

Expense-Type Factory Overhead Analysis Sheets. A form of factory overhead subsidiary ledger that provides a separate amount column for each department, which makes it possible to distribute overhead costs to the departments as the costs are recorded.

Fixed Cost. A cost that does not vary in amount from month to month. Examples include insurance, property taxes, and depreciation.

Direct Method. A method of allocating service department costs to just producing departments.

Step Method. A method of allocating service department costs to other service departments, as well as to producing departments.

QUESTIONS FOR REVIEW

1. Identify some common factory overhead costs.
2. Is it possible to have a separate general ledger account for each factory overhead cost? Explain.
3. What are two ways of maintaining a subsidiary ledger for factory overhead costs if a single control account is maintained in the general ledger?
4. What is an expense-type overhead analysis sheet?
5. Do all factory overhead costs require a cash payment? Explain.
6. What is a fixed cost?
7. What is the source document that is often used as a basis to record fixed costs?
8. The Factory Overhead Control account is debited for what type of overhead costs?
9. How do service departments differ from producing departments?
10. Why are service department costs allocated to producing departments?
11. Are service department costs allocated to other service departments? Explain.
12. Differentiate between the direct method and the step method of allocating service department costs.
13. Describe the work sheet used to facilitate allocating service department costs.
14. What journal entries are needed to record the allocation of service department costs?

NOTE Unless told otherwise in Exercises and Problems, record transactions in general journal form.

EXERCISES

6–1. Learning Objective 4. Allocating Overhead Costs.

Global Products Company allocates factory rent on the basis of floor space occupied by the producing departments. Based on the following breakdown of the area of the plant, allocate the firm's $3,000 monthly rent.

Department	Square Feet
Cutting	9,240
Sanding	10,500
Painting	8,400
Finishing	13,860

6–2. Learning Objectives 1 & 4. Recording Factory Overhead Costs.

Record the journal entries for the following selected factory overhead costs incurred by Spencer Company during February (date all entries February 28):

a. Indirect materials issued to production, $33,600.
b. Indirect labor charged to production, $23,400.

c. Factory utilities paid, $6,700.
d. Depreciation of factory building, $4,500.
e. Depreciation of factory machinery, $12,000.
f. Factory insurance expired, $1,200.
g. Accrued property taxes on factory building and land, $2,400.

6–3. Learning Objective 5. Allocating Service Department Costs.

Michigan Metal Products Company allocates the costs of its Building Services Department on the basis of floor space occupied by the producing departments. The Melting Department occupies 3,000 square feet; the Forming Department occupies 4,000 square feet; the Cutting Department occupies 6,000 square feet; and the Finishing Department occupies 2,000 square feet. Determine the amount that should be allocated to each of these departments during March if the Building Service Department accumulated costs of $38,500. (Round rates to four places, if necessary.)

6–4. Learning Objective 5. Allocating Service Department Costs.

The Good Earth Nut Butter Company allocates the costs of its General Factory Department on the basis of the direct labor costs incurred in its producing departments. Using the following breakdown of direct labor costs, determine the amount to be distributed to each producing department if the General Factory Department incurred $45,600 in overhead costs during September. (Round rates to four places, if necessary.)

Department	Direct Labor Cost
Cleaning	$18,900
Grinding	21,400
Baking	16,800
Finishing	12,400

6–5. Learning Objective 5. Recording the Allocation of Service Department Costs.

Using the data from Exercise 6–4, record the journal entry to allocate the costs of the General Factory Department to the producing departments, assuming that the Factory Overhead Control account has been closed to departmental overhead accounts.

6–6. Learning Objective 5. Recording the Allocation of Service Department Costs.

The departmental overhead analysis sheets for Augusta Wood Products Company showed the following amounts for November:

Maintenance	$10,400
General Factory	12,200
Cutting	18,600
Sanding	16,350
Finishing	15,210

A work sheet showed that the service departments were allocated as follows:

Maintenance Department:
    22% to General Factory
    27% to Cutting
    25% to Sanding
    26% to Finishing

General Factory:
    41% to Cutting
    28% to Sanding
    31% to Finishing

1. Make a journal entry to close the Factory Overhead to departmental overhead accounts.
2. Make journal entries to allocate the service department costs.

GROUP A PROBLEMS

6–1A. Learning Objectives 1 & 3. Recording Factory Overhead Costs.

Speer Company incurred the following factory overhead costs during April:

a. Requisitioned indirect materials to production, $12,800.
b. Charged indirect labor to production, $14,600.
c. Requisitioned factory supplies to production, $1,200.
d. Paid factory rent, $3,500.
e. Paid factory utilities, $8,658.
f. Recorded depreciation of machinery and equipment, $4,000.
g. Recorded depreciation of factory building, $2,500.
h. Recorded employer's payroll taxes for the month: OASDI, $10,900; HIP, $2,549; FUTA, $1,406; SUTA, $4,747.
i. Recorded expired factory insurance, $1,700.
j. Paid for repairs to factory machinery, $2,450.
k. Paid salaries of product inspectors, $12,300 (ignore payroll deductions).
l. Applied factory overhead to production, $45,700.

Required:
Record these transactions. Date each entry April 30.

6–2A. Learning Objectives 5. Allocating Service Department Costs.

A-1 Baking Company is divided into two service departments (Maintenance and Factory Office) and three producing departments (Mixing, Cooking, and Finishing). During June, A-1 incurred factory overhead costs as follows:

Maintenance	$ 9,000
Factory Office	8,400
Mixing	18,000
Cooking	16,000
Finishing	21,000

The basis for allocating service department costs to the other departments follows:

   Maintenance: On the basis of floor space occupied by the other departments, as follows:

Factory office	2,500 square feet
Mixing	8,200 square feet
Cooking	6,800 square feet
Finishing	3,500 square feet

   Factory office: On the basis of direct labor costs in the producing departments, as follows:

Mixing	$10,200
Cooking	6,800
Finishing	5,000

Required

Using the step method, prepare a schedule showing the allocation of the service department costs.

6–3A. Learning Objective 5. Allocating Service Department Costs and Making Journal Entries.

March data for allocating service department costs for the Kingsley Company follows:

Department	Overhead Costs	Allocation of Personnel Department	Allocation of Building Services
Personnel	$12,200		
Building Ser.	10,800	20%	
Cutting	10,200	22%	36%
Shaping	9,400	28%	35%
Forming	8,800	30%	29%

Required: *51400*

1. Prepare a work sheet to allocate service department costs.
2. Make journal entries to close:
   a. the balance of the Factory Overhead Control account to departmental overhead accounts.
   b. overhead costs of the Personnel Department to the other departments.
   c. overhead costs of the Building Services Department to the producing departments.

6–4A. Learning Objectives 1, 3, 5. Allocating Service Department Costs, Making Journal Entries, and Posting.

The following data relate to Bluff City Products Company for the month ending May 31:

Department	Overhead Costs	Allocation of Maintenance Department	Allocation of General Factory Department
Maintenance	$ 3,670		
General Factory	3,890	20%	
Cutting	6,200	25%	30%
Shaving	7,200	30%	40%
Finishing	7,000	25%	30%
Totals	$27,960	100%	100%

Required:

1. Open a general ledger account for Factory Overhead Control, 501. Enter a debit balance of $27,960 as of May 31.
2. Open a general ledger account for each of the following departmental overhead accounts:

Account	Number
Factory Overhead—Maintenance Dept.	502
Factory Overhead—General Factory Dept.	503
Factory Overhead—Cutting Dept.	504
Factory Overhead—Shaving Dept.	505
Factory Overhead—Finishing Dept.	506

3. Complete a work sheet for allocating service department costs.

4. Make journal entries to:
   a. close the Factory Overhead Control account to the departmental overhead accounts.
   b. allocate the Maintenance Department costs to the other departments.
   c. allocate the General Factory Department costs to the producing departments.
5. Post journal entries to the ledger accounts.

GROUP B PROBLEMS

6–1B. Learning Objectives 1 & 3. Recording Factory Overhead Costs.

Rodriguez Company incurred the following factory overhead costs during July:

a. Requisitioned indirect materials to production, $10,900.
b. Charged indirect labor to production, $12,400.
c. Requisitioned factory supplies to production, $1,250.
d. Paid factory rent, $5,000.
e. Paid factory utilities, $9,300.
f. Recorded depreciation of factory machinery, $6,000.
g. Recorded depreciation of factory building, $3,000.
h. Recorded employer's payroll taxes for the month: OASDI, $9,500; HIP, $2,222; FUTA, $1,226; SUTA, $9,500.
i. Recorded expired factory insurance, $1,800.
j. Paid for repairs to factory machinery, $1,800.
k. Paid salaries of product inspectors, $11,800 (ignore payroll deductions).
l. Applied factory overhead to production, $42,500.

Required:
Record these transactions. Date each entry July 31.

6–2B. Learning Objective 5. Allocating Service Department Costs.

Simpson Company is divided into two service departments (Maintenance and Personnel) and three producing departments (Cutting, Shaping, and Finishing). During October, the Simpson factory incurred overhead costs as follows:

Maintenance	$ 9,200
Personnel	8,500
Cutting	16,000
Shaping	14,400
Finishing	18,300

The basis for allocating service department costs to the other departments are as follows:

Maintenance: On the basis of floor space occupied by the other departments, as follows:

Personnel	2,000 square feet
Cutting	8,000 square feet
Shaping	6,000 square feet
Finishing	4,000 square feet

Personnel: On the basis of direct labor costs in the producing departments, as follows:

Cutting $10,800
Shaping   7,100
Finishing   6,000

Required:
Using the step method, prepare a schedule showing the allocation of the service department costs.

6–3B. Learning Objective 5. Allocating Service Department Costs and Making Journal Entries.

August data for allocating service department costs for Iowa Manufacturing Company follows:

Department	Overhead Costs	Allocation of Personnel Department	Allocation of Building Services
Factory Office	$10,300		
Building Services	9,200	22%	
Cutting	10,200	20%	35%
Forming	9,800	30%	36%
Finishing	8,500	28%	29%

Required:

1. Prepare a work sheet to allocate service department costs.
2. Record journal entries to close:
   a. the balance of the Factory Overhead Control account to departmental overhead accounts.
   b. overhead costs of the Factory Office Department to the other departments.
   c. overhead costs of the Building Services Department to the producing departments.

6–4B. Learning Objectives 1, 3, 5. Allocating Service Department Costs, Making Journal Entries, and Posting.

The following data relate to Twin Cities Products Company for the month ending November 30:

Department	Overhead Costs	Allocation of Maintenance Department	Allocation of General Factory Department
Maintenance	$ 4,200		
General Factory	4,500	18%	
Cutting	6,800	27%	40%
Assembling	7,400	30%	30%
Finishing	7,200	25%	30%
Totals	$30,100	100%	100%

Required:

1. Open a general ledger account for Factory Overhead Control, 501. Enter a debit balance of $30,100 as of November 30.
2. Open a general ledger account for each of the following departmental overhead accounts:

Account	Number
Factory Overhead—Maintenance Dept.	502
Factory Overhead—General Factory Dept.	503
Factory Overhead—Cutting Dept.	504
Factory Overhead—Assembling Dept.	505
Factory Overhead—Finishing Dept.	506

3.   Complete a work sheet for allocating service department costs.
4.   Make journal entries to:
    a.   close the Factory Overhead Control account to the departmental overhead accounts.
    b.   allocate the Maintenance Department costs to the other departments.
    c.   allocate the General Factory Department costs to the producing departments.
5.   Post journal entries to the ledger accounts.

CASE FOR CRITICAL THINKING

Factory overhead was once considered to be a lesser cost of production. In recent years, however, it has become a significant cost of production. Write a paragraph explaining why this has happened.

ANSWERS TO SELF-STUDY QUIZ 6–1

1	Mar.	31	Factory Overhead Control			6 9 9 2 00				1
2			Prepaid Insurance						7 3 9 00	2
3			Property Taxes Payable						8 6 8 00	3
4			Accum. Depr.—Building					1 8 0 0 00		4
5			Accum. Depr.—Machinery					3 5 8 5 00		5

ANSWERS TO SELF-STUDY QUIZ 6–2

Mixing Dept.:	3,000	= .25 × $92,000 =	$23,000
Shaping Dept.:	6,000	= .50 × $92,000 =	$46,000
Finishing Dept.:	3,000	= .25 × $92,000 =	$23,000
	12,000		$92,000

ANSWERS TO SELF-STUDY QUIZ 6–3

(a)

1	Sept.	30	Factory Overhead—General Fact. Dept.	9 000 00	1
2			Factory Overhead—Stores Dept.	9 800 00	2
3			Factory Overhead—Cutting Dept.	12 200 00	3
4			Factory Overhead—Assembling Dept.	8 850 00	4
5			Factory Overhead—Finishing Dept.	9 400 00	5
6			Factory Overhead Control		49 250 00	6

(b)

7		30	Factory Overhead—Stores Dept.	1 980 00	7
8			Factory Overhead—Cutting Dept.	2 250 00	8
9			Factory Overhead—Assembling Dept.	2 340 00	9
10			Factory Overhead—Finishing Dept.	2 430 00	10
11			Factory Overhead—Gen. Fact. Dept.		9 000 00	11

(c)

12		30	Factory Overhead—Cutting Dept.	4 712 00	12
13			Factory Overhead—Assembling Dept.	3 769 60	13
14			Factory Overhead—Finishing Dept.	3 298 40	14
15			Factory Overhead—Stores Dept.		11 780 00	15

Chapter 7
Applying Overhead
to Production

LEARNING OBJECTIVES

After studying Chapter 7, you should be able to:

1. Discuss why factory overhead is applied to production.
2. Compute predetermined factory overhead rates using various bases.
3. Compute departmental overhead rates.
4. Enter applied overhead on job cost sheets.
5. Make journal entries to record applied overhead.
6. Determine under- and overapplied overhead.
7. Analyze under- and overapplied overhead into volume and spending variances.

In Chapter 6, we started our study of factory overhead by examining how actual factory overhead costs are accumulated and recorded. Due to the high cost of modern production and the large number of unlike overhead costs—ranging from grease used on the machinery to the fringe benefit costs of factory workers—it is vital that a firm have an accounting system that accurately and efficiently records actual overhead costs. In most manufacturing firms, however, it is not the actual factory overhead costs that are charged to production. Instead, overhead costs are *applied* (assigned) to jobs through an allocation process. In this chapter, we will study why and how overhead costs are applied to production, and how to analyze differences that exist between actual factory overhead costs and applied overhead costs.

APPLICATION OF FACTORY OVERHEAD

LEARNING OBJECTIVE 1

There are some factory overhead costs that occur on somewhat of a regular basis (such as indirect labor, factory utilities, and rent). However, there are many factory overhead costs that will not be known until the end of the accounting period (such as depreciation and accrued expenses). There are still other factory costs such as repairs that tend to be heavy in some periods and light in others.

This somewhat inconsistent occurrence of overhead costs presents a problem for management—because management cannot wait until the end of an accounting period to determine the total amount of overhead that should be charged to production. To be useful, the cost accounting system must provide accurate cost data as each job is completed, regardless of when it is completed. To illustrate this problem, let's assume that TurboFlex received an order for 200 TurboFlex II's from Champ's Sports. Let's further assume that TurboFlex was able to manufacture all 200 units in eight working days. During those eight days, some overhead costs would certainly have been recorded—utilities, repairs, indirect labor, indirect materials, etc. But other overhead costs probably would *not* have been recorded; for example, depreciation, accrued property taxes, expired insurance, and other overhead costs that are typically recorded by adjusting entries at the end of the accounting period.

Even common overhead costs such as utilities and repairs can present a problem. Utility costs are an ever present cost of operating any business. But how can the actual power used during an eight-day period be charged to production when the power bill will not arrive until the end of the month? Even with the power bill in hand, how can it be broken down and charged to a specific job when many jobs are going on simultaneously?

Similar problems are encountered with repair costs. Repair costs tend to be erratic in that a firm could experience huge repair bills as machinery ages, and far less when machinery has been recently replaced. If actual overhead costs were charged to production, products completed during periods of heavy repair costs would have a higher assigned cost than identical products completed during periods of light repair costs.

In order to overcome the shortcomings of charging actual overhead costs to production and to provide management with timely cost data, factory overhead costs are assigned or applied to production by using a predetermined rate. The rate is referred to as "predetermined" because it is calculated before the start of an accounting period and is based entirely on estimated data. Common bases for computing the rate are discussed next.

PREDETERMINED FACTORY OVERHEAD RATE

LEARNING OBJECTIVE 2   The calculation of the **predetermined factory overhead rate** can be a relatively simple task. Management must relate the estimated amount of factory overhead for a period to an *activity base*. The activity base should have a cause-and-effect relationship to the actual incurrence of overhead. That is, the activity base chosen should be directly related to the actual occurence of overhead in the firm. Stated another way, the activity base should act as a *cost driver* in the incurrence of overhead costs. A **cost driver** is any activity that causes overhead to occur. Common cost drivers in a manufacturing firm include machine hours, direct materials cost, direct labor hours, and direct labor cost. In nonmanufacturing firms, cost drivers include such activities as miles driven, computer operation, beds occupied, and hours in flight.

It is vital that the activity base chosen actually drive costs. If a base is chosen that does not drive costs, the result will be inaccurate product costing and unreliable information. For example, with automation has come *computer-integrated manufactuing (CIM) systems*, which require very little, if any, direct labor input. In plants using such systems, direct labor would not be an appropriate activity base because it does not represent a significant part of production costs. On the other hand, in plants where direct labor remains a significant cost of production, it is a logical base for computing overhead rates and applying overhead to production.

Computing the Overhead Rate

In the previous section, we stated that a firm must choose an appropriate activity base in order to compute an overhead application rate. It is also necessary for a firm to select a period of time to serve as a basis for computing the rate. Most manufacturing firms use an annual period. Periods shorter than one year are usually not satisfactory because most industries experience seasonal fluctuations in activity.

To illustrate how to calculate a predetermined rate, assume that the Alaska Boat Company estimates that its factory overhead costs for 19X2 will be $100,000. Further assume that the firm estimates that the following activities will occur in 19X2:

Activity Base	Estimated Activity for 19X2
Machine hours	8,000 hours
Materials costs	$200,000
Direct labor costs	$250,000
Direct labor hours	20,000 hours

Esr FO = $100,000
for yr 19x2

Machine Hours. If machines are in operation, overhead is certainly occurring: power, repairs, depreciation, maintenance, etc. Thus, machine hours is an appropriate activity base for firms where work is performed primarily by machines. If the Alaska Boat Company chose this base, the predetermined overhead application for 19X2 would be computed as follows:

$$\frac{\text{Estimated factory overhead costs}}{\text{Estimated machine hours}} = \frac{\$100,000}{8,000} = \$12.50 \text{ per machine hour}$$

This rate would be used to apply overhead costs to all jobs completed during 19X2. For example, if a job required 100 machine hours to complete, overhead costs of $1,250 (100 hours × $12.50) would be applied to the job and thus added to the job cost sheet. This cost, along with the costs of direct materials and direct labor, would make up the total cost of the job.

Direct Materials Costs. An appropriate activity base in firms where materials constitute a signficant cost of production is direct materials costs. If the Alaska Boat Company used this base, the predetermined overhead application rate for 19X2 would be calculated as follows:

$$\frac{\text{Estimated factory overhead costs}}{\text{Estimated direct materials costs}} = \frac{\$100,000}{\$200,000} = 50\% \text{ of direct materials costs}$$

Thus, if a job required the use of $10,000 of direct materials costs, the overhead applied to that job would be $5,000 ($10,000 × 50%).

Direct Labor Costs. Historically, direct labor costs has been the most widely used activity base. As mentioned earlier, highly automated plants, with very little direct labor input, would not use direct labor as an activity base. For many other companies, however, direct labor costs remains the most popular base for applying overhead because it is simple and easy to use. If the Alaska Boat Company used this base, its overhead application rate would be:

$$\frac{\text{Estimated factory overhead costs}}{\text{Estimated direct labor costs}} = \frac{\$100,000}{\$250,000} = 40\% \text{ of direct labor costs}$$

Under this method, if $12,000 in direct labor costs were charged to a job, the overhead applied to that job would be $4,800 ($12,000 × 40%).

Direct Labor Hours. Direct labor hours is an appropriate activity base in firms where labor is a significant part of production and where the wages paid to workers vary considerably from worker to worker. In such a situation, direct labor hours would be a more realistic base than direct labor costs—because the hours devoted to jobs would be more uniform than the wages of direct labor employees. Had Alaska Boat Company used this base, the overhead application rate would be:

$$\frac{\text{Estimated factory overhead costs}}{\text{Estimated direct labor hours}} = \frac{\$100,000}{20,000} = \$5 \text{ per direct labor hour}$$

Under this method, $5 in factory overhead would be applied for each one hour that direct labor employees worked on a job. Thus, if 2,000 direct labor hours were devoted to completing a job, the overhead applied to that job would be $10,000 (2,000 hours × $5).

SELF-STUDY QUIZ 7–1 Estimated data for the Alliance Manufacturing Group for the year follows:

Factory overhead costs	$240,000
Machine hours	8,000 hours
Direct materials costs	$300,000
Direct labor costs	$320,000
Direct labor hours	16,000 hours

Use each of the following activity bases to compute the overhead application rate.

a. Machine hours
b. Direct materials costs
c. Direct labor costs
d. Direct labor hours

Answers at end of chapter.

Choosing the Activity Base

An activity base is the common denominator that links the costs of all products. Consequently, the base chosen should be the best possible measure of the cause-and-effect relationship between overhead costs and the volume of production. Following are some of the factors that must be considered when choosing a base:

- The base chosen must be a cost driver.
- The base chosen must provide a rate that yields realistic results.
- The base chosen must be one that can be easily measured for each job.
- Different bases must be available to calculate departmental rates if the nature of activity varies from department to department.

Determining Departmental Rates

Notice that the last factor listed above addresses the need for departmental overhead rates if production activity varies considerably from department to department. Rarely can a single "blanket" overhead rate be used for an entire firm. Since different departments incur costs differently, a single overhead rate for the entire firm does not provide an adequate cause-and-effect relationship for a realistic charge of overhead to production. The make-up of each department must therefore be studied to determine cost drivers for that particular department. For example, some departments may be made up mostly of machines, with only a small amount of labor input needed to operate the machinery. In such a department, direct labor would not be a good base for applying overhead. Machines hours, instead, would be a more appropriate base.

At TurboFlex, a separate overhead rate is computed for each producing department because the activities of each department differ considerably. The base chosen for each department is direct labor hours because labor makes up the largest cost of each department, and the hourly wages differ considerably within each department. (Usually, when hourly wages vary in a department, direct labor hours—not direct labor costs—is selected as the activity base.)

TurboFlex uses a period of one year as a basis to compute overhead application rates. In December of each year, a budget is developed that shows estimated overhead costs by departments for the coming year. Figure 7–1 shows TurboFlex's budget of factory overhead costs for 19X6.

TurboFlex Corporation
Budgeted Overhead
19X6

Cost	Shaping Dept.	Assembling Dept.	Finishing Dept.	Mainten. Dept.	Gen. Fact. Dept.	Total
Indirect Materials	2975 00	4500 00	4800 00	3000 00	1500 00	16775 00
Indirect Labor	12000 00	18000 00	15000 00	48000 00	93600 00	186600 00
Payroll Taxes	900 00	1350 00	1125 00	3600 00	7020 00	13995 00
Property Taxes	2850 00	800 00	875 00	2000 00	4000 00	10525 00
Factory Insurance	900 00	820 00	860 00	2020 00	3600 00	8200 00
Depreciation	18760 00	2520 00	5400 00	18000 00	7320 00	52000 00
Utilities	16000 00	9200 00	7800 00	18500 00	7700 00	59200 00
Repair	4000 00	2500 00	1200 00	3200 00	2600 00	13500 00
Miscellaneous	1275 00	825 00	800 00	550 00	1850 00	5300 00
Totals	59660 00	40515 00	37860 00	98870 00	129190 00	366095 00
Estimated direct labor hours	24000	21000	18000			

FIGURE 7–1
*Budgeted
Overhead Costs*

TurboFlex Corporation
Worksheet for Allocating Estimated Overhead Costs
For year ending December 31, 19X6

	Mainten-ance	General Factory	Shaping	Assembling	Finishing	Total
Budgeted Costs	98 870 00	129 190 00	59 660 00	40 515 00	37 860 00	366 095 00
Allocation of Maintenance Dept.	(98 870 00)	19 774 00	29 661 00	26 695 00	22 740 00	
		(148 964 00)	53 627 00	55 117 00	40 220 00	
			142 948 00	122 327 00	100 820 00	366 095 00

FIGURE 7–2
Work Sheet for
Allocating
Estimated
Overhead Costs

Notice that budgeted overhead costs are shown for each of the two service departments, as well as the three producing departments. The cost accountant now prepares a work sheet to allocate estimated service department costs to the producing departments. The work sheet, shown in Figure 7–2, is identical to the work sheet we prepared in Chapter 6, except that the data are estimated. All amounts were rounded to the nearest whole dollar (because we are working with estimated amounts) and the following rates were used:

Maintenance: 20% to General Factory
                            30% to Shaping
                            27% to Assembling
                            23% to Finishing

General Factory: 36% to Shaping
                            37% to Assembling
                            27% to Finishing

Each department's rate is now computed by dividing the department's total estimated overhead costs by its estimated direct labor hours, as follows:

Shaping Department

$$\frac{\$142,948}{24,000} = \$5.96$$

Assembling Department

$$\frac{\$122,327}{21,000} = \$5.83$$

Finishing Department

$$\frac{\$100,820}{18,000} = \$5.60$$

Show if on the FOA of the JCS.

Entry made @ EOJ or EOM

APPLYING FACTORY OVERHEAD

Since TurboFlex uses direct labor hours as a basis for applying overhead, the amount of overhead to be charged to each job is computed by multiplying the number of hours each department worked on a job by that department's predetermined overhead rate. The amount of applied overhead is then entered in the Factory Overhead Applied section of the job cost sheet. This entry is made when a job is completed, or at the end of the month if the job is still in production (some firms apply overhead at the end of each week).

At TurboFlex, overhead is applied when a job is completed, or at the end of the month if the job is still in production. For example, Job 118 was completed on January 19. The direct labor hours needed to complete the job are recorded on the daily time tickets. These hours are totaled and sent to the cost accountant as follows:

Shaping Department	260 hours
Assembling Department	230 hours
Finishing Department	275 hours

Using the predetermined departmental overhead rates we computed earlier, the overhead applied to this job follows:

Shaping Department	260 × $5.96 = $1,549.60
Assembling Department	230 × $5.83 = $1,340.90
Finishing Department	275 × $5.60 = $1,540.00

LEARNING OBJECTIVE 4 These amounts are entered in the appropriate columns of the Factory Overhead Applied section of the job cost sheet, as shown in Figure 7–3.

JOB COST SHEET

Customer ___Sports World___ Job # ___118___
Job Description ___On file___ Date Started ___1–2–X6___
Quantity ___18___ Date Completed _____

MATERIALS			DIRECT LABOR									FACTORY OVERHEAD APPLIED										
					SHAPING		ASSEMBLING		FINISHING					SHAPING			ASSEMBLING			FINISHING		
DATE	REQ. NO.	AMOUNT	DATE	REF.	HR	AMOUNT	HR	AMOUNT	HR	AMOUNT	DATE	REF.	HR	RATE	AMOUNT	HR	RATE	AMOUNT	HR	RATE	AMOUNT
1–4	701	500 00	1–6	TTA	50	612 00	180	162 0 00	—		1–19		260	5.96	154 9 60	230	5.83	134 0 90	275	5.60	154 0 00
1–5	RM 12	(500)	1–13	TTA	210	2415 00	50	450 00	90	810 00											
1–8	759	1528 00	1–19	TTA					185	1665 00											
1–9	763	211 00																			
1–15	780	51 00																			
1–17	792	112 00																			

FIGURE 7–3
*Job Cost Sheet
Showing Applied
Overhead*

SELF-STUDY QUIZ 7–2 At the beginning of the year, Rollins Company estimates that factory overhead for the Grinding Department will be $140,000 for the year. Direct labor cost, which is used as a basis for applying overhead in the Grinding Department, is estimated to be $200,000 for the year. Compute the amount of overhead to be applied to Job 101 if the job required $10,000 in direct labor costs to complete.
Answers at end of chapter.

Recording Applied Overhead

LEARNING OBJECTIVE 5

Overhead entered on the individual job cost sheets must also be entered in the general ledger. TurboFlex does this by making a month-end journal entry of the total of the overhead entries that have been made on the job cost sheets during the month. For example, at the end of January, TurboFlex's cost accountant totaled the overhead entered during the month and made the following journal entry:

Page 18

1	Jan.	31	Work in Process Inventory	3 1 8 3 1 28	**1**
2			Factory Overhead—Shaping Dept.	1 2 5 6 3 68	**2**
3			Factory Overhead—Assembling Dept.	1 0 0 2 7 60	**3**
4			Factory Overhead—Finishing Dept.	9 2 4 0 00	**4**
5			Recognized applied overhead for month.		**5**

Notice in this entry that the amount of applied overhead is debited to the Work in Process Inventory account. This, as we discussed in Chapter 2, is done so that Work in Process Inventory will show total production costs for the month, factory overhead as well as direct materials and direct labor. Also notice that each department's applied overhead is credited to the departmental overhead account.

After the above entry is posted to the general ledger, the departmental overhead accounts appear as follows:

ACCOUNT Factory Overhead—Shaping Department						**ACCOUNT NO.** 504		
							BALANCE	
DATE		ITEM	P.R.	DEBIT	CREDIT	DEBIT	CREDIT	
19X6 Jan.	31		GJ10	6 2 1 2 00		6 2 1 2 00		
	31		GJ10	3 1 2 2 55		9 3 3 4 55		
	31		GJ10	4 5 9 4 73		1 3 9 2 9 28		
	31		GJ18		1 2 5 6 3 68	1 3 6 5 60		

ACCOUNT	Factory Overhead—Assembling Department			ACCOUNT NO. 505		

					BALANCE	
DATE	ITEM	P.R.	DEBIT	CREDIT	DEBIT	CREDIT
19X6 Jan. 31		GJ10	3 1 7 4 65		3 1 7 4 65	
31		GJ10	2 8 1 0 30		5 9 8 4 95	
31		GJ10	4 7 5 4 58		10 7 3 9 53	
31		GJ18		10 0 2 7 60	7 1 1 93	

ACCOUNT	Factory Overhead—Finishing Department			ACCOUNT NO. 506		

					BALANCE	
DATE	ITEM	P.R.	DEBIT	CREDIT	DEBIT	CREDIT
19X6 Jan . 31		GJ10	2 4 5 6 85		2 4 5 6 85	
31		GJ10	2 3 9 3 95		4 8 5 0 80	
31		GJ10	3 3 8 0 39		8 2 3 1 19	
31		GJ18		9 2 4 0 00		1 0 0 8 81

The $1,365.60 debit balance in the Factory Overhead—Shaping Department account represents *underapplied overhead*. This happened because the actual overhead for the month, $13,929.28, exceeded the applied overhead. In other words, the Work in Process Inventory account was undercharged for the costs of overhead incurred during the month. This same situation occurs in the Factory Overhead—Assembling Department account because the actual overhead, $10,739.53, exceeded the applied overhead, $10,027.60. However, the $1,008.81 credit balance in the Factory Overhead—Finishing Department account means that overhead was *overapplied* for the month—the amount of applied overhead, $9,240.00, was more than the actual overhead, $8,231.19. This means that more overhead was applied to production than was actually incurred during the month.

Applied Overhead Accounts

Instead of crediting the amount of applied overhead to the departmental overhead accounts, some accountants prefer to use separate departmental accounts entitled Factory Overhead Applied. This way, there would be a separate record of the actual factory overhead (recorded on the debit side of the departmental overhead accounts) and the applied overhead (recorded on the credit side of the departmental overhead applied accounts). Had TurboFlex followed this practice, three additional overhead accounts would appear in the general ledger, as follows:

ACCOUNT Factory Overhead Applied—Shaping Department				ACCOUNT NO. XX			
DATE	ITEM	P.R.	DEBIT	CREDIT	BALANCE		
					DEBIT	CREDIT	
19X6 Jan. 31		GJ18		12 56 3 68		12 56 3 68	

ACCOUNT Factory Overhead Applied—Assembling Department				ACCOUNT NO. XX			
DATE	ITEM	P.R.	DEBIT	CREDIT	BALANCE		
					DEBIT	CREDIT	
19X6 Jan. 31		GJ18		10 02 7 60		10 02 7 60	

ACCOUNT Factory Overhead Applied—Finishing Department				ACCOUNT NO. XX			
DATE	ITEM	P.R.	DEBIT	CREDIT	BALANCE		
					DEBIT	CREDIT	
19X6 Jan. 31		GJ18		9 24 0 00		9 24 0 00	

At the end of the accounting period, the balances in the overhead applied accounts are closed to the departmental overhead accounts, thus yielding the exact same end result as initially crediting applied overhead to the departmental overhead accounts.

ACCOUNTING FOR UNDER- AND OVERAPPLIED FACTORY OVERHEAD

LEARNING OBJECTIVE 6   Since predetermined factory overhead rates are based on estimated data, the amount of overhead applied to production will rarely (if ever) equal the amount of actual overhead incurred during the month. Over the course of a year, however, applied overhead and actual overhead should be very close in amounts (if realistic overhead rates have been used). Overhead overapplied one month is expected to be offset by overhead underapplied in another month.

To keep track of under- or overapplied overhead on a monthly basis, TurboFlex starts each month with a zero balance in the departmental overhead accounts. This is accomplished by transferring the month-end balances of the departmental overhead accounts to a special account entitled **Under- or**

Overapplied Factory Overhead. For example, looking back at the January 31 balances in the departmental overhead accounts (pages 157 and 158), we see the following information:

Account	Balance	Representing
Factory Overhead—Shaping Dept.	$1,365.60 Dr.	Underapplied overhead
Factory Overhead—Assembling Dept.	711.93 Dr.	Underapplied overhead
Factory Overhead—Finishing Dept.	1,008.81 Cr.	Overapplied overhead

These balances are closed to the Under- or Overapplied Factory Overhead account, as follows:

Page 20

1	Jan. 31	Under- or Overapplied Factory Overhead	2077 53		1
2		Factory Overhead—Shaping Dept.		1365 60	2
3		Factory Overhead—Assembling Dept.		711 93	3
4					4
5		Factory Overhead—Finishing Dept.	1008 81		5
6		Under- or Overapplied Factory Overhead		1008 81	6

After these entries are posted, the departmental overhead accounts will have zero balances and the Under- or Overapplied Factory Overhead account appears as follows:

ACCOUNT Under- or Overapplied Factory Overhead					ACCOUNT NO. 507		
						BALANCE	
DATE	ITEM	P.R.	DEBIT	CREDIT	DEBIT	CREDIT	
19X6 Jan. 31		GJ20	2077 53		2077 53		
31		GJ20		1008 81	1068 72		

The $1,068.72 debit balance in the Under- or Overapplied Factory Overhead account represents the amount by which actual overhead costs for January exceeded the amount of overhead applied to production during January. This account will remain open all year to accumulate the month-to-month differences between actual and applied overhead. If the account has a debit balance at the end of a month, as here, it is reported on the interim balance sheet as a deferred charge (asset). If, on the other hand, there is a credit balance in the account, it is reported on the interim balance sheet as a deferred credit (liability).

At the end of the year, the balance of the Under- or Overapplied Factory Overhead account must be eliminated, usually in one of two ways:

1. The balance is closed to the Cost of Goods Sold account.
2. The balance is allocated among Work in Process Inventory, Finished Goods Inventory, and Cost of Goods Sold.

Closed to Cost of Goods Sold. The most common practice closes the balance of the Under- or Overapplied Factory Overhead account to Cost of Goods Sold. This practice is justified because it is quick, and the amount of any underapplied or overapplied overhead at year-end is usually relatively small. The following journal entry closes a debit balance (underapplied overhead) at the end of the year:

1	Dec.	31	Cost of Goods Sold	X X X X XX		1
2			Under- or Overapplied Factory Overhead		X X X X XX	2

Notice that Cost of Goods Sold is debited (increased) for the amount of underapplied overhead. This is done because underapplied overhead means that not enough overhead was applied to production during the year. For example, assume that actual overhead for the year amounted to $300,000 and applied overhead amounted to $290,000. Here, overhead was *under*applied by $10,000. Thus, production costs were *under*stated by $10,000, and Cost of Goods Sold must be increased to correct the problem.

When an overapplied overhead balance occurs at the end of the year, the following journal entry closes the balance of the Under- or Overapplied Factory Overhead account:

1	Dec.	31	Under- or Overapplied Factory Overhead	X X X X XX		1
2			Cost of Goods Sold		X X X X XX	2

In this case, Cost of Goods Sold is credited (decreased) by the amount of overapplied overhead. Overapplied overhead means that too much overhead was charged to production during the year. For example, assume that actual overhead costs for the year amounted to $400,000; however, $420,000 in factory overhead was applied to production. Here, overhead was *over*applied by $20,000. Thus, production was *over*charged by $20,000. To correct this problem, the Cost of Goods Sold account is decreased (credited) by $20,000.

Balance Is Allocated to Production Accounts. If the amount of underapplied or overapplied overhead is material, it should be allocated to the period's production costs. That is, the underapplied or overapplied overhead is allocated among the accounts through which overhead costs flow during the year: Work in

Process Inventory, Finished Goods Inventory, and Cost of Goods Sold. Though theoretically sound, this procedure is very difficult and time-consuming. Consequently, it is not widely used.

ANALYSIS OF UNDERAPPLIED OR OVERAPPLIED OVERHEAD

LEARNING OBJECTIVE 7   From a costing viewpoint, underapplied or overapplied overhead represents an error in assigning overhead costs to production. A small underapplied or overapplied amount is to be expected, and large amounts sometimes occur. Regardless of whether the amount is large or small, however, management wants to know why applied overhead costs differ from actual overhead costs. To explain the difference, accountants often analyze under- or overapplied overhead into *volume* and *spending variances*, which are discussed next.

NOTE Underapplied or overapplied overhead is also analyzed into variances in a standard cost system, which is discussed in detail in Chapter 19. Variance analysis is introduced here to help explain why applied overhead costs differ from actual overhead costs.

Volume and Spending Variances

To analyze under- or overapplied overhead into variances, it is necessary to classify overhead costs as *fixed* or *variable*. You will recall from Chapter 6 that fixed overhead costs do not change (in total) as production levels change. In contrast to fixed costs are **variable costs**, which do change (in total) as production levels change.

A **volume variance** results when the fixed overhead applied during a period differs from the fixed overhead budgeted for the same period. This variance measures the effect of a change in the volume of production. A **spending variance** results when the actual overhead for a period differs from the amount that should have been spent for the number of hours worked.

To illustrate how to compute these variances, let's look again at the actual and applied overhead for TurboFlex for January:

Department	Actual Costs	Applied Costs	Underapplied or Overapplied
Shaping	$13,929.28	$12,563.68	$1,365.60 under.
Assembling	10,739.53	10,027.60	711.93 under.
Finishing	8,231.19	9,240.00	1,008.81 over.

Shaping Department. To analyze the $1,365.60 underapplied overhead in the Shaping Department, we must classify the department's overhead costs as fixed and variable. To do this, let's look again at the overhead application rate for the department:

examine the numerator

$$\frac{\text{Budgeted factory overhead}}{\text{Budgeted direct labor hours}} = \frac{\$142,948}{24,000} = \$5.96$$

An examination of the budgeted overhead of the Shaping Department shows that $62,400 is fixed. The remaining $80,548 ($142,948 − $62,400) is variable. The overhead application rate of $5.96 can now be broken down as follows:

$$\frac{\text{Budgeted fixed factory overhead}}{\text{Budgeted direct labor hours}} = \frac{\$62,400}{24,000} = \$2.60 \text{ fixed overhead per direct labor hour.}$$

$$\frac{\text{Budgeted variable factory overhead}}{\text{Budgeted direct labor hours}} = \frac{\$80,548}{24,000} = \$3.36 \text{ variable overhead per direct labor hour.}$$

As we can see, the Shaping Department has budgeted (estimated) 24,000 direct labor hours for the year. Thus, the average monthly direct labor hours for this department is 2,000 (24,000 divided by 12 months). If the actual number of direct labor hours worked in a month were exactly 2,000, the amount of fixed overhead charged to production would be equal to the fixed costs budgeted (estimated).

To illustrate this, first multiply 2,000 hours by the fixed overhead rate per hour: 2,000 × $2.60 = $5,200. This gives us the amount of fixed overhead that would have been applied during the month had the actual number of direct hours worked in the Shaping Department been exactly 2,000. Now, divide the department's budgeted fixed overhead by 12 months: $62,400 ÷ 12 = $5,200. As we can see, the two figures are the same. However, the actual number of direct labor hours worked during the month was not 2,000. According to payroll records, the actual direct labor hours worked were 2,108. Thus, since the actual number of direct labor hours worked during the month differs from the estimated number of direct labor hours used in determining the overhead application rate, an overhead volume variance exists.

The overhead volume variance accounts for only part of the reason that the applied overhead in the Shaping Department differed from the actual overhead. The remainder of the difference is due to a spending variance. We can analyze the variances as follows:

Volume Variance:
Fixed overhead applied (2,108 × $2.60)	$ 5,480.80	
Fixed overhead budgeted ($62,400 ÷ 12)	5,200.00	
Volume Variance (favorable)		$ 280.80

Spending Variance:
Total actual overhead for the month	$13,929.28	
Budgeted overhead for hours worked:		
Fixed $5,200.00		
Variable (2,108 × $3.36) 7,082.88		
Total budgeted	12,282.88	
Spending Variance (unfavorable)		(1,646.40)

Total variance (unfavorable)		$1,365.60

From this we can see that the volume variance of $280.80 is favorable. It is favorable because the department actually worked 2,108 direct labor hours without an increase in fixed costs, which had been budgeted based on 2,000 hours. In other words, the department received a benefit from operating at a level above that budgeted.

The spending variance is unfavorable because the actual overhead costs incurred during the month exceeded the budgeted overhead for the number of hours actually worked. The total variance of $1,365.60 is unfavorable because the $1,646.40 unfavorable spending variance exceeded the $280.80 favorable volume variance. Had both variances been favorable (or both unfavorable), they would have been added to obtain the total variance.

NOTE Since the volume variance relates to fixed costs, another way to calculate it is to multiply the difference between the number of actual hours worked and the number of hours budgeted by the fixed factory overhead rate per hour: $2,108 - 2,000 = 108 \times \$2.60 = \$280.80$.

Assembling Department. If we look back to page 158, we will see that overhead was also underapplied (by $711.93) in the Assembling Department. To explain why this happened, we can again analyze into volume and spending variances. An examination of the Assembling Department's budgeted overhead shows that $55,650 is fixed. The remaining $66,677 ($122,327 − $55,650) is variable. Looking back to page 155, we see that the department's overhead application rate is $5.83 based on estimated direct labor hours of 21,000. We can break this rate down as follows:

$$\frac{\text{Budgeted fixed factory overhead}}{\text{Budgeted direct labor hours}} = \frac{\$55,650}{21,000} = \$2.65 \text{ fixed overhead per direct labor hour.}$$

$$\frac{\text{Budgeted variable factory overhead}}{\text{Budgeted direct labor hours}} = \frac{\$66,677}{21,000} = \$3.18 \text{ variable overhead per direct labor hour.}$$

To compute the volume variance, we now compare the number of direct labor hours budgeted for the month with the number of direct labor hours actually worked in the department. The number of direct labor hours budgeted is 1,750 (21,000 ÷ 12 months). An examination of the payroll records shows that 1,720 direct labor hours were actually worked by the department. Since there is a difference between the two, there is a volume variance. But the volume variance alone does not account for the $711.93 underapplied overhead; there was also a spending variance.

Compare budgetted hours to actual hours.

Volume Variance:

Fixed overhead applied (1,720 × $2.65)	$ 4,558.00	
Fixed overhead budgeted ($55,650 ÷ 12)	4,637.50	
Volume Variance (unfavorable)		$ 79.50

Spending Variance:

Total actual overhead for the month	$10,739.53	
Budgeted overhead for hours worked:		
Fixed $4,637.50		
Variable (1,720 × $3.18) 5,469.60		
Total budgeted	10,107.10	
Spending Variance (unfavorable)		632.43
Total variance (unfavorable)		$711.93

Unfavorable = when they work < what was budgeted

The volume variance is unfavorable because the direct labor hours that were budgeted (1,750) for the month exceeded the hours actually worked (1,720). This means that the department operated at a level below the numbers of hours budgeted. The spending variance is unfavorable because the actual overhead for the month exceeded the amount budgeted for the number of hours worked.

Finishing Department. Overhead in the Finishing Department was overapplied by $1,008.81. This amount, too, can be analyzed into volume and spending variances. An examination of the budgeted overhead in the department revealed that $48,600 is fixed and the remaining $52,220 ($100,820 − $48,600) is variable. As before, our first task is to break down the department's $5.60 (page 155) hourly overhead application rate into a fixed rate per hour and a variable rate per hour, as follows:

$$\frac{\text{Budgeted fixed factory overhead}}{\text{Budgeted direct labor hours}} = \frac{\$48,600}{18,000} = \$2.70 \text{ fixed overhead per direct labor hour.}$$

$$\frac{\text{Budgeted variable factory overhead}}{\text{Budgeted direct labor hours}} = \frac{\$52,220}{18,000} = \$2.90 \text{ variable overhead per direct labor hour.}$$

The number of direct labor hours budgeted for the month is 1,500 (18,000 ÷ 12). However, payroll records show that the actual direct labor hours worked during the month totaled 1,650. Using these data, we can analyze the department's overapplied overhead into variances, as follows:

Volume Variance:

Fixed overhead applied (1,650 × $2.70)	$4,455.00	
Fixed overhead budgeted ($48,600 ÷ 12)	4,050.00	
Volume Variance (favorable)		$ 405.00

Spending Variance:

Total actual overhead for the month		$8,231.19
Budgeted overhead for hours worked:		
Fixed $4,050.00		
Variable (1,650 × $2.90) . . . . _4,785.00_		
Total budgeted	8,835.00	
Spending Variance (favorable)		_603.81_
Total variance (favorable)		$1,008.81

The volume variance is favorable because the actual direct labor hours worked exceeded those budgeted. The spending variance is favorable because the actual overhead was less than the amount budgeted.

SELF-STUDY QUIZ 7–3 From the following data, analyze the under- or over-applied factory overhead into volume and spending variances.

	Budgeted Data for the Year	Actual Data for the Year
Direct labor hours	72,000	74,400
Factory overhead:		
Fixed	$ 50,400	$ 50,400
Variable	151,200	155,000
Totals	$201,600	$205,400

Answers at end of chapter.

SELF-STUDY PROBLEM

Selected data for Lancaster Products Company follow for the year:

	Budgeted Data	Actual Data
Direct labor hours	70,000	72,000
Factory overhead:		
Fixed	$ 49,000	$ 49,000
Variable	147,000	155,000
Totals	$196,000	$204,000

Required:

1. Compute the overhead application rate.
2. Determine the amount of overhead applied during the year.
3. Compute the under- or overapplied overhead for the year.
4. Analyze the under- or overapplied overhead into volume and spending variances.
5. Close the under- or overapplied overhead to Cost of Goods Sold.

SOLUTION TO SELF-STUDY PROBLEM

1. $\dfrac{\$196,000}{70,000} = \$2.80$

2. $72,000 \times \$2.80 = \$201,600$

3. $\begin{array}{r} \$204,000 \text{ actual factory overhead} \\ -201,600 \text{ applied factory overhead} \\ \hline \$ \ \ 2,400 \text{ underapplied} \end{array}$

4. $\dfrac{\$49,000}{70,000} = \$.70$ fixed overhead per direct labor hour.

   $\dfrac{\$147,000}{70,000} = \$2.10$ variable overhead per direct labor hour.

Volume Variance:

Fixed overhead applied ($.70 × 72,000)	$ 50,400	
Fixed overhead budgeted	49,000	
Volume Variance (favorable)		$1,400

Spending Variance:

Total actual overhead		$204,000	
Budgeted overhead for hours worked:			
Fixed	$ 49,000		
Variable (72,000 × $2.10)	151,200		
Total budgeted overhead		200,200	
Spending Variance (unfavorable)			(3,800)

Total variance (unfavorable) $2,400

5.

1	Dec.	31	Cost of Goods Sold	2 4 0 0 0 0		1
2			Under- or Overapplied Factory Overhead		2 4 0 0 0 0	2
3			Closed underapplied overhead to			3
4			Cost of Goods Sold.			4

SUMMARY

Factory overhead costs are a present and ongoing part of producing any product. However, actual overhead costs are rarely, if ever, used in product costing. This is because many actual overhead costs are not available until the end of the accounting period (depreciation, expired insurance, accrued expenses, etc.). This is too late for management to consider them when computing the unit cost of products manufactured during the period. Also, some overhead costs occur on an inconsistent basis. For example, repair costs may be very heavy in one period, but light in another period. As a result of these factors, overhead costs are charged to jobs in production based on a predetermined rate. The rate is referred to as "predetermined" because it is calculated before a period starts and is based entirely on estimated data.

The **predetermined factory overhead rate** is computed by dividing the budgeted (estimated) factory overhead costs for a period by an estimated *activity base* for the same period. The activity base selected should have a cause-and-effect relationship to the actual incurrence of overhead. This means that the activity base should act as a cost driver. **A cost driver** is any activity that causes overhead to occur. For example, in most firms direct labor is a cost driver because the occurence of factory overhead costs is directly related to direct labor (if employees are working, overhead is occurring because utilities are being used, machinery is operating, repairs are being made, etc.).

Common cost drivers in a manufacturing firm include machine hours, direct materials cost, direct labor hours, and direct labor cost. Cost drivers in nonmanufacturing firms include activities such as total miles driven, hours of computer operations, and number of beds occupied.

The period of time used to compute the overhead application rate is usually one year. Periods of less than a year are usually susceptible to seasonal fluctuations and variations, thus making them improper to use as a base for applying overhead.

Once an overhead application rate has been computed, it is used for the entire period. If, for example, a firm uses direct labor cost as a base for applying overhead, the amount of overhead to be charged to each job completed during the period is calculated by multiplying the direct labor costs charged to the job by the overhead application rate. The applied overhead is posted to the job cost sheet, where it is added to the cost of direct materials and direct labor to obtain the total cost of the job.

Applied overhead is recorded by debiting the Work in Process Inventory account and crediting Factory Overhead Control (or departmental overhead accounts if a firm is departmentalized). Since the applied overhead is based on estimated data, the amount of overhead applied during a month will typically be different from the amount of actual overhead incurred during the month. Over the course of a year, however, applied overhead and actual overhead should be close in amount because overhead overapplied during one month should be offset by overhead underapplied during another month.

Overhead that is under- or overapplied at the end of each month can be transferred to an account entitled **Under- or Overapplied Factory Overhead.** At the end of the year, the balance of this account is usually closed to Cost of Goods Sold.

To determine why overhead was under- or overapplied for a period, cost accountants often analyze the difference into volume and spending variances. To calcuate these variances, it is necessary to classify overhead costs as *fixed* and *variable*. **Fixed overhead costs** do not change (in total) as production levels change. **Variable overhead costs** do change (in total) as production levels vary.

A **volume variance** results when the fixed overhead applied during a period differs from the fixed overhead budgeted for the same period. A volume variance is favorable when the number of hours actually worked exceed the number of hours budgeted. On the other hand, a volume variance is unfavorable when the number of hours actually worked are less than those budgeted (estimated).

A **spending variance** results when the actual overhead for the period differs from the amount of overhead that should have been spent for the hours that were actually worked. A spending variance is favorable when the actual overhead during a period is less than that budgeted; it is unfavorable when the actual overhead exceeds that budgeted.

APPENDIX 7A: ACTIVITY-BASED COSTING (ABC)

The most difficult task in product costing is to determine how much factory overhead to apply to a job. In this chapter, we worked with departmental overhead rates when applying factory overhead for TurboFlex Corporation. The use of departmental rates involves two stages: (1) costs are assigned to individual departments, and (2) costs are allocated from the departments to individual jobs. Each department uses an application rate related to cost drivers in that department.

While the use of departmental overhead rates offers many advantages over the use of a single blanket rate for an entire firm, departmental rates are not equitable for all situations. If large departmental differences exist in the volume of activity, or complexity of operations, the use of departmental overhead rates could distort product costing. In these situations, *activity-based costing* would be more realistic. An **activity-based costing (ABC) system** is also a two-stage allocation process (as described earlier). In activity-based costing, however, costs are *not* initially traced to departments. Instead, costs are first traced to activities, and then to products. Cost drivers (activities) causing overhead to occur are identified. These activities (called **activity drivers** in an ABC system) are later used as a basis for allocating overhead costs to products. Examples of activity drivers include the amount of power used, the number of machine setups required, the amount of power consumed, the total number of direct labor hours needed, the number of miles driven, the amount of inventory movements, and hours of computer time logged. In the second stage, costs are assigned to individual jobs based on the number of these activites that were necessary to complete the job.

To illustrate the application of activity-based costing, assume that Winegar Company manufactures two products known as Product J and Product L. Product J is a low-volume item with sales of about 10,000 units a year. Product L is a high-volume item with sales of about 30,000 units a year. The production of these products requires four overhead activities—power, machine setups, maintenance, and quality inspections. Expected overhead costs to be allocated to Products J and L follow:

Power	$240,000
Machine setups	72,000
Maintenance	80,000
Quality inspections	60,000
Total	$452,000

Now, activity drivers must be identified, that is, the overhead activities must be analyzed to determine how the costs for the activities are incurred. Winegar identified the following activity drivers:

Cost	Activity Driver
Power	Kilowatt-hours
Machine setups	Number of setups
Maintenance	Machine hours
Quality inspections	Number of inspections

Next, the amounts of activity drivers required to complete each product are determined, as follows:

	Kilowatt-Hours	Number of Setups	Machine Hours	Number of Inspections
Product J	200,000	198	10,000	400
Product K	800,000	702	40,000	600
Totals	1,000,000	900	50,000	1,000

Rates for each activity driver are now determined as follows:

Item	Cost		Activity Driver		Rate
Power	$240,000	÷	1,000,000 kwh	=	$ 0.24 per kwh
Machine setups	72,000	÷	900 setups	=	80.00 per setup
Maintenance	80,000	÷	50,000 mach. hours	=	1.60 per hour
Quality inspections	60,000	÷	1,000 inspections	=	60.00 per inspection

The $452,000 in overhead costs are now allocated to Products J and L as follows:

Overhead costs	Rate			Product J	Product L
Power:					
200,000 kwh	×	$ 0.24	=	$ 48,000	
800,000	×	$ 0.24	=		$192,000
Machine setups:					
198	×	$80.00	=	15,840	
702	×	$80.00	=		56,160
Maintenance:					
10,000 hours	×	$ 1.60	=	16,000	
40,000 hours	×	$ 1.60	=		64,000
Quality Inspections:					
400 inspections	×	$60.00	=	24,000	
600 inspections	×	$60.00	=		36,000
Totals				$103,840	+ $348,160 = $452,000

As we can see, activity-based costing focuses on identifying and measuring activities that cause overhead costs to occur. The related costs are then traced to the specific products based on the activities. Winegar Company used a different activity driver for each overhead activity. This could be very time consuming for large companies because many different overhead activities could be identified. As a result, overhead activities may be grouped together in cost pools. Each cost pool would then be allocated using a primary cost driver related to the costs within that pool.

KEY TERMS

Cost Driver. A factor that has a cause-and-effect relation to the occurence of factory overhead costs.

Predetermined Factory Overhead Rate. A rate determined at the beginning of an accounting period and used to apply (charge) overhead to production during the period.

Under- or Overapplied Factory Overhead Account. An account used to record the amount of under- or overapplied factory overhead at the end of each month. At year-end, its balance is usually closed to Cost of Goods Sold.

Spending Variance. A variance that results when the actual factory overhead costs for a period differs from the amount that should have been spent for the number of hours actually worked.

Variable Overhead Costs. Overhead costs that vary (in total) as production levels change. Examples include indirect materials, indirect labor, utilities, and repairs.

Volume Variance. A variance that results when the fixed factory overhead applied during a period differs from the fixed overhead budgeted for the same period.

APPENDIX

Activity-Based Costing. A method of accumulating and allocating factory overhead costs by activities rather than by departments.

Activity Driver. Any activity base used to allocate overhead costs to jobs in production.

QUESTIONS FOR REVIEW

1. Why are actual factory overhead costs rarely (if ever) charged to production?
2. Why is the factory overhead application rate referred to as "predetermined?"
3. What is a cost driver?
4. Is direct labor always a cost driver? Explain.
5. How is a predetermined overhead application rate determined?
6. What are some common bases used in establishing overhead application rates in (a) a manufacturing firm and (b) a nonmanufacturing firm?
7. How is the overhead application rate determined when the activity base used is machine hours?
8. When would machine hours be an appropriate base for applying overhead?
9. Direct labor remains a cost driver for many manufacturing firms. Under what circumstances would direct labor hours be a more appropriate base than direct labor cost?
10. Historically, direct labor cost has been the most popular base for applying overhead. Why?
11. What is meant by (a) underapplied overhead; (b) overapplied overhead?
12. What is the interim financial statement presentation of (a) underapplied overhead; (b) overhead applied overhead?

13. What are two methods of handling any underapplied or overapplied factory overhead at the end of a year? Which method is the most popular? Why?
14. Differentiate between a volume variance and a spending variance.
15. When is a volume variance favorable? When is it unfavorable?
16. When is a spending variance favorable? When is it unfavorable?
17. (Appendix) What is meant by activity-based costing?
18. (Appendix) What is an activity driver?

NOTE Unless told otherwise in Exercises and Problems, record transactions in general journal form.

EXERCISES

7–1. Learning Objectives 1, 2. Calculating Overhead Application Rates.

At the beginning of the year, Simmons Company estimates that factory overhead costs for the year will be $198,000. The company also estimates that 55,000 direct labor hours will be worked during the year. What is the overhead application rate based on direct labor hours?

7–2. Learning Objectives 2, 3, 4. Applying Overhead to Jobs.

Johnson Corporation is divided into five production departments. Departmental overhead rates are used because the activites in each department are different. The Cutting Department estimates that its overhead for the year will be $294,000 and that its direct labor cost will be $490,000. During July, the Cutting Department worked on three jobs: Job 101 on which $12,800 in direct labor was charged; Job 104 on which $10,400 in direct labor was charged; Job 105 on which $4,000 of direct labor was charged. What is the amount of overhead that should be applied to each job?

7–3. Learning Objective 3. Computing Overhead Rates.

Using the following data, determine the amount of factory overhead to charge Job 308 if (a) direct labor hours are used as a base for applying overhead and (b) direct labor costs are used as a base for applying overhead.

Estimated factory overhead costs for the year	$573,440
Estimated direct labor hours for the year	112,000 hours
Estimated direct labor costs for the year	$688,128

Job 308:
Direct labor hours used	1,510
Direct labor charged	$7,776.50

7–4. Learning Objective 4. Applying Factory Overhead Costs.

Fitzpatrick Company records applied overhead on job cost sheets as each job is completed, or at the end of the month if the job is still in production. During March, the firm completed Jobs 114, 118, and 121, while Jobs 119 and 122 were still in production. The Molding Department worked on these jobs as follows:

Job	Direct Labor Hours
114	156
118	142
119	112
121	138
122	43

The current overhead application rate in the Molding Department is $4.12 per direct labor hour. How much factory overhead should be added to each job's cost sheet?

7–5. Learning Objective 5. Journalizing Factory Overhead Costs.

The following overhead costs were added to the job cost sheets by Birmingham Steel Company during June:

Cutting Department	$25,890.00
Stamping Department	34,560.90
Finishing Department	22,345.10

Make the journal entry to record these costs assuming that the firm uses departmental overhead accounts.

7–6. Learning Objective 6. Journalizing Underapplied or Overapplied Factory Overhead.

After all posting was completed during September, the following account balances appear in the ledger of Destin Products Company:

Factory Overhead—Cutting Department	$1,540.70 Cr.
Factory Overhead—Grinding Department	1,215.90 Dr.
Factory Overhead—Baking Department	1,155.60 Cr.
Factory Overhead—Finishing Department	925.00 Dr.

Close these balances to the Under- or Overapplied Factory Overhead account.

7–7. Learning Objective 6. Journalizing Underapplied or Overapplied Factory Overhead.

Jacobs Company is a small manufacturing firm with one producing department. During March, the company incurred $22,600 in actual factory overhead costs. Overhead was applied to production at the rate of $4.65 per direct labor hour.

a. What is the under- or overapplied factory overhead if 4,950 direct labor hours were worked during the month.
b. Make the journal entry to transfer the balance of the Factory Overhead Control account to the Under- or Overapplied Factory Overhead account.

7–8. Learning Objective 6. Closing Year-end Under- or Overapplied Factory Overhead.

Close the balance of the Under- or Overapplied Factory Overhead account under each of the following independent assumptions:

a. The account has a year-end debit balance of $3,215.12.
b. The account has a year-end credit balance of $2,346.47.

7–9. Learning Objective 7. Computing a Volume Variance.

The following data relate to the Biggers Corporation. Compute the volume variance.

	Budgeted Data	Actual Data
Direct labor hours	80,000 hours	82,300 hours
Factory overhead costs:		
Fixed	$240,000	$240,000
Variable	260,000	264,000

7–10. Learning Objective 7. Computing a Spending Variance.
Using the data from Exercise 9, calculate the spending variance for Biggers Corporation.

7–11. Learning Objective 7. Activity-Based Costing (Appendix).
Plitt Company manufactures two products, X and Y, which involve the following over-head activities: power, factory supervision, and maintenance. The expected costs for these activities follow:

Power	$181,000
Factory supervision	125,000
Maintenance	90,000

Activity drivers for each product:

Cost	Activity Driver
Power	Kilowatt hours
Factory supervision	Number of employees
Maintenance	Square footage

Amounts of activity drivers for each product:

Product	Kilowatt Hours	Number of Employees	Square Footage
X	81,450	32	8,000
Y	99,550	68	12,000

Allocate the overhead costs to each product.

GROUP A PROBLEMS

7–1A. Learning Objective 2. Computing Overhead Application Rates.
Estimated data for Pyramid Products Company for the year follow:

Factory overhead costs	$281,000
Machine hours	9,000 hours
Direct materials costs	$325,000
Direct labor costs	$300,000
Direct labor hours	21,000 hours

Required:
Use each of the following activity bases to compute an overhead application rate:

a. Machine hours
b. Direct materials costs
c. Direct labor costs
d. Direct labor hours

7–2A. Learning Objectives 2, 4. Determining Total Job Costs Using Predetermined Overhead Rates.

Chi Gaming Company applies overhead to production on the basis of direct labor costs. At the beginning of the year, the firm's cost accountant computed an overhead application rate of 80% for the year. The following list of jobs completed during June shows charges for direct materials and direct labor.

Job	Direct Materials	Direct Labor
098	$ 6,200	$12,800
101	9,500	16,700
102	10,300	19,200
104	7,800	14,500

Required:

1. Compute the amount of overhead to be added to the cost of each job completed during the month.
2. Compute the total cost of each job completed during the month.
3. Compute the total cost of producing all jobs completed during the month.

7–3A. Learning Objectives 2, 3, 4, 5, 6. Computing Overhead Rates and Applying Overhead.

Calico Company is a small manufacturer of wood products with one producing department. The following data relate to Calico:

Estimated data for the year

Factory overhead costs	$60,000
Direct labor costs	$80,000
Direct labor hours	12,000
Machine hours	8,000

Actual data for June

Job	Materials Costs	Direct Labor Costs	Direct Labor Hours	Machine Hours	Date Job Completed
211	$2,000	$1,380	200	80	June 12
212	2,500	1,408	204	72	June 18
213	3,000	1,512	212	70	June 25
215	1,200	800	115	30	In process
216	1,820	1,210	175	42	In process

Required:

1. Compute the predetermined overhead application rate based on the following:
   a. Direct labor cost
   b. Direct labor hours
   c. Machine hours
2. Using each of these bases, calculate the total cost of each job at the end of the month.
3. Make the general journal entry to record applied overhead for the month assuming that direct labor cost is used as a base for applying overhead.
4. Determine the under- or overapplied factory overhead at the end of the month under each method.

7–4A. Learning Objective 6. Closing the Balance of Under- or Overapplied Factory Overhead.
At the end of 19X8, the Under- or Overapplied Factory Overhead account in the ledger
of Ring-Around Products Company appeared as follows:

ACCOUNT	Under–Overapplied Factory Overhead				ACCOUNT NO. 507	
					BALANCE	
DATE	ITEM	P.R.	DEBIT	CREDIT	DEBIT	CREDIT
19X8 Dec. 31		GJ8	4 3 1 0 00		4 3 1 0 00	
31		GJ12		4 0 0 0 00	3 1 0 00	

Required:

1. What is the actual factory overhead for the period?
2. Was overhead under- or overapplied?
3. Close the balance of the account to Cost of Goods Sold.
4. Under what conditions would the entry made in number 3 above been reversed?
   Explain.

7–5A. Learning Objective 7. Computing Volume and Spending Variances.
Selected data for Lanier Company for the year follow:

	Budgeted Data	Actual Data
Direct labor hours	90,000	91,800
Factory Overhead:		
Fixed	$252,000	$252,000
Variable	288,000	291,000
Totals	$540,000	$543,000

Required:

1. Compute the overhead application rate.
2. Determine the amount of overhead that was applied during the year.
3. Compute the under- or overapplied overhead for the year.
4. Analyze the under- or overapplied overhead into volume and spending variances.
5. Close the under- or overapplied overhead to Cost of Goods Sold.

7–6A. Activity-Based Costing (Appendix).
Plant Company manufactures two products, X-1 and X-2. The following overhead
activities are involved: power, maintenance, factory supervision, and quality inspections. The expected costs for these activities follow:

Power	$220,000
Maintenance	200,000
Factory supervision	160,000
Quality inspections	90,000

The activity drivers for each product follow:

Overhead Cost	Activity Driver
Power	Kilowatt hours
Maintenance	Square footage
Factory supervision	Number of employees
Quality inspections	Number of inspections

The amounts of activity drivers for each product follow:

Product	Kilowatt Hours	Square Footage	Number of Employees	Number of Inspections
X-1	400,000	8,750	48	144
X-2	600,000	16,250	72	216

Required:

1. Compute an overhead application rate for each activity.
2. Allocate the overhead costs to each product.

GROUP B PROBLEMS

7–1B. Learning Objective 2. Computing Overhead Application Rates.
Estimated data for Pyramid Products Company for the year follows:

Factory overhead costs	$272,000
Machine hours	8,000 hours
Direct materials costs	$408,000
Direct labor costs	515,800
Direct labor hours	16,000 hours

Required:
Use each of the following activity bases to determine an overhead application rate:

a. Machine hours
b. Direct materials costs
c. Direct labor costs
d. Direct labor hours

7–2B. Learning Objectives 2 & 4. Determining Total Job Costs Using Predetermined Overhead Rates.
Santos Company applies overhead to production on the basis of direct labor hours. At the beginning of the year, the firm's cost accountant computed an overhead application

rate of 70% for the year. The following list of jobs completed during May shows charges for direct materials and direct labor.

Job	Direct Materials	Direct Labor
070	$ 5,600	$10,400
085	9,000	12,400
090	12,600	18,200
102	5,700	9,980

Required:

1. Compute the amount of overhead to be added to the cost of each job completed during the month.
2. Compute the total cost of each job completed during the month.
3. Compute the total cost of producing all jobs completed during the month.

7–3B. Learning Objectives 2, 3, 4, 5, 6. Computing Overhead Rates and Applying Overhead.

Caro Manufacturing Company is a small manufacturer of metal products with one producing department. The following data relate to Caro:

Estimated data for the year

Factory overhead costs	$72,000
Direct labor costs	90,000
Direct labor hours	9,000
Machine hours	6,000

Actual data for August

Job	Materials Costs	Direct Labor Costs	Direct Labor Hours	Machine Hours	Date Job Completed
109	$2,200	$1,250	190	70	Aug. 10
112	2,400	1,400	200	68	Aug. 17
115	3,200	2,450	208	72	Aug. 28
116	1,820	1,610	140	31	In process
117	900	625	38	22	In process

Required:

1. Compute the predetermined overhead application rate based on the
   a. Direct labor cost.
   b. Direct labor hours.
   c. Machine hours.
2. Using each of these bases, compute the total cost of each job at the end of the month.
3. Make the general journal entry to record applied overhead for the month assuming that direct labor cost is used as a base for applying overhead.
4. Determine the under- or overapplied factory overhead at the end of the month under each method.

7–4B. Learning Objective 6. Closing the Balance of Under- or Overapplied Factory Overhead.

At the end of 19X3, the Under- or Overapplied Factory Overhead account in the ledger of Pike Products Company appeared as follows:

ACCOUNT Under–Overapplied Factory Overhead					ACCOUNT NO. 507	
					BALANCE	
DATE	ITEM	P.R.	DEBIT	CREDIT	DEBIT	CREDIT
19X3 Dec. 31		GJ12	89 31 5 00		89 31 5 00	
31		GJ16		91 29 0 00		1 97 5 00

Required:

1. What is the actual factory overhead for the period?
2. Was overhead under- or overapplied?
3. Close the balance of the account to Cost of Goods Sold.
4. Under what conditions would the entry made in number 3 above been reversed? Explain.

7–5B. Learning Objective 7. Computing Volume and Spending Variances.

Selected data for Gainesville Company for the year follow:

	Budgeted Data	Actual Data
Direct labor hours	80,000	82,200
Factory Overhead:		
Fixed	$244,800	$244,800
Variable	284,800	290,000
Totals	$529,600	$534,800

if act hrs 7 budget hrs then fav.

Required:

1. Compute the overhead application rate.
2. Determine the amount of overhead that was applied during the year.
3. Compute the under- or overapplied overhead for the year.
4. Analyze the under- or overapplied overhead into volume and spending variances.
5. Make the journal entry to close the under- or overapplied overhead to Cost of Goods Sold.

7–6B. Activity-Based Costing (Appendix).

Savannah Products Company manufactures two products, L-1 and L-2. The following overhead activities are involved: power, maintenance, factory supervision, and quality inspections. The expected costs for these activities follow:

Power	$200,000
Maintenance	175,000
Factory supervision	150,000
Quality inspections	60,000

The activity drivers for each product follow:

Overhead Cost   **Activity Driver**

Power   Kilowatt hours
Maintenance   Square footage
Factory supervision   Number of employees
Quality inspections   Number of inspections

The amounts of activity drivers for each product follow:

Product	Kilowatt Hours	Square Footage	Number of Employees	Number of Inspections
L-1	200,000	7,200	48	96
L-2	600,000	10,800	112	204

Required:

1. Compute an overhead application rate for each activity.
2. Allocate the overhead costs to each product.

CASE FOR CRITICAL THINKING

Ben Turner is studying accounting at Coastal Community College. Ben is having some difficulty with the concept of applying overhead. Ben reasons that it makes no sense for a firm to charge estimated overhead to production when actual overhead occurs everyday, even on days when the plant is closed. Write a paragraph explaining why overhead is applied to production.

ANSWERS TO SELF-STUDY QUIZ 7–1

a. $\dfrac{\$240,000}{8,000} = \$30$

b. $\dfrac{\$240,000}{\$300,000} = 80\%$

c. $\dfrac{\$240,000}{\$320,000} = 75\%$

d. $\dfrac{\$240,000}{16,000} = \$15$

ANSWERS TO SELF-STUDY QUIZ 7–2

$$\frac{\$140,000}{\$200,000} = 70\% \text{ overhead application rate}$$

$\$10,000 \times .70 = \$7,000$ in overhead applied to Job 101.

ANSWERS TO SELF-STUDY QUIZ 7–3

Volume Variance:
Fixed overhead applied (74,400 × $0.70*) . . . . $ 52,080
Fixed overhead budgeted   50,400
   Volume Variance (favorable) . . . . $ 1,680

Spending Variance:
Total actual overhead $205,400
Budgeted overhead for hours worked:
   Fixed . . . . $ 50,400
   Variable (74,400 × $2.10**)   156,240
     Total budgeted 206,640
      Spending Variance (favorable).   1,240

Total variance (favorable) . . . . $ 2,920

$*\ \dfrac{\$50,400}{72,000} = \$0.70$

$**\ \dfrac{\$151,200}{72,000} = \$2.10$

Job
Completion

Aug 18/69

9 2 8 1 6 8 u d
f j u 0 8 8 4 0 7
1 8 2 t 1 0 9

Chapter 8
Completing the Cost Cycle

LEARNING OBJECTIVES

After studying Chapter 8, you should be able to:

1. Record the cost of completed jobs.
2. Prove the job cost ledger.
3. Record the sale of finished goods.
4. Prove the stock ledger.
5. Prepare financial statements showing manufacturing costs.

n the last five chapters, we learned how the elements of manufacturing costs (direct materials, direct labor, and factory overhead) are accounted for in a job-order costing system. When jobs are completed, the finished goods are moved from the production floor to the finshed goods warehouse, where they will remain until sold. To match the flow of costs with the physical flow of these goods, the cost of all units completed during the month must be transferred from the Work in Process Inventory account to the Finished Goods Inventory account. When the finished goods are sold, their cost must be transferred from the Finished Goods Inventory account to the Cost of Goods Sold account.

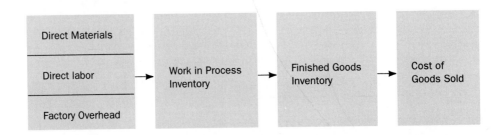

In this chapter, we will discuss and illustrate how these entries are made. We will also examine how subsidiary ledgers are proved, and how cost data are presented on financial statements.

RECORDING THE COST OF COMPLETED JOBS

LEARNING OBJECTIVE 1

During a month's operations, the cost of raw materials placed in production is accounted for through materials requisitions, the direct labor charged to jobs is accumulated on time tickets, and factory overhead is applied to production using predetermined rates. These costs are posted to the individual job cost sheets throughout the month. When a job is completed, the related job cost sheet is totaled, summarized, and transferred from the in-process category to a finished work file. Figure 8–1 illustrates the completed job cost sheet for job number 118.

JOB COST SHEET

Customer __Sports World__
Job Description __On file__
Quantity __18__

Job # ____118____
Date Started __1–2–X6__
Date Completed __1–19–X6__

MATERIALS DATE	REQ. NO.	AMOUNT	DL DATE	REF.	SHAPING HRS.	SHAPING AMOUNT	ASSEMBLING HRS.	ASSEMBLING AMOUNT	FINISHING HRS.	FINISHING AMOUNT	OH DATE	REF.	SHAPING HRS.	RATE	SHAPING AMOUNT	ASSEMBLING HRS.	RATE	ASSEMBLING AMOUNT	FINISHING HRS.	RATE	FINISHING AMOUNT
1–4	701	500 00	1–6	TTA	50	612 00	180	1620 00	—		1–19		260	5.96	1549 60	230	5.83	1340 90	275	5.60	1540 00
1–5	RM12	(5 00)	1–13	TTA	210	2415 00	50	450 00	90	810 00											
1–8	759	1528 00	1–19	TTA					185	1665 00											
1–9	763	211 00																			
1–15	780	51 00																			
1–17	792	112 00																			
Totals		2352 00			260	3027 00	230	2070 00	275	2475 00			260		1549 60	230		1340 90	275		1540 00

Total Costs $ __14,354.50__
Units Produced   __18__
Cost Per Unit $ __797.47__
Contract Price $ __18,540.00__

FIGURE 8–1
*Completed Job
Cost Sheet*

At the end of the month, all completed job cost sheets are totaled. The total is debited to the Finished Goods Inventory account and credited to the Work in Process Inventory account. To illustrate, TurboFlex made the following general journal entry to record the cost of goods completed during January:

Page 21

1	Jan.	31	Finished Goods Inventory	143 32 5 00		1
2			Work in Process Inventory		143 32 5 00	2
3			Transferred cost of completed units.			3
4						4
5						5
6						6

After posting this entry, the Work in Process Inventory account appears as follows:

ACCOUNT Work in Process Inventory					ACCOUNT NO. 122	
					BALANCE	
DATE	ITEM	P.R.	DEBIT	CREDIT	DEBIT	CREDIT
19X6 Jan. 1	Balance	✓			6400000	
31	Direct Materials	GJ12	3720000		10120000	
31	Direct Labor	GJ16	3564800		13684800	
31	Applied Overhead	GJ18	3183128		16867928	
31	Returned Materials	GJ15		62000	16805928	
31	Completed Jobs	GJ21		14333250	2473428	

The debits to the Work in Process Inventory account represent the *total* factory cost for the month's operations. The first credit, $620, is for materials returned to the storeroom. The second credit, as we just saw, represents the cost of goods completed during the month. The balance of the account represents the total of all costs charged to the jobs that are still in production at the end of the month, i.e., ending work in process.

Proving the Job Cost Ledger

LEARNING OBJECTIVE 2

The Work in Process Inventory account is a controlling account. The related subsidiary ledger, the **job cost ledger**, is made up of the job cost sheets. The month-end balance of the Work-in-Process Inventory account must equal the total cost of all uncompleted jobs. To verify that these two amounts are in agreement, TurboFlex's cost accountant prepared the **Schedule of Work in Process** illustrated in Figure 8–2.

FIGURE 8–2
Schedule of Work in Process

TURBOFLEX CORPORATION Schedule of Work in Process January 31, 19X6				
Job	Direct Materials	Direct Labor	Factory Overhead	Total
121	$3,245.00	$2,810.00	$2,416.00	$ 8,471.00
122	3,050.00	2,623.00	2,255.78	7,928.78
123	2,115.00	1,861.20	1,582.02	5,558.22
124	1,110.51	971.70	694.07	2,776.28
Totals	$9,520.51	$8,265.90	$6,947.87	$24,734.28

Stock Ledger

As we have seen, completion of a job results in a debit to the Finished Goods Inventory account and a credit to the Work in Process Inventory account. If a job is completed for the purpose of replenishing the stock level, its cost is recorded in a **stock ledger** (also called a **finished goods ledger**), as well as the general ledger. The stock ledger, a subsidiary ledger for the Finished Goods Inventory account, is made up of ledger cards for each type of product manufactured for stock. TurboFlex makes only one product, the TurboFlex II; however, it comes in several versions. A ledger card is thus maintained for each version. Figure 8–3 illustrates the stock ledger card for the heavy duty version of the TurboFlex II (called the TurboFlex II Plus).

ITEM TurboFlex II Plus		NUMBER 1128875									
DATE	REFERENCE	RECEIVED			SOLD			BALANCE			
		UNITS	PRICE	AMOUNT	UNITS	PRICE	AMOUNT	UNITS	PRICE	AMOUNT	
19X6 Jan. 1	Bal.							5	940 00	4700 00	
2	J–119	30	975 00	29250 00				*5 30	940 00 975 00	4700 00 29250 00	

*Balance is shown on two lines because the units were manufactured at two different costs.

FIGURE 8–3
Stock Ledger Card

The stock ledger only shows goods available for sale. Thus, special order goods manufactured to a customer's specifications are not entered in the stock ledger. TurboFlex ships special order goods immediately to the customers and does not enter them in the stock ledger. For example, TurboFlex regularly manufactures the TurboFlex II for the SaveMore Department Store chain. However, the SaveMore units are a different color and bear the name of SaveMore, not TurboFlex. These units are only manufactured when an order is received from SaveMore. When a job for these units is completed, TurboFlex ships the units immediately without making an entry in the stock ledger.

RECORDING SALES OF FINISHED GOODS

LEARNING OBJECTIVE 3   The sale of finished units requires two journal entries. The first entry records the selling price of the units; the second entry transfers the cost of the units from Finished Goods Inventory to Cost of Goods Sold. For example, on January 27, TurboFlex sold 25 of the TurboFlex II Plus units on account to Wilk's Department Store. The selling price of each unit was $1,575. The following entry records the sale:

Page 22

1	Jan.	27	Accounts Receivable	39 3 7 5 00	1
2			Sales	39 3 7 5 00	2
3			Sold finished units ($1,575 x 25).		3

This entry is necessary to record the selling price of the units. And since the 25 units have been sold, the Finished Goods Inventory account and the stock ledger must be updated immediately. Thus the stock ledger card for the TurboFlex II Plus is reduced and a journal entry is made to transfer the cost of the 25 units from the Finished Goods Inventory account to the Cost of Goods Sold account. To determine the cost of the 25 units, look again at the stock ledger card (Figure 8–3).

The cost of the 25 units sold is computed as follows:

$$
\begin{array}{lr}
5 \text{ units} \times \$940 = & \$\ 4,700 \\
\underline{20} \text{ units} \times\ \ 975 = & \underline{19,500} \\
\underline{\underline{25}} & \$24,200
\end{array}
$$

The following entry records the cost of the units sold:

1	Jan.	27	Cost of Goods Sold	24 2 0 0 00	1
2			Finished Goods Inventory	24 2 0 0 00	2
3			Transferred cost of units sold.		3

Recording Credit Sales in a Sales Journal

Manufacturing firms make most sales on a credit basis. As a result, many firms use a specially designed sales journal to record more efficiently the high volume of credit sales. TurboFlex uses the sales journal illustrated in Figure 8–4. Notice that it is used to record both the selling price of the units, as well as to transfer the cost of the units from Finished Goods Inventory to Cost of Goods Sold. Thus, at month-end, only four postings to the general ledger are required.

FIGURE 8–4
Sales Journal

			SALES JOURNAL			

Date		Inv. No.	Customer's Name	✔	Accounts Rec. Dr. Sales Cr.	Cost of Goods Sold Dr. Fin. Goods Cr.
19X6 Jan.	3	1003	Tri-State Fitness		25 2 0 0 00	18 3 0 0 00
	5	1004	King Sporting Goods		18 7 5 0 00	12 6 0 0 00
	27	1015	Wilk's Department		39 3 7 5 00	24 2 0 0 00
	31		Totals		198 2 1 0 00	101 3 1 8 00
					(112) (411)	(415) (123)

Proving the Stock Ledger

LEARNING OBJECTIVE 4   After posting all January transactions, the Finished Goods Inventory account appears as follows:

ACCOUNT Finished Goods Inventory   **ACCOUNT NO.** 123

DATE		ITEM	P.R.	DEBIT	CREDIT	BALANCE DEBIT	BALANCE CREDIT
19X6 Jan.	1	Balance	✔			87 0 0 0 00	
	31	Completed Jobs	GJ21	143 3 2 5 00		230 3 2 5 00	
	31	Cost of Goods Sold	S18		138 6 0 0 00	91 7 2 5 00	

The Finished Goods Inventory account is a controlling account for the stock ledger. Thus, at the end of the month, the balance of the Finished Goods Inventory account must agree with the total of the individual balances of the stock ledger cards. To prove this, TurboFlex's cost accountant prepared the **Schedule of Finished Goods** illustrated in Figure 8–5.

FIGURE 8–5
Schedule of Finished Goods

	TURBOFLEX CORPORATION			
	Schedule of Finished Goods			
	January 31, 19X6			
Item	Stock Number	Quantity	Unit Cost	Total Cost
TurboFlex II	1386206	50	$810	$40,500
TurboFlex II Plus	1128875	10	975	9,750
Total				$91,725

SELF-STUDY QUIZ 8–1 For the month of May, the Russell Corporation sold goods that had manufacturing costs of $144,560. The selling price of the goods was $205,800 and all sales were on account. Record the sales and cost of goods sold for May.
Answers at end of chapter.

FINANCIAL STATEMENTS

LEARNING OBJECTIVE 5 In Chapter 1 we discussed that, in addition to an income statement and balance sheet, manufacturing firms prepare a statement of cost of goods manufactured in order to compute the total cost of goods manufactured during the period. The cost of goods manufactured figure then becomes a part of the calculation of cost of goods sold.

In addition to formal year-end financial statements, TurboFlex prepares financial statements at the end of each month. Management uses these interim statements for planning, controlling, and analysis. Turboflex's statement of cost of goods manufactured and income statement are illustrated below. A balance sheet is not shown since the only manufacturing accounts appearing on the balance sheet are the ending balances of the inventory accounts.

NOTE The statement of cost of goods manufactured shows only manufacturing costs. Selling, general, and other expenses are reported on the income statement.

Statement of Cost of Goods Manufactured

Figure 8–6 illustrates TurboFlex's statement of cost of goods manufactured for the month ending January 31.

TurboFlex Corporation
Statement of Cost of Goods Manufactured
For Month Ended January 31, 19X6

1	Work in process inventory, Jan. 1		$ 6400000
2	Raw materials:		
3	Raw materials inventory, Jan. 1	$5000000	
4	Raw materials purchases	3240000	
5	Cost of materials available for use	$8240000	
6	Less raw materials inventory, Jan. 31	4442000	
7	Total cost of raw materials used	$3798000	
8	Less indirect materials used	140000	
9	Direct materials used	$3658000	
10	Direct labor	3564800	
11	Factory overhead applied	3183128	
12	Total manufacturing costs		10405928
13	Total goods in production		$16805928
14	Less work in process inventory, Jan. 31		2473428
15	Cost of goods manufactured		$14332500

Notice that the amount of indirect materials used during the month, $1,400, is subtracted from the total cost of materials used to obtain the cost of direct materials used. Since indirect materials are a part of factory overhead, including their cost in the cost of materials used would amount to double counting.

Also notice that only factory overhead applied is shown on the statement of cost of goods manufactured—because it was the applied overhead that was charged to production during the month. To show the actual overhead for the month, a supplementary schedule of factory overhead costs is prepared, as illustrated in Figure 8–7.

FIGURE 8–7
Schedule of Factory Overhead Costs

	TurboFlex Corporation Schedule of Factory Overhead Costs For Month Ended January 31, 19X6			
1	Actual factory overhead costs during month:			1
2				2
3	Indirect materials	$ 1 4 0 0 00		3
4	Indirect labor	1 3 9 8 0 00		4
5	Property taxes	8 1 0 00		5
6	Factory insurance	1 0 0 0 00		6
7	Depreciation	3 7 5 0 00		7
8	Utilities	2 7 6 0 00		8
9	Payroll taxes	3 8 0 0 00		9
10	Repairs	3 2 0 0 00		10
11	Miscellaneous	2 2 0 0 00		11
12				12
13	Total actual overhead costs		$32 9 0 0 00	13
14	Less underapplied overhead for month		1 0 6 8 72	14
15	Factory overhead applied		$31 8 3 1 28	15
16				16
17				17
18				18
19				19
20				20
21				21
22				22
23				23
24				24
25				25

Income Statement

Having computed cost of goods manufactured for January, $143,325, we can now prepare an income statement, as illustrated in Figure 8–8.

FIGURE 8–8
*Income
Statement*

should go here as a line item
what happened to the 106,872? Probably done at EOY.

	TurboFlex Corporation Income Statement For Month Ended January 31, 19X6			
1	Sales	$263 500 00		1
2	Less sales returns and allowances	2 500 00		2
3	Net sales		$261 000 00	3
4	Cost of goods sold:			4
5	Finished goods inventory, Jan. 1	$ 87 000 00		5
6	Add cost of goods manufactured	143 325 00		6
7	Goods available for sale	$230 325 00		7
8	Less finished goods inventory, Jan. 31	91 725 00		8
9	Cost of goods sold		138 600 00	9
10	Gross profit		$122 400 00	10
11	Operating expenses:			11
12	Selling expenses	$ 25 416 45		12
13	General expenses	21 345 50		13
14	Total operating expenses		46 761 95	14
15	Net income from operations		$ 75 638 05	15
16	Other expenses:			16
17	Interest expense		1 890 00	17
18	Net income before income taxes		$ 73 748 05	18
19	Provision for income taxes		16 224 00	19
20	Net income after income taxes		$ 57 524 05	20

SELF-STUDY QUIZ 8–2   The following data pertain to Milo Company for the year ended December 31:

Raw materials inventory, Jan. 1	$ 38,000
Raw materials purchases during the year	192,000
Raw materials inventory, Dec. 31	36,400
Work in process inventory, Jan. 1	42,000
Work in process inventory, Dec. 31	43,900
Direct labor incurred during the year	188,000
Factory overhead applied	150,400
Finished goods inventory, Jan. 1	37,500
Finished goods inventory, Dec. 31	35,000
Sales during the year	994,000
Operating expenses incurred during the year	386,700

Compute: (a) cost of goods manufactured; (b) cost of goods sold; (c) gross profit; (d) net income (or loss) from operations
Answers at end of chapter.

JOB-ORDER COSTING IN SERVICE BUSINESSES

In Chapter 2, we stated that job-order costing is used extensively in service organizations such as law firms, printing shops, advertising agencies, movie studios, hospitals, and auto repair shops. In a law firm, for example, each case represents a "job" and the costs of the job are accumulated on a job cost sheet. The amount of time attorneys spent working on the case represents the direct labor. Paper and supplies represent direct materials for the job; and the cost of paralegals, secretaries, depreciation, rent, etc. represents factory overhead costs.

In a printing shop, each order accepted is a "job." The costs of direct materials (paper, ink, binding, etc.) and direct labor (wages of typesetters, photo copier operators, etc.) are charged to each job cost sheet. A proportionate share of the shop's overhead costs (rent, utilities, depreciation, etc.) is also charged to each job. The job cost sheet is then totaled to determine the total charge to the customer.

SELF-STUDY PROBLEM

Nature's Way produces natural cosmetics. The firm's transactions for June follow.

a. Purchased raw materials on credit, $28,000.
b. Issued raw materials to production as follows:

Direct materials	$25,600
Indirect materials	4,500

c. Recorded factory labor during the month totaling $29,600. Payroll deductions were as follows:

FICA—OASDI	$ 1,866
FICA—HIP	436
Federal income taxes	6,020

d. Allocated factory payroll as follows:

Direct labor	$24,700
Indirect labor	6,200

e. Paid miscellaneous factory overhead costs, $3,920.
f. Computed depreciation for the month, $3,800 for the factory building and $1,290 for factory equipment.
g. Recorded expired factory insurance for the month, $412.
h. Recorded factory utilities for the month, $1,250.
i. Recorded accrued properety taxes on the factory building, $875.
j. Computed employer's payroll taxes:

FICA—OASDI	$ 1,866
FICA—HIP	466
FUTA	240
SUTA	810

k. Applied overhead to production at 90% of direct labor cost.
l. Recorded cost of jobs completed during the month, $48,900.
m. Sold goods having manufacturing costs of $56,700 on credit for $82,500.

Required:
Record these transactions in general journal form.

SOLUTION TO SELF-STUDY PROBLEM

a.	June	30	Raw Materials Inventory	2800000		**1**
			Accounts Payable		2800000	**2**
						3
b.		30	Work in Process Inventory	2560000		**4**
			Factory Overhead Control	450000		**5**
			Raw Materials Inventory		3010000	**6**
						7
c.		30	Factory Payroll Clearing	2960000		**8**
			FICA Tax Payable—OASDI		186600	**9**
			FICA Tax Payable—HIP		43600	**10**
			Federal Income Taxes Payable		602000	**11**
			Salaries and Wages Payable		2127800	**12**
						13
d.		30	Work in Process Inventory	2470000		**14**
			Factory Overhead Control	620000		**15**
			Factory Payroll Clearing		3090000	**16**
						17
e.		30	Factory Overhead Control	392000		**18**
			Cash		392000	**19**
						20
f.		30	Factory Overhead Control	509000		**21**
			Accumulated Depreciation—Building		380000	**22**
			Accumulated Depreciation—Equipment		129000	**23**
						24
g.		30	Factory Overhead Control	41200		**25**
			Prepaid Insurance		41200	**26**
						27
h.		30	Factory Overhead Control	125000		**28**
			Cash		125000	**29**
						30
i.		30	Factory Overhead Control	87500		**31**
			Property Taxes Payable		87500	**32**
						33
j.		30	Factory Overhead Control	338200		**34**
			FICA Tax Payable—OASDI		186600	**35**
			FICA Tax Payable—HIP		46600	**36**
			FUTA Tax Payable		24000	**37**
			SUTA Tax Payable		81000	**38**

k.	30	Work in Process Inventory	2223000		**40**
		Factory Overhead Control		2223000	**41**
					42
l.	30	Finished Goods Inventory	4890000		**43**
		Work in Process Inventory		4890000	**44**
					45
m.	30	Accounts Receivable	8250000		**46**
		Sales		8250000	**47**
					48
	30	Cost of Goods Sold	5670000		**49**
		Finished Goods Inventory		5670000	**50**
					51

SUMMARY

While goods are in production, manufacturing costs accumulate on job costs sheets. When a job is completed, the related job cost sheet is totaled and summarized. It is then moved from the in-process category to a finished work file. To match the cost flow with work flow, an entry is made debiting the cost of all jobs finished during a month to the Finished Goods Inventory account and crediting the credit to the Work in Process Inventory account. After this entry is made, the Work in Process Inventory account shows the cost of all incomplete units at month end.

Since the Work in Process Inventory account is the controlling account for the **job cost ledger,** its month-end balance must equal the total cost of all uncompleted jobs. To verify that these amounts agree, the cost accountant prepares a **Schedule of Work in Process,** which is a listing of costs charged to incomplete job cost sheets.

The cost of a job completed for the purpose of replenishing the firm's stock level is recorded in a **stock ledger** (also called **finished goods ledger**), as well as the general ledger. The stock ledger is made up of ledger cards for each type of product that the firm produces.

Because the stock ledger shows only goods available for sale, special order goods manufactured to a customer's specifications are not entered in the stock ledger. Since special order goods are immediately shipped to the customer, and are not available for sale out of stock, their cost is not picked up in the stock ledger.

Two journal entries are needed when finished units are sold. The first entry records the selling price of the units, while the second entry transfers the cost of the units from Finished Goods Inventory to Cost of Goods Sold.

Since the Finished Goods Inventory account is the controlling account for the stock ledger, its month-end balance must agree with the total of the individual balances of the stock ledger cards. To verify this, a **Schedule of Finished Goods** is prepared.

In addition to formal year-end financial statements, most manufacturing firms prepare interim financial statements at the end of each month. These statements are used by management for planning, analysis, and cost control.

APPENDIX 8A: COST FLOWS IN A JIT SYSTEM

In Chapter 4, we mentioned that, to keep inventories to a minimum and increase operating efficiency, some firms have adopted *just-in-time (JIT) inventory systems*. When a firm utilizes JIT inventory methods, its cost flows are greatly simplified from those we discussed in conventional job-order costing systems. JIT eliminates the need for separate accounts for Raw Materials Inventory and Work in Process Inventory. Typically, only two inventory accounts are used. One of these accounts is entitled **Raw and In-Process Inventory**; the other is the Finished Goods Inventory account that we worked with in our discussion of conventional job-order costing. Costs are added to products only when the products are completed and ready for shipment. This eliminates the need for detailed cost tracking and job cost sheets.

In this section, we will illustrate cost flows in a JIT system, and compare JIT entries with conventional job-order costing entries.

Transaction 1:

Purchased direct materials on account, $500,000, of which $50,000 are for inventory.

Entry 1:

Conventional System

1	Raw Materials Inventory	50 00 0 0 00		1
2	Accounts Payable		50 00 0 0 00	2

JIT System

1	Raw and In-Process Inventory	45 00 0 0 00		1
2	Accounts Payable		45 00 0 0 00	2

Comments:

Under JIT, just enough materials are purchased for the day's production. Thus, only $450,000 ($500,000 – $50,000) of materials would be purchased because no materials would be left over to go into inventory. Under conventional systems, a minimum level of inventory is maintained on hand ($50,000 in this case).

Transaction 2

Issued raw materials to production, $450,000.

Entry 2:

Conventional System

1		Work in Process Inventory	45000000		1
2		Raw Materials Inventory		45000000	2

JIT System
(No entry needed)

Comments:

Under a conventional job-order costing system, an entry is needed when raw materials are purchased (Entry 1) and when raw materials are issued to production (Entry 2). Under a JIT system, however, raw materials are purchased for immediate entry into production. As a result, a separate entry is not needed to record the cost of materials issued to production. Instead, the entry made when materials are purchased (Entry 1) shows not only that materials have been purchased, but that they have been entered into production. This greatly simplifies the recordkeeping process because there are no requisition forms to be prepared and no perpetual inventory records to maintain.

Transaction 3:

Incurred direct labor cost $60,000.

Entry 3:

Conventional System

1		Work in Process Inventory	6000000		1
2		Salaries and Wages Payable		6000000	2

JIT System
(No entry needed)

Comments:

In a JIT system, direct labor is not treated as a separate component of manufacturing costs; instead, it is recorded as factory overhead. Having gone through a conventional job-order costing system, you may find this strange, but there are two reasons for this treatment. First, it simplifies the costing process. Second, many plants that use the JIT system are highly automated. Consequently, direct labor is not a significant cost in such plants.

Transaction 4:

Incurred factory overhead costs on account, $150,000.

Entry 4:

Conventional System

1		Factory Overhead Control	150 00 0 00		1
2		Accounts Payable		150 0 0 0 00	2

JIT System

1		Factory Overhead Control	210 00 0 00		1
2		Salaries and Wages Payable		60 0 0 0 00	2
3		Accounts Payable		150 0 0 0 00	3

Comments:

Notice that the JIT Entry 4 records direct labor as part of factory overhead. As we discussed earlier, direct labor is not considered a separate cost of production in a JIT system.

Transaction 5:

Applied factory overhead to production, $120,000.

Entry 5:

Conventional System

1		Work in Process Inventory	120 00 0 00		1
2		Factory Overhead Control		120 0 0 0 00	2

JIT System
(No entry needed)

Comments:

No entry is needed under JIT because factory overhead costs are applied to production *only* when the goods are finished.

Transaction 6:

Cost of goods completed during the period, $630,000.

Entry 6:

Conventional System

1		Finished Goods Inventory	63000000		1
2		Work in Process Inventory		63000000	2

JIT System

1		Finished Goods Inventory*	63000000		1
2		Raw and In-Process Inventory		45000000	2
3		Factory Overhead Control		18000000	3

Comments:

Under JIT, materials costs and conversion costs (direct labor and factory overhead) *are not* added to the goods until the goods are completed. At the completion of goods, costs are transferred from the Raw and In-Process Inventory and Factory Overhead Control accounts into the Finished Goods Inventory account. In Entry 6 (for JIT), the $630,000 debit to Finished Goods Inventory is the result of combining two amounts: (1) the $450,000 balance of the Raw and In-Process Inventory account and (2) $180,000, which is determined as follows:

Direct labor added to overhead	$ 60,000
Other overhead applied to production (Transaction 5)	120,000
Total overhead applied	$180,000

BACKFLUSH COSTING

Traditional cost accounting systems use what is called **sequential tracking** to keep up with production costs. This method records journal entries in the accounting system as goods physically move through the production process. Stated another way, costs are tracked sequentially with the movement of the products from direct materials, through work in process, to finished goods. Due to the large amount of paperwork involved, sequential tracking is often expensive.

*In a pure JIT system, goods are sold as soon as they are completed. As a result, the debit to Finished Goods Inventory (in Entry 6) would be replaced by a debit to Cost of Goods Sold. The entry would then appear as follows:

1		Cost of Goods Sold	63000000		1
2		Raw and In-Process Inventory		45000000	2
3		Factory Overhead Control		18000000	3

An alternative to sequential tracking, called **backflush costing,** delays recording journal entries until after goods have moved through the production process (manufacturing costs are "flushed" out of the system *after* the goods are completed). Backflush costing is usually used with JIT systems, although backflush can be used with any production system.

We saw an application of backflush costing in Entry 6 above. Under JIT, costs *were not* accumulated while the goods were in production; this was delayed until the finished units appeared. Then, the system worked "backward" to assign manufacturing costs to the units produced.

It should be stressed that backflush costing is appropriate *only* in a true JIT system. If either a raw materials inventory or a work in process inventory exist at the end of the period, backflush costing will be difficult and expensive. The existence of inventories means that there will have to be frequent and expensive physical counts to determine the amount of raw materials on hand and the amount of partially completed goods still in production. Further, with no materials requisitions or job cost sheets, it would be difficult to identify how much cost should be allocated to the various inventories (raw materials, work in process and finished goods). As a result, unless a true JIT system is in operation, backflush costing could be less efficient and more expensive than a conventional costing system.

KEY TERMS

Finished Goods Ledger. Another name for the **stock ledger.**

Job Cost Ledger. The subsidiary ledger to the Work in Process Inventry account. It consists of the individual job cost sheets for each job in production.

Schedule of Finished Goods. A listing of the cost of all items that are in stock (in the warehouse) and awaiting sale to customers.

Schedule of Work in Process. A month-end listing of the balances of job cost sheets for uncompleted jobs.

Stock Ledger. The subsidiary ledger to the Finished Goods Inventory account. It is made up of stock ledger cards for each product that a firm manufactures for stock (to go in the warehouse). The stock ledger is also called the **finished goods ledger.**

APPENDIX

Sequential Tracking. Method which records journal entries as goods move through the production process.

Backflush Costing. Method which delays recording journal entries until after goods have moved through the production process.

QUESTIONS FOR REVIEW

1. What general ledger account is debited for the cost of units completed during the month?
2. The Work in Process Inventory account is a controlling account for what subsidiary ledger?

3. What is the job cost ledger and how is it proved?
4. What is the controlling account for the stock ledger?
5. Where are the cost of completed units recorded?
6. How is the stock ledger proved?
7. Are all completed units entered in the stock ledger? Explain.
8. The sale of finished units requires two entries. Explain.
9. What is another name for the stock ledger?
10. Why do firms prepare interim financial statements?
11. What factory overhead (actual or applied) is entered on an interim statement of cost of goods manufactured? Why?
12. Do nonmanufacturing firms use job-order costing systems? Explain.
13. (Appendix) How is the purchase and issue of materials to production handled in a JIT system?
14. (Appendix) Why is direct labor often recorded as overhead in a JIT system?
15. (Appendix) What is meant by backflush costing?
16. (Appendix) Is backflush costing appropriate for all costing systems? Explain.

NOTE Unless told otherwise in Exercises and Problems, record transactions in general journal form.

EXERCISES

8–1. Learning Objective 1. Recording the Cost of Completed Jobs.
During May, Mathis Company completed jobs costing $455,800. Record the cost of these jobs.

8–2. Learning Objective 1. Recording the Cost of Completed Jobs and Determining the Cost of Unfinished Jobs.
The following account appears in the ledger of O'Malley Company on May 31 (all postings *have not* been completed).

Work in Process Inventory

Balance, May 1	8,000	
Direct materials	32,600	
Direct labor	48,000	
Factory overhead	43,200	

The following jobs were completed during May.

Job 212	$23,700
Job 214	17,900
Job 215	18,500
Job 216	28,950

a. Record the cost of jobs completed.
b. Determine the cost of unfinished jobs at May 31.

8–3. Learning Objective 3. Recording Sales and Cost of Goods Sold.

During June, Jarrel Corporation sold goods for $287,000 that had manufacturing costs of $207,500. Terms of sales were 2/10,n/30. Record the sales and cost of goods sold for the month.

8–4. Learning Objectives 1, 3. Recording Entries in a Job-Order Costing System.

Champion Company completed the following transactions during July. Record these transactions.

a. Purchased materials on account, $75,000.
b. Issued materials to production: direct, $45,000; indirect, $7,000.
c. Recorded payroll: gross amount, $62,000; FICA taxes, 6.2% OASDI, 1.45% HIP; federal withholding taxes, 20%.
d. Distributed payroll costs to production: direct, $44,000; indirect, $18,900.
e. Paid various factory overhead costs, $15,000.
f. Applied factory overhead to production at 80% of direct labor cost.
g. Completed jobs costing $78,000.
h. Sold goods costing $74,500 on account for $138,500.

8–5. Learning Objective 5. Computing Cost of Goods Manufactured, Cost of Goods Sold, Gross Profit, and Net Income from Operations.

The following data relate to Gregory Company for March:

Raw materials inventory, March 1	$37,000
Materials purchases during March	93,000
Raw materials inventory, March 31	35,000
Work in process inventory, March 1	41,000
Work in process inventory, March 31	40,500
Direct labor incurred during March	106,000
Factory overhead applied during March	84,800
Finished goods inventory, March 1	38,000
Finished goods inventory, March 31	39,500
Operating expenses incurred during March	212,000
Sales during March	741,000

Compute: (a) Cost of goods manufactured; (b) Cost of goods sold; (c) Gross profit; and (d) Net income (or loss) from operations.

8–6. Comparison of Costing Systems (Appendix).

The following selected transactions were incurred by Trevor Steel Products Company during its first month of operation.

a. Purchased raw materials on account, $400,000.
b. Issued direct materials from the storeroom to production, $380,000.
c. Incurred direct labor cost during the month, $60,000.
d. Incurred actual factory overhead costs during the month, $195,000 (credit Various Accounts).
e. Applied factory overhead to production, $200,000.
f. Completed and transferred goods to finished goods, $640,000.

1. Record these transactions assuming the firm uses a conventional job-order costing system.
2. Record these transactions assuming the firm uses JIT inventory system.

GROUP A PROBLEMS

8–1A. Learning Objectives 1, 3. Recording Manufacturing Costs.

Best Products Company completed the following transactions during February:

a. Purchased materials on account, $18,000.
b. Issued materials to production as follows: direct, $9,510; indirect, $1,230.
c. Incurred payroll: gross amount, $15,400; FICA taxes, 6.2% OASDI, 1.45% HIP; federal withholding, 20%; group insurance, $980.
d. Distributed labor to production as follows: direct, $14,250; indirect, $1,920.
e. Paid various factory overhead costs, $1,890.
f. Recognized factory depreciation as follows: factory building, $2,050; factory equipment, $810.
g. Accrued property taxes for the month, $415.
h. Recognized expired insurance for the month, $240.
i. Incurred employer's payroll taxes: OASDI, 6.2%; HIP, 1.45%; FUTA, 0.8%; SUTA, 2.5% (no employee has exceeded the OASDI taxable base).
j. Applied factory overhead to production at 80% of direct labor cost.
k. Completed jobs costing $23,500 during the month.
l. Sold goods costing $19,600 on account for $27,900.

Required:

1. Record these transactions.
2. What is the balance of the Factory Payroll Clearing account? What does this balance represent?
3. (a) What is the balance of the Factory Overhead Control account? (b) What does this balance represent? (c) How will this balance be reported on the interim financial statements prepared for February?

8–2A. Learning Objectives 1 & 3. Recording Manufacturing Costs.

Eagle Wood Products Company completed the following transactions during April, 19X6, the firm's first month of operation.

a. Purchased materials on account, $32,000.
b. Materials requisitioned and factory labor used:

	Materials	Factory Labor
Job 1.	$4,200	$2,800
Job 2.	3,150	2,400
Job 3.	3,925	2,780
Job 4.	6,255	4,600
Job 5.	1,560	1,275
General factory use	860	978

c. Various factory overhead costs incurred on account, $4,800.
d. Depreciation: machinery, $800; equipment, $650.
e. Expired factory insurance, $225.
f. Applied factory overhead to production at 70% of direct labor cost.
g. Completed Jobs 1, 2, and 4.
h. Jobs 1 and 2 were shipped and customers were billed for $12,800 and $11,700 respectively.

Required:

1. Open T accounts for Work in Process Inventory and Finished Goods Inventory.
2. Record the firm's April transactions.
3. Post to the accounts opened in number 1.
4. Prepare a schedule of work in process.
5. Prepare a schedule of finished goods.

8–3A. Learning Objective 1. Completing a Job Cost Sheet.

Michaels Corporation manufactures lawn and garden furniture. On August 15, 19X7, Michaels received an order for 300 model K-8 tables. The job was started on August 16 and completed on August 26. The following costs are associated with the job.

Materials:

Date	Requisition Number	Amount
Aug. 16	1102	$1,250
Aug. 18	1134	890
Aug. 24	1187	560
Aug. 25	1212	310

Returned Materials:

Date	Returned Materials Report	Amount
Aug. 26	128	$45

Labor:

Date	Department	Number of Hours	Amount
Week ending Aug. 19	Cutting	112	$714
	Assembling	31	218
Week ending Aug. 26	Cutting	28	203
	Assembling	112	836
	Finishing	140	992

Factory Overhead Applied:

Date	Department	Rate
Aug. 26	Cutting	$5.10 per direct labor hour
Aug. 26	Assembling	5.30 per direct labor hour
Aug. 26	Finishing	6.40 per direct labor hour

Required:
Complete the job cost sheet presented in the Study Guide/Working Papers.

8–4A. Learning Objectives 1, 3, 5. Recording and Posting Transactions.

Blankenship Company's ledger contained the following account balances on June 1, 19X1:

Raw Materials Inventory	$25,600
Work in Process Inventory	18,200
Finished Goods Inventory	21,640

June transactions:

a. Purchased materials on account, $30,200.
b. Materials requisitioned to production as follows: direct, $26,400; indirect, $4,800.
c. Factory wages totaled $34,000; deductions were made as follows: FICA—OASDI, 6.2%; FICA—HIP, 1.45%; federal income taxes, 20%; group health insurance, $569. (All wages were subject to OASDI.)
d. Labor charged to production: direct, $24,900; indirect, $9,200.
e. Paid for repairs, $300.
f. Recorded depreciation as follows: building, $850; equipment, $630.
g. Recorded employer payroll taxes on June wages: FICA—OASDI, 6.2%; FICA—HIP, 1.45%; FUTA, 0.8%; SUTA, 2.7%.
h. Factory insurance expired, $195.
i. Accrued property taxes, $225.
j. Paid for various factory overhead costs, $1,200.
k. Factory overhead applied to production at 80% of direct labor cost.
l. Cost of jobs completed during the month, $71,300.
m. Goods costing $65,400 to manufacture were sold on account for $81,750.

Required:

1. Open general ledger accounts for Raw Materials Inventory 121, Work in Process Inventory 122, Finished Goods Inventory 123, Sales 411, Cost of Goods Sold 415, Factory Payroll Clearing 500, and Factory Overhead Control, 511.
2. Enter the balances of the manufacturing accounts given at the beginning of the problem.
3. Record Blankenship's June transactions.
4. Post to the selected accounts opened in number 1.
5. Prepare a statement of cost of goods manufactured.
6. Prepare a schedule of factory overhead costs.
7. Prepare an income statement for the month, assuming selling expenses of $12,400, general expenses of $11,800, and an income tax rate of 34%.

8–5A. Comparison of Costing Systems (Appendix).

Integrated Products Company completed the following transactions during its first month of operation:

a. Purchased raw materials on account, $500,000.
b. Issued direct materials to production, $475,000.
c. Incurred direct labor during the month, $65,000.
d. Incurred actual factory overhead costs during the month, $215,000 (credit Various Accounts).

e. Applied factory overhead to production, $220,000.
f. Completed goods during the month, $760,000.
g. Sold goods costing $580,000 on account for $725,000.

Required:

1. Assuming the firm uses a conventional job-order cost system, record these transactions.
2. Assuming the firm uses a JIT inventory system, record these transactions.
3. Related to materials, explain how JIT provides a cost savings.
4. Related to Transaction (g), explain why product costing under JIT is sometimes referred to as backflush costing.

GROUP B PROBLEMS

8–1B. Learning Objectives 1 & 3. Recording Manufacturing Costs.
Jay Products Company completed the following transactions during January, 19X2:

a. Purchased materials on account, $20,000.
b. Issued materials to production as follows: direct, $9,800; indirect, $1,420.
c. Incurred payroll: gross amount, $16,000; FICA taxes, 6.2% OASDI, 1.45% HIP; federal withholding, 20%; group insurance, $860.
d. Distributed labor to production as follows: direct, $14,950; indirect, $2,120.
e. Paid various factory overhead costs, $1,936.
f. Recognized factory depreciation as follows: factory building, $2,200; factory equipment, $875.
g. Accrued property taxes for the month, $490.
h. Recognized expired insurance for the month, $250.
i. Incurred employer's payroll taxes: OASDI, 6.2%; HIP, 1.45%; FUTA, 0.8%; SUTA, 2.5% (no employee has exceeded the OASDI taxable base).
j. Applied factory overhead to production at 80% of direct labor cost.
k. Completed jobs costing $23,800 during the month.
l. Sold goods costing $20,600 on account for $28,000.

Required:

1. Record these transactions.
2. What is the balance of the Factory Payroll Clearing account? What does this balance represent?
3. a. What is the balance of the Factory Overhead Control account?
   b. What does this balance represent?
   c. How will this balance be reported on the interim financial statements prepared for January?

8–2B. Learning Objectives 1 & 3. Recording Manufacturing Costs.
Eagle Wood Products Company completed the following transactions during May, 19X5, the firm's first month of operation.

a. Purchased materials on account, $33,000.
b. Materials requisitioned and factory labor used:

	Materials	Factory Labor
Job 1.	$4,000	$2,700
Job 2.	3,200	2,500
Job 3.	3,810	2,850
Job 4.	6,400	4,800
Job 5.	1,250	850

18,660   *$13,700*

c. Various factory overhead costs incurred on account, $4,500.
d. Depreciation: machinery, $900; equipment, $700.
e. Expired factory insurance, $240.
f. Applied factory overhead to production at 80% of direct labor cost.   *13,700 x 80%*
g. Completed Jobs 1, 2, and 4.   *4000 + 2700 + 2160*
h. Jobs 1 and 2 were shipped and customers were billed for $14,500 and $12,800 respectively.

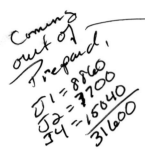

Coming out of Prepaid,
J1 = 8860
J2 = 7700
J4 = 16040
31600

Required:

1. Open T accounts for Work in Process Inventory and Finished Goods Inventory.
2. Record the firm's May transactions.
3. Post to the accounts opened in number 1.
4. Prepare a schedule of work in process.
5. Prepare a schedule of finished goods.

8–3B. Learning Objective 1. Completing a Job Cost Sheet.

Mitchell Corporation manufactures wood products. On July 16, the firm received an order for 250 Model 10 end-tables. The job was started on July 17 and completed on July 27. The following costs are associated with the job.

Materials:

Date	Requisition Number	Amount
July 11	1002	$1,290
July 19	1038	900
July 25	1062	590
July 27	1077	425

Labor:

Date	Department	Number of Hours	Amount
Week ending July 20	Cutting	110	$665
	Assembling	40	272
Week ending July 27	Cutting	32	200
	Assembling	114	775
	Finishing	138	938

Factory Overhead Applied:

Date	Department	Rate
July 27	Cutting	$4.90 per direct labor hour
July 27	Assembling	5.25 per direct labor hour
July 27	Finishing	5.90 per direct labor hour

Required:
Complete the job cost sheet presented in the Study Guide/Working Papers.

8–4B. Learning Objectives 1, 3, 5. Recording and Posting Transactions.
Boswell Company's ledger contained the following account balances on May 1, 19X3:

Raw Materials Inventory	$31,000
Work in Process Inventory	22,500
Finished Goods Inventory	20,800

May transactions:

a. Purchased materials on account, $32,000.
b. Materials requisitioned to production as follows: direct, $27,200; indirect, $5,100.
c. Factory wages totaled $36,000; deductions were made as follows: FICA—OASDI, 6.2%; FICA—HIP, 1.45%; federal income taxes, 20%; group health insurance, $601. (All wages were subject to OASDI.)
d. Labor charged to production: direct, $25,600; indirect, $9,800.
e. Paid for repairs, $345.
f. Recorded depreciation as follows: building, $900; equipment, $600.
g. Recorded employer payroll taxes on May wages: FICA—OASDI, 6.2%; FICA—HIP, 1.45%; FUTA, 0.8%; SUTA, 2.7%.
h. Factory insurance expired, $230.
i. Accrued property taxes, $230.
j. Paid for various factory overhead costs, $1,250.
k. Factory overhead applied to production at 80% of direct labor cost.
l. Cost of jobs completed during the month, $63,400.
m. Goods costing $58,600 to manufacture were sold on account for $72,500.

Required:

1. Open general ledger accounts for Raw Materials Inventory 121, Work in Process Inventory 122, Finished Goods Inventory 123, Sales 411, Cost of Gods Sold 415, Factory Payroll Clearing 500, and Factory Overhead Control, 511.
2. Enter the balances of the manufacturing accounts given at the beginning of the problem.
3. Record Boswell's May transactions.
4. Post to the selected accounts opened in number 1.
5. Prepare a statement of cost of goods manufactured.
6. Prepare a schedule of factory overhead costs.
7. Prepare an income statement for the month, assuming selling expenses of $12,800, general expenses of $12,200, and an income tax rate of 34%.

8–5B. Comparing of Costing Systems (Appendix).
Grady Products Company completed the following transactions during its first month of operation:

a. Purchased raw materials on account, $300,000.
b. Issued direct materials to productions, $260,000.
c. Incurred direct labor during the month, $52,000.
d. Incurred actual factory overhead costs incurred during the month, $201,000 (credit Various Accounts).

e. Applied factory overhead to production, $175,000.
f. Completed goods during the month, $487,000.
g. Sold goods costing $325,000 on account for $415,000.

Required:

1. Assuming the firm uses a conventional job-order cost system, record these transactions.
2. Assuming the firm uses a JIT inventory system, record these transactions.
3. Related to materials, explain how JIT provides a cost savings.
4. Related to Transaction (g), explain why product costing under JIT is sometimes referrred to as backflush costing.

CASE FOR CRITICAL THINKING

The job-order costing system is used in many different types of organizations (manufacturing, service, merchandising, not-for-profit, and governmental agencies). However, some accountants believe that this system is difficult to operate because of the paper work involved. From the viewpoint of those accountants, explain how paper work in a job-order system could be time consuming. Suggest ways to improve this.

ANSWERS TO SELF-STUDY QUIZ 8–1

1	May	31	Accounts Receivable	205 80 0 00		1
2			Sales		205 80 0 00	2
3						3
4		31	Cost of Goods Sold	144 56 0 00		4
5			Finished Goods Inventory		144 56 0 00	5

ANSWERS TO SELF-STUDY QUIZ 8–2

a.	Work in process inventory, Jan. 1			$ 42 000 00	**1**
	Raw materials inventory, Jan. 1		$ 38 000 00		**2**
	Raw materials purchases		192 000 00		**3**
	Materials available for use		$230 000 00		**4**
	Less raw materials inventory, Dec. 31		36 400 00		**5**
	Cost of raw materials used		$193 600 00		**6**
	Direct labor		188 000 00		**7**
	Factory overhead applied		150 400 00		**8**
	Total manufacturing costs			532 000 00	**9**
	Total goods in production			$574 000 00	**10**
	Less work in process inventory, Dec. 31			43 900 00	**11**
	Cost of goods manufactured			$530 100 00	**12**
					13
b.	Finished goods inventory, Jan. 1			$ 37 500 00	**14**
	Cost of goods manufactured			530 100 00	**15**
	Goods available for sale			$567 600 00	**16**
	Finished goods inventory, Dec. 31			35 000 00	**17**
	Cost of goods sold			$532 600 00	**18**
					19
c.	Sales	$994 000 00			**20**
	Cost of goods sold	532 600 00			**21**
	Gross profit	$461 400 00			**22**
					23
d.	Gross profit	$461 400 00			**24**
	Operating expenses	386 700 00			**25**
	Net Income from operations	$ 74 400 00			**26**

Chapter 9
Accounting for Scrap, Spoiled, and Defective Units

LEARNING OBJECTIVES

After studying Chapter 9, you should be able to:

1. Define scrap and show several different ways to account for it.
2. Explain the nature of spoiled goods and the different methods of accounting for them.
3. Explain the nature of defective goods and how to account for them.

In the first eight chapters, we learned job-order costing, including how to account for materials. We assumed that waste and spoilage did not occur. However, in the real world, wastage, spoilage, and defective units occur as a normal part of the manufacturing process. In this chapter you will learn how to account for these things.

ACCOUNTING FOR SCRAP

LEARNING OBJECTIVE 1

Scrap is the remnant or residual that remains after the primary product has been manufactured. Scrap is an expected by-product from the production of a valued product. For example, in a lumber mill, scrap would be bark, shavings, end pieces, and sawdust. This scrap can be accumulated and later sold to individuals or to other businesses who need this scrap as a raw material for manufacturing their product. The method of accounting for scrap depends primarily upon its value and how readily the value can be determined.

If the scrap value is small, no journal entry is made until the scrap is sold. Assume that a business sells scrap for $300 (small value). The following journal entry records the sale:

1	Jan.	15	Cash (or Accounts Receivable)	300 00		1
2			Miscellaneous Income		300 00	2
3			Sold scrap.			3

In some manufacturing processes, the scrap has a large dollar value. When this happens, an inventory card should be prepared, and the scrap transferred to a secured storage area. Several methods of accounting for this scrap exist depending upon how readily the value can be determined.

If the market value of the scrap is known, debit Scrap Inventory account. Assume for illustrative purposes that scrap has a market value of $2,500 and is identified with job no. 147. The following journal entry recognizes the scrap value:

1	Jan.	15	Scrap Inventory	2500 00		1
2			Work in Process—job no. 147		2500 00	2
3			Recognized scrap value.			3

If the scrap cannot be identified with a particular job, then credit Factory Overhead Control. Crediting the Factory Overhead Control account spreads the value of the scrap over all the jobs.

1	Jan.	15	Scrap Inventory	2 5 0 0 00		1
2			Factory Overhead Control		2 5 0 0 00	2
3			Charged scrap value.			3

Assume a buyer will pay $2,500 for the scrap on January 30. The following journal entry records the sale:

1	Jan.	30	Cash or Accounts Receivable	2 5 0 0 00		1
2			Scrap Inventory		2 5 0 0 00	2
3			Sold scrap.			3

It is not always possible to sell the scrap for the same amount that was charged to the Scrap Inventory account. When this happens, the difference between the amount received and the amount recorded in the Scrap Inventory account must be adjusted to the account originally credited (Work in Process or Factory Overhead Control). Assume that Scrap Inventory was originally debited for $2,500. On January 30 the scrap was sold on account for only $2,200. The following journal entry records the sale:

1	Jan.	30	Accounts Receivable	2 2 0 0 00		1
2			Work in Process or Factory Overhead Control	3 0 0 00		2
3			Scrap Inventory		2 5 0 0 00	3
4			Sold scrap for less than estimated.			4

Assume instead that the scrap was sold on account for $2,800. The following journal entry records the sale:

1	Jan.	30	Accounts Receivable	2 8 0 0 00		1
2			Scrap Inventory		2 5 0 0 00	2
3			Work in Process or Factory Overhead Control		3 0 0 00	3
4			Sold scrap for more than estimated.			4

If the market value of the scrap cannot be determined, no journal entry is made until the scrap is sold. Assume that scrap is sold for $3,000 on February 15. The following journal entry records the sale:

1	Feb.	15	Cash (or Accounts Receivable)	300000		1
2			Work in Process or Factory Overhead Control		300000	2
3			Sold scrap at current market value.			3

SELF-STUDY QUIZ 9–1 Kennington Enterprises manufactures a primary product that results in several by-products that are sold as scrap. Make the general journal entries under the following situations:

a. February 23, sold the scrap value for $250 on account and credited to Miscellaneous Income.
b. March 19, estimated the scrap value to be worth $4,000 and charged to Scrap Inventory account. Identified the scrap with job number 227.
c. Same as (b) above, but spread the value of the scrap over all the jobs worked on during the period.

Answers at end of chapter.

ACCOUNTING FOR SPOILED GOODS

LEARNING OBJECTIVE 2   **Spoiled goods** can be the result of improper workmanship or perhaps a result of equipment malfunctioning. In any case, the spoiled goods cannot be economically corrected and are sold as damaged goods or "seconds."

The accountant must decide if the loss associated with the spoiled goods should be charged to a specific job or to the Factory Overhead Control account which spreads the cost over all the jobs worked on during the period.

If the spoiled goods are considered a normal part of the production process, then debit the Factory Overhead Control account for the loss. If the spoiled goods are the result of a special order and considered unique to this order, then the loss should be charged to this job. In either event, a Spoiled Goods inventory account should be debited for the expected sales value.

For illustrative purposes, assume Cascade Manufacturing Company specializes in team sportswear. One of its special orders, job no. 159, involved the production of 400 warm-up jackets completed on March 18. The cost of the special order came to $20,000, or $50 per jacket. Later, on March 25, just before delivery, Cascade discovered that 20 of the jackets were of inferior quality and were classified as irregulars or seconds. If the jackets will sell for only

$20 each and the loss should be charged to Factory Overhead Control, then the following journal entry recognizes the loss:

1	Mar.	25	Spoiled Goods Inventory	40000		1
2			Factory Overhead Control	60000		2
3			Work in Process—job no. 159		100000	3
4			Recognized loss.			4

As you can see, Factory Overhead Control is debited for $600, the difference between the cost of 20 jackets (20 × $50), and the market value of the spoiled goods (20 × $20). Work in Process—job no. 159—was credited for the entire amount of spoiled goods.

If it is decided that the loss associated with the spoiled goods should be charged to job no. 159, the following journal entry records the loss.

1	Mar.	25	Spoiled Goods Inventory	40000		1
2			Work in Process—job no. 159		40000	2
3			Charged loss to job no. 159			3

In this case, job no. 159 is credited for $400, the market value of the spoiled goods. However, the total cost of job no. 159 includes the $600 loss ($1,000 – $400). The total unit cost will increase because this $600 remains in job no. 159.

As in the case involving scrap inventory, if the spoiled goods inventory cannot be sold for the amount of the expected sales value, then the difference between the amount received and the amount charged to spoiled goods inventory is adjusted to the account originally credited (Work in Process or Factory Overhead Control). Assume in the above example that on April 5, $300 was received for the spoiled goods. The following journal entry records the sale:

1	Apr.	5	Cash	30000		1
2			Work in Process or Factory Overhead Control	10000		2
3			Spoiled Goods Inventory		40000	3
4			Sold scrap for less than estimated.			4

If $500 were received for the spoiled goods, then the following journal entry records the sale:

1	Apr.	5	Cash	50000			1
2			Work in Process or Factory Overhead Control		10000		2
3			Spoiled Goods Inventory		40000		3
4			Sold scrap for more than estimated.				4

SELF-STUDY QUIZ 9–2 Hansen Manufacturing Company completed job no. 313, which involved the production of 1,000 units. Each unit cost $80 to manufacture. During final inspection, Hansen determined that 30 units were spoiled and could not be economically corrected. Hansen estimated that the spoiled units could sell for $30 each, and on August 11, created a Spoiled Goods Inventory account. Make the general journal entries under each of the following situations:

a. The loss should be charged to Factory Overhead Control.
b. The loss should be charged to job no. 313.

Answers at end of chapter.

ACCOUNTING FOR DEFECTIVE UNITS

LEARNING OBJECTIVE 3

Defective units have imperfections but can be economically corrected with additional materials, labor, and factory overhead costs. It is worth the time and effort to correct the defects because the sales value of the finished product exceeds the expense of correcting the defects.

The accounting procedures for recording defective units resemble the way we recorded spoiled goods except that we do not create an inventory account. Instead, the additional costs associated with reworking the defective units are charged either to Work in Process or to Factory Overhead Control.

For illustrative purposes, assume that job number 159 (used in an earlier example) involving the special order for 400 warm-up jackets have regular pockets instead of zipper pockets. If the customer requested this change after the order was completed, then the additional costs of adding these zippers should be charged to the job. Assuming that it would cost an additional $2 for materials, $2 for labor, and $1 of factory overhead to correct this defect, the following journal entry shows the additional costs:

1	Mar.	25	Work in Process—job no. 159	2 0 0 0 00		1
2			Materials Inventory (400 x $2)		8 0 0 00	2
3			Factory Payroll Clearing (400 x $2)		8 0 0 00	3
4			Factory Overhead Control (400 x $1)		4 0 0 00	4
5			Charged job no. 159 for additional costs.			5

The total cost of job no. 159 will be higher because of the costs of materials, labor, and factory overhead added to the job. The unit cost for each jacket will increase from $50 ($20,000/400) to $55 ($22,000/400) because of the additional costs charged to this job.

Assume instead that the 400 jackets that lack the zipper pockets are management's error and not the customer's error. In this situation, spread the cost over all the jobs worked on during the accounting period and not just job no. 159. Factory Overhead Control is debited for the cost of reworking the jackets instead of Work in Process—job no. 159. The following journal entry charges the cost to factory overhead:

1	Mar.	25	Factory Overhead Control	2 0 0 0 00		1
2			Materials Inventory (400 x $2)		8 0 0 00	2
3			Factory Payroll Clearing (400 x $2)		8 0 0 00	3
4			Factory Overhead Control (400 x $1)		4 0 0 00	4
5			Charged additional costs to all jobs.			5

As you can see, Factory Overhead Control is debited for the cost of reworking the defective units. The unit cost of job no. 159 will remain at $50.

NOTE Scrap is the residual that remains after the primary product has been manufactured. Scrap is sold at its current market value. Spoiled goods are the result of improper workmanship or equipment malfunctioning and cannot be economically corrected. Spoiled goods are sold as damaged goods or "seconds." Defective units are units that have imperfections but can be economically corrected with additional materials, labor, and factory overhead costs. Defective units can be sold at their regular sales price.

SELF-STUDY QUIZ 9–3 Janikowski Equipment Company completed job no. 631, which involved the manufacturing of 1,000 machines costing $200 in materials, labor, and factory overhead. Janikowski discovered upon final inspection 100 defective machines. It will cost the following to rework these machines in order to sell them at the regular sales price:

Materials, $20 per unit.
Labor, $10 per unit.
Applied factory overhead, $5 per unit.

Janikowski corrected the defective units on May 8. Make the general journal entries under each of the following situations:

a. Charge the cost of correcting the defects to job no. 631.
b. Charge the cost of correcting the defects to Factory Overhead Control.

Answers at end of chapter.

SELF-STUDY PROBLEM

Mueller Company manufactures a variety of products. Three of the products include the following:

1. One of the primary products manufactured by Mueller Company also creates several by-products that Mueller sells as scrap. Make the general journal entries under each of the following situations:
   a. On February 12, sold scrap for $350 and credited Miscellaneous Income for the cash sale.
   b. Mueller estimated the market value of the scrap to be $5,000 and prepared an inventory card on March 3. Credit the scrap to job no. 415.
   c. Same as (b) above except credit the scrap to Factory Overhead Control.
   d. On March 21, sold scrap inventory recorded at $5,000 on account for $4,800. When the Scrap Inventory was originally recorded, Factory Overhead Control was credited.
2. Another product manufactured by Mueller Company involved the production of 500 units job no. 518, at a total cost of $35,000 or $70 per unit. Just before delivery on May 16, Mueller discovered that 40 of the units were spoiled and could be sold for only $40 each. A Spoiled Goods Inventory account is used to record the sales value. Make the general journal entries under each of the following situations:
   a. The loss associated with the spoiled goods should be charged to Factory Overhead Control.
   b. The loss associated with the spoiled goods should be charged to job no. 518.
   c. On June 3, sold the spoiled goods on account for $1,200. Originally charged the loss associated with the spoiled goods to job no. 518.
3. A third product manufactured by Mueller Company involved the production of 2,000 units at a cost of $60 each. On July 15, just before delivery, Mueller discovered that 100 of the units were defective. Mueller determines that the units can be reworked and made ready for the following unit costs: materials $3, labor $5, factory overhead $2. Make the general journal entries under each of the following situations:

    a. Charge the costs of reworking these defective units to job no. 279.

    b. Charge the costs of reworking these defective units to Factory Overhead Control.

SOLUTION TO SELF-STUDY PROBLEM

1.

a.	Feb.	12	Cash	35000		1
			Miscellaneous Income		35000	2
						3
b.	Mar.	3	Scrap Inventory	500000		4
			Work in Process—job no. 415		500000	5
						6
c.	Mar.	3	Scrap Inventory	500000		7
			Factory Overhead Control		500000	8
						9
d.	Mar.	21	Accounts Receivable	480000		10
			Factory Overhead Control	20000		11
			Scrap Inventory		500000	12

2.

a.	May	16	Spoiled Goods Inventory	160000		1
			Factory Overhead Control	120000		2
			Work in Process—job no. 518		280000	3
						4
b.	May	16	Spoiled Goods Inventory	160000		5
			Work in Process—job no. 518		160000	6
						7
c.	Jun.	3	Accounts Receivable	120000		8
			Work in Process—job no. 518	40000		9
			Spoiled Goods Inventory		160000	10

3.

a.	Jul.	15	Work in Process—job no. 279	100000		1
			Materials Inventory		30000	2
			Payroll		50000	3
			Factory Overhead Control		20000	4
						5
b.	Jul.	15	Factory Overhead Control	100000		6
			Materials Inventory		30000	7
			Payroll		50000	8
			Factory Overhead Control		20000	9

SUMMARY

Scrap is the remnant or residual that remains after the primary product has been manufactured. If the scrap value is small, no journal entry is made until the scrap is sold. If the scrap has a large dollar value, then Scrap Inventory is debited for the market value. Either Work in Process or Factory Overhead Control is credited.

Spoiled goods can result from improper workmanship or equipment malfunctioning. The spoiled goods cannot be economically corrected and are sold as damaged goods or seconds. The market value of the spoiled goods are debited to Spoiled Goods Inventory. If the spoiled goods are considered a normal part of the production process, then Factory Overhead Control is debited for the difference between the Spoiled Goods Inventory and Work in Process accounts. If the spoiled goods are the result of a special order and unique to this order, then the loss should be charged to Work in Process.

Defective units have imperfections but can be economically corrected with additional cost to materials, labor, and factory overhead. If the defective units are the result of a special order and the customer is to be charged for the costs, then Work in Process is debited. If the costs of reworking the defective units are charged against all the jobs worked on during the period, then Factory Overhead Control is debited.

KEY TERMS

Defective Units. Units that have imperfections but can be economically corrected with additional materials, labor, and factory overhead costs.

Scrap. The remnant or residual that remains after the primary product has been manufactured. Scrap is an expected by-product from the production of a valued product.

Spoiled Goods. The result of improper workmanship or equipment malfunctioning.

QUESTIONS FOR REVIEW

1. Define scrap and explain how scrap with a low value is entered in the general journal.
2. What account is debited when the market value of the scrap is known?
3. If scrap has a large dollar value and is identified with a particular job, describe the journal entry to record the market value of the scrap.
4. If scrap has a large dollar value and it is determined that the scrap value should be spread over all the jobs, describe the journal entry to record the market value of the scrap.
5. If scrap inventory cannot be sold for the same amount charged to the Scrap Inventory account, to which account is the difference adjusted?
6. Define spoiled goods.
7. What are the methods of accounting for spoiled goods if (1) the spoiled goods are considered a normal part of the production process and (2) the loss should be charged to a special order?

8. If the amount received for the spoiled goods inventory is different than the amount recorded, what account(s) are adjusted?
9. Define defective units.
10. Describe the different methods of accounting for defective units assuming that (1) the costs of reworking the defective units is charged against a specific job or (2) the costs of reworking the defective units are charged against all jobs worked on during the period.

NOTE Unless told otherwise in Exercises and Problems, record transactions in general journal form.

EXERCISES

9–1. Learning Objective 1. Journalizing Scrap of Low Market Value.
Steiner Company sold some scrap with low market value. On May 16, Steiner sold scrap on account for $275. Make the journal entry to record this sale.

9–2. Learning Objective 1. Journalizing Scrap of High Market Value Using Work in Process Account.
Rahberger Manufacturing has scrap of high market value. On July 22, Rahberger estimated market value of scrap of $6,000, identified with job no. 412, using a Scrap Inventory account. On August 8, Rahberger sold the scrap on account for $6,000. Make the journal entries to record these two events.

9–3. Learning Objective 1. Journalizing Scrap of High Market Value Using Factory Overhead Control Account.
Newton Enterprises has scrap of high market value. Newton determined that the value of the scrap should be spread over all the jobs worked on during the period. On September 27, Newton estimated the market value of scrap is $5,300. On October 21, Newton sold the scrap for cash for $5,300. Make the journal entries to record these two events.

9–4. Learning Objective 1. Journalizing Scrap of High Market Value Followed by a Change in Market Price.
Stamps Corporation has scrap with an estimated value of $7,300. Stamps determined that the scrap should be credited to job no. 187. On February 13, Stamps created a Scrap Inventory account to store the scrap. On March 5, Stamps sold the scrap but only received $7,100 in cash. Make journal entries to record these two events.

9–5. Learning Objective 2. Journalizing Spoiled Goods Inventory Using Factory Overhead Control Account.
Weber Company completed job no. 269, which involved the production of 800 units. Each unit cost $120 to manufacture. During final inspection Weber discovered that 40 units were spoiled and could not be economically corrected. On March 16, Weber created a Spoiled Goods Inventory account to record the estimated market value of the spoiled goods at $50 each. Weber determined that the loss should be charged to Factory Overhead Control. Make the journal entry to record this.

9–6. Learning Objective 2. Journalizing Spoiled Goods Inventory Using Work in Process Account.

Roy Manufacturing completed job no. 429, which involved the production of 500 units. Each unit cost $90 to manufacture. Just before delivery Roy discovered that 30 units were spoiled and could not be economically corrected. On May 23, Roy created a Spoiled Goods Inventory account to record the estimated market value of $40 each. The loss should be charged to job no. 429. On June 21, Roy received $1,000 in cash for the spoiled goods. Make the journal entries to record these events.

9–7. Learning Objective 3. Accounting for Defective Units Using Work in Process Account.

Auskaps Company completed job no. 542, which involved the manufacturing of 700 machines costing $300 each. Auskaps discovered upon final inspection that 20 of the machines were defective. It will cost the following to rework these units in order to sell at the regular sales price:

> Materials, $15 per unit.
> Labor, $8 per unit.
> Factory overhead, $4 per unit.

On October 21, Auskaps corrected the defects. Auskaps decided that the cost of correcting the defects should be charged against job no. 542. Make the journal entry to record the correction of the defective units.

9–8. Learning Objective 3. Accounting for Defective Units Using Factory Overhead Control Account.

The same as exercise 9–7, except that the cost of correcting the defects should be charged to Factory Overhead Control.

GROUP A PROBLEMS

9–1A. Learning Objective 1. Accounting for Scrap.

Baldwin Company produces three primary products, called product A, B, and C, that create scrap.

a. Product A scrap has low market value. On April 7, Baldwin Sold scrap on account for $210.
b. Product B scrap has high market value. On July 17, Baldwin estimated market value of scrap of $7,600, identified with job no. 187, and recorded using a Scrap Inventory account. On July 30, Baldwin sold the scrap on account for $7,600.
c. Product C scrap has high market value. On August 4, Baldwin estimated market value of scrap of $6,800, and recorded using a Scrap Inventory account. The market value of the scrap should be spread over all the jobs worked on during the period. Due to a shortage of this scrap on the market, on August 19, Baldwin received $7,100 cash.

Required:
Record the scrap for all three products.

9–2A. Learning Objective 2. Accounting for Spoiled Goods Using Factory Overhead Control Account.

Brooks Corporation completed job no. 275, which involved the production of 900 units. Each unit cost $80 to manufacture. During final inspection Brooks discovered that 30 units were spoiled and could not be economically corrected. On November 8, Brooks created a Spoiled Goods Inventory account to record the estimated market value of the spoiled goods at $20 each. Brooks determined that the loss should be charged to Factory Overhead Control. On December 3, Brooks sold the spoiled goods on account for $530.

Required:
Record the two transactions.

9–3A. Learning Objective 2. Accounting for Spoiled Goods Using Work in Process Account.

Dyche Manufacturing completed job no. 391, which involved the production of 1,000 units. Each unit cost $110 to manufacture. Just before delivery Dyche discovered that 60 units were spoiled and could not be economically corrected. On January 17, Dyche created a Spoiled Goods Inventory account to record the estimated market value of $60 each. Dyche determined that the loss should be charged to job no. 391. On February 4, Dyche received $4,000 cash for the spoiled goods.

Required:
Record the two transactions.

9–4A. Learning Objective 3. Accounting for Defective Units.

Gammiere Company completed job no. 739, which involved the production of 500 machines at a cost of $100 each. Gammiere discovered upon final inspection that 25 of the machines were defective. It will cost the following to rework these units in order to sell at the regular sales price:

Materials, $6 per unit.
Labor, $10 per unit.
Factory overhead, $2 per unit.

On September 15, Gammiere corrected the defects.

Required:

1. Record the cost of correcting the defective units assuming that the cost should be charged against job no. 739.
2. Record the cost of correcting the defective units assuming that the cost should be charged to Factory Overhead Control.

GROUP B PROBLEMS

9–1B. Learning Objective 1. Accounting for Scrap.

Gsell Company produces three primary products, called product A, B, and C, that create scrap.

a. Product A scrap has low market value. On April 15, Gsell sold scrap for cash, $195.
b. Product B scrap has high market value. On July 25, Gsell estimated market value scrap of $8,200, identified with job no. 207, and recorded using a Scrap Inventory account. On August 14, Gsell sold the scrap on account for $8,200.
c. Product C scrap has high market value. On August 11, Gsell estimated market value of scrap of $5,400, and recorded using a Scrap Inventory account. The market value of the scrap should be spread over all the jobs worked on during the period. Due to a shortage of this scrap, on August 28, Gsell received cash, $5,900.

Required:
Make journal entries to record the scrap for all three products.

9–2B. Learning Objective 2. Accounting for Spoiled Goods Using Factory Overhead Control Account.

Melton Corporation completed job no. 186, which involved the production of 1,200 units. Each unit cost $60 to manufacture. During final inspection Melton discovered that 40 units were spoiled and could not be economically corrected. On November 15, Melton created a Spoiled Goods Inventory account to record the estimated market value of the spoiled goods at $35 each. Melton determined that the loss should be charged to Factory Overhead Control. On December 11, Melton sold the spoiled goods on account for $1,500.

Required:
Record the two transactions.

9–3B. Learning Objective 2. Accounting for Spoiled Goods Using Work in Process Accounts.

McDonald Manufacturing completed job no. 601, which involved the production of 1,500 units. Each unit cost $80 to manufacture. Just before delivery McDonald discovered that 70 units were spoiled and could not be economically corrected. On January 20, McDonald created a Spoiled Goods Inventory account to record the estimated market value of $50 each. McDonald determined that the loss should be charged to job no. 601. On February 20, McDonald received cash, $3,000 for the spoiled goods.

Required:
Record the two transactions.

9–4B. Learning Objective 3. Accounting for Defective Units.

Minsker Company completed job no. 274, which involved the production of 300 machines at a cost of $120 each. Minsker discovered upon final inspection that 15 of the machines were defective. It will cost the following to rework these units in order to sell at the regular sales price:

Materials, $15 per unit.
Labor, $20 per unit.
Factory overhead, $10 per unit.

On September 21, Minsker corrected the defects.

Required:

1. Record the cost of correcting the defective units assuming that the cost should be charged against job no. 274.
2. Record the cost of correcting the defective units assuming that the cost should be charged against Factory Overhead Control.

CASE FOR CRITICAL THINKING

The accountant for Dexter Manufacturing Company has been crediting a revenue account when selling spoiled goods associated with a given job. Management is concerned that the company is losing business because their bids for new jobs are not price competitive. Explain why the system currently being used to account for spoiled goods provides misleading information to management.

ANSWERS TO SELF-STUDY QUIZ 9–1

a.	Feb.	23	Accounts Receivable		250 00		1
			Miscellaneous Income			250 00	2
							3
b.	Mar.	19	Scrap Inventory		4000 00		4
			Work in Process—job no. 227			4000 00	5
							6
c.	Mar.	19	Scrap Inventory		4000 00		7
			Factory Overhead Control			4000 00	8

ANSWERS TO SELF-STUDY QUIZ 9–2

a.	Aug.	11	Spoiled Goods Inventory		900 00		1
			Factory Overhead Control		1500 00		2
			Work in Process—job no. 313			2400 00	3
							4
b.	Aug.	11	Spoiled Goods Inventory		900 00		5
			Work in Process—job no. 313			900 00	6

ANSWERS TO SELF-STUDY QUIZ 9–3

a.	May	8	Work in Process—job no. 631	350000		1
			Materials Inventory		200000	2
			Payroll		100000	3
			Factory Overhead Control		50000	4
						5
b.	May	8	Factory Overhead Control	350000		6
			Materials Inventory		200000	7
			Payroll		100000	8
			Factory Overhead Control		50000	9

PROJECT 1—JOB-ORDER COSTING

The first eight chapters covered transactions for TurboFlex Corporation for the month of January. We will continue to analyze selected transactions for TurboFlex Corporation for the month of February. All the required forms can be found in the Study Guide/Working Papers.

Task 1—Completing a Materials Ledger Card

During February, 19X6, one of the materials used by TurboFlex is leg support braces.

Feb. 1 Balance; 50 units at $3.20 and 900 units at $3.30; total cost $3,130.
    7 Purchased 1,000 units on account at $3.40 each (P.O. 152); total cost, $3,400.
   14 Issued 1,200 units to production on Materials Requisition 114.
   19 Purchased 1,000 units on account at $3.50 each (P.O. 171); total cost, $3,500.
   25 Issued 900 units to production on Material Requisition 133.
   28 Prepared Returned Materials Report 21 for the return of 100 units to the storeroom. These units were issued to production on February 25 (Materials Requisition 114).

Requirements:

1. Prepare materials ledger cards to determine the cost of materials used and the cost of the February 28 inventory under each of the following methods: (a) FIFO, (b) LIFO, and (c) Moving Average.
2 Assuming the use of FIFO, record transactions in general journal form.

Task 2—Accounting for Labor

The monthly payroll for February for TurboFlex Company follows:

EARNINGS:

Regular earnings	$ 39,900
Overtime earnings	4,600
Gross earnings	$ 44,500

TAXABLE EARNINGS:

FICA—OASDI	$44,500
FICA—HIP	44,500
FUTA	38,000
SUTA	38,000

TAX RATES:

Federal income tax rate (assumed)	15%
FICA—OASDI rate	6.2%
FICA—HIP rate	1.45%
FUTA	.8%
SUTA	3.0%

LABOR ALLOCATION:

Direct labor	$38,000
Indirect labor	6,500

OPTIONAL DEDUCTIONS:

U.S. Savings Bonds	$ 1,200
Medical Insurance	4,700
Union Dues	800

Prepare general journal entries (dated February 28) to record:

a. Payroll.
b. Payment of the payroll.
c. Distribution of the payroll to production.
d. Employer's payroll taxes.

Task 3—Completing a Job Cost Sheet

One of the jobs that TurboFlex has been working on is job no. 119. The following information relates to the job cost sheet.

> Customer name: Chamberlain Fitness Spa
> Job Description: On file
> Quantity: 100
> Job no. 119
> Date Started: 2–3–X6

Materials

Date	Req. No.	Amount
2–5	803	600.00
2–6	RM 14	(75.00)
2–9	821	1,615.00
2–10	826	300.00
2–16	831	25.00
2–17	834	35.00

Direct Labor

Shaping			Assembling			Finishing		
Date	Hours	Amount	Date	Hours	Amount	Date	Hours	Amount
2–6	50	$625.00	2–7	180	$1,710.00	2–15	90	$900.00
						2–19	30	300.00

1. Enter the above information onto a job cost sheet. Assign job number 119.
2. Factory overhead is applied on the basis of direct labor hours. Use the following table of department overhead rates:

Shaping:	$6.00 per direct labor hour.
Assembling Department:	5.75 per direct labor hour.
Finishing Department:	5.25 per direct labor hour.

3. Complete the job cost sheet by entering the applied factory overhead for each department.

Task 4—Recording Applied Overhead and Determining Under- or Overapplied Overhead

At the end of February, the total overhead applied for the month follows:

Factory Overhead—Shaping Dept.   2,500 hours at $6.00 = $15,000.00
Factory Overhead—Assembling Dept.   1,920 hours at $5.75 =   11,040.00
Factory Overhead—Finishing Dept.   2,100 hours at $5.25 =   11,025.00

1. Prepare the month-end journal entry to record the applied overhead.
2. Post the applied overhead amounts to the Department Factory Overhead accounts.

   The actual factory overhead for the month follows:

   Factory Overhead—Shaping Dept. $15,890.00
   Factory Overhead—Assembling Dept.   10,980.00
   Factory Overhead—Finishing Dept.   11,110.00

3. Post the actual overhead amounts to the Department Factory Overhead accounts.
4. Determine the amount of over- or underapplied overhead in each Department Factory Overhead account.
5. Close the amount of Departmental over- or underapplied overhead into the Under- or Overapplied Factory Overhead account.
6. Close the balance of the Under- or Overapplied Factory Overhead account to the Cost of Goods Sold account.

Task 5—Analyzing Under- and Overapplied Overhead into Volume and Spending Variances

The following information was taken from the annual budget for TurboFlex Corporation:

   Budgeted annual Fixed Factory Overhead by Department:

      Shaping Department: $89,856/28,800 = $3.12 per hour
      Assembling Department: $59,940/22,200 = $2.70 per hour
      Finishing Department: $68,640/26,400 = $2.60 per hour

   Budgeted Variable Factory Overhead by Department:

      Shaping Department: $82,944/28,800 = $2.88 per hour
      Assembling Department: $67,710/22,200 = $3.05 per hour
      Finishing Department: $69,960/26,400 = $2.65 per hour

Budgeted Direct Labor Hours by Department:

Shaping Department:	28,800
Assembling Department:	22,200
Finishing Department:	26,400

1. Using the information in task 4, calculate the volume and spending overhead variances for each department for the month of February. Indicate whether the variances are favorable or unfavorable.

Task 6—Accounting for Defective Units

TurboFlex discovered upon final inspection, two defective machines. It will cost the following to rework these machines in order to sell them at the regular sales price:

Materials, $200 per unit
Labor, $120 per unit
Applied Factory overhead, $50 per unit

1. Charge the cost of correcting the defects to job no. 120, assuming the job was completed on Feb. 28.
2. Charge the cost of correcting the defects to factory overhead control.

Task 7—Preparing Summary Journal Entries

Record the below summary transactions for the last few days in February in general journal form:

February 26

1. Purchased materials on credit, $60,000
2. Issued credit memo for the return of damaged merchandise; $300.

February 27

1. Issued materials to production as follows: Direct $52,000; indirect, $6,600.
2. Incurred factory overhead costs on account, $3,000.
3. Recognized other factory overhead costs as follows: depreciation of equipment, $4,600; depreciation of building, $6,000; expired insurance, $800; accrued property taxes, $2,200.

February 28

1. Completed jobs costing $130,700.
2. Sold finished goods costing $127,400 to various customers; billed customers for $203,840 (make two entries).
3. Summary entry from the cash receipts journal; collected cash from customers previously billed, $198,270.
4. Paid selling and general expense; $5,310–Selling expense, $3,400–General expense.
5. Paid accounts payable, $63,000.

Task 8—Preparing Financial Statements

At the end of February, balances in selected accounts for TurboFlex appear as follows:

	Ending Balance
Direct labor	$ 38,000
Factory overhead applied	35,265
Finished Goods Inventory	92,000
General Expense	22,000
Indirect materials used	1,500
Interest Expense	1,950
Raw Materials Inventory	48,000
Raw Material Purchases	33,000
Sales	265,000
Sales Returns and Allowances	3,000
Selling Expense	26,000
Work in Process Inventory	28,000

Additional Information:

	Beginning Balance
Finished Goods Inventory	91,725
Raw Materials Inventory	44,420
Work in Process Inventory	24,750

Income Tax expense is 20%

1. Prepare a Statement of Cost of Goods Manufactured for the month ending February 28, 19X6.
2. Prepare a classified Income Statement for the month ending February 28, 19X6.

Part II

Process
Cost
Accounting

Chapter 10
Overview of Process Costing

LEARNING OBJECTIVES

After studying Chapter 10, you should be able to:

1. Identify types of businesses that use process costing systems.
2. Identify similarities and differences between job-order and process costing systems.
3. Identify the accounts used to accumulate and control costs in a process costing system.
4. Make journal entries to record the flow of costs through a process costing system.
5. Apply factory overhead to production.
6. Compute the unit cost of finished goods.

In Part I, we covered two principal types of cost accounting systems: the job-order costing system and the process costing system. A job-order costing system is used by businesses that manufacture products that can be separately identified and usually have a high cost per unit—such as ships, aircraft, highways, buildings, and specialized equipment.

LEARNING OBJECTIVE 1

In Part II, we will study the process costing system. Process costing is used in industries that mass produce like-kind products on a continuous basis—such as cement, peanut butter, bricks, automobiles, breakfast cereal, steel, petroleum, glass, mining, and canneries. The process costing system is also used in the production of utilities—such as gas, water, and electricity. In addition, process costing systems are used in nonmanufacturing businesses such as food preparation in fast-food restaurants, mail sorting in post offices, check processing in banks, and student registration in college.

Cost accumulation is generally simpler in a process costing system than in a job-order costing system, because costs are identified by departments (or processes), not by the individual job. Thus, in a process costing system, it is not necessary to maintain job cost sheets for goods in production. Instead, costs are accumulated on a department-by-department basis as goods move through the production process.

In Chapter 10, we will start our study of process costing by overviewing the system and looking at how it operates. We will continue our study of process costing through Chapter 13, and then in Chapter 14, we will look at joint products and by-products.

PROCESS COSTING—AN OVERVIEW

The process system is used by firms that manufacture **homogeneous products.** That is, the products are all very much alike. If you saw several of them, you would not be able to tell them apart. The products are usually produced in a continuous process and a large number of units or volume of output is produced in a given time period, such as a month. Before we get into a discussion of how the process costing systems works, let's look at a comparison of job-order and process costing systems.

Comparison of Job-Order and Process Costing Systems

LEARNING OBJECTIVE 2

In some ways process costing is very similar to job-order costing, and in other ways it is very different. In this section, we will look at the similarities and differences between the two costing systems.

Similarities. As we look at the similarities between the two systems, keep in mind that most of what you learned about job-order costing will also apply to process costing. The similarities can be summarized as follows:

1. Both systems are designed to accumulate costs for materials, labor, and factory overhead so that unit costs of products can be calculated.
2. Both systems produce cost data that is used by management in planning, controlling, and directing the operations of the business.
3. Both sytems use the same basic manufacturing accounts, including Raw Materials Inventory, Work in Process Inventory, Factory Overhead Control, and Finished Goods Inventory.
4. Both systems normally use a perpetual inventory system where materials, work in process, and finished goods inventories are maintained in subsidiary ledgers.

Differences. The main difference between job-order and process costing is in the manner in which costs are assigned to the products produced. Under process costing, costs are accumulated *by department*, rather than by individual jobs as in job-order costing. No attempt is made to identify production costs (materials, labor, and factory overhead) with a particular order from a customer—because each order is just one of many that continously flow through the production process. For example, what if the manufacturer of Jiffy peanut butter received an order for 500 cases of smooth peanut butter from Save-More Stores. Jiffy would not set up a special production run just for this order. Instead, the order would be filled from the flow of units that continuously come off the production line.

A second difference between the two costing systems is that the job cost sheet has no function in a process costing system—because costs are accumulated by departments, not by individual jobs. Instead, a form known as a **cost of production report** is prepared for each department in which work is done on the products. This report, discussed in detail later, has two main functions: (1) it shows a summary of the number of units moving through a department during a specific period and (2) it shows what costs were charged to the department during the period. Figure 10–1 shows a summary of the differences between job-order and process costing systems.

Figure 10–2 shows a comparison of job-order and process cost systems.

Flow of Costs in a Process Costing System

LEARNING OBJECTIVE 3

In our study of job-order costing, we learned that production costs (direct materials, direct labor, and applied factory overhead) are charged to production by debiting the Work in Process Inventory account. In process costing systems, production costs are likewise charged to production by debiting the Work in Process Inventory account. How this is done, however, depends on the complexity of a firm's operations. If a firm has only one producing department (remember, a producing department is any location in the factory where

FIGURE 10–1
Differences between Job-Order and Process Costing

Job-Order Costing

1. Many different jobs with different production requirements are worked on during each period. Each unit of product can be separately identified and often has a high cost.

2. Most jobs are manufactured for specific customers.

3. Costs are accumulated for each job in production.

4. Each job uses a job-cost sheet to accumulate and summarize the costs necessary to complete the job.

5. Unit costs are calculated for each job.

Process Costing

1. A single product is continuously produced during a period of time, such as a month. All units produced are identical.

2. Most units are manufactured for stock.

3. Costs are accumulated by departments.

4. Units passing through a department and costs charged to the department are summarized on a cost of production report.

5. Unit costs are calculated for each department.

FIGURE 10–2
Comparison of Job-Order and Process Costing Systems

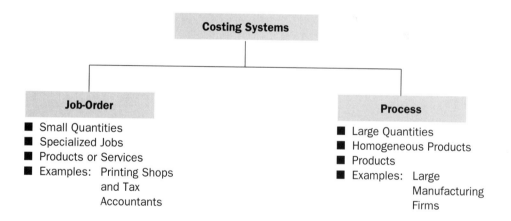

Costing Systems

Job-Order
- Small Quantities
- Specialized Jobs
- Products or Services
- Examples: Printing Shops and Tax Accountants

Process
- Large Quantities
- Homogeneous Products
- Products
- Examples: Large Manufacturing Firms

materials, labor, or overhead costs are added to the products), or continuously produces a single product, it is possible to use a single Work in Process Inventory account for the entire plant. However, the activity of most firms using the process costing system requires products in production to pass through several different departments before the units emerge as finished goods. Each department has a specific function, and separate cost figures are usually accumulated on a department-by-department basis. It is thus necessary for each producing department to have a Work in Process Inventory account.

You are already familiar with the use of a single Work in Process Inventory account (from our study of job-order costing). Since the second approach—departmental Work in Process Inventory accounts—is very common, we will focus on it in our discussion. Under this approach, a firm with three producing departments would have the following general ledger accounts:

122   Work in Process Inventory—Dept. 1
123   Work in Process Inventory—Dept. 2
124   Work in Process Inventory—Dept. 3

Costs are charged to production as follows:

1. The cost of direct materials issued to each department is debited to the departmental Work in Process Inventory account, and credited to the Raw Materials Inventory account. The cost of indirect materials used is debited to the Factory Overhead Control account, and credited to the Raw Materials Inventory account.

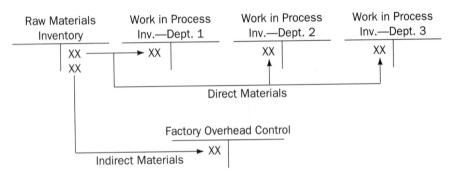

2. From monthly summaries of factory payroll, direct labor costs are debited to the departmental Work in Process Inventory accounts, and credited to the Factory Payroll Clearing account. Indirect labor costs are debited to the Factory Overhead Control account, and credited to the Factory Payroll Clearing account.

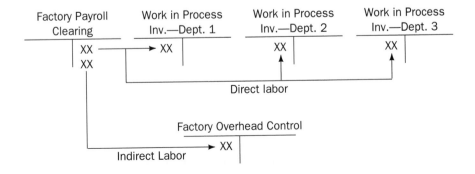

3. Actual factory overhead costs are debited to the Factory Overhead Control account and posted to departmental overhead analysis sheets. However, the actual factory overhead cost *is not* charged to production. Instead, overhead is applied to production using predetermined departmental overhead rates. Overhead is applied to production by debiting the departmental Work in Process Inventory accounts, and crediting the Factory Overhead Control account.

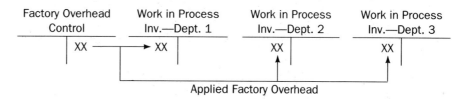

4. Production costs accumulated in each department are summarized and an average cost per unit is calculated. Costs are transferred from one department (or process) to the next as the units move through the production process.

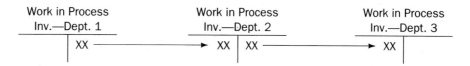

5. When finished units are transferred to the warehouse to await sale, their cost is transferred to the Finished Goods Inventory account.

6. When finished goods are sold, their cost is debited to the Cost of Goods Sold account, and credited to Finished Goods Inventory. The selling price of the units is debited to Accounts Receivable (or Cash) and credited to Sales.

PROCESS COSTING SYSTEM ILLUSTRATED

To illustrate how a process costing system works, we will use South Company as our example. South manufactures T-shirts for distribution to retail stores who sell them to the general public. The T-shirts are produced in three different departments (or processes). Production starts in the Cutting Department where materials (cloth) are cut into sections. The cut sections are then transferred to the Sewing Department where they are sewn together. To match cost flow with work flow, all production costs accumulated in the Cutting Department are transferred to the Sewing Department. After the Sewing Department has completed sewing the cut sections together, the T-shirts are transferred to the Dyeing Department where they are finished. The costs incurred in the Sewing Department, along with the costs transferred from the Cutting Department, are transferred to the Dyeing Department.

When the Dyeing Department is finished, the completed T-shirts are transferred to finished goods storage. The total cost accumulated in the production of the completed units is transferred to the Finished Goods Inventory account. Figure 10–3 shows a floor plan of South Company's plant.

FIGURE 10–3
Floor Plan of South Company

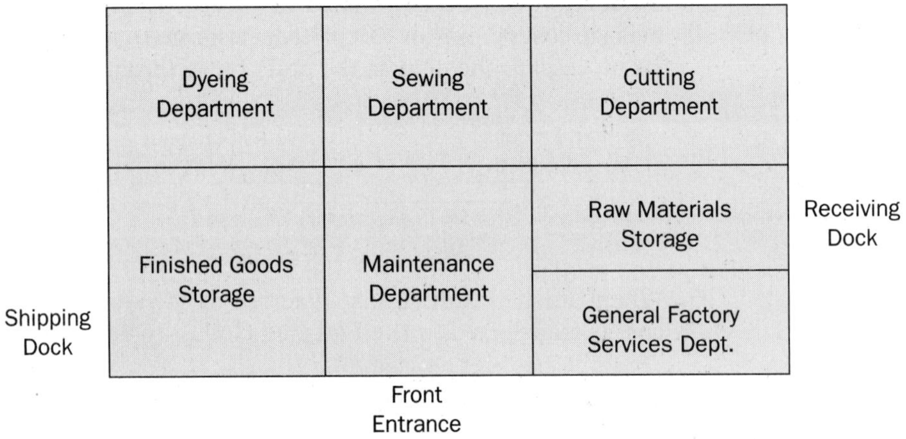

The Raw Materials Storage Department receives and stores materials until requisitioned. The General Factory Services Department is a service department responsible for purchasing, issuing materials to production, timekeeping, payroll, and factory accounting. The Maintenance Department is a service department reponsible for the maintenance and repair of the factory building, grounds, machinery and equipment, as well as the janitorial services and heating and lighting. The Cutting, Sewing, and Dyeing Departments are producing departments that manufacture the T-shirts. The Finished Goods Storage Department stores the finished T-shirts until they are sold.

South Company's first step in the production of T-shirts is to determine the quantity that will be produced and how much labor, materials, and factory overhead are needed to produce the desired quantity. To make our example as easy as possible, we will assume that each of the three producing departments had no beginning inventory of work in process (we will deal with beginning inventories in Chapter 11). Figure 10–4 shows a flowchart of the costs of production at South Company.

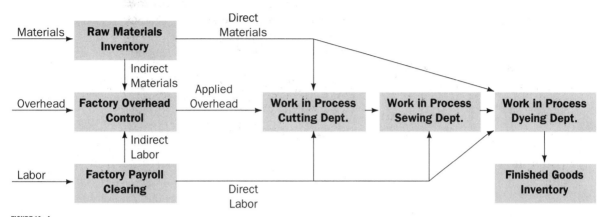

FIGURE 10–4
*Flowchart of the
Costs of Production*

Accounting for Raw Materials Costs

LEARNING OBJECTIVE 4   In Part I, we studied the procedures for purchasing and storing materials in a job-order costing system. A firm using a process costing system would follow the same basic procedures. At South Company, the General Factory Services Department is responsible for ordering and receiving all materials and supplies. In response to purchase requisition forms received from production supervisors, the purchasing agent chooses a supplier (vendor) and sends a purchase order. When materials arrive and are counted, a receiving report is prepared at the Receiving Dock.

During June South Company purchased $200,000 of materials on credit. Journal entry (A) records the purchase.

(A)

1	Jun.	30	Raw Materials Inventory	200 000 00		1
2			Accounts Payable		200 000 00	2
3			Purchased materials.			3

When materials are needed in production, the production supervisor in the department needing the materials issues a materials requisition to the storeroom clerk, who fills the order and delivers the materials to production. As you have already learned, direct materials can be traced directly to the final product. As you have also learned, not all materials issued to production can be traced directly to the final products (or can be traced only at great expense or inconvenience). Such materials are called indirect materials and are recorded as Factory Overhead Control. An analysis of South's materials requisitions for June showed that $150,000 of direct materials were issued to the Cutting Department, $30,000 were issued to the Dyeing Department, and $20,000 were indirect materials. Journal entry (B) shows how these materials were charged to production.

(B)

1	Jun.	30	Work in Process Inventory—Cutting Dept.	150 00 0 00		1
2			Work in Process Inventory—Dyeing Dept.	30 00 0 00		2
3			Factory Overhead Control	20 00 0 00		3
4			Raw Materials Inventory		200 0 0 0 00	4
5			Issued materials to production.			5

Notice from this entry, and from Figure 10–4, that the Sewing Department does not requisition direct materials. It would be difficult to trace the type of materials (thread, patches, sewing machine needles, etc.) used by the Sewing Department directly to the finished product. As a result, all materials used by this department are recorded as factory overhead.

SELF-STUDY QUIZ 10–1 A summary of materials costs for Byner Company for June, shows the following costs. Make a general journal entry to charge these costs to production.

Direct materials—Hulling Dept. $25,000
Direct materials—Grinding Dept.   12,000
Direct materials—Finishing Dept.   18,000
Indirect materials   15,000

Answers at end of chapter.

Accounting for Labor Costs

In our study of job-order costing systems, we learned that direct labor costs are debited to the Work in Process Inventory account, and indirect labor costs are debited to the Factory Overhead Control account. In process costing systems, labor is recorded the same way except that direct labor is charged to departments, rather than to job-cost sheets. The total factory labor cost for South Company during June was $180,000. Journal entry (C) shows how the payroll is recorded.

(C)

1	Jun.	30	Factory Payroll Clearing	1800000		1
2			FICA Tax Payable—OASDI		1116000	2
3			FICA Tax Payable—HIP		261000	3
4			Federal Income Tax Payable		270000	4
5			Health Insurance Payable		54000	5
6			Wages Payable		1338300	6
7			Incurred June payroll.			7

An analysis of time tickets for June shows labor costs as follows:

Direct labor—Cutting Dept.	$40,000
Direct labor—Sewing Dept.	60,000
Direct labor—Dyeing Dept.	20,000
Indirect labor	60,000

Journal entry (D) shows how labor was distributed to production.

(D)

1	Jun.	30	Work in Process Inventory—Cutting Dept.	400000		1
2			Work in Process Inventory—Sewing Dept.	600000		2
3			Work in Process Inventory—Dyeing Dept.	200000		3
4			Factory Overhead Control	600000		4
5			Factory Payroll Clearing		1800000	5
6			Distributed June payroll.			6

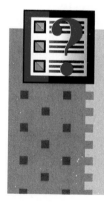

SELF-STUDY QUIZ 10–2 A summary of factory wages at Bibb Company for July shows the following labor costs. Make a general journal entry to charge these costs to production.

Cutting Dept.	$28,000
Assembling Dept.	21,000
Finishing Dept.	24,000
Indirect labor	18,000

Answers at end of chapter.

Accounting for Factory Overhead

In process costing systems, as in job-order costing systems, all costs of operating the factory other than direct materials and direct labor are considered factory overhead. In addition to the indirect materials and indirect labor costs we have already recorded, South Company incurred the following indirect costs during June:

Factory rent	$ 6,000
Factory utilities	12,000
Repairs	10,000
Expired factory insurance	4,000
Accrued wages	15,000
Depreciation Expense	25,000
Payroll taxes	20,000
Miscellaneous overhead	28,000
Total	$120,000

Journal entry (E) shows the recording of these costs.

(E)

1	Jun.	30	Factory Overhead Control	120 00 0 00		1
2			Cash (rent, utilities, and repairs)		28 00 0 00	2
3			Prepaid Insurance		4 00 0 00	3
4			Wages Payable		15 00 0 00	4
5			Accumulated Depreciation		25 00 0 00	5
6			Payroll Taxes Payable		20 00 0 00	6
7			Various Accounts		28 00 0 00	7
8			Recognized factory overhead costs.			8

Applying Factory Overhead to Production

LEARNING OBJECTIVE 5   In Chapter 7, you learned that factory overhead is applied to production using predetermined overhead rates. You also learned that overhead application rates are computed at the beginning of a year and are based on some activity that has a cause-and-effect relationship to factory overhead, such as direct labor cost, direct materials cost, or machine hours. South Company uses direct labor cost as a base for applying overhead. The following rates were determined at the beginning of the current year.

Department	Overhead Application Rate
Cutting	150% of direct labor cost
Sewing	200% of direct labor cost
Dyeing	100% of direct labor cost

Using these rates, the June allocation of factory overhead to the three producing departments follows:

Cutting Dept.: 150% × $40,000 = $60,000
Sewing Dept.: 200% × $60,000 = $120,000
Dyeing Dept.: 100% × $20,000 = $20,000

Journal entry (F) records the applied factory overhead for June.

(F)

1	Jun.	30	Work in Process Inventory—Cutting Dept.	60 00 00 0				1
2			Work in Process Inventory—Sewing Dept.	120 00 00 0				2
3			Work in Process Inventory—Dyeing Dept.	20 00 00 0				3
4			Factory Overhead Control			200 00 0 00 0		4
5			Recorded applied overhead for June.					5

NOTE Actual factory overhead costs are debited to the Factory Overhead account; applied factory overhead is credited to the Factory Overhead account. At the end of the period, any over- or under-applied factory overhead is closed to the Cost of Goods Sold account.

SELF-STUDY QUIZ 10–3 Bibb Company, from Self-Study Quiz 10–2, applies factory overhead to production on the basis of direct labor cost. Based on the following predetermined factory overhead rates, make a journal entry, dated July 31, to apply overhead to production.

Cutting Dept.   80%
Assembling Dept.   90%
Finishing Dept.   70%

Answers at end of chapter.

Transferring Costs between Processing Department

As we stated earlier, when the Cutting Department completes its work on the units, the partially completed units are physically transferred to the Sewing Department. To match cost flow with work flow, an entry must be made to transfer the costs accumulated in the Cutting Department to the Sewing Department. Likewise, when the partially completed units move from the Sewing Department to the Dyeing Department, an entry is needed to record the transfer of costs. And, as the completed units are transferred to finished goods storage, an entry is needed to record the transfer of costs from the Dyeing Department to Finished Goods Inventory. Each of these entries is illustrated shortly. Before looking at the entries, however, let's look at the Work in Process Inventory—Cutting Dept. account.

Work in Process Inventory—Cutting Dept.

Materials	(B)	150,000	
Labor	(D)	40,000	
Overhead	(F)	60,000	
Balance		250,000	

As we can see, production costs totaling $250,000 have been added to the units by the Cutting Department during the month. Journal entry (G) shows how these costs were transferred to the Sewing Department.

(G)

1	Jun.	30	Work in Process Inventory—Sewing Dept.	250 00 0 00		1
2			Work in Process Inventory—Cutting Dept.		250 00 0 00	2
3			Transferred partial units to Sewing Dept.			3

After this entry is posted, the Work in Process Inventory—Cutting Dept. account will have a zero balance, and the Work in Process Inventory—Sewing Dept. account will look like this:

Work in Process Inventory—Sewing Dept.

Labor	(D)	60,000	
Overhead	(F)	120,000	
Transferred in	(G)	250,000	
Balance		430,000	

As we can see, the Work in Process Inventory—Sewing Dept. account has **transferred-in costs** of $250,000 and added costs of $60,000 and $120,000. Now, journal entry (H) shows how the costs of the Sewing Department are transferred to the Dyeing Department.

(H)

1	Jun.	30	Work in Process Inventory—Dyeing Dept.	430 00 0 00		1
2			Work in Process Inventory—Sewing Dept.		430 00 0 00	2
3			Transferred costs to Dyeing Dept.			3

After this entry is posted, the Work in Process Inventory—Sewing Dept. account will have a zero balance, and the Work in Process Inventory—Dyeing Dept. account will appear as follows.

Work in Process Inventory—Dyeing Dept.

Materials	(B)	30,000	
Labor	(D)	20,000	
Overhead	(F)	20,000	
Transferred in	(H)	430,000	
Balance		500,000	

Journal entry (I) shows how the $500,000 in costs accumulated in the Dyeing Department are transferred to Finished Goods Inventory.

(I)

1	Jun. 30	Finished Goods Inventory	50000000		1
2		Work in Process Inventory—Dyeing Dept.		50000000	2
3		Transferred completed units to storage.			3

After this entry is posted, the Finished Goods Inventory account will have a $500,000 debit balance, and the Work in Process Inventory—Dyeing Dept. account will have a zero balance.

SELF-STUDY QUIZ 10–4 At Janus Company, the last department in the production process is the Finishing Department. During October, the Finishing Department accumulated production costs as follows:

Direct materials	$40,000
Direct labor	60,000
Applied overhead	30,000

Assuming no beginning or ending inventories in the Finishing Department, record the transfer of costs to Finished Goods Inventory.
Answers at end of chapter.

Calculating Unit Costs

LEARNING OBJECTIVE 6   Assuming that a total of 50,000 units were completed in June, at a total cost of $500,000, the cost per T-shirt is:

$$\frac{\$500,000}{50,000} = \$10.00$$

Recording the Sale of Finished Goods

During June, South Company sold 45,000 T-shirts on account for $15 each. Remember that when units are sold, two entries are needed—one to transfer the cost of the units sold to the Cost of Goods Sold account, and the other to record the selling price. Journal entry (J) shows how the cost of 45,000 T-shirts (with a unit cost of $10) is transferred to Cost of Goods Sold.

(J)

1	Jun.	30	Cost of Goods Sold	45 00 0 000		1
2			Finished Goods Inventory		45 00 0 000	2
3			Transferred finished goods to cost of			3
4			goods sold (45,000 x $10).			4

Our last entry is journal entry (K), which records the selling price of the 45,000 T-shirts sold during June.

(K)

1	Jun.	30	Accounts Receivable	67 50 0 000		1
2			Sales		67 50 0 000	2
3			Sold 45,000 units at $15.			3

NOTE In our example of South Company, we assumed that there were no June 1 beginning inventories in the producing departments. We also assumed that there were no June 30 ending inventories in the producing departments. While this is the objective of JIT systems, most firms have both beginning and ending inventories in producing departments. In Chapter 11, we will see how beginning and ending inventories affect our calculations.

SELF-STUDY PROBLEM

West Company manufactures women's dresses. During July, West incurred the following costs:

a. Raw materials purchased on account, $400,000.
b. Direct materials issued to Cutting Department, $250,000.
c. Direct materials issued to Dyeing Department, $40,000.
d. Labor incurred as follows:

Cutting Dept.	$100,000
Sewing Dept.	150,000
Dyeing Dept.	80,000
Indirect labor	120,000

e.   Indirect materials used, $80,000.

f.   Factory overhead applied to production as follows:

Cutting Dept., 80% of direct labor cost
Sewing Dept., 100% of direct labor cost
Dyeing Dept., 75% of direct labor cost

g.   Other factory overhead costs incurred, $100,000.

h.   Transferred costs from the Cutting Department to the Sewing Department; there was no ending inventory.

i.   Transferred costs from the Sewing Department to the Dyeing Department; there was no ending inventory.

j.   Transferred cost of finished units from the Dyeing Department to Finished Goods Inventory. A total of 50,000 dresses was completed; there was no ending inventory in the Dyeing Department.

k.   Sold 45,000 dresses on account for $30 each.

Required:

Record these transactions in general journal form. To simplify the problem, assume that there were no payroll deductions.

SOLUTION TO SELF-STUDY PROBLEM

			Debit	Credit	
a.		Raw Materials Inventory	400 00 0 00		1
		Accounts Payable		400 00 0 00	2
					3
b.		Work in Process Inventory—Cutting Dept.	250 00 0 00		4
		Raw Materials Inventory		250 00 0 00	5
					6
c.		Work in Process Inventory—Dyeing Dept.	40 00 0 00		7
		Raw Materials Inventory		40 00 0 00	8
					9
d.		Work in Process Inventory—Cutting Dept.	100 00 0 00		10
		Work in Process Inventory—Sewing Dept.	150 00 0 00		11
		Work in Process Inventory—Dyeing Dept.	80 00 0 00		12
		Factory Overhead Control	120 00 0 00		13
		Factory Payroll Clearing		450 00 0 00	14
					15
e.		Factory Overhead Control	80 00 0 00		16
		Raw Materials Inventory		80 00 0 00	17
					18
f.		Work in Process Inventory—Cutting Dept.	80 00 0 00		19
		Work in Process Inventory—Sewing Dept.	150 00 0 00		20
		Work in Process Inventory—Dyeing Dept.	60 00 0 00		21
		Factory Overhead Control		290 00 0 00	22

					23
g.		Factory Overhead Control	100 00 000		24
		Various Accounts		100 00 000	25
					26
h.		Work in Process Inventory—Sewing Dept.	430 00 000		27
		Work in Process Inventory—Cutting Dept.		430 00 000	28
					29
i.		Work in Process Inventory—Dyeing Dept.	730 00 000		30
		Work in Process Inventory—Sewing Dept.		730 00 000	31
					32
j.		Finished Goods Inventory	910 00 000		33
		Work in Process Inventory—Dyeing Dept.		910 00 000	34
					35
k.		Cost of Goods Sold (45,000 x $18.20*)	819 00 000		36
		Finished Goods Inventory		819 00 000	37
					38
		Accounts Receivable (45,000 x $30)	1350 00 000		39
		Sales		1350 00 000	40

*Unit cost of each dress is calculated as follows:

Work in Process Inventory—Dyeing Department

Direct materials	(c.)	40,000
Direct labor	(d.)	80,000
Applied overhead	(f.)	60,000
Transferred in	(i.)	730,000
Total		910,000

$$\frac{\$910,000}{50,000} = \$18.20$$

SUMMARY

Process costing is a system of assigning costs to **homogeneous products** that are mass produced in a continuous series of steps (called processes). Mass production firms produce large numbers of identical units, such as gallons of gasoline, cases of Coca-Cola, boxes of breakfast cereal, and hunderds of typewriters. Process costing is also used in non-manufacturing firms that prepare products or services in a series of steps, such as food preparation in fast food restaurants, claims processing in an insurance office, and registration in college.

In a process costing firm, units usually flow through several different departments (processes). Each producing department has a specific function that brings the units closer to being finished. Job cost sheets are not used because costs are accumulated in each department for a week or a month. Each department has a Work in Process Inventory account that shows the total production costs charged to the department during the period. When a department has completed work on a production run, the cost of the partially completed units is transferred to the next department. When the units are completed, their total cost is transferred to Finished Goods Inventory.

Total manufacturing cost is the sum of all costs added in the processing departments during the period. Unit cost is computed by dividing the total manufacturing cost by the number of units completed during the period. A **cost of production report** is prepared for each department to show a summary of the number of units moving through the department during the month and the total costs that were charged to the department.

KEY TERMS

Cost of Production Report. A report that summarizes production costs and quantities for a period for each departmnet and provides information necessary for costing and inventory valuation.

Homogeneous Products. Products identical to other products in production.

Transferred-in Costs. Costs added to the units of product in a prior processing department(s).

QUESTIONS FOR REVIEW

1. Under what conditions would a process costing system be appropriate?
2. What are some similarities between the job-order and process costing systems?
3. What are some differences between the job-order and process costing systems?
4. Why are job cost sheets not needed in a process costing system?
5. How are costs accumulated in a process costing system?
6. Cost accumulation is usually easier under a process costing system than a job-order costing system. Explain why.
7. How many Work in Process Inventory accounts would be needed by a firm that has five producing departments? Explain your answer.
8. Mother Earth Bakery Products Company has two producing departments—Mixing and Baking. What journal entry is needed to show a transfer of partially completed units from the Mixing Department to the Baking Department?
9. Do all producing departments use direct materials? Explain.
10. Most firms using a process costing system will have more than one Work in Process Inventory account. Under what conditions could a firm use a single Work in Process Inventory account?
11. The East Company charged $100,000 of direct labor to the Finishing Department during August. If the firm's overhead application rate is 175% of direct labor cost, how much overhead could be charged to the Finishing Department for August?
12. How are unit costs determined in a process costing system?

NOTE Unless told otherwise in Exercises and Problems, record transactions in general journal form.

EXERCISES

10–1. Learning Objective 4. Recording Materials Transactions.

On May 15, Rodgers Company purchased materials costing $125,000 with terms of 2/10,n/30. The invoice was paid in full on May 25. Record these transactions.

10–2. Learning Objectives 3, 4. Recording Raw Materials Issued to Production.

During July, the following materials were requisition by producing departments at Northup Company. Make a summary entry to record these costs.

Department	Requisition
Assembling	$24,000
Painting	15,000
Finishing	10,000
Indirect materials	15,000

10–3. Learning Objectives 3, 4. Recording Labor Costs.

During June, Sun Coast Products Company incurred total payroll costs of $150,000 broken down as follows:

Assembling Dept.	$40,000
Painting Dept.	30,000
Finishing Dept.	50,000
Indirect labor	30,000

a. Make a journal entry to record the payroll (ignore payroll deductions).
b. Make a journal entry to transfer the labor cost to production.

10–4. Learning Objectives 4, 5. Applying Factory Overhead to Production.

Maple Company applies factory overhead to production based on direct labor cost. During August, the company incurred total factory overhead costs of $150,000 and uses the following overhead application rates. Make a journal entry, dated August 31, to record the application of overhead to production.

Department	Overhead Rate	Direct labor for June
Assembling	75%	$50,000
Cutting	100%	40,000
Finishing	125%	60,000

10–5. Learning Objective 4. Recording Transfer Costs.

During January, the following transactions occurred for the Holt Company. Record these transactions.

a. Transferred costs from Dept. 1 to Dept. 2, $45,000.
b. Transferred costs from Dept. 2 to Dept. 3, $75,000.
c. Transferred costs from Dept. 3 to finished goods storage, $125,000.

10–6. Learning Objectives 4, 5. Recording Factory Overhead Costs.

During June, Wilson Company incurred the following factory overhead costs. Make a summary entry, dated June 30, to record these costs.

Factory rent paid	$12,000
Depreciation	10,000
Expired insurance	6,000
Indirect materials	18,000
Indirect labor	20,000
Repairs	5,000

10–7. Learning Objective 4. Recording Sales and Cost of Goods Sold.

During September, Mantabe Company sold goods for $450,000 that cost $375,000 to produce. Record both transactions.

GROUP A PROBLEMS

10–1A. Learning Objectives 4, 5. Recording and Posting Process Cost Transactions.

Williams Company produces cloth that is used in making clothing. Williams uses two departments, Spinning and Weaving. Materials are issued to the Spinning Department where materials are spun into thread, which is sent to the Weaving Department. The thread is woven into cloth and moved into finished goods storage. Following are production accounts and their balances at the beginning of January:

Raw Materials Inventory	$15,000
Work in Process Inventory—Spinning Dept.	-0-
Work in Process—Weaving Dept.	-0-
Finished Goods Inventory	75,000
Cost of Goods Sold	-0-
Factory Payroll Clearing	-0-
Factory Overhead Control	-0-

The following transactions occurred during January:

a. Purchased materials on account, $144,000.
b. Issued materials to production as follows:

Spinning Dept.	$120,000
Weaving Dept.	10,000
Indirect materials	12,000

c. Incurred payroll costs, $215,000.
d. Allocated labor costs as follows:

Spinning Dept. $125,000
Weaving Dept.   55,000
Indirect labor   35,000

e. Incurred factory overhead costs, $60,000 (make a credit to Various Accounts).
f. Applied overhead to production as follows:

Spinning Dept., 80% of direct labor cost.
Weaving Dept., 120% of direct labor cost.

g. Transferred costs from the Spinning Department to the Weaving Department.
h. Transferred cost of goods completed to Finished Goods Inventory.
i. Sold on account $600,000 of finished goods that cost $340,000 to manufacture.

Required:

1. Set up T accounts for each account listed at the beginning of the problem. Record the opening balance in Raw Materials Inventory and Finished Goods Inventory.
2. Record the January transactions.
3. Post to the T accounts and balance each account.

10–2A. Learning Objectives 4, 5. Recording and Posting Transactions and Applying Overhead.

Taylor Mills, a manufacturer of breakfast cereal, completed the following transactions during November:

a. Purchased materials on account, $260,000.
b. Incurred payroll costs, $220,000 (ignore payroll deductions).
c. Allocated payroll as follows:

Dept. 1 . . . . $100,000
Dept. 2   80,000
Indirect labor   40,000

d. Issued materials to production as follows:

Dept. 1 . . . . $120,000
Dept. 2   100,000
Indirect materials   30,000

e. Incurred factory overhead as follows:

Depreciation of machinery . . . . $ 25,000
Depreciation of factory building   15,000
Property taxes accrued on factory   5,000
Factory insurance expired   5,000

f. Applied factory overhead to the producing departments based on the percentage of materials used in each department to total direct materials used.
g. Transferred out all costs incurred in Department 1 and Department 2.
h. Produced 550,000 units in November.
i. Sold 500,000 units in June for $1.25 each.

Required:

1. Set up T accounts for Raw Materials Inventory, Work in Process Inventory—Dept. 1, Work in Process Inventory—Dept. 2, Finished Goods Inventory, Cost of Goods Sold, Factory Payroll Clearing, and Factory Overhead Control.
2. Record and post the November transactions.

10–3A. Learning Objectives 4, 6. Recording Costs and Computing the Unit Cost of Finished Goods.

Mason Company manufactures bricks used in construction. During August, Mason incurred the following costs:

a. Purchased materials on account, $440,000; terms, 2/10,n/30.
b. Paid for materials purchases within the discount period.
c. Incurred payroll, $555,000.
d. Allocated payroll as follows:

Mixing Dept.	$200,000
Drying Dept.	180,000
Indirect labor	175,000

e. Issued materials as follows:

Mixing Dept.	$350,000
Indirect materials	60,000

f. Incurred factory overhead costs as follows:

Machinery depreciation	$ 55,000
Factory building depreciation	40,000
Accrued property taxes	10,000
Expired insurance	20,000

g. Incurred selling and general expenses on account as follows:

Selling expenses	$ 25,000
General expenses	65,000

h. Applied factory overhead based as follows:

Mixing Dept.: 100% of direct labor cost.
Drying Dept.: 90% of direct labor cost.

i. Transferred costs from the Mixing Department to the Drying Department.
j. Completed 1,500,000 bricks.

Required:

1. Record the August transactions.
2. Compute the unit cost of finished goods.

GROUP B PROBLEMS

10–1B. Learning Objectives 4, 5. Recording and Posting Process Cost Transactions.

Rodgers Company, a producer of cloth used in the manufacture of clothing, consists of two departments, Spinning and Weaving. Materials sent to the Spinning Department are spun into thread and sent to the Weaving Department where the thread is woven into cloth. The cloth is then sent to finished goods storage. Following are production accounts and their balances at the beginning of June:

Raw Materials Inventory	$30,000
Work in Process Inventory—Spinning Dept.	-0-
Work in Process Inventory—Weaving Dept.	-0-
Finished Goods Inventory	80,000
Cost of Goods Sold	-0-

Factory Payroll Clearing . . . .   -0-
Factory Overhead Control . . . .   -0-

The following transactions occurred during June:

a. Purchased materials on account, $150,000.
b. Issued materials to production as follows:

Spinning Dept. $130,000
Weaving Dept.   15,000
Indirect materials   14,000

c. Recorded payroll costs, $225,000.
d. Allocated labor costs as follows:

Spinning Dept. $125,000
Weaving Dept.   55,000
Indirect labor   45,000

e. Incurred factory overhead costs, $70,000 (make a credit to Various Accounts).
f. Applied overhead to production as follows:

Spinning Dept. $108,000
Weaving Dept.   106,000

g. Transferred costs from the Spinning Department to the Weaving Department.
h. Transferred cost of goods completed to Finished Goods Inventory.
i. Sold on account $615,000 of finished goods that cost $350,000 to manufacture.

Required:

1. Set up T accounts for each account listed at the beginning of the problem. Record
    the opening balance in Raw Materials Inventory and Finished Goods Inventory.
2. Record the January transactions in general journal form.
3. Post to the T accounts and balance each account.

10–2B. Learning Objectives 4, 5. Recording and Posting Transactions and Applying Overhead.

Trigg's Bread Company, a manufacturer of breakfast cereal, completed the following
transactions during October:

a. Purchased materials on account, $340,000.
b. Incurred payroll costs, $420,000 (ignore payroll deductions).
c. Allocated payroll as follows:

Dept. 1 . . . . $150,000
Dept. 2   110,000
Indirect labor   160,000

d. Issued materials to production as follows:

Dept. 1 . . . . $160,000
Dept. 2   120,000
Indirect materials   50,000

e. Incurred factory overhead costs as follows:

Depreciation of machinery	$ 35,000
Depreciation of factory building	20,000
Property taxes accrued on factory	8,000
Factory insurance expired	6,000

f. Applied factory overhead to the producing departments based on the percentage of materials used in each department to total direct materials used.

g. Transferred out all costs incurred in Department 1 and Department 2.

h. Produced 600,000 units in October.

i.   Sold 525,000 units for $1.40 each.

Required:

1. Set up T accounts for Raw Materials Inventory, Work in Process Inventory—Dept. 1, Work in Process Inventory—Dept. 2, Finished Goods Inventory, Cost of Goods Sold, Factory Payroll Clearing, and Factory Overhead Control.

2. Record and post the November transactions.

10–3B. Learning Objectives 4, 6. Recording Cost and Calculating the Unit Cost of Finished Goods.

Jason Company manufactures bricks used in construction. During May, 19X6, Jason incurred the following costs:

a. Purchased materials on account, $540,000.

b. Paid for materials purchases within the discount period.

c. Incurred payroll, $625,000.

d. Allocated payroll as follows:

Mixing Dept.	$235,000
Drying Dept.	195,000
Indirect labor	195,000

e. Issued materials as follows:

Mixing Dept.	$425,000
Indirect materials	75,000

f. Incurred factory overhead as follows:

Machinery depreciation	$ 55,000
Factory building depreciation	45,000
Accrued property taxes	5,000
Expired insurance	15,000

g. Applied factory overhead to production as follows:

Mixing Dept., 80% of direct labor costs.
Drying Dept., 110% of direct labor costs.

h. Transferred costs from the Mixing Department to the Drying Department.

i.   Produced 1,575,000 bricks.

Required:

1. Record the transactions for May.
2. Compute the unit cost of finished goods.

CASE FOR CRITICAL THINKING

William Rodman and a small group of investors are about to start a business manufacturing swim suits. You have been commissioned to set up the cost accounting system. What type, job-order or process costing, system do you recommend? Why?

ANSWERS TO SELF-STUDY QUIZ 10–1

1	Jun.	30	Work in Process Inventory—Hulling Dept.	25 00 000		1
2			Work in Process Inventory—Grinding Dept.	12 00 000		2
3			Work in Process Inventory—Finishing Dept.	18 00 000		3
4			Factory Overhead Control	15 00 000		4
5			Raw Materials Inventory		70 00 000	5

ANSWERS TO SELF-STUDY QUIZ 10–2

1	Jul.	31	Work in Process Inventory—Cutting Dept.	28 00 000		1
2			Work in Process Inventory—Assembling Dept.	21 00 000		2
3			Work in Process Inventory—Finishing Dept.	24 00 000		3
4			Factory Overhead Control	18 00 000		4
5			Factory Payroll Clearing		91 00 000	5

ANSWERS TO SELF-STUDY QUIZ 10–3

1	Jul.	31	Work in Process Inventory—Cutting Dept.	2240000		1
2			Work in Process Inventory—Assembling Dept.	1890000		2
3			Work in Process Inventory—Finishing Dept.	1680000		3
4			Factory Overhead Control		5810000	4

ANSWERS TO SELF-STUDY QUIZ 10–4

| 1 | Oct. | 31 | Finished Goods Inventory | 13000000 | | 1 |
| 2 | | | Work in Process Inventory—Finishing Dept. | | 13000000 | 2 |

Chapter 11
Equivalent Production— Weighted Average Costing of Work in Process

LEARNING OBJECTIVES

After studying Chapter 11, you should be able to:

1. Describe the two most common inventory flow methods used in a process costing system.
2. Define equivalent units of production.
3. Calculate the equivalent units produced in each department using the weighted average cost method.
4. Calculate the unit cost of goods produced each month using the weighted average cost method.
5. Calculate the amount of cost to transfer to the next department or to finished goods using a cost of production report.

We learned in Chapter 10 the differences between job-order and process costing systems, how costs flow through a process costing system, and how transactions are recorded in such a system. We also explored the application of overhead to various departments and the calculation of the cost of units completed and transferred to finished goods inventory. To simplify our calculations, we assumed that there were no beginning or ending balances in the Work in Process Inventory account. This assumption, however, is not realistic. In a real situation, the Work in Process Inventory account will likely have both beginning and ending balances. In this chapter, we will see how having a beginning and ending inventory in the Work in Process Inventory account will affect our calculations.

INVENTORY VALUATION METHODS

LEARNING OBJECTIVE 1   There are two alternative methods of determining and accounting for cost flows in a process costing system: (1) *the weighted average cost method* and (2) *the first-in-first-out (FIFO) method.* The **weighted average process costing method** (also called the *average cost method) does not* differentiate between the units in production at the start of a month and the units started during the month. Under this method, the work in process at the beginning of the month (both units and cost) is merged with new production started during the month (both units and cost), and an average cost per unit of production is determined.

The **first-in-first-out (FIFO) process costing method,** which more realistically reflects how goods flow through the production process, requires that units in production at the beginning of the month be treated differently than the units started in production during the month. Under this method, we assume that the first costs recorded in the month are incurred to complete the units that were already in production when the month started. Subsequent costs are then charged to the new units started into production during the month. We will work with the average cost method in this chapter, and then in Chapter 12, we will study the FIFO method.

EQUIVALENT UNITS OF PRODUCTION

In Chapter 10, we learned that costs in a process costing system are transferred from one producing department to the next, and that a final unit cost is calculated when the units are completed. But remember, in Chapter 10 we assumed that there were no beginning or ending inventories in work in process. In other words, there were no goods in production when the month started and no goods in production when the month ended. Thus, all costs incurred in a month related *only* to units started and completed during the same month. Consequently, unit costs could be calculated by dividing the total cost of production by the number of units completed.

The situation changes, however, when there are partially completed units on hand at the end of the month. A partially completed unit must carry a lower cost than a completed unit (because there is work still to be done). Thus, it naturally follows that where inventories remain in work in process, unit production costs cannot be calculated simply by dividing the total cost of production by the number of units actually completed.

In reality, the task in process costing consists of two parts. First, we must account for the cost of units that have been completed in one department and sent to the next department. Second, we must account for the cost of unfinished units, which remain in the department at the end of the month. How do we calculate cost per unit when the total cost added during the month applies to *both* finished and unfinished units? This question is answered by calculating *equivalent units of production.*

LEARNING OBJECTIVE 2, 3   **Equivalent units of production** is a measure of the number of units that *could have been completed* using the costs incurred during the period. Equivalent units are calculated by multiplying the actual number of units in production by their estimated stage of completion. For example, if you have two units, each one-half complete, you could have completed one whole unit with the materials, labor, and overhead used in those two partially completed units. Likewise, 10,000 units that are 25% complete are equivalent to 2,500 units fully completed, as follows:

Actual Number of Units	×	Estimated Stage of Completion	=	Equivalent Units of Production
10,000	×	.25	=	2,500

In most firms, the estimated stage of completion is determined by a supervisor or an engineer who has experience in estimating the average degree of completion of units in the ending work in process inventory. The units could be in varying stages of completion—some could be 50% complete, others 60% complete, etc.—but an average percentage of completion of all units is generally used for convenience.

AVERAGE COST METHOD ILLUSTRATED WITH ONE DEPARTMENT

Company with No Beginning Work in Process Inventory

To simplify our first illustration, we will use a firm that did not have a beginning inventory of work in process. Alpha Company manufactures a product that can be produced in one department. Materials, labor, and overhead are added evenly throughout the production process. Alpha had the following production and cost data for August.

Units to account for:

Units in beginning work in process inventory	-0-
Units started into production during August	55,000
Total units to account for	55,000
Units in ending work in process inventory (40% complete as to materials and 40% complete as to conversion)	<5,000>
Units completed and transferred out during August	50,000

Costs to account for:

	Materials	Conversion	Total
Costs in beginning work in process inventory	-0-	-0-	-0-
Current costs added in August	$156,000	$182,000	$338,000
Total costs to account for	$156,000	$182,000	$338,000

NOTE Remember, conversion costs = direct labor + factory overhead.

As you can see, Alpha completed 50,000 units during the month and is still working on 5,000 units at month-end. Our task is to determine the unit cost of the 50,000 units transferred to finished goods inventory, and determine the unit cost of the 5,000 units remaining in production at the end of the month. To do this, we first need to calculate equivalent units of production for materials costs and conversion costs, as follows (remember, the ending work in process inventory is only 40% complete as to materials costs and conversion costs):

Equivalent units of production:

Materials

Transferred to finished goods: 50,000 x 100%	=	50,000
In ending work in process inventory: 5,000 x 40%	=	2,000
Equivalent units for materials		52,000

Conversion

Transferred to finished goods: 50,000 x 100%	=	50,000
In ending work in process inventory: 5,000 x 40%	=	2,000
Equivalent units for labor and overhead		52,000

NOTE Units completed and transferred are always 100% complete.

LEARNING OBJECTIVE 4 From this calculation, we see that Alpha Company produced 52,000 equivalent units in August. However, this does not tell us the cost of the 50,000 units finished and transferred to finished goods inventory. Nor does it tell us the cost of the 5,000 units in ending work in process inventory. In order to determine these costs, we calculate a cost per equivalent unit for materials costs and for conversion costs, as follows:

Materials cost per equivalent unit:

$$\frac{\text{Materials costs}}{\text{Equivalent units}} = \frac{\$156,000}{52,000} = \$3.00$$

Conversion cost per equivalent unit:

$$\frac{\text{Conversion costs}}{\text{Equivalent units}} = \frac{\$182,000}{52,000} = \$3.50$$

Total equivalent unit cost $6.50

We can now compute the cost of the finished units and the cost of the ending work in process inventory.

Cost of finished units:
  50,000 units × $6.50 per unit $325,000
Cost of the ending work in process inventory:
  Materials: 5,000 × 40% × $3.00 . . . . $6,000
  Conversion costs: 5,000 × 40% × $3.50   7,000
Total cost of ending work in process inventory   13,000
Total cost accounted for $338,000

As you can see, we use the unit equivalent cost to compute the cost of the finished units and the cost of the ending work in process inventory. The accounting department uses the total cost of the finished units, $325,000, to make the following journal entry.

1	Aug.	31	Finished Goods Inventory	325 00 0 00		1
2			Work in Process Inventory		325 00 0 00	2
3			Transferred 50,000 completed units.			3

After this entry is posted, the Work in Process Inventory account appears as follows. Notice that the ending balance, $13,000, equals the costs assigned the units still in production at month-end.

| ACCOUNT Work in Process Inventory | | | | | ACCOUNT NO. 122 | | |
| | | | | | **BALANCE** | | |
DATE	ITEM	P.R.	DEBIT	CREDIT	DEBIT	CREDIT
19X3 Aug. 31	Materials	X	156 00 0 00		156 00 0 00	
31	Conversion	X	182 00 0 00		338 00 0 00	
31	Finished units	X		325 00 0 00	13 00 0 00	

NOTE In this illustration, we assumed that materials, labor, and overhead were all incurred evenly throughout the manufacturing process. This, however, is not always the case. Typically, materials are at one stage of completion, while direct labor and conversion costs are at another stage. All of the materials could be added at the beginning of the process, or one-half at the beginning and the other half at some other point in the production process. Labor and overhead, on the other hand, are usually incurred evenly throughout the process. As far as the calculation of the equivalent units is concerned, the stage at which the materials, labor, and overhead are added is not important except in determining the degree of completion of the ending work in process inventory.

Cost of Production Report

LEARNING OBJECTIVE 5   As you can see from our calculations for Alpha Company, determining unit costs in a process costing systems involves several steps. This information can be combined into one report called a *Cost of Production Report* (Figure 11–1), which summarizes the information into a more condensed format. This report is used to compute the cost of transfer to another producing department (or to Finished Goods Inventory) and to compute the cost of the ending work in process inventory. It is also used as a source for summary journal entries.

ALPHA CO.
Cost of Production Report—Weighted Average
For August 19X3

Quantities

1. Units to account for:
   From beginning work in process. . . . .   –0–
   Started into production this month. 55,000
   Total units to account for 55,000

2. Units accounted for:
   Completed and transferred out 50,000
   From ending work in process (40% complete as to materials and 40% complete as
     to conversion). 5,000
   Total units accounted for 55,000

3. Equivalent production:

	Equivalent Units	
	Materials	**Conversion**
Completed and transferred out	50,000	50,000
Ending work in process inventory:		
Materials (5,000 × 40%).	2,000	
Conversion (5,000 × 40%).		2,000
Total equivalent units.	52,000	52,000

Costs

4. Costs to account for:

	Total Costs	**Equivalent Units**	**Unit Cost**
Materials	$156,000 ÷	52,000 =	$3.00
Conversion	182,000 ÷	52,000 =	3.50
Totals	$338,000		$6.50

5. Costs accounted for:
   Completed and transferred out (50,000 × $6.50) $325,000
     Work in process—August 31, 19X3:
     Materials (5,000 × 40% × $3.00) $6,000
     Conversion (5,000 × 40% × $3.50) 7,000   13,000
   Total costs accounted for (52,000 × $6.50) $338,000

FIGURE 11–1
*Cost of Production
Report—Alpha Company*

SELF-STUDY QUIZ 11–1 Short, Inc. had the following production and cost data for April.

Units to account for:

Units in beginning work in process inventory	-0-
Units started into production during April	55,000
Total units to account for	55,000
Units in ending work in process inventory (30% complete as to materials and 30% complete as to conversion)	<10,000>
Units completed and transferred out during April	45,000

Costs to account for:

	Materials	Conversion	Total
Costs in beginning work in process inventory	-0-	-0-	-0-
Current costs added during April	$162,720	$204,000	$366,720
Total costs to account for	$162,720	$204,000	$366,720

a. Prepare a cost of production report for April.
b. Make the general journal entry transferring costs out of Work in Process Inventory.

Answers at end of chapter.

Company with Beginning and Ending Work in Process Inventory

To simplify our calculations in the preceding example, we assumed that Alpha Company did not have a beginning inventory of work in process. Most actual companies, however, will have both a beginning and an ending inventory of work in process. In this situation, the cost of the work in process at the beginning of the month is added to the production costs incurred during the month. An average unit cost for the period is then calculated by dividing the total of these costs by the equivalent units of production. We can show this in formula form as follows:

$$\frac{\text{Beginning cost} + \text{Current cost}}{\text{Equivalent units of production}} = \text{Average cost per unit}$$

To illustrate this, we will use the example of Beta, Inc. Beta manufactures a product in one department. Labor and overhead are added evenly throughout the production process, while materials are added unevenly. Beta had the following production and cost data for August.

Units to account for:

Units in beginning work in process inventory (40% complete as to materials and 60% complete as to conversion)	5,000
Units started into production during August	60,000
Total units to account for	65,000

Units in ending work in process inventory (40% complete as to materials and 60% complete as to conversion)	<15,000>
Units completed and transferred out during August	50,000
Units in beginning work in process inventory	<5,000>
Units started and completed during August	45,000

Costs to account for:

	Materials	Conversion	Total
Costs in beginning work in process inventory	$ 6,000	$ 7,000	$ 13,000
Current costs added in August	176,000	205,400	381,400
Total costs to account for	$182,000	$212,400	$394,400

Notice that a total of 50,000 units was completed during the month. By subtracting the 5,000 units in beginning work in process inventory, we get the number of units actually started and finished during August, 45,000 units. In other words, of the 50,000 units completed during August, 5,000 units were in production when the month started, and 45,000 units were started and completed during the month.

Equivalent units for materials costs and conversion costs can now be calculated, as follows. (Remember that the units in ending work in process inventory are 40% complete as to materials and 60% complete as to conversion costs.)

Materials:

Units in beginning work in process inventory: 5,000 × 100%	5,000
Units started and completed in August: 45,000 × 100%	45,000
Units in ending work in process inventory: 15,000 × 40%	6,000
Equivalent units for materials	56,000

Conversion costs:

Units in beginning work in process inventory: 5,000 × 100%	5,000
Units started and completed in August: 45,000 × 100%	45,000
Units in ending work in process inventory: 15,000 × 60%	9,000
Equivalent units for conversion costs	59,000

NOTE We always assume that the beginning work in process units are finished during the month. Thus, the beginning 5,000 units are now 100% complete. And, as stated earlier, the units started and completed during the month are always 100% complete.

We now compute cost per equivalent unit, as follows:

Materials cost per equivalent unit:

$$\frac{\text{Beginning cost} + \text{Current cost}}{\text{Equivalent units of production}} = \frac{\$6,000 + \$176,000}{56,000} = \frac{\$182,000}{56,000} = \$3.25$$

Conversion cost per equivalent unit:

$$\frac{\text{Beginning cost} + \text{Current cost}}{\text{Equivalent units of production}} = \frac{\$7,000 + \$205,400}{59,000} = \frac{\$212,400}{59,000} = \underline{3.60}$$

Total equivalent unit cost for August $6.85

The cost of the finished goods and the ending work in process inventory are computed as follows:

Cost of finished units:		
50,000 units × $6.85		$342,500
Cost of the ending work in process inventory:		
Materials: 15,000 × 40% × $3.25	$19,500	
Conversion costs: 15,000 × 60% × $3.60	32,400	
Cost of ending work in process inventory		51,900
Total cost accounted for		$394,400

In computing the cost of the finished units, 50,000, we always assume that the beginning work in process units are finished and that the cost associated with them is added to the cost incurred in the current month to compute total manufacturing cost for the month. The $6.85 cost per equivalent unit is an average cost and the 50,000 units would be inventoried at that amount. Figure 11–2 shows Beta's cost of production report for August. The following journal entry transfers the cost of the completed units to Finished Goods Inventory.

1	Aug.	30	Finished Goods Inventory	34250000		1
2			Work in Process Inventory		34250000	2
3			Transferred 50,000 completed units.			3

BETA, INC.
Cost of Production Report—Weighted Average
For August 19X3

Quantities

1. Units to account for:
   From beginning work in process. 5,000
   Started into production this month. 60,000
   Total units to account for 65,000

2. Units accounted for:
   From beginning work in process. 5,000
   Started and completed 45,000
   From ending work in process (40% complete as to materials and 60% complete as
   to conversion) 15,000
   Total units accounted for. 65,000

3. Equivalent production:

	Equivalent Units	
	Materials	**Conversion**
Beginning work in process inventory	5,000	5,000
Started and completed.	45,000	45,000
Ending work in process inventory:		
Materials (15,000 × 40%)	6,000	
Conversion (15,000 × 60%)		9,000
Total equivalent units.	56,000	59,000

FIGURE 11–2
*Cost of Production
Report—Beta, Inc.*

(Continued)

4. Costs to account for:

Costs

	Total Costs		Equivalent Units		Unit Cost
Materials.	$182,000	÷	56,000	=	$3.25
Conversion.	212,400	÷	59,000	=	3.60
Totals.	$394,400				$6.85

5. Costs accounted for:

Completed and transferred out (50,000 × $6.85).		$342,500
Work in process—August 31, 19X3:		
Materials (15,000 × 40% × $3.25)	$19,500	
Conversion (15,000 × 60% × $3.60).	32,400	51,900
Total costs accounted for		$394,400

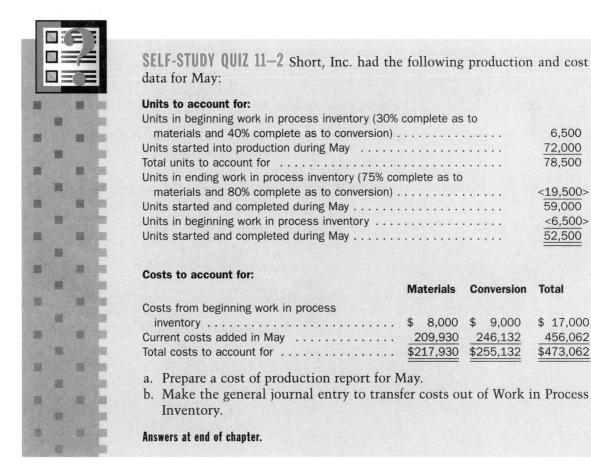

SELF-STUDY QUIZ 11–2 Short, Inc. had the following production and cost data for May:

Units to account for:

Units in beginning work in process inventory (30% complete as to materials and 40% complete as to conversion)	6,500
Units started into production during May	72,000
Total units to account for	78,500
Units in ending work in process inventory (75% complete as to materials and 80% complete as to conversion)	<19,500>
Units started and completed during May	59,000
Units in beginning work in process inventory	<6,500>
Units started and completed during May	52,500

Costs to account for:

	Materials	Conversion	Total
Costs from beginning work in process inventory	$ 8,000	$ 9,000	$ 17,000
Current costs added in May	209,930	246,132	456,062
Total costs to account for	$217,930	$255,132	$473,062

a. Prepare a cost of production report for May.
b. Make the general journal entry to transfer costs out of Work in Process Inventory.

Answers at end of chapter.

AVERAGE COST METHOD ILLUSTRATED WITH TWO DEPARTMENTS

Most manufacturing operations have more than one department or process. The following illustration will demonstrate how the calculation of equivalent units, cost per equivalent unit, cost of finished units, and the cost of the ending work in process inventory would be made in a company with two producing departments.

Grant Company manufactures a product in two producing departments (Department 1 and Department 2). Labor and overhead (conversion costs) are added evenly throughout the production process, while materials are added unevenly.

Department 1

Department 1 had the following production and cost data for August:

Units to account for:

Units in beginning work in process inventory (75% complete as to materials and 40% complete as to conversion)	10,000
Units started into production during August	50,000
Total units to account for	60,000
Units in ending work in process inventory (80% complete as to materials and 50% complete as to conversion)	<8,000>
Units completed and transferred out during August	52,000
Units in beginning work in process inventory	<10,000>
Units started and completed during August	42,000

Costs to account for:

	Materials	Conversion	Total
Costs in beginning work in process inventory	$ 23,780	$ 20,000	$ 43,780
Current costs added in August	221,500	274,000	495,500
Total costs to account for	$245,280	$294,000	$539,280

Equivalent units of production are computed as follows:

Materials:

Units in beginning work in process inventory:	10,000 × 100% = 10,000
Units started and completed during August:	42,000 × 100% = 42,000
Units in ending work in process inventory:	8,000 × 80% = 6,400
Equivalent units for materials	58,400

Conversion Costs:

Units in beginning work in process inventory:	10,000 × 100% = 10,000
Units started and completed during August:	42,000 × 100% = 42,000
Units in ending work in process inventory:	8,000 × 50% = 4,000
Equivalent units for conversion costs	56,000

We now compute cost per equivalent unit, as follows:

Materials cost per equivalent unit:

$$\frac{\text{Beginning cost + Current cost}}{\text{Equivalent units of production}} = \frac{\$23,780 + \$221,500}{58,400} = \frac{\$245,280}{58,400} = \$4.20$$

Conversion cost per equivalent unit:

$$\frac{\text{Beginning cost + Current cost}}{\text{Equivalent units of production}} = \frac{\$20,000 + \$274,000}{56,000} = \frac{\$294,000}{56,000} = \underline{\$5.25}$$

Total equivalent unit cost for August $\underline{\$9.45}$

We can now compute the cost of the 52,000 units transferred to Department 2, and the cost added to the 8,000 partially completed units in ending inventory.

Cost of units transferred to Department 2:
  52,000 units × $9.45 . . . . $491,400
Ending work in process inventory:
  Materials: 8,000 × 80% × $4.20 . . . . $26,880
  Conversion: 8,000 × 50% × $5.25   21,000
Cost of ending work in process inventory 47,880
Total cost accounted for $539,280

Figure 11–3 shows the cost of production report for Department 1. The following journal entry records the transfer of the 52,000 units to Department 2.

1	Aug.	31	Work in Process Inventory—Dept. 2	491 4 0 0 00			1
2			Work in Process Inventory—Dept. 1		491 4 0 0 00		2
3			Transferred 52,000 units				3
4			to Department 2.				4

Department 2

The first department in a manufacturing operation will add materials costs and conversion costs. The units then flow into other departments where conversion costs will be added; however, materials costs may or may not be added depending on the function of the department. As we just saw, during August Grant Company transferred 52,000 partially completed units from Department 1 to Department 2. The costs added to these units by Department 1 ($491,400) are also transferred to Department 2 where additional materials, labor, and overhead will be added.

GRANT CO.—Department 1
Cost of Production Report—Weighted Average
For August 19X3

Quantities

1. Units to account for:
   From beginning work in process.. 10,000
   Started into production this month... 50,000
   Total units to account for... 60,000

2. Units accounted for:
   From beginning work in process   10,000
   Started and completed   42,000
   From ending work in process (80% complete as to materials and 50% complete as
   to conversion)... 8,000
   Total units accounted for... 60,000

3. Equivalent production:

| | Equivalent Units | |
	Materials	Conversion
Beginning work in process inventory.....................	10,000	10,000
Started and completed	42,000	42,000
Ending work in process inventory:		
Materials (8,000 × 80%)................................	6,400	
Conversion (8,000 × 50%)		4,000
Total equivalent units	58,400	56,000

Costs

4. Costs to account for:

	Total Costs		Equivalent Units		Unit Cost
Materials...............................	$245,280	÷	58,400	=	$4.20
Conversion	294,000	÷	56,000	=	5.25
Totals	$539,280				$9.45

5. Costs accounted for:
   Completed and transferred out (52,000 × $9.45) $491,400
   Work in process—August 31, 19X3:
   Materials (8,000 × 80% × $4.20)................................ $26,880
   Conversion (8,000 × 50% × $5.25).............................. 21,000   47,880
   Total costs accounted for $539,280

FIGURE 11–3
*Cost of Production
Report—Grant
Company,
Department 1*

Department 2 had the following production and cost data for August:

Units to account for:

Units in beginning work in process inventory (60% complete as to materials and 50% complete as to conversion)	12,000
Units transferred in from Department 1 and started into production during August	52,000
Total units to account for	64,000
Units in ending work in process inventory (60% complete as to materials and 40% complete as to conversion	<14,000>
Units completed and transferred out during August	50,000
Units in beginning work in process inventory	<12,000>
Units started and completed during August	38,000

Costs to account for:

	Transferred In	Materials	Conversion	Total
Costs in beginning work in process inventory	$116,600	$ 28,800	$ 30,000	$ 175,400
Current costs added in August	491,400	210,640	261,900	963,940
Total costs to account for	$608,000	$239,440	$291,900	$1,139,340

Notice that in Department 2 you have three costs to deal with, instead of only two. In any producing department other than the first, you will have transferred-in cost from another department, as well as production costs added by the department.

To compute the unit production cost in Department 2 for August, we first compute the equivalent units of production, as follows. (Remember, the ending work in process units are 60% complete for materials and 40% complete for conversion costs.)

	Transferred In	Materials	Conversion
Units in beginning work in process inventory: 12,000 × 100%	12,000	12,000	12,000
Units started and transferred out in August: 38,000 × 100%	38,000	38,000	38,000
Units in ending work in process inventory:			
Transferred-in: 14,000 × 100%	14,000		
Materials: 14,000 × 60%		8,400	
Conversion: 14,000 × 40%			5,600
Equivalent units of production	64,000	58,400	55,600

NOTE Transferred-in units are considered 100% complete because they are treated as if they were started and completed during the month.

Costs per equivalent unit are computed as follows:

Transferred-in costs:

$$\frac{\$116{,}600 + \$491{,}400}{64{,}000} = \frac{\$608{,}000}{64{,}000} = \$ \ 9.50$$

Materials costs:

$$\frac{\$28{,}800 + \$210{,}640}{58{,}400} = \frac{\$239{,}440}{58{,}400} = \$ \ 4.10$$

Conversion costs:

$$\frac{\$30{,}000 + \$261{,}900}{55{,}600} = \frac{\$291{,}900}{55{,}600} = \underline{\$ \ 5.25}$$

Total cost per equivalent single unit . . . $\underline{\$18.85}$

We can now compute the cost of the 50,000 units transferred to finished goods inventory, and the cost added to the 14,000 partially completed units in ending work in process inventory.

Units transferred to finished goods inventory:
50,000 × \$18.85 . . . .   \$ 942,500

Ending work in process inventory:
Transferred-in costs (14,000 × \$9.50) \$133,000
Materials (14,000 × 60% × \$4.10)   34,440
Conversion (14,000 × 40% × \$5.25)   29,400   196,840
Total costs accounted for \$1,139,340

NOTE Remember that in any department other than the first department, all units will have costs added by another department(s)—transferred-in costs—as well as costs added by the current department.

Figure 11–4 shows the cost of production report for Department 2. The following entry shows the transfer of the 50,000 units to Finished Goods Inventory.

1	Aug.	31	Finished Goods Inventory	942 50 0 00		1
2			Work in Process Inventory—Dept. 2		942 50 0 00	2
3			Transferred 50,000 completed units.			3

NOTE By referring to the cost of production reports for Departments 1 and 2 (Figures 11–3 and 11–4), notice the following:

1. The units transferred out of Department 1 (52,000) must be equal to the number of units transferred into Department 2.
2. The total costs of \$491,400 transferred out of Department 1 are the same costs transferred into Department 2.

GRANT CO.—Department 2
Cost of Production Report—Weighted Average
For August 19X3

Quantities

1. Units to account for:
   From beginning work in process 12,000
   Started into production this month 52,000
   Total units to account for 64,000

2. Units accounted for:
   From beginning work in process 12,000
   Started and completed 38,000
   From ending work in process (60% complete as to materials and 40% complete as
   to conversion) 14,000
   Total units accounted for. 64,000

3. Equivalent production:

	Equivalent Units		
	Transferred In	Materials	Conversion
Beginning work in process inventory	12,000	12,000	12,000
Started and completed	38,000	38,000	38,000
Ending work in process inventory:			
Transferred in (14,000 × 100%)	14,000		
Materials (14,000 × 60%)		8,400	
Conversion (14,000 × 40%)			5,600
Total equivalent units	64,000	58,400	55,600

Costs

4. Costs to account for:

	Total Costs	Equivalent Units	Unit Cost
Transferred in	$ 608,000 ÷ 64,000	= $ 9.50	
Materials	239,440 ÷ 58,400	= 4.10	
Conversion	291,900 ÷ 55,600	= 5.25	
Totals	$1,139,340		$18.85

5. Costs accounted for:
   Completed and transferred out (50,000 × $18.85). . . . . $ 942,500
   Work in process—August 31, 19X3:
   Transferred in (14,000 × $9.50) $133,000
   Materials (14,000 × 60% × $4.10). 34,440
   Conversion (14,000 × 40% × $5.25) 29,400   196,840
   Total costs accounted for. $1,139,340

FIGURE 11–4
Cost of Production Report—
Grant Company, Department 2

SELF-STUDY PROBLEM

South Company, which manufactures T-shirts and was introduced in Chapter 10, had the following costs and production information by department for August:

Cutting Department	Materials	Conversion	Total
Beginning work in process inventory costs ...	$ 15,110	$ 4,895	$ 20,005
Current costs added in August	183,250	61,150	244,400
Total costs to be accounted for	$198,360	$66,045	$264,405

Units in beginning work in process inventory (65% complete as to materials and 40% complete as to conversion	11,000
Units started into production during August	50,000
Total units to be accounted for	61,000
Units in ending work in process inventory (70% complete as to materials and 45% complete as to conversion)	<10,000>
Units completed and transferred out during August	51,000
Units in beginning work in process inventory	<11,000>
Units started and completed during August	40,000

Sewing Department	Transferred In	Conversion	Total
Beginning work in process inventory costs ...	$33,050	$ 21,462	$54,512
Current costs added in August	?	223,120	?
Total costs to be accounted for	$?	$244,582	$?

Units in beginning work in process inventory (55% complete as to conversion)	13,000
Units in ending work in process inventory (65% complete as to conversion)	12,000

Dyeing Department	Transferred In	Materials	Conversion	Total
Beginning work in process inventory costs	$66,690	$ 5,425	$ 7,144	$79,259
Current costs added in August	?	38,600	54,550	?
Total costs to be accounted for	$?	$44,025	$61,694	$?

Units in beginning work in process inventory (55% complete as to materials and 55% complete as to conversion)	13,000
Units in ending work in process inventory (55% complete as to materials and 40% complete as to conversion)	14,000

Required:

1. Prepare weighted-average cost of production reports for August 19X3.
2. Make the journal entry to transfer costs out of work in process inventory at August 31 for each department.

SOLUTION TO SELF-STUDY PROBLEM

1.

SOUTH COMPANY—Cutting Department
Cost of Production Report—Weighted Average
For August 19X3

Quantities

1. Units to account for:
   From beginning work in process 11,000
   Started into production this month 50,000
   Total units to account for 61,000

2. Units accounted for:
   From beginning work in process 11,000
   Started and completed 40,000
   From ending work in process (70% complete as to materials and 45% complete as
     to conversion) 10,000
   Total units accounted for 61,000

3. Equivalent production:

| | Equivalent Units | |
	Materials	Conversion
Beginning work in process inventory	11,000	11,000
Started and completed	40,000	40,000
Ending work in process inventory:		
Materials (10,000 × 70%)	7,000	
Conversion (10,000 × 45%)		4,500
Total equivalent units	58,000	55,500

4. Costs to account for:

Costs

	Total Costs	Equivalent Units	Unit Cost
Materials	$198,360 ÷ 58,000		= $3.42
Conversion	66,045 ÷ 55,500		= 1.19
Totals	$264,405		$4.61

5. Costs accounted for:
   Completed and transferred out (51,000 × $4.61) $235,110
   Work in process—August 31, 19X3:
     Materials (10,000 × 70% × $3.42) $23,940
     Conversion (10,000 × 45% × $1.19) 5,355   29,295
   Total costs accounted for $264,405

2.

	19X3					
1	Aug.	31	Work in Process Inventory—Sewing Dept.	235 1 1 0 00		1
2			Work in Process Inventory—Cutting Dept.		235 1 1 0 00	2

1.

SOUTH COMPANY—Sewing Department
Cost of Production Report—Weighted Average
For August 19X3

Quantities

1. Units to account for:
   From beginning work in process 13,000
   Started into production this month 51,000
   Total units to account for 64,000

2. Units accounted for:
   From beginning work in process 13,000
   Started and completed 39,000
   From ending work in process (65% complete as to conversion) 12,000
   Total units accounted for 64,000

3. Equivalent production:

	Equivalent Units	
	Transferred In	**Conversion**
Beginning work in process inventory...............................	13,000	13,000
Started and completed	39,000	39,000
Ending work in process inventory:		
Transferred (12,000 × 100%)	12,000	
Conversion (12,000 × 65%)...................................		7,800
Total equivalent units	64,000	59,800

Costs

4. Costs to account for:

	Total Costs	**Equivalent Units**	**Unit Cost**
Transferred in	$268,160 ÷ 64,000	= $4.19
Conversion..	244,582 ÷ 59,800	= 4.09
Totals	$512,742		$8.28

5. Costs accounted for:
   Completed and transferred out (52,000 × $8.28)...................................... $430,560
   Work in process—August 31, 19X3:
   Transferred in (12,000 × $4.19) $50,280
   Conversion (12,000 × 65% × $4.09) 31,902   82,182
   Total costs accounted for $512,742

2.

	19X3					
1	Aug.	31	Work in Process Inventory—Dyeing Dept.	430 56 0 00		1
2			Work in Process Inventory—Sewing Dept.		430 56 0 00	2

1.

SOUTH COMPANY—Dyeing Department
Cost of Production Report—Weighted Average
For August 19X3

Quantities

1. Units to account for:
   From beginning work in process 13,000
   Started into production this month 52,000
   Total units to account for. 65,000

2. Units accounted for:
   From beginning work in process 13,000
   Started and completed 38,000
   From ending work in process (55% complete as to materials and 40% complete as
      to conversion) 14,000
   Total units accounted for 65,000

3. Equivalent production:

	Equivalent Units		
	Transferred In	**Materials**	**Conversion**
Beginning work in process inventory	13,000	13,000	13,000
Started and completed	38,000	38,000	38,000
Ending work in process inventory:			
Transferred in (14,000 × 100%)	14,000		
Materials (14,000 × 55%)		7,700	
Conversion (14,000 × 40%)			5,600
Total equivalent units	65,000	58,700	56,600

4. Costs to account for:

Costs

	Total Costs		**Equivalent Units**		**Unit Cost**
Transferred in	$497,250	÷	65,000	=	$7.65
Materials	44,025	÷	58,700	=	.75
Conversion	61,694	÷	56,600	=	1.09
Totals	$602,969				$9.49

5. Costs accounted for:
   Completed and transferred out (51,000 × $9.49). $483,990
   Work in process—August 31, 19X3:
   Transferred in (14,000 × $7.65) $107,100
   Materials (14,000 × 55% × $0.75)   5,775
   Conversion (14,000 × 40% × $1.09)   6,104   118,979
   Total costs accounted for $602,969

1.

	19X3						
1	Aug.	31	Finished Goods Inventory	483 99 0 00			1
2			Work in Process Inventory—Dyeing Dept.		483 99 0 00		2

SUMMARY

In Chapter 11, we continued our study of process cost accounting by introducing two alternative methods of determining and accounting for cost flows in a process costing system: (1) the **weighted average process costing method** and (2) the **first-in-first-out (FIFO) process costing method.** Under the weighted average method, units in production at the start of a month are added to units started in production during the month. An average unit cost is then calculated and used to assign a cost to units completed during the month, and units remaining in ending work in process inventory. As a result of averaging costs, each unit completed during the month is assumed to have the same cost, regardless of when it was started.

Under the FIFO method, units in production at the start of a month are kept separate from new units started during the month. It is assumed that first costs recorded in the month are incurred to complete the beginning units, with subsequent costs charged to new units started in the current month.

When there are ending inventories in work in process, unit costs of production *cannot* be determined by dividing total production costs for the period by the number of units produced. This is because the costs incurred relate not only to the units completed, but also to the ending inventories in work in process at the end of the period. To equitably assign costs when there are ending work in process inventories, equivalent units of production must be calculated. **Equivalent units of production** is a measure of the number of units that could have been completed using the costs incurred during the period. Equivalent units are calculated by multiplying the actual number of units in production by their estimated stage of completion. For example, 2,000 units 75% complete equal 1,500 units fully completed (2,000 × 75%). This means that there were enough materials, labor, and overhead added to the 2,000 units to have fully completed 1,500 units.

In order to calculate a unit product cost for a period, it is necessary to calculate a cost per equivalent unit for each cost element (materials, labor, and overhead). The individual costs per equivalent units are then added to obtain a total cost per equivalent unit of production. For example, the cost per equivalent unit for materials is determined by *adding* the materials cost in the beginning work in process inventory to the cost of materials issued into production during the period. This total is then *divided* by the equivalent units for materials to determine an average unit cost for materials. The same thing is done for conversion costs (labor and overhead). The individual costs per equivalent unit are then combined to calculate an average product cost for the period.

Because the calculation of unit costs in a process costing system involves many steps, a summary of activity for the month is prepared. This summary is called the *cost of production report* and is prepared for each producing department. The cost of production report is divided into two main sections. The first section shows the quantity of units that the department must account for during the month. The other section shows the costs charged to the department for the month. The cost of production report serves as a managerial tool and as a source document for summary journal entries.

APPENDIX 11–A : ALTERNATIVE FORMAT FOR WEIGHTED AVERAGE COST OF PRODUCTION REPORT

In actual practice, the format of the cost of production varies from company to company. This appendix presents the cost of production reports for South Company (presented in the Self-Study Problem) in an alternative format.

SOUTH COMPANY—Cutting Department
Cost of Production Report—Weighted Average
For August 19X3

Equivalent units and costs of production:

Materials:

	Total Units				Equivalent Units	Costs	Unit Cost
Beginning inventory	11,000	×	1.00	=	11,000	$ 37,620	
Started and completed	40,000	×	1.00	=	40,000	136,800	
Ending inventory	10,000	×	.70	=	7,000	23,940	
Totals	61,000				58,000	$198,360	$3.42

Conversion:

	Total Units				Equivalent Units	Costs	Unit Cost
Beginning inventory	11,000	×	1.00	=	11,000	$ 13,090	
Started and completed	40,000	×	1.00	=	40,000	47,600	
Ending inventory	10,000	×	.45	=	4,500	5,355	
Totals	61,000				55,500	$ 66,045	$1.19

Accounting for total costs:

Total cost of units transferred out		$235,110
Work in process—August 31, 19X3:		
Materials	$23,940	
Conversion	5,355	$ 29,295
Total costs accounted for		$264,405

SOUTH COMPANY—Sewing Department
Cost of Production Report—Weighted Average
For August 19X3

Equivalent units and costs of production:

Transferred in:

	Total Units				Equivalent Units	Costs	Unit Cost
Beginning inventory	13,000	×	1.00	=	13,000	$ 54,470	
Started and completed	39,000	×	1.00	=	39,000	163,410	
Ending inventory	12,000	×	1.00	=	12,000	50,280	
Totals	64,000				64,000	$268,160	$4.19

Conversion:

	Total Units				Equivalent Units	Costs	Unit Cost
Beginning inventory	13,000	×	1.00	=	13,000	$ 53,170	
Started and completed	39,000	×	1.00	=	39,000	159,510	
Ending inventory	12,000	×	.65	=	7,800	31,902	
Totals	64,000				59,800	$244,582	$4.09

Accounting for total costs:

Total cost of units transferred out		$430,560
Work in process—August 31, 19X3:		
Transferred in	$50,280	
Conversion	31,902	82,182
Total costs accounted for		$512,742

SOUTH COMPANY—Dyeing Department
Cost of Production Report—Weighted Average
For August 19X3

Equivalent units and costs of production:

Transferred in:

	Total Units				Equivalent Units	Costs	Unit Cost
Beginning inventory	13,000	×	1.00	=	13,000	$ 99,450	
Started and completed	38,000	×	1.00	=	38,000	290,700	
Ending inventory	14,000	×	1.00	=	14,000	107,100	
Totals	65,000				65,000	$497,250	$7.65

(Continued)

Materials:

	Total Units				Equivalent Units	Costs	Unit Cost
Beginning inventory...............	13,000	×	1.00	=	13,000	$ 9,750	
Started and completed	38,000	×	1.00	=	38,000	28,500	
Ending inventory	14,000	×	.55	=	7,700	5,775	
Totals	65,000				58,700	$ 44,025	$ .75

Conversion:

	Total Units				Equivalent Units	Costs	Unit Cost
Beginning inventory...............	13,000	×	1.00	=	13,000	$ 14,170	
Started and completed	38,000	×	1.00	=	38,000	41,420	
Ending inventory	14,000	×	.40	=	5,600	6,104	
Totals	65,000				56,600	$ 61,694	$1.09

Accounting for total costs:

Total cost of units transferred out		$483,990
Work in process—August 31, 19X3:		
Transferred in	$107,100	
Materials	5,775	
Conversion	6,104	118,979
Total costs accounted for		$602,969

KEY TERMS

Equivalent Units of Production. As estimation of the number of complete units that could have been produced during a period.

First-In-First-Out (FIFO) Process Costing Method. The method of process costing that keeps beginning work in process units separate from the started and completed units.

Weighted Average Process Costing Method. The method of process costing that requires that the units in work in process at the beginning of the current month be treated the same as the units started and completed during the month.

QUESTIONS FOR REVIEW

1. What is meant by equivalent units of production?
2. How does the weighted average process costing method differ from the FIFO process costing method?

3. Which one of the two process costing methods more accurately depicts the actual flow of units through a production process?
4. What is a cost of production report and how is it used?
5. How are the units started and completed in the current period computed?
6. What is the transferred-in cost and how is it determined?
7. What additional costs do subsequent departments have that the first department does not have?
8. What is conversion cost?

NOTE Unless told otherwise in Exercises and Problems, record transactions in general journal form.

EXERCISES

11–1. Learning Objective 2. Calculating Equivalent Units of Production for Materials.

Blue Co. began the month with 20,000 units in process which were 30% complete as to materials, and started another 80,000 units during the month. Ending work in process was 60% complete as to materials and consisted of 25,000 units, while 75,000 units were transferred to finished goods.

Assuming Blue Co. uses the weighted average process costing method, calculate the equivalent units of production for materials.

11–2. Learning Objective 2. Calculating the Number of Units Transferred.

Jones Co. had 45,000 units 50% complete in beginning work in process, started 120,000 units during the month, and had 35,000 units 75% complete in ending work in process.

Assuming Jones Co. uses the weighted average process costing method, calculate the number of units transferred to finished goods during the month.

11–3. Learning Objectives 2. Calculating Equivalent Units of Production for Conversion.

Smith Co. began the month with 40,000 units in process which were 35% complete as to conversion, and started another 110,000 units during the month. Ending work in process was 60% complete as to conversion and consisted of 30,000 units, while 120,000 units were transferred to finished goods.

Assuming Smith Co. uses the weighted average process costing method, calculate the equivalent units of production for conversion.

11–4. Learning Objective 2. Calculating Equivalent Units of Production for a Company with One Department.

Star Co. produces a product in one department. During August, the company had the following units of production:

Units in beginning work in process inventory
  (75% complete as to materials and 60% complete
  as to conversion) 20,000
Units started into production during August 90,000
Total units to be accounted for 110,000
Units in ending work in process inventory (50% complete
  as to materials and 70% complete as to conversion) .... <25,000>
Units completed and transferred out during August 85,000
Units in beginning work in process inventory .... <20,000>
Units started and completed during August 65,000

Assuming Star Co. uses the weighted average process costing method, calculate the equivalent units of production for materials and conversion.

11–5. Learning Objective 2. Calculating Equivalent Units of Production for a Company with Two Departments.

Sun Co. produces a product in two departments. During September, the company had the following units of production:

Department 1:

Units in beginning work in process inventory
  (100% complete as to materials and 70% complete
  as to conversion) 30,000
Units started into production during September 110,000
Total units to be accounted for 140,000
Units in ending work in process inventory (100% complete
  as to materials and 60% complete as to conversion) .... <35,000>
Units completed and transferred out during September 105,000
Units in beginning work in process inventory .... <30,000>
Units started and completed during September 75,000

Department 2:

Units in beginning work in process inventory
  (85% complete as to materials and 65% complete
  as to conversion) 25,000
Units transferred in from Department 1 and
  started into production during September 105,000
Total units to be accounted for 130,000
Units in ending work in process inventory (75% complete
  as to materials and 50% complete as to conversion) .... <20,000>
Units completed and transferred out during September 110,000
Units in beginning work in process inventory .... <25,000>
Units started and completed during September 85,000

Assuming Sun Co. uses the weighted average process costing method, calculate the equivalent units of production for materials and conversion for both departments.

11–6. Learning Objectives 2, 3. Calculating Equivalent Units and Costs of Production for Materials for a Company with One Department.

Green Co. began in September with 40,000 units in process which were 20% complete as to materials, and started another 120,000 units during the month. Ending work in process was 50% complete as to materials and consisted of 50,000 units. Green Co. had the following materials costs for the month:

Beginning work in process inventory costs	$ 30,000
Current costs added during September	240,000
Total materials costs to be accounted for	$270,000

Assuming Green Co. uses the weighted average process costing method, calculate the equivalent units and costs of production for materials.

11–7. Learning Objectives 2, 3, 4, 5. Preparing a Cost of Production Report and Making the Journal Entry Transferring Costs Out of Work In Process Inventory for a Company with One Department.

Red Co. had the following costs and production information for October, 19X3:

	Materials	Conversion	Total
Beginning work in process inventory costs	$ 22,500	$ 30,000	$ 52,500
Current costs added in October	151,500	192,000	343,500
Total costs to be accounted for	$174,000	$222,000	$396,000

Units in beginning work in process inventory (50% complete as to materials and 50% complete as to conversion)	30,000
Units started into production during October	110,000
Total units to be accounted for	140,000
Units in ending work in process inventory (40% complete as to materials and 40% complete as to conversion)	<40,000>
Units completed and transferred out during October	100,000
Units in beginning work in process inventory	<30,000>
Units started and completed during October	70,000

1. Prepare a cost of production report for October 19X3 using the weighted average method.
2. Make the journal entry transferring costs out of work in process inventory at October 31.

GROUP A PROBLEMS

11–1A. Learning Objectives 2, 3, 4, 5. Preparing a Cost of Production Report and Making the Journal Entry to Transfer Costs Out of Work In Process Inventory for a Company with One Department.

Parts, Inc. had the following costs and production information for September 19X3:

	Materials	Conversion	Total
Beginning work in process inventory costs	$100,000	$ 50,000	$150,000
Current costs added in September ...	380,000	462,500	842,500
Total costs to be accounted for	$480,000	$512,500	$992,500

Units in beginning work in process inventory (100% complete as to materials and 10% complete as to conversion)	25,000
Units started into production during September	95,000
Total units to be accounted for	120,000
Units in ending work in process inventory (100% complete as to materials and 50% complete as to conversion)	<35,000>
Units completed and transferred out during September	85,000
Units in beginning work in process inventory	<25,000>
Units started and completed during September	60,000

Required:

1. Prepare a cost of production report for September 19X3 using the weighted average method.
2. Make the journal entry transferring costs out of work in process inventory at September 30.

11–2A. Learning Objectives 2, 3, 4, 5. Preparing Cost of Production Reports and Making the Journal Entries to Transfer Costs Out of Work In Process Inventories for a Company with Two Departments.

Iota, Inc., which manufactures its product in two departments, had the following costs and production information for October 19X3:

Cutting Department. Labor and overhead are added evenly throughout the production process, while materials are added at the beginning of production. Iota's Cutting Department had the following costs and production information for October:

	Materials	Conversion	Total
Beginning work in process inventory costs	$ 60,000	$ 15,000	$ 75,000
Current costs added in October	512,600	247,400	760,000
Total costs to be accounted for	$572,600	$262,400	$835,000

Units in beginning work in process inventory (100% complete as to materials and 30% complete as to conversion)	15,000
Units started into production during October	125,000
Total units to be accounted for	140,000
Units in ending work in process inventory (100% complete as to materials and 60% complete as to conversion)	<30,000>
Units completed and transferred out during October	110,000
Units in beginning work in process inventory	<15,000>
Units started and completed during October	95,000

Finishing Department. Labor and overhead are added evenly throughout the production process, while materials are also added evenly throughout production. Iota's Finishing Department had the following costs and production information for October:

	Transferred In	Materials	Conversion	Total
Beginning work in process inventory costs	$102,410	$ 8,500	$ 12,750	$123,660
Current costs added in October	?	116,350	168,850	?
Total costs to be accounted for	$?	$124,850	$181,600	$?

Units in beginning work in process inventory (60% complete as to materials and 60% complete as to conversion)	17,000
Units transferred in from the Cutting Department and started into production during October	110,000
Total units to be accounted for	127,000
Units in ending work in process inventory (50% complete as to materials and 50% complete as to conversion)	<27,000>
Units completed and transferred out during October	100,000
Units in beginning work in process inventory	<17,000>
Units started and completed during October	83,000

Required:
For each department:

1. Prepare a cost of production report for October 19X3 using the weighted average method.
2. Make the journal entry transferring costs out of work in process inventory at October 31.

11–3A. Learning Objectives 2, 3, 4, 5. Preparing Cost of Production Reports and Making the Journal Entries Transferring Costs Out of Work In Process Inventories for a Company with Three Departments.
Bell, Inc., which manufactures its product in three departments, had the following costs and production information for November 19X3:

Cutting Department	Materials	Conversion	Total
Beginning work in process inventory costs	$ -0-	$ -0-	$ -0-
Current costs added in November	687,500	495,125	1,182,625
Total costs to be accounted for	$687,500	$495,125	$1,182,625

Units in beginning work in process inventory (100% complete as to materials and 20% complete as to conversion)	-0-
Units started into production during November	125,000
Total units to be accounted for	125,000
Units in ending work in process inventory (100% complete as to materials and 50% complete as to conversion)	<17,000>
Units completed and transferred out during November	108,000
Units in beginning work in process inventory	<-0->
Units started and completed during November	108,000

Assembling Department	Transferred In	Materials	Conversion	Total
Beginning work in process inventory costs	$120,600	$ 12,000	$ 9,000	$141,600
Current costs added in November .	?	233,250	290,750	?
Total costs to be accounted for ...	$?	$245,250	$299,750	$?

Units in beginning work in process inventory (55% complete as to materials and 55% complete as to conversion)	12,000
Units in ending work in process inventory (50% complete as to materials and 50% complete as to conversion)	22,000

Finishing Department	Transferred In	Conversion	Total
Beginning work in process inventory costs ..	$210,280	$ 11,200	$221,480
Current costs added in November	?	286,575	?
Total costs to be accounted for	$?	$297,775	$?

Units in beginning work in process inventory (55% complete as to conversion)	14,000
Units in ending work in process inventory (50% complete as to conversion)	9,000

Required:

For each department:

1. Prepare a cost of production report for November 19X3 using the weighted average method.
2. Make the journal entry transferring costs out of work in process inventory at November 30.

GROUP B PROBLEMS

11–1B. Learning Objectives 2, 3, 4, 5. Preparing a Cost of Production Report and Making the Journal Entry to Transfer Costs Out of Work in Process Inventory for a Company with One Department.

April, Inc. had the following costs and production information for September 19X3:

	Materials	Conversion	Total
Beginning work in process inventory costs	$120,000	$ 60,000	$180,000
Current costs added in September	344,800	419,750	764,550
Total costs to be accounted for	$464,800	$479,750	$944,550

Units in beginning work in process inventory (100% complete as to materials and 20% complete as to conversion)	30,000
Units started into production during September	82,000
Total units to be accounted for	112,000
Units in ending work in process inventory (100% complete as to materials and 50% complete as to conversion)	<22,000>
Units completed and transferred out during September	90,000
Units in beginning work in process inventory	<30,000>
Units started and completed during September	60,000

Required:

1. Prepare a cost of production report for September 19X3 using the weighted average method.
2. Make the journal entry transferring costs out of work in process inventory at September 30.

11–2B. Learning Objectives 2, 3, 4, 5. Preparing of Cost of Production Reports and Making the Journal Entries Transferring Costs Out of Work In Process Inventories for a Company with Two Departments.

Gala, Inc., which manufactures its product in two departments, had the following costs and production information for October 19X3:

Cutting Department. Labor and overhead are added evenly throughout the production process, while materials are added at the beginning of production. Gala's Cutting Department had the following costs and production information for October:

	Materials	Conversion	Total
Beginning work in process inventory costs	$ 80,000	$ 22,000	$ 102,000
Current costs added in October	578,750	367,125	945,875
Total costs to be accounted for	$658,750	$389,125	$1,047,875

Units in beginning work in process inventory (100% complete as to materials and 40% complete as to conversion)	20,000
Units started into production during October	135,000
Total units to be accounted for	155,000
Units in ending work in process inventory (100% complete as to materials and 50% complete as to conversion)	<27,000>
Units completed and transferred out during October	128,000
Units in beginning work in process inventory	<20,000>
Units started and completed during October	108,000

Finishing Department. Labor and overhead are added evenly throughout the production process, while materials are also added evenly throughout production. Gala's Finishing Department had the following costs and production information for October:

	Transferred In	Materials	Conversion	Total
Beginning work in process inventory costs	$283,550	$ 8,500	$ 12,750	$304,800
Current costs added in October . . .	?	116,600	169,340	?
Total costs to be accounted for . . .	$?	$125,100	$182,090	$?

Units in beginning work in process inventory (60% complete as to materials and 60% complete as to conversion)	27,000
Units transferred in from the Cutting Department and started into production during October	128,000
Total units to be accounted for	155,000
Units in ending work in process inventory (50% complete as to materials and 50% complete as to conversion)	<32,000>
Units completed and transferred out during October	123,000
Units in beginning work in process inventory	<27,000>
Units started and completed during October	96,000

Required:
For each department:

1. Prepare a cost of production report for October 19X3 using the weighted average method.
2. Make the journal entry transferring costs out of work in process inventory at October 31.

11–3B. Learning Objectives 2, 3, 4, 5. Preparing Cost of Production Reports and Making the Journal Entries Transferring Costs Out of Work In Process Inventories for a Company with Three Departments.

Dell, Inc., which manufactures its product in three departments, had the following costs and production information for November 19X3:

Cutting Department	Materials	Conversion	Total
Beginning work in process inventory costs ..	$ 15,750	$ 17,500	$ 33,250
Current costs added in November	627,375	413,750	1,041,125
Total costs to be accounted for	$643,125	$431,250	$1,074,375

Units in beginning work in process inventory (100% complete as to materials and 30% complete as to conversion)	7,500
Units started into production during November	115,000
Total units to be accounted for	122,500
Units in ending work in process inventory (100% complete as to materials and 50% complete as to conversion)	<15,000>
Units completed and transferred out during November	107,500
Units in beginning work in process inventory	<7,500>
Units started and completed during November	100,000

Assembling Department	Transferred In	Materials	Conversion	Total
Beginning work in process inventory costs	$134,810	$ 9,450	$ 8,000	$152,260
Current costs added in November	?	235,220	304,950	?
Total costs to be accounted for ..	$?	$244,670	$312,950	$?

Units in beginning work in process inventory (45% complete as to materials and 45% complete as to conversion)	13,500
Units in ending work in process inventory (60% complete as to materials and 60% complete as to conversion)	18,000

Finishing Department	Transferred In	Conversion	Total
Beginning work in process inventory costs ..	$288,570	$ 13,200	$301,770
Current costs added in November	?	360,550	?
Total costs to be accounted for	$?	$373,750	$?

Units in beginning work in process inventory (60% complete as to conversion)	17,000
Units in ending work in process inventory (50% complete as to conversion)	10,000

Required:

For each department:

1. Prepare a cost of production report for November 19X3 using the weighted average method.
2. Make the journal entry transferring costs out of work in process inventory at November 30.

CASE FOR CRITICAL THINKING

Meri Robinson is a new employee in the accounting department at Bi-City Products Company. Meri is confused why it is often possible to combine direct labor cost and factory overhead costs into a single conversion cost when calculating cost per equivalent unit. After all, Meri reasons, the two components have to be separated when costs are accumulated, recorded in the ledger, and reported on financial statements. Explain why it is very often possible for direct labor cost and factory overhead costs to be combined into a single figure when determining product costs.

ANSWERS TO SELF-STUDY QUIZ 11–1

SHORT, INC.
Cost of Production Report—Weighted Average
For April 19X4

Quantities

1. Units to account for:

From beginning work in process	–0–
Started into production this month	55,000
Total units to account for	55,000

2. Units accounted for:

Completed and transferred out	45,000
From ending work in process (30% complete as to materials and 30% complete as to conversion)	10,000
Total units accounted for	55,000

3. Equivalent production:

	Equivalent Units	
	Materials	**Conversion**
Completed and transferred out	45,000	45,000
Ending work in process inventory:		
Materials (10,000 × 30%)	3,000	
Conversion (10,000 × 30%)		3,000
Total equivalent units	48,000	48,000

(Continued)

Costs

4. Costs to account for:

	Total Costs		Equivalent Units		Unit Cost
Materials	$162,720	÷	48,000	=	$3.39
Conversion	204,000	÷	48,000	=	4.25
Totals	$366,720				$7.64

5. Costs accounted for:

Completed and transferred out (45,000 × $7.64)......................		$343,800
Work in process—April 30, 19X4:		
Materials (10,000 × 30% × $3.39)................................	$10,170	
Conversion (10,000 × 30% × $4.25).............................	12,750	22,920
Total costs accounted for (48,000 × $7.64)		$366,720

	19X4					
1	Apr.	30	Finished Goods Inventory	343 80 000		1
2			Work in Process Inventory		343 80 000	2

ANSWERS TO SELF-STUDY QUIZ 11–2

SHORT, INC.
Cost of Production Report—Weighted Average
For May 19X4

Quantities

1. Units to account for:

From beginning work in process	6,500
Started into production this month	72,000
Total units to account for	78,500

2. Units accounted for:

From beginning work in process	6,500
Started and completed	52,500
From ending work in process (75% complete as to materials and 80% complete as to conversion)	19,500
Total units accounted for	78,500

(Continued)

3. Equivalent production:

	Equivalent Units	
	Materials	**Conversion**
Beginning work in process inventory	6,500	6,500
Started and completed.	52,500	52,500
Ending work in process inventory:		
Materials (19,500 × 75%).	14,625	
Conversion (19,500 × 80%).		15,600
Total equivalent units.	73,625	74,600

Costs

4. Costs to account for:

	Total Costs	**Equivalent Units**	**Unit Cost**
Materials.	$217,930 ÷ 73,625	= $2.96
Conversion	255,132 ÷ 74,600	= 3.42
Totals	$473,062	$6.38

5. Costs accounted for:

Completed and transferred out (59,000 × $6.38).		$376,420
Work in process—May 31, 19X4:		
Materials (19,500 × 75% × $2.96).	$43,290	
Conversion (19,500 × 80% × $3.42).	53,352	96,642
Total costs accounted for.		$473,062

	19X4					
1	May	31	Finished Goods Inventory	376 42 0 00		**1**
2			Work in Process Inventory		376 42 0 00	**2**

Chapter 12
FIFO Costing of Work in Process

LEARNING OBJECTIVES

After studying Chapter 12, you should be able to:

1. Differentiate between weighted average cost method and FIFO cost method.
2. Calculate the equivalent units produced in each department using the FIFO cost method.
3. Calculate the unit cost of goods produced each month using the FIFO cost method.
4. Calculate the amount of cost to transfer to the next department or to finished goods using a cost of production report.

In Chapter 11, we learned that there are two basic methods used in a process costing system to compute the cost of units transferred to other departments or to finished goods inventory: (1) the weighted average process costing method and (2) the first-in-first-out (FIFO) process costing method. These methods were defined and the weighted average cost method was illustrated. In this chapter, we will illustrate and discuss the FIFO method and show how it differs from the weighted average cost method.

DIFFERENCES BETWEEN WEIGHTED AVERAGE COST METHOD AND FIFO COST METHOD

LEARNING OBJECTIVE 1

You will recall that, under the weighted average cost method, the cost of the beginning work in process inventory is added to the cost of new production started during the month. As a result, we treat units in beginning work in process inventory the same as units started and completed during the month. Costing under the FIFO method is more complex because units completed in a month must be divided into parts. Units from the beginning work in process inventory must be kept separate from new units started in production during the current month. The first costs incurred during the month are assumed to go toward completing the units that were in production when the month started. All other costs incurred during the month are assumed to go toward completing the new units started in production during the month.

FIFO ILLUSTRATIONS WITH ONE DEPARTMENT

Company with No Beginning Work in Process Inventory

FIFO costing differs from weighted average costing *only* if there are units in process at the start of the period. If there is no beginning work in process inventory, both methods will produce the *same* results. For example, in the last chapter, we started our discussion of weighted average costing by illustrating a company (Alpha Company) that did not have a beginning work in process inventory. Since there were no beginning units in process, a cost of production report under FIFO would yield results identical to a cost of production report using weighted average costing. The only slight difference would be in the "Costs accounted for" section because FIFO separates beginning units from new units started during the period.

To illustrate this, Figure 12–1 shows Alpha's August cost of production report using FIFO. Compare the "Costs accounted for" section in the weighted average report (Figure 11–1) with the "Costs accounted for" section in the FIFO report (Figure 12–1). In Figure 11–1, the 50,000 units completed are simply multiplied by the $6.50 unit cost. Whereas, the FIFO report in Figure 12–1 shows a distinction between the cost of beginning units ($0 in this example) and the cost of units started and completed during August.

ALPHA CO.
Cost of Production Report—FIFO
For August 19X3

Quantities

1. Units to account for:
   From beginning work in process . . . . –0–
   Started into production this month 55,000
   Total units to account for 55,000

2. Units accounted for:
   Completed and transferred out 50,000
   From ending work in process (40% complete as to materials and 40% complete as
      to conversion) 5,000
   Total units accounted for 55,000

3. Equivalent production:

	Equivalent Units	
	Materials	**Conversion**
Completed and transferred out	50,000	50,000
Ending work in process inventory:		
Materials (5,000 × 40%)	2,000	
Conversion (5,000 × 40%)		2,000
Total equivalent units	52,000	52,000

Costs

4. Costs to account for:

	Total Costs	Equivalent Units	Unit Cost
Materials	$156,000 ÷	52,000 =	$3.00
Conversion	182,000 ÷	52,000 =	3.50
Totals	$338,000		$6.50

5. Costs accounted for:
   Transferred out:
      Work in process—August 1, 19X3 . . . . $ –0–
   Started and completed:
      Materials (50,000 × $3.00) $150,000
      Conversion (50,000 × $3.50) 175,000   325,000
   Total cost of units transferred out   325,000
   Work in process—August 31, 19X3 . . . .
      Materials (5,000 × 40% × $3.00) . . . . $ 6,000
      Conversion (5,000 × 40% × $3.50)   7,000   13,000
   Total costs accounted for (52,000 × $6.50) $338,000

FIGURE 12–1
Cost of Production
Report—Alpha
Company

SELF-STUDY QUIZ 12–1 In Self-Review Quiz 11–1 you prepared a weighted average cost of production report for Short, Inc. Short had the following production and cost data for April, 19X4.

Units to account for:

Units in beginning work in process inventory	-0-
Units started into production during April	55,000
Total units to account for	55,000
Units in ending work in process inventory (30% complete as to materials and 30% complete as to conversion)	<10,000>
Units completed and transferred out during April	45,000
Units in beginning work in process inventory	-0-
Units started and completed during April	45,000

Costs to account for:

	Materials	Conversion	Total
Cost in beginning work in process inventory	-0-	-0-	-0-
Costs added in April	$162,720	$204,000	$366,720
Total costs to account for	$162,720	$204,000	$366,720

a. Prepare a cost of production report for April using the FIFO method.
b. Make the general journal entry to transfer costs out of work in process inventory.

Answers at end of chapter.

Company with Beginning and Ending Work in Process Inventory

In Chapter 11, we prepared a weighted average cost of production for Beta, Inc. Beta, as you recall, manufactures a product in one department with labor and overhead added evenly throughout the production process, while materials are added unevenly. Beta's production and cost data for August follows:

Units to account for:

Units in beginning work in process inventory (40% complete as to materials and 60% complete as to conversion)	5,000
Units started into production during August	60,000
Total units to account for	65,000
Units in ending work in process inventory (40% complete as to materials and 60% complete as to conversion)	<15,000>
Units completed and transferred out during August	50,000
Units in beginning work in process inventory	<5,000>
Units started and completed during August	45,000

Costs to account for:

	Materials	Conversion	Total
Costs in beginning work in process inventory . . .	$ 6,000	$ 7,000	$ 13,000
Current costs added in August	176,040	205,520	381,560
Total cost to account for	$182,040	$212,520	$394,560

LEARNING OBJECTIVE 2

As with weighted average costing, the first thing we need to do is calculate Beta's equivalent units of production for August. However, the calculation of equivalent units under FIFO differs somewhat from the calculation under weighted average costing because the units in beginning work in process inventory are *not* merged with new units started during the period. To illustrate, equivalent units calculation for materials follows. (Remember, the beginning units were 40% complete as to materials costs and 60% complete as to conversion costs.)

Materials

Units from beginning work in process inventory: 5,000 × 60%	3,000
Units started and completed in August: 45,000 × 100%	45,000
Units in ending work in process inventory: 15,000 × 40%	6,000
Equivalent units for materials	54,000

Notice that the 5,000 units in beginning work in process inventory were multiplied by 60% to determine the equivalent whole units. The 60% rate was obtained by subtracting the percentage of completion that these units were in at the beginning of the month from 100% (100% − 40% = 60%). The 60% is the amount of work completed on the beginning units during the current month, and it is the amount completed *during the current month* that determines the equivalent units of production for beginning work in process inventory. This may seem a bit complicated, but think of it this way: When the month started, 40% of the materials had already been added to the beginning units. As a result, the remaining 60% of materials must be added this month in order to finish them.

The units started and finished during the month are always 100% complete for all costs. The units in the ending work in process inventory are multiplied by their percentage of completion (40% in this case).

Now, let's look at the equivalent unit calculation for conversion costs:

Conversion costs:

Units from beginning work in process inventory: 5,000 × 40%	2,000
Units started and completed in August: 45,000 × 100%	45,000
Units in ending work in process inventory: 15,000 × 60%	9,000
Equivalent units for conversion costs	56,000

Again, notice that we multiplied the beginning units by the percentage remaining to be finished this month. Since the beginning units had 60% of the conversion costs added in the previous month, they will require the remaining 40% of conversion costs to be added during the current month in order to be completed.

As always, the units started and completed during the month are 100% complete. And the units in ending work in process inventory are multiplied by their percentage of completion (60% in this case).

LEARNING OBJECTIVE 3   Now that we have calculated equivalent units for both materials and conversion costs, we compute cost per equivalent unit:

Materials cost per equivalent unit:

$$\frac{\text{Current cost}}{\text{Equivalent units}} = \frac{\$176{,}040}{54{,}000} = \$3.26$$

Conversion cost per equivalent unit:

$$\frac{\text{Current cost}}{\text{Equivalent units}} = \frac{\$205{,}520}{56{,}000} = \underline{\$3.67}$$

Total cost per equivalent unit $= \underline{\$6.93}$

Notice that under FIFO the unit costs are computed using *only* the current period costs. Unlike the weighted average method, which averages beginning costs and current costs, FIFO uses only costs incurred in the current month. By doing this, a better comparison of cost changes between production periods can be determined. The question of how much more or how much less did it cost the company to produce an equivalent unit this period compared to last period can be determined. Because of this, the FIFO method is widely used even though the weighted average method is generally considered easier.

Let's now determine Beta's production costs for August. Since the FIFO method keeps the units in beginning inventory separate from new units started during the period, the costs incurred during the current month relate to three different activities:

1. Costs necessary to complete the beginning work in process inventory.
2. Costs necessary to complete the units started and completed in the current month.
3. Costs necessary to start the unfinished units in the ending inventory.

August costs follow:

Units in beginning work in process inventory:

Costs from prior period	$ 13,000	
Materials (5,000 × 60% × $3.26)	9,780	
Conversion (5,000 × 40% × $3.67)	7,340	
Total		$ 30,120

Cost of units started and completed in August:

Materials: 45,000 × $3.26	$146,700	
Conversion: 45,000 × $3.67	165,150	
Total		311,850
Total cost of units transferred out		$341,970

Units in ending work in process inventory:

Materials: 15,000 × 40% × $3.26	$ 19,560
Conversion: 15,000 × 60% × $3.67	33,030
Total	52,590
Total cost accounted for	$394,560

LEARNING OBJECTIVE 4

Notice how the FIFO method keeps the beginning work in process inventory cost ($13,000) as a separate figure. Costs necessary to complete these beginning units were added to this figure to obtain the total cost of the units. Units started and finished during the month have their own cost which, when added to the cost of the beginning work in process inventory, yields the total cost of units finished and transferred out.

Figure 12–2 on pages 306 and 307 shows Beta's FIFO cost of production report for August. The following entry records the cost of units transferred out.

1	Aug.	31	Finished Goods Inventory	34197000		1
2			Work in Process Inventory		34197000	2
3			Transferred 45,000 completed units.			3

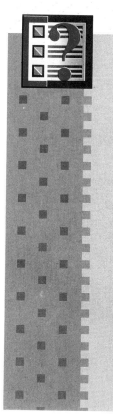

SELF-REVIEW QUIZ 12–2   Assume that Short, Inc. had the following production and cost data for May, 19X4.

Units to account for:

Units in beginning work in process inventory (30% complete as to materials and 40% complete as to conversion)	6,500
Units started into production during May	72,000
Total units to account for	78,500
Units in ending work in process inventory (75% complete as to materials and 80% complete as to conversion)	<19,500>
Units completed and transferred out during May	59,000
Units in beginning work in process inventory	<6,500>
Units started and completed during May	52,500

Costs to account for:

	Materials	Conversion	Total
Costs in beginning work in process inventory	$ 8,000	$ 9,000	$ 17,000
Costs added in May	209,291	246,240	455,531
Total costs to account for	$217,291	$255,240	$472,531

a. Prepare a cost of production report for May using the FIFO method.
b. Prepare the general journal entry to transfer costs out of work in process inventory.

Answers at end of chapter.

BETA, INC.
Cost of Production Report—FIFO
For August 19X3

Quantities

1. Units to account for:
   From beginning work in process 5,000
   Started into production this month 60,000
   Total units to account for 65,000

2. Units accounted for:
   From beginning work in process (40% complete as to materials and 60% complete as
      to conversion) 5,000
   Started and completed 45,000
   From ending work in process (40% complete as to materials and 60% complete as
      to conversion) 15,000
   Total units accounted for 65,000

3. Equivalent production:

	Equivalent Units	
	Materials	**Conversion**
Beginning work in process inventory:		
Materials (5,000 × 60%)	3,000	
Conversion (5,000 × 40%)		2,000
Started and completed	45,000	45,000
Ending work in process inventory:		
Materials (15,000 × 40%)	6,000	
Conversion (15,000 × 60%)		9,000
Total equivalent units	54,000	56,000

Costs

4. Costs to account for:

	Total Costs	Equivalent Units	Unit Cost
Materials:			
From beginning work in process	$ 6,000		
Current month's costs	176,040 ÷	54,000	= $3.26
Conversion:			
From beginning work in process	7,000		
Current month's costs	205,520 ÷	56,000	= 3.67
Totals	$394,560		$6.93

FIGURE 12–2
Cost of Production
Report—Beta, Inc.

(Continued)

5. Costs accounted for:
   Transferred out:
      Work in process—August 1, 19X3:

Beginning work in process inventory		$ 13,000	
Materials (5,000 × 60% × $3.26)		9,780	
Conversion (5,000 × 40% × $3.67)		7,340	$ 30,120
Started and completed:			
Materials (45,000 × $3.26)		146,700	
Conversion (45,000 × $3.67)		165,150	311,850
Total costs of units transferred out			341,970
Work in process—August 31, 19X3:			
Materials (15,000 × 40% × $3.26)		$ 19,560	
Conversion (15,000 × 60% × $3.67)		33,030	52,590
Total costs accounted for			$394,560

FIFO ILLUSTRATION WITH TWO DEPARTMENTS

In Chapter 11, we introduced Grant Company to illustrate weighted average costing in a firm with two producing departments. Grant, as you recall, adds labor and overhead evenly throughout the process, while adding materials unevenly. Grant's Department 1 had the following production and cost data for August. (The figures have been modified slightly from those in Chapter 11 to make calculations come out evenly.)

Units to account for:

Units in beginning work in process inventory (75% complete as to materials and 40% complete as to conversion)	10,000
Units started into production during August	50,000
Total units to account for	60,000
Units in ending work in process inventory (80% complete as to materials and 50% complete as to conversion)	<8,000>
Units completed and transferred out during August	52,000
Units in beginning work in process inventory	<10,000>
Units started and completed during August	42,000

Costs to account for:

	Materials	Conversion	Total
Costs in beginning work in process inventory	$ 23,780	$ 20,000	$ 43,780
Current costs added in August	221,415	274,040	495,455
Total costs to account for	$245,195	$294,040	$539,235

We compute equivalent units of production for Department 1 as follows:

Materials:
Units in beginning work in process inventory: 10,000 × 25% = ... 2,500
Units started and completed during August: 42,000 × 100% = ... 42,000
Units in ending work in process inventory: 8,000 × 80% = ... 6,400
Equivalent units for materials 50,900

Conversion Costs:
Units in beginning work in process inventory: 10,000 × 60% = ... 6,000
Units started and completed during August: 42,000 × 100% = ... 42,000
Units in ending work in process inventory: 8,000 × 50% 4,000
Equivalent units for conversion costs 52,000

NOTE Again, notice that the units in beginning work in process inventory are multiplied by the percent of work needed to be done in order to complete them, while the units in ending work in process inventory are multiplied by their stage of completion.

We compute costs per equivalent unit as follows:

Materials cost per equivalent unit:

$$\frac{\text{Current costs}}{\text{Equivalent units}} = \frac{\$221,415}{50,900} = \$4.35$$

Conversion cost per equivalent unit:

$$\frac{\text{Current costs}}{\text{Equivalent units}} = \frac{\$274,040}{52,000} = \underline{\$5.27}$$

Total cost per equivalent unit $9.62

August costs can be accounted for as follows.

Units in beginning work in process inventory:
Costs from prior period . . . . $ 43,780
Materials: 10,000 × 25% × $4.35 10,875
Conversion: 10,000 × 60% × $5.27 31,620
Total . . . . $ 86,275

Costs of units started and completed in August:
Materials: 42,000 × $4.35 . . . .$182,700
Conversion: 42,000 × $5.27 221,340
Total   404,040
Total cost of units transferred out $490,315

Units in ending work in process inventory:
Materials: 8,000 × 80% × $4.35 . . . . $ 27,840
Conversion: 8,000 × 50% × $5.27 21,080
Total   48,920
Total costs accounted for $539,235

Figure 12–3 shows the cost of production report for Department 1. The following journal entry shows the transfer of costs into Department 2.

1	Work in Process Inventory—Dept. 2	490 3 1 5 00		1
2	Work in Process Inventory—Dept. 1		490 3 1 5 00	2
3	Transferred 52,000 units from Dept. 1 to			3
4	Dept. 2.			4

GRANT CO.—Department 1
Cost of Production Report—FIFO
For August 19X3

Quantities

1. Units to account for:
   From beginning work in process 10,000
   Started into production this month 50,000
   Total units to account for 60,000

2. Units accounted for:
   From beginning work in process (75% complete as to materials and 40% complete as
      to conversion) 10,000
   Started and completed 42,000
   From ending work in process (80% complete as to materials and 50% complete as
      to conversion) 8,000
   Total units accounted for 60,000

3. Equivalent production:

	Equivalent Units	
	Materials	**Conversion**
Beginning work in process inventory:		
Materials (10,000 × 25%)	2,500	
Conversion (10,000 × 60%)		6,000
Started and completed	42,000	42,000
Ending work in process inventory:		
Materials (8,000 × 80%)	6,400	
Conversion (8,000 × 50%)		4,000
Total equivalent units	50,900	52,000

FIGURE 12–3
*Cost of Production
Report—Grant
Company*

(*Continued*)

Costs

4. Costs to account for:

	Total Costs	Equivalent Units	Unit Cost
Materials:			
From beginning work in process	$ 23,780		
Current month's costs	221,415 ÷	50,900	= $4.35
Conversion:			
From beginning work in process	20,000		
Current month's costs	274,040 ÷	52,000	= 5.27
Totals	$539,235		$9.62

5. Costs accounted for:
    Transferred out:
      Work in process—August 1, 19X3:

Beginning work in process inventory	$ 43,780	
Materials (10,000 × 25% × $4.35)	10,875	
Conversion (10,000 × 60% × $5.27)	31,620	$ 86,275
Started and completed:		
Materials (42,000 × $4.35)	182,700	
Conversion (42,000 × $5.27)	221,340	404,040
Total costs of units transferred out		490,315
Work in process—August 31, 19X3:		
Materials (8,000 × 80% × $4.35)	$ 27,840	
Conversion (8,000 × 50% × $5.27)	21,080	48,920
Total costs accounted for		$539,235

Department 2

Department 2 had the following production and cost data for August.

Units to account for:

Units in beginning work in process inventory (60% complete as to materials and 50% complete as to conversion)	12,000
Units transferred in from Department 1 and started into production during August	52,000
Total units to account for	64,000
Units in ending work in process inventory (60% complete as to materials and 40% complete as to conversion)	<14,000>
Units completed and transferred out during August	50,000
Units in beginning work in process inventory	<12,000>
Units started and completed during August	38,000

Costs to account for:

	Transferred In	Materials	Conversion	Total
Costs in beginning work in process inventory	$116,600	$ 28,800	$ 30,000	$ 175,400
Current costs added	490,315	210,432	261,888	962,635
Costs to account for	$606,915	$239,232	$291,888	$1,138,035

We calculate equivalent units of production for Department 2 as follows:

	Transferred In	Materials	Conversion
Beginning work in process inventory:			
Transferred in: 12,000 × 0%	-0-		
Materials: 12,000 × 40%		4,800	
Conversion: 12,000 × 50%			6,000
Units started and completed	38,000	38,000	38,000
Ending work in process inventory:			
Transferred in: 14,000 × 100%	14,000		
Materials: 14,000 × 60%		8,400	
Conversion: 14,000 × 40%			5,600
Total equivalent units	52,000	51,200	49,600

NOTE The beginning transferred-in units are multiplied by 0% percent because these units were transferred in July, so they cannot be considered in the equivalent unit calculation for August. The 14,000 units in ending work in process inventory are multiplied by 100% because they were transferred during August. In the calculation of equivalent units for next month (September), these units will be multiplied by 0%.

We calculate costs per equivalent unit as follows.

Transferred-in cost per equivalent unit:

$$\frac{\text{Current costs}}{\text{Equivalent units}} = \frac{\$490,315}{52,000} = \$ \ 9.4291346$$

Materials cost per equivalent unit:

$$\frac{\text{Current costs}}{\text{Equivalent units}} = \frac{\$210,432}{51,200} = \ 4.1100000$$

Conversion cost per equivalent unit:

$$\frac{\text{Current costs}}{\text{Equivalent units}} = \frac{\$261,888}{49,600} = \ 5.2800000$$

Total cost per equivalent unit $18.8191346

We can now account for Department 2's August costs, as follows.

Units in beginning work in process inventory:
Costs in beginning work in process inventory	$175,400	
Transferred-in costs	-0-	
Materials: 12,000 × 40% × $4.11	19,728	
Conversion: 12,000 × 50% × $5.28	31,680	
Total		$ 226,808

Costs of units started and completed in August:
Transferred in: 38,000 × $9.4291346	$358,307*	
Materials: 38,000 × $4.11	156,180	
Conversion: 38,000 × $5.28	200,640	
Total		715,127
Total cost of units transferred out		$ 941,935

Units in ending work in process inventory:
Transferred in: 14,000 × $9.4291346	$132,008*	
Materials: 14,000 × 60% × $4.11	34,524	
Conversion: 14,000 × 40% × $5.28	29,568	
Total		196,100
Total costs accounted for		$1,138,035

*rounded

Figure 12–4 shows the August cost of production report for Department 2. The following journal entry records the transfer of costs from Department 2 to Finished Goods Inventory.

1	Aug.	31	Finished Goods Inventory	941 9 3 5 00		1
2			Work in Process Inventory—Dept. 2		941 9 3 5 00	2
3			Transferred 50,000 completed units.			3

GRANT CO.—Department 2
Cost of Production Report—FIFO
For August 19X3

Quantities

1. Units to account for:
From beginning work in process	12,000
Started into production this month	52,000
Total units to account for	64,000

2. Units accounted for:
From beginning work in process (60% complete as to materials and 50% complete as to conversion)	12,000
Started and completed	38,000
From ending work in process (60% complete as to materials and 40% complete as to conversion)	14,000
Total units accounted for	64,000

FIGURE 12–4
Cost of Production
Report—Grant Company

(*Continued*)

3. Equivalent production:

	Equivalent Units		
	Transferred in	Materials	Conversion
Beginning work in process inventory:			
Transferred in (12,000 × 0%)	–0–		
Materials (12,000 × 40%).		4,800	
Conversion (12,000 × 50%)			6,000
Started and completed	38,000	38,000	38,000
Ending work in process inventory:			
Transferred in (14,000 × 100%)	14,000		
Materials (14,000 × 60%)		8,400	
Conversion (14,000 × 40%)			5,600
Total equivalent units	52,000	51,200	49,600

Costs

4. Costs to account for:

	Total Costs	Equivalent Units	Unit Cost
Transferred in:			
From beginning work in process	$ 116,600		
Current month's costs	490,315 ÷ 52,000	=	$ 9.4291346
Materials:			
From beginning work in process	28,800		
Current month's costs.	210,432 ÷ 51,200	=	4.1100000
Conversion:			
From beginning work in process	30,000		
Current month's costs.	261,888 ÷ 49,600	=	5.2800000
Totals	$1,138,035		$18.8191346

5. Costs accounted for:
   Transferred out:
   Work in process—August 1, 19X3:

Beginning work in process inventory	$175,400	
Transferred in (–0– × $9.4291346)	–0–	
Materials (12,000 × 40% × $4.11).	19,728	
Conversion (12,000 × 50% × $5.28)	31,680	$ 226,808
Started and completed:		
Transferred in (38,000 × $9.4291346).	358,307	
Materials (38,000 × $4.11).	156,180	
Conversion (38,000 × $5.28).	200,640	715,127
Total costs of units transferred out		941,935
Work in process—August 31, 19X3:		
Transferred in (14,000 × $9.4291346)	$132,008	
Materials (14,000 × 60% × $4.11)	34,524	
Conversion (14,000 × 40% × $5.28)	29,568	196,100
Total costs accounted for		$1,138,035

SELF-STUDY PROBLEM

Assume that South Company, which manufactures T-shirts and was introduced in Chapter 10, had the following costs and production information by department for August 19X3.

Cutting Department	Materials	Conversion	Total
Beginning work in process inventory costs	$ 15,110	$ 4,895	$ 20,005
Current costs added in August	183,060	61,320	244,380
Total costs to be accounted for	$198,170	$66,215	$264,385

Units in beginning work in process inventory (65% complete as to materials and 40% complete as to conversion)	11,000
Units started into production during August	50,000
Total units to be accounted for	61,000
Units in ending work in process inventory (70% complete as to materials and 45% complete as to conversion)	<10,000>
Units completed and transferred out during August	51,000
Units in beginning work in process inventory	<11,000>
Units started and completed during August	40,000

Sewing Department	Transferred In	Conversion	Total
Beginning work in process inventory costs	$ 33,050	$ 21,462	$54,512
Current costs added in August	?	223,236	?
Total costs to be accounted for	$?	$ 244,698	$?

Units in beginning work in process inventory (55% complete as to conversion)	13,000
Units in ending work in process inventory (65% complete as to conversion)	12,000

Dyeing Department	Transferred In	Materials	Conversion	Total
Beginning work in process inventory costs	$66,690	$ 5,425	$ 7,144	$79,259
Current costs added in August	?	39,178	54,395	?
Total costs to be accounted for	$?	$44,603	$61,539	$?

Units in beginning work in process inventory (55% complete as to materials and 55% complete as to conversion)	13,000
Units in ending work in process inventory (55% complete as to materials and 40% complete as to conversion)	14,000

Required:
For each department:

1. Prepare a cost of production report for August 19X3.
2. Make the general journal entry to transfer costs out of work in process inventory at August 31 using the FIFO method.

SOLUTION TO SELF-STUDY PROBLEM

1.

SOUTH COMPANY—Cutting Dept.
Cost of Production Report—FIFO
For August 19X3

Quantities

1. Units to account for:
   From beginning work in process.   11,000
   Started into production this month   50,000
   Total units to account for.   61,000

2. Units accounted for:
   From beginning work in process (65% complete as to materials and 40% complete as
      to conversion).   11,000
   Started and completed   40,000
   From ending work in process (70% complete as to materials and 45% complete as
      to conversion).   10,000
   Total units accounted for   61,000

3. Equivalent production:

	Equivalent Units	
	Materials	**Conversion**
Beginning work in process inventory:		
Materials (11,000 × 35%).	3,850	
Conversion (11,000 × 60%).		6,600
Started and completed.	40,000	40,000
Ending work in process inventory:		
Materials (10,000 × 70%)	7,000	
Conversion (10,000 × 45%).		4,500
Total equivalent units.	50,850	51,100

Costs

4. Costs to account for:

	Total Costs	Equivalent Units	Unit Cost
Materials:			
From beginning work in process	$ 15,110		
Current month's costs.	183,060 ÷	50,850	= $3.60
Conversion:			
From beginning work in process	4,895		
Current month's costs.	61,320 ÷	51,100	= 1.20
Totals	$264,385		$4.80

5. Costs accounted for:
  Transferred out:
    Work in process—August 1:
      Beginning work in process inventory . . . . $ 20,005
      Materials (11,000 × 35% × $3.60) 13,860
      Conversion (11,000 × 60% × $1.20) . . . . 7,920 $ 41,785
    Started and completed:
      Materials (40,000 × $3.60) 144,000
      Conversion (40,000 × $1.20) 48,000   192,000
    Total costs of units transferred out 233,785
    Work in process—August 31:
      Materials (10,000 × 70% × $3.60) . . . . $ 25,200
      Conversion (10,000 × 45% × $1.20) 5,400   30,600
  Total costs accounted for $264,385

2.

	19X3					
1	Aug.	31	Work in Process Inventory—Sewing Dept.	233 78 500		1
2			Work in Process Inventory—Cutting Dept.		233 78 500	2

1.

SOUTH COMPANY—Sewing Dept.
Cost of Production Report—FIFO
For August 19X3

Quantities

1. Units to account for:
  From beginning work in process. 13,000
  Started into production this month. 51,000
  Total units to account for. 64,000

2. Units accounted for:
  From beginning work in process (55% complete as to conversion) 13,000
  Started and completed 39,000
  From ending work in process (65% complete as to conversion) 12,000
  Total units accounted for. 64,000

(Continued)

3. Equivalent production:

	Equivalent Units	
	Materials	**Conversion**
Beginning work in process inventory:		
Transferred in (13,000 × 0%)	–0–	
Conversion (13,000 × 45%)		5,850
Started and completed	39,000	39,000
Ending work in process inventory:		
Transferred in (12,000 × 100%)	12,000	
Conversion (12,000 × 65%)		7,800
Total equivalent units	51,000	52,650

Costs

4. Costs to account for:

	Total Costs	Equivalent Units	Unit Cost
Transferred in:			
From beginning work in process.	$ 33,050		
Current month's costs	233,785 ÷ 51,000		= $4.5840196
Conversion:			
From beginning work in process	21,462		
Current month's costs	233,236 ÷ 52,650		= 4.2400000
Totals	$511,533		$8.8240196

5. Costs accounted for:
  Transferred out:
   Work in process—August 1:

Beginning work in process inventory	$ 54,512	
Transferred in (–0– × $4.5840196)	–0–	
Conversion (5,850 × $4.24)	24,804	$ 79,316
Started and completed:		
Transferred in (39,000 × $4.5840196)	178,777	
Conversion (39,000 × $4.24)	165,360	344,137
Total costs of units transferred out		423,453
Work in process—August 31:		
Transferred in (12,000 × $4.5840196)	55,008	
Conversion (7,800 × $4.24)	33,072	88,080
Total costs accounted for		$511,533

2.

	19X3					
1	Aug.	31	Work in Process Inventory—Dyeing Dept.	423 45 3 00		1
2			Work in Process Inventory—Sewing Dept.		423 45 3 00	2

1.

SOUTH COMPANY—Dyeing Dept.
Cost of Production Report—FIFO
For August 19X3

Quantities

1. Units to account for:
   From beginning work in process 13,000
   Started into production this month 52,000
   Total units to account for 65,000

2. Units accounted for:
   From beginning work in process (55% complete as to materials and 55% complete as
       to conversion)   13,000
   Started and completed 38,000
   From ending work in process (55% complete as to materials and 40% complete as
       to conversion) 14,000
   Total units accounted for 65,000

3. Equivalent production:

	Equivalent Units		
	Transferred In	**Materials**	**Conversion**
Beginning work in process inventory:			
Transferred in (13,000 × 0%)	–0–		
Materials (13,000 × 45%)		5,850	
Conversion (13,000 × 45%)			5,850
Started and completed	38,000	38,000	38,000
Ending work in process inventory:			
Transferred in (14,000 × 100%)	14,000		
Materials (14,000 × 55%)		7,700	
Conversion (14,000 × 40%)			5,600
Total equivalent units	52,000	51,550	49,450

Costs

4. Costs to account for:

	Total Costs	**Equivalent Units**		**Unit Cost**
Transferred in:				
From beginning work in process.	$ 66,690			
Current month's costs	423,453	÷ 52,000	=	$ 8.1433269
Materials:				
From beginning work in process	5,425			
Current month's costs	39,178	÷ 51,550	=	.7600000
Conversion:				
From beginning work in process	7,144			
Current month's costs	54,395	÷ 49,450	=	1.1000000
Totals	$596,285			$10.0033269

(Continued)

5. Costs accounted for:
  Transferred out:
    Work in process—August 1:
      Beginning work in process inventory . . . . $ 79,259
      Transferred in (–0– × $8.1433269) . . . . –0–
      Materials (13,000 × 45% × $0.76) 4,446
      Conversion (13,000 × 45% × $1.10) . . . . 6,435 $ 90,140
    Started and completed:
      Transferred in (38,000 × $8.1433269) 309,446
      Materials (38,000 × $0.76) 28,880
      Conversion (38,000 × $1.10) 41,800   380,126
    Total costs of units transferred out 470,266
  Work in process—August 31:
    Transferred in (14,000 × $8.1433269) $114,007
    Materials (14,000 × 55% × $0.76) 5,852
    Conversion (14,000 × 40% × $1.10) 6,160   126,019
  Total costs accounted for $596,285

	19X3				
1	Aug.	31	Finished Goods Inventory	470 26600	1
2			Work in Process Inventory—Dyeing Dept.	470 26600	2

SUMMARY

In this chapter, we discussed the FIFO method of assigning costs to units in manufacturing departments producing substantial quantities of homogeneous products. The difference between the application of FIFO and the weighted average method can be found exclusively in the treatment of the beginning work in process inventory. The weighted average method combines the costs and equivalent units of the beginning inventory with the current period's costs and equivalent units. Under this method, equivalent whole units are simply the number of completed units transferred out plus the equivalent whole units in the ending work in process inventory. The same unit cost is assigned regardless of whether a unit was started and completed during the month, or was carried into the month in the beginning inventory.

The FIFO method keeps separate the costs of the beginning work in process inventory and the costs of production started during the current month. Under FIFO, equivalent whole units represent only the current month's activity. The first costs incurred are assumed to go toward completing the beginning units. All other costs are assumed to go toward completing units started in the current month.

APPENDIX 12A: ALTERNATIVE FORMAT FOR FIFO COST OF PRODUCTION REPORT

An alternative cost of production report format for South Company (See SELF-STUDY PROBLEM) is presented.

SOUTH COMPANY—Cutting Dept.
Cost of Production Report—FIFO
For August 19X3

Equivalent units and costs of production:

Materials:	Total Units				Equivalent Units	Costs	Unit Cost
Beginning inventory.	11,000	×	.35	=	3,850	$ 13,860	
Started and completed	40,000	×	1.00	=	40,000	144,000	
Ending inventory	10,000	×	.70	=	7,000	25,200	
Totals	61,000				50,850	$183,060	$3.60

Conversion:	Total Units				Equivalent Units	Costs	Unit Cost
Beginning inventory	11,000	×	.60	=	6,600	$ 7,920	
Started and completed	40,000	×	1.00	=	40,000	48,000	
Ending inventory	10,000	×	.45	=	4,500	5,400	
Totals	61,000				51,100	$ 61,320	$1.20

Accounting for total costs:
Transferred out:
  Work in process—August 1:

Beginning inventory.	$ 20,005	
Materials.	13,860	
Conversion.	7,920	$ 41,785

  Started and completed:

Materials.	144,000	
Conversion.	48,000	192,000
Total cost of units transferred out		$233,785

Work in process—August 31:

Materials.	25,200	
Conversion.	5,400	30,600
Total costs accounted for		$264,385

	19X3						
1	Aug.	31	Work in Process Inventory—Sewing Dept.	233 78 500			**1**
2			Work in Process Inventory—Cutting Dept.		233 78 500		**2**

SOUTH COMPANY—Sewing Dept.
Cost of Production Report—FIFO
For August 19X3

Equivalent units and costs of production:

Transferred in:	Total Units				Equivalent Units	Costs	Unit Cost
Beginning inventory	13,000	×	0.00	=	–0–	$ –0–	
Started and completed.	39,000	×	1.00	=	39,000	178,777	
Ending inventory	12,000	×	1.00	=	12,000	55,008	
Totals	64,000				51,000	$233,785	$4.5840196

Conversion:	Total Units				Equivalent Units	Costs	Unit Cost
Beginning inventory	13,000	×	.45	=	5,850	$ 24,804	
Started and completed.	39,000	×	1.00	=	39,000	165,360	
Ending inventory	12,000	×	.65	=	7,800	33,072	
Totals	64,000				52,650	$223,236	$4.24

Accounting for total costs:
  Transferred out:
    Work in process—August 1:

Beginning inventory.	$ 54,512	
Conversion.	24,804	$ 79,316
Started and completed:		
Transferred in.	178,777	
Conversion.	165,360	344,137
Total cost of units transferred out		$423,453
Work in process—August 31:		
Transferred in.	55,008	
Conversion.	33,072	88,080
Total costs accounted for		$511,533

	19X3						
1	Aug.	31	Work in Process Inventory—Dyeing Dept.	423 45 300			**1**
2			Work in Process Inventory—Sewing Dept.		423 45 300		**2**

SOUTH COMPANY—Dyeing Dept.
Cost of Production Report—FIFO
For August 19X3

Equivalent units and costs of production:

Transferred in:	Total Units				Equivalent Units	Costs	Unit Cost
Beginning inventory	13,000	×	0.00	=	–0–	$ –0–	
Started and completed	38,000	×	1.00	=	38,000	309,446	
Ending inventory	14,000	×	1.00	=	14,000	114,007	
Totals	65,000				52,000	$423,453	$8.1433269

Materials:	Total Units				Equivalent Units	Costs	Unit Cost
Beginning inventory	13,000	×	.45	=	5,850	$ 4,446	
Started and completed	38,000	×	1.00	=	38,000	28,800	
Ending inventory	14,000	×	.55	=	7,700	5,852	
Totals	65,000				51,550	$ 39,178	$ .76

Conversion:	Total Units				Equivalent Units	Costs	Unit Cost
Beginning inventory	13,000	×	.45	=	5,850	$ 6,435	
Started and completed	38,000	×	1.00	=	38,000	41,800	
Ending inventory	14,000	×	.40	=	5,600	6,160	
Totals	65,000				49,450	$ 54,395	$1.10

Accounting for total costs:
  Transferred out:
    Work in process—August 1:

Beginning inventory	$ 79,259	
Materials	4,446	
Conversion	6,435	$ 90,140
Started and completed:		
Transferred in	309,446	
Materials	28,880	
Conversion	41,800	380,126
Total cost of units transferred out		470,266
Work in process—August 31:		
Transferred in	114,007	
Materials	5,852	
Conversion	6,160	126,019
Total costs accounted for		$596,285

	19X3						
1	Aug.	31	Finished Goods Inventory	470 26 6 00			**1**
2			Work in Process Inventory—Dyeing Dept.		470 26 6 00		**2**

QUESTIONS FOR REVIEW

1. How does the FIFO process costing method differ from the weighted average process costing method?
2. How are equivalent units of production calculated using the FIFO method?
3. Is the FIFO method more accurate than the weighted average method? Discuss fully.
4. If a company has more than one processing department, why is the computation of equivalent units of production more challenging?
5. Will the number of equivalent units of production be greater or less with FIFO as opposed to the weighted average method?
6. Is the FIFO method or the weighted average method more difficult to apply?
7. Under what condition will the equivalent units of production be the same under FIFO as under weighted average?
8. How are the unit costs for each cost component assigned to the units produced during the current period under the FIFO method?

EXERCISES

12–1. Learning Objective 2. Calculating Equivalent Units of Production for Materials.
Blue Co. began the month with 20,000 units in process which were 30% complete as to materials, and started another 80,000 units during the month. Ending work in process was 60% complete as to materials and consisted of 25,000 units, while 75,000 units were transferred to finished goods.

Assuming Blue Co. uses the FIFO process costing method, calculate the equivalent units of production for materials.

12–2. Learning Objectives 2, 3. Calculating the Number of Units Transferred.
Jones Co. had 50,000 units 50% complete in beginning work in process, started 100,000 units during the month, and had 25,000 units 75% complete in ending work in process.

Assuming Jones Co. uses the FIFO process costing method, calculate the number of units transferred to finished goods during the month.

12–3. Learning Objective 2. Calculating Equivalent Units of Production for Conversion.
Smith Co. began the month with 40,000 units in process which were 35% complete as to conversion, and started another 110,000 units during the month. Ending work in process was 60% complete as to conversion and consisted of 30,000 units, while 120,000 units were transferred to finished goods.

Assuming Smith Co. uses the FIFO process costing method, calculate the equivalent units of production for conversion for the month.

12–4. Learning Objective 2. Calculating Equivalent Units of Production for a Company with One Department.

Star Co. produces a product in one department. During August the company had the following units of production:

Units in beginning work in process inventory (75% complete as to materials and 60% complete as to conversion)	20,000
Units started into production during August	90,000
Total units to be accounted for	110,000
Units in ending work in process inventory (50% complete as to materials and 70% complete as to conversion)	<25,000>
Units completed and transferred out during August	85,000
Units in beginning work in process inventory	<20,000>
Units started and completed during August	65,000

Assuming Star Co. uses the FIFO process costing method, calculate the equivalent units of production for materials and conversion for August.

12–5. Learning Objectives 2, 3. Calculating Equivalent Units of Production for a Company with Two Departments.

Sun Co. produces a product in two departments. During September the company had the following units of production:

Department 1:

Units in beginning work in process inventory (100% complete as to materials and 70% complete as to conversion)	30,000
Units started into production during September	110,000
Total units to be accounted for	140,000
Units in ending work in process inventory (100% complete as to materials and 60% complete as to conversion)	<35,000>
Units completed and transferred out during September	105,000
Units in beginning work in process inventory	<30,000>
Units started and completed during September	75,000

Department 2:

Units in beginning work in process inventory (85% complete as to materials and 65% complete as to conversion)	25,000
Units transferred in from Department 1 during September	105,000
Total units to be accounted for	130,000
Units in ending work in process inventory (75% complete as to materials and 50% complete as to conversion)	<20,000>
Units completed and transferred out during September	110,000
Units in beginning work in process inventory	<25,000>
Units started and completed during September	85,000

Assuming Sun Co. uses the FIFO process costing method, calculate the equivalent units of production for materials and conversion for both departments for September.

12–6. Learning Objectives 2, 3, 4. Calculating Equivalent Units and Costs of Production for Materials for a Company with One Department.

Green Co. began September with 40,000 units in process which were 20% complete as to materials, and started another 120,000 units during the month. Ending work in process was 50% complete as to materials and consisted of 50,000 units. Green Co. had the following materials costs for the month:

Beginning work in process inventory costs	$ 30,000
Current costs added during September	240,030
Total materials costs to be accounted for	$270,030

Assuming Green Co. uses the FIFO process costing method, calculate the equivalent units and costs of production for materials.

12–7. Learning Objectives 1, 2, 4. Preparing a Cost of Production Report and Making the Journal Entry Transferring Costs Out of Work In Process Inventory for a Company with One Department.

Red Co. had the following costs and production data for October 19X3.

	Materials	Conversion	Total
Beginning work in process inventory costs	$ 22,500	$ 30,000	$ 52,500
Current costs added in October	151,200	192,150	343,350
Total costs to be accounted for	$173,700	$222,150	$395,850

Units in beginning work in process inventory (50% complete as to materials and 50% complete as to conversion)	30,000
Units started into production during October	110,000
Total units to be accounted for	140,000
Units in ending work in process inventory (40% complete as to materials and 40% complete as to conversion)	<40,000>
Units completed and transferred out during October	100,000
Units in beginning work in process inventory	<30,000>
Units started and completed during October	70,000

1. Prepare a cost of production report for October using the FIFO method.
2. Make the journal entry transferring costs out of work in process inventory at October 31.

GROUP A PROBLEMS

12–1A. Learning Objectives 2, 3, 4. Preparing a Cost of Production Report and Making the Journal Entry Transferring Costs Out of Work In Process Inventory for a Company with One Department.

Parts, Inc. had the following costs and production information for September 19X3:

	Materials	Conversion	Total
Beginning work in process inventory costs	$100,000	$ 50,000	$150,000
Current costs added in September	380,000	463,000	843,000
Total costs to be accounted for	$480,000	$513,000	$993,000

Units in beginning work in process inventory (100% complete as to materials and 10% complete as to conversion)	25,000
Units started into production during September	95,000
Total units to be accounted for	120,000
Units in ending work in process inventory (100% complete as to materials and 50% complete as to conversion)	<35,000>
Units completed and transferred out during September	85,000
Units in beginning work in process inventory	<25,000>
Units started and completed during September	60,000

Required:

1. Prepare a cost of production report for September using the FIFO method.
2. Make the journal entry transferring costs out of work in process inventory at September 30.

12–2A. Learning Objectives 2, 3, 4. Preparing Cost of Production Reports and Making the Journal Entries Transferring Costs Out of Work In Process Inventories for a Company with Two Departments.

Iota, Inc., which manufactures its product in two departments, had the following costs and production data for October 19X3:

Cutting Department. Labor and overhead are added evenly throughout the production process, while materials are added at the beginning of production. Iota's Cutting Department had the following costs and production data for October:

	Materials	Conversion	Total
Beginning work in process inventory costs	$ 60,000	$ 15,000	$ 75,000
Current costs added in October	512,500	247,000	759,500
Total costs to be accounted for	$572,500	$262,000	$834,500

Units in beginning work in process inventory (100% complete as to materials and 30% complete as to conversion)	15,000
Units started into production during October	125,000
Total units to be accounted for	140,000
Units in ending work in process inventory (100% complete as to materials and 60% complete as to conversion)	<30,000>
Units completed and transferred out during October	110,000
Units in beginning work in process inventory	<15,000>
Units started and completed during October	95,000

Finishing Department. Labor and overhead are added evenly throughout the production process, while materials are also added evenly throughout production. Iota's Finishing Department had the following costs and production data for October:

	Transferred In	Materials	Conversion	Total
Beginning work in process inventory costs	$102,410	$ 8,500	$ 12,750	$123,660
Current costs added in October . . .	?	116,729	169,412	?
Total costs to be accounted for . . .	$?	$125,229	$182,162	$?

Units in beginning work in process inventory (60% complete as to materials and 60% complete as to conversion)	17,000
Units transferred in from the Cutting Department and started into production during October	110,000
Total units to be accounted for	127,000
Units in ending work in process inventory (50% complete as to materials and 50% complete as to conversion)	<27,000>
Units completed and transferred out during October	100,000
Units in beginning work in process inventory	<17,000>
Units started and completed during October	83,000

Required:

1. Prepare a cost of production report for October using the FIFO method.
2. Make the journal entry transferring costs out of work in process inventory at October 31.

12–3A. Learning Objectives 2, 3, 4. Preparing Cost of Production Reports and Making the Journal Entries Transferring Costs Out of Work In Process Inventories for a Company with Three Departments.

Bell, Inc., which manufactures its product in three departments, had the following costs and production data for November 19X3:

Cutting Department	Materials	Conversion	Total
Beginning work in process inventory costs	$ -0-	$ -0-	$ -0-
Current costs added in November	687,500	495,125	1,182,625
Total costs to be accounted for	$687,500	$495,125	$1,182,625

Units in beginning work in process inventory	-0-
Units started into production during November	125,000
Total units to be accounted for	125,000
Units in ending work in process inventory (100% complete as to materials and 50% complete as to conversion)	<17,000>
Units completed and transferred out during November	108,000
Units in beginning work in process inventory	-0-
Units started and completed during November	108,000

Assembling Department	Transferred In	Materials	Conversion	Total
Beginning work in process inventory costs	$120,600	$ 12,000	$ 9,000	$141,600
Current costs added in November .	?	233,472	290,816	?
Total costs to be accounted for . . .	$?	$245,472	$299,816	$?

Units in beginning work in process inventory (55% complete as to materials and 55% complete as to conversion)	12,000
Units in ending work in process inventory (50% complete as to materials and 50% complete as to conversion)	22,000

Finishing Department	Transferred In	Conversion	Total
Beginning work in process inventory costs . . .	$210,280	$ 11,200	$221,480
Current costs added in November	?	286,426	?
Total costs to be accounted for	$?	$297,626	$?

Units in beginning work in process inventory (55% complete as to conversion)	14,000
Units in ending work in process inventory (50% complete as to conversion)	9,000

Required:

For each department:

1. Prepare a cost of production report for November using the FIFO method.
2. Make the journal entry transferring costs out of work in process inventory at November 30.

GROUP B PROBLEMS

12–1B. Learning Objectives 2, 3, 4. Preparing a Cost of Production Report and Making the Journal Entry Transferring Costs Out of Work In Process Inventory for a Company with One Department.

April, Inc. had the following costs and production data for September 19X3:

	Materials	Conversion	Total
Beginning work in process inventory costs	$120,000	$ 60,000	$180,000
Current costs added in September	344,400	419,900	764,300
Total costs to be accounted for	$464,400	$479,900	$944,300
Units in beginning work in process inventory (100% complete as to materials and 20% complete as to conversion)			30,000
Units started into production during September			82,000
Total units to be accounted for			112,000
Units in ending work in process inventory (100% complete as to materials and 50% complete as to conversion)			<22,000>
Units completed and transferred out during September			90,000
Units in beginning work in process inventory			<30,000>
Units started and completed during September			60,000

Required:

1. Prepare a cost of production report for September using the FIFO method.
2. Make the journal entry transferring costs out of work in process inventory at September 30.

12–2B. Learning Objectives 2, 3, 4. Preparing Cost of Production Reports and Making the Journal Entries Transferring Costs Out of Work In Process Inventories for a Company with Two Departments.

Gala, Inc., which manufactures its product in two departments, had the following costs and production data for October 19X3:

Cutting Department. Labor and overhead are added evenly throughout the production process, while materials are added at the beginning of production. Gala's Cutting Department had the following costs and production data for October:

	Materials	Conversion	Total
Beginning work in process inventory costs	$ 80,000	$ 22,000	$ 102,000
Current costs added in October	579,150	367,125	946,275
Total costs to be accounted for	$659,150	$389,125	$1,048,275

Units in beginning work in process inventory (100% complete as to materials and 40% complete as to conversion)	20,000
Units started into production during October	135,000
Total units to be accounted for	155,000
Units in ending work in process inventory (100% complete as to materials and 50% complete as to conversion)	<27,000>
Units completed and transferred out during October	128,000
Units in beginning work in process inventory	<20,000>
Units started and completed during October	108,000

Finishing Department. Labor and overhead are added evenly throughout the production process, while materials are also added evenly throughout production. Gala's Finishing Department had the following costs and production data for October 19X3:

	Transferred In	Materials	Conversion	Total
Beginning work in process inventory costs	$283,550	$ 8,500	$ 12,750	$304,800
Current costs added in October . .	?	116,660	169,464	?
Total costs to be accounted for . . .	$?	$125,160	$182,214	$?

Units in beginning work in process inventory (60% complete as to materials and 60% complete as to conversion)	27,000
Units transferred in from the Cutting Department and started into production during October	128,000
Total units to be accounted for	155,000
Units in ending work in process inventory (50% complete as to materials and 50% complete as to conversion)	<32,000>
Units completed and transferred out during October	123,000
Units in beginning work in process inventory	<27,000>
Units started and completed during October	96,000

Required:
For each department:

1. Prepare a cost of production report for October using the FIFO method.
2. Make the journal entry transferring costs out of work in process inventory at October 31.

12–3B. Learning Objectives 2, 3, 4. Preparing Cost of Production Reports and Making the Journal Entries Transferring Costs Out of Work In Process Inventories for a Company with Three Departments.

Dell Inc., which manufactures its product in three departments, had the following costs and production information for November 19X3.

Cutting Department

	Materials	Conversion	Total
Beginning work in process inventory costs	$ 15,750	$ 17,500	$ 33,250
Current costs added in November	627,900	414,920	1,042,820
Total costs to be accounted for	$643,650	$432,420	$1,076,070

Units in beginning work in process inventory (100% complete as to materials and 30% complete as to conversion)	7,500
Units started into production during November	115,000
Total units to be accounted for	122,500
Units in ending work in process inventory (100% complete as to materials and 50% complete as to conversion) . . . . : . . .	<15,000>
Units completed and transferred out during November	107,500
Units in beginning work in process inventory	<7,500>
Units started and completed during November	100,000

Assembling Department	Transferred In	Materials	Conversion	Total
Beginning work in process inventory costs	$134,810	$ 9,450	$ 8,000	$152,260
Current costs added in November	?	236,995	305,939	?
Total costs to be accounted for .	$?	$246,445	$313,939	$?

Units in beginning work in process inventory (45% complete as to materials and 45% complete as to conversion)	13,500
Units in ending work in process inventory (60% complete as to materials and 60% complete as to conversion)	18,000

Finishing Department	Materials	Conversion	Total
Beginning work in process inventory costs	$288,570	$ 13,200	$301,770
Current costs added in November	?	$360,512	?
Total costs to be accounted for	$?	$373,712	$?

Units in beginning work in process inventory (60% complete as to conversion)	17,000
Units in ending work in process inventory (50% complete as to conversion)	10,000

Required:

For each department:

1. Prepare a cost of production report for November using the FIFO method.
2. Make the journal entry transferring costs out of work in process inventory at November 30.

CASE FOR CRITICAL THINKING

After taking a cost accounting course at Star Community College, Marge Jones wonders why the FIFO method is generally preferred over the weighted average cost method. Marge reasons that the weighted average method is easier to apply and results in an averaging of beginning costs and current costs. Explain why the FIFO method is preferred by many accountants.

ANSWERS TO SELF-STUDY QUIZ 12–1

SHORT, INC.
Cost of Production Report—FIFO
For April 19X4

Quantities

1. Units to account for:
   From beginning work in process . . . . –0–
   Started into production this month 55,000
   Total units to account for 55,000

2. Units accounted for:
   Completed and transferred out 45,000
   From ending work in process (30% complete as to materials and 30% complete as
     to conversion) 10,000
   Total units accounted for 55,000

3. Equivalent production:

	Equivalent Units	
	Materials	**Conversion**
Completed and transferred out	45,000	45,000
Ending work in process inventory:		
Materials (10,000 × 30%)	3,000	
Conversion (10,000 × 30%)		3,000
Total equivalent units	48,000	48,000

4. Costs to account for:

Costs

	Total Costs		Equivalent Units		Unit Cost
Materials	$162,720	÷	48,000	=	$3.39
Conversion	204,000	÷	48,000	=	4.25
Totals	$366,720				$7.64

5. Costs accounted for:
   Transferred out:
     Work in process—April 1, 19X4 . . . . $ –0–
   Started and completed:
     Materials (45,000 × $3.39) $152,550
     Conversion (45,000 × $4.25) 191,250   343,800
   Total cost of units transferred out   343,800
   Work in process—April 30, 19X4:
     Materials (10,000 × 30% × $3.39) . . . . $ 10,170
     Conversion (10,000 × 30% × $4.25) 12,750   22,920
   Total costs accounted for (48,000 × $7.64) $366,720

	19X4					
1	Apr.	30	Finished Goods Inventory	34380000		1
2			Work in Process Inventory		34380000	2

ANSWERS TO SELF-STUDY QUIZ 12–2

SHORT, INC.
Cost of Production Report—FIFO
For May 19X4

Quantities

1. Units to account for:
   From beginning work in process 6,500
   Started into production this month 72,000
   Total units to account for 78,500

2. Units accounted for:
   From beginning work in process (30% complete as to materials and 40% complete as
     to conversion) 6,500
   Started and completed 52,500
   From ending work in process (75% complete as to materials and 80% complete as
     to conversion) 19,500
   Total units accounted for 78,500

3. Equivalent production:

	Equivalent Units	
	Materials	**Conversion**
Beginning work in process inventory:		
Materials (6,500 × 70%)	4,550	
Conversion (6,500 × 60%)		3,900
Started and completed	52,500	52,500
Ending work in process inventory:		
Materials (19,500 × 75%)	14,625	
Conversion (19,500 × 80%)		15,600
Total equivalent units	71,675	72,000

(Continued)

Costs

4. Costs to account for:

	Total Costs	Equivalent Units	Unit Cost
Materials:			
From beginning work in process...........................	$ 8,000		
Current month's costs	209,291 ÷ 71,675		= $2.92
Conversion:			
From beginning work in process...........................	9,000		
Current month's costs	246,240 ÷ 72,000		= 3.42
Totals...	$472,531		$6.34

5. Costs accounted for:
   Transferred out:
   Work in process—May 1, 19X4:

Beginning work in process inventory	$ 17,000	
Materials (6,500 × 70% × $2.92)	13,286	
Conversion (6,500 × 60% × $3.42)	13,338	$ 43,624

   Started and completed:

Materials (52,500 × $2.92)	153,300	
Conversion (52,500 × $3.42)	179,550	332,850
Total cost of units transferred out		376,474

   Work in process—May 31, 19X4:

Materials (19,500 × 75% × $2.92)	$ 42,705	
Conversion (19,500 × 80% × $3.42)	53,352	96,057
Total costs accounted for		$472,531

	19X4					
1	May	31	Finished Goods Inventory	376 47 4 00		1
2			Work in Process Inventory		376 47 4 00	2

Chapter 13
Units Lost or Increased in Production

LEARNING OBJECTIVES

After studying Chapter 13, you should be able to:

1. Explain the difference between normal and abnormal spoilage.
2. Compute how normal spoilage affects the computation of unit cost, cost transferred to the next department (or to finished goods inventory), and the cost of ending work in process inventory.
3. Compute how abnormal spoilage affects the computation of unit cost, cost transferred to the next department (or to finished goods inventory), and the cost of ending work in process inventory.
4. Compute how the addition of direct materials in subsequent departments (resulting in an increase in the number of units produced) affects the calculation of product costs.

n Chapters 11 and 12, we worked with the two principal costing methods used in process costing systems: (1) the weighted average cost method and (2) the FIFO cost method. In every example we used, we assumed that there were no units lost or spoiled during the production process. That is, we assumed that all units placed in production were completed in a salable form. In reality, some units are lost or spoiled during most production processes.

In this chapter, we will discuss how the introduction of lost or spoiled units will affect the costing of units transferred to the next department (or to finished goods inventory) and the costing of the ending work in process inventory. We will also discuss how the addition of direct materials in subsequent departments, which results in an increase in the number of units produced, will affect the computation of the costs of completed and transferred units and the costs of ending work in process inventory.

TYPES OF LOST OR SPOILED UNITS

Since production in a process costing environment is done on a continuous basis and usually with the use of high speed machinery, the production process may occasionally produce units that do not meet the quality standards that have been established for good units. Also, production workers occasionally make mistakes which result in finished units that cannot be considered good units.

Such units may be lost due to spoilage or other factors such as evaporation, shrinkage, leakage, condensation, seepage, defects, or other factors in the production process. A *defective unit* can be economically reworked to bring it up to standard. However, a *spoiled unit* is so unacceptable that it cannot be economically reworked to be brought up to standard.

The accounting for lost units depends on two factors:

1. Whether the lost units resulted from normal or abnormal spoilage.
2. Whether the lost units were discovered in the first producing department or in subsequent departments.

LEARNING OBJECTIVE 1   **Normal spoilage** is defined as spoilage expected (because of the type of production process) and within the tolerance limits set by the company for human and machine error. One would expect to lose these units under efficient operating conditions.

Abnormal spoilage is defined as spoilage in excess of normal spoilage. A company does not expect such spoilage during efficient operating conditions and can more likely prevent abnormal spoilage than normal spoilage. Abnormal spoilage would occur, for example, if production machinery were set incorrectly for a particular process and the units produced before the error was discovered did not meet established quality standards.

Accounting for normal spoilage is different from accounting for abnormal spoilage. The cost of normal spoilage is absorbed by the good units produced, while the cost of abnormal spoilage is charged out as a current period expense or loss.

NORMAL SPOILAGE IN A COMPANY WITH ONE PRODUCING DEPARTMENT

LEARNING OBJECTIVE 2   When a company has only one producing department or process, the cost of normal spoilage is simply spread over the good units transferred to finished goods inventory and the units in ending work in process inventory. This results in a higher cost for these units since fewer units exist to spread the total cost over. To illustrate, we will again use our example of Alpha Company (introduced in Chapter 10). During May, Alpha had the following production and cost data:

Units to account for:

Units in beginning work in process inventory	-0-
Units started into production during May	50,000
Total units to account for	50,000
Units in ending work in process inventory (60% complete for materials and 50% complete for conversion)	<5,000>
Units lost due to normal spoilage	<3,000>
Units completed and transferred out during May	42,000

Costs to account for:

	Materials	Conversion	Total
Costs in beginning work in process inventory . . .	-0-	-0-	-0-
Current costs added in May	$157,500	$200,250	$357,750
Total costs to account for	$157,500	$200,250	$357,750

Notice that Alpha placed 50,000 units into production during May. Of these units, 5,000 were still being worked on at month-end, and 3,000 units had been lost in the production process due to normal spoilage. This leaves 42,000 units (50,000 – 8,000) actually transferred to finished goods inventory. To assign a cost to the finished units, and the units in ending work in process inventory, we first compute equivalent units of production.

Materials:

Units transferred to finished goods: 42,000 × 100%	42,000
Units in ending work in process inventory: 5,000 × 60%	3,000
Units spoiled: 3,000 × 0%	-0-
Equivalent units for materials	45,000

Conversion:

Units transferred to finished goods: 42,000 × 100%	42,000
Units in ending work in process inventory: 5,000 × 50%	2,500
Units spoiled: 3,000 × 0%	-0-
Equivalent units for conversion	44,500

Notice that a finished equivalent of 0% is assumed for the 3,000 spoiled units, which means that the cost associated with these units will be allocated between the 42,000 good units completed and the 5,000 units in ending work in process inventory. We now compute Alpha's cost per equivalent unit for May, as follows:

Materials cost per equivalent unit:

$$\frac{\text{Materials cost}}{\text{Equivalent units}} = \frac{\$157,500}{45,000} = \$3.50$$

Conversion cost per equivalent unit:

$$\frac{\text{Conversion cost}}{\text{Equivalent units}} = \frac{\$200,250}{44,500} = \underline{\$4.50}$$

Total equivalent unit cost for May . . $\underline{\$8.00}$

We can now compute the cost of the finished units and the cost of units remaining in ending work in process inventory, as follows:

Cost of finished units:		
42,000 units × $8.00		$336,000
Cost of the ending work in process inventory:		
Materials: 5,000 × 60% × $3.50	$10,500	
Conversion: 5,000 × 50% × $4.50	11,250	
Cost of ending work in process inventory		21,750
Total cost accounted for		$357,750

Figure 13–1 shows Alpha's cost of production report for May. The following journal entry transfers the cost of the completed units to Finished Goods Inventory.

1	May	31	Finished Goods Inventory	336 00 0 00		1
2			Work in Process Inventory		336 00 0 00	2
3			Transferred 42,000 completed units.			3

NOTE In the preceding example, Alpha Company did not have a beginning work in process inventory. Had there been a beginning inventory, the calculations would be the same, except that the beginning costs would have been added to the current costs before dividing by the number of equivalent units (assuming the use of the weighted average cost method).

ALPHA CO.
Cost of Production Report
For May

Quantities

1. Units to account for:
   From beginning work in process . . . .   –0–
   Started into production this month   50,000
   Total units to account for   50,000

2. Units accounted for:
   Completed and transferred out   42,000
   From ending work in process (60% complete as to materials and 50% complete as
      to conversion)   5,000
   Units lost due to normal spoilage   3,000
   Total units accounted for   50,000

3. Equivalent production:

	Equivalent Units	
	Materials	**Conversion**
Completed and transferred out	42,000	42,000
Ending work in process inventory:		
Materials (5,000 × 60%)	3,000	
Conversion (5,000 × 50%)		2,500
Total equivalent units	45,000	44,500

Costs

4. Costs to account for:

	Total Costs		**Equivalent Units**		**Unit Cost**
Materials	$157,500	÷	45,000	=	$3.50
Conversion	200,250	÷	44,500	=	4.50
Totals	$357,750				$8.00

5. Costs accounted for:
   Completed and transferred out (42,000 × $8.00) $336,000
   Work in process—
     Materials (5,000 × 60% × $3.50) $10,500
     Conversion (5,000 × 50% × $4.50)   11,250   21,750
   Total costs accounted for $357,750

FIGURE 13–1
Cost of
Production Report—
Alpha Company

SELF-STUDY QUIZ 13–1 Arnold Company had the following production and cost data for April:

Units to account for:

Units in beginning work in process inventory	-0-
Units started into production during April	70,000
Total units to account for	70,000
Units in ending work in process inventory (100% complete for	
materials and 50% complete for conversion)	<10,000>
Units lost due to normal spoilage	<2,000>
Units completed and transferred out during April	58,000

Costs to account for:

	Materials	Conversion	Total
Costs in beginning work in			
process inventory	-0-	-0-	-0-
Current costs added in April	$267,920	$325,710	$593,630
Total costs to account for	$267,920	$325,710	$593,630

Prepare a cost of production report for April.
Answers at end of chapter.

NORMAL SPOILAGE IN A COMPANY WITH TWO PRODUCING DEPARTMENTS

When a company has two or more producing departments where units of product are spoiled or lost in subsequent departments, the calculations are more complicated—due to the costs transferred in from the prior department. When prior department costs are initially transferred in, a specific number of units are identified with the costs. If some of the transferred-in units are lost or spoiled, the transferred-in unit cost must be recalculated based on the reduced number of goods units, causing an increase in unit cost. To illustrate this, we will use a slightly modified version of our earlier example of Grant Company. In this example, we will use weighted average costing and assume that Grant had the following production and cost data for August:

Department 1

Units to account for:

Units in beginning work in process inventory (75% complete as to	
materials and 40% complete as to conversion)	10,000
Units started into production during August	50,000
Total units to account for	60,000

Units in ending work in process inventory (80% complete as to
  materials and 50% complete as to conversion) . . . .   <8,000>
Units lost due to normal spoilage . . . .   <1,000>
Units completed and transferred out during August   51,000
Units in beginning work in process inventory . . . .   <10,000>
Units started and completed during August   41,000

Costs to account for:

	Materials	**Conversion**	**Total**
Costs in beginning work in process inventory	$ 23,780	$ 20,000	$ 43,780
Current costs added in August	221,318	274,250	495,568
Total costs to account for	$245,098	$294,250	$539,348

We can now compute Department 1's equivalent units for August:

Materials:
Units in beginning work in process inventory: 10,000 × 100%   10,000
Units started and completed during August: 41,000 × 100%   41,000
Units in ending work in process inventory: 8,000 × 80%   6,400
Units spoiled: 1,000 × 0% . . . .   -0-
Equivalent units for materials   57,400

Conversion:
Units in beginning work in process inventory: 10,000 × 100%   10,000
Units started and completed during August: 41,000 × 100%   41,000
Units in ending work in process inventory: 8,000 × 50%   4,000
Units spoiled: 1,000 × 0% . . . .   -0-
Equivalent units for conversion   55,000

We now compute cost per equivalent unit using the weighted average cost
method.

Materials cost per equivalent unit:

$$\frac{\text{Beginning cost + Current cost}}{\text{Equivalent units of production}} = \frac{\$23,780 + \$221,318}{57,400} = \frac{\$245,098}{57,400} = \$4.27$$

Conversion cost per equivalent unit:

$$\frac{\text{Beginning cost + Current cost}}{\text{Equivalent units of production}} = \frac{\$20,000 + \$274,250}{55,000} = \frac{\$294,250}{55,000} = \$5.35$$

Total equivalent unit cost for August $9.62

We account for Department 1's costs for August as follows:

Cost of units transferred to Dept. 2:
  51,000 units × $9.62 . . . . $490,620
Ending work in process inventory:
  Materials: 8,000 × 80% × $4.27 . . . . $27,328
  Conversion: 8,000 × 50% × $5.35   21,400
Cost of ending work in process inventory   48,728
Total cost accounted for $539,348

Figure 13–2 shows Department 1's weighted average cost of production report for August. The following journal entry shows the total cost of units transferred to Department 2.

1	Aug.	31	Work in Process Inventory—Dept. 2		490 62 000		1
2			Work in Process Inventory—Dept. 1			490 62 000	2
3			Transferred 51,000 units to Dept. 2.				3

Department 2

Department 2 had the following production and cost data for August.

Units to account for:

Units in beginning work in process inventory (60% complete as to materials and 50% complete as to conversion)	12,000
Units transferred in from Dept. 1	51,000
Total units to account for	63,000
Units in ending work in process inventory (60% complete as to materials and 40% complete as to conversion)	<11,000>
Units lost due to normal spoilage	<2,000>
Units completed and transferred out during August	50,000
Units in beginning work in process inventory	<12,000>
Units started and completed during August	38,000

Costs to account for:

	Transferred in	Materials	Conversion	Total
Costs in beginning work in process inventory	$116,330	$ 28,800	$ 30,000	$ 175,130
Current costs added in August	490,620	210,618	262,128	963,366
Total costs to account for	$606,950	$239,418	$292,128	$1,138,496

We can now compute Department 2's equivalent units for August:

	Transferred In	Materials	Conversion
Units in beginning work in process inventory: 12,000 × 100%	12,000	12,000	12,000
Units started and transferred out in August: 38,000 × 100%	38,000	38,000	38,000
Units in ending work in process			
Transferred in: 11,000 × 100%	11,000		
Materials: 11,000 × 60%		6,600	
Conversion: 11,000 × 40%			4,400
Total equivalent units	61,000	56,600	54,400

GRANT CO.—Dept. 1
Cost of Production Report—Weighted Average
For August 19X3

Quantities

1. Units to account for:
   From beginning work in process 10,000
   Started into production this month 50,000
   Total units to account for 60,000

2. Units accounted for:
   From beginning work in process 10,000
   Started and completed 41,000
   From ending work in process (80% complete as to materials and 50% complete as
       to conversion) 8,000
   Units lost due to normal spoilage 1,000
   Total units accounted for 60,000

3. Equivalent production:

	Equivalent Units	
	Materials	**Conversion**
Beginning work in process inventory	10,000	10,000
Started and completed	41,000	41,000
Ending work in process inventory:		
Materials (8,000 × 80%)	6,400	
Conversion (8,000 × 50%)		4,000
Total equivalent units	57,400	55,000

Costs

4. Costs to account for:

	Total Costs	**Equivalent Units**	**Unit Cost**
Materials	$245,098	÷ 57,400	= $4.27
Conversion	294,250	÷ 55,000	= 5.35
Totals	$539,348		$9.62

5. Costs accounted for:
   Completed and transferred out (51,000 × $9.62) $490,620
       Work in process—August 31, 19X3:
       Materials (8,000 × 80% × $4.27) $27,328
       Conversion (8,000 × 50% × $5.35)   21,400   48,728
   Total costs accounted for $539,348

FIGURE 13–2
Cost of Production
Report—Grant
Company Dept. 1

We compute costs per equivalent unit as follows:

Transferred-in costs:

$$\frac{\$116{,}330 + \$490{,}620}{61{,}000} = \frac{\$606{,}950}{61{,}000} = \quad \$9.95$$

Materials costs:

$$\frac{\$28{,}800 + \$210{,}618}{56{,}600} = \frac{\$239{,}418}{56{,}600} = \quad \$4.23$$

Conversion costs:

$$\frac{\$30{,}000 + \$262{,}128}{54{,}400} = \frac{\$292{,}128}{54{,}400} = \quad \underline{\$5.37}$$

Total cost per equivalent unit . . . . $\underline{\$19.55}$

We account for Department 2's costs for August as follows:

Units transferred to finished goods inventory:		
50,000 × $19.55		$ 977,500
Ending work in process inventory:		
Transferred-in costs: 11,000 × $9.95	$109,450	
Materials: 11,000 × 60% × $4.23	27,918	
Conversion: 11,000 × 40% × $5.37	23,628	160,996
Total cost accounted for		$1,138,496

Figure 13–3 shows the August cost of production report for Department 2. Notice that the calculation of equivalent units does not include spoiled units which decreases the total number of equivalent units and thus increases the cost per equivalent unit. The following journal entry records the total cost of units transferred to Finished Goods Inventory.

1	Aug.	31	Finished Goods Inventory	97 7 5 0 00 0		1
2			Work in Process Inventory—Dept. 2		97 7 5 0 00 0	2
3			Transferred 50,000 completed units.			3

GRANT CO.—Dept. 2
Cost of Production Report—Weighted Average
For August 19X3
Quantities

1. Units to account for:

From beginning work in process	12,000
Started into production this month	51,000
Total units to account for	63,000

2. Units accounted for:

From beginning work in process	12,000
Started and completed	38,000
From ending work in process (60% complete as to materials and 40% complete as to conversion)	11,000
Units lost due to normal spoilage	2,000
Total units accounted for	63,000

3. Equivalent production:

	Equivalent Units		
	Transferred In	Materials	Conversion
Beginning work in process inventory	12,000	12,000	12,000
Started and completed	38,000	38,000	38,000
Ending work in process inventory:			
Transferred in (11,000 × 100%)	11,000		
Materials (11,000 × 60%)		6,600	
Conversion (11,000 × 40%)			4,400
Total equivalent units	61,000	56,600	54,400

Costs

4. Costs to account for:

	Total Costs		Equivalent Units		Unit Cost
Transferred in	$ 606,950	÷	61,000	=	$ 9.95
Materials	239,418	÷	56,600	=	4.23
Conversion	292,128	÷	54,400	=	5.37
Totals	$1,138,496				$19.55

5. Costs accounted for:

Completed and transferred out (50,000 × $19.55)		$ 977,500
Work in process—August 31, 19X3:		
Transferred in (11,000 × $9.95)	$109,450	
Materials (11,000 × 60% × $4.23)	27,918	
Conversion (11,000 × 40% × $5.37)	23,628	160,996
Total costs accounted for		$1,138,496

FIGURE 13–3

Cost of Production Report—Grant Company Dept. 2

SELF-STUDY QUIZ 13–2 The Finishing Department of Janson Company had the following production data for July:

Units in beginning work in process inventory (70% complete as to materials and 50% complete as to conversion)	8,000
Units transferred in from the Assembly Department	53,000
Total units to account for	61,000
Units in ending work in process inventory (60% complete as to materials and 45% complete as to conversion)	<10,000>
Units lost due to normal spoilage	<1,000>
Units completed and transferred out during July	50,000
Units in beginning work in process inventory	<8,000>
Units started and completed during July	42,000

Using the weighted average cost method, calculate the June equivalent units of production for the Finishing Department.
Answers at end of chapter.

ABNORMAL SPOILAGE

LEARNING OBJECTIVE 3   When units are lost or spoiled during production due to unusual circumstances that *could have* been avoided, the resulting abnormal loss *should not* be assigned to the remaining goods units. Instead, the cost of such units should be recorded as a loss in the current period. To illustrate abnormal spoilage, we will use the example of Omega Company, which has two producing departments. Assume that Omega's Department 1 had the following production and cost data for June:

Units to account for:

Units in beginning work in process inventory (100% complete as to materials and 50% complete as to conversion)	10,000
Units started into production during June	50,000
Total units to account for	60,000
Units in ending work in process inventory (100% complete as to materials and 50% complete as to conversion)	<5,000>
Units lost due to normal spoilage	<2,000>
Units lost due to abnormal spoilage	<3,000>
Units completed and transferred out during June	50,000
Units in beginning work in process inventory	<10,000>
Units started and completed during June	40,000

Costs to account for:

	Materials	Conversion	Total
Costs in beginning work in process inventory	$ 21,000	$ 33,000	$ 54,000
Current costs added in June	173,300	250,050	423,350
Total costs to be accounted for	$194,300	$283,050	$477,350

We compute equivalent units of production as follows:

	Materials	Conversion
Beginning work in process inventory: 10,000 × 100% ...	10,000	10,000
Units started and finished: 40,000 × 100%	40,000	40,000
Ending work in process inventory:		
Materials: 5,000 × 100%	5,000	
Conversion: 5,000 × 50%		2,500
Normal spoilage: 2,000 × 0%	-0-	-0-
Abnormal spoilage	3,000	3,000
Total equivalent units	58,000	55,500

Notice that the calculation of equivalent units *does not* include the number of units lost due to normal spoilage. This, as you recall, results in the cost of these units being absorbed by the good units completed. Notice, however, that the calculation of equivalent units *does include* the number of units due to abnormal spoilage. This takes place because we must determine a cost for these units so that a journal entry can be made charging the lost to the current period. We can now compute Omega's costs per equivalent unit for June.

Materials:

$$\frac{\$21,000 + \$173,300}{58,000} = \frac{\$194,300}{58,000} = \$3.35$$

Conversion:

$$\frac{\$33,000 + \$250,050}{55,500} = \frac{\$283,050}{55,500} = \underline{\$5.10}$$

Total cost for equivalent unit . . . . $\underline{\$8.45}$

We can now account for costs as follows:

Costs transferred to Dept. 2:		
Total cost of goods units: 50,000 × $8.45		$422,500
Cost of abnormal spoilage:		
Materials: 3,000 × $3.35	$10,050	
Conversion: 3,000 × $5.10	15,300	25,350
Total cost of units transferred out		$447,850
Cost of ending work in process inventory:		
Materials: 5,000 × 100% × $3.35	$16,750	
Conversion: 5,000 × 50% × $5.10	12,750	29,500
Total costs accounted for		$477,350

Figure 13–4 shows the cost of production report for Omega's Department 1 for June. Notice that the 3,000 abnormally spoiled units are assigned a cost of $25,350. The entry on page 349 records this abnormal spoilage loss and the total cost of units transferred to Department 2.

OMEGA CO.—Dept. 1
Cost of Production Report—Weighted Average
For June 19X4

Quantities

1. Units to account for:
   From beginning work in process 10,000
   Started into production this month 50,000
   Total units to account for 60,000

2. Units accounted for:
   From beginning work in process 10,000
   Started and completed 40,000
   From ending work in process (100% complete as to materials and 50% complete as
     to conversion) 5,000
   Units lost due to normal spoilage 2,000
   Units lost due to abnormal spoilage 3,000
   Total units accounted for 60,000

3. Equivalent production:

	Equivalent Units	
	Materials	Conversion
Beginning work in process inventory	10,000	10,000
Started and completed	40,000	40,000
Ending work in process inventory:		
Materials (5,000 × 100%)	5,000	
Conversion (5,000 × 50%)		2,500
Abnormal spoilage	3,000	3,000
Total equivalent units	58,000	55,500

Costs

4. Costs to account for:

	Total Costs	Equivalent Units	Unit Cost
Materials	$194,300 ÷	58,000	= $3.35
Conversion	283,050 ÷	55,500	= 5.10
Totals	$477,350		$8.45

FIGURE 13–4
Cost of
Production Report
—Omega
Company, Dept. 1

(Continued)

5. Costs accounted for:
   Transferred out:
     To Department 2:
       Total cost of good units (50,000 × $8.45) $422,500
     Abnormal spoilage cost:
       Materials (3,000 × $3.35) $10,050
       Conversion (3,000 × $5.10)   15,300   25,350
     Total cost of units transferred out   447,850
   Work in process—August 31, 19X3:
     Materials (5,000 × $3.35)   16,750
     Conversion (5,000 × 50% × $5.10)   12,750   29,500
   Total costs accounted for $477,350

1	June	30	Work in Process Inventory—Dept. 2	422 50 0 00		1
2			Loss from Abnormal Spoilage	25 35 0 00		2
3			Work in Process Inventory—Dept. 1		447 85 0 00	3
4			Recorded abnormal spoilage and cost			4
5			of units transferred to Dept. 2.			5

The above entry would be made whenever the abnormal spoilage occurred. The department in which the spoilage occurs does not matter. If the spoilage occurred in the second department, the amount of the loss would be determined at that time and the entry to record the loss would be made when the good units were transferred out of that department.

Having completed this example, we should emphasize three points. First, the calculation of Department 1's equivalent units for June did not include the 2,000 units lost due to normal spoilage. This results in the 50,000 completed good units having a higher unit cost to absorb the costs associated with the normal spoilage. Second, the calculation of equivalent units for June included abnormal spoilage of 3,000 units. Third, they were assigned a cost so that a loss could be charged to the month in which the units were spoiled.

INCREASES IN PRODUCTION

LEARNING OBJECTIVE 4   In some production processes, the addition of materials in subsequent departments causes the number of units produced to increase. This occurs often in the chemical industry. The accounting difficulties encountered in such a situation are the opposite of those created by lost units. The total costs are applied to a greater number of units, causing the unit cost to decrease. Stated another way, there are more units to spread total costs over, which results in a lower unit product cost.

To illustrate how the accounting for an increase in production differs from the accounting for lost units due to spoilage, we will use the example of Apex Chemical Company. Apex produces a chemical in a two-department process. Additional materials added in Department 2 cause the total number of units to increase beyond those started in Department 1. Department 2 had the following production and cost data for September:

Units to account for:

Units in beginning work in process inventory (100% complete as to materials and 40% complete as to conversion)	12,000
Units transferred in from Dept. 1	48,000
Units added by the production process	25,000
Total units to account for	85,000
Units in ending work in process inventory (100% complete as to materials and 50% complete as to conversion)	<15,000>
Units completed and transferred out during September	70,000
Units in beginning work in process inventory	<12,000>
Units started and completed during September	58,000

Costs to account for:

	Transferred In	Materials	Conversion	Total
Costs in beginning work in process inventory	$ 96,000	$ 24,000	$12,000	$132,000
Current costs added in September . .	414,000	146,000	57,750	617,750
Total costs to account for	$510,000	$170,000	$69,750	$749,750

As you know, we must first compute equivalent units of production in order to calculate Department 2's unit costs for September.

	Transferred In	Materials	Conversion
Beginning work in process inventory:			
12,000 × 100%	12,000	12,000	12,000
Started and completed	58,000	58,000	58,000
Ending work in process inventory:			
Transferred in: 15,000 × 100%	15,000		
Materials: 15,000 × 100%		15,000	
Conversion: 15,000 × 50%			7,500
Total equivalent units	85,000	85,000	77,500

We compute costs per equivalent unit as follows:

Transferred in:

$$\frac{\$96,000 + \$414,000}{85,000} = \frac{\$510,000}{85,000} = \$6.00$$

Materials:

$$\frac{\$24,000 + \$146,000}{85,000} = \frac{\$170,000}{85,000} = 2.00$$

Conversion:

$$\frac{\$12,000 + \$57,750}{77,500} = \frac{\$69,750}{77,500} = .90$$

Total cost per equivalent unit . . . $\underline{\$8.90}$

We account for Department 2's September costs as follows:

Costs transferred out:
   70,000 × $8.90 . . . . $623,000
Cost of ending work in process inventory:
   Transferred in: 15,000 × $6.00 . . . . $90,000
   Materials: 15,000 × $2.00   30,000
   Conversion: 15,000 × 50% × $.90   6,750   126,750
Total costs accounted for $749,750

     Figure 13–5 shows Department 2's cost of production report for September. Notice that the calculation of the units to account for includes an increase of 25,000 units caused by the addition of materials in Department 2. We compute this figure by taking the total units to account for (85,000), and subtracting the units in beginning work in process inventory and the units transferred in from Department 1:

Total units to account for   85,000
Units in beginning work in process inventory . . . .   <12,000>
Units transferred in from Dept. 1 . . . .   <48,000>
Units added by the production process   25,000

     The following entry records the total cost of units transferred to Finished Goods Inventory.

1	Sept.	30	Finished Goods Inventory	623 00 000		1
2			Work in Process Inventory—Dept. 2		623 00 000	2
3			Transferred 70,000 completed units.			3

SELF-STUDY QUIZ 13–3 The Blending Department of Hathaway Chemicals had the following production data for December:

Total units to account for   60,000
Units in beginning work in process inventory   15,000
Units transferred in from the Mixing Department   42,000

Calculate the number of units added by the production process.
Answers at end of chapter.

APEX CHEMICAL CO.—Dept. 2
Cost of Production Report—Weighted Average
For September

Quantities

1. Units to account for:
   From beginning work in process 12,000
   Started into production this month 73,000
   Total units to account for 85,000

2. Units accounted for:
   From beginning work in process 12,000
   Started and completed 58,000
   From ending work in process (100% complete as to materials and 50% complete as
      to conversion) 15,000
   Total units accounted for 85,000

3. Equivalent production:

	Equivalent Units		
	Transferred in	Materials	Conversion
Beginning work in process inventory	12,000	12,000	12,000
Started and completed	58,000	58,000	58,000
Ending work in process inventory:			
Transferred in (15,000 × 100%)	15,000		
Materials (15,000 × 100%)		15,000	
Conversion (15,000 × 50%)			7,500
Total equivalent units	85,000	85,000	77,500

Costs

4. Costs to account for:

	Total Costs		Equivalent Units		Unit Cost
Transferred in	$510,000	÷	85,000	=	$ 6.00
Materials	170,000	÷	85,000	=	2.00
Conversion	69,750	÷	77,500	=	.90
Totals	$749,750				$ 8.90

5. Costs accounted for:
   Completed and transferred out (70,000 × $8.90) $623,000
   Work in process—August 31, 19X3:
      Transferred in (15,000 × $6.00) $90,000
      Materials (15,000 × $2.00) 30,000
      Conversion (15,000 × 50% × $0.90) 6,750   126,750
   Total costs accounted for $749,750

FIGURE 13–5
*Cost of Production
Report—Apex
Chemical Company
Dept. 2*

SELF-STUDY PROBLEM

Assume that South Company—which has been covered in Chapters 10, 11, and 12—had the following costs and production information, by department, for August 19X3.

Cutting Department	Materials	Conversion	Total
Beginning work in process inventory costs . .	$ 15,110	$ 5,090	$ 20,200
Current costs added in August	183,378	61,150	244,528
Total costs to be accounted for	$198,488	$66,240	$264,728

Units in beginning work in process inventory (65% complete as to materials and 40% complete as to conversion)	11,000
Units started into production during August	50,000
Total units to be accounted for	61,000
Units in ending work in process inventory (70% complete as to materials and 45% complete as to conversion)	<10,000>
Units lost due to normal spoilage	<300>
Units lost due to abnormal spoilage	<1,000>
Units completed and transferred out during August	49,700
Units in beginning work in process inventory	<11,000>
Units started and completed during August	38,700

Sewing Department	Transferred In	Conversion	Total
Beginning work in process inventory costs . .	$33,142	$ 21,740	$54,882
Current costs added in August	?	223,120	?
Total costs to be accounted for	$?	$244,860	$?

Units in beginning work in process inventory (55% complete as to conversion)	13,000
Units in ending work in process inventory (65% complete as to conversion)	12,000
Units lost due to normal spoilage	200
Units lost due to abnormal spoilage	800

Dyeing Department	Transferred In	Materials	Conversion	Total
Beginning work in process inventory costs	$66,902	$ 5,425	$ 7,374	$79,701
Current costs added in August	?	38,388	54,550	?
Total costs to be accounted for	$?	$43,813	$61,924	$?

Units in beginning work in process inventory (55% complete as to materials and 55% complete as to conversion)	13,000
Units in ending work in process inventory (55% complete as to materials and 40% complete as to conversion)	14,000
Units lost due to normal spoilage	500
Units lost due to abnormal spoilage	2,000

Required:
1. Prepare cost of production reports for August.
2. Make the general journal entry to transfer costs out of work in process inventory at August 31 for each department using the weighted average method.

SOLUTION TO SELF-STUDY PROBLEM

SOUTH COMPANY—Cutting Dept.
Cost of Production Report—Weighted Average
For August 19X3

Quantities

1. Units to account for:
   From beginning work in process 11,000
   Started into production this month. 50,000
   Total units to account for. 61,000

2. Units accounted for:
   From beginning work in process 11,000
   Started and completed 38,700
   From ending work in process (70% complete as to materials and 45% complete as
      to conversion) 10,000
   Units lost due to normal spoilage 300
   Units lost due to abnormal spoilage 1,000
   Total units accounted for. 61,000

3. Equivalent production:

	Equivalent Units	
	Materials	**Conversion**
Beginning work in process inventory	11,000	11,000
Started and completed	38,700	38,700
Ending work in process inventory:		
Materials (10,000 × 70%)	7,000	
Conversion (10,000 × 45%)		4,500
Abnormal spoilage	1,000	1,000
Total equivalent units	57,700	55,200

Costs

4. Costs to account for:

	Total Costs		Equivalent Units		Unit Cost
Materials	$198,488	÷	57,700	=	$3.44
Conversion	66,240	÷	55,200	=	1.20
Totals	$264,728				$4.64

(*Continued*)

5. Costs accounted for:
    Transferred out:
      To Sewing Dept.:

Total cost of good units (49,700 × $4.64)......................		$230,608
Abnormal spoilage cost:		
Materials (1,000 × $3.44)......................	$ 3,440	
Conversion (1,000 × $1.20).....................	1,200	4,640
Total cost of units transferred out		235,248
Work in process—August 31:		
Materials (10,000 × 70% × $3.44)......................	24,080	
Conversion (10,000 × 45% × $1.20)	5,400	29,480
Total costs accounted for...........................		$264,728

	19X3				
1	Aug.	31	Work in Process—Sewing Dept.	230 60 800	1
2			Loss from Abnormal Spoilage	4 64 000	2
3			Work in Process—Cutting Dept.	235 24 800	3

SOUTH COMPANY—Sewing Dept.
Cost of Production Report—Weighted Average
For August 19X3

Quantities

1. Units to account for:

From beginning work in process..	13,000
Started into production this month..	49,700
Total units to account for...	62,700

2. Units accounted for:

From beginning work in process..	13,000
Started and completed	36,700
From ending work in process (65% complete as to conversion)	12,000
Units lost due to normal spoilage	200
Units lost due to abnormal spoilage	800
Total units accounted for...	62,700

3. Equivalent production:

	Transferred in	Conversion
Beginning work in process inventory	13,000	13,000
Started and completed..	36,700	36,700
Ending work in process inventory:		
Transferred in (12,000 × 100%)	12,000	
Conversion (12,000 × 65%)		7,800
Abnormal spoilage..	800	800
Total equivalent units...	62,500	58,300

(Continued)

Costs

4. Costs to account for:

	Total Costs		Equivalent Units		Unit Cost
Transferred in	$263,750	÷	62,500	=	$4.22
Conversion	244,860	÷	58,300	=	4.20
Totals	$508,610				$8.42

5. Costs accounted for:
   Transferred out:
   To Dyeing Dept.:

Total cost of good units (49,700 × $8.42)		$418,474
Abnormal spoilage cost:		
Transferred in (800 × $4.22)	$ 3,376	
Conversion (800 × $4.20)	3,360	6,736
Total cost of units transferred out		425,210
Work in process—August 31:		
Transferred in (12,000 × $4.22)	50,640	
Conversion (12,000 × 65% × $4.20)	32,760	83,400
Total costs accounted for		$508,610

	19X3					
1	Aug.	31	Work in Process Inventory—Dyeing Dept.	418 4 7 4 00		1
2			Loss from Abnormal Spoilage	6 7 3 6 00		2
3			Work in Process Inventory—Sewing Dept.		425 2 1 0 00	3

SOUTH COMPANY—Dyeing Dept.
Cost of Production Report—Weighted Average
For August 19X3

Quantities

1. Units to account for:

From beginning work in process	13,000
Started into production this month	50,700
Total units to account for	63,700

2. Units accounted for:

From beginning work in process	13,000
Started and completed	34,200
From ending work in process (55% complete as to materials and 40% complete as to conversion)	14,000
Units lost due to normal spoilage	500
Units lost due to abnormal spoilage	2,000
Total units accounted for	63,700

(Continued)

3. Equivalent production:

	Equivalent Units		
	Transferred In	**Materials**	**Conversion**
Beginning work in process inventory	13,000	13,000	13,000
Started and completed	34,200	34,200	34,200
Ending work in process inventory:			
Transferred in (14,000 × 100%).........................	14,000		
Materials (14,000 × 55%)..............................		7,700	
Conversion (14,000 × 40%)			5,600
Abnormal spoilage......................................	2,000	2,000	2,000
Total equivalent units	63,200	56,900	54,800

Costs

4. Costs to account for:

	Total Costs		Equivalent Units		Unit Cost
Transferred in	$485,376	÷	63,200	=	$7.68
Materials...	43,813	÷	56,900	=	.77
Conversion	61,924	÷	54,800	=	1.13
Totals	$591,113				$9.58

5. Costs accounted for:
   Transferred out:
   To finished goods:

Total cost of good units (47,200 × $9.58)		$452,176
Abnormal spoilage cost:		
Transferred in (2,000 × $7.68)	$ 15,360	
Materials (2,000 × $0.77)	1,540	
Conversion (2,000 × $1.13).....................................	2,260	19,160
Total cost of units transferred out		471,336
Work in process—August 31:		
Transferred in (14,000 × $7.68)	$107,520	
Materials (14,000 × 55% × $0.77)	5,929	
Conversion (14,000 × 40% × $1.13).............................	6,328	119,777
Total costs accounted for		$591,113

	19X3				
1	Aug.	31	Finished Goods Inventory	452 176 00		1
2			Loss from Abnormal Spoilage	19 160 00		2
3			Work in Process Inventory—Dyeing Dept.		471 336 00	3

SUMMARY

In this chapter, we concluded our study of process costing by examining units lost or increased in production. We learned that units in production can be lost due to normal and abnormal spoilage. **Normal spoilage** is expected based on the nature of the process and falls within the tolerance range set by company management for human and machine error. **Abnormal spoilage** is spoilage in excess of normal spoilage. Such spoilage is not expected during efficient operating conditions and can more likely be prevented than normal spoilage.

Costs associated with normal spoilage are absorbed by the goods units produced, resulting in an increase in unit product cost. Costs associated with abnormal spoilage are charged to a loss account in the period in which the spoilage occurred.

Some production processes cause materials added in a department other than the first to increase the number of units produced. When this happens, the accounting is the opposite of that for normal spoilage. Whereas, normal spoilage results in a decrease in the number of units produced with a resulting higher unit cost, an increase in the number of units produced results in a lower unit cost.

KEY TERMS

Abnormal Spoilage. Spoilage in excess of the expected normal amount or rate. It could have been avoided.

Normal Spoilage. Spoilage expected to be incurred in the production process under regular conditions. It can be caused by human or machine error; or it can be due to such factors as evaporation, shrinkage, leakage, condensation, seepage, or defects.

QUESTIONS FOR REVIEW

1. What is normal spoilage and how does it differ from abnormal spoilage?
2. How does normal spoilage affect the computation of equivalent units?
3. How does abnormal spoilage affect the computation of equivalent units?
4. What could cause the number of units to increase during the production process?
5. Does normal spoilage affect transferred in costs differently than do material and conversion costs?
6. How is the increase in the number of units produced computed?
7. If a company started the month with 12,000 units in beginning work in process, started 55,000 units in production, transferred 60,000 out, and had 5,000 units remaining in ending work in process, how many units were lost?
8. If a company that adds materials in the second department starts the month with 10,000 units in beginning work in process, transferred in 50,000 units, had 15,000 remaining in ending work in process, and transferred out 70,000 units, how many additional units were added in production?
9. What effect does an increase in the number of units produced have on the equivalent unit cost?

EXERCISES

13–1. Learning Objective 2. Computing Equivalent Units of Production for Materials.

Green Co. began the month with 12,000 units in process (100% complete as to materials) and started into production another 55,000 units during the month. Ending work in process (80% complete as to materials) consisted of 15,000 units, while 50,000 units were transferred to finished goods inventory.

Assuming Green Co. uses the weighted average process costing method and that all spoilage is considered normal, calculate the equivalent units of production for materials.

13–2. Learning Objective 2. Computing Equivalent Units and Costs of Production for Materials for a Company with One Department.

Grand Co. had the following materials costs and production information for May 19X4.

	Materials
Beginning work in process inventory costs	$ 16,000
Current costs added in May	200,000
Total costs to be accounted for	$216,000
Units in beginning work in process inventory	
(70% complete as to materials)	10,000
Units started into production during May	50,000
Total units to be accounted for	60,000
Units in ending work in process inventory	
(60% complete as to materials)	<10,000>
Units lost due to normal spoilage	<2,000>
Units completed and transferred out during May	48,000
Units in beginning work in process inventory	<10,000>
Units started and completed during May	38,000

Assuming Grand Co. uses the weighted average process costing method, calculate the equivalent units and costs of production for materials.

13–3. Learning Objectives 2, 3. Preparing a Cost of Production Report and Making the Journal Entry Transferring Costs Out of Work in Process Inventory for a Company with Two Departments and Abnormal Spoilage.

Fairchild Co.'s Department 2 had the following costs and production information for June 19X4.

Department 2	Transferred In	Materials	Conversion	Total
Beginning work in process				
inventory costs	$ -0-	$ -0-	$ -0-	$ -0-
Current costs added in June	209,000	42,350	157,500	408,850
Total costs to be accounted for	$209,000	$42,350	$157,500	$408,850
Units in beginning work in process inventory				-0-
Units started into production during June				55,000
Total units to be accounted for				55,000
Units in ending work in process inventory (100% complete as to				
materials and 50% complete as to conversion)				<5,000>
Units lost due to abnormal spoilage				<2,000>
Units started and completed during June				48,000

1. Prepare a cost of production report for June 19X4.
2. Make the general journal entry to transfer costs out of work in process inventory at June 30 for Department 2 using the weighted average method.

13–4. Learning Objectives 2, 3. Preparing a Cost of Production Report and Making the Journal Entry Transferring Costs Out of Work in Process Inventory for a Company with Two Departments and an Increase in Units.

Wallace Co. produces a product in two departments. Additional materials were added in the second department that caused the units produced to increase. During June 19X4, the company's Department 2 had the following costs and units of production.

Department 2	Transferred In	Materials	Conversion	Total
Beginning work in process inventory costs	$ -0-	$ -0-	$ -0-	$ -0-
Current costs added in June	126,000	78,300	122,120	326,420
Total costs to be accounted for	$126,000	$78,300	$122,120	$326,420

	Total
Units in beginning work in process inventory	-0-
Units transferred in from Dept. 1 and started into production during June	60,000
Units added by the production process	30,000
Total units to be accounted for	90,000
Units in ending work in process inventory (100% complete as to materials and 60% complete as to conversion)	<10,000>
Units started and completed during June	80,000

1. Prepare a cost of production report for June.
2. Make the general journal entry to transfer costs out of work in process inventory at June 30 for Department 2 using the weighted average method.

13–5. Learning Objectives 2, 3. Preparing a Cost of Production Report and Making the Journal Entry Transferring Costs Out of Work in Process Inventory for a Company with One Department and Normal and Abnormal Spoilage.

West Co. had the following costs and production information for July 19X4.

	Materials	Conversion	Total
Beginning work in process inventory costs	$ 36,000	$ 40,000	$ 76,000
Current costs added in July	179,820	192,320	372,140
Total costs to be accounted for	$215,820	$232,320	$448,140

	Total
Units in beginning work in process inventory (80% complete as to materials and 60% complete as to conversion)	12,000
Units started into production during July	60,000
Total units to be accounted for	72,000
Units in ending work in process inventory (60% complete as to materials and 40% complete as to conversion)	<10,000>
Units lost due to normal spoilage	<2,000>
Units lost due to abnormal spoilage	<2,000>
Units completed and transferred out during July	58,000
Units in beginning work in process inventory	<12,000>
Units started and completed during July	46,000

1. Prepare a cost of production report for July.
2. Make the general journal entry to transfer costs out of work in process inventory at July 31 for West Co. using the weighted average method.

13–6. Learning Objective 4. Computing Equivalent Units for a Company with Three Departments and an Increase In Units Produced.

Black Co.'s Department 3 had the following units of production for October 19X3.

Units in beginning work in process inventory (100% complete as to materials and 50% complete as to conversion)	11,000
Units transferred in from Dept. 2 and started into production during October	54,000
Units added by the production process	25,000
Total units to be accounted for	90,000
Units in ending work in process inventory (100% complete as to materials and 60% complete as to conversion)	<10,000>
Units completed and transferred out during October	80,000
Units in beginning work in process inventory	<11,000>
Units started and completed during October	69,000

Assuming Black Co. uses the weighted average process costing method, compute the equivalent units of production.

GROUP A PROBLEMS

13–1A. Learning Objectives 2, 3. Preparing a Cost of Production Report and Making the Journal Entry to Transfer Costs Out of Work in Process Inventory for a Company with One Department Having Normal and Abnormal Spoilage and Using the Weighted Average Method.

Parts, Inc. had the following costs and production information for September 19X3.

	Materials	Conversion	Total
Beginning work in process inventory costs	$100,000	$ 50,000	$150,000
Current costs added in September	380,260	462,550	842,810
Total costs to be accounted for	$480,260	$512,550	$992,810

Units in beginning work in process inventory (100% complete as to materials and 10% complete as to conversion)	25,000
Units started into production during September	95,000
Total units to be accounted for	120,000
Units in ending work in process inventory (100% complete as to materials and 50% complete as to conversion)	<35,000>
Units lost due to normal spoilage	<2,000>
Units lost due to abnormal spoilage	<1,000>
Units completed and transferred out during September	82,000
Units in beginning work in process inventory	<25,000>
Units started and completed during September	57,000

Required:

1. Prepare a cost of production report for September using the weighted average method.
2. Make the general journal entry transferring costs out of work in process inventory at September 30.

13–2A. Learning Objectives 2,3. Preparing Cost of Production Reports and Making Journal Entries Transferring Costs Out of Work in Process Inventories for a Company with Two Departments Having Normal and Abnormal Spoilage and Using the Weighted Average Method.

Iota, Inc., which manufactures its product in two departments, had the following costs and production information for October 19X3.

Cutting Department. Labor and overhead are added evenly throughout the production process, while materials are added at the beginning of production in Iota's Cutting Department, which had the following costs and production information for October 19X3.

	Materials	Conversion	Total
Beginning work in process inventory costs	$ 60,000	$ 15,000	$ 75,000
Current costs added in October	512,005	246,855	758,860
Total costs to be accounted for	$572,005	$261,855	$833,860

	Total
Units in beginning work in process inventory (100% complete as to materials and 30% complete as to conversion)	15,000
Units started into production during October	125,000
Total units to be accounted for	140,000
Units in ending work in process inventory (100% complete as to materials and 60% complete as to conversion)	<30,000>
Units lost due to normal spoilage	<1,500>
Units lost due to abnormal spoilage	<900>
Units completed and transferred out during October	107,600
Units in beginning work in process inventory	<15,000>
Units started and completed during October	92,600

Finishing Department. Labor and overhead are added evenly throughout the production process, while materials are also added evenly throughout production in Iota's Finishing Department, which had the following costs and production information for October 19X3.

	Transferred In	Materials	Conversion	Total
Beginning work in process inventory costs	$102,908	$ 8,500	$ 12,750	$124,158
Current costs added in October . . .	?	115,913	168,915	?
Total costs to be accounted for	$?	$124,413	$181,665	$?

	Total
Units in beginning work in process inventory (60% complete as to materials and 60% complete as to conversion)	17,000
Units transferred in from the Cutting Dept. and started into production during October	107,600
Total units to be accounted for	124,600
Units in ending work in process inventory (50% complete as to materials and 50% complete as to conversion)	<27,000>
Units lost due to normal spoilage	<1,000>
Units lost due to abnormal spoilage	<600>
Units completed and transferred out during October	96,000
Units in beginning work in process inventory	<17,000>
Units started and completed during October	79,000

Required:
For each department:

1. Prepare a cost of production report for October, using the weighted average method.
2. Make the general journal entry transferring costs out of work in process inventory at October 31.

13–3A. Learning Objectives 2, 3. Preparing Cost of Production Reports and Making the Journal Entries Transferring Costs Out of Work in Process Inventories for a Company with Two Departments and Increases in Units Produced.

Bell, Inc., which manufactures its product in two departments, had the following costs and production information for November 19X3.

Mixing Department	**Materials**	**Conversion**	**Total**
Beginning work in process inventory costs	$ 35,000	$ 15,000	$ 50,000
Current costs added in November	687,850	494,760	1,182,610
Total costs to be accounted for	$722,850	$509,760	$1,232,610

Units in beginning work in process inventory (100% complete as to materials and 20% complete as to conversion)	12,500
Units started into production during November	125,000
Units added by the production process	15,000
Total units to be accounted for	152,500
Units in ending work in process inventory (100% complete as to materials and 50% complete as to conversion)	<17,000>
Units completed and transferred out during November	135,500
Units in beginning work in process inventory	<12,500>
Units started and completed during November	123,000

Finishing Department	**Transferred In**	**Materials**	**Conversion**	**Total**
Beginning work in process inventory costs	$120,560	$ 12,000	$ 9,000	$141,560
Current costs added in November . .	?	232,755	290,700	?
Total costs to be accounted for	$?	$244,755	$299,700	$?

Units in beginning work in process inventory (55% complete as to materials and 55% complete as to conversion)	12,000
Units transferred in from the Mixing Dept. and started into production during November	135,500
Units added by the production process	30,000
Total units to be accounted for	177,500
Units in ending work in process inventory (50% complete as to materials and 50% complete as to conversion)	<22,000>
Units completed and transferred out during November	155,500
Units in beginning work in process inventory	<12,000>
Units started and completed during November	143,500

Required:
For each department:

1. Prepare a cost of production report for November using the weighted average method.
2. Make the general journal entry transferring costs out of work in process inventory at November 30.

GROUP B PROBLEMS

13–1B. Learning Objectives 2, 3. Preparing a Cost of Production Report and Making the Journal Entry Transferring Costs Out of Work In Process Inventory for a Company with One Department Having Normal and Abnormal Spoilage and Using the FIFO Method.

Parts, Inc. had the following costs and production information for September 19X3.

	Materials	Conversion	Total
Beginning work in process inventory costs	$100,000	$ 50,000	$150,000
Current costs added in September	380,370	462,560	842,930
Total costs to be accounted for	$480,370	$512,560	$992,930

Units in beginning work in process inventory (100% complete as to materials and 10% complete as to conversion)	25,000
Units started into production during September	95,000
Total units to be accounted for	120,000
Units in ending work in process inventory (100% complete as to materials and 50% complete as to conversion)	<35,000>
Units lost due to normal spoilage	<2,000>
Units lost due to abnormal spoilage	<1,000>
Units completed and transferred out during September	82,000
Units in beginning work in process inventory	<25,000>
Units started and completed during September	57,000

Required:

1. Prepare a cost of production report for September using the FIFO method.
2. Make the general journal entry transferring costs out of work in process inventory at September 30.

13–2B. Learning Objectives 2, 3. Preparing Cost of Production Reports and Making Journal Entries Transferring Cost Out of Work in Process Inventories for a Company with Two Departments Having Normal and Abnormal Spoilage and Using the FIFO Method.

Iota, Inc., which manufactures its product in two departments, had the following costs and production information for October 19X3.

Cutting Department. Labor and overhead are added evenly throughout the production process, while materials are added at the beginning of production in Iota's Cutting Department, which had the following costs and production information for October 19X3.

	Materials	Conversion	Total
Beginning work in process inventory costs	$ 60,000	$ 15,000	$ 75,000
Current costs added in October	512,525	246,440	758,965
Total costs to be accounted for	$572,525	$261,440	$833,965

Units in beginning work in process inventory (100% complete as to materials and 30% complete as to conversion)	15,000
Units started into production during October	125,000
Total units to be accounted for	140,000
Units in ending work in process inventory (100% complete as to materials and 60% complete as to conversion)	<30,000>
Units lost due to normal spoilage	<1,500>
Units lost due to abnormal spoilage	<900>
Units completed and transferred out during October	107,600
Units in beginning work in process inventory	<15,000>
Units started and completed during October	92,600

Finishing Department. Labor and overhead are added evenly throughout the production process, while materials are also added evenly throughout production in Iota's Finishing Department, which had the following costs and production information for October 19X3.

	Transferred In	Materials	Conversion	Total
Beginning work in process inventory costs	$102,908	$ 8,500	$ 12,750	$124,158
Current costs added in October ..	?	115,884	168,831	?
Total costs to be accounted for . . .	$?	$124,384	$181,581	$?

Units in beginning work in process inventory (60% complete as to materials and 60% complete as to conversion)	17,000
Units transferred in from the Cutting Dept. and started into production during October	107,600
Total units to be accounted for	124,600
Units in ending work in process inventory (50% complete as to materials and 50% complete as to conversion)	<27,000>
Units lost due to normal spoilage	<1,000>
Units lost due to abnormal spoilage	<600>
Units completed and transferred out during October	96,000
Units in beginning work in process inventory	<17,000>
Units started and completed during October	79,000

Required:

For each department:

1. Prepare a cost of production report for October using the FIFO method.
2. Make the general journal entry transferring costs out of work in process inventory at October 31.

13–3B. Learning Objectives 2, 3. Preparing Cost of Production Reports and Making the Journal Entries Transferring Costs Out of Work in Process Inventories for a Company with Two Departments and Increases in Units Produced

Bell, Inc., which manufactures its product in two departments, had the following costs and production information for November 19X3.

Mixing Department	Materials	Conversion	Total
Beginning work in process inventory costs	$ 35,000	$ 15,000	$ 50,000
Current costs added in November	687,400	495,250	1,182,650
Total costs to be accounted for	$722,400	$510,250	$1,232,650

Units in beginning work in process inventory (100% complete as to materials and 20% complete as to conversion)	12,500
Units started into production during November	125,000
Units added by the production process	15,000
Total units to be accounted for	152,500
Units in ending work in process inventory (100% complete as to materials and 50% complete as to conversion)	<17,000>
Units completed and transferred out during November	135,500
Units in beginning work in process inventory	<12,500>
Units started and completed during November	123,000

Finishing Department	Transferred in	Materials	Conversion	Total
Beginning work in process inventory costs	$120,560	$ 12,000	$ 9,000	$141,560
Current costs added in November .	?	233,454	291,018	?
Total costs to be accounted for ...	$?	$245,454	$300,018	$?

Units in beginning work in process inventory (55% complete as to materials and 55% complete as to conversion)	12,000
Units transferred in from the Mixing Dept. and started into production during November	135,500
Units added by the production process	30,000
Total units to be accounted for	177,500
Units in ending work in process inventory (50% complete as to materials and 50% complete as to conversion)	<22,000>
Units completed and transferred out during November	155,500
Units in beginning work in process inventory	<12,000>
Units started and completed during November	143,500

Required:
For each department:

1. Prepare a cost of production report for November using the FIFO method.
2. Make the general journal entry transferring costs out of work in process inventory at November 30.

CASE FOR CRITICAL THINKING

Bill Morrow is working on a paper for a production management class. Bill wonders why most firms accept that some spoilage (normal spoilage) will occur and set limits on what is acceptable. After all, Bill reasons, if you know spoilage is going to occur, why not do something to stop it. Explain why this is not an option for most manufacturing firms.

ANSWERS TO SELF-STUDY QUIZ 13–1

ARNOLD COMPANY
Cost of Production Report
For April

Quantities

1. Units to account for:
   From beginning work in process. . . . .   –0–
   Started into production this month . . . .   <u>70,000</u>
   Total units to account for. . . . .   <u>70,000</u>

2. Units accounted for:
   Completed and transferred out   58,000
   From ending work in process (100% complete as to materials and 50% complete as
      to conversion)   10,000
   Units lost due to normal spoilage . . . .   <u>2,000</u>
   Total units accounted for. . . . .   <u>70,000</u>

3. Equivalent production:

	Equivalent Units	
	Materials	**Conversion**
Completed and transferred out	58,000	58,000
Ending work in process inventory:		
Materials (10,000 × 100%)	10,000	
Conversion (10,000 × 50%)		<u>5,000</u>
Total equivalent units	<u>68,000</u>	<u>63,000</u>

Costs

4. Costs to account for:

	Total Costs	**Equivalent Units**	**Unit Cost**
Materials.	$267,920	÷ 68,000	= $3.94
Conversion	$325,710	÷ 63,000	= <u>5.17</u>
Totals.	<u>$593,630</u>		<u>$9.11</u>

5. Costs accounted for:
   Completed and transferred out (58,000 × $9.11) $528,380
   Work in process—
     Materials (10,000 × $3.94). $39,400
     Conversion (10,000 × 50% × $5.17) . . . . $25,850   <u>65,250</u>
   Total costs accounted for . . . .   <u>$593,630</u>

ANSWERS TO SELF-STUDY QUIZ 13–2

	Transferred In	Materials	Conversion
Units in beginning work in process inventory: 8,000 × 100%	8,000	8,000	8,000
Units started and transferred out in July: 42,000 × 100%	42,000	42,000	42,000
Units in ending work in process Transferred-in: 10,000 × 100%	10,000		
Materials: 10,000 × 60%		6,000	
Conversion: 10,000 × 45%			4,500
Total equivalent units	60,000	56,000	54,500

ANSWERS TO SELF-STUDY QUIZ 13–3

Total units to account for	60,000
Units in beginning work in process inventory	<15,000>
Units transferred in from Mixing Dept.	<42,000>
Units added by production process	3,000

Chapter 14
Accounting for Joint Products and By-Products

LEARNING OBJECTIVES

After studying Chapter 14, you should be able to:

1. Differentiate between joint products and by-products.
2. Explain the meaning of joint costs.
3. Allocate joint cost based on the following methods:
    a. Relative sales value method.
    b. Physical unit method.
    c. Assigned weight method.
4. Account for by-products not needing further processing.
5. Account for by-products needing further processing.

Thus far in our discussion of costing systems, we have worked primarily with two companies, TurboFlex Corporation and South Corporation. Each of these companies produced only one product. There are many industries, however, whose manufacturing process simultaneously produces two or more distinct products from a single process. Examples of these industries include chemical companies, petroleum refineries, lumber mills, flour mills, coal mines, dairies, meat packing plants, and many others. In the processing of logs, for example, a lumber mill produces several different grades of lumber, as well as scrap wood and salable sawdust. In the processing of cattle, the meat packer produces a variety of cuts of meat (steaks, roasts, hamburger), hides, and other products.

LEARNING OBJECTIVE 1

Different products produced as a result of a common process are divided into two categories: joint products and by-products. **Joint products** arise when two or more products with nearly equal value are produced from a single input of raw materials. For example, the processing of crude oil yields gasoline, kerosene, paraffin, and benzine. The processing of soap yields lanolin and other cosmetic oils, as well as soap.

Unlike joint products, which are primary to the production process, **by-products** are incidental to the production of a main product. Thus, by-products are the "left over" materials that result when producing the main or joint products. For example, sawdust and scrap wood are left over after processing lumber. Likewise, meat scraps and bones are left over after processing meat products. By-products normally have low sales value compared with the sales of the main or joint product(s).

NOTE In the preceding paragraph, we described by-products as left over materials that result from the production of a main product or joint products. While the term "left over" is certainly applicable to most by-products, we should note that some by-products are separated from the main product at the beginning of the production process. For example, cottonseed is separated from raw cotton before the cotton is processed into cloth.

ACCOUNTING FOR JOINT PRODUCTS

LEARNING OBJECTIVE 2

Throughout most of the manufacturing process, joint products *cannot* be identified as separate products. Only at a particular point in the production process, called the **split-off point,** separate products become identifiable. Costs incurred in processing before the split-off point is reached are called **joint costs.** Since joint costs relate to the entire production process, and not to individual products, they must be allocated to the final products. Figure 14–1 illustrates the problem with joint cost allocation. Here we assume that the joint cost of processing 60,000 gallons of gasoline and liquid natural gas is $54,000.

FIGURE 14-1
Joint Product
Cost Allocation

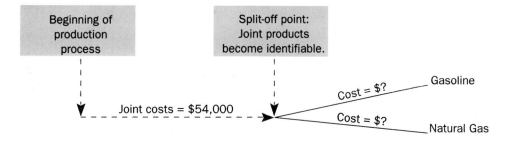

As we can see, joint production costs of $54,000 have been incurred up to the split-off point. Since this amount relates to the production of *both* products, and not to either product individually, it must be allocated between the two products. There are three principal methods of allocating joint costs: (1) the relative sales value method, (2) the physical unit method, and (3) the assigned weight method.

Allocation by the Relative Sales Value Method

LEARNING OBJECTIVE 3   The **relative sales value method** is a commonly used method that allocates joint costs based on the sales value of each product at the split-off point. This method is based on the theory that the higher the selling price of a product, the more joint costs should be allocated to that product. To illustrate, let's assume that the sales value of the gasoline in Figure 14-1 is $1.20 per gallon and the sales value of the natural gas is $2.00 per gallon. The allocation of the joint costs follows:

Step 1. Compute the total sales value of the products:

Joint Costs	Joint Products	Gallons Produced	Sales Value per Unit	Total Sales Value
	Gasoline	50,000	$1.20	$60,000
$54,000	Natural gas	10,000	2.00	20,000
Total sales value				$80,000

Step 2. Allocate joint costs based on the rate of each product's sales value to the total:

Gasoline: $\dfrac{\$60,000}{\$80,000}$ = 75% × $54,000 = $40,500

Natural gas: $\dfrac{\$20,000}{\$80,000}$ = 25% × $54,000 = $13,500

Total allocated $54,000

Step 3. Compute unit costs:

Gasoline: $40,500 ÷ 50,000 gallons = $0.81 per gallon
Natural gas: 13,500 ÷ 10,000 gallons = $1.35 per gallon

Allocation by Adjusted Sales Value

LEARNING OBJECTIVE 3   In the above example, we assumed that both joint products could be sold at the split-off point. While many joint products can be sold at the split-off point, some products require further processing to make them marketable. The additional processing costs must be deducted from the sales value of these products before making the cost allocation. To illustrate, let's assume that the sales price of the gasoline in the previous example remains at $1.20 per gallon, but that the liquid natural gas must undergo additional processing (bleaching and filtering) before it can be sold for $2.00 per gallon. Let's further assume that the additional processing costs consist of $4,000 in direct labor costs and $1,000 in factory overhead costs. Joint costs would now be allocated as follows:

Step 1. Compute the total sales value of the products:

Joint Products	Gallons Produced	Sales Value per Unit	Total Sales Value	Additional Pro. Costs	Adjusted Sales Value
Gasoline	50,000	$1.20	$60,000	–0–	$60,000
Natural gas	10,000	2.00	20,000	$5,000	15,000
Total sales value					$75,000

Step 2. Allocate joint costs based on the rate of each product's sales value to the total:

Gasoline: $\dfrac{\$60,000}{\$75,000}$ =   80% × $54,000   = $43,200

Natural gas: $\dfrac{\$15,000}{\$75,000}$ =   20% × $54,000   = $10,800

Total allocated $54,000

Step 3. Compute unit costs:

Gasoline: $43,200 ÷ 50,000 gallons = $0.864 per gallon
Natural gas: 10,800 ÷ 10,000 gallons = $1.08 per gallon

SELF-STUDY QUIZ 14–2 Break-A-Way Products Company produces two joint products from a single raw material. One of the products, Product A, can be sold at the split-off point for $1.25 each. The other product, Product B, can be sold for $3.00 each after further processing. During June, Break-A-Way incurred joint costs of $80,000 in producing 50,000 units of Product A and 20,000 units of Product B. Break-A-Way incurred additional processing costs of $9,000 to get Product B ready to sell. Compute the total and unit cost of the two products.
Answers at end of chapter.

Allocation by the Physical Unit Method

LEARNING OBJECTIVE 3

The relative sales value method discussed in the previous section has two main advantages: (1) it is simple to use and (2) costs are allocated based on the revenue-generating power of the individual products. While these advantages are significant, the relative sales value method is not suitable when the sales values of joint products are highly volatile. The **physical unit method** uses a common physical unit of measure, such as weight or volume, as a basis to allocate joint costs at the split-off point. To illustrate, let's return to our example of gasoline and natural gas. Using gallons as the common unit of measure, we can allocate the $54,000 in joint costs as follows:

Step 1: Compute the total gallons produced:

```
Gasoline:     50,000 gallons
Natural gas:  10,000 gallons
Total  . . . . . .  60,000 gallons
```

Step 2: Allocate joint costs based on the rate of each unit to the total:

NOTE For this example, our calculations will be easier if we use fractions, rather than decimals.

$$\text{Gasoline:} \quad \frac{50,000}{60,000} = \frac{5}{6} \times \$54,000 = \$45,000$$

$$\text{Natural gas:} \quad \frac{10,000}{60,000} = \frac{1}{6} \times \$54,000 = \underline{\$\ 9,000}$$

Total allocated $54,000

Step 3: Compute unit costs:

Gasoline: $45,000 ÷ 50,000 gallons = $0.90 per gallon
Natural gas: $ 9,000 ÷ 10,000 gallons = $0.90 per gallon

A disadvantage of the physical unit method is that the physical units used for allocating joint costs may have no relationship to the revenue-producing capacity of the individual products. For example, if the joint costs of processing beef were assigned to the various products on the basis of weight, trimmings, scrap meat, etc. would have the same cost per pound as T-bone steaks.

SELF-STUDY QUIZ 14–3 Bovee Manufacturing Company incurred joint costs of $65,000 in the production of 80,000 pounds of Joint Product A and 20,000 pounds of Joint Product B. Using pounds as a common unit of measure, allocate the joint costs between the two products.
Answers at end of chapter.

Allocation by Assigned Weights

LEARNING OBJECTIVE 3

In many industries, the allocation methods we have discussed thus far do not provide a satisfactory solution to the joint cost allocation problem. As an alternative, some firms use the **assigned weight method.** Under this method, firms develop their own formulas for apportionment. Such formulas usually involve assigning *weight factors* to each product produced. Products assigned a higher weight factor will receive a greater allocation of joint costs. The weight factors assigned can be based on many considerations, such as the physical size of the product, the difficulty of manufacturing, the time involved in making the product, the variety of materials used, the type of labor employed, and the marketing system used.

To illustrate this method, let's return once again to our example of gasoline and liquid natural gas. Management could decide to assign a weight of 2 points to each gallon of gasoline produced. But since the natural gas is more difficult to work with, management could assign it a weight of 6 points for each gallon produced. Based on these point values, we can allocate the $54,000 in joint costs as follows:

Step 1. Compute the total production weight:

Product	Gallons Produced	Assigned Weight	Weight Production
Gasoline	50,000	2	100,000
Natural gas	10,000	6	60,000
Total production weight			160,000

Step 2. Allocate joint costs based on the rate of each unit to the total:

Gasoline: $\dfrac{100,000}{160,000}$ =   62.5% × $54,000   = $33,750

Natural gas: $\dfrac{60,000}{160,000}$ =   37.5% × $54,000   = $20,250

Total allocated $54,000

Step 3. Compute the unit costs:

Gasoline: $33,750 ÷ 50,000 gallons = $0.675 per gallon
Natural gas: $20,250 ÷ 10,000 gallons = $2.025 per gallon

Notice that the higher point value assigned to the natural gas resulted in a higher unit cost (compared to the other methods).

The main advantage of the assigned weight method is that it often yields a more logical cost allocation than other methods. Its main disadvantage is that the determination of weights is often complicated and time-consuming, especially when many products are involved.

SELF-STUDY QUIZ 14–4 For a joint cost of $80,000, Murphy Corporation produced 90,000 pounds of Product H and 7,500 pounds of Product J. Allocate the joint cost between the two products if 3 points are assigned to Product H and 4 points are assigned to Product J.
Answers at end of chapter.

ACCOUNTING FOR BY-PRODUCTS

LEARNING OBJECTIVE 4   How to account for a by-product depends on whether it can be sold "as is" after it is separated from the main product, or whether it must undergo further processing after separation to get it ready to sell. In this section, we will look at how to account for by-products that require no further processing, and how to account for by-products that require further processing to make them salable.

By-Products Not Needing Further Processing

There are two popular methods of accounting for by-products that do not need additional processing after separation:

1. Record the proceeds from the sale of the by-product as other income and charge all manufacturing costs to the main products.
2. Record the estimated selling price of the by-product as a reduction in the cost of the main product.

Proceeds Recorded as Other Income. Under this method, no costs are assigned or allocated to the by-product, and the sale of the by-product has no effect on the cost of the main product. Further, no entry is made in the accounting records until the by-product is sold. At the time of sale, an entry is made debiting Cash (or Accounts Receivable) and crediting Miscellaneous Income. To illustrate, we will use the example of Allied Chemical Company. Allied's main activity is the production of environmentally safe products. Allied had been paying a local farmer to haul off residue that was left over after producing non-toxic glue. The farmer noticed that the grass really grew quickly in the areas where he had dumped the residue. As a result, Allied started selling the residue to a local fertilizer company to market as lawn fertilizer. On June 23, Allied sold on account 9,000 pounds of residue for $0.12 per pound. The following general journal entry records the sale:

1	June	23	Accounts Receivable		1 0 8 0 00		1
2			Miscellaneous Income			1 0 8 0 00	2
3			Sold by-product (9,000 × $0.12).				3

This method is simple and requires no computation of by-product cost. However, it does not relate the sales value of the by-product with the main product. Consequently, it is usually used only when the proceeds from the sale of a by-product are small.

By-Product Recorded as a Reduction in the Main Product. Let's now assume that Allied records the estimated sales value of its by-product as a reduction in the cost of the main product. Under this method, the estimated sales value at separation (or the proceeds from a sale) is accounted for by debiting an asset account entitled **By-Products Inventory**, and crediting Work in Process Inventory, as follows:

1	June	23	By-Products Inventory		1 0 8 0 00		1
2			Work in Process Inventory			1 0 8 0 00	2
3			Recognized estimated sales value of				3
4			by-product (9,000 × $0.12)				4

As we can see, an inventory account has been increased by $1,080 and the cost of the main product has been reduced by the same amount. When the by-product is sold later, the By-Products Inventory account is credited and Cash or Accounts Receivable is debited. If the by-product is sold for more or less than the estimated sales value, the difference may be credited or debited to an account entitled **Gain or Loss on Sales of By-Products.** For example, assume that on June 25 Allied sold its by-product on account for $1,200. The following general journal entry records the sale:

1	June	25	Accounts Receivable		1 2 0 0 0 0			1
2			By-Products Inventory			1 0 8 0 0 0		2
3			Gain or Loss on Sales of By-Products			1 2 0 0 0		3
4			Sold by-product for more than recorded					4
5			value.					5

Here, the by-product was sold for $120 more than its recorded sales value. This amount was *credited* to the Gain or Loss on Sales of By-Product account. Had the by-product been sold for less than its recorded sales value, the amount would be *debited* to the Gain or Loss on Sales of By-Product account. A period-end credit balance in this account is reported on the income statement as *other income*; a period-end debit balance is reported on the income statement as *other expense*.

SELF-REVIEW QUIZ 14–5 Baker Company, a manufacturer of steel products, sells metal shavings without further processing for $0.03 per pound. On May 12, Baker had accumulated 8,000 pounds of shavings.

a. Record the credit sale of the shavings assuming that the proceeds are recorded as other income.
b. Record the sales value of the shavings assuming that their estimated sales value is recorded as a reduction in the cost of the main product.
c. Record the credit sale of the shavings for $0.04 per pound assuming that their cost had been recorded as a reduction in the cost of the main product.

Answers at end of chapter.

By-Products Needing Further Processing after Separation

LEARNING OBJECTIVE 5   In some cases, the manufacturer may find that additional processing is needed to make a by-product salable, or that additional processing will increase the sales value of the by-product. Let's assume that Allied Chemical Company further processes its glue residue to increase its sales value. The residue is filtered to remove solid lumps and is then mixed with ground bone meal to create a finished product. (NOTE: bone meal is a by-product of meat processing and has many uses, which include fertilizer, a food supplement for humans and animals, and a base for many common products such as lipstick and toothpaste.) The finished product is then sold in bulk to fertilizer companies for $0.25 per pound. Additional production costs for June follow:

Direct materials	$1,800
Direct labor	200
Factory overhead	400
Total	$2,400

These costs are debited to a special account entitled **By-Products in Process** (also called *Work in Process—By-Products*), as follows:

1	June	23	By-Products in Process	2 4 0 0 0 0		1
2			Raw Materials Inventory		1 8 0 0 0 0	2
3			Factory Payroll Clearing		2 0 0 0 0	3
4			Factory Overhead Control		4 0 0 0 0	4
5			Recognized additional by-product			5
6			processing costs.			6

Let us now assume that these units are completed on June 25. The final output consisted of 16,000 pounds of bulk fertilizer. The following entry records the transfer of costs from the in-process account to an inventory account:

1	June	25	By-Products Inventory	2 4 0 0 0 0		1
2			By-Products in Process		2 4 0 0 0 0	2
3			Completed 16,000 pounds of by-product.			3

Our final assumption is that Allied makes a cash sale of the fertilizer on June 26 for $0.25 per pound (16,000 × $.25 = $4,000). The following journal entry records the sale:

1	June	26	Cash	4 0 0 0 0 0		1
2			By-Products Inventory		2 4 0 0 0 0	2
3			Gain or Loss on Sales of By-Products		1 6 0 0 0 0	3
4			Sold by-product for cash.			4

As we have already learned, the Gain or Loss on Sales of By-Products account will be reported on the income statement as other income (credit balance) or other expense (debit balance).

Since by-product revenue is usually insignificant in relation to revenue from the sale of the main product, some firms do not maintain a separate account to record gains or losses on the sale of by-products. If we assume that Allied did not maintain a separate account, the above $4,000 sale would be recorded as follows:

1	June	26	Cash		400000		1
2			By-Products Inventory			400000	2
3			Sold by-product for cash.				3

The By-Product Inventory account would then appear as follows:

ACCOUNT By-Products Inventory					ACCOUNT NO. 501	
					BALANCE	
DATE	ITEM	P.R.	DEBIT	CREDIT	DEBIT	CREDIT
June 25	Costs	X	240000		240000	
26	Sale	X		400000		160000

The $1,600 credit balance in the By-Products Inventory is reported on the income statement as other income, or as a reduction in cost of goods sold. The final year-end balance of the account would be closed to Income Summary during the closing process.

SELF-STUDY QUIZ 14–6 Good Earth Grain Company does not immediately sell the wheat germ taken from the wheat berry in the production of flour. Instead, sugar and honey are added and the finished product is sold to be boxed as breakfast cereal. In July, the following costs were incurred to process 6,000 pounds of wheat germ after it was separated from the main product:

Materials	$1,400
Direct labor	800
Factory overhead	600
Total	$2,800

a. Record the additional processing costs.
b. Record the sale of the final product at $0.60 per pound assuming the company maintains a separate account to record gains or losses on the sale of by-products.

Answers at end of chapter.

NOTE Remember:

1. When two or more products are produced as a result of a single process and each product has a significant sales value, the products are referred to as joint products and the cost of production must be allocated between them.
2. Sometimes one or more products with relatively little sales value are produced unavoidably as a result of producing the main product(s). These products are referred to as by-products since they are incidental to the production of the main product.
3. Assigning a final cost to joint products and by-products is, oftentimes, a difficult task because the same production costs produced both, or all, products. In other words, the cost to produce two joint products is the same up to the split-off point because one cannot be produced without the other.

SELF-STUDY PROBLEM

Scientific Products, Inc. produces two joint products from a single raw material. One of the products, Product J, can be sold at the split-off point for $1.00 per pound. The other product, Product K, can be sold for $2.50 per pound after further processing. During May, Scientific Products incurred joint costs of $30,000 in producing 30,000 pounds of Product J and 10,000 pounds of Product K. Additional processing costs of $5,000 were incurred to get Product K ready to sell.

Required:
Compute the following:

a. Total and unit cost of each product using the relative sales value method.
b. Total and unit cost of each product using the physical unit method.
c. Total and unit cost of each product using the assigned weight method assuming that Product J has an assigned weight factor of 2 and Product K has an assigned weight factor of 3.

SOLUTION TO SELF-STUDY PROBLEM

a.

Product	Pounds Produced	Sales Value Per Unit	Total Sales Value	Additional Pro. Costs	Adjusted Sales Value
J	30,000	$1.00	$30,000	-0-	$30,000
K	10,000	2.50	25,000	$5,000	20,000
Total sales value					$50,000

Product J: $\dfrac{\$30,000}{\$50,000}$ = 60% × $30,000 = $18,000

Product K: $\dfrac{\$20,000}{\$50,000}$ = 40% × $30,000 = $12,000

Unit cost: Product J: $18,000 ÷ 30,000 pounds = $0.60 cost per pound
                  Product K: $12,000 ÷ 10,000 pounds = $1.20 cost per pound

b. Product J: 30,000 pounds
    Product K: 10,000 pounds
    Total   40,000 pounds

    Product J: $\dfrac{30,000}{40,000}$ = 75% × $30,000 = $22,500

    Product K: $\dfrac{10,000}{40,000}$ = 25% × $30,000 = $7,500

    Unit cost:
        Product J: $22,500 ÷ 30,000 pounds = $0.75 cost per pound
        Product K: $7,500 + $5,000* = $12,500 ÷ 10,000 pounds = $1.25 cost
                      per pound

*additional processing cost necessary to complete Product K.

c.

Product	Pounds Produced	Assigned Weight	Weight Production
J	30,000	2	60,000
K	10,000	3	30,000
Total production weight			90,000

    Product J: $\dfrac{60,000}{90,000} = \dfrac{2}{3}$ × $30,000 = $20,000

    Product K: $\dfrac{30,000}{90,000} = \dfrac{1}{3}$ × $30,000 = $10,000

    Unit cost:
        Product J: $20,000 ÷ 30,000 pounds = $0.6667 (or $0.67) per pound.
        Product K: $10,000 + $5,000 = $15,000 ÷ 10,000 pounds = $1.50 cost
                      per pound.

SUMMARY

Many manufacturing companies produce two or more products from a single process. For example, the processing of beef renders a variety of end products—such as roasts, steaks, and ground beef.

Different products produced as a result of a common process are divided into two categories: joint products and by-products. **Joint products** are the major outputs of a joint process, with each joint product normally having a high sales value. By contrast, **by-products** are minor outputs of a joint process and normally have a lower sales value than joint products.

Throughout most of the manufacturing process, joint products cannot be identified as separate products. The point in time at which by-products become distinguishable as separate products is known as the **split-off point.** Costs incurred in processing before the split-off point is reached are called **joint costs.** Since joint costs relate to the entire manufacturing process, they must be allocated to the final products.

Companies use various methods for allocating joint costs to the final products. Three common methods include: (1) the relative sales value method, (2) the physical unit method, and (3) the assigned weight method. The **relative sales value method** results in an allocation based on the sale value of each joint-product at the split-off point. The higher the selling price of a product, the more joint costs are allocated to the product.

The **physical unit method** is often used for joint cost allocations when the sales values of joint products are highly volatile. Under this method, a common physical unit of measure, such as weight or volume, is used as a basis to allocate joint costs. A disadvantage of this method is that the physical units used for cost allocation may have no relationship to the revenue-producing capacity of the individual products.

Under the **assigned weight method,** firms develop their own formulas for allocating joint costs. These formulas usually assign weight factors to each product. Products with a higher assigned weight factor receive a greater allocation of joint costs. The weight factors are assigned based on factors such as the size of the products, the difficulty of manufacturing, the time involved in making the products, the variety and amount of materials used, and the amount and type of labor involved.

How to account for a by-product depends on how it can be sold after its separation from the main product. Some by-products can be sold "as is" after separation from the main product. Other by-products will require further processing.

Two popular methods of accounting for by-products that do not require additional processing after separation include: (1) record the proceeds from the sale of the by-product as other income and charge all manufacturing costs to the main product and (2) record the estimated selling price of the by-product as a reduction in the cost of the main product.

Some by-products will need additional processing to make them salable (or additional processing will increase the sales value). Additional processing costs are usually debited to a special account entitled **By-Products in Process** (or Work in Process—By-Products). When processing is complete, the **By-Products Inventory** account is debited and the By-Products in Process account is credited. When the by-product is sold, the Cash (or Accounts Receivable) account is debited for the selling price, and the By-Products Inventory account is credited for its balance (cost). The difference between the by-product's selling price and its cost is recorded in an account entitled **Gain or Loss on Sales of By-Products.** This account is credited if the by-product is sold for more than its cost; it is debited if the by-product is sold for less than its cost.

KEY TERMS

Assigned Weight Method. A method used to assign joint costs to joint products based on an assignment of weight factors to the joint products. Products with a high weight factor will be assigned more costs.

By-Products. Secondary products with a relatively low sales value that are incidentally produced as a result of producing the primary product.

By-Products in Process Account. An account used to record additional production costs needed to make a by-product salable.

By-Products Inventory Account. An asset account used to record the estimated sales value of a by-product.

Gain or Loss on Sales of By-Products Account. An account used to record the difference between the selling price of a by-product and the amount assigned as the by-product's inventory value.

Joint Costs. Manufacturing costs that are incurred before reaching the split-off point in producing joint products.

Joint Products. Two or more products with nearly equal value equal produced from a single input of raw materials.

Physical Unit Method. A method used to allocate joint costs to joint products based on a common unit of measure, such as weight or volume.

Relative Sales Value Method. A method used to allocate joint costs to joint products based on the sales value of each joint product.

Split-off Point. The point in the production of joint products where separate products become identifiable.

QUESTIONS FOR REVIEW

1. How do joint products differ from by-products?
2. What are joint costs?
3. What is meant by the split-off point?
4. Why must joint costs be allocated among joint products?
5. How does the relative sales value method of allocating joint costs differ from the adjusted sales value method?
6. Under what conditions would the physical unit method of allocating joint costs be used?
7. How are weight factors determined in the assigned weight method?
8. When would it be appropriate to record the proceeds of a by-product as other income?
9. What is the purpose of the By-Products Inventory account?
10. What is the purpose of the Gain or Loss on Sales of By-Products account?
11. How would a period-end credit balance in the Gain or Loss on Sales of By-Products account be reported? How would a debit balance be reported?
12. Why are some by-products processed further after separation from the primary product?

NOTE Unless told otherwise in Exercises and Problems, record transactions in general journal form. Where applicable, round rates correct to one decimal place and dollar amounts correct to three decimal places.

EXERCISES

14–1. Learning Objective 3. Allocating Joint Costs Using the Relative Sales Value Method.
During May, Baker Company produced 15,000 units of Product H and 10,000 units of Product J at a total joint cost of $30,000. Using the relative sales value method, compute the total and unit cost of each product if Product H has a sales value of $1.00 per unit and Product J has a sales value per unit of $2.00.

14–2. Learning Objective 3. Allocating Joint Costs Using the Adjusted Sales Value Method.
Halter Industries produces two joint products from a single raw material. One of the products, Product X, can be sold at the split-off point for $1.20 each. The other product, Product Y, can be sold for $3.00 each after further processing. During April, Halter incurred joint costs of $90,000 in producing 40,000 units of Product X and 15,000 units of Product B. Additional processing costs of $6,000 were incurred to get Product Y ready to sell. Compute the total and unit costs of the two products.

14–3. Learning Objective 3. Allocating Joint Costs Using the Physical Unit Method.
Ortiz Products Company incurred joint costs of $70,000 in the production of 60,000 pounds of Joint Product A-1 and 40,000 pounds of Joint Product A-2. Using pounds as a common unit of measure, allocate the joint costs between the two products.

14–4. Learning Objective 3. Allocating Joint Costs Using the Assigned Weight Method.
Singer Corporation produced 60,000 pounds of Product J and 20,000 pounds of Product K for joint costs of $60,000. Allocate the joint costs between the two products if 2 weight factor points are assigned to Product J and 3 weight factor points are assigned to Product K.

14–5. Learning Objective 4. Recording By-Products Not Needing Further Processing.
Hall Company, a manufacturer of steel products, sells metal shavings without further processing for $0.04 per pound. During July, Hall accumulated 12,000 pounds of shavings.

a. Record the sale of the shavings assuming that the proceeds are recorded as other income.
b. Record the sales value of the shavings assuming that their estimated sales value is recorded as a reduction in the cost of the main product.
c. Record the sale of the shavings for $0.03 per pound assuming that their cost had been recorded as a reduction in the cost of the main product.

14–6. Learning Objective 5. Recording By-Products Needing Further Processing.
Nature's Best Company does not immediately sell the rice bran that is left over after rice grain is processed. The bran is further processed by adding flavorings and sugar, and then sold as cereal. The following costs were incurred to process 9,000 pounds of bran after it was separated from the main product.

Direct materials	$1,800
Direct labor	1,200
Factory overhead	960
Total	$3,960

a. Record the additional processing costs.
b. Record the sale of the final product at $0.69 per pound assuming the company maintains a separate account to record gains or losses on the sale of by-products.

GROUP A PROBLEMS

14–1A. Learning Objective 3. Allocating Joint Costs Using the Relative Sales Value Method.

Coastal Drilling Company owns a lease on an off-shore well that produces both crude oil and natural gas. During 19X8, the well produced 10,000 barrels of oil and 200,000 cubic feet of natural gas for a total cost of $40,000.

Required:
Compute the total and unit cost of each product if the oil has a sales value of $12.00 per barrel and the natural gas has a sales value of $2.00 per cubic foot.

14–2A. Learning Objective 3. Allocating Joint Costs Using the Adjusted Sales Value Method.

Ring-Around-Products Company manufactures three joint products from a single raw material. One of the products, Product X, can be sold as is at the split-off point. The other products, Y and Z, require additional processing. During July, the firm incurred joint costs of $90,000 in producing 30,000 units of Product X, 20,000 units of Product Y, and 15,000 units of Product Z. Product Y required $6,000 in additional processing costs and Product Z required $9,000. The unit sales value of each product follows:

Product X	$1.25
Product Y	3.00
Product Z	3.50

Required:

a. Allocate the joint costs among the three products.
b. Compute the unit cost of each product.

14–3A. Learning Objectives 3 & 4. Allocating Joint Costs Using the Relative Sales Value Method and Accounting for By-Products.

During April, the following costs were recorded in the Work in Process Inventory—Finishing Department account:

Transferred from the Assembly Department	$130,000
Direct labor	25,000
Factory overhead	10,200

These costs led to the production of 4,000 units of Joint Product A, 10,000 units of Joint Product B, and 1,000 units of By-product C. The Finishing Department had no beginning or ending inventories. Unit sales values of the products follow:

Joint Product A	$25.00
Joint Product B	15.00
By-product C	1.00

Required:

a. Using the relative sales value method, allocate the joint costs between the two joint products and compute a unit cost for each.
b. Record the sale of the by-product as other income.

14–4A. Learning Objective 3. Allocating Joint Costs Using Three Methods.

Anderson Company produces two joint products from a single raw material. One of the products, Product D, can be sold at the split-off point for $1.25 per pound. The other product, Product E, can be sold for $2.75 per pound after further processing. During December, Anderson incurred joint costs of $40,000 in producing 70,000 pounds of Product D and 30,000 pounds of Product E. Additional processing costs of $10,000 were incurred to get Product E ready to sell.

Required:
Compute the following:

a. Total and unit cost of each product using the relative sales value method.
b. Total and unit cost of each product using the physical unit method, using pounds as the common unit of measure.
c. Total and unit cost of each product using the assigned weight method assuming that Product D has an assigned weight factor of 2 and Product E has an assigned weight factor of 3.

14–5A. Learning Objectives 4 & 5. Recording By-product Transactions.

Allied Chemical Company produces household cleaning products. Allied's production process leaves a by-product residue that is further processed and sold as an industrial cleaning compound. During August, 19X5, the following costs were incurred to process 12,000 pounds of the by-product after it was separated from the main products:

Direct materials	$8,000
Direct labor	1,200
Factory overhead	800

Required:

a. Record the additional processing costs.
b. Record the sale of the final product at $1.50 per pound assuming the company maintains a separate account to record gains or losses on the sale of by-products.
c. Record the sale of the final product at $1.50 per pound assuming the company *does not* maintain a separate account for gains or losses on the sale of by-products.

GROUP B PROBLEMS

14–1B. Learning Objective 3. Allocating Joint Costs Using the Relative Sales Value Method.

King Refinery produces gasoline and liquid natural gas from a common process. During 19X6, the firm produced 60,000 gallons of gasoline and 10,000 gallons of liquid natural gas for a joint cost of $63,000.

Required:

Compute the total and unit cost of each product if the gasoline has a sales value of $0.90 per gallon and the liquid natural gas has a sales value of $2.10 per gallon.

14–2B. Learning Objective 3. Allocating Joint Costs Using the Adjusted Sales Value Method.

Maine Products Company manufactures three joint products from a single raw material. One of the Products, Product A, can be sold as is at the split-off point. The other products, C and D, require additional processing. During May, the firm incurred joint costs of $80,000 in producing 25,000 units of Product A, 18,000 units of Product B, and 12,000 units of Product C. Product B required $4,000 in additional processing costs and Product C required $6,000. The unit sales value of each product follows:

Product A	$1.20
Product B	2.80
Product C	3.00

Required:

a. Allocate the joint costs among the three products.
b. Compute the unit cost of each product.

14–3B. Learning Objectives 3 & 4. Allocating Joint Costs Using the Relative Sales Value Method and Accounting for By-products.

During May, the following costs were recorded in the Work in Process Inventory—Finishing Department account:

Transferred from the Assembly Department	$140,000
Direct labor	30,000
Factory overhead	12,000

These costs led to the production of 5,000 units of Joint Product A, 12,000 units of Joint Product B, and 1,000 units of By-product C. The Finishing Department had no beginning or ending inventories. Unit sales values of the products follow:

Joint Product A	$30.00
Joint Product B	20.00
By-product C	1.25

Required:

a. Using the relative sales value method, allocate the joint costs between the two joint products and compute a unit cost for each.
b. Record the sale of the by-product as other income.

14–4B. Learning Objective 3. Allocating Joint Costs Using Three Methods.

Roark Company produces two joint products from a single raw material. One of the products, Product A, can be sold at the split-off point for $1.00 per pound. The other product, Product B, can be sold for $2.75 per pound after further processing. During July, Roark incurred joint costs of $32,000 in producing 28,000 pounds of Product A and 12,000 pounds of Product B. Additional processing costs of $6,000 were incurred to get Product B ready to sell.

Required:
Compute the following:

a.   Total and unit cost of each product using the relative sales value method.
b.   Total and unit cost of each product using the physical unit method.
c.   Total and unit cost of each product using the assigned weight method assuming
     that Product A has an assigned weight factor of 2 and Product B has an assigned
     weight factor of 3.

14–5B. Learning Objectives 4 & 5. Recording By-product Transactions.

Madison Company is a producer of meat products. Madison's production process leaves
beef bones as a by-product. The bones are steamed, sterilized, and ground into meal,
which is sold as a mineral supplement to the human diet. During June, the following
costs were incurred to process 25,000 pounds of the by-product after separation from
the main product.

Direct materials	$1,200
Direct labor	4,000
Factory overhead	3,600

Required:

a.   Record the additional processing costs.
b.   Record the sale of the final product at $0.65 per pound assuming the company
     maintains a separate account to record gains or losses on the sale of by-products.
c.   Record the sale of the final product at $0.65 per pound assuming the company *does
     not* maintain a separate account for gains or losses on the sale of by-products.

CASE FOR CRITICAL THINKING

James Cannon is working on an associates degree in accounting at Golden Coast
Community College. After studying joint costs in a cost accounting course, James is
wondering why allocating joint costs between joint products is an issue. James thinks
that the total joint cost should be divided by the total number of all joint products produced, thus assigning all products the same unit cost. Write a paragraph explaining
why this procedure will usually not result in a proper allocation of costs. Is there a situation where this would result in a logical allocation of joint costs? If so, identify that
situation.

ANSWERS TO SELF-STUDY QUIZ 14–1

Joint Costs	Joint Products	Units Produced	Sales Value per Unit	Total Sales Value
$81,000	X	15,000	$1.20	$ 18,000
	Y	50,000	$2.00	100,000
Total sales value				$118,000

Product X: $\dfrac{\$18,000}{\$118,000}$ = 15.3% × $81,000 = $12,393

Product Y: $\dfrac{\$100,000}{\$118,000}$ = 84.7% × $81,000 = $68,607

Total allocated $81,000

Unit costs:

Product X: $12,393 ÷ 15,000 units = $0.826 per unit.
Product Y: $68,607 ÷ 50,000 units = $1.372 per unit.

ANSWERS TO SELF-STUDY QUIZ 14–2

Joint Product	Units Produced	Sales Value per Unit	Total Sales Value	Additional Pro. Costs	Adjusted Sales Value
A	50,000	$1.25	$62,500	-0-	$ 62,500
B	20,000	$3.00	$60,000	$9,000	51,000
Total sales value					$113,500

Product A: $\dfrac{\$\ 62,500}{\$113,500}$ = 55.1% × $80,000 = $44,080

Product B: $\dfrac{\$\ 51,000}{\$113,500}$ = 44.9% × $80,000 = $35,920

Total allocated $80,000

Unit costs:

Product A: $44,080 ÷ 50,000 units = $0.882 per unit.
Product B: $35,920 ÷ 20,000 units = $1.796 per unit.

ANSWERS TO SELF-STUDY QUIZ 14–3

Total pounds produced:
   Joint Product A   80,000
   Joint Product B   20,000
Total   100,000

Joint Product A: $\dfrac{80,000}{100,000}$ = 80% × $65,000 = $52,000

Joint Product B: $\dfrac{20,000}{100,000}$ = 20% × $65,000 = $13,000

Total allocated $65,000

ANSWERS TO SELF-STUDY QUIZ 14—4

Product	Pounds Produced	Assigned Weight	Weight Production
H	90,000	3	270,000
J	7,500	4	30,000
Total weight production			300,000

Product H: $\dfrac{270,000}{300,000}$ = 90% × $80,000 = $72,000

Product J: $\dfrac{30,000}{300,000}$ = 10% × $80,000 = $ 8,000

Total allocated $80,000

ANSWERS TO SELF-STUDY QUIZ 14—5

1	a.	Accounts Receivable	24000	
2		Miscellaneous Income		24000
3	b.	By-Product Inventory	24000	
4		Work in Process Inventory		24000
5	c.	Accounts Receivable	32000	
6		By-Product Inventory		24000
7		Gain or Loss on Sales of By-Product		8000

ANSWERS TO SELF-REVIEW QUIZ 14—6

1	a.	By-Products in Process	280000	
2		Raw Materials Inventory		140000
3		Factory Payroll Clearing		80000
4		Factory Overhead Control		60000
5	b.	Cash	360000	
6		By-Product Inventory		280000
7		Gain or Loss on Sales of By-Product		80000

PROJECT 2—PROCESS COSTING

In Chapters 10 through 14 we covered process costing, including accounting for units lost and accounting for joint products and by-products. We will review these chapters in the form of a comprehensive problem, continuing with South Company for the month of September. All the required forms can be found in the Study Guide/Working Papers. When necessary, carry unit cost to the seventh decimal place.

Task 1—Process Costing Using the Weighted Average Cost Method

South Company had the following costs and production information by department for September, 19X3.

Cutting Department	Materials	Conversion	Total
Beginning work in process inventory costs	$ 23,940	$ 5,355	$ 29,295
Current costs added in September	179,610	61,845	241,455
Total costs to be accounted for	$203,550	$67,200	$270,750

Units in beginning work in process inventory (70% complete as to materials and 45% complete as to conversion)	10,000
Units started into production during September	55,000
Total units to be accounted for	65,000
Units in ending work in process inventory (60% complete as to materials and 40% complete as to conversion)	(15,000)
Units completed and transferred out during September	50,000
Units in beginning work in process inventory	10,000
Units started and completed during September	40,000

Sewing Department	Transferred In	Conversion	Total
Beginning work in process inventory costs	$27,900	$ 16,980	$44,880
Current costs added in September	?	220,000	?
Total costs to be accounted for	$?	$236,980	$?

Units in beginning work in process inventory (65% complete as to conversion)	12,000
Units in ending work in process inventory (70% complete as to conversion)	14,000

Dyeing Department	Transferred In	Materials	Conversion	Total
Beginning work in process inventory costs	$85,440	$ 7,110	$ 7,460	$100,010
Current costs added in September . .	?	37,396	53,812	?
Total costs to be accounted for	$?	$44,506	$61,272	$?

Units in beginning work in process inventory (55% complete as to materials and 55% complete as to conversion)	15,000
Units in ending work in process inventory (60% complete as to materials and 40% complete as to conversion)	13,000

Required:

1. Prepare a cost of production report for September 19X3.
2. Make the journal entry to transfer costs out of work in process inventory at September 30 for each department using the weighted average method.

Task 2—Process Costing Using the FIFO Cost Method

South Company had the following costs and production information by department for September, 19X3.

Cutting Department	Materials	Conversion	Total
Beginning work in process inventory costs	$ 16,100	$ 5,355	$ 21,455
Current costs added in September	188,240	63,860	252,100
Total costs to be accounted for	$204,340	$69,215	$273,555

Units in beginning work in process inventory (70% complete as to materials and 45% complete as to conversion)	10,000
Units started into production during September	55,000
Total units to be accounted for	65,000
Units in ending work in process inventory (60% complete as to materials and 40% complete as to conversion)	(15,000)
Units completed and transferred out during September	50,000
Units in beginning work in process inventory	10,000
Units started and completed during September	40,000

Sewing Department	Transferred In	Conversion	Total
Beginning work in process inventory costs	$40,130	$ 23,510	$63,640
Current costs added in September	?	212,500	?
Total costs to be accounted for	$?	$236,010	$?

Units in beginning work in process inventory (65% complete as to conversion)	12,000
Units in ending work in process inventory (70% complete as to conversion)	14,000

Dyeing Department	Transferred In	Materials	Conversion	Total
Beginning work in process inventory costs	$68,320	$ 7,110	$ 9,470	$84,900
Current costs added in September . .	?	40,404	51,744	?
Total costs to be accounted for	$?	$47,514	$61,214	$?

Units in beginning work in process inventory (40% complete as to materials and 60% complete as to conversion)	15,000
Units in ending work in process inventory (60% complete as to materials and 40% complete as to conversion	13,000

Required:

1. Prepare a cost of production report for September 19X3.
2. Make the journal entry to transfer costs out of work in process inventory at September 30 for each department using the FIFO method.

Task 3—Accounting for Units Lost in Production

South Company had the following costs and production information by department for September, 19X3.

Cutting Department	Materials	Conversion	Total
Beginning work in process inventory costs	$ 15,220	$ 4,910	$ 20,130
Current costs added in September	188,360	62,800	251,160
Total costs to be accounted for	$203,580	$67,710	$271,290

	Total
Units in beginning work in process inventory (70% complete as to materials and 45% complete as to conversion)	10,000
Units started into production during September	55,000
Total units to be accounted for	65,000
Units in ending work in process inventory (60% complete as to materials and 40% complete as to conversion)	(15,000)
Units lost due to normal spoilage	(500)
Units lost due to abnormal spoilage	(1,500)
Units completed and transferred out during September	48,000
Units in beginning work in process inventory	10,000
Units started and completed during September	38,000

Sewing Department	Transferred In	Conversion	Total
Beginning work in process inventory costs	$27,952	$ 24,076	$52,028
Current costs added in September	?	210,000	?
Total costs to be accounted for	$?	$234,076	$?

	Total
Units in beginning work in process inventory (65% complete as to conversion)	12,000
Units in ending work in process inventory (70% complete as to conversion)	14,000
Units lost due to normal spoilage	200
Units lost due to abnormal spoilage	1,000

Dyeing Department	Transferred In	Materials	Conversion	Total
Beginning work in process inventory costs	$78,400	$ 8,200	$10,850	$97,450
Current costs added in September . . .	?	33,611	46,537	?
Total costs to be accounted for	$?	$41,811	$57,387	$?

	Total
Units in beginning work in process inventory (55% complete as to materials and 55% complete as to conversion	15,000
Units in ending work in process inventory (60% complete as to materials and 40% complete as to conversion	13,000
Units lost due to normal spoilage	300
Units lost due to abnormal spoilage	1,000

Required:

1. Prepare a cost of production report for September 19X3.
2. Make the journal entry to transfer costs out of work in process inventory at September 30 for each department using the weighted average method.

Task 4—Accounting for Joint Products and By-Products

South Company has a division called Precision Molding that manufactures two joint products and one by-product from a soft clay. The two joint products are figurines and pottery. Figurines can be sold at the split-off point for $5.00 per pound. Pottery can be sold for $12.00 per pound after further processing. During September, Precision Molding incurred joint costs of $60,000 in producing 20,000 pounds of figurines and 40,000 pounds of pottery. Additional processing costs of $80,000 were incurred to get the pottery ready to sell. Pottery scraps can be crushed into pellets and sold for $.50 per pound. On September 30, Precision Molding had accumulated 1,000 pounds of crushed pellets.

Required:

1. Compute the total and unit cost of each product using the relative sales value method.
2. Compute the total and unit cost of each product using the physical unit method.
3. Compute the total and unit cost of each product using the assigned weight method assuming that figurines have an assigned weight factor of 4 and pottery has an assigned weight factor of 6.
4. Record the credit sale as of September 30 of the crushed pellets assuming that the proceeds are recorded as other income.
5. Record the sales value as of September 30 of the crushed pellets assuming that their estimated sales value is recorded as a reduction in the cost of pottery.
6. Record the credit sale as of September 30 of the crushed pottery for $.60 per pound assuming that their cost had been recorded as a reduction in the cost of pottery.

Part III
Use of Cost
Accounting
in Planning
and Control

Chapter 15
Cost Behavior

LEARNING OBJECTIVES

After studying Chapter 15, you should be able to:

1. Define a variable cost and show how a change in output affects total variable cost and per unit variable cost.
2. Define a fixed cost and show how a change in output affects total fixed cost and per unit fixed cost.
3. Separate a mixed cost into its variable and fixed elements by the scattergraph method.
4. Separate a mixed cost into its variable and fixed elements by the high-low method.
5. Separate a mixed cost into its variable and fixed elements by the least-squares method.

n this chapter we will learn how to separate costs based upon the behavior in relationship to a change in output or to a change in a given activity level. In previous chapters, the emphasis on defining costs was based more on its function or use within the organization. In our discussion of variable, fixed, and mixed costs, it is assumed that the given levels of production fall within the relevant range of activity. The relevant range is the normal range of production between the high and low levels of activity that occurs during a year.

VARIABLE COST

LEARNING OBJECTIVE 1   A **variable cost** is a cost that varies directly with a change in output or with the number of units produced. A variable cost will change in total based upon a change in output, but will always stay constant on a per unit basis. Figure 15–1 gives examples of variable costs.

FIGURE 15–1
*Examples of
Variable Costs*

Type of Organization	Variable Costs

Manufacturing company	Direct materials
	Direct labor
	Variable portion of:
	    Indirect materials
	    Indirect labor
	    Supplies
	    Utilities

Merchandising company	Cost of goods sold

Both manufacturing and
    merchandising companies
	Salespersons commissions
	Clerical costs such as:
	    Invoicing
	    Freight-out
	    Office supplies

Service organizations	Office supplies Travel

Let's assume that we manufacture electric golf carts. Each golf cart requires a battery that costs $100 each. If only ten golf carts are manufactured, the total variable cost for batteries is $1,000 (10 × $100). However, if 100 golf carts are manufactured, the total variable cost for batteries would be $10,000 (100 × $100). Notice that the total variable costs for batteries changes in direct proportion to the number of golf carts manufactured, but the unit cost per battery remains constant at $100. Figure 15–2 shows the behavior of a purely variable cost.

FIGURE 15–2
Analysis of Variable Cost Behavior

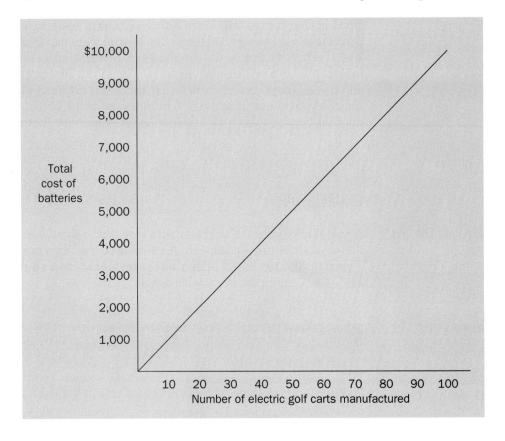

Notice in Figure 15–2 that a purely variable cost (battery) is directly proportional to the output (number of electric golf carts manufactured), resulting in a line that runs directly through the origin and extends upward in a straight line.

FIXED COST

LEARNING OBJECTIVE 2   A **fixed cost** is a cost that is constant in total but will change on a per unit basis depending upon the output or the number of units produced. A fixed cost is not affected by changes in production within the relevant range of activity. Figure 15–3 shows examples of fixed costs.

Let's assume that the annual depreciation on the factory building where electric golf carts are manufactured is $10,000. If only ten electric golf carts are produced, the per unit cost for the annual depreciation assigned to one electric golf cart is $1,000 ($10,000/10). However, if 100 electric carts are produced, the annual depreciation per unit decreases to $100 ($10,000/100). Figure 15–4 shows the behavior of a fixed cost.

FIGURE 15–3
*Examples of
Fixed Costs*

Type of Organization	Fixed Costs
Manufacturing	Straight-line depreciation on: 　　Factory building 　　Machinery and equipment
Manufacturing, merchandising and service	Salaries of: 　　President, 　　Managers, 　　Supervisors Advertising, Insurance Fixed portion of utility costs Maintenance

FIGURE 15–4
*Analysis of Fixed
Cost Behavior*

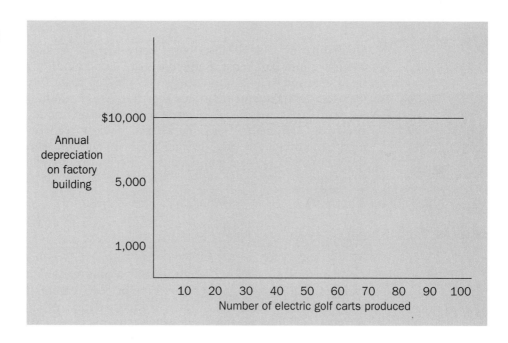

Notice in Figure 15–4 that the annual depreciation on the factory building remains constant at $10,000 no matter how many electric golf carts are produced. This results in a straight line that runs horizontal to the number of units produced. However, the fixed cost per unit will increase when fewer units are produced, and will decrease when greater units are produced.

Figure 15–5 presents a summary of variable and fixed costs.

FIGURE 15–5
Summary of Variable and Fixed Cost Behavior

Cost	Cost Behavior	
	In Total	**Per Unit**
Variable Cost	Changes in total depending upon the number of units produced.	Constant on a per unit basis.
Fixed cost	Constant in total	Changes per unit depending upon the number of units produced.

SEMIVARIABLE COST

Unfortunately, not all costs come conveniently packaged as a true variable cost or a pure fixed cost. Some costs are a combination of both variable and fixed, referred to as a *semivariable* or a **mixed cost.** These costs have both a variable and fixed portion mixed together. A good example of this type of cost is the monthly utility bill. Even if a manufacturer shuts off all the gas, electricity, etc., there will still be a fixed hook-up charge that appears in the monthly billing. An organization needs to separate these mixed costs into their variable and fixed components. Later in this chapter you will learn how to do this.

STEP-VARIABLE COST

Another type of cost that is not exactly a pure variable cost is called a **step-variable** or a *stair-step* cost. This type of cost remains constant for a small range of activity or output, but will increase in large chunks or steps as the activity level increases. A good example of this is the cost of a machine maintenance worker. Assume that only one maintenance worker, who earns $25,000 per year, is required when 50 electric golf carts are produced. However, if production increases to more than 50, a second maintenance worker is required in order to keep up with the increased production. Figure 15–6 shows a step-variable cost.

For purposes of planning and control, a step-variable cost is normally treated as a variable cost, even though it is not directly proportional (constant per unit) to changes in output.

FIGURE 15–6
Step-Variable Cost

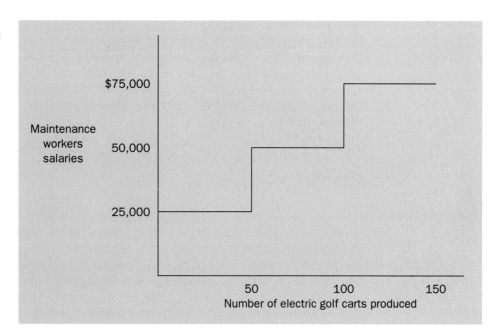

SELF-STUDY QUIZ 15–1   Classify the following as variable cost (vc), fixed cost (fc), or mixed cost (mc):

a. President's salary.
b. Direct labor.
c. Straight-line depreciation on factory building.
d. Utility cost.
e. Commissions paid to salespersons.

Answers at end of chapter.

ANALYSIS OF MIXED COST

In order to use cost accounting data for purposes of planning and control, all costs need to be classified as variable or fixed. Many costs will be easy to classify, such as direct materials (variable) and straight-line depreciation on equipment (fixed). However, some costs are **mixed,** such as a utility cost, and the variable portion has to be separated from the fixed portion. Three widely used methods of separating a mixed cost include: (1) scattergraph method, (2) high-low method, and (3) least squares method. The first two methods (scattergraph and high-low) are considered non-scientific and may not be mathematically precise but are easy to do. The last method, least squares, is more scientific and mathematically precise, but more difficult to do. All three methods have one thing in common—they use past accounting data to predict future costs.

SCATTERGRAPH METHOD

LEARNING OBJECTIVE 3   One easy method to separate a mixed cost requires plotting data points on graph paper and drawing a line (called a trend line or regression line) through the middle of all the data points. This procedure is known as the **scattergraph method.** This visually fitted line, although not scientific, can be a very close approximation to the actual variable and fixed costs. For example, assume that a manufacturer has collected the last six months of electric bills. It is reasonable to assume that a high correlation exists between the total machine hours used during the month and the monthly electric bill. Let's arrange our data in the following table:

Month	Machine Hours	Utility Bill
April	400	$1,100
May	425	1,150
June	390	975
July	450	1,200
August	300	900
September	375	950

Figure 15–7 shows the machine hours on the x axis (horizontal line) and the utility bill costs on the y axis (vertical line). Each dot represents a monthly utility bill on the graph.

Now that the points have been plotted as shown in Figure 15–7, the next step requires drawing a line through the middle of all the dots. This means using a ruler and visually attempting to draw the best fitted line through the middle of all the dots. Figure 15–8 shows the scattergraph with the trend line added.

Notice in Figure 15–8 that where the trend line crosses the total cost line (also called the y axis or vertical axis) is the amount of fixed cost. In our example, the fixed cost appears to be about $250. Once the fixed cost is known, do the following steps to figure the variable cost:

1. Select any point along the trend line and determine the total cost. For example at 400 machine hours the total cost is $1,100. This is a coinci-

FIGURE 15–7
*Data Points
Plotted on Graph*

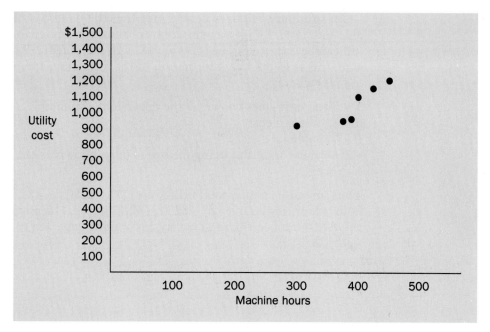

FIGURE 15–8
Scattergraph

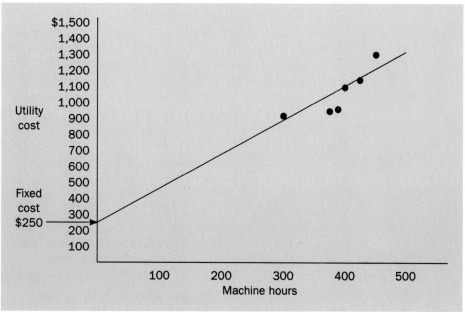

dence because in Figure 15–8, the trend line just happens to go through this dot.

2. Since we know that the estimated fixed cost is $250, then total variable cost at 400 machine hours must be $850 ($1,100 – $250). The variable rate must be $2.125 ($850/400) per machine hour.

In summary, we have determined that the fixed cost is $250 and the variable rate is $2.125 per machine hour. Thus, for any given month, the utility bill can be expected to be $250 plus $2.125 per machine hour. Another way to state this is to put the information in the following equation or formula: $Y = a + b(x)$ where:

Y = Total cost (also known as the dependent variable)
a = Total fixed cost
b = Variable rate
x = Activity or output being measured (also known as the independent variable)

Thus, in our example, total utility cost (Y) = $250 (a) + $2.125 (b) per machine hour (x); or, restated as $Y = \$250 + \$2.125(x)$. If 410 machine hours are budgeted for October, the total utility cost can be expected to be $ 1,121.25 ($250 + $2.125 (410)).

HIGH-LOW METHOD

LEARNING OBJECTIVE 4 Another method of separating a mixed cost, considered non-scientific but easy to use, is called the **high-low method.**

The high-low method requires selecting the high and low points from the observed data and then determining the fixed and variable cost. Let's use the same data that we used in the scattergraph method. The following table presents this data again:

Month	Machine Hours	Utility Bill
April	400	$1,100
May	425	1,150
June	390	975
July	450	1,200
August	300	900
September	375	950

As you can see from the above table, the highest number of machine hours is 450 (July) and the lowest is 300 (August). Rearrange the data as follows:

		Machine Hours	Utility Cost
	High	450	$1,200
	Low	300	900
Difference		150	$ 300

The difference in the utility cost divided by the difference in machine hours will yield the variable rate per machine hour.

$$\frac{\text{Difference in cost}}{\text{Difference in hours}} = \frac{\$300}{150} = \$2.00 \text{ per machine hour.}$$

Once the variable rate is known, the next step is to compute the fixed cost. Either the high point or low point can be used. Using the high point, the fixed cost would be computed as follows:

Total cost at the high point	=	$1,200
Total variable cost at the high point		
(450 × $2.00 per machine hour)	=	900
Total fixed cost	=	$ 300

Or using the low point, the fixed cost would be calculated as follows:

Total cost at the low point	=	$900
Total variable cost at the low point		
(300 × $2.00 per machine hour)	=	600
Total fixed cost	=	$300

As you can see, the fixed cost is $300 using either the high point or low point. Thus, the formula for utility cost is $Y = \$300 + \$2.00$ per machine hour; or, restated as $Y = \$300 + \$2.00(x)$. If 410 machine hours are budgeted for October, the total utility cost is expected to be $1,120.00 (300 + $2.00 (410)).

Note that the scattergraph method yields a different cost equation than the high-low method. This will be true when the high and low points in the collected data are not representative of all the observed data points. In other words, if the high and low points in our observed data do not represent all the data, a distortion will result.

LEAST-SQUARES METHOD

LEARNING OBJECTIVE 5   The third and last method of separating mixed costs, called the **least-squares method,** is the most precise but, unfortunately, the most difficult to do. The term, least-squares, derives its name from a mathematical technique of fitting the trend line exactly in the middle of the squared deviations from each data point plotted on the graph.

In order to arrive at our cost formula $Y = a + b(x)$, we will need to solve two equations with two unknowns. The two equations are listed below:

(1) $\Sigma XY = \Sigma X(a) + \Sigma X^2(b)$
(2) $\Sigma Y = n(a) + \Sigma X(b)$

where

Σ = Sum of (e.g. ΣY = sum of all Y's)
n = Number of observations
x = Activity or output being measured (also known as the independent variable)

Y = Total cost (also known as the dependent variable)
a = Total fixed cost
b = Variable rate

We will *array* our data so that the above two equations can be solved.

Month	Machine Hours X	Utility Bill Y	$X(X)$	$X(Y)$
April	400	$1,100	160,000	440,000
May	425	1,150	180,625	488,750
June	390	975	152,100	380,250
July	450	1,200	202,500	540,000
August	300	900	90,000	270,000
Sept.	375	950	140,625	356,250
Totals	2,340	6,275	925,850	2,475,250

Substituting the above totals into the two equations yields the following results:

equation (1) $2,475,250 = 2,340a + 925,850b$
equation (2) $6,275 = 6a + 2,340b$

Now we have a situation which includes two unknowns: a and b. In order to solve for one unknown, we must eliminate one of the unknowns. Since the number next to a is the smallest, let's eliminate a. First multiply equation (1) by 6 (the coefficient of a in equation (2)) and multiply equation (2) by 2,340 (the coefficient of a in equation (1)). This gives

equation (1) $14,851,500 = 14,040a + 5,555,100b$
equation (2) $14,683,500 = 14,040a + 5,475,600b$

Subtracting equation (2) from equation (1) gives

$168,000 = 79,500b$
   $b = \$2.113$ (rounded to the nearest thousandth)

The value of b is the variable rate. We can now substitute the value of b in either equation. Substituting \$2.113 in equation (2) yields the following:

equation (2) $6,275 = 6a + 2,340(\$2.113)$
                   $6,275 = 6a + 4,944.42$
              $1,330.58 = 6a$
                    $a = \$221.76$

The value of a or the fixed cost is \$221.76. The cost formula for the expected utility cost gives:

$Y = \$221.76 + \$2.113(x)$

If 410 machine hours are budgeted for October, the total utility cost is expected to be \$1,088.09 (\$221.76 + (\$2.113 (410)).

Figure 15–9 presents a summary of the three methods.

FIGURE 15–9
*Summary of
Three Methods*

Total cost = fixed cost + variable rate times (hours, units, miles, etc.)

$$Y = a + b \text{ times } (x)$$

Method	Cost Formula
Scattergraph	$Y = \$250.00 + \$2.125\,(x)$
High–low	$Y = \$300.00 + \$2.00\,(x)$
Least Squares	$Y = \$221.76 + \$2.113\,(x)$

As you can see in Figure 15–9, we have arrived at a different cost formula using each of the three methods: scattergraph, high-low, and least-squares. The first two methods are non-scientific and the results can vary. The least-squares method is the mathematically precise way of determining the cost equation and will normally yield a different set of numbers.

SELF-STUDY QUIZ 15–2 Johnson Company has reviewed the past six months of shipping bills and has noticed a high degree of fluctuation in its shipping expense. The data has been assembled in the following table. Using the high-low method, determine the cost formula for shipping expense.

Month	Units Shipped	Total Shipping Expense
January	5	$35
February	7	50
March	4	30
April	3	25
May	6	45
June	8	52

Answers at end of chapter.

NOTE The scattergraph method and the high-low method are non-scientific procedures designed to separate variable and fixed costs. The least-squares method, considered more scientific and accurate, is a mathematically designed procedure that separates variable and fixed costs.

SELF-STUDY PROBLEM

Precision Parts Company manufactures a product that goes through a glazing process. Management has noticed cost fluctuations during the past six quarters and would like to gain an understanding of this cost. The data for this glazing process appears below:

Quarter	Units Produced	Total Glazing Cost
1	6	52
2	9	70
3	12	94
4	8	61
5	10	75
6	4	38

Required:

1. Using the scattergraph method, separate the glazing cost into its variable and fixed cost portions. Put the cost formula in the format of $Y = a + b(x)$

2. Using the high-low method, separate the glazing cost into its variable and fixed cost portions. Put the cost formula in the format of $Y = a + b(x)$.

3. Using the least-squares method, separate the glazing cost into its variable and fixed cost portions. Round the variable rate to the nearest 1,000th of a decimal point, and the fixed cost to the 100th of a decimal point. Put the cost formula in the format of $Y = a + b(x)$.

SOLUTION TO SELF-STUDY PROBLEM

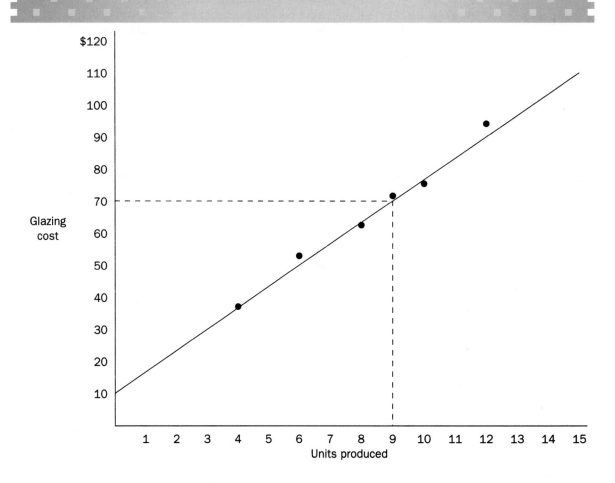

Fixed cost (a) = $10.00
Total cost at 9 units produced = $70.00
Less: Fixed cost   10.00
          Total variable cost $60.00

Variable rate = $\dfrac{\$60}{9}$ = $6.667

Cost formula Y = $10.00 + $6.667(x)

2.

	Units Produced	Glazing Cost
High	12	$94
Low	4	38
Difference	8	$56

$\dfrac{\text{Difference in cost}}{\text{Difference in units}}$ = $\dfrac{\$56}{8}$ = $7.00 per unit (variable rate)

Total cost at the high point   = $94
Total variable cost at the high point
   (12 × $7.00 per machine hour)   =   84
Total fixed cost   = $10
       Cost formula: Y = $10.00 + $7.00(x).

3.

Quarter	Units Produced X	Glazing Cost Y	X2	XY
1	6	52	36	312
2	9	70	81	630
3	12	94	144	1,128
4	8	61	64	488
5	10	75	100	750
6	4	38	16	152
Totals	49	390	441	3,460

(1) $\Sigma XY = \Sigma X(a) + \Sigma b(X^2)$
(2) $\Sigma Y = n(a) + b(\Sigma X)$

equation (1)	3,460	=	49a	+	441b
equation (2)	390	=	6a	+	49b

Multiply equation (1) by 6 and multiply equation (2) by 49.

equation (1)	20,760	=	294a	+	2,646b
equation (2)	19,110	=	294a	+	2,401b
subtract equation (2)					
from equation (1)	1,650	=			245b
	b	=	6.735		

Substituting b in
equation (2):	390	=	6a	+	49(6.735)
	390	=	6a	+	3,300.015
	6a	=	59.985		
	a	=	10.00		

Cost formula: Y = 10.00 + $6.735 (x)

SUMMARY

A **variable cost** varies directly with an activity such as the number of units produced. A variable cost will change in total based upon a change in output, but will always stay constant on a per unit basis. Examples of variable costs include direct materials and direct labor. A **fixed cost** remains constant in total but will vary on a per unit basis depending upon the output or the number of units produced. An example of a fixed cost is the straight line depreciation on the factory building.

A **semivariable** or a **mixed cost** has both a variable and fixed portion mixed together. A good example of a mixed cost is the monthly utility bill.

A **step-variable cost** varies in large increments, and not in a proportional or direct relationship with the activity being measured. It is treated as a variable cost for planning and control purposes. A good example of a step-variable cost is the cost of maintenance workers.

For planning and control purposes, mixed costs must be separated into their variable and fixed components. There are three methods of separating mixed costs; **scattergraph method, high-low method,** and **least-squares method.** The scattergraph method involves plotting the data on graph paper and visually fitting a trend line in the middle of the observed data points. The high-low method assumes that the high and low points of observation are representative of all the data. A formula computes the variable rate and the fixed cost once the difference between the high and low points in activity and cost are measured. The least-squares method is the most accurate and precise of the three methods. This method uses a statistical technique of fitting a mathematically exact trend line between all of the observed data points.

KEY TERMS

Fixed Cost. A cost constant in total but varies on a per unit basis depending upon the output or quantity produced.

High-low Method. A non-scientific method of separating a mixed cost by selecting the high and low data points. A formula is then used to calculate the variable rate and the total fixed costs.

Least-squares Method. A scientific method of fitting a mathematically precise trend line in the middle of all plotted points on a graph.

Scattergraph Method. A non-scientific method of separating a mixed cost by visually fitting a trend line in the middle of all the data points plotted on a graph.

Semivariable Cost or Mixed Cost. A cost that includes both a variable and fixed cost.

Step-variable Cost. A cost that remains constant for a small range of activity or output but increases in steps as the activity level increases.

Variable Cost. A cost constant on a per unit basis but varies in total depending upon the output or quantity produced.

QUESTIONS FOR REVIEW

1. Define a variable cost and give an example.
2. What happens to the per-unit variable cost when output increases?
3. What happens to total variable cost when output increases?
4. Define a fixed cost and give an example.
5. What happens to the per-unit fixed cost when output decreases?
6. What happens to total fixed cost when output decreases?
7. Define a mixed cost and give an example.
8. What is another term for a semivariable cost?
9. What is the nature of a step-variable cost?
10. Describe the scattergraph method of separating a mixed cost.
11. Define each of the letters in the cost formula $Y = a + bx$.
12. In the high-low method, how do you determine the variable rate?
13. What does the term least-squares mean?
14. Of the three methods of analyzing mixed costs, which method is considered the most accurate and precise?

EXERCISES

15–1. Learning Objectives 1, 2, 3. Identifying Costs.
Classify the following costs as being variable (v), fixed (f), or mixed (m).

a. Salespersons' commissions.
b. President's salary.
c. Electricity bill.
d. Advertising.
e. Rental on warehouse.
f. Direct materials.
g. Straight-line depreciation of equipment.
h. Office supplies used.
i. Direct labor.
j. Shipping expense that costs $20,000 per year, plus $2.00 per item shipped.

15–2. Learning Objective 2. Calculating Unit Cost for Depreciation.
The annual depreciation for the factory building is $20,000. Determine the unit cost for depreciation under the following situations:

a. 1,000 units are produced.
b. 10,000 units are produced.

15–3. Learning Objective 1. Calculating Variable Costs for Direct Materials.
For each truck that Davis Company manufactures, it adds a radiator that costs $200 during the manufacturing process. Determine the total direct material cost for radiators under the following situations:

a.   500 trucks are manufactured.

b.   1,000 trucks are manufactured.

15–4. Learning Objectives 1, 2. Analyzing Variable and Fixed Costs in Total and Per Unit.

Guild Company manufactures and sells one product. The production can vary from 20,000 to 60,000 units. A partially completed schedule of the company's total and per unit costs for the coming year follows:

	Units produced and sold		
	20,000	**40,000**	**60,000**
Total Costs:			
Variable costs	$ 80,000	?	?
Fixed costs	100,000	?	?
Total costs	$180,000	?	?
Cost per unit:			
Variable cost	?	?	?
Fixed cost	?	?	?
Total cost per unit	?	?	?

a.   Complete the schedule for Guild Company's total and per unit costs.

b.   Determine the cost formula in the format of $Y = a + bx$.

15–5. Learning Objectives 3, 4, 5. Using the Cost Formula.

The monthly cost formula for shipping expense is $1,200 plus $3.25 per unit shipped. Calculate the expected total shipping expense for the month of March if:

a.   Shipped 230 units.

b.   Shipped 470 units.

15–6. Learning Objective 4. Using the High-Low Method.

Lee Company has analyzed their monthly maintenance costs and have determined the following from their accounting records: During the month of August their direct labor hours totaled 20,000 and their maintenance costs for this month totaled $36,000. During the month of March their direct labor hours totaled only 10,000 and their maintenance costs totaled $30,000. Using the high-low method determine the following:

a.   Variable rate per direct labor hour.

b.   Total fixed cost for the month.

c.   Cost formula for maintenance costs $(Y = a + b(x))$.

d.   Total expected maintenance cost for a month in which 12,000 direct labor hours are worked.

GROUP A PROBLEMS

15–1A. Learning Objectives 3. Using the Scattergraph Method.

Providence Hospital has kept records of their x-ray costs and the number of x-rays taken for the last nine months. This information appears on the following page:

Month	X-Rays Taken	X-Ray Costs
January	4,100	$26,000
February	5,000	27,000
March	3,000	21,000
April	2,250	18,000
May	2,500	20,000
June	1,000	14,000
July	1,750	16,000
August	3,500	22,000
September	3,750	24,000

Required:

1. Prepare a scattergraph. Plot the x-ray cost on the vertical axis or y axis, and the number of x-rays taken on the horizontal or x axis. Fit a trend line in the middle of all the data points that have been plotted.
2. What is the approximate monthly fixed cost for x-rays? The approximate variable cost per x-ray taken?
3. State the variable and fixed costs in the formula $Y = a + b(x)$.

15–2A. Learning Objectives 4. Using the High-Low Method.
Refer to the data in problem 15–1A.
Required:

1. Using the high-low method, determine the cost formula for x-ray costs.
2. State the variable and fixed costs in the formula $Y = a = b(x)$.
3. How much x-ray costs would be expected to be incurred during a month in which 2,600 x-rays are taken?

15–3A. Learning Objectives 4. Using the High-Low Method.
Mercury Delivery Service operates a fleet of delivery trucks. The cost accountant has determined that if a truck is driven 100,000 miles during the year, the operating cost is 12.5 cents per mile or a total of $12,500. If a truck is driven only 80,000 miles during a year, the operating cost increases to 13 cents per mile or a total of $10,400.
Required:

1. Using the high-low method, determine the variable cost per mile and the total fixed costs for the year.
2. Express the variable and fixed costs in the form $Y = a + b(x)$.
3. If a truck were driven 90,000 miles during a year, what total cost would you expect to be incurred?

15–4A. Learning Objectives 5. Using the Least-Squares Method.
A product that Wray Company manufactures goes through a polishing process. The company has observed polishing costs over the last six quarters as follows:

Quarter	Units Produced	Total Polishing Cost
1	9	$30
2	6	22
3	12	36
4	5	20
5	8	28
6	10	33

The management of Wray Company would like to separate the variable and fixed costs.

Required:

1. Using the least-squares method, determine the variable polishing cost per unit and the total fixed polishing cost per quarter. Round to the nearest 1,000 of a decimal point for the variable rate, and the nearest cent for fixed cost.
2. State the variable and fixed costs in the formula $Y = a + b(x)$.
3. If the company processes seven units next quarter, what is the expected total polishing cost?

GROUP B PROBLEMS

15–1B. Learning Objectives 3. Using the Scattergraph Method.

St. Joseph Hospital has kept records of their x-ray costs and the number of x-rays taken for the last nine months. This information appears below:

Month	X-Rays Taken	X-Ray Costs
January	7,000	$28,000
February	8,000	30,000
March	6,000	24,000
April	5,250	22,000
May	5,750	23,000
June	4,000	16,000
July	4,750	18,000
August	6,500	25,000
September	6,750	27,000

Required:

1. Prepare a scattergraph. Plot the x-ray cost on the vertical axis or y axis, and the number of x-rays taken on the horizontal or x axis. Fit a trend line in the middle of all the data points that have been plotted.
2. What is the approximate monthly fixed cost for x-rays? The approximate variable cost per x-ray taken?
3. State the variable and fixed costs in the formula $Y = a + b(x)$.

15–2B. Learning Objectives 4. Using the High-Low Method.

Refer to the data in problem 15-1B.
Required:

1. Using the high-low method, determine the cost formula for x-ray costs.
2. State the variable and fixed costs in the formula $Y = a = b(x)$.
3. How much x-ray costs would be expected to be incurred during a month in which 5,600 x-rays are taken?

15–3B. Learning Objectives 4. Using the High-Low Method.

Speedy Delivery Service operates a fleet of delivery trucks. The cost accountant has determined that if a truck is driven 80,000 miles during the year, the operating cost is 9 cents per mile or a total of $7,200. If a truck is driven only 50,000 miles during a year, the operating cost increases to 12 cents per mile or a total of $6,000.

Required:

1. Using the high-low method, determine the variable cost per mile and the total fixed costs for the year.
2. Express the variable and fixed costs in the form $Y = a + b(x)$.
3. If a truck were driven 70,000 miles during a year, what total cost would you expect to be incurred?

15–4B. Learning Objectives 5. Using the Least-Squares Method.

A product that Hansen Company manufactures goes through a polishing process. The company has observed polishing costs over the last six quarters as follows:

Quarter	Units Produced	Total Polishing Cost
1	8	$40
2	5	30
3	12	58
4	4	20
5	9	42
6	10	45

The management of Hansen Company would like to separate the variable and fixed costs.

Required:

1. Using the least-squares method, determine the variable polishing cost per unit and the total fixed polishing cost per quarter. Round to the nearest 1,000 of a decimal point for the variable rate, and the nearest cent for fixed cost.
2. State the variable and fixed costs in the formula $Y = a + b(x)$.
3. If the company processes 6 units next quarter, what is the expected total polishing cost?

CASE FOR CRITICAL THINKING

McGregor Corporation, a small manufacturer of office furniture, has requested your assistance in helping them control costs. After reviewing their financial statements, you ask the president if anyone has ever separated costs between variable and fixed. The president is interested and asks you what the difference is between a variable and fixed cost. Explain this to the president and also explain the advantages and disadvantages of using scattergraph, high-low, and least–squares method to separate a mixed cost.

ANSWERS TO SELF-STUDY QUIZ 15–1

a. fc
b. vc
c. fc
d. mc
e. vc

ANSWERS TO SELF-STUDY QUIZ 15–2

	Units Shipped	**Shipping Expense**
High	8	$52
Low	3	25
Difference	5	$27

$$\frac{\text{Difference in cost}}{\text{Difference in units}} = \frac{\$27}{5} = \$5.40 \text{ per unit (variable rate)}$$

Total cost at the high point	=	$52.00
Total variable cost at the high point		
(8 × $5.40 per unit shipped)	=	43.20
Total fixed cost	=	$ 8.80

Cost formula: $Y = \$8.80 + \$5.40(x)$.

Chapter 16
Direct Costing: Cost-Volume-Profit Relationships

LEARNING OBJECTIVES

After studying Chapter 16, you should be able to:

1. Explain the difference between direct costing and absorption costing and compute the unit product cost under each method.
2. Prepare income statements using both direct costing and absorption costing and explain why the net income is different.
3. Compute the break-even point by the unit contribution method.
4. Estimate the sales necessary to earn a desired profit.
5. Prepare a break-even chart.

In Chapter 15 we learned how to separate costs based upon their cost behavior in relationship to a change in output or volume. We also learned how to separate a mixed cost into its variable and fixed elements. In this chapter we are going to continue using costs based upon this analysis. First, we will learn how to calculate the unit product cost under the direct (variable) costing method and the absorption (traditional) costing method. Next, we will learn how to prepare income statements under the direct costing method and the absorption costing method. Finally, once costs are categorized as variable and fixed, we can perform some basic cost-volume-profit analysis.

DIRECT COSTING

LEARNING OBJECTIVE 1

The term **direct costing** describes the method of accounting that uses only direct or variable production costs in the calculation of the product cost. The fixed production costs are treated as a period cost (similar to selling and administration cost) and deducted in total in the year that they are incurred. In order to demonstrate the direct costing method, let's assume that Collier Company manufactures a single product where 20,000 units were produced in a year. Figure 16–1 shows the production data.

FIGURE 16–1
Production Data Using Direct Costing

**Collier Company
Production Data
(Direct Costing)**

Units produced: 20,000

Variable production cost per unit:	Total Cost/Units produced	Unit Cost
Direct materials	$100,000/20,000	$ 5
Direct labor	160,000/20,000	8
Variable factory overhead	40,000/20,000	2
Variable production cost per unit	$300,000/20,000	$15

Fixed factory overhead: $100,000

As you can see in Figure 16–1, under the direct costing method, the calculation of the unit product cost includes only the variable production costs. The fixed factory overhead is deducted in total on the income statement, similar to the way selling and administrative expenses are deducted. Direct costing is useful for internal reporting. It allows management to analyze costs by behavior and provides needed input for break-even analysis, which is covered later in the chapter.

ABSORPTION COSTING

LEARNING OBJECTIVE 1

The term **absorption costing** describes the method of accounting that absorbs all production costs (both variable and fixed) in the calculation of the production cost. The fixed production costs (fixed factory overhead) appear as part of the unit product cost. In order to demonstrate the absorption costing method, let's use Collier Company again. Let's assume that the fixed factory overhead amounted to $100,000 for the year. Figure 16–2 shows the production data.

FIGURE 16–2
Production Data Using Absorption Costing

Collier Company
Production Data
(Absorption Costing)

Units produced: 20,000

Variable production cost per unit:	Total Cost/Units Produced	Unit Cost
Direct materials	$100,000/20,000	$ 5
Direct labor	160,000/20,000	8
Variable factory overhead	40,000/20,000	2
Variable production cost per unit	$300,000/20,000	$15
Fixed factory overhead cost per unit:	100,000/20,000	5
Total production cost per unit:	$400,000/20,000	$20

As you can see in Figure 16–2, the product cost per unit includes both variable and fixed production costs. If you compare Figure 16–1 with 16–2 you will see that the difference between the product cost under direct costing and the product cost under absorption costing appears in the accounting for the fixed factory overhead. Under direct costing, the fixed factory overhead of $100,000 is deducted in total as a period cost and does not appear as part of the unit product cost. Under absorption costing, the fixed factory overhead is added to the product cost. Under absorption costing, the unit product cost is $20, $5 higher than under direct costing. This $5 represents the fixed factory overhead ($100,000/20,000) that has been assigned to each unit produced. Generally Accepted Accounting Principles (GAAP) requires absorption costing for external reporting. Absorption costing is also known as "full costing" since all factory overhead (variable and fixed) is assigned to cost of goods sold and inventory.

SELF-STUDY QUIZ 16–1 Calculate the unit product cost under (a) direct costing method, and (b) absorption costing method using the following production cost data:

Units produced	10,000
Direct materials	$50,000
Direct labor	60,000
Variable factory overhead	30,000
Fixed factory overhead	40,000
Variable selling & administrative expense	50,000
Fixed selling & administrative expense	60,000

Answers at end of chapter.

DIRECT COSTING INCOME STATEMENT

LEARNING OBJECTIVE 2

Now that we have learned how to calculate the product costs for direct costing and absorption costing, let's prepare income statements. An income statement prepared under the direct costing approach emphasizes the separation of **all** variable and fixed costs. Continuing with our example of Collier Company, let's assume this additional data:

Units sold:	15,000 ($40 each)
Variable selling and administrative expenses:	$90,000 ($ 6 each)
Fixed selling and administrative expenses:	$60,000

Figure 16–3 shows an income statement prepared under the direct costing method.

FIGURE 16–3
Income Statement Under Direct Costing

Collier Company
Income Statement
(Direct Costing)
For Year Ended December 31, 19XX

1	Sales (15,000 x $40)		$600 0 0 0 00
2	Less variable expenses:		
3	Variable cost of goods sold (15,000 x $15)	$225 0 0 0 00	
4	Variable selling and administrative		
5	expense (15,000 x $6)	90 0 0 0 00	
6	Total variable expenses		315 0 0 0 00
7	Contribution margin		$285 0 0 0 00
8	Less fixed expenses:		
9	Fixed factory overhead	$100 0 0 0 00	
10	Fixed selling and administrative expense	60 0 0 0 00	
11	Total fixed expenses		160 0 0 0 00
12	Net income		$125 0 0 0 00

As you can see in Figure 16–3, under the direct costing method, the income statement shows all variable expenses deducted from sales to arrive at the contribution margin. The **contribution margin,** the amount remaining after deducting all variable expenses from sales, applies (or contributes) toward fixed expenses and net income. Also notice in Figure 16–3, that all fixed expenses, including fixed factory overhead, are deducted from the contribution margin to arrive at net income. The format of a direct costing income statement emphasizes the presentation of costs based upon their cost behavior. In Figure 16–3, note that the total fixed factory overhead is deducted on the income statement. None of the fixed factory overhead appears in the cost of goods sold or in the ending inventory. Next we will compare and contrast the direct costing format of an income statement with the absorption costing format of an income statement.

ABSORPTION COSTING INCOME STATEMENT

LEARNING OBJECTIVE 2

You will recognize the absorption costing format of an income statement. This is similar to the format used in previous chapters when preparing an income statement. This costing method absorbs or applies all manufacturing costs, including the fixed factory overhead to units of product. If any of the units produced during a period of time remain unsold at the end of the period then the fixed factory overhead attached to these unsold units will become a part of the cost of the ending inventory. In Figure 16–4, an absorption costing income statement has been prepared using the same data that was used for the direct costing income statement appearing in Figure 16–3.

FIGURE 16–4
Income Statement Under Absorption Costing

Collier Company
Income Statement
(Absorption Costing)
For Year Ended December 31, 19XX

1	Sales (15,000 x $40)	$600 000 00	1
2	Less cost of goods sold (15,000 x $20)	300 000 00	2
3	Gross profit	$300 000 00	3
4	Operating expenses:		4
5	Variable selling and administrative expense	$90 000 00	5
6	Fixed selling and administrative expense	60 000 00	6
7	Total operating expenses	150 000 00	7
8	Net income	$150 000 00	8
9			9
10			10
11			11
12			12

Notice in Figure 16–4 that the cost of goods sold uses $20 per unit (see Figure 16–2). This figure includes the fixed factory overhead of $5 per unit. You will also notice that after deducting the cost of goods sold, we arrived at the gross profit. All selling and administrative expenses were deducted from gross profit in order to arrive at net income. The absorption costing format divides expenses based upon their function or use within the organization. The unit product cost includes all production costs (variable and fixed). If you compare direct costing to absorption costing net income, you will see that absorption costing net income is $25,000 higher. This can be explained by examining more closely the application of fixed factory overhead to units of product. In Figure 16–3, all $100,000 of fixed factory overhead was deducted from the contribution margin to arrive at net income. In Figure 16–4, only $75,000 of fixed factory overhead (15,000 × $5) was deducted from sales to arrive at gross profit. The ending inventory includes the remaining 5,000 units with each unit having $5 of fixed factory overhead attached. Therefore, under the absorption costing method, $25,000 of the fixed factory overhead has not been released on the income statement because it is attached to the ending inventory. The net income figures under direct costing and absorption costing can be reconciled as shown in Figure 16–5.

FIGURE 16–5
Reconciliation of Net Income

1	Net income under absorption costing	$150 00 0 00		1
2	Less fixed factory overhead cost deferred or			2
3	attached to the ending inventory (5,000 x $5)	25 00 0 00		3
4	Net income under direct costing	$125 00 0 00		4

As you can see in Figure 16–5, whenever the units produced exceed the number of units sold, net income under absorption costing will be higher than net income under direct costing. The difference will always be in the amount of fixed overhead attached to each unit produced under the absorption costing method. Because of the ending inventory, some of the fixed factory overhead cost will not be released on the income statement. However, the opposite will occur whenever the number of units sold exceeds the number of units produced. Net income under absorption costing will be less than net income under direct costing. Again the reason is the fixed factory overhead attached to the units produced. Under absorption costing, when sales exceed production, the fixed factory overhead deferred in the ending inventory from a previous period will now be released on the income statement in a following period.

When sales are exactly the same as the number of units produced, net income under absorption costing will be identical to the net income under direct costing. In this situation, there will not be an increase in the ending inventory. All fixed factory overhead, for this time period, will be charged against sales on the absorption income statement. Fixed factory overhead is always deducted from the contribution margin to arrive at net income on the direct costing method. Therefore, the net income under the two methods will be the same.

NOTE Variable costing is useful for internal reporting. It allows management to analyze costs by behavior. Management can determine if a department covers its direct or variable expenses. Generally Accepted Accounting Principles (GAAP) requires absorption costing for external reporting. The financial statements must be prepared using the absorption costing method.

SELF-STUDY QUIZ 16–2 Prepare an income statement for R.J. Goodman Co., for the year ending December 31, 19X5, under direct costing and absorption costing methods using the below sales and production data.

Sales Data:		Production Data:	
Variable selling and admin. exps.	$2 per unit	Direct materials	$4 per unit
		Direct labor	$3 per unit
Fixed selling and admin. exps.	$20,000	Variable factory overhead	$1 per unit
		Fixed factory overhead	$60,000
Unit sales price:	$20		
Units sold:	18,000	Units produced:	20,000

Answers at end of chapter.

COST-VOLUME-PROFIT RELATIONSHIPS

LEARNING OBJECTIVE 3 One of the more interesting tools that a cost accountant can use is referred to as break-even analysis. This type of analysis can be done after all costs have been separated into their variable and fixed elements. The term break-even refers to the point (**break-even point**) where total sales dollars equal total fixed costs and variable costs. Let's use as an example, the production and cost data from Harris Manufacturing Co. (see Figure 16–6).

Harris Manufacturing Co.

	Per Unit	Percent		
Sale price	$40	100%		
Variable costs:			Fixed costs:	
Direct materials	$7			
Direct labor	6		Fixed factory overhead	$100,000
Variable factory overhead	3		Fixed selling and	
Variable selling and			administrative expense	60,000
administrative expense	4		Total fixed costs	$160,000
Total variable costs	20	50%		
Contribution margin	$20	50%		

FIGURE 16–6
*Break-even
Analysis*

The formula for break-even in units is:

$$\text{Break-even in units} = \frac{\text{Fixed costs}}{\text{Unit contribution margin}}$$

In our example, Figure 16–6, the break-even in units for Harris Manufacturing Co. shows:

$$\text{Break-even} = \frac{\$160,000}{\$20} = 8,000 \text{ units}$$

The break-even point means that when 8,000 units are sold, all fixed and variable costs have been covered and net income equals zero. If 8,001 units are sold, net income will equal $20 ($40 –20). Since the fixed costs have been covered, net income will increase by the unit contribution margin for each unit sold above break-even.

The break-even in sales dollars would be $320,000 (8,000 × $40). Another formula for the break-even in sales dollars is:

$$\text{Break-even in sales dollars} = \frac{\text{Fixed costs}}{\text{Contribution margin ratio}}$$

$$\text{Contribution margin ratio} = \frac{\text{Contribution margin per unit}}{\text{Sales price per unit}}$$

As you can see, the contribution margin ratio equals the percentage amount after dividing the unit contribution margin by the unit sales price. In our example it equals 50 percent. To use this formula in our example, the answer would be

$$\text{Break-even in sales dollars} = \frac{\$160,000}{50\%} = \$320,000$$

ESTIMATE THE SALES NECESSARY TO EARN A DESIRED PROFIT

LEARNING OBJECTIVE 4

Now that we have learned how to compute the break-even point in units and in sales dollars, it is easy to compute the sales in units and dollars required to earn a desired profit or *target profit*. We can use the same two formulas that were used earlier and simply add the desired profit in the numerator of the fraction. The formula for calculating the number of units to be sold to earn a desired profit becomes:

$$\text{Sales in units required to earn a desired profit} = \frac{\text{Fixed costs} + \text{Desired profit}}{\text{Unit contribution margin}}$$

For example, assume that Harris Manufacturing Co. desires a profit of $40,000. The required calculation is:

$$\text{Sales in units required to earn a profit of }\$40,000 = \frac{\$160,000 + \$40,000}{\$20}$$

$$\text{Sales in units required to earn a profit of }\$40,000 = 10,000 \text{ units}$$

Or, the formula for finding the sales dollars required to earn a desired profit becomes:

$$\text{Sales in dollars required to earn a desired profit} = \frac{\text{Fixed costs} + \text{Desired profit}}{\text{Contribution margin ratio}}$$

In our example, the sales dollars required for Harris Manufacturing Co. to earn a desired profit of $40,000 is calculated with the following formula:

$$\text{Sales in dollars required to earn a profit of }\$40,000 = \frac{\$60,000 + \$40,000}{50\%}$$

$$\text{Sales in dollars required to earn a profit of }\$40,000 = \$400,000$$

BREAK-EVEN CHART

LEARNING OBJECTIVE 5

A **break-even chart** can easily be prepared that highlights the break-even point. Below the break-even point is the loss area, and above the break-even point is the profit area. Figure 16–7 shows a break-even chart for Harris Manufacturing Co.

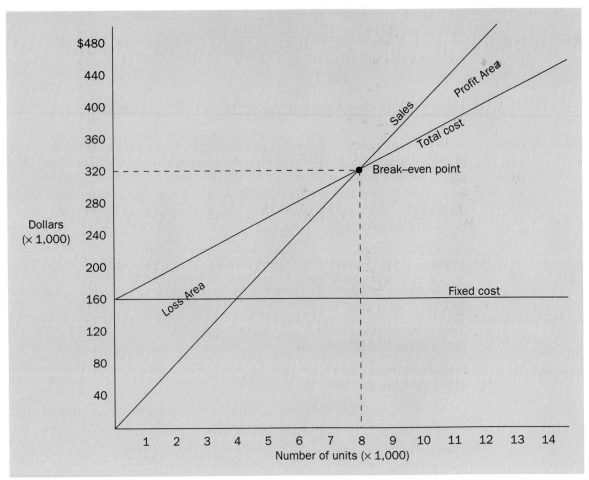

FIGURE 16–7
Break-Even Chart

As you can see in Figure 16–7, dollars are on the vertical axis and units sold are on the horizontal axis. The following steps are necessary in order to draw a break-even chart:

1. Determine the break-even in sales dollars and the break-even in units. In Figure 16–7, a dot was placed at the intersection of $320,000 in sales dollars and 8,000 in units. Label this point the break-even point.
2. Draw a line through the origin and the break-even point. This line represents the total sales dollars.
3. From the place where fixed costs cross the vertical axis, draw a line from this point through the break-even point. This line represents the total cost (variable + fixed). In Figure 16–7, a line is drawn from $160,000, on the vertical axis, through the break-even point.
4. The area below the break-even point represents the loss area. The area above the break-even point represents the profit area.

SELF-STUDY QUIZ 16–3 The following sales and production information came from the records of Drysdale Company:

Drysdale Company

	Per Unit	Percent
Sales price	$25	100%
Variable costs:		
Direct materials	$ 9	
Direct labor	5	
Variable factory overhead	4	
Variable selling and administrative expense	2	
Total variable costs	20	80%
Contribution margin	$ 5	20%

Fixed costs:

Fixed factory overhead	$40,000
Fixed selling and administrative expense	20,000
Total fixed costs	$60,000

a. Compute the break-even point in units and sales dollars for Drysdale Company.

b. Compute the dollar amount of sales necessary to earn a desired profit of $30,000.

Answers at end of chapter.

SELF-STUDY PROBLEM

The production and sales data for Kennington Corporation for the year ending December 31, 19X5, follow:

	Per Unit	Percent
Sales price	$40	100%
Variable costs:		
Direct materials	9	
Direct labor	8	
Variable factory overhead	6	
Variable selling and administrative expense	7	
Total variable costs	30	75%
Contribution Margin	$10	25%
Units produced: 20,000		
Units sold: 18,000		

Fixed costs:

Fixed factory overhead	$ 80,000
Fixed selling and administrative expense	50,000
Total fixed costs	$130,000

Required:

1. Compute the unit product cost under the direct costing method.
2. Compute the unit product cost under the absorption costing method.

3. Prepare an income statement under the direct costing method.
4. Prepare an income statement under the absorption costing method.
5. Reconcile the difference between the net income under direct costing and the net income under absorption costing.
6. Compute the break-even point in units and sales dollars.
7. Prepare a break-even chart for Kennington Corporation.
8. Compute the dollar amount of sales necessary to earn a desired profit of $90,000.

SOLUTION TO SELF-STUDY PROBLEM

1. Unit product cost under direct costing:

Direct materials	$ 9
Direct labor	8
Variable factory overhead	6
Total product cost	$23

2. Unit product cost under absorption costing:

Direct materials	$ 9
Direct labor	8
Variable factory overhead	6
Fixed factory overhead ($80,000/20,000)	4
Total product cost	$27

3. Income Statement prepared under the direct costing method:

Kennington Corporation
Income Statement
(Direct Costing)
For Year Ended December 31, 19X5

1	Sales (18,000 x $40)		$720 000 00
2	Less Variable expenses:		
3	Variable cost of goods sold (18,000 x $23)	$414 000 00	
4	Variable selling and administrative		
5	expense (18,000 x $7)	126 000 00	
6	Total variable expenses		540 000 00
7	Contribution margin		$180 000 00
8	Less Fixed expenses:		
9	Fixed factory overhead	$ 80 000 00	
10	Fixed selling and administrative expense	50 000 00	
11	Total fixed expenses		130 000 00
12	Net income		$ 50 000 00

4.   Income Statement prepared under the absorption costing method:

	Kennington Corporation Income Statement (Absorption Costing) For Year Ended December 31, 19X5				
1	Sales (18,000 x $40)			$720 00 000	1
2	Less: Cost of goods sold (18,000 x $27)			486 00 000	2
3	Gross profit			$234 00 000	3
4	Operating expenses:				4
5	Variable selling and administrative expense	$126 00 000			5
6	Fixed selling and administrative expense	50 00 000			6
7	Total operating expenses			176 00 000	7
8	Net income			$ 58 00 000	8
9					9
10					10
11					11
12					12
13					13
14					14

5.   Reconciliation of net income under absorption costing and direct costing:

1	Net income under absorption costing	$58 00 000		1
2	Less: fixed factory overhead cost deferred or			2
3	attached to the ending inventory (2,000 x $4)	8 00 000		3
4	Net income under direct costing	$50 00 000		4
5				5
6				6
7				7
8				8
9				9

6.   Break-even point in units and sales dollars.

$$\text{Break-even in units} = \frac{\$130{,}000}{\$10} = \$13{,}000$$

$$\text{Break-even in sales dollars} = \frac{\$130{,}000}{25\%} = \$520{,}000$$

7. Break-even chart.

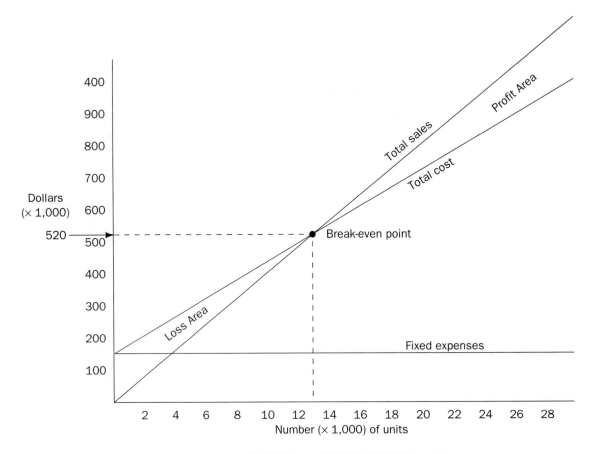

8. Dollar amount of sales necessary to earn a desired profit of $90,000.

Sales in dollars required to $130,000 + $90,000
earn a profit of $90,000   = ───────────────────
                                        25%

Sales in dollars required to
earn a desired profit of $90,000 = $880,000

SUMMARY

After costs have been separated into their variable and fixed elements, one interesting use of this information is to prepare a direct costing income statement. The term **direct costing** refers to the method of assigning only direct or variable production costs to the cost of goods sold and ending inventory. The fixed production cost, or factory overhead, is deducted in total on the income statement. **Contribution margin** equals total variable costs subtracted from sales. The contribution margin should be enough to cover all fixed expenses and contribute toward net income.

The **absorption costing** format of an income statement assigns all production costs (both variable and fixed) to the cost of goods sold and ending inventory. The absorption costing format of an income statement will show a higher net income than the direct costing format when the number of units produced exceed the number of units sold. The reason is in the fixed factory overhead cost assigned to the units produced. When production exceeds sales, some of the fixed overhead is deferred into the ending inventory under the absorption costing method, and is not released on the income statement. Just the opposite occurs when the number of units sold exceed the number of units produced.

Break-even analysis is another concept that makes use of the separation of variable and fixed costs. **Break-even** is the point where total sales equal the total of fixed costs and variable costs up to the break-even point. A **break-even chart** is a graphical representation of fixed costs, variable costs, total costs, total sales revenue, and the break-even point.

KEY TERMS

Absorption Costing. A method of accounting that uses all production costs (both variable and fixed) in the calculation of the product cost.

Break-even. The point where total sales dollars equal the total of fixed costs and variable costs up to the break-even point.

Break-even Chart. A graph that highlights fixed costs, variable costs, total sales volume, total cost, and the break-even point.

Contribution Margin. The amount remaining after deducting all variable expenses from sales on the direct costing format of an income statement.

Direct Costing. A method of accounting that uses only direct or variable production costs in the calculation of the product cost.

QUESTIONS FOR REVIEW

1. What is meant by the term direct costing?
2. What is meant by the term absorption costing?
3. What does contribution margin mean?
4. What is the basic difference between net income under direct costing and net income under absorption costing?
5. When the number of units produced exceed the number of units sold, will net income under direct costing be higher or lower than net income under absorption costing?
6. What does break-even point mean?
7. How much will net income be at the break-even point? Why?
8. What is the formula for computing the break-even point in number of units?

9. What is the formula for computing the break-even point in the amount of sales dollars?
10. When estimating the sales necessary to earn a desired profit, where do you put the dollar amount of desired profit in the formula?
11. What is the purpose of the break-even chart?
12. What is the point, on the break-even chart, where total fixed costs and total variable costs equal total sales?

EXERCISES

Data for Exercises 1–7

	Per Unit	Percent		
Sales price	$50	100%		
Variable costs:			Fixed costs:	
Direct materials	11			
Direct labor	9		Fixed factory overhead	$128,000
Variable factory overhead	6		Fixed selling and	
Variable selling and			administrative expense	72,000
administrative expense	4		Total fixed costs	$200,000
Total variable costs	30	60%		
Contribution margin	$20	40%		
Units produced: 16,000				
Units sold: 14,000				

Compute the unit product cost under the direct costing method.

16–1. Learning Objective 1. Computing Direct Cost.
Calculate the unit product cost under the direct costing method.

16–2. Learning Objective 1. Computing Absorption Cost.
Calculate the unit product cost using the absorption costing method.

16–3. Learning Objective 2. Preparing a Direct Costing Income Statement.
Prepare a direct costing income statement for Henderson Manufacturing Company, for the year ending December 31, 19X5.

16–4. Learning Objective 3. Preparing an Absorption Costing Income Statement.
Prepare an absorption costing income statement for Henderson Manufacturing Company, for the year ending December 31, 19X5.

16–5. Learning Objective 3. Computing Break-even Point.
Calculate the break-even point in units and sales dollars.

16–6. Learning Objective 4. Estimating the Sales Necessary to Earn a Desired Profit.
How much sales in dollars and in units is required to earn a profit of $60,000?

16–7. Learning Objective 5. Preparing a Break-even Chart.
Prepare a break-even chart for the Henderson Manufacturing Company.

GROUP A PROBLEMS

16–1A. Learning Objective 1. Computing Unit Product Cost Under Direct Costing and Absorption Costing.

The production and sales data for Pitcher Company follow:

Units sold:	14,000
Units produced:	15,000
Direct materials:	$120,000
Direct labor:	90,000
Variable factory overhead:	45,000
Variable selling and administrative expense:	28,000 or $2 per unit.
Fixed selling and administrative expense:	50,000
Fixed factory overhead:	60,000

Required:

1. Compute the unit product cost under direct costing.
2. Compute the unit product cost under absorption costing.

16–2A. Learning Objective 2. Preparing Direct Costing and Absorption Costing Income Statements.

In addition to the production and sales data in problem 16–1A, Pitcher Company's unit sales price is $30.

Required:

1. Prepare a direct costing income statement for Pitcher Company for the year ending December 31, 19X5.
2. Prepare an absorption costing income statement for Pitcher Company for the year ending December 31, 19X5.
3. Reconcile the difference between the net income under direct costing and the net income under absorption costing.

16–3A. Learning Objectives 3, 4. Computing Break-even Point.

The following sales and production information came from the records of Himes Company:

	Per Unit	Percent		
Sales price	$50	100%		
Variable costs:			Fixed costs:	
Direct materials	12			
Direct labor	9		Fixed factory overhead	$ 66,000
Variable factory overhead	5		Fixed selling and	
Variable selling and			administrative expense	34,000
administrative expense	4		Total fixed costs	$100,000
Total variable costs	30	60%		
Contribution margin	$20	40%		
Units produced: 12,000				
Units sold: 10,000				

Required:

1. Compute the break-even point in number of units and sales dollars.
2. Compute the number of units and dollar amount of sales necessary to earn a desired profit of $50,000.

16–4A. Learning Objective 5. Preparing a Break-even Chart.
Refer to the production and sales data in problem 16–3A. Prepare a break-even chart for the Himes Company.

GROUP B PROBLEMS

16–1B. Learning Objective 1. Computing Unit Product Cost Under Direct Costing and Absorption Costing.
The production and sales data for Johnson Manufacturing Company follow:

Units sold:	23,000
Units produced:	25,000
Direct materials:	$ 75,000
Direct labor:	100,000
Variable factory overhead:	50,000
Variable selling and administrative expense:	69,000 or $3 per unit.
Fixed selling and administrative expense:	60,000
Fixed factory overhead:	25,000

Required:

1. Compute the unit product cost under direct costing.
2. Compute the unit product cost under absorption costing.

16–2B. Learning Objective 2. Preparing Direct Costing and Absorption Costing Income Statements.
In addition to the production and sales data in problem 16–1B, Johnson Manufacturing Company's unit sales price is $20.

Required:

1. Prepare a direct costing income statement for Johnson Manufacturing Company for the year ending December 31, 19X5.
2. Prepare an absorption costing income statement for Johnson Manufacturing Company for the year ending December 31, 19X5.
3. Reconcile the difference between the net income under direct costing and the net income under absorption costing.

16–3B. Learning Objectives 3, 4. Computing Break-even Point.
The following sales and production information came from the records of Guild Company:

	Per Unit	Percent
Sales price	$60	100%
Variable costs:		
Direct materials	14	
Direct labor	12	
Variable factory overhead	8	
Variable selling and administrative expense	5	
Total variable costs	$39	65%
Contribution margin	$21	35%
Units produced: 15,000		
Units sold: 12,000		

Fixed costs:

Fixed factory overhead	$150,000
Fixed selling and administrative expense	60,000
Total fixed costs	$210,000

Required:

1. Compute the break-even point in number of units and sales dollars.
2. Compute the number of units and dollar amount of sales necessary to earn a desired profit of $80,000.

16-4B. Learning Objective 5. Preparing A Break-even Chart.

Refer to the production and sales data in problem 16-3B. Prepare a break-even chart for the Guild Company.

CASE FOR CRITICAL THINKING

You have been hired by the management of Fulton Company, a small manufacturer, to prepare their annual financial statements. In addition to preparing their statements using the absorption costing method, you also prepared their financial statements using the direct costing method. Fixed overhead for the year was $100,000. Fulton Company produced 20,000 units of product and sold 18,000 units. Management noticed that net income was $10,000 higher under absorption costing than under direct costing, and asks you why this happened. Explain to management the difference between the absorption costing and direct costing methods, and why net income was $10,000 higher under the absorption costing method.

ANSWERS TO SELF-STUDY QUIZ 16-1

a. Direct costing method: $14
b. Absorption costing method: $18

ANSWERS TO SELF-STUDY QUIZ 16–2

R.J. Goodman Co.
Income Statement
(Direct Costing)
For Year Ended December 31, 19X5

1	Sales (18,000 x $20)		$360 000 00
2	Less Variable expenses:		
3	Variable cost of goods sold (18,000 x $8)	$144 000 00	
4	Variable selling and administrative		
5	expense (18,000 x $2)	36 000 00	
6	Total variable expenses		180 000 00
7	Contribution margin		$180 000 00
8	Less Fixed expenses:		
9	Fixed factory overhead	$ 60 000 00	
10	Fixed selling and administrative expense	20 000 00	
11	Total fixed expenses		80 000 00
12	Net income		$100 000 00

R.J. Goodman Co.
Income Statement
(Absorption Costing)
For Year Ended December 31, 19X5

1	Sales (18,000 x $20)		$360 000 00
2	Less: Cost of goods sold (18,000 x $11)		198 000 00
3	Gross profit		$162 000 00
4	Operating expenses:		
5	Variable selling and administrative expense	$36 000 00	
6	Fixed selling and administrative expense	20 000 00	
7	Total operating expenses		56 000 00
8	Net income		$106 000 00

ANSWERS TO SELF-STUDY QUIZ 16–3

a. Break-even in units: $\dfrac{\$60,000}{\$5}$ = 12,000

Break-even in sales dollars: $\dfrac{\$60,000}{20\%}$ = $300,000

b. Sales necessary to earn a desired profit of $30,000:

$\dfrac{\$60,000 + \$30,000}{20\%}$ = $450,000

Chapter 17
Essentials of Budgeting

LEARNING OBJECTIVES

After studying Chapter 17, you should be able to:

1. Define and explain how budgeting relates to budgetary control.
2. Prepare a sales budget, and show the expected collection of cash receipts.
3. Prepare a production budget.
4. Prepare a direct materials budget, and show the expected cash payments for direct materials.
5. Prepare a direct labor budget.
6. Prepare a manufacturing overhead budget.
7. Prepare a manufacturing costs budget.
8. Prepare a selling and administrative expense budget.
9. Prepare a cash budget.
10. Prepare a budgeted income statement.
11. Prepare a flexible budgeted income statement.

This chapter presents the essentials of budgeting for a manufacturing company. The term **budget** refers to the company's financial plan. Once the budget has been finalized, the company has a means of comparing actual results to its financial plan. **Budgetary control** means taking corrective action when things get out of line. Think of budgetary control as the follow-up to the planning process. Management first maps out its strategy in the financial plan or budget, and then follows up with corrective action when things deviate from what was planned.

For most businesses, the process of budgeting involves the entire company. Each department prepares its own budget. The individual budgets are collected and summarized, and eventually a master budget is put together.

A **master budget** summarizes all the department budgets. Typically, a master budget consists of a series of budgets as shown in Figure 17–1.

FIGURE 17–1
Master Budget

MASTER BUDGET

1. Sales Budget
2. Production Budget
3. Direct Materials Budget
4. Direct Labor Budget
5. Manufacturing Overhead Budget
6. Manufacturing Costs Budget
7. Selling and Administrative Expense Budget
8. Cash Budget
9. Budgeted Income Statement

As Figure 17–1 indicates, the sales budget has to be prepared before the other budgets can be finalized. The sales budget represents the sales forecast. From the sales forecast, a production budget can be prepared, which shows the total amount to be produced. All other production costs, including direct materials, direct labor, and manufacturing overhead* are then finalized in accordance to the desired level of production.

For purposes of illustration, let's assume that Cascade Company manufactures a recreational game for home or commercial use. Each game requires 10 pounds of raw material and sells for $400.

SALES BUDGET

As mentioned earlier, the starting point in formulating a master budget begins with a sales budget. Forecasting sales is a critical step in preparing the sales budget. Input from the sales force, past sales experience, general economic

---

*The terms "manufacturing overhead" and "factory overhead" may be used interchangeably.

conditions, and industry competition are among the many variables considered when making a sales forecast.

Schedule A presents the sales budget for Cascade Company.

Cascade Company
Sales Budget
For the Year Ending December 31, 19X6

	Quarter				
	1	**2**	**3**	**4**	**Year**
Budgeted sales in units	250	400	800	550	2,000
Selling price per unit	× $300	× $300	× $300	× $300	× $300
Total budgeted sales	$75,000	$120,000	$240,000	$165,000	$600,000

Schedule of Budgeted Cash Collections*

Accounts rec., 12–31–X5	$37,500				$ 37,500
Quarter 1 sales ($75,000)	56,250	$ 18,750			75,000
Quarter 2 sales ($120,000)		90,000	$ 30,000		120,000
Quarter 3 sales ($240,000)			180,000	$ 60,000	240,000
Quarter 4 sales ($165,000)				123,750	123,750
Total cash collections	$93,750	$108,750	$210,000	$183,750	$596,250

*Seventy-five (75) percent of a quarter's sales is collected in the quarter of sale; the remaining 25 percent is collected in the following quarter.

Schedule A
Sales Budget

Notice that the sales budget is initially set in units then converted to dollars by quarter. Total sales for the year is estimated to be 2,000 units. Also, *a schedule of budgeted cash collections* appears at the bottom of the sales budget. This information will be helpful when preparing a cash budget.

PRODUCTION BUDGET

LEARNING OBJECTIVE 3   Once the sales budget has been finalized, the production budget can now be completed. From the sales budget we know the estimated number of units to sell. The production budget shows the number of units to be produced based upon the budgeted sales. A production budget for Cascade Company appears in Schedule B.

Cascade Company
Production Budget
For the Year Ending December 31, 19X6

	Quarter				Year
	1	**2**	**3**	**4**	**Year**
Budgeted sales (Schedule A)	250	400	800	550	2,000
Add **desired ending finished goods** inventory*	80	160	110	50**	50
Total budgeted needs	330	560	910	600	2,050
Less **beginning finished goods** inventory	50	80	160	110	50
Budgeted production	280	480	750	490	2,000

*20 percent of next quarter's sales
**Estimated 1st quarter sales of 19X7 is 250 units

Schedule B
Production
Budget

Note in the production budget, the ending finished goods inventory is added to the budgeted sales in units to compute the total budgeted needs. Then the beginning finished goods inventory is subtracted from total budgeted needs to compute budgeted production. When completing the "Year column," the desired ending finished goods inventory equals the Quarter 4 desired ending finished goods inventory. The beginning finished goods inventory for the "Year column" equals the Quarter 1 beginning finished goods inventory.

NOTE   When preparing the production budget: (1) add the desired ending finished goods inventory to budgeted sales to compute total budgeted needs and (2) subtract the beginning finished goods inventory from total budgeted needs to compute budgeted production.

DIRECT MATERIALS BUDGET

LEARNING OBJECTIVE 4   After the production budget has been prepared, we can prepare a direct materials budget. The direct materials budget will show the amount of direct materials needed to be purchased. At this point, the cost of the direct materials can be estimated based upon the amount to be purchased. The format of this budget is similar to the production budget. Schedule C shows a direct materials budget for Cascade Company.

Cascade Company
Direct Materials Budget
For the Year Ending December 31, 19X6

	Quarter				
	1	**2**	**3**	**4**	**Year**
Budgeted production (Schedule B)	280	480	750	490	2,000
Direct materials per unit (lbs)	× 10	× 10	× 10	× 10	× 10
Production needs (lbs)	2,800	4,800	7,500	4,900	20,000
Add desired ending inventory of direct materials*	480	750	490	250	250
Total budgeted needs	3,280	5,500	7,990	5,150	20,250
Less beginning inventory of direct materials (lbs)	**250	480	750	490	250
Direct materials to be purchased (lbs)	3,030	5,070	7,240	4,660	20,000
Cost of direct materials to be purchased at $5 per pound	$15,150	$25,350	$36,200	$23,300	$100,000

*Desired ending inventory is ten (10) percent of the next quarter's budgeted production needs, in pounds. The fourth quarter's ending inventory is estimated.
**First quarter's beginning inventory is assumed to be given.

Schedule of budgeted cash payments for materials

Accounts Payable, 12/31/X5	$ 6,125				$ 6,125
Quarter 1 purchases**	7,575	$ 7,575			15,150
Quarter 2 purchases		12,675	$12,675		25,350
Quarter 3 purchases			18,100	$18,100	36,200
Quarter 4 purchases				11,650	11,650
Total cash payments	$13,700	$20,250	$30,775	$29,750	$94,475

**Fifty (50) percent of a quarter's purchases is paid for in the same quarter, the remaining 50 percent is paid for in the following quarter.

Schedule C
Direct Materials
Budget

Notice in the "Year column," the desired ending inventory of direct materials equals the Quarter 4 ending inventory. Also, notice that the beginning inventory for the "Year column" equals the beginning inventory in Quarter 1. The schedule of budgeted cash payments for materials will help us when we prepare the cash budget.

NOTE When preparing the direct materials budget: (1) add the desired ending inventory of direct materials to compute total needs and (2) subtract the beginning direct materials inventory from total needs to compute direct materials to be purchased.

DIRECT LABOR BUDGET

LEARNING OBJECTIVE 5   Our master budget is beginning to fall into place. Next, we are going to prepare a direct labor budget, again based upon the budgeted production of units, from Schedule B. Schedule D presents a direct labor budget for Cascade Company.

Cascade Company
Direct Labor Budget
For the Year Ending December 31, 19X6

	Quarter				
	1	**2**	**3**	**4**	**Year**
Budgeted production (Schedule B)	280	480	750	490	2,000
Direct labor hours per unit	× 4	× 4	× 4	× 4	× 4
Total budgeted direct labor hours needed	1,120	1,920	3,000	1,960	8,000
Direct labor cost per hour	× $10	× $10	× $10	× $10	× $10
Total direct labor cost	$11,200	$19,200	$30,000	$19,600	$80,000

Schedule D
Direct Labor
Budget

In Schedule D, the direct labor budget shows the total budgeted direct labor hours needed and the total direct labor cost. This information will help us when we prepare the manufacturing overhead budget and cash budget.

SELF-STUDY QUIZ 17–1 Complete the below production budget for Johnson Manufacturing Company given the following information:

Johnson Manufacturing Company
Production Budget
For the Year Ending December 31, 19X7

	Quarter				
	1	2	3	4	Year
Budgeted sales in units	150	200	500	350	1,200
Add desired ending finished goods inventory	a.	b.	c.	d.	e.
Total budgeted needs	f.	g.	h.	i.	j.
Less beginning finished goods inventory	k.	l.	m.	n.	o.
Budgeted production	p.	q.	r.	s.	t.

Desired finished goods inventory is 20 percent of the next quarter's sales.
Estimated first quarter sales of 19X8 is 200 units.
Beginning finished goods inventory is 20 units.

Answers at end of chapter.

MANUFACTURING OVERHEAD BUDGET

LEARNING OBJECTIVE 6

We have completed the direct materials and direct labor budgets. We are now ready to produce the manufacturing overhead budget. Recall the three manufacturing costs: direct materials, direct labor, and manufacturing overhead. In our example, Cascade Company applies manufacturing overhead on the basis of direct labor hours. As you review Schedule E, note that the manufacturing costs are separated between variable and fixed. The completed manufacturing overhead budget for Cascade Company appears in Schedule E.

Schedule E presents the total budgeted overhead for each quarter and for the year. Depreciation expense, a non-cash expense, is deducted to show the actual cash expenditures for manufacturing overhead. This will help us when we prepare the cash budget.

Cascade Company
Manufacturing Overhead Budget
For the Year Ending December 31, 19X6

	Quarter				
	1	**2**	**3**	**4**	**Year**
Budgeted direct labor hours needed (Schedule D)	1,120	1,920	3,000	1,960	8,000
Variable overhead rate	× $5	× $5	× $5	× $5	× $5
Budgeted variable overhead	$ 5,600	$ 9,600	$15,000	$ 9,800	$ 40,000
Budgeted fixed overhead	25,000	25,000	25,000	25,000	100,000
Total budgeted overhead	$30,600	$34,600	$40,000	$34,800	$140,000
Less depr. expense	5,000	5,000	5,000	5,000	20,000
Cash payments for overhead	$25,600	$29,600	$35,000	$29,800	$120,000

Schedule E
Manufacturing
Overhead Budget

MANUFACTURING COSTS BUDGET

LEARNING OBJECTIVE 7

Now we can prepare the manufacturing costs budget. This budget will show the total of direct materials, direct labor, manufacturing overhead, and their per unit cost. This information will be helpful when we prepare an income statement. Schedule F presents a manufacturing costs budget for Cascade Company.

Schedule F shows that the unit manufacturing cost is $160.00. Later Schedule F manufacturing costs will be used to prepare an income statement for Cascade Company.

Schedule F
Manufacturing
Costs Budget

Cascade Company
Manufacturing Costs Budget
For the Year Ending December 31, 19X6

Direct materials purchased and used (Schedule C)	$100,000
Direct labor cost (Schedule D)	80,000
Manufacturing overhead (Schedule E)	140,000
Cost of goods manufactured*	$320,000
Cost per unit	
Direct materials ($100,000/2,000)	$ 50.00
Direct labor ($80,000/2,000)	40.00
Manufacturing overhead ($140,000/2,000)	70.00
Total unit manufacturing cost	$ 160.00

*Work-in-process inventories are negligible and can be ignored.

SELLING AND ADMINISTRATIVE EXPENSE BUDGET

LEARNING OBJECTIVE 8   Let's continue the master budget by preparing the selling and administrative expense budget. Note again the separation of these costs between variable and fixed. Schedule G shows the completed selling and administrative expense budget for Cascade Company.

Cascade Company
Selling and Administrative Expense Budget
For the Year Ending December 31, 19X6

| | Quarter | | | | |
	1	2	3	4	Year
Budgeted sales in units (Schedule A)	250	400	800	550	2,000
Varialble selling and admin. expense per unit*	× $20	× $20	× $20	× $20	× $20
Budgeted variable expense	$ 5,000	$ 8,000	$16,000	$11,000	$ 40,000
Budgeted fixed selling and admin. expense	25,000	25,000	25,000	25,000	100,000
Total budgeted selling and admin. expense	$30,000	$33,000	$41,000	$36,000	$140,000

*Assumed rate.

Schedule G
Selling and
Administrative
Expense Budget

Notice that the selling and administrative expense budget begins with the budgeted sales in units from Schedule A, multiplied by the variable cost rate. Completion of the selling and administrative expense budget will help us when we prepare the cash budget and the budgeted income statement.

We have just two budgets remaining to complete our example of the formulation of a master budget. Next we will produce the cash budget which shows the total inflow and outflow of cash. The budget also indicates whether additional financing is needed and when the money should be borrowed.

CASH BUDGET

LEARNING OBJECTIVE 9   One of the last budgets to be prepared when completing the master budget is the cash budget. The analysis of cash is of critical importance to management. Among the many uses of cash that must be planned for in advance include cash payments for materials, cash needed to make payroll, and cash needed for overhead. If there appears to be a cash shortage during the year, management must open up a line of credit at a bank in order to ensure that bills will be paid on time. In addition, banks appreciate an early notification that a company needs cash. The bank can also plan to have additional cash available.

Schedule H shows a cash budget prepared for Cascade Company. Note the following assumptions: (1) Cascade Company desires to purchase equipment of $20,000 and $30,000 in Quarters 1 and 4 respectively, and (2) Cascade Company budgeted $10,000 cash dividends per quarter.

Cascade Company
Cash Budget
For the Year Ending December 31, 19X6

	Schedule	Quarter 1	2	3	4	Year
Beginning cash balance		$ 20,000	$ 20,750	$ 20,950	$ 22,015	$ 20,000
Cash Inflows:						
Budgeted cash collections	A	93,750	108,750	210,000	183,750	596,250
Total budgeted cash available		$113,750	$129,500	$230,950	$205,765	$616,250
Cash Outflows:						
Direct materials	C	13,700	20,250	30,775	29,750	94,475
Direct labor cost	D	11,200	19,200	30,000	19,600	80,000
Manufacturing overhead	E	25,600	29,600	35,000	29,800	120,000
Selling and admin. expense	G	30,000	33,000	41,000	36,000	140,000
Purchase of equipment		20,000			30,000	50,000
Income tax expense	I	12,500	12,500	12,500	12,500	50,000
Cash dividends paid		10,000	10,000	10,000	10,000	40,000
Total budgeted cash outflow		$123,000	$124,550	$159,275	$167,650	$574,475
Excess (deficiency) of cash inflow over cash outflow		(9,250)	4,950	71,675	38,115	41,775
Financing:						
Amount borrowed (beginning of Qtr.)		30,000*	16,000			46,000
Amount of principal paid				(46,000)		(46,000)
Amount of interest paid (end of Qtr.)				(3,660)		(3,660)
Total amount financed		30,000	16,000	(49,660)		(3,660)**
Ending cash balance		$ 20,750	$ 20,950	$ 22,015	$ 38,115	$ 38,115

*Management requires a minimum cash balance of $20,000. In order to end the quarter with a minimum cash balance of $20,000, a total of $30,000 must be borrowed at the beginning of Quarter 1, and 16,000 must be borrowed at the beginning of Quarter 2. It is also management's policy to borrow in increments of $1,000. Any amount repaid is assumed to be at the end of the quarter.

**Interest is at 12% per year: $30,000 × .12 × 9/12 = $2,700
                                  16,000 × .12 × 6/12 =   960
        Total amount of interest paid $3,660

Schedule H
Cash Budget

As Schedule H shows, the cash flow is not uniform throughout the year. Cascade Company will have to borrow during Quarters 1 and 2 and will repay the loans in Quarter 3. Also, the cash budget indicates that additional equipment can be purchased in Quarter 4 because of the large cash surplus generated from the previous quarter sales.

BUDGETED INCOME STATEMENT

LEARNING OBJECTIVE 10   The last budget in the master budget is the budgeted income statement. The information needed has already been presented in earlier budgets. We will summarize this information and produce an income statement. Schedule I shows a budgeted income statement for Cascade Company.

Schedule I
Budgeted Income
Statement

Cascade Company
Budgeted Income Statement
For the Year Ending December 31, 19X6

Revenue		
Sales (Schedule A)		$600,000
Cost of goods sold:		
Finished goods inventory, Jan. 1*	$ 8,000	
Add cost of goods manufactured (Schedule F)	320,000	
Goods available for sale	$328,000	
Less finished goods inventory, Dec. 31	8,000	
Cost of goods sold		320,000
Gross profit		$280,000
Operating expenses:		
Selling and admin. expense (Schedule G)		140,000
Income before income taxes and interest expense		$140,000
Interest expense		3,660
Income before taxes		$136,340
Provision for income taxes (Schedule H)		50,000
Net income after income taxes		$ 86,340

*Beginning finished goods inventory is $8,000.

Schedule I shows that net income after taxes is $86,340. This budgeted income statement can now be used internally by management as well as externally by outside parties, such as a banker, who is interested in the future profitability of the business.

This completes our example of a master budget. Other budgets could be prepared within the master budget such as a capital (long-term assets) expenditure budget, budgeted statement of cash flows, and a budgeted balance sheet. However, these budgets do not directly relate to manufacturing costs so they will not be presented.

FLEXIBLE BUDGETED INCOME STATEMENT

LEARNING OBJECTIVE 11   The last topic of this chapter covers a flexible budgeted income statement using the direct costing format. Chapter 16 presented the direct costing format of an income statement. This format will be used in preparing a flexible budgeted income statement for Cascade Company. This income statement can be very useful to management if sales differ from what was planned. Schedule J presents a flexible budgeted income statement for Cascade Company.

Cascade Company
Flexible Budgeted Income Statement
For the Year Ending December 31, 19X6

	Per unit cost					
Budgeted sales (in units)		1,000	1,500	2,000	2,500	3,000
Sales price		× $300	× $300	× $300	× $300	× $300
Total revenue		$300,000	$450,000	$600,000	$750,000	$900,000
Variable costs:	**Per unit cost**					
Direct materials	$50	50,000	75,000	100,000	125,000	150,000
Direct labor	40	40,000	60,000	80,000	100,000	120,000
Variable mfg. overhead	20	20,000	30,000	40,000	50,000	60,000
Variable selling and						
admin. expense	20	20,000	30,000	40,000	50,000	60,000
Total variable costs		$130,000	$195,000	$260,000	$325,000	$390,000
Fixed costs:						
Fixed mfg. overhead		100,000	100,000	100,000	100,000	100,000
Fixed selling and						
admin. expense		100,000	100,000	100,000	100,000	100,000
Total fixed costs		$200,000	$200,000	$200,000	$200,000	$200,000
Total costs		$330,000	$395,000	$460,000	$525,000	$590,000
Net income (loss) before						
taxes and interest expense		($ 30,000)	$ 55,000	$140,000	$225,000	$310,000

Schedule J
Flexible Budgeted
Income Statement

To arrive at the variable manufacturing overhead per unit sold, review Schedule E. The variable manufacturing overhead rate per direct labor hour is $5. The total variable manufacturing overhead for the year on Schedule E is $40,000. Since 2,000 units were sold, the variable overhead rate per unit sold is $20 ($40,000/2,000).

NOTE To prepare a flexible budgeted income statement, costs must be separated between variable and fixed, then a direct costing format of an income statement can be prepared for different levels of sales.

From the flexible budget presented in Schedule J, management can see at a glance what the net income (before tax and interest expense) will be for various sales levels. This can be very helpful for planning purposes.

SELF-STUDY QUIZ 17–2   In this chapter, nine budgets have been presented that make up the master budget.

a. What must always be the first budget prepared before any other budget can be prepared in the master budget?
b. List the remaining eight budgets that comprise the master budget.

Answers at end of chapter.

SELF-STUDY PROBLEM

The following information has been assembled by Darwin Company for the purposes of preparing a master budget for the year ending December 31, 19X8.

1. Budgeted sales in units Quarter 1, 100; Quarter 2, 200; Quarter 3, 400; Quarter 4, 300.
2. Sales price per unit, $300.
3. Beginning balance of Accounts Receivable account, $ 20,000.
4. Collection of Accounts Receivable is 60% in the quarter of sale, 40% in the following quarter.
5. Desired ending inventory of finished goods is 10% of the following quarter's sales in units.
6. Beginning finished goods inventory, 20 units
7. Budgeted sales for Quarter 1 of 19X9, 200 units
8. Direct materials per unit, 5 gallons
9. Desired, ending inventory of direct materials, 20% of the next quarter's production needs
10. Beginning inventory of direct materials, 100 gallons
11. Beginning balance of Accounts Payable account, $2,500
12. Cost of direct materials to be purchased, $10 per gallon
13. Cash payments for purchases are 50% in the quarter of purchase and the remaining 50% in the following quarter.
14. Direct labor hours per unit, 3
15. Direct labor cost per hour, $10
16. Variable manufacturing overhead rate of $3 is applied on the basis of budgeted direct labor hours. The variable manufacturing overhead rate is $9 per unit produced.
17. Budgeted fixed manufacturing overhead, $40,000 per year
18. Depreciation expense related to manufacturing overhead, $24,000 per year
19. Budgeted variable selling and admin. expense per unit, $15
20. Budgeted fixed selling and admin. expense, $80,000 per year.
21. Income tax expense and amount paid, $5,000 per quarter
22. Cash dividends paid, $2,000 per quarter

23. Equipment is budgeted to be purchased in Quarter 1 for $20,000 and Quarter 4 for $40,000.
24. Beginning cash balance, $30,000
25. A minimum cash balance of $20,000 must be maintained.
26. Money is borrowed in increments of $1,000. Borrowed money is always considered received at the beginning of a quarter and the principal is repaid in full or in increments at the end of each quarter when there is enough cash flow.
27. The annual interest rate on borrowed funds, 12%
28. Beginning finished goods inventory, $2,600

Required:

1. Prepare the following budgets:
   a. Sales budget and a schedule of budgeted cash collections.
   b. Production budget.
   c. Direct materials budget and a schedule of budgeted cash payments for materials.
   d. Direct labor budget.
   e. Manufacturing overhead budget.
   f. Manufacturing costs budget.
   g. Selling and administrative expense budget.
   h. Cash budget.
   i. Budgeted income statement.
2. Prepare flexible budgeted income statements for Darwin Company assuming sales in units are 500, 1,000, 1,500, 2,000 and 2,500.

SOLUTION TO SELF-STUDY PROBLEM

1. a.

Darwin Company
Sales Budget
For the Year Ending December 31, 19X8

| | Quarter | | | | |
	1	2	3	4	Year
Budgeted sales in units	100	200	400	300	1,000
Sale price per unit	× $300	× $300	× $300	× $300	× $300
Total budgeted sales	$30,000	$60,000	$120,000	$ 90,000	$300,000

Schedule of Budgeted Cash Collections*

Accounts rec., 12–31–X7	$20,000				$ 20,000
Quarter 1 sales ($30,000)	18,000	$12,000			30,000
Quarter 2 sales ($60,000)		36,000	$ 24,000		60,000
Quarter 3 sales ($120,000)			72,000	$ 48,000	120,000
Quarter 4 sales ($90,000)				54,000	54,000
Total Cash Collections	$38,000	$48,000	$ 96,000	$102,000	$284,000

b.

Darwin Company
Production Budget
For the Year Ending December 31, 19X8

	Quarter				
	1	**2**	**3**	**4**	**Year**
Budgeted sales in units	100	200	400	300	1,000
Add desired ending finished goods inventory*	20	40	30	20	20
Total budgeted needs	120	240	430	320	1,020
Less beginning finished goods inventory	20	20	40	30	20
Budgeted production	100	220	390	290	1,000

*Desired finished goods inventory is 10% of the following quarter's sales in units.

c.

Darwin Company
Direct Materials Budget
For the Year Ending December 31, 19X8

	Quarter				
	1	**2**	**3**	**4**	**Year**
Budgeted production in units	100	220	390	290	1,000
Direct materials per unit (gal.)	× 5	× 5	× 5	× 5	× 5
Production needs (gal.)	500	1,100	1,950	1,450	5,000
Add desired ending inventory of direct materials*	220	390	290	200	200
Total budgeted needs	720	1,490	2,240	1,650	5,200
Less beginning inventory of direct materials (gal.)	100	220	390	290	100
Direct materials to be purchased (gal.)	620	1,270	1,850	1,360	5,100
Cost of direct materials to be purchased at $10 per gallon	$6,200	$12,700	$18,500	$13,600	$51,000

*Twenty (20) percent of next quarter's production needs.

Schedule of Budgeted Cash Payments for Materials

Accounts Payable, 12/31/X7	$2,500				$ 2,500
Quarter 1 purchases	3,100	$3,100			6,200
Quarter 2 purchases		6,350	$ 6,350		12,700
Quarter 3 purchases			9,250	$ 9,250	18,500
Quarter 4 purchases				6,800	6,800
Total cash payments	$5,600	$9,450	$15,600	$16,050	$46,700

d.

Darwin Company
Direct Labor Budget
For the Year Ending December 31, 19X8

	Quarter				
	1	**2**	**3**	**4**	**Year**
Budgeted production	100	220	390	290	1,000
Direct labor hours per unit	× 3	× 3	× 3	× 3	× 3
Total budgeted direct labor hours needed	300	660	1,170	870	3,000
Direct labor cost per hour	× $10	× $10	× $10	× $10	× $10
Total direct labor cost	$3,000	$6,600	$11,700	$8,700	$30,000

e.

Darwin Company
Manufacturing Overhead Budget
For the Year Ending December 31, 19X8

	Quarter				
	1	**2**	**3**	**4**	**Year**
Budgeted direct labor hours needed	300	660	1,170	8,70	3,000
Variable overhead rate	× $3	× $3	× $3	× $3	× $3
Budgeted variable overhead	$ 900	$ 1,980	$ 3,510	$ 2,610	$ 9,000
Budgeted fixed overhead	10,000	10,000	10,000	10,000	40,000
Total budgeted overhead	$10,900	$11,980	$13,510	$12,610	$49,000
Less depr. expense	6,000	6,000	6,000	6,000	24,000
Cash payments for overhead	$ 4,900	$ 5,980	$ 7,510	$ 6,610	$25,000

f.

Darwin Company
Manufacturing Costs Budget
For the Year Ending December 31, 19X8

Direct materials purchased and used	$ 51,000
Direct labor cost	30,000
Manufacturing overhead	49,000
Cost of goods manufactured*	$130,000
Cost per unit	
Direct materials ($51,000/1,000)	$ 51.00
Direct labor ($30,000/1,000)	30.00
Manufacturing overhead ($49,000/1,000)	49.00
Total unit manufacturing cost	$ 130.00

g.

Darwin Company
Selling and Administrative Expense Budget
For the Year Ending December 31, 19X8

	Quarter				
	1	**2**	**3**	**4**	**Year**
Budgeted sales in units	100	200	400	300	1,000
Variable selling and admin. expense per unit	× $15	× $15	× $15	× $15	× $15
Budgeted variable expense	$ 1,500	$ 3,000	$ 6,000	$ 4,500	$15,000
Budgeted fixed selling and admin. expense	20,000	20,000	20,000	20,000	80,000
Total budgeted selling and admin. expense	$21,500	$23,000	$26,000	$24,500	$95,000

h.

Darwin Company
Cash Budget
For the Year Ending December 31, 19X8

	Quarter				
	1	2	3	4	Year
Beginning cash balance	$30,000	$20,000	$ 20,970	$ 28,600	$ 30,000
Cash Inflows:					
Budgeted cash collections	38,000	48,000	96,000	102,000	284,000
Total budgeted cash available	$68,000	$68,000	$116,970	$130,600	$314,000
Cash Outflows:					
Direct materials	5,600	9,450	15,600	16,050	46,700
Direct labor cost	3,000	6,600	11,700	8,700	30,000
Manufacturing overhead	4,900	5,980	7,510	6,610	25,000
Selling and admin. expense	21,500	23,000	26,000	24,500	95,000
Purchase of equipment	20,000			40,000	60,000
Income tax expense	5,000	5,000	5,000	5,000	20,000
Cash dividends paid	2,000	2,000	2,000	2,000	8,000
Total budgeted cash outflow	$62,000	$52,030	$ 67,810	$102,860	$284,700
Excess (deficiency) of cash available over cash outflow	6,000	15,970	49,160	28,160	29,300
Financing:					
Amount borrowed (beginning of Qtr.)	14,000	5,000			19,000
Amount of principal paid			(19,000)		(19,000)
Amount of interest paid (end of Qtr.)			(1,560)*		(1,560)
Total amount financed	14,000	5,000	(20,560)		(1,560)
Ending cash balance	$20,000	$20,970	$ 28,600	$ 27,740	$ 27,740

* Interest is at 12% per year: $14,000 × .12 × 9/12 = $1,260
                                    5,000 × .12 × 6/12 =   300
      Total amount of interest paid $1,560

1.

Darwin Company
Budgeted Income Statement
For the Year Ending December 31, 19X8

Revenue		
Sales		$300,000
Cost of goods sold:		
Finished goods inventory, Jan. 1*	$ 2,600	
Add cost of goods manufactured	130,000	
Goods available for sale	$132,600	
Less finished goods inventory, Dec. 31	2,600	
Cost of goods sold		130,000
Gross profit		$170,000
Operating expenses:		
Selling and admin. expense		95,000
Income before income taxes and interest expense		$ 75,000
Interest expense		1,560
Income before income taxes		$ 73,440
Provision for income taxes		20,000
Net income after income taxes		$ 53,440

*Beginning finished goods inventory is $2,600.

2.

Darwin Company
Flexible Budgeted Income Statement
For the Year Ending December 31, 19X8

	Per unit cost					
Budgeted sales (in units)		500	1,000	1,500	2,000	2,500
Sales price		× $300	× $300	× $300	× $300	× $300
Total revenue		$150,000	$300,000	$450,000	$600,000	$750,000
Variable costs:						
Direct materials	$51	25,500	51,000	76,500	102,000	127,500
Direct labor	30	15,000	30,000	45,000	60,000	75,000
Variable mfg. overhead	9	4,500	9,000	13,500	18,000	22,500
Variable selling and admin. expense	15	7,500	15,000	22,500	30,000	37,500
Total variable costs		$ 52,500	$105,000	$157,500	$210,000	$262,500
Fixed costs:						
Fixed mfg. overhead		40,000	40,000	40,000	40,000	40,000
Fixed selling and admin. expense		80,000	80,000	80,000	80,000	80,000
Total fixed costs		$120,000	$120,000	$120,000	$120,000	$120,000
Total costs		$172,500	$225,000	$277,500	$330,000	$382,500
Net income (loss) before taxes and interest expense		($ 22,500)	$ 75,000	$172,500	$270,000	$367,500

SUMMARY

Most manufacturing companies will spend the time to formulate a financial plan called a **budget. Budgetary control** is the process of following up and correcting operations when the actual results deviate from what was planned. The budget process involves the entire company. Each department submits a budget. Eventually, all the individual budgets are collected and summarized into the **master budget.**

The master budget includes: (1) sales budget, (2) production budget, (3) direct materials budget, (4) direct labor budget, (5) manufacturing overhead budget, (6) manufacturing costs budget, (7) selling and administrative expense budget, (8) cash budget, and (9) budgeted income statement. The sales budget must always be prepared first in the preparation of the master budget.

A flexible budgeted income statement uses the direct costing format for an income statement. Costs are divided into variable costs and fixed costs. The net income, before tax and interest expense, is shown at several different sales levels. This can be very beneficial to management since the income statement is flexible to several different sets of sales figures. Management can see at a glance the effect of different sales levels on the income statement.

KEY TERMS

Budget. The manufacturing company's financial plan.

Budgetary Control. The management process of taking corrective action when actual results deviate from the financial plan.

Flexible Budgeted Income Statement. An income statement that uses the direct costing format. All expenses are separated as either variable or fixed. The effect on net income is shown at several different sales levels.

Master Budget. A summary of all the departmental budgets. The master budget typically includes a (1) sales budget, (2) production budget, (3) direct materials budget, (4) direct labor budget, (5) manufacturing overhead budget, (6) manufacturing costs budget, (7) selling and administrative expense budget, (8) cash budget, (9) budgeted income statement.

QUESTIONS FOR REVIEW

1. What does the term budget mean?
2. How does budgetary control relate to budgeting?
3. What is a master budget?
4. What budget is always prepared first in a master budget?
5. Name the nine budgets this chapter presents as composing the master budget.
6. A schedule of budgeted cash collections appears as a part of which budget?

7. A schedule of budgeted cash payments appears as a part of which budget?
8. What are the three manufacturing costs?
9. How does management use a flexible budgeted income statement?

EXERCISES

17–1. Learning Objective 2. Preparing a Sales Budget.

Prepare a sales budget and a schedule of budgeted cash collections for Lopez Company for the year ending December 31, 19X5, given the following data:

a. Sales in units by quarter:
   Quarter 1 19X5   600
   Quarter 2 19X5   800
   Quarter 3 19X5 1,300
   Quarter 4 19X5   900
   Quarter 1 19X6   700
b. Sales price per unit, $50.
c. Accounts Receivable balance December 31, 19X4, $12,000.
d. All sales are on account.
e. Accounts receivable is collected 70% in the quarter of sale, 30% in the following quarter.

17–2. Learning Objective 3. Preparing a Production Budget.

Prepare a production budget for Sandberg Company for the year ending December 31, 19X6, given the following data:

	19X6 Quarter				19X7 Qtr.
	1	2	3	4	1
Budgeted sales	300	600	900	800	400

a. Desired ending finished goods inventory is 20 percent of next quarter's sales.
b. Beginning inventory of finished goods is 40.

17–3. Learning Objective 4. Preparing a Direct Materials Budget.

Prepare a direct materials budget and a schedule of budgeted cash payments for Grace Company, for the year ending December 31, 19X6, given the following data:

	19X6 Quarter				19X7 Qtr.
	1	2	3	4	1
Budgeted production	400	550	900	600	500

a. Direct materials per unit, 5 lbs
b. Desired ending inventory is 10% of the next quarter's budgeted production needs.
c. Beginning inventory of direct materials, 250 lbs
d. Accounts Payable balance December 31, 19X5, $10,000

e. Cost of direct materials, $10 per lb.

f. Fifty (50) percent of a quarter's purchase is paid for in the quarter of purchase. The remainder is paid in the following quarter.

17–4. Learning Objective 5. Preparing a Direct Labor Budget.

Prepare a direct labor budget for Johnson Company for the year ending June 30, 19X7, given the following data:

Quarter

1	2	3	4	Year
500	900	400	600	2,400

a. Budgeted production (units)
b. Direct labor hours per unit, 6
c. Direct labor cost per hour, $20

17–5. Learning Objective 6. Preparing a Manufacturing Overhead Budget.

Prepare a manufacturing overhead budget for Justice Corporation for the year ending September 30, 19X8, given the following data:

	Quarter				
	1	2	3	4	Year
a. Budgeted direct labor hours needed	4,000	6,000	9,000	7,000	26,000

b. Variable overhead rate per direct labor hour, $3
c. Budgeted fixed overhead per quarter, $30,000.
d. Depreciation expense per quarter, $4,000

17–6. Learning Objective 7. Preparing a Manufacturing Costs Budget.

Prepare a manufacturing costs budget for Murphy Company for the year ending December 31, 19X2, given the following data:

a. Direct materials purchased and used, $200,000.
b. Direct labor cost, 350,000.
c. Manufacturing overhead, 160,000.
d. Number of units produced, 10,000.

17–7. Learning Objective 8. Preparing a Selling and Administrative Expense Budget.

Prepare a selling and administrative expense budget for Glenn Company for the year ending November 30, 19X3, given the following data:

	Quarter				
	1	2	3	4	Year
a. Budgeted sales in units	1,000	2,600	4,800	3,400	11,800

b. Variable selling and admin. expense per unit, $10.
c. Budgeted fixed selling and admin. expense, per year $200,000.

17–8. Learning Objective 9. Preparing a Cash Budget.

Prepare a cash budget for Bonds Company for the year ending December 31, 19X7 given the following data:

		Quarter				
		1	**2**	**3**	**4**	**Year**
a.	Budgeted cash collections	$46,800	51,400	185,600	130,200	414,000
b.	Cash outflows:					
	Direct materials	4,600	5,100	12,200	11,300	
	Direct labor cost	8,000	9,000	16,000	12,000	
	Manufacturing overhead	5,000	7,000	11,000	9,000	
	Selling and admin. expense	20,000	22,000	33,000	21,000	
	Purchase of equipment	20,000			40,000	
	Income tax expense	4,000	4,000	4,000	4,000	
	Cash dividends paid	10,000	10,000	10,000	10,000	

c. A minimum cash balance of $20,000 is required.
d. Borrowing must be in increments of $1,000.
e. All borrowing is done at the beginning of a quarter, and the repayments are made at the end of a quarter.
f. Annual interest rate on borrowed funds, 12%
g. Beginning cash balance, $20,000

17–9. Learning Objective 10. Preparing a Budgeted Income Statement.

Prepare a budgeted income statement for Garvey Company for the year ending December 31, 19X6 given the following data:

a. Revenue from sales, $700,000.
b. Beginning finished goods inventory, $35,400.
c. Ending finished goods inventory, $55,100.
d. Cost of goods manufactured, $380,000.
e. Selling and admin. expense, $160,000.
f. Interest expense, $2,190.
g. Income tax expense, 40% of net income before tax

17–10. Learning Objective 11. Preparing a Flexible Budgeted Income Statement.

Prepare a flexible budgeted income statement for Larkin Corporation for the year ending June 30, 19X8 given the following data:

a. Budgeted sales in units: 2,000, 3,000, 4,000, 5,000, 6,000
b. Sales price per unit, $200.
c. Variable costs per unit:
   Direct materials, $30.
   Direct labor, $25.
   Variable mfg. overhead, $20.
   Variable selling and admin. expense, $15.
d. Fixed costs:
   Fixed mfg. overhead, $220,000.
   Fixed selling and admin. expense, $90,000.

GROUP A PROBLEMS

17–1A. Learning Objectives 2, 3, 8. Preparing a Sales Budget, Production Budget, and a Selling and Administrative Expense Budget.
Stewart Corporation has assembled the following information to help them in preparing budgets for the year ending December 31, 19X3:

a. Sales in units by quarter:
    Quarter 1   19X3   700
    Quarter 2   19X3   900
    Quarter 3   19X3 1,300
    Quarter 4   19X3 1,100
    Quarter 1   19X4   800
b. Sales price, $100.
c. Accounts Receivable balance 12/31/X2, $24,000.
d. Collection of accounts receivable is 60% in quarter of sale, the remaining 40% in the following quarter. All sales are on account.
e. Desired ending inventory of finished goods is 20% of the next quarter's sales.
f. Beginning inventory of finished goods, 120 units.
g. Variable selling and admin. expense per unit, $30.
h. Budgeted fixed selling and admin. expense, $20,000 per quarter.

Required:

1. Prepare a sales budget, including a schedule of budgeted cash collections.
2. Prepare a production budget.
3. Prepare a selling and administrative expense budget.

17–2A. Learning Objectives 4, 5, 6, 7. Preparing a Direct Materials Budget, Direct Labor Budget, Manufacturing Overhead Budget, and a Manufacturing Costs Budget.
Gomez Company is preparing various budgets for the year ending December 31, 19X4. The following information has been assembled to aid them:

a. Budgeted production in units by quarter:
    Quarter 1   19X4   300
    Quarter 2   19X4   500
    Quarter 3   19X4   700
    Quarter 4   19X4   500
    Quarter 1   19X5   320
b. Direct materials required per unit, 5 gallons.
c. Desired ending inventory of direct materials is 20% of the next quarter's production needs.
d. Beginning inventory of direct materials, 280 gallons
e. Cost of direct materials to be purchased, $8 per gallon
f. Beginning balance of accounts payable, $5,600
g. Schedule of cash payments for materials is 50% paid for in the quarter of purchase, the remaining 50 percent is paid for in the following quarter.
h. It takes 6 direct labor hours to produce one unit.
i. Direct labor cost per hour, $10

j. Variable overhead rate, $4 per direct labor hour needed.
k. Budgeted fixed overhead, $40,000 per quarter
l. Amount of depr. expense in the manufacturing overhead, $2,500 per quarter.

Required:

1. Prepare a direct materials budget including a schedule of budgeted cash payment for materials.
2. Prepare a direct labor budget.
3. Prepare a manufacturing overhead budget.
4. Prepare a manufacturing costs budget.

17–3A. Learning Objective 9. Preparing a Cash Budget.

Steinbach Company is in the process of preparing budgets for the next year. The following information will be used to prepare a cash budget for the year ending December 31, 19X2.

a. Beginning cash balance, $22,000.
b. Budgeted cash collections by quarter for 19X2:

Quarter 1 $ 82,000
Quarter 2   93,400
Quarter 3   215,600
Quarter 4   206,800

c. Budgeted cash outflows by quarter for 19X2:

	Quarter			
	1	2	3	4
Direct materials	$18,475	$16,250	$32,420	$35,680
Direct labor cost	12,300	19,100	29,375	31,200
Manufacturing overhead	20,000	23,000	28,000	26,000
Selling and admin. expense	30,000	35,000	45,000	36,000
Purchase of equipment	20,000			20,000
Income tax expense	10,000	10,000	10,000	10,000
Cash dividends paid	5,000	5,000	5,000	5,000

d. A minimum cash balance of $20,000 must be maintained.
e. Financing is available at 12% per year. Money must be borrowed in $1,000 increments. Money is borrowed at the beginning of a quarter and is repaid at the end of a quarter, when there is adequate cash flow.

Required:
Prepare a cash budget for the year ending December 31, 19X2.

17–4A. Learning Objectives 2, 3, 4, 5, 6, 7, 8, 9, 10, 11. Preparing a Master Budget and a Flexible Budgeted Income Statement.

Sheffield Company has assembled the following information for the purposes of preparing a master budget for the year ending December 31, 19X4.

1. Budgeted sales in units: Quarter 1, 150; Quarter 2, 200; Quarter 3, 800; Quarter 4, 350.
2. Sales price per unit, $325.

3. Beginning balance of Accounts Receivable, $21,000
4. Collection of Accounts Receivable is 60% in the quarter of sale, 40% in the following quarter. All sales are on account.
5. Desired ending inventory of finished goods is 10% of the following quarter's sales in units.
6. Beginning finished goods inventory, 20 units.
7. Budgeted sales for Quarter 1 of 19X5 is 200 units, and budgeted production needs for quarter 1 of 19X5 is 1,000 lbs.
8. Direct materials per unit, 5 pounds.
9. Desired ending inventory of direct materials is 20% of the next quarter's production needs.
10. Beginning inventory of direct materials, 100 pounds
11. Beginning balance of Accounts Payable, $2,600
12. Cost of direct materials to be purchased, $12 per pound
13. Cash payments for purchases are 50% in the quarter of purchase and the remaining 50% in the following quarter.
14. Direct labor hours per unit, 4
15. Direct labor cost per hour, $10
16. Variable overhead rate of $4 is applied on the basis of budgeted direct labor hours. The variable overhead rate is $16 per unit sold.
17. Budgeted fixed overhead, $20,000 per quarter
18. Depr. expense related to manufacturing overhead, $5,000 per quarter
19. Budgeted variable selling and admin. expense per unit, $14
20. Budgeted fixed selling and admin. expense, $7,000 per quarter
21. Income tax expense, $6,000 per quarter
22. Cash dividends paid, $3,000 per quarter
23. Equipment is budgeted to be purchased in Quarter 1 for $30,000 and Quarter 4 for $80,000.
24. Beginning cash balance, $25,000.
25. A minimum cash balance of $20,000 must be maintained.
26. Money is borrowed in increments of $1,000. Borrowed money is always considered received at the beginning of a quarter and the principal is repaid in full or in increments at the end of each quarter when there is enough cash flow.
27. Annual interest rate on borrowed funds, 12%
28. Beginning and ending finished goods inventory, $2,700

Required:

1. Prepare the following budgets:
   a. Sales budget and a schedule of budgeted cash collections.
   b. Production budget.
   c. Direct materials budget and a schedule of budgeted cash payments for materials.
   d. Direct labor budget.
   e. Manufacturing overhead budget.
   f. Manufacturing costs budget.
   g. Selling and administrative expense budget.
   h. Cash budget.
   i. Budgeted income statement.
2. Prepare a flexible budgeted income statement for Sheffield Company assuming sales in units: 500, 1,000, 1,500, 2,000 and 2,500.

GROUP B PROBLEMS

17–1B. Learning Objectives 2, 3, 8. Preparing a Sales Budget, Production Budget, and a Selling and Administrative Expense Budget.

Puckett Corporation has assembled the following information to help them in preparing budgets for the year ending December 31, 19X3:

a. Sales in units by quarter:

Quarter 1	19X3	800
Quarter 2	19X3	1,100
Quarter 3	19X3	1,800
Quarter 4	19X3	1,200
Quarter 1	19X4	900

b. Sales price, $200.
c. Accounts Receivable balance 12/31/X2, $38,000.
d. Collection of accounts receivable is 70% in quarter of sale, the remaining 30% in the following quarter. All sales are on account.
e. Desired ending inventory of finished goods is 10% of the next quarter's sales.
f. Beginning inventory of finished goods, 100 units
g. Variable selling and administrative expense per unit, $40.
h. Budgeted fixed selling and admin. expense, $30,000 per quarter

Required:

1. Prepare a sales budget, including a schedule of budgeted cash collections.
2. Prepare a production budget.
3. Prepare a selling and administrative expense budget.

17–2B. Learning Objectives 4, 5, 6, 7. Preparing a Direct Materials Budget, Direct Labor Budget, Manufacturing Overhead Budget, and a Manufacturing Costs Budget.

Griffey Company is preparing various budgets for the year ending December 31, 19X4. The following information has been assembled to aid them:

a. Budgeted production in units by quarter:

Quarter 1	19X4	400
Quarter 2	19X4	700
Quarter 3	19X4	1,200
Quarter 4	19X4	800
Quarter 1	19X5	500

b. Direct materials required per unit, 6 gallons.
c. Desired ending inventory of direct materials is 20% of the next quarter's production needs.
d. Beginning inventory of direct materials, 840 gallons
e. Cost of direct materials to be purchased, $10 per gallon
f. Beginning balance of accounts payable, $21,000.
g. Schedule of cash payments for materials is 50% paid for in the quarter of purchase, the remaining 50 percent is paid for in the following quarter.

h. It takes 7 direct labor hours to produce one unit.
i. Direct labor cost per hour, $12
j. Variable overhead rate, $5 per direct labor hour needed
k. Budgeted fixed overhead, $50,000 per quarter
l. Amount of depr. expense in the manufacturing overhead, $5,000 per quarter

Required:

1. Prepare a direct materials budget including a schedule of budgeted cash payment for materials.
2. Prepare a direct labor budget.
3. Prepare a manufacturing overhead budget.
4. Prepare a manufacturing costs budget.

17–3B. Learning Objective 9. Preparing a Cash Budget.

Ripken Company is in the process of preparing budgets for the next year. The following information will be used to prepare a cash budget for the year ending December 31, 19X2.

a. Beginning cash balance is $24,000.
b. Budgeted cash collections by quarter for 19X2:
    Quarter 1, $ 83,000
    Quarter 2,   94,100
    Quarter 3,   212,300
    Quarter 4,   203,400
c. Budgeted cash outflows by quarter for 19X2:

| | Quarter | | | |
	1	2	3	4
Direct materials	$19,350	$17,140	$31,475	$33,250
Direct labor cost	14,200	18,500	28,275	30,840
Manufacturing overhead	21,000	22,000	26,000	23,000
Selling and admin. expense	32,000	36,000	38,000	35,000
Purchase of equipment	30,000			20,000
Income tax expense	11,000	11,000	11,000	11,000
Cash dividends paid	6,000	6,000	6,000	6,000

d. A minimum cash balance of $20,000 must be maintained.
e. Financing is available at 12% per year. Money must be borrowed in $1,000 increments. Money is borrowed at the beginning of a quarter and is repaid at the end of a quarter, when there is adequate cash flow.

Required:

Prepare a cash budget for the year ending December 31, 19X2.

17–4B. Learning Objectives 2, 3, 4, 5, 6, 7, 8, 9, 10, 11. Preparing a Master Budget and a Flexible Budgeted Income Statement.

Clark Company has assembled the following information for the purposes of preparing a master budget for the year ending December 31, 19X4:

1. Budgeted sales in units: Quarter 1, 175; Quarter 2, 225; Quarter 3, 850; Quarter 4, 250.

2. Sales price per unit, $310.
3. Beginning balance of Accounts Receivable, $18,500
4. Collection of Accounts Receivable is 50% in the quarter of sale, 50% in the following quarter. All sales are on account.
5. Desired ending inventory of finished goods is 20% of the following quarter's sales in units.
6. Beginning finished goods inventory, 25 units.
7. Budgeted sales for Quarter 1 of 19X5 is 125 units, and budgeted production needs for quarter 1 of 19X5 is 600 pounds.
8. Direct materials per unit, 6 pounds
9. Desired ending inventory of direct materials is 10% of the next quarter's production needs.
10. Beginning inventory of direct materials, 60 pounds
11. Beginning balance of Accounts Payable, $2,800
12. Cost of direct materials to be purchased, $10 per gallon
13. Cash payments for purchases are 50% in the quarter of purchase and the remaining 50% in the following quarter.
14. Direct labor hours per unit, 5
15. Direct labor cost per hour, $8
16. Variable overhead rate of $5 is applied on the basis of budgeted direct labor hours. The variable overhead rate is $25 per unit sold.
17. Budgeted fixed overhead, $26,250 per quarter
18. Depr. expense related to manufacturing overhead, $15,000 per quarter
19. Budgeted variable selling and admin. expense per unit, $15
20. Budgeted fixed selling and admin. expense, $8,000 per quarter
21. Income tax expense, $7,000 per quarter
22. Cash dividends paid, $4,000 per quarter
23. Equipment is budgeted to be purchased in Quarter 4 for $65,000.
24. Beginning cash balance, $22,000
25. A minimum cash balance of $20,000 must be maintained.
26. Money is borrowed in increments of $1,000. Borrowed money is always considered received at the beginning of a quarter and the principal is repaid in full or in increments at the end of each quarter when there is enough cash flow.
27. Annual interest rate on borrowed funds, 12%
28. Beginning and ending finished goods inventory, $4,875

Required:

1. Prepare the following budgets:
   a. Sales budget and a schedule of budgeted cash collections.
   b. Production budget.
   c. Direct materials budget and a schedule of budgeted cash payments for materials.
   d. Direct labor budget.
   e. Manufacturing overhead budget.
   f. Manufacturing costs budget.
   g. Selling and administrative expense budget.
   h. Cash budget.
   i. Budgeted income statement.
2. Prepare a flexible budgeted income statement for Clark Company assuming sales in units: 500, 1,000, 1,500, 2,000 and 2,500.

CASE FOR CRITICAL THINKING

McNary Company completed a master budget for 19X8, based on projected total unit sales of 50,000. At the end of the year, when comparing the budget to actual sales and production, large discrepancies were noted. Upon further investigation it was noted that actual sales were 10,000 units higher than budgeted. Explain to management a method of dealing with this type of problem, and how you would design the report.

ANSWERS TO SELF-STUDY QUIZ 17–1

a.   40; b. 100; c. 70; d. 40; e. 40; f. 190; g. 300; h. 570; i. 390; j. 1240; k. 20; l. 40; m. 100; n. 70; o. 20; p. 170; q. 260; r. 470; s. 320; t. 1220

ANSWERS TO SELF-STUDY QUIZ 17–2

a.   Sales budget.
b.   1. Production budget.
     2. Direct materials budget.
     3. Direct labor budget.
     4. Manufacturing overhead budget.
     5. Manufacturing costs budget.
     6. Selling and administrative expense budget.
     7. Cash budget.
     8. Budgeted income statement.

Chapter 18
Standard Costs—
Materials and Labor

LEARNING OBJECTIVES

After studying Chapter 18, you should be able to:

1. Define a standard cost system.
2. Explain the difference between theoretical standards and practical standards.
3. Compute the direct materials cost and quantity variances and show how these variances are recorded in the accounting records.
4. Compute the direct labor rate and efficiency variances and show how these variances are recorded in the accounting records.
5. Close the four variance accounts into Cost of Goods Sold.

LEARNING OBJECTIVE 1

In Chapter 17, we learned the essentials of budgeting, including the concept of budgetary control—taking corrective action when conditions deviate from what was planned. We will continue the theme of budgetary control by introducing the concept of standard costs for materials and labor. A standard resembles a bench mark in that it will show at a glance whether the price paid or the quantity used for materials and labor are favorable or unfavorable. A **standard cost system** is an accounting method that uses standard costs for materials, labor, and manufacturing overhead. During the year, the standard costs become the basis of journal entries in recording the flow of costs through the accounting system. Figure 18–1 diagrams the flow of manufacturing costs through an accounting system.

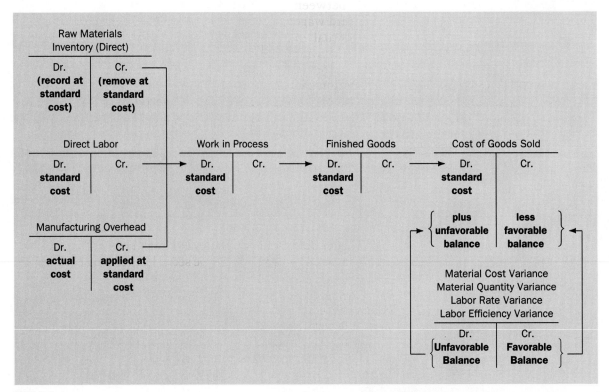

FIGURE 18–1
Flow of Manufacturing

As Figure 18–1 shows, the three manufacturing costs (direct materials inventory, direct labor, and manufacturing overhead) flow into the work in process inventory. When the work is completed, the costs flow from the Work in Process Inventory into the Finished Goods Inventory. When the product is sold, the costs flow from the Finished Goods Inventory into the Cost of Goods Sold account. All the above account balances will show standard costs instead of actual costs, except for manufacturing overhead. In Chapter 19, we will cover the application of manufacturing overhead using a standard cost system. However, when analyzing direct materials and direct labor, when actual costs differ from standard, the differences will appear in "variance" accounts. Figure 18–1 showed that four types of variances relate to direct materials and direct labor.

The **material cost variance** is the difference between the actual cost paid for materials and the standard cost. The **material quantity variance** is the difference between the actual quantity of materials used and the standard quantity allowed given the actual level of production. The **labor rate variance** is the difference between the actual wage rate paid to the production workers and the standard wage rate. The **labor efficiency variance** is the difference between the actual number of labor hours used and the standard quantity allowed given the actual level of production. A **variance** shows up whenever a difference exists between the actual cost and the predetermined standard. Corrective action can be taken during the year when things get out of line. Then at the end of the year, these variance accounts are closed into the Cost of Goods Sold account so that the financial statements reflect actual costs.

SETTING STANDARDS

LEARNING OBJECTIVE 2

When management decides to adopt a standard cost system, it becomes necessary to analyze costs and determine a fair standard for materials, labor, and overhead. Basically, two types of standards can be set: (1) a theoretical standard or (2) a practical standard. A **theoretical standard** can be achieved only if conditions are perfect. It does not allow for wastage, breakdowns, downtime, or spoilage. The problem with setting standards too high is that they are rarely, if ever, met. This can become a morale problem for the workers if they feel that the standards are set too high and can never be achieved.

On the other hand, a **practical standard** allows for a normal amount of wastage, breakdown, downtime, and spoilage. It can be met when operations are running efficiently, but a practical standard is not set so high that it becomes idealistic or unattainable. Most standard cost systems, including the examples in this chapter, use practical standards rather than theoretical standards.

In this chapter we will examine material and labor standards. In the next chapter we will analyze manufacturing overhead standards.

MATERIAL COSTS

In our discussion of material costs, we will separate the cost of buying the materials from the amount or quantity of materials used. This is beneficial because the purchasing of materials is a different activity and involves a different department than the use of materials in production. Also, it is important to separate a material price variance from a material quantity variance because the time when these variances appear will be different. A material cost variance can be computed when the materials are purchased. A material quantity variance will be computed later when the materials are used in production.

A group effort is required to set a material cost standard. For example, this activity typically involves a purchasing manager, production supervisor, and cost accountant. Once the grade of material, method of delivery, purchase price, and all other material purchase factors have been agreed upon, a material cost standard is set. The purchasing manager or representative will be the primary person to contact when a large favorable or unfavorable price variance occurs. Both types of variances need to be investigated. A large favorable variance could indicate shoddy or lower grade materials have been purchased. This can create additional problems when the material is used in production. Of course, a material price standard must be updated as conditions change. For example, if the price paid for materials has permanently increased, then the material price standard must be adjusted immediately.

A group effort is also required when setting a material quantity standard. This activity typically involves a production supervisor, design engineer, and cost accountant. Once a consensus has been reached among the various parties, a material quantity standard is set. When a large favorable or unfavorable material quantity variance occurs, the production supervisor is contacted. Material quantity standards can be adjusted during the year when conditions warrant it. For example, if the design engineer changes the specifications for a product, the material quantity standard may need to be adjusted.

Figure 18–2 shows a basic format to analyze material and labor variances and the required general journal entries that can be developed to aid the cost accountant.

Notice in Figure 18–2 that the amount on line (A) (Standard Cost × Standard Quantity) represents the amount that will be debited to Work in Process Inventory. The standard quantity represents the quantity allowed given the actual level of production. This amount can be computed by multiplying the units produced times the standard quantity allowed per unit. Line (C) (Actual Cost × Actual Quantity) represents the amount that will be credited to accounts or salaries payable. We debit all unfavorable variances and credit all favorable variances. In the calculation of either the cost or quantity variance, a negative amount represents an unfavorable variance. A positive

		General Journal			
	Date	**Description**	**P.R.**	**Debit**	**Credit**
(A) Standard Cost × Standard Quantity → (SC × SQ)		Work in Process Inventory		X X X X XX	
Quantity Variance = (A) − (B)		Material Quantity Variance		X X X X XX	X X X X XX
Materials quantity variance		or Labor Efficiency Variance		X X X X XX	X X X X XX
Labor efficiency variance				(U)	(F)
(B) Standard Cost × Actual Quantity used (SC × AQ)					
Cost Variance = (B) − (C)		Material Cost Variance		X X X X XX	X X X X XX
Materials cost variance		or Labor Rate Variance		X X X X XX	X X X X XX
Labor rate variance				(U)	(F)
(C) Actual Cost × Actual Quantity → (AC × AQ)		Accounts/Salaries Payable			X X X X XX
Total Variance = (A) − (C)					

F = Favorable
U = Unfavorable

FIGURE 18–2
*Basic Format of
Variance Analysis*

amount represents a favorable variance. To compute the total variance, subtract line (C) from line (A).

LEARNING OBJECTIVE 3   To illustrate the application of this basic format for variance analysis and to show the required journal entries to record the purchase and the material quantity and cost variances, let's assume the following data for Rock Creek Company:

	Standard Cost Per Lb.		**Standard Quantity Per Unit**		**Standard Cost Per Unit**
Direct Material	$5.00	×	2 pounds	=	$10.00

During the month of August, Rock Creek Company purchased 4,200 pounds of material at a cost of $4.80 per pound to immediately manufacture 2,000 units of product. Using the basic format for variance analysis, Figure 18–3 presents this data.

		General Journal			
	Date	**Description**	**P.R.**	**Debit**	**Credit**

Purchase of Raw Materials

(A) Standard Cost × Actual Quantity purchased → Raw Materials Inventory | 21 00 0 00 |
 ($5.00 × 4,200 lbs)
 $21,000

Cost Variance = (A) − (B)   Material Cost Variance | | 8 40 0 00
 $840 F

(B) Actual Cost × Actual Quantity purchased → Accounts Payable | | 20 16 0 00
 ($4.80 × 4,200)
 $20,160

Usage of Raw Materials in Production

(C) Standard Cost × Standard Quantity → Work in Process Inventory | 20 00 0 00 |
 ($5.00 × 4,000 lbs*)
 $20,000

Quantity Variance = (C) − (D)   Material Quantity Variance | 1 00 0 00 |
 −$1,000 U

(D) Standard Cost × Actual Quantity used → Raw Materials Inventory | | 21 00 0 00
 ($5.00 × 4,200 lbs)
 $21,000

*Standard Quantity = 2,000 units × 2.0 pounds per unit = 4,000 lbs.
F = Favorable
U = Unfavorable

FIGURE 18–3
*Basic Format for Material
Variance Analysis*

To arrive at the standard quantity allowed for this level of production, on line (A), multiply the number of units produced times the standard quantity allowed per unit. In our example, the standard quantity per unit is 2.0 pounds. If 2,000 units are to be produced, then 4,000 pounds (2.0 lbs × 2,000) is the required standard quantity.

The journal entry to record the purchase of direct materials appears in Figure 18–3. This information is repeated in general journal form below:

			Debit	Credit	
1		Raw Materials Inventory	21 00 0 00		1
2		Material Cost Variance		8 40 0 00	2
3		Accounts Payable		20 16 0 00	3
4		Record material purchase and			4
5		cost variance			5

The journal entry to record the usage of materials in production appears in general journal form below:

1		Work in Process Inventory	2000000		1
2		Material Quantity Variance	100000		2
3		Raw Materials Inventory		2100000	3
4		Record material usage and			4
5		quantity variance			5

We debit the Work in Process Inventory account for the standard cost of the direct materials, $20,000. Another way to arrive at the amount to charge the Work in Process Inventory is to multiply the total standard material cost per unit, $10, times the number of units produced, 2,000, which equals $20,000.

As mentioned earlier, we debit unfavorable variances and credit favorable variances. We credit Accounts Payable for the actual cost times the actual quantity purchased, $20,160 ($4.80 × 4,200).

Using the same example, assume instead that the materials were purchased long before the production of the product. In this situation, a two-step procedure is necessary to calculate the variances and make the journal entries. Figure 18–4 shows only the purchase of materials and the price variance.

(A) Standard Cost × Actual Quantity purchased
($5.00 × 4,200 lbs)
$21,000

Cost Variance = (A) − (B)
$840 F

(B) Actual Cost × Actual Quantity purchased
($4.80 × 4,200 lbs)
$20,160

| General Journal | | | | | |
Date	Description	P.R.	Debt	Credit
→	Raw Materials Inventory		2100000	
	Material Cost Variance			84000
	Accounts Payable			2016000

FIGURE 18–4
*Purchase of
Materials and Cost
Variance*

The material cost variance could be investigated immediately upon the purchase of the materials. The purchasing manager should be contacted. Assuming that a cheaper grade of material was purchased, this may account for the favorable material cost variance.

The general journal entry to record the purchase of materials and the favorable cost variance follows:

1	Raw Materials Inventory	2100000		1
2	Material Cost Variance		84000	2
3	Accounts Payable		2016000	3
4	Purchased materials and recog.			4
5	cost variance.			5

Later when the materials are issued into production, Figure 18–5 shows the issuance of materials and the unfavorable quantity variance.

(A) Standard Cost × Standard Quantity
($5.00 × 4,000 lbs*)
$20,000

Quantity Variance = (A) – (B)
–$1,000 U

(B) Standard Cost × Actual Quantity used
$21,000

	General Journal				
Date	Description	P.R.	Debit		Credit
	Work in Process Inventory		2000000		
	Material Quantity Variance		100000		
	Raw Materials Inventory				2100000

* Standard Quantity = 2,000 units × 2.0 pounds per unit = 4,000 lbs.
F = Favorable
U = Unfavorable

FIGURE 18–5
Use of Materials and Cost Variance

The general journal entry to record use of materials and the unfavorable material quantity variance appears as follows:

1	Work in Process Inventory	2000000		1
2	Material Quantity Variance	100000		2
3	Raw Materials Inventory		2100000	3
4	Recog. material usage and quantity			4
5	variance.			5

The production supervisor should be contacted regarding the unfavorable material quantity variance. Perhaps, production required more materials because of the cheaper grade of material that was purchased. This could explain the unfavorable material quantity variance.

SELF-STUDY QUIZ 18–1 Stockwell Company uses a standard cost system. Their standard costs for direct material cost and quantity follow:

Standard Costs

Standard cost per gallon:	$3.00
Standard quantity per unit:	10 gallons

During the month of June, Stockwell purchased 950 gallons at $3.20 per gallon. All the material was used to manufacture 100 units of product.

1. Compute the material cost and quantity variances.
2. Make general journal entries as of June 30, to Record (1) the purchase of the materials and the material cost variance, and (2) the usage of materials in production and the material quantity variance.

Answers at end of chapter.

LABOR COSTS

LEARNING OBJECTIVE 4   The analysis of direct labor costs is very similar to the methods used in analyzing direct materials cost. In our discussion of direct labor costs we will separate the hourly rate paid to direct labor workers, called the **labor rate variance,** from the quantity of hours used, called the **labor efficiency variance.** The primary person responsible for these two variances is the production supervisor. However, just as there was a group effort in setting material price and material quantity standards, a group effort is required to set labor rate and labor efficiency standards. This activity typically involves the production supervisor, personnel manager, and cost accountant. Once a consensus has been reached among the various parties, a labor rate and labor efficiency standard are set. Of course, these standards can be adjusted if conditions warrant it. For example, if the wage rates have increased, or the production methods have changed, the labor rate and labor efficiency variances will need to be adjusted.

The labor rate relates to the average wage paid to the production workers. An unfavorable labor rate variance can appear when higher skilled workers are doing a job that had required lower skilled workers to complete.

The labor efficiency relates to the quantity of hours used. If more labor hours are required to complete a job than was called for at standard rate, an unfavorable labor efficiency variance is created. The production supervisor should be contacted regarding a large favorable or unfavorable direct labor variance.

To illustrate the application of the basic format to analyze direct labor variances and to make journal entries to record labor costs and the labor efficiency and labor rate variances, let's continue to use the data for Rock Creek Company:

	Standard Rate Per Hour		Standard Hours Per Unit		Standard Cost Per Unit
Direct Labor	$12.00	×	3 hours	=	$36.00

During the month of August, Rock Creek Company recorded 5,950 hours of direct labor time, at an average wage rate of $12.50, to manufacture 2,000 units of product. Using the basic format to analyze variances, Figure 18–6 presents this data.

	General Journal			
Date	**Description**	**P.R.**	**Debit**	**Credit**
	Work in Process Inventory		72 00 0 00	
	Labor Efficiency Variance			6 00 00
	Labor Rate Variance		2 97 5 00	
	Salaries Payable			74 37 5 00

(A) Standard Rate × Standard Hours
($12.00 × 6,000 hrs*)
$72,000

Labor Efficiency Variance = (A) – (B)
$600 F

(B) Standard Rate × Actual Hours used
($12.00 × 5,950 hrs)
$71,400

Labor Rate Variance = (B) – (C)
–$2,975 U

(C) Actual Rate × Actual Hours
($12.50 × 5,950)
$74,375

Total Variance = (A) – (C)
–$2,375 U

*Standard Quantity = 2,000 units × 3 hours per unit = 6,000 hrs.
F = Favorable
U = Unfavorable

FIGURE 18–6
*Direct Labor Rate
and Efficiency
Variances*

As Figure 18–6 shows, the labor efficiency variance is $600 favorable, but the labor rate variance is $2,975 unfavorable. This created a net, direct labor, unfavorable variance of $2,375. It appears that 50 fewer hours were worked than the 6,000 standard called for. A favorable labor efficiency variance of $600 appears. However, the average wage rate paid to the production workers was $12.50, which is higher than the standard wage rate, $12.00. This created an unfavorable labor rate variance of $2,975. In summary, it appears that higher skilled workers were paid to do work usually performed by lower skilled workers. However, fewer hours were required to complete the work, probably because higher skilled labor was being used.

Figure 18–6 shows the journal entry to record the payment of direct labor at a standard rate and quantity and to record the direct labor rate and efficiency variances. It appears in general journal form:

1	Work in Process Inventory	72000 00	1
2	Labor Rate Variance	2975 00	2
3	Labor Efficiency Variances		600 00	3
4	Salaries Payable		74375 00	4

As the journal entry shows, we debit the Work in Process Inventory for the standard cost of direct labor. We debit the unfavorable Labor Rate Variance and credit the favorable Labor Efficiency Variance. We credit Salaries Payable for the actual cost of direct labor.

The production supervisor, who is in charge of scheduling work and personnel to complete a job, should be contacted regarding the labor rate and labor efficiency variances.

NOTE The purchasing manager should be contacted regarding the material cost variance. The production supervisor should be contacted regarding the material quantity variance, labor rate variance, and labor efficiency variance.

CLOSING VARIANCES INTO COST OF GOODS SOLD

LEARNING OBJECTIVE 5   At the end of the year, the balances in the four variance accounts will be closed into the Cost of Goods Sold account. Let's assume in our example that the balances in the four variance accounts represent the end of the year balances. Of course, during the year, each variance account can be either debited or credited and the ending balance of any variance account can be a debit or credit balance. Using T accounts, the four variance account balances, before closing, appear as follows:

Material Cost Variance		Material Quantity Variance	
Dr.	Cr.	Dr.	Cr.
	840	1,000	

Labor Rate Variance		Labor Efficiency Variance	
Dr.	Cr.	Dr.	Cr.
2,975			600

The general journal entry to close the four variance accounts into Cost of Goods Sold follows:

1		Cost of Goods Sold	2535 00		1
2		Material Cost Variance	840 00		2
3		Labor Efficiency Variance	600 00		3
4		Material Quantity Variance		1000 00	4
5		Labor Rate Variance		2975 00	5
6		Closing Variances into Cost of			6
7		Goods Sold			7

At the end of the year, the variance accounts will all be closed out, and the Cost of Goods Sold will be increased or decreased by the net amount of the four variances. After posting the closing entries, the four variance accounts will have zero balances and Cost of Goods Sold will increase by $2,535, as follows:

Material Cost Variance		Material Quantity Variance	
Dr.	Cr.	Dr.	Cr.
840	840	1,000	**1,000**
Balance 0		Balance 0	

Labor Rate Variance		Labor Efficiency Variance	
Dr.	Cr.	Dr.	Cr.
2,975	**2,975**	**600**	600
Balance 0		Balance 0	

Cost of Goods Sold	
Dr.	Cr.
2,535	

SELF-STUDY QUIZ 18–2 Baker Company uses a standard cost system. Their standard costs for direct labor rate and hours follow:

Standard Costs

Standard rate per hour: $15.00
Standard hours per unit: 4 hours

During the month of September, 400 units of product were manufactured. Actual hours worked were 1,620 at an average wage rate of $14.75.

1. Compute the direct labor efficiency and rate variances.
2. Make general journal entries as of September 30, to record the payment of the labor and to record the direct labor efficiency and rate variances.

Answers at end of chapter.

SELF-STUDY PROBLEM

Foxworth Company uses a standard cost system. The standard costs for direct materials and direct labor follow:

	Standard Cost or Standard Rate		Standard Quantity or Standard Hours		Standard Cost per Unit
Direct Material	$ 2.00	×	6 pounds	=	$12.00
Direct Labor	10.00		3 hours		30.00

During the month of March, Foxworth Company produced 1,000 units of product using the following amounts of materials and labor:

5,920 pounds of material were purchased at $2.20 per pound.
3,070 hours were worked at an average wage rate of $9.80 per hour.

Required:

1. Compute the direct materials cost and quantity variances.
2. Make general journal entries to record (1) the purchase and the material cost variance, and (2) the usage of materials and the material quantity variances. Date the journal entry March 31, 19—.
3. Compute the direct labor efficiency and rate variances.
4. Make general journal entries to record the payment of the direct labor and the amount charged to production, and to record the labor efficiency and rate variances. Date the journal entry March 31, 19—.
5. Make a general journal entry to close the four variance accounts into Cost of Goods Sold, as of March 31, 19—.

SOLUTION TO SELF-STUDY PROBLEM

1.

			General Journal			
Purchase of Raw Materials	**Date**	**Description**	**P.R.**	**Debit**		**Credit**
(A) Standard Cost × Actual Quantity purchased →		Raw Materials Inventory		1184000		
($2.00 × 5,920 lbs) $11,840						
Cost Variance = (A) − (B) **−$1,184**		Material Cost Variance		118400		
(B) Actual Cost × Actual Quantity purchased →		Accounts Payable				1302400
($2.20 × 5,920) $13,024						
Usage of Raw Materials in Production						
(C) Standard Cost × Standard Quantity →		Work in Process Inventory		1200000		
($2.00 × 6,000 lbs*) $12,000						
Quantity Variance = (A) − (B) $160 F		Material Quantity Variance				16000
(D) Standard Cost × Actual Quantity used →		Raw Materials Inventory				1184000
($2.00 × 5,920 lbs) $11,840						

*Standard Quantity = 1,000 units × 6.0 pounds per unit = 6,000 lbs.
F = Favorable
U = Unfavorable

2.

	19XX						
1	Mar.	31	Raw Materials Inventory	1184000			1
2			Material Cost Variance	118400			2
3			Accounts Payable		1302400		3

1		31	Work in Process Inventory	1200000			1
2			Material Quantity Variance		16000		2
3			Raw Materials Inventory		1184000		3

3.

(A) Standard Rate × Standard Hours
($10.00 × 3,000 hrs*)
$30,000

Labor Efficiency Variance = (A) − (B)
−$700 U

(B) Standard Rate × Actual Hours used
($10.00 × 3,070 hrs)
$30,700

Labor Rate Variance = (B) − (C)

(C) Actual Rate × Actual Hours
($9.80 × 3,070 hrs)
$30,086

Total Variance = (A) − (C)
−$86 U

	General Journal				
Date	Description	P.R.	Debit		Credit
	Work in Process Inventory		3000000		
	Labor Efficiency Variance		70000		
	Labor Rate Variance				61400
	Salaries Payable				3008600

*Standard Quantity = 1,000 units × 3 hours per unit = 3,000 hrs.

4.

	19XX						
1	Mar.	31	Work in Process Inventory	3000000			1
2			Labor Efficiency Variance	70000			2
3			Labor Rate Variance		61400		3
4			Salaries Payable		3008600		4

5.

	19XX						
1	Mar.	31	Cost of Goods Sold	1 1 1 0 00			1
2			Material Quantity Variance	1 6 0 00			2
3			Labor Rate Variance	6 1 4 00			3
4			Material Cost Variance		1 1 8 4 00	4
5			Labor Efficiency Variance		7 0 0 00	5

SUMMARY

In this chapter we learned that using a standard cost system helps management control costs and improve operating efficiency. A **standard cost system** is an accounting method that sets standards for manufacturing costs. The accounting records reflect standard costs instead of actual costs. A variance occurs when the actual cost differs from the predetermined standard. When actual costs and quantity used differ from standard costs and quantity allowed, the differences are collected in variance accounts. The two variance accounts for materials include: (1) **Material Cost Variance** and (2) **Material Quantity Variance.** The two variance accounts for labor include: (1) **Labor Efficiency Variance** and (2) **Labor Rate Variance.** The purchasing manager should be contacted when a large favorable or unfavorable material cost variance occurs. The production supervisor should be contacted when a large favorable or unfavorable material quantity variance, labor efficiency variance, or labor rate variance occurs.

Two types of standards, theoretical standards and practical standards, may be used. A **theoretical standard** is set so high that it can only be reached if operations run perfectly, with no downtime, spoilage, or work interruptions. A **practical standard** is attainable but allows for normal downtime, spoilage, and work interruptions.

When preparing the journal entry using a standard cost system, we always debit the Work in Process Inventory account for the standard costs of direct materials and direct labor. We always debit an unfavorable variance and always credit a favorable variance. We credit Accounts Payable and Salaries Payable for the actual costs of direct materials and direct labor respectively.

KEY TERMS

Labor Efficiency Variance. The difference between the actual number of labor hours used and the standard quantity allowed given the actual level of production.

Labor Rate Variance. The difference between the actual wage rate paid to the production workers and the standard wage rate.

Material Cost Variance. The difference between the actual cost paid for materials and the standard cost.

Material Quantity Variance. The difference between the actual quantity of materials used and the standard quantity allowed given the actual level of production.

Practical Standard. An attainable level of output that allows for a normal amount of wastage, breakdown, downtime, and spoilage.

Standard Cost System. An accounting method that uses standard costs for materials, labor, and manufacturing overhead.

Theoretical Standard. An ideal level of output that can only be achieved if conditions are perfect.

Variance. The difference between the actual cost and the predetermined standard.

QUESTIONS FOR REVIEW

1. What is a standard cost system?
2. Describe the flow of manufacturing costs through an accounting system using a standard cost system.
3. What is a variance?
4. What is the difference between a theoretical standard and a practical standard?
5. Define each of these variances:
    a. Material cost variance.
    b. Material quantity variance.
    c. Labor rate variance.
    d. Labor efficiency variance.
6. Who is the primary person responsible for a material cost variance?
7. Who is the primary person responsible for a material quantity variance, labor rate variance, and a labor efficiency variance?
8. The work in process inventory account is always debited with which of the following?
    a. Standard Cost × Standard Quantity.
    b. Actual Cost × Actual Quantity.
9. All unfavorable variances are debited/credited? (select one).
10. All favorable variances are debited/credited? (select one).
11. When there is a material cost variance, is it appropriate to investigate the variance immediately or later when the materials are used in production?
12. At the end of the year, the variance accounts are closed into what account title?

NOTE Unless told otherwise in Exercises and Problems, record transactions in general journal form.

EXERCISES

18–1. Learning Objective 3. Computing Direct Materials Cost and Quantity Variances.

Maxwell Company uses a standard cost system to help control costs. The following material standards have been established for their product:

Standard Cost per Pound	Standard Quantity in Pounds per Unit Produced
$2.50	4 pounds

During the month of May, 11,960 pounds were purchased at $2.60 per pound. All the material was used to produce 3,000 units of product.

1. What was the standard quantity of materials allowed for this level of production?
2. Compute the material and quantity cost variances and indicate whether they are favorable (f), or unfavorable (u).

18–2. Learning Objective 3. Making General Journal Entry to Record Direct Material Purchase and Cost Variance.

From the information presented in Exercise 18–1, make the journal entry to record the purchase and material cost variance. Use May 31, 19— as the date of journal entry.

18–3. Learning Objective 3. Making General Journal Entry to Record Material Usage and Quantity Variance.

From the information presented in Exercise 18–1, make the general journal entry to record the material usage and quantity variance. Use June 18, 19— as the date of journal entry.

18–4. Learning Objective 4. Computing Direct Labor Efficiency and Rate Variances.

Sanders Company uses a standard cost system to help control costs. The following labor standards have been established for their product:

Standard Rate per Hour	Standard Hours per Unit
$12.00	2 hours

During the month of August, Sanders Company recorded 20,400 direct labor hours at an average wage rate of $12.20 in the production of 10,000 units of product.

1. What was the standard quantity of hours allowed for this level of production?
2. Compute the direct labor efficiency variance and rate variance, and indicate whether it is favorable (f), or unfavorable (u).

18–5. Learning Objective 4. Making General Journal Entries to Record Labor Rate and Efficiency Variances.

From the information presented in Exercise 18–4, make the general journal entries to record the payment of direct labor, the amount charged to production, and the direct labor rate and efficiency variances. Use August 31, 19— as the date of journal entry.

18–6. Learning Objective 5. Closing Variance Accounts into Cost of Goods Sold.

Strong Company uses a standard cost system to control costs. At the end of the year, the variance accounts have the following balances:

Material Cost Variance		Material Quantity Variance	
Dr.	Cr.	Dr.	Cr.
670			1,450

Labor Rate Variance		Labor Efficiency Variance	
Dr.	Cr.	Dr.	Cr.
	1,130	1,240	

Cost of Goods Sold	
Dr.	Cr.
400,200	

1. Close the four variance accounts into Cost of Goods Sold. Use December 31, 19— for the date of entry.
2. What is the balance of cost of goods sold after the variance accounts have been closed into it?

GROUP A PROBLEMS

18–1A. Learning Objective 3. Computing Direct Material Cost Price and Quantity Variances and Journal Entries to Record the Purchase, Use, and Variances.

Mills Company uses a standard cost system to control costs. The following direct material standards have been established by the company:

	Standard Cost per Gallon	Standard Quantity per Unit
Direct Materials	$1.80	3 gallons

During October Mills Company purchased 15,120 gallons at $1.75 per gallon. All the material was used to produce 5,000 units of product.

Required:

1. Compute the direct material quantity and cost variances.
2. Make general journal entries to record (1) the purchase of materials and material cost variance, and (2) use of materials in production and the material quantity variance. Use October 31, 19— for the date of both entries.

18–2A. Learning Objective 4. Computing Direct Labor Rate and Efficiency Variances and Making Journal Entries to Record the Payment, Amount Charged to Production, and the Variances.

Stephens Company uses a standard cost system to control costs. The following direct labor standards have been established by the company:

	Standard Rate per Hour	Standard Hours per Unit
Direct Labor	$15.00	1.5

During January Stephens Company recorded a total of 8,870 hours at an average wage rate of $15.70 to produce 6,000 units of product.

Required:

1. Compute the direct labor efficiency and rate variances.
2. Make journal entries to record the payment of direct labor, the amount charged to production, and the variances. Use January 31, 19— for the date of entry.

18–3A. Learning Objectives 3, 4. Computing Direct Material Cost and Direct Labor Variances and Making Journal Entries.

Jackson Corporation has established the following standards for direct materials and direct labor:

	Standard Cost or Standard Rate		Standard Quantity or Standard Hours		Standard Cost per Unit
Direct Material	$ 6.00	×	3 pounds	=	$18.00
Direct Labor	$14.00		2 hours		28.00

During the month of April, Jackson Corporation produced 4,000 units of product using the following amounts of materials and labor:

12,150 pounds of material were purchased and used at $5.90 per pound.
7,920 hours were worked at an average wage rate of $14.25 per hour.

Required:

1. Compute the direct materials cost and quantity variances.
2. Make general journal entries to record (1) the purchase of direct materials and the material cost variance, and (2) the amount charged to production and the material quantity variance. Date both journal entries April 30, 19—.
3. Compute the direct labor efficiency and rate variances.
4. Make journal entries to record the payment of the direct labor, the amount charged to production, and to record the labor efficiency and rate variances. Date the journal entry April 30, 19—.

18–4A. Learning Objectives 3, 4, 5. Computing Direct Material Cost and Direct Labor Variances, Making Journal Entries, and Closing the Variance Accounts into Cost of Goods Sold.

Davidson Company has established the following standards for direct materials and direct labor:

	Standard Cost or Standard Rate		Standard Quantity or Standard Hours		Standard Cost per Unit
Direct Material	$ 2.50	×	4 pounds	=	$10.00
Direct Labor	$12.00		3 hours		36.00

During the month of December, Davidson Company produced 8,000 units of product using the following amounts of materials and labor:

33,200 pounds of material were purchased and used at $2.30 per pound.
24,625 hours were worked at an average wage rate of $11.90 per hour.

Required:

1. Compute the direct materials cost and quantity variances.
2. Make general journal entries to record (1) the purchase of direct materials and the material cost variance, and (2) the usage of materials in production and the material quantity variance. Date both journal entries December 31, 19—.
3. Compute the direct labor efficiency and rate variances.
4. Make journal entries to record the payment of direct labor, the amount charged to production, and the labor efficiency and rate variances. Date the journal entry December 31, 19—.
5. Close the variances into Cost of Goods Sold. Date the journal entry December 31, 19—.

GROUP B PROBLEMS

18–1B. Learning Objective 3. Computing Direct Material Cost and Quantity Variances and Making Journal Entries to Record the Purchase, Use, and Variances.
Chin Company uses a standard cost system to control costs. The following direct material standards have been established by the company:

	Standard Cost per Gallon	Standard Quantity per Unit
Direct Materials	$2.25	4 gallons

During October Chin Company purchased 31,600 gallons at $2.30 per gallon. All the material was used to produce 8,000 units of product.

Required:

1. Compute the direct material cost and quantity variances.
2. Make general journal entries to record (1) the purchase and material cost variance, and (2) usage of materials in production and the material quantity variance. Use October 31, 19— for both journal entries.

18–2B. Learning Objective 4. Computing Direct Labor Rate and Efficiency Variances and Making Journal Entries to Record the Payment, Amount Charged to Production, and the Variances.
Gonzalez Company uses a standard cost system to control costs. The following direct labor standards have been established by the company:

	Standard Rate per Hour	Standard Hours per Unit
Direct Labor	$13.00	2.0

During January Gonzalez Company recorded a total of 18,120 hours at an average wage rate of $12.85 to produce 9,000 units of product.

Required:

1. Compute the direct labor rate and efficiency variances.
2. Make journal entries to record the payment of direct labor, the amount charged to production, and the variances. Use January 31, 19— for the date of entry.

18–3B. Learning Objective 3, 4. Computing Direct Material Cost and Direct Labor Rate Variances and Making Journal Entries.

Himes Corporation has established the following standards for direct materials and direct labor:

	Standard Cost or Standard Rate		Standard Quantity or Standard Hours		Standard Cost per Unit
Direct Material	$ 2.40	×	5 pounds	=	$12.00
Direct Labor	$11.00		3 hours		33.00

During the month of April, Himes Corporation produced 2,600 units of product using the following amounts of materials and labor:

13,180 pounds of material were purchased and used at $2.55 per pound.
7,915 hours were worked at an average wage rate of $11.10 per hour.

Required:

1. Compute the direct materials cost and quantity variances.
2. Make general journal entries to record (1) the purchase of direct materials and the material cost variance, and (2) the amount charged to production and material quantity variance. Date both journal entries April 30, 19—.
3. Compute the direct labor rate and efficiency variances.
4. Make journal entries to record the payment of the direct labor, the amount charged to production, and to record the labor rate and efficiency variances. Date the journal entry April 30, 19—.

18–4B. Learning Objectives 3, 4, 5. Computing Direct Material Cost and Direct Labor Variances, Making Journal Entries, and Closing the Variance Accounts into Cost of Goods Sold.

Pike Company has established the following standards for direct materials and direct labor:

	Standard Cost Or Standard Rate		Standard Quantity Or Standard Hours		Standard Cost Per Unit
Direct Material	$ 4.60	×	6 pounds	=	$27.60
Direct Labor	$18.00		2.5 hours		45.00

During the month of December, Pike Company produced 3,000 units of product using the following amounts of materials and labor:

18,610 pounds of material were purchased and used at $4.45 per pound.
7,715 hours were worked at an average wage rate of $17.80 per hour.

Required:

1. Compute the direct materials cost and quantity variances.
2. Make general journal entries to record (1) the purchase of direct materials and the material cost variance, and (2) the amount charged to production and the material quantity variance. Date both journal entries December 31, 19—.
3. Compute the direct labor rate and efficiency variances.

4. Make journal entries to record the payment of direct labor, the amount charged to production, and the labor efficiency and rate variances. Date the journal entry December 31, 19—.

5. Close the variances into Cost of Goods Sold. Date the journal entry December 31, 19—

CASE FOR CRITICAL THINKING

Becket Company, a small appliance manufacturer, has been preparing a master budget for three years. The president of the company appreciates having a financial plan to compare actual results to a budget. However the president has read about other companies using a standard cost system for direct materials and direct labor. The president has asked you to explain to him the advantages of setting up a standard cost system for materials and labor. Include in your analysis the use of material and labor variances to help control costs, and who would be responsible for each of the variances.

ANSWERS TO SELF-STUDY QUIZ 18–1

1.

			General Journal			
	Date	**Description**	**P.R.**	**Debit**	**Credit**	

Purchase of Raw Materials

(A) Standard Cost × Actual Quantity purchased → ($3.00 × 950 gals.) $2,850
| | | Raw Materials Inventory | | 2850 00 | | |

Cost Variance = (A) – (B)
| | | Material Cost Variance | | 190 00 | | |

(B) Actual Cost × Actual Quantity purchased → ($3.20 × 950) $3,040
| | | Accounts Payable | | | 3040 00 | |

Usage of Raw Materials in Production

(C) Standard Cost × Standard Quantity → ($3.00 × 1,000 lbs*) $3,000
| | | Work in Process Inventory | | 3000 00 | | |

Quantity Variance = (A) – (B) $150 F
| | | Material Quantity Variance | | | 150 00 | |

(D) Standard Cost × Actual Quantity used → ($3.00 × 950 lbs) $2,850
| | | Raw Materials Inventory | | | 2850 00 | |

*Standard Quantity = 100 units × 10 gallons per unit = 1,000 gallons
F = Favorable
U = Unfavorable

2.

	19XX				
1	Mar. 31	Raw Materials Inventory	285000		1
2		Material Cost Variance	19000		2
3		Accounts Payable		304000	3

1	31	Work in Process Inventory	300000		1
2		Material Quantity Variance		15000	2
3		Raw Materials Inventory		285000	3

ANSWERS TO SELF-STUDY QUIZ 18–2

1.

(A) Standard Rate × Standard Hours
($15.00 × 1,600 hours*)
$24,000

Labor Efficiency Variance = (A) – (B)
–$300 U

(B) Standard Rate × Actual Hours used
($15.00 × 1,620 hours)
$24,300

Labor Rate Variance = (B) – (C)

(C) Actual Rate × Actual Hours
($14.75 × 1,620)
$23,895

Total Variance = (A) – (C)
$105 F

*Standard Quantity = 400 units × 4 hours per unit = 1,600 hrs.

General Journal

Date	Description	P.R.	Debit	Credit
	Work in Process Inventory		2400000	
	Labor Efficiency Variance		30000	
	Labor Rate Variance			40500
	Salaries Payable			2389500

2.

	19XX				
1	Sep. 30	Work in Process Inventory	2400000		1
2		Labor Efficiency Variance	30000		2
3		Labor Rate Variance		40500	3
4		Salaries Payable		2389500	4

Chapter 19
Standard Costs—
Manufacturing Overhead

LEARNING OBJECTIVES

After studying Chapter 19, you should be able to:

1. Explain the nature of using a standard cost system to apply manufacturing overhead to production.
2. Compute the variable overhead spending and efficiency variances and prepare the journal entries to close the Variable Overhead Control account, and to record any variances.
3. Close the variable overhead spending and efficiency variances into the Cost of Goods Sold account.
4. Compute the fixed budget and volume variances and prepare the journal entries to close the Fixed Overhead Control account, and to record any variances.
5. Close the fixed overhead budget and volume variances into the Cost of Goods Sold account.

Chapter 18 covered how to use a standard cost system to apply direct materials and direct labor to production. In this chapter, we will learn how to apply variable and fixed overhead to production using a standard cost system.

Let's review the application of factory overhead using an activity measure such as direct labor hours, machine hours, units produced, etc., in the predetermined overhead application rate. In our examples we will use direct labor hours as the activity measure. Previously we learned to keep track of the activity measure, such as actual direct labor hours, and multiply this number times the predetermined overhead rate. At the end of the year, a debit balance in Factory Overhead Control represented underapplied factory overhead and a credit balance in Factory Overhead Control represented overapplied factory overhead. If the under- or overapplied factory overhead balance was immaterial, the balance was closed to Cost of Goods Sold. If the balance in Factory Overhead Control was large, the amount was prorated among Cost of Goods Sold, Work in Process Inventory, and Finished Goods Inventory.

In this chapter we will learn how to apply factory overhead to production using standard direct labor hours allowed, given the actual level of production. Factory overhead will be applied based on the standard direct labor hours allowed to produce a product, not on the actual number of direct labor hours used. By using this approach, we can analyze the difference between the standard cost allowed and the actual cost, and compute four overhead variances.

Figure 19–1 shows the flow of manufacturing costs through an accounting system. In this diagram we will emphasize manufacturing overhead costs.

Most companies which adopt a standard cost system account for manufacturing overhead differently than the way they handle direct materials and direct labor. When overhead costs are paid, amounts are debited to the Variable and Fixed Overhead Control accounts. When overhead is applied based on the standard hours allowed, the overhead is credited to Variable and Fixed Overhead applied accounts. Most companies do not set up variance accounts for variable and fixed overhead until the end of the year, or until they complete a project or job. A variance is the difference between the actual cost and a predetermined standard. At the end of the year, the variable and fixed overhead can be analyzed and the variance accounts set up to record the differences between actual overhead and the standard cost allowed, given the actual level of production. Also, at the end of the year, the variance accounts are closed to Cost of Goods Sold if immaterial. If material, the variances are closed into Costs of Goods Sold, Finished Goods Inventory, and Work in Process Inventory.

Figure 19–1 shows four variance accounts relating to manufacturing overhead.

The **Variable Overhead Spending Variance** account represents the difference between the budgeted variable overhead and the actual amount of variable overhead spent during the period. This variance relates to the cost and

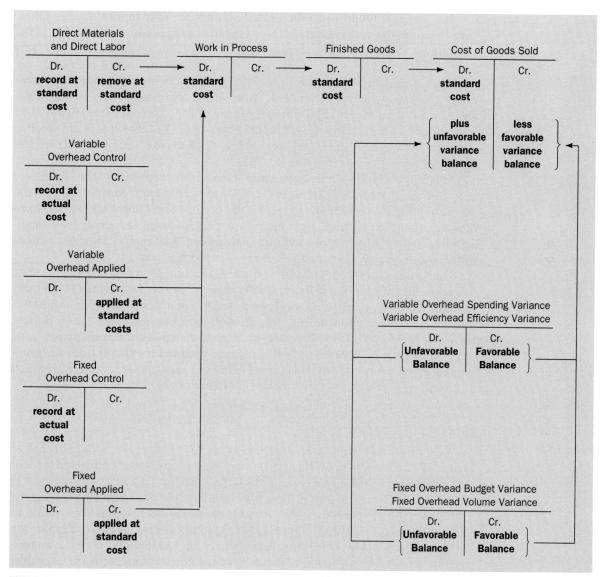

FIGURE 19–1
*Flow of
Manufacturing
Costs*

usage of variable overhead items such as indirect materials and indirect labor. This very useful variance measures the amount of variable overhead paid and used in production. If variable overhead items are being wasted, or if variable overhead items cost more than the standard cost allowed, an unfavorable or debit balance will result. The reverse situation will cause a favorable or credit balance.

The **Variable Overhead Efficiency Variance** account represents the difference between the budgeted variable overhead at actual hours and the budgeted variable overhead at the standard hours allowed. This variance measures how accurately the budget process determined the correct number of hours allowed for the actual level of production. The production manager does not have direct control over this variance. If more direct labor hours are worked than are allowed at standard, then the variable overhead efficiency variance will be unfavorable to reflect this inefficiency. If fewer direct labor hours are worked than are allowed at standard, the variable overhead efficiency variance will be favorable.

The **Fixed Overhead Budget Variance** account represents the difference between the actual fixed overhead costs incurred during the period and the amount of fixed overhead budgeted for the period. The budget variance resembles the variable overhead spending variance. However, the production manager has little, if any, control over fixed overhead. The budget variance is used more to call attention to changes in fixed overhead costs.

The **Fixed Overhead Volume Variance** account represents the difference between the amount of fixed overhead budgeted for the period and the amount of fixed overhead applied to work in process based upon the standard hours allowed given the actual level of production. It measures plant utilization. A favorable fixed overhead volume variance indicates that the company operated at an activity level greater than the amount planned for the period. An unfavorable fixed overhead volume variance indicates that the company operated at an activity level below the amount planned for the period.

VARIABLE OVERHEAD

Figure 19–2 shows a basic format to analyze variable overhead spending and efficiency variances and the required journal entries.

Notice in Figure 19–2 that the amount on line (A) (Standard Hours Allowed × Standard Rate) represents the amount that has been debited to Work in Process Inventory. This amount of applied factory overhead is based upon the standard hours allowed for the actual level of production. If any variance amount is negative, the variance is unfavorable. Positive variances are favorable.

LEARNING OBJECTIVE 2   To illustrate the application of this basic format to analyze variable overhead variances, let's assume the following data for Rock Creek Company:

	Standard Rate Per Hour		Standard Hours Per Unit		Standard Cost Per Unit
Variable Overhead	$4.00	×	3 hours	=	$12.00

During the month of August, Rock Creek Company recorded 5,950 hours of direct labor time to manufacture 2,000 units of product. It incurred $24,400 of actual variable overhead. Figure 19–3 presents the data using the basic format to analyze variable overhead variances.

General Journal

Date	Description	P.R.	Debit	Credit
	Work in Process Inventory		X X X X XX	
	Variable OH Efficiency			
	Variance		X X X X XX	X X X X XX
			(U)	(F)
	Variable OH Spending			
	Variance		X X X X XX	X X X X XX
			(U)	(F)
	Accounts Payable			X X X X XX

(A) Standard Hours Allowed
   × Standard Rate (SH × SR)

Variable Overhead Efficiency Variance
   = (A) − (B)

(B) Actual Hours × Standard Rate (AH × SR)

Variable Overhead Spending Variance
   = (B) − (C)

(C) Actual Variable Overhead

Total Variance = (A) − (C)
F = Favorable   U = Unfavorable

FIGURE 19–2
*Basic Format to
Analyze Variable
Overhead*

General Journal

Date	Description	P.R.	Debit	Credit
	Work in Process Inventory		$24 00 0 00	
	Variable OH Efficiency			2 0 0 00
	Variance			
	Variable OH Spending			
	Variance		6 0 0 00	
	Accounts Payable			24 4 0 0 00

(A) Standard Hours Allowed × Standard Rate
   (6,000* × 4.00)
   $24,000

Variable Overhead Efficiency Variance
   = (A) − (B)
   $200 F

(B) Actual Hours × Standard Rate
   (5,950 × 4.00)
   $23,800

Variable Overhead Spending Variance
   = (B) − (C)
   −$600 U

(C) Actual Variable Overhead $24,400

Total Variance = $400 (U)
   (A) − (C) = −$400

* Standard hours allowed = 6,000 (2,000 units of product times 3 hours allowed per unit)

FIGURE 19–3
*Variable Overhead
Variances*

As Figure 19–3 shows, the variable overhead efficiency variance is $200 favorable, because fewer hours were worked than the standard allowed to produce 2,000 units of product. The variable overhead spending variance is $600 unfavorable, because more variable overhead was spent than was allowed at standard cost. Production managers have control over only the variable overhead spending variance. An unfavorable variable overhead spending variance could represent higher prices paid for variable overhead or perhaps more variable overhead was used than was allowed at standard.

NOTE The production manager is responsible for the variable overhead spending variance. The variance measures how responsibly the production supervisor spent on items such as indirect labor and indirect materials. The production manager is not responsible for the variable overhead efficiency variance. This variance measures how efficiently the budget process determined the number of hours allowed for the actual level of production.

LEARNING OBJECTIVE 3

The journal entry to record the variable overhead spending and efficiency variances differs from the journal entries to record direct materials and direct labor variances. Variable overhead is being applied at standard rates and is being credited to the Variable Overhead Applied account. The actual variable overhead is paid and debited to the Variable Overhead Control account. The variance analysis is not normally done until the end of the year or until a job or project is completed. Before the variable overhead variances are analyzed, the Variable Overhead Control and Applied accounts appear as follows:

Variable Overhead Control		Variable Overhead Applied	
Dr.	Cr.	Dr.	Cr.
24,400			24,000

The first step in the closing process closes Variable Overhead Applied into the Variable Overhead Control account. The general journal entry appears below:

1		Variable Overhead Applied	24 00 00 0		1
2		Variable Overhead Control		24 00 00 0	2
3		Closed Variable Overhead Applied.			3

The Variable Overhead Control account, after closing the Variable Overhead Applied account, appears below in T account form:

Variable Overhead Control	
Dr.	Cr.
24,400	24,000
balance 400	

The next step in the closing process closes the Variable Overhead Control account into the variable overhead efficiency and variable overhead spending variances. These variances appear in Figure 19–3. The general journal entry appears below.

1	Variable Overhead Spending Variance	60000		1
2	Variable Overhead Efficiency Variance		20000	2
3	Variable Overhead Control		40000	3
4	Closed Variable Overhead Control.			4

The last step in the closing process closes the variable overhead variances into Cost of Goods Sold. This journal entry appears below:

1	Cost of Goods Sold	40000		1
2	Variable Overhead Efficiency Variance	20000		2
3	Variable Overhead Spending Variance		60000	3
4	Closed Variable Overhead Spending			4
5	and Efficiency Variances into Cost of			5
6	Goods Sold.			6

SELF-STUDY QUIZ 19–1 Newman Company uses a standard cost system. Their standard cost for variable overhead follows:

	Standard Rate Per Hour		Standard Hours Per Unit		Standard Cost Per Unit
Variable Overhead	$6.00	×	1 hours	=	$6.00

During the month of December, Newman Company recorded 5,130 hours of direct labor time to manufacture 5,000 units of product. The actual amount of variable overhead incurred was $29,800.

Compute the variable overhead efficiency and spending variances.

Answers at end of chapter.

FIXED OVERHEAD

LEARNING OBJECTIVE 4　We can analyze fixed overhead in much the same manner as we analyzed variable overhead. We debit the Fixed Overhead Control account for fixed overhead. When the fixed overhead is applied to work in process, we credit the Fixed Overhead Applied account. The fixed overhead variances are not normally analyzed until the end of the year or until the job or project is completed. The format to analyze fixed manufacturing overhead appears in Figure 19–4.

	General Journal				
Date	**Description**	**P.R.**	**Debit**		**Credit**
	Work in Process Inventory		X X X X XX		
	Fixed OH Volume Variance		X X X X XX (U)		X X X X XX (F)
	Fixed OH Budget Variance		X X X X XX (U)		X X X X XX (F)
	Accounts Payable				X X X X XX

(A) Fixed Overhead Cost Applied to Work in Process

Standard Hours Allowed* × Standard Rate

Fixed Overhead Volume Variance = (A) − (B)

(B) Budget Fixed Overhead Cost

Fixed Overhead Budget Variance = (B) − (C)

(C) Actual Fixed Overhead

Total Variance = (A) − (C)

*Standard hours allowed = Actual units produced times standard hours per unit.

FIGURE 19–4
Basic Format to Analyze Fixed Overhead

Notice in Figure 19–4 that the amount on line (A) (Standard Hours Allowed × Standard Rate) represents the amount debited to Work in Process Inventory. This amount of applied factory overhead is based upon the standard hours allowed for the actual level of production.

To illustrate the application of this basic format to analyze fixed overhead variances, let's assume the following data for Rock Creek Company:

	Standard Rate Per Hour		Standard Hours Per Unit		Standard Cost Per Unit
Fixed Overhead	$10.00	×	3 hours	=	$30.00

Budgeted Fixed Overhead $63,000

During the month of August, Rock Creek Company recorded 5,950 hours of direct labor time to manufacture 2,000 units of product. The actual amount of fixed overhead incurred was $61,500. Using the basic format to analyze fixed overhead variances, the data is presented in Figure 19–5.

General Journal				
Date	**Description**	**P.R.**	**Debit**	**Credit**
	Work in Process Inventory		60 00 0 00	
	Fixed OH Volume Variance		30 00 0 00	
	Fixed OH Budget Variance			15 00 0 00
	Accounts Payable			61 50 0 00

(A) Fixed Overhead Cost Applied to Work in Process

Standard Hours Allowed × Standard Rate
(6,000* × 10.00) = $60,000

Fixed Overhead Volume Variance
= (A) – (B) = –$3,000

(B) Budget Fixed Overhead Cost = $63,000
Fixed Overhead Budget Variance
= (B) – (C) = 1,500

(C) Actual Fixed Overhead = $61,500

Total Variance = (A) – (C) = –$1,500
*Standard hours allowed = 6,000 (2,000 units produced × 3 hours per unit).

FIGURE 19–5
Fixed Overhead Variances

As Figure 19–5 shows, the fixed overhead volume variance is unfavorable because the budgeted fixed overhead is based on 2,100 units to be produced ($63,000/$30 = 2,100), but only 2,000 units were actually produced. Since the plant is under utilized, the volume variance is unfavorable.

The fixed overhead budget variance is favorable because less fixed overhead was spent than was budgeted for the period.

NOTE The production manager is not responsible for either the fixed overhead budget variance or the fixed overhead volume variance. In the case of the fixed overhead budget variance, the production manager has little if any control over items such as property tax and insurance on the factory building. In the case of the fixed overhead volume variance, the variance measures plant utilization. If the plant is overutilized, there will be a favorable volume variance. If the plant is underutilized, there will be an unfavorable volume variance.

Before any variances are journalized, the Fixed Overhead Control and Fixed Overhead Applied accounts appear as follows:

Fixed Overhead Control		Fixed Overhead Applied	
Dr.	Cr.	Dr.	Cr.
61,500			60,000

The first step in the closing process closes the Fixed Overhead Applied into the Fixed Overhead Control account. The general journal entry to record this appears below:

1		Fixed Overhead Applied	60 00 00		1
2		Fixed Overhead Control		60 00 00	2
3		Closed Fixed Overhead Applied.			3

The Fixed Overhead Control account, after closing the Fixed Overhead Applied account, appears below in T account form:

Fixed Overhead Control

Dr.		Cr.
	61,500	60,000
balance	1,500	

The next step in the closing process closes the Fixed Overhead Control account into the fixed overhead budget and volume variances. These variances appear in Figure 19–5. This step appears in general journal form as follows:

1		Fixed Overhead Volume Variance	30 00 00		1
2		Fixed Overhead Budget Variance		15 00 00	2
3		Fixed Overhead Control		15 00 00	3
4		Closed Fixed Overhead Control into			4
5		volume and budget variances.			5

LEARNING OBJECTIVE 5 The last step in the closing process closes the fixed overhead variances into Cost of Goods Sold. This general journal entry appears below:

1		Cost of Goods Sold	15 00 00		1
2		Fixed Overhead Budget Variance	15 00 00		2
3		Fixed Overhead Volume Variance		30 00 00	3
4		Closed Fixed Overhead Variances into			4
5		Cost of Goods Sold.			5

SELF-STUDY QUIZ 19–2

Redford Company uses a standard cost system. Their standard costs for fixed overhead follow:

	Standard Rate Per Hour		Standard Hours Per Unit		Standard Cost Per Unit
Fixed Overhead	$20.00	×	2 hours	=	$40.00

Budgeted Fixed Overhead = $164,000

During the month of February, Redford Company recorded 3,980 hours of direct labor time to manufacture 4,000 units of product. It incurred $162,300 of actual fixed overhead.

Required:
   Compute the fixed overhead volume and budget variances.
Answers at end of chapter.

SELF-STUDY PROBLEM

McQueen Company uses a standard cost system. The standard costs for variable and fixed overhead follow:

	Standard Rate Per Hour		Standard Hours Per Unit		Standard Cost Per Unit
Variable Overhead	$5.00	×	4 hours	=	$20
Fixed Overhead	8.00		4 hours		32

Budgeted Fixed Overhead = $96,000

During the month of March, McQueen Company recorded 12,300 direct labor time to manufacture 3,100 units of product. It incurred actual variable and fixed overhead as follows:

Actual Variable Overhead:	$ 64,000
Actual Fixed Overhead:	102,400

Required:

1. Compute variable overhead efficiency and spending variances.
2. Close the Variable Overhead Applied into the Variable Overhead Control account.
3. Close the Variable Overhead Control account into the efficiency and spending variances.
4. Close the variable overhead efficiency and spending variances into Cost of Goods Sold account.

5. Compute the fixed overhead volume and budget variances.
6. Close the Fixed Overhead Applied account into the Fixed Overhead Control account.
7. Close the Fixed Overhead Control account into the volume and budget variances.
8. Close the fixed overhead volume and budget variances into Cost of Goods Sold.

SOLUTION TO SELF-STUDY PROBLEM

1. **Variable Overhead Variances**

		General Journal			
Date	Description	P.R.	Debit	Credit	
	Work in Process Inventory		6200000		
	Variable OH Efficiency			50000	
	Variance				
	Variable OH Spending				
	Variance		250000		
	Accounts Payable			6400000	

(A) Standard Hours Allowed × Standard Rate
(12,400* × 5.00)
$62,000

Variable Overhead Efficiency Variance
= (A) − (B)
$500 F

(B) Actual Hours × Standard Rate
(12,300 × 5.00)
$61,500

Variable Overhead Spending Variance
= (B) − (C)
−$2,500 U

(C) Actual Variable Overhead $64,000

Total Variance = −$2,000 (U)

*Standard hours allowed = 12,400 (3,100 units of product times 4 hours allowed per unit)

2.

1	Variable Overhead Applied	6200000		1
2	Variable Overhead Control		6200000	2

3.

1	Variable Overhead Spending Variance	250000		1
2	Variable Overhead Efficiency Variance		50000	2
3	Variable Overhead Control		200000	3

4.

1		Cost of Goods Sold	200000		1
2		Variable Overhead Efficiency Variance	50000		2
3		Variable Overhead Spending Variance		250000	3

5.

(A) Fixed Overhead Cost Applied to
Work in Process
Standard Hours Allowed × Standard Rate
(12,400* × 8.00) = $99,200

Fixed Overhead Volume Variance
= (A) − (B) = $3,200 F

(B) Budget Fixed Overhead Cost = $96,000

Fixed Overhead Budget Variance
= (B) − (C) = −$6,400 U

(C) Actual Fixed Overhead = $102,400

Total Variance = (A) − (C) = −$3,200 (U)

	General Journal				
Date	Description	P.R.	Debit	Credit	
	Work in Process Inventory		9920000		
	Fixed OH Volume Variance			320000	
	Fixed OH Budget Variance		640000		
	Accounts Payable			10240000	

*Standard hours allowed = 12,400 (3,100 units produced × 4 hours per unit).

6.

1		Fixed Overhead Applied	9920000		1
2		Fixed Overhead Control		9920000	2

7.

1		Fixed Overhead Budget Variance	640000		1
2		Fixed Overhead Volume Variance		320000	2
3		Fixed Overhead Control		320000	3

8.

1		Cost of Goods Sold	320000		1
2		Fixed Overhead Volume Variance	320000		2
3		Fixed Overhead Budget Variance		640000	3

SUMMARY

When a manufacturing company adopts a standard cost system for overhead costs, the Work in Process account is debited for the standard costs allowed given the actual level of production. The Overhead Applied account is credited for the same amount. A variance is the difference between the actual cost and a predetermined standard. Variance analysis for variable and fixed overhead is normally not done until the end of the year or until a job or project is completed.

The first step in analyzing overhead closes the Variable Overhead Applied and the Fixed Overhead Applied accounts into their respective overhead control accounts.

The next step analyzes and records the variance amounts for variable and fixed overhead. The variable overhead variances include the **Variable Overhead Spending Variance** and the **Variable Overhead Efficiency Variance.** The fixed overhead variances include the **Fixed Overhead Budget Variance** and the **Fixed Overhead Volume Variance.**

The last step in the closing process closes the variable and fixed overhead variances into the Cost of Goods Sold account.

KEY TERMS

Fixed Overhead Budget Variance Account. Represents the difference between the actual fixed overhead costs incurred during the period and the amount of fixed overhead budgeted for the period.

Fixed Overhead Volume Variance Account. Represents the difference between the fixed overhead budgeted for the period and the amount of fixed overhead applied to work in process, using standard hours allowed, given the actual level of production.

Variable Overhead Efficiency Variance Account. Represents the difference between the budgeted variable overhead at actual hours and the budgeted variable overhead at the standard hours allowed.

Variable Overhead Spending Variance Account. Represents the difference between the amount of actual variable overhead used and spent and the amount of variable overhead that should have been used and spent, given the actual amount of direct labor hours used.

QUESTIONS FOR REVIEW

1. Describe the process of applying factory overhead to work in process, without using a standard cost system.
2. When using a standard cost system to apply factory overhead to work in process, how are the accounts Factory Overhead Control and Factory Overhead Applied used?

3. Describe the flow of manufacturing overhead costs through an accounting system using a standard cost system.
4. Define each of these variances:
   a. Variable overhead spending variance.
   b. Variable overhead efficiency variance.
   c. Fixed overhead budget variance.
   d. Fixed overhead volume variance.
5. Assuming the overhead variances are immaterial, to what account are the overhead variances closed in to at the end of an accounting period, or upon the completion of a job or project?
6. At what point in time are overhead variances normally analyzed and recorded?
7. How do you arrive at "standard hours allowed" in the basic format to analyze overhead variances?
8. To what account titles are large, material overhead variances closed in to at the end of an accounting period, or upon the completion of a job or project?
9. What is the first step in the closing process in order to analyze variable and fixed overhead variances?
10. A credit balance in an overhead control account represents (under/over) applied factory overhead?

NOTE Unless told otherwise in Exercises and Problems, record transactions in general journal form.

EXERCISES

19–1. Learning Objective 2. Calculating Variable Overhead Efficiency and Spending Variances.
Douglass Company uses a standard cost system for overhead costs. The following variable overhead standards have been established for their product:

	Standard Rate Per Hour		Standard Hours Per Unit		Standard Cost Per Unit
Variable Overhead	$7.00	×	2 hours	=	$14.00

During the month of April, Douglass Company recorded 10,350 hours of direct labor time to manufacture 5,000 units of product. It incurred $68,900 of actual variable overhead.

1. What was the standard hours allowed for this level of production?
2. Compute the variable overhead efficiency and spending variances and indicate whether they are favorable (f) or unfavorable (u).

19–2. Learning Objective 3. Making General Journal Entries to Record Variable Overhead Variances.
From the information presented in Exercise 19–1, make the following journal entries:

1. Close the Variable Overhead Applied into the Variable Overhead Control account.
2. Close the Variable Overhead Control account into the efficiency and spending variances.
3. Close the variable overhead efficiency and spending variances into the Cost of Goods Sold account.

19–3. Learning Objective 4. Computing Fixed Overhead Volume and Budget Variances.

Strong Company uses a standard cost system to account for overhead costs. The following fixed overhead standards have been established:

	Standard Rate Per Hour	Standard Hours Per Unit	Standard Cost Per Unit
Fixed Overhead	$40.00 ×	2 hours =	$80.00

Budgeted Fixed Overhead = $240,000

During the month of July, Strong Company recorded 5,910 hours of direct labor time to manufacture 2,900 units of product. It incurred $237,500 of actual fixed overhead.

1. What was the standard hours allowed for this level of production?
2. Compute the fixed overhead volume and budget variances and indicate whether they are favorable (f) or unfavorable (u).

19–4. Learning Objective 5. Making Journal Entries to Record Fixed Overhead Variances.

From the information presented in Exercise 19–3, make the following journal entries.

1. Close the Fixed Overhead Applied into the Fixed Overhead Control account.
2. Close the Fixed Overhead Control account into the volume and budget variances.
3. Close the fixed overhead volume and budget variances into the Cost of Goods Sold account.

19–5. Learning Objectives 3, 5. Closing Overhead Variance Accounts into Cost of Goods Sold.

Knox Company uses a standard cost system to control overhead costs. At the end of the year, the overhead variance accounts have the following balances:

Variable OH Efficiency Variance		Variable OH Spending Variance	
Dr.	Cr.	Dr.	Cr.
1,450			3,100

Fixed OH Volume Variance		Fixed OH Budget Variance	
Dr.	Cr.	Dr.	Cr.
2,620		1,810	

Cost of Goods Sold	
Dr.	Cr.
500,300	

1. Close the four variance accounts into Cost of Goods Sold. Use December 31, 19— for the date of entry.
2. What is the balance of Cost of Goods Sold after the variance accounts have been closed?

GROUP A PROBLEMS

19–1A. Learning Objectives 2, 3. Computing Variable Overhead Variances and Making Journal Entries.

Eisenreich Company uses a standard cost system to account for variable overhead. The standard costs for variable overhead follow:

	Standard Rate Per Hour		Standard Hours Per Unit		Standard Cost Per Unit
Variable Overhead	$3.00	×	5 hours	=	$15.00

For the year ending September 30, 19—, Eisenreich Company's records show 102,100 direct labor hours were worked to produce 19,800 units of product. Actual variable overhead for the year was $302,600. The balance in the Cost of Goods Sold account, before any closing entries, is $960,300.

Required:

1. Compute the variable overhead efficiency and spending variances.
2. Close the Variable Overhead Applied into the Variable Overhead Control account.
3. Close the Variable Overhead Control account into the efficiency and spending variances.
4. Close the variable overhead efficiency and spending variances into the Cost of Goods Sold account.
5. Compute the balance in the Cost of Goods Sold account, after recording the closing entries.

19–2A. Learning Objectives 4, 5. Computing Fixed Overhead Variances and Making Journal Entries.

Olson Company uses a standard cost system to account for fixed overhead. The standard costs for fixed overhead follow:

	Standard Rate Per Hour		Standard Hours Per Unit		Standard Cost Per Unit
Fixed Overhead	$6.00	×	2 hours	=	$12.00

Budgeted Fixed Overhead = $480,000

For the year ending June 30, 19—, Olson's accounting records show that 81,200 direct labor hours were recorded to manufacture 39,500 units of product. The Fixed Overhead Control account indicates a debit balance of $483,900. The balance in the Cost of Goods Sold account, before any closing entries, is $890,300.

Required:

1. Compute the fixed overhead volume and budget variances.
2. Close the Fixed Overhead Applied into the Fixed Overhead Control account.

3. Close the Fixed Overhead Control account into the budget and volume variances.
4. Close the fixed overhead budget and volume variances into the Cost of Goods Sold account.
5. Compute the balance in the Cost of Goods Sold account after recording the closing entries.

19–3A. Learning Objectives 2, 3, 4, 5. Computing Variable and Fixed Overhead Variances and Making Journal Entries.

Justice Corporation uses a standard cost system to account for overhead. The following standards for variable and fixed overhead have been established:

	Standard Rate Per Hour		Standard Hours Per Unit		Standard Cost Per Unit
Variable Overhead	$7.00	×	3 hours	=	$21.00
Fixed Overhead	9.00	×	3 hours	=	27.00

Budgeted Fixed Overhead = $270,000

For the year ending December 31, 19—, Justice Corporation recorded the following in their accounting records:

Actual direct labor hours worked:	30,500
Actual fixed overhead:	$271,800
Actual variable overhead:	$196,300
Number of units produced:	9,900

Required:

1. Compute the variable overhead efficiency and spending variances.
2. Close the Variable Overhead Applied into the Variable Overhead Control account.
3. Close the Variable Overhead Control account into the efficiency and spending variances.
4. Close the variable overhead efficiency and spending variances into the Cost of Goods Sold account.
5. Compute the Fixed Overhead Volume and budget variances.
6. Close the Fixed Overhead Applied into the Fixed Overhead Control account.
7. Close the Fixed Overhead Control account into the budget and volume variances.
8. Close the fixed overhead budget and volume variances into the Cost of Goods Sold account.

19–4A. Learning Objectives 3, 5. Making Journal Entries Relating to Variable and Fixed Overhead Accounts.

Goodman Company uses a standard cost system to account for their overhead. The following selected account titles and balances appear in their accounting records, as of December 31, 19—.

Variable OH Efficiency Variance		Variable OH Spending Variance	
Dr.	Cr.	Dr.	Cr.
	3,160		4,500

Fixed OH Volume Variance		Fixed OH Budget Variance	
Dr.	Cr.	Dr.	Cr.
	3,180		2,410

Cost of Goods Sold	
Dr.	Cr.
718,000	

Required:

1. Compute the balance in the Variable Overhead Control account before the balance was closed into the variable overhead efficiency and spending variances. Indicate a debit or credit balance.
2. Compute the balance in the Fixed Overhead Control account before the balance was closed into the fixed overhead budget and volume variances. Indicate a debit or credit balance.
3. Close the four variance accounts into the Cost of Goods Sold.
4. Compute the ending balance in the Cost of Goods Sold account, after the closing entries have been recorded.

GROUP B PROBLEMS

19–1B. Learning Objectives 2, 3. Computing Variable Overhead Variances and Making Journal Entries.

Hansen Company uses a standard cost system to account for variable overhead. The standard costs for variable overhead follow:

	Standard Rate Per Hour		Standard Hours Per Unit		Standard Cost Per Unit
Variable Overhead	$5.00	×	2 hours	=	$10.00

For the year ending December 31, 19—, Hansen Company's records shows 41,100 direct labor hours were worked to produce 20,300 units of product. Actual variable overhead for the year was $205,200. The balance in the Cost of Goods Sold account, before any closing entries, is $875,600.

Required:

1. Compute the variable overhead efficiency and spending variances.
2. Close the Variable Overhead Applied into the Variable Overhead Control account.
3. Close the Variable Overhead Control account into the efficiency and spending variances.
4. Close the variable overhead efficiency and spending variances into the Cost of Goods Sold account.
5. Compute the balance in the Cost of Goods Sold account, after recording the closing entries.

19–2B. Learning Objectives 4, 5. Computing Fixed Overhead Variances and Making Journal Entries.

Smoltz Company uses a standard cost system to account for fixed overhead. The standard costs for fixed overhead follow:

	Standard Rate Per Hour		Standard Hours Per Unit		Standard Cost Per Unit
Fixed Overhead	$10.00	×	2 hours	=	$20.00

Budgeted Fixed Overhead = $300,000

For the year ending December 31, 19—, Smoltz's accounting records show that 30,900 direct labor hours were recorded to manufacture 15,800 units of product. The Fixed Overhead Control account indicates a debit balance of $319,300. The balance in the Cost of Goods Sold account, before any closing entries, is $918,250.

Required:

1. Compute the fixed overhead volume and budget variances.
2. Close the Fixed Overhead Applied into the Fixed Overhead Control account.
3. Close the Fixed Overhead Control account into the budget and volume variances.
4. Close the fixed overhead budget and volume variances into the Cost of Goods Sold account.
5. Compute the balance in the Cost of Goods Sold account, after recording the closing entries.

19–3B. Learning Objectives 2, 3, 4, 5. Computing Variable and Fixed Overhead Variances and Making Journal Entries.

Murphy Corporation uses a standard cost system to account for overhead. The following standards for variable and fixed overhead have been established:

	Standard Rate Per Hour		Standard Hours Per Unit		Standard Cost Per Unit
Variable Overhead	$4.00	×	4 hours	=	$16.00
Fixed Overhead	12.00	×	4 hours	=	48.00

Budgeted Fixed Overhead = $480,000

For the year ending July 31, 19—, Murphy Corporation recorded the following in their accounting records:

Actual direct labor hours worked:	40,100
Actual fixed overhead:	$486,200
Actual variable overhead:	$165,300
Number of units produced:	10,200

Required:

1. Compute the variable overhead efficiency and spending variances.
2. Close the Variable Overhead Applied into the Variable Overhead Control account.
3. Close the Variable Overhead Control account into the efficiency and spending variances.
4. Close the variable overhead efficiency and spending variances into the Cost of Goods Sold account.
5. Compute the fixed overhead volume and budget variances.
6. Close the Fixed Overhead Applied into the Fixed Overhead Control account.
7. Close the Fixed Overhead Control account into the budget and volume variances.
8. Close the fixed overhead budget and volume variances into the Cost of Goods Sold account.

19–4B. Learning Objectives 3, 5. Making Journal Entries Relating to Variable and Fixed Overhead Accounts.

Carey Company uses a standard cost system to account for their overhead. The following selected account titles and balances appear in their accounting records, as of December 31, 19—.

Variable OH Efficiency Variance		Variable OH Spending Variance	
Dr.	Cr.	Dr.	Cr.
2,530			3,165

Fixed OH Volume Variance		Fixed OH Budget Variance	
Dr.	Cr.	Dr.	Cr.
4,150		2,450	

Cost of Goods Sold	
Dr.	Cr.
891,600	

Required:

1. Compute the balance in the Variable Overhead Control account before the balance was closed into the variable overhead efficiency and spending variances. Indicate a debit or credit balance.
2. Compute the balance in the Fixed Overhead Control account before the balance was closed into the fixed overhead budget and volume variances. Indicate a debit or credit balance.

3. Close the four variance accounts into the Cost of Goods Sold.
4. Compute the ending balance in the Cost of Goods Sold account, after the closing entries have been recorded.

CASE FOR CRITICAL THINKING

Weber Company, a medium size manufacturer of farm equipment, has adopted a standard cost system. The production supervisor noticed that an unfavorable volume variance occurs whenever actual production is less than budgeted production. Explain to the production supervisor why this will always be the case.

ANSWERS TO SELF-STUDY QUIZ 19–1

General Journal					
Date	Description	P.R.	Debit	Credit	
	Work in Process Inventory		30 00 00 0		
	Variable OH Efficiency		7 80 00		
	Variance				
	Variable OH Spending				
	Variance			9 80 00	
	Accounts Payable			29 80 00 0	

(A) Standard Hours Allowed × Standard Rate ⟶ Work in Process Inventory
(5,000* × 6.00)
$30,000

Variable Overhead Efficiency Variance
= (A) − (B)
−$780 U

(B) Actual Hours × Standard Rate
(5,130 × 6.00)
$30,780

Variable Overhead Spending Variance
= (B) − (C)
$980 F

(C) Actual Variable Overhead ⟶ Accounts Payable
$29,800

Total Variance = $200 F
*Standard hours allowed = 5,000 (5,000 units of product times 1 hour allowed per unit).

ANSWERS TO SELF-STUDY QUIZ 19–2

(A) Fixed Overhead Cost Applied to
Work in Process
Standard Hours Allowed × Standard Rate
(8,000* × 20.00) = $160,000

Fixed Overhead Volume Variance
= (A) − (B) = $4,000 U

(B) Budget Fixed Overhead Cost = $164,000
Fixed Overhead Budget Variance
= (B) − (C) = 1,700 F

(C) Actual Fixed Overhead = $162,300

Total Variance = (A) − (C) = −$2,300

*Standard hours allowed = 8,000 (4,000 units produced × 2 hours per unit).

		General Journal			
Date	Description	P.R.	Debit		Credit
	Work in Process Inventory		160000 00		
	Fixed OH Volume Variance		4000 00		
	Fixed OH Budget Variance				1700 00
	Accounts Payable				162300 00

Chapter 20
Relevant Costs for Decision Making

LEARNING OBJECTIVES

After studying Chapter 20, you should be able to:

1. Describe important cost terms that are used in decision making situations.
2. Identify the relevant costs in a decision to purchase a new machine in replacement of an old machine, and prepare an analysis.
3. Identify the relevant costs in a decision to add or drop a product line and prepare an analysis.
4. Identify the relevant costs in a decision to make or buy a part and prepare an analysis.
5. Identify the relevant costs in a decision to special price a product and prepare an analysis.

Making a decision is one of the basic functions of a manager. A manager faces many types of decisions, such as whether to purchase a new machine in replacement of an old machine, add or drop a product line, make or buy a part, or special price a product. All of these decisions have one thing in common—they all involve an analysis of cost. A manager must compare the cost of one alternative to the cost of another alternative and decide which one is the most desirable. In this chapter you will learn how to separate a relevant cost from an irrelevant cost and you will examine the general tools of analysis that help in making an informed decision.

COST TERMS

A **relevant cost** is a cost that applies to a particular situation and should be included in the decision framework. Another way to select a relevant cost is to determine if the cost is avoidable. An **avoidable cost** is a cost that can be eliminated when comparing one alternative to another. In a sense, all costs are considered avoidable except for sunk costs and future costs that do not differ.

A **sunk cost** is a historical cost that has already been incurred and cannot be avoided in the near future. A common example of a sunk cost is the book value of a depreciable asset. If the asset, such as old equipment, is sold, generally accepted accounting principles (GAAP), requires that the book value of the equipment be removed from the accounting records and the resulting gain or loss be recognized. If the asset is not sold, then the remaining book value is depreciated over its useful life. Therefore, the book value of a depreciable asset is an unavoidable cost, and is always treated as a sunk cost in our analysis.

Opportunity costs are the benefits or earnings foregone because one alternative was selected over another alternative. For example, assume that a decision has been made to purchase a new machine rather than use the same amount of money to invest in stocks and bonds. The amount of money that could have been earned on an investment in stocks and bonds equals the opportunity cost of making the decision to purchase the new machine.

A **differential cost** is the difference in cost between two alternatives. For example, the difference in the purchase price between machine A and machine B is a differential cost. In most decisions situations, a differential cost is considered a relevant cost.

A **differential revenue** is the difference in revenue between two alternatives, similar to differential cost. In a decision situation, if the amount of revenue differs between two alternatives, then the difference is relevant to the decision.

Before leaving this section on cost terms, one other term should be discussed. All of the terms we have covered to this point involve cost or quantitative data. Non-cost data should also be considered when making a decision. **Non-cost data** is information that does not have a cost basis because it is difficult to measure. Such things as customer relations and employee morale should be considered in any decision situation. Our emphasis in this chapter is on cost data because it can be more easily measured, but you should be aware that decision situations exist where non-cost data can also be important.

PURCHASE A NEW MACHINE

LEARNING OBJECTIVE 2   In our first decision situation, we are going to analyze the costs associated with replacing an old machine with a new machine. Assume the following data:

	If Machine Is Not Bought	If Machine Is Bought
Annual sales	10,000 units	10,000 units
Sales price per unit	$ 30.00	$ 30.00
Variable costs per unit to operate		
Direct materials	$ 8.00	$ 8.00
Direct labor	10.00	8.00
Variable overhead	4.00	4.00
Fixed costs per year to operate	$50,000	$60,000*
Original cost of machine	$30,000	$40,000
Remaining book value of old machine	$10,000	
Expected life	4 years	4 years
Salvage value at end of expected life	0	0

*Includes depreciation on new machine of $10,000 ($40,000/4) but does not include depreciation on old machine.

Should the new machine be purchased to replace the old machine?

The book value of the old machine is a sunk cost and can be ignored in our analysis. In Figure 20–1 an analysis has been prepared comparing the two alternatives.

FIGURE 20–1
Analysis of Proposed Purchase of Machine

	If Machine Is Not Bought	Difference	If Machine Is Bought
Annual sales	$300,000		$300,000
Less Variable costs:			
Direct materials	80,000		80,000
Direct labor	100,000	$20,000	80,000
Variable overhead	40,000		40,000
Total variable costs	$220,000		$200,000
Contribution margin	$ 80,000		$100,000
Fixed costs	50,000	(10,000)	60,000
Net income	$ 30,000	$10,000	$ 40,000

In Figure 20–1, the analysis indicates that there will be an annual savings of $10,000 if we purchase the new machine. Another way to analyze this decision is to concentrate on only the costs that differ between the two alternatives. In Figure 20–2 an analysis shows only the relevant costs for this decision.

FIGURE 20–2
*Analysis
of Relevant
Costs*

Annual savings in direct labor costs (10,000 × $2)	$20,000
Less increase in fixed costs per year	10,000
Net annual costs savings if new machine is purchased	$10,000

As Figure 20–2 shows, if we consider only the relevant costs in this decision, an annual savings of $10,000 or a total of $40,000 ($10,000 × 4) over the life of the machine results.

NOTE The book value of the old asset is considered a sunk cost and is never considered in a decision to purchase a new asset.

SELF-STUDY QUIZ 20–1 The following data relates to a decision involving the replacement of an old machine for a new machine:

	If Machine is Not Bought	If Machine is Bought
Annual sales	5,000 units	5,000 units
Sales price per unit	$ 20.00	$ 20.00
Variable costs per unit to operate		
Direct materials	$ 5.00	$ 5.00
Direct labor	7.00	5.00
Variable overhead	3.00	3.00
Fixed costs per year to operate	$40,000	$55,000*
Original cost of machine	$20,000	$60,000
Remaining book value of old machine	$ 5,000	
Expected life	4 years	4 years
Salvage value at end of expected life	0	0

*Includes depreciation on new machine of $15,000 ($60,000/4).

Compute the following:

a. Annual savings in direct labor costs.
b. Change in fixed costs per year.
c. Net annual increase (decrease) in net income if new machine is purchased.

Answers at end of chapter.

ADDING OR DROPPING A PRODUCT LINE

LEARNING OBJECTIVE 3   A decision involving whether to add or drop a product line is one of the most difficult decisions a manager must face. The decision should be based on a sound analysis and only the relevant costs should be considered.

For illustrative purposes, assume that the management of Dougherty Manufacturing considers dropping Product Z after reviewing an income statement prepared under the absorption costing method. Figure 20–3 presents this information.

Dougherty Manufacturing
Income Statement
(Absorption Costing)
For the Year Ended, December 31, 19X2

	Total	Product X	Product Y	Product Z
Sales	$200,000	$60,000	$100,000	$ 40,000
Cost of goods sold	150,000	38,000	70,000	42,000
Gross margin	$ 50,000	$22,000	$ 30,000	($2,000)
Operating expenses	31,000	5,500	22,500	3,000
Net income (loss)	$ 19,000	$16,500	$ 7,500	($5,000)
Additional data:				
Units sold		2,000	10,000	1,000
Sales price per unit		$30	$10	$40
Variable manufacturing cost per unit		10	4	30
Variable operating expenses per unit		2	2	2
Fixed manufacturing costs		$18,000	$30,000	$12,000
Fixed operating expenses		1,500	2,500	1,000

FIGURE 20–3
Absorption Costing
Income Statement

From the information presented in Figure 20–3 it would appear that discontinuing Product Z would raise overall company profits by $5,000. Before deciding to eliminate Product Z, let's redo the income statement using the direct costing format. In Figure 20–4, an income statement has been prepared for Dougherty Manufacturing using the direct costing method.

Both the fixed manufacturing costs and the fixed operating costs were allocated on the basis of total sales dollars. If all of the fixed manufacturing and operating costs continue after eliminating Product Z, then the total net income for Dougherty Manufacturing will be reduced by $8,000. If any of the fixed manufacturing costs could have been eliminated, then these costs should have been subtracted from the contribution margin to see if Product Z covers

Dougherty Manufacturing
Income Statement
(Direct Costing)
For the Year Ended, December 31, 19X2

	Total	Product X	Product Y	Product Z
Sales	$200,000	$60,000	$100,000	$40,000
Less variable costs				
Variable manufacturing	90,000	20,000	40,000	30,000
Variable operating	26,000	4,000	20,000	2,000
Total variable costs	$116,000	$24,000	$ 60,000	$32,000
Contribution margin	$ 84,000	$36,000	$ 40,000	$ 8,000
Less total fixed costs	65,000			
Net income	$ 19,000			

FIGURE 20–4
Direct Costing
Income Statement

all of its direct expenses. Another way compares the loss of contribution margin with the fixed expenses that could be avoided. Figure 20–5 shows a comparison of contribution margin and fixed expenses.

FIGURE 20–5
Analysis
of Relevant
Costs

Contributed margin lost if Product Z is discontinued	($8,000)
Less fixed expenses that can be avoided if Product Z is discontinued	0
Decrease in overall company profits	($8,000)

In order to prove that the total company profits will decrease $8,000, let's redo the direct costing income statement after Product Z has been eliminated.

As Figure 20–6 shows, net income decreased from $19,000 to $11,000, or a decrease of $8,000 because Product Z was discontinued.

NOTE In a decision to add or drop a product line, the relevant costs include the variable costs and any fixed costs that could be avoided. Compare the contribution margin lost to the amount of variable and fixed costs avoidable. If more contribution margin is lost than variable and fixed costs avoided, then keep the product line.

FIGURE 20–6
*Direct Costing
Income Statement
after Elimination of
Product Z*

Dougherty Manufacturing
Income Statement
(Direct Costing)
For the Year Ended, December 31, 19X2

	Total	Product X	Product Y
Sales	$160,000	$60,000	$100,000
Less variable costs			
Variable manufacturing	60,000	20,000	40,000
Variable operating	24,000	4,000	20,000
Total variable costs	$ 84,000	$24,000	$ 60,000
Contribution margin	$ 76,000	$36,000	$ 40,000
Less total fixed costs	65,000		
Net income	$ 11,000		

SELF-STUDY QUIZ 20–2   The following data relates to a decision involving whether to add a product line:

	Product A
Estimated sales	$90,000
Cost of goods sold	63,000
Gross profit	$27,000
Operating expenses	30,000
Net income (loss)	$(3,000)
Additional data:	
Estimated sales in units	6,000
Sales price per unit	$15
Variable manufacturing cost per unit	8
Variable operating expenses per unit	3
*Allocated fixed manufacturing costs	$15,000
*Allocated fixed operating expenses	12,000

*All allocated fixed costs will continue whether Product A is produced or not.

Prepare an analysis in a direct costing format that shows the advantage or disadvantage of adding this product line.
Answers at end of chapter.

MAKING OR BUYING A PART

LEARNING OBJECTIVE 4

Sometimes a manager must make a decision as to whether it's more economical to continue to buy a part from an outside supplier or to make the same part using its own facilities. For illustrative purposes, assume that Poole Company faces this decision. The cost data showing the per unit cost and the total annual cost of making the part has been assembled in Figure 20–7.

FIGURE 20–7

Per Unit and Total Annual Cost to Make

	Per Unit	10,000 Units
Direct materials	$ 6	$ 60,000
Direct labor	4	40,000
Variable overhead	2	20,000
Supervisor's salary	3	30,000
Allocated general overhead	5	50,000
	$20	$200,000

An outside supplier has offered to provide this part for only $17 each. Should this offer be accepted? To answer this question let's first take a closer look at our cost data. All of the costs shown in Figure 20–6 are avoidable, therefore relevant, except the allocated general overhead. This general overhead will continue whether the part is manufactured or purchased, therefore this cost is not relevant. Figure 20–8 shows the relevant costs in this decision.

As Figure 20–8 shows, a savings of $2 per part results from Poole Company continuing to make the part. The direct materials, direct labor, variable overhead, and supervisor's salary are all avoidable costs, and therefore relevant costs,

FIGURE 20–8

Relevant Cost to Make

	Per Unit	10,000 Units
Direct materials	$ 6	$ 60,000
Direct labor	4	40,000
Variable overhead	2	20,000
Supervisor's salary	3	30,000
	$ 15	$150,000
Cost to buy	$ 17	
Cost to make	15	
Difference in favor of making	$ 2	
	× 10,000	
Annual difference in favor of making	$ 20,000	

if the part is purchased from an outside supplier. Since the allocated general overhead cannot be avoided, it should not be included in our analysis.

What if the floor space used to make this part could be used to make another product that would provide an annual contribution margin of $30,000? Should the part continue to be made? In this case an opportunity cost, or revenue foregone, of $30,000 a year results from the part continuing to be made. In our analysis this opportunity cost should be added to the cost of making the part. Figure 20–9 includes this opportunity cost.

FIGURE 20–9
Analysis of Cost to Make including Opportunity Cost

	Cost to Make	Cost to Buy
Number of units	10,000	10,000
	× $15	× $17
	$150,000	$170,000
Opportunity cost of lost revenue	30,000	
Total	$180,000	$170,000

As Figure 20–9 shows, a $10,000 advantage results from buying the part from an outside supplier and using the floor space to manufacture another product that provides a $30,000 annual contribution margin.

NOTE Never include an allocated fixed cost in a decision to make or buy. An opportunity cost should be included if it involves potential revenue lost if the part is made and the facilities could earn money from other sources.

SELF-STUDY QUIZ 20–3 The following data relates to a decision involving whether to make or buy a part from an outside supplier. An outside supplier has offered to provide 20,000 parts for $12 each.

	Per Unit	20,000 Units
Direct materials	$ 4	$80,000
Direct labor	3	60,000
Variable overhead	4	80,000
Supervisor's salary	2	40,000
Allocated general overhead	3	60,000
	$16	$320,000

Prepare an analysis showing the per unit and total net advantage or disadvantage of continuing to make this part.
Answers at end of chapter.

SPECIAL PRICING OF A PRODUCT

A manager might face a decision involving whether to price specially a product. If a company operates below capacity and receives an offer from a customer to buy a part below its normal sales price, a manager should give this consideration. If the company operates above the break-even point, then only the variable costs need to be covered. As you may recall, once a company oper-ates above break-even, the fixed costs have all been covered so only the vari-able costs remain.

LEARNING OBJECTIVE 5

It is important that a special price will not hurt the existing sales. This can be avoided if the sale is made outside the normal market. For example, assume we receive a special price from a customer from overseas where the domestic market will not be affected.

For illustrative purposes, assume that a New Zealand company has made an offer to buy 5,000 units of a product from Fernandez Company for $30. The regular sales price is $50 per unit. Fernandez currently manufactures 60,000 units with a normal operating capacity of 80,000 units. Figure 20–10 shows the standard cost for this product.

FIGURE 20–10
Standard Cost Sheet

Fernandez Company Standard Cost Sheet		
Direct materials		$ 8.00
Direct labor		12.00
Manufacturing overhead		
Variable overhead	$8.00	
Fixed overhead	5.00	13.00
Total standard cost per unit		$33.00

If you compare the price offered, $30, to the standard cost of manufactur-ing the product, $33, it would appear that Fernandez Company will lose $3 on each unit sold. Assume that Fernandez Company operates above the break-even point. In this case, the fixed overhead is not a relevant cost because all the fixed costs have been covered. Therefore, in this special price decision, the relevant costs are the variable costs. Figure 20–11 shows an analysis compar-ing the special price offer to the variable costs.

As Figure 20–11 shows, Fernandez Company can improve its total contri-bution margin by $10,000 if it accepts the special order. Remember, a special order should be accepted when the company operates below capacity, above the break-even point, and the regular sales will not be affected.

FIGURE 20–11
Relevant Costs to Make

Fernandez Company Special Price Analysis		
Special price offer		$ 30
Variable costs		
Direct materials	$ 8	
Direct labor	12	
Variable manufacturing overhead	8	
Total variable costs		28
Increase in contribution margin per unit from accepting the special offer		$ 2
		× 5,000 units
Total increase in contribution margin from accepting the special offer		$10,000

SELF-STUDY QUIZ 20–4   A special sales price has been offered for a product. The customer, located outside the normal sales territory, has offered to purchase 30,000 units of this product for $12 per unit. The standard cost sheet for this product appears below.

Standard Cost Sheet

Direct materials		$ 3
Direct labor		4
Manufacturing overhead		
Variable overhead	$2	
Fixed overhead	5	7
Total standard cost per unit		$14

The manufacturer operates above the break-even point and has excess capacity.

Prepare an analysis showing the net advantage or disadvantage of selling at this special price.

Answers at end of chapter.

SELF-STUDY PROBLEM

McNaughton Company faces several decisions. The first involves a decision as to whether a new machine should be purchased to replace an older machine.

DECISION 1—PURCHASING A NEW MACHINE TO REPLACE AN OLD MACHINE

	If Machine Is Not Bought	If Machine Is Bought
Annual sales	20,000 units	19,000 units
Sales price per unit	$ 34.00	$ 36.00
Variable costs per unit to operate		
Direct materials	$ 9.00	$ 7.00
Direct labor	14.00	15.00
Variable overhead	7.00	6.00
Fixed costs per year to operate	$40,000	$60,000*
Original cost of machine	$20,000	$80,000
Remaining book value of old machine	$10,000	
Expected life	4 years	4 years
Salvage value at end of expected life	0	0

*Includes depreciation on new machine of $20,000 ($80,000/4).

Required:
Prepare an analysis showing the net advantage or disadvantage in purchasing the new machine.

SOLUTION TO SELF-STUDY PROBLEM (DECISION 1)

	If Machine Is Not Bought	If Machine Is Bought
Annual sales	20,000	19,000
Sales price per unit	× $ 34	× $ 36
Total revenue	$680,000	$684,000
Variable costs		
Direct materials	180,000	133,000
Direct labor	280,000	285,000
Variable overhead	140,000	114,000
Total variable costs	$600,000	$532,000
Contribution margin	80,000	$152,000
Less Fixed expenses	40,000	60,000
Net income	$ 40,000	$ 92,000

The net advantage of purchasing the new machine increases net income $52,000.
Alternative analysis, using only differential costs:

	If Machine Is Bought
Differential revenue	$ 4,000
Differential variable costs savings	68,000
Differential fixed costs (increase)	(20,000)
Increase in net income	$52,000

DECISION 2—ADDING A PRODUCT LINE

McNaughton Company is considering a new product line called product Q. The company accountant prepared the following information:

	Product Q
Estimated sales	$130,000
Cost of goods sold	87,000
Gross profit	$ 43,000
Operating expenses	50,000
Net income (loss)	$ (7,000)

Additional data:	
Estimated sales in units	5,000
Sales price per unit	$ 26
Variable manufacturing cost per unit	15
Variable operating expenses per unit	7
*Allocated fixed manufacturing costs	$ 12,000
*Allocated fixed operating expenses	15,000

*All allocated fixed costs will continue whether Product Q is produced or not.

Required:
Prepare an analysis using the direct costing format of an income statement that shows the advantage or disadvantage of adding this product line.

SOLUTION TO SELF-STUDY PROBLEM (DECISION 2)

	Product Q
Estimated sales	$130,000
Total variable costs	110,000
Contribution margin	$ 20,000

McNaughton Company is better off by $20,000 to add this product line. The fixed costs are not relevant since they will continue whether this produce line is added or not.

DECISION 3—MAKING OR BUYING A PART

McNaughton Company receives an offer from an outside supplier to provide 5,000 parts for $27 per part. A company accountant has assembled the following data relating to this decision:

	Per Unit	5,000 Units
Direct materials	$ 8	$40,000
Direct labor	6	30,000
Variable overhead	5	25,000
Supervisor's salary	5	25,000
Allocated general overhead	6	30,000
	$30	$150,000

Required:
Prepare an analysis showing the per unit and total net advantage or disadvantage of continuing to make this part.

SOLUTION TO SELF-STUDY PROBLEM (DECISION 3)

	Per Unit Relevant Costs to Make:
Direct materials	$ 8
Direct labor	6
Variable overhead	5
Supervisor's salary	5
	$ 24
Cost to buy	$ 27
Cost to make	24
Net advantage per unit to continue to make	$ 3
	× 5,000
Total net advantage to continue to make	$15,000

DECISION 4—SPECIAL PRICING A PRODUCT

McNaughton Company has been offered a special sales price for one of its products. The customer, located overseas, has offered to purchase 10,000 units of this product for

$18 per unit. A company accountant assembled the following information relating to the standard cost for this product.

McNaughton Company
Standard Cost Sheet

Direct materials		$ 5.00
Direct labor		9.00
Manufacturing overhead		
Variable overhead	$2.00	
Fixed overhead	6.00	8.00
Total standard cost per unit		$22.00

McNaughton Company operates above the break-even point and has excess capacity.

Required:
Prepare an analysis showing the net advantage or disadvantage of selling at this special price.

SOLUTION TO SELF-STUDY PROBLEM (DECISION 4)

McNaughton Company
Special Price Analysis

Special price offer		$ 18
Variable costs		
Direct materials	$5	
Direct labor	9	
Variable overhead	2	
Total variable costs		16
Increase in contribution margin per unit from accepting the special offer		$ 2
		× 10,000 units
Total increase in contribution margin from accepting the special offer		$20,000

SUMMARY

The job of being a manager means making decisions. A good manager uses only relevant costs to make a decision. A **relevant cost** is avoidable when comparing alternatives. All costs are considered **avoidable costs** except for **sunk costs** and future costs that do not differ. The book value of an old machine is always considered a sunk cost.

Opportunity costs are the benefits or earnings foregone because one alternative was selected over another alternative. A **differential cost** is the difference in cost between two alternatives. A **differential revenue** is the difference in revenue between two alternatives.

Non-cost data does not have a cost basis because it is difficult to measure. Such things as customer relations and employee morale should be considered in any decision situation.

In every decision situation, only the relevant costs should be considered. An allocated fixed cost should not be included in the decision framework. These costs will continue whether or not a decision is made. When an organization operates above the break-even point and has excess capacity, fixed costs should not be considered in the decision analysis. When making a decision to eliminate a product line, the direct costing format of an income statement is helpful. If a product line shows a contribution margin, then eliminating this product line will reduce over-all company profits.

In a decision to special price a product, the special price should not affect the existing market. If the company operates above the break-even point, only the variable manufacturing costs need to be considered.

KEY TERMS

Avoidable Cost. A cost that can be eliminated when comparing one alternative to another.

Differential Cost. The difference in cost between two alternatives.

Differential Revenue. The difference in revenue between two alternatives.

Non-cost Data. Information that does not have a cost basis because it is difficult to measure.

Opportunity Costs. The benefits or earnings foregone because one alternative was selected over another alternative.

Relevant Cost. A cost that applies to a particular situation and should be included in the decision framework.

Sunk Cost. A historical cost that has already been incurred and cannot be avoided in the near future.

QUESTIONS FOR REVIEW

1. How are a relevant cost and an avoidable cost similar?
2. Give an example of a sunk cost.
3. Define the following cost terms:
   a. Opportunity cost
   b. Differential cost
   c. Differential revenue

4. What is non-cost data and give an example.
5. How are fixed expenses treated in a decision situation when the organization is operating above the break-even point and has excess capacity?
6. How are allocated fixed expenses treated in a decision situation involving the elimination of a product line?
7. When analyzing the data involving the elimination of a product line, what should one do when the fixed expenses that could be avoided are larger than the contribution margin lost if the product line is discontinued?
8. What costs are relevant in a decision situation about making a part or buying the part from an outside supplier?
9. When a special sales price is offered to a customer that is below the regular sales price, what other factor is an important consideration in this decision?
10. Under what condition would it be advisable to buy a part from an outside supplier rather than continuing to make the part?
11. How is opportunity cost used in a decision to make or buy?

EXERCISES

20–1. Learning Objective 1. Describing Cost Terms.

Match the description with the list of cost terms on the right. A cost term may be used more than once.

1. Benefits or earnings foregone because one alternative was selected over another
2. Difference in revenue between two alternatives
3. A cost that can be eliminated when comparing one alternative to another
4. Customer relations
5. A cost that applies to a particular situation and should be included in the decision framework
6. A historical cost that has already been incurred and cannot be avoided in the near future
7. Difference in cost between two alternatives
8. Employee morale
9. A future cost that does not differ
10. Book-value of a depreciable asset

a. relevant cost
b. avoidable cost
c. sunk cost
d. opportunity costs
e. differential cost
f. differential revenue
g. non-cost data

20–2 Learning Objective 2. Identifying Relevant Costs.

Mills Company has listed a number of items that may or may not be relevant in two independent cases.

Item	Case 1		Case 2	
	Relevant	Not Relevant	Relevant	Not Relevant
a. Sales revenue				
b. Direct materials				
c. Direct labor				
d. Variable production overhead				
e. Depreciation—machine X				
f. Depreciation—machine Y				
g. Fixed production overhead				
h. Variable selling expense				
i. Fixed selling expense				
j. General administrative salaries				
k. Book value—machine X				
l. Market value—machine X				
m. Cost of machine Y				
n. Rate of return available from outside investments				

Copy the above information onto your answer sheet and place a check mark under the appropriate column to indicate whether each item is relevant or not relevant in the following independent cases:

Case 1   Mills Company is interested in buying machine Y to replace machine X. Machine X will be sold. Both machines produce the same number of units and have the same estimated life. Machine Y will reduce direct materials and direct labor costs by 15%. Other production costs will remain the same.

Case 2   Mills Company is interested in buying machine Y to increase both production and sales. Machine X will continue to be used.

20–3. Learning Objective 2. Purchasing a New Machine.

Edgerton Company is trying to decide whether to replace an old machine with a new one. The accompany accountant has assembled the following information:

	If Machine Is Not Bought	If Machine Is Bought
Annual sales	30,000 units	30,000 units
Sales price per unit	$ 15.00	$ 15.00
Variable costs per unit to operate		
Direct materials	$ 6.00	$ 6.00
Direct labor	5.00	4.00
Variable overhead	2.00	2.00
Fixed costs per year to operate	$35,000	$45,000*
Original cost of machine	$15,000	$40,000
Remaining book value of old machine	$ 5,000	
Expected life	4 years	4 years
Salvage value at end of expected life	0	0

*Includes depreciation on new machine of $10,000 ($40,000/4).

Prepare an analysis showing the net advantage or disadvantage in purchasing the new machine.

20–4. Learning Objective 3. Adding a Product Line.

Schaeffner Company is considering a new product line called Product Alpha. The company accountant prepared the following data:

Product Alpha

Estimated sales	$600,000
Cost of goods sold	420,000
Gross profit	$180,000
Operating expenses	190,000
Net income (loss)	$ (10,000)

Additional data:

Estimated sales in units	20,000
Sales price per unit	$ 30
Variable manufacturing cost per unit	20
Variable operating expenses per unit	8
*Allocated fixed manufacturing costs	$ 20,000
*Allocated fixed operating expenses	30,000

*All allocated fixed costs will continue whether Product Alpha is produced or not.

Prepare an analysis using the direct costing format of an income statement that shows the advantage or disadvantage of adding this product line.

20–5. Learning Objective 4. Making or Buying a Part.

Masterman Company receives an offer from an outside supplier to provide 10,000 parts for $23 per part. A company accountant has assembled the following data.

Prepare an analysis showing the per unit and total net advantage or disadvantage of continuing to make this part.

	Per Unit	10,000 Units
Direct materials	$ 8	$ 40,000
Direct labor	6	30,000
Variable overhead	5	25,000
Supervisor's salary	5	25,000
Allocated general overhead	6	30,000
	$30	$150,000

20–6. Learning Objective 5. Special Pricing a Product.

Auskaps Company has been offered a special sales price for one of its products. The customer, located overseas, has offered to purchase 5,000 units of this product for $20 per unit. A company accountant has assembled the following information relating to the standard cost for this product.

Auskaps Company		
Standard Cost Sheet		
Direct materials		$ 8.00
Direct labor		6.00
Manufacturing overhead		
Variable overhead	$4.00	
Fixed overhead	5.00	9.00
Total standard cost per unit		$23.00

Auskaps Company operates above the break-even point and has excess capacity.
Prepare an analysis showing the net advantage or disadvantage of selling at this special price.

GROUP A PROBLEMS

20–1A. Learning Objective 2. Purchasing a New Machine to Replace an Old Machine.

Hahn Company considers replacing a new machine for an old machine. The following data has been assembled by the company accountant.

	If Machine is Not Bought	If Machine Is Bought
Annual sales	10,000 units	9,000 units
Sales price per unit	$ 40.00	$ 43.00
Variable costs per unit to operate		
Direct materials	$ 14.00	$ 12.00
Direct labor	12.00	10.00
Variable overhead	4.00	4.00
Fixed costs per year to operate	$60,000	$80,000*
Original cost of machine	$30,000	$60,000
Remaining book value of old machine	$10,000	
Expected life	3 years	3 years
Salvage value at end of expected life	0	0

*Includes depreciation on new machine of $20,000 ($60,000/3).

Required:

1. Compute the differential revenue per year between the two alternatives.
2. Compute the differential variable cost savings per year between the two alternatives.

3. Compute the differential fixed costs per year between the two alternatives.
4. Compute the net advantage or disadvantage from purchasing the new machine.
5. Prepare a direct costing income statement assuming the machine is not bought, for the year ending December 31, 19XX.
6. Prepare a direct costing income statement assuming Hahn buys the machine, for the year ending December 31, 19XX.

20–2A. Learning Objective 3. Dropping a Product Line.

The management of Hollar Manufacturing considers dropping Product X after reviewing an income statement prepared by the company accountant.

Hollar Manufacturing
Income Statement
(Absorption Costing)
For the Year Ended, December 31, 19X2

	Total	Product X	Product Y	Product Z
Sales	$325,000	$80,000	$120,000	$125,000
Cost of goods sold	178,000	72,000	56,000	50,000
Gross margin	$147,000	$ 8,000	$ 64,000	$ 75,000
Operating expenses	93,000	11,600	46,400	35,000
Net income (loss)	$ 54,000	$ (3,600)	$ 17,600	$ 40,000
Additional data:				
Units sold		2,000	8,000	5,000
Sales price per unit		$40	$15	$25
Variable manufacturing cost per unit		33	4	7
Variable operating expenses per unit		4	4	4
*Fixed manufacturing costs		$6,000	$24,000	$15,000
*Fixed operating expenses		3,600	14,400	$15,000

*Both the fixed manufacturing costs and the fixed operating expenses were allocated on the basis of the total number of units sold. If Product X is eliminated, 30 percent of the fixed manufacturing and operating operating expenses allocated to Product X can be avoided.

Required:

1. Redo the income statement presented in the problem into a direct costing format, showing all three product lines and the total for the company.
2. Eliminate Product X and prepare a direct costing income statement for the remaining two product lines and for the company in total.
3. Determine the net advantage or disadvantage from eliminating Product X.
4. Prepare an analysis showing the contribution margin lost compared to the amount of fixed expenses avoided if Product X is eliminated.

20–3A. Learning Objective 4. Making or Buying a Part.

Steiner Company receives an offer from an outside supplier to provide 20,000 parts at $18 per part. An accountant for Steiner Company has prepared the following data relating to the cost of making the part:

	Per Unit	20,000 Units
Direct materials	$ 6	$120,000
Direct labor	4	80,000
Variable overhead	2	40,000
Supervisor's salary	3	60,000
Allocated general overhead	5	100,000
	$20	$400,000

Required:

1. Compute the relevant cost to make the part.
2. Compute the per unit and the total advantage to make or buy the part.
3. Assuming that the space now being used to make the part can be used to manufacture another product that would bring an annual contribution margin of $80,000, compute the total advantage or disadvantage of making or buying the part, including this opportunity cost.

20–4A. Learning Objective 5. Special Pricing a Product.

Weber Company has been offered a special sales price for one of its products. The customer, located in Australia, has offered to purchase 20,000 units of this product for $20 per unit. An accountant from Weber Company has prepared a standard cost sheet for this product:

Weber Company Standard Cost Sheet		
Direct materials		$ 9.00
Direct labor		5.00
Manufacturing overhead		
Variable overhead	$4.00	
Fixed overhead	5.00	9.00
Total standard cost per unit		$23.00

Weber Company operates above the break-even point and has excess capacity.

Required:

1. Compute the relevant cost to make the product.
2. Compute the total advantage or disadvantage from accepting the special offer.
3. Prepare a special price analysis and show the effect on the contribution margin from accepting the special offer.

GROUP B PROBLEMS

20–1B. Learning Objective 2. Purchasing a New Machine to Replace an Old Machine.

Shorb Company considers replacing a new machine for an old machine. The following data has been assembled by the company accountant:

	If Machine Is Not Bought	If Machine Is Bought
Annual sales	20,000 units	18,000 units
Sales price per unit	$ 25.00	$ 30.00
Variable costs per unit to operate		
Direct materials	$ 9.00	$ 7.00
Direct labor	8.00	9.00
Variable overhead	4.00	4.00
Fixed costs per year to operate	$50,000	$70,000*
Original cost of machine	$40,000	$80,000
Remaining book value of old machine	$ 6,000	
Expected life	4 years	4 years
Salvage value at end of expected life	0	0

*Includes depreciation on new machine of $20,000 ($80,000/4).

Required:

1. Compute the differential revenue per year between the two alternatives.
2. Compute the differential variable cost savings per year between the two alternatives.
3. Compute the differential fixed costs per year between the two alternatives.
4. Compute the net advantage or disadvantage from purchasing the new machine.
5. Prepare a direct costing income statement assuming the machine is not bought, for the year ending December 31, 19XX.
6. Prepare a direct costing income statement assuming Shorb buys the machine, for the year ending December 31, 19XX.

20–2B. Learning Objective 3. Dropping a Product Line.

The management of Stamps Manufacturing considers dropping Product Z after reviewing an income statement prepared by the company accountant.

Stamps Manufacturing
Income Statement
(Absorption Costing)
For the Year Ended, December 31, 19X2

	Total	Product X	Product Y	Product Z
Sales	$720,000	$300,000	$300,000	$120,000
Cost of goods sold	404,000	152,000	146,400	105,600
Gross margin	$316,000	$148,000	$153,600	$ 14,400
Operating expenses	151,000	70,000	84,000	21,000
Net income (loss)	$141,000	$ 78,000	$ 69,600	$ (6,600)
Additional data:				
Units sold		10,000	12,000	3,000
Sales price per unit		$30	$25	$40
Variable manufacturing cost per unit		12	9	32
Variable operating expenses per unit		5	5	5
*Fixed manufacturing costs		$32,000	$38,400	$9,600
*Fixed operating expenses		20,000	24,000	6,000

*Both the fixed manufacturing costs and the fixed operating expenses were allocated on the basis of the total number of units sold. If Product Z is eliminated, 30 percent of the fixed manufacturing and operating expenses allocated to Product Z can be avoided.

Required:

1. Redo the income statement presented in the problem into a direct costing format, showing all three product lines and the total for the company.
2. Eliminate Product Z and prepare a direct costing income statement for the remaining two product lines and for the company in total.
3. Determine the net advantage or disadvantage from eliminating Product Z.
4. Prepare an analysis showing the contribution margin lost compared to the amount of fixed expenses avoided if Product Z is eliminated.

20–3B. Learning Objective 4. Making or Buying a Part.

Nehring Company receives an offer from an outside supplier to provide 30,000 parts at $14 per part. An accountant for Nehring Company has prepared the following data relating to the cost of making the part:

	Per Unit	30,000 Units
Direct materials	$ 5	$150,000
Direct labor	4	120,000
Variable overhead	1	30,000
Supervisor's salary	2	60,000
Allocated general overhead	6	180,000
	$18	$540,000

Required:

1. Compute the relevant cost to make the part.
2. Compute the per unit and the total advantage to make or buy the part.
3. Assuming that the space now being used to make the part can be used to manufacture another product that would bring an annual contribution margin of $50,000. Compute the total advantage or disadvantage of making or buying the part, including this opportunity cost.

20–4B. Learning Objective 5. Special Pricing a Product.

Popp Company has been offered a special sales price for one of its products. The customer, located in the Philippines, has offered to purchase 50,000 units of this product for $19 per unit. An accountant from Popp Company has prepared a standard cost sheet for this product:

Popp Company **Standard Cost Sheet**		
Direct materials		$ 7.00
Direct labor		4.00
Manufacturing overhead		
Variable overhead	$5.00	
Fixed overhead	8.00	13.00
Total standard cost per unit		$24.00

Popp Company operates above the break-even point and has excess capacity.

Required:

1. Compute the relevant cost to make the product.
2. Compute the total advantage or disadvantage from accepting the special offer.
3. Prepare a special price analysis and show the effect on the contribution margin from accepting the special offer.

CASE FOR CRITICAL THINKING

Last year, the president of a mid-size company authorized the purchase of a main-frame computer costing $100,000. The computer had an expected life of five years, and would be depreciated by the straight-line method.

You have been called in as a consultant regarding the possible purchase of a new computer costing $60,000. The new computer would save labor and processing costs of $20,000 a year. All other costs would be the same. The new computer would be depreciated over four years. The old computer has no salvage value and has a book value of $80,000.

The president does not want to purchase the new computer because it would involve a loss of $80,000 book value on the old computer. The vice-president of finance would rather invest the $60,000 in stocks and bonds that would yield a 10% return. Evaluate each of their arguments.

ANSWERS TO SELF-STUDY QUIZ 20–1

a. $10,000
b. ($15,000)
c. ($5,000)

ANSWERS TO SELF-STUDY QUIZ 20–2

	Product A
Estimated sales	$90,000
Total variable costs	66,000
Contribution margin	$24,000

The company is better off by $24,000 to add this product line. The fixed costs are not relevant since they will continue whether this product line is added or not.

ANSWERS TO SELF-STUDY QUIZ 20–3

	Per Unit Relevant Costs to Make
Direct materials	$ 4
Direct labor	3
Variable overhead	4
Supervisor's salary	2
	$13
Cost to buy	$ 12
Cost to make	13
Net advantage per unit to buy	$1
	× 20,000
Total net advantage to buy	$20,000

ANSWERS TO SELF-STUDY QUIZ 20–4

Special Price Analysis

Special price offer	$12	
Variable costs		
Direct materials	$ 3	
Direct labor	4	
Variable overhead	2	
Total variable costs		9
Increase in contribution margin per unit from accepting the special offer		$ 3
		× 30,000 units
Total increase in contribution margin from accepting the special offer		$90,000

Chapter 21
Capital Budgeting

LEARNING OBJECTIVES

After studying Chapter 21, you should be able to:

1. Explain the payback period method and apply it to a capital budgeting decision.
2. Explain the accounting rate of return method and apply it to a capital budgeting decision.
3. Explain the net present value method and apply it to a capital budgeting decision.
4. Explain the time adjusted rate of return method and apply it to a capital budgeting decision.

Chapter 20 covered identifying relevant costs as they related to several management decisions. In Chapter 21 we will continue our analysis of relevant costs as they relate to capital expenditures.

A **capital expenditure** involves the use of a large amount of cash that will be tied up for a long period of time. Decisions which consider capital expenditures include purchasing a new machine, expanding the size of the plant, or introducing a new product line. Most companies experience a competition for funds between deserving projects. In order for management to evaluate the worthiness of these requests, they must have some guidelines.

This chapter will introduce four techniques for evaluating a capital expenditure. The first two techniques are less scientific because they do not include the time value of money. The last two techniques are more scientific because they factor in the time value of money. The **time value of money** is a concept that states money received today is worth more than the same amount of money received in future years. This concept will be explained later in the chapter.

PAYBACK PERIOD

LEARNING OBJECTIVE 1

One method of evaluating a capital expenditure computes the payback period. The **payback period** method is the number of years it takes for an investment project to repay the initial cost of the investment. A company might use a guideline that considers only those investments that have a payback of less than four years. This might be appropriate for a company short on cash and needing a faster return on its investment. The payback period has one major drawback. If an investment has larger returns occurring after four years from the date of investment, the project will not be considered.

The formula for computing the payback period divides the initial cost of the investment by the net annual cash inflow generated by the investment. This net annual cash inflow could be either the annual cash earnings or annual cash savings derived from the investment.

$$\text{Payback period} = \frac{\text{Initial cost of investment}}{\text{Net annual cash inflow}}$$

To illustrate the use of the payback period to evaluate a capital budgeting decision, let's review a decision situation from Chapter 20. The first decision we covered in Chapter 20 concerned whether to purchase a new machine to replace an old machine (see Figure 20–1, Chapter 20). The new machine cost $40,000. The net annual cash savings was $20,000 (reduced direct labor costs). The payback period in this example is 2 years ($40,000/$20,000).

Let's take another example of a situation that has uneven cash flows. Assume that two capital projects require an initial cash outlay of $50,000. Figure 21–1 presents the data for projects A and B.

FIGURE 21–1
*Data for Projects
A and B*

Annual Cash Flows	Project A	Project B
Year 1	$12,000	$15,000
Year 2	8,000	18,000
Year 3	16,000	6,000
Year 4	10,000	3,000
Year 5	10,000	4,000
Year 6	20,000	8,000
Payback period	4.40 years	5.50 years

In Figure 21–1, we computed the payback for Project A by adding the cash flows from years 1 through 4, which total $46,000. To reach $50,000, $4,000 more was needed. During year 5, we reached the $50,000 investment at .40 during the year ($4,000/$10,000). We used the same procedure to calculate the payback for project B. If Project B requires a payback period of five years or less, Project A would be acceptable but Project B would not.

SELF-STUDY QUIZ 21–1 Vickers Company is considering an investment in a capital project. The company will accept an investment if it has a payback period of less than four years. The following data relate to this investment:

Cost of investment: $30,000

Cash flow:

Year 1	$ 8,000
Year 2	10,000
Year 3	7,000
Year 4	10,000
Year 5	6,000

1. Compute the payback period.
2. Is this an acceptable investment for Vickers Company?

Answers at end of chapter.

ACCOUNTING RATE OF RETURN

LEARNING OBJECTIVE 2   Another evaluation technique, called the accounting rate of return, ignores the time value of money but remains a popular method. This method does not focus on net cash inflows but rather on accounting net income. The **accounting rate of return** method follows the conventional financial statements and emphasizes a profitability index. The major weakness of the accounting rate of return method is that it does not consider the time value of money. Money is worth more today than if it is received several years into the future. The accounting rate of return method does not factor this concept into the formula.

The following formula is for computing the accounting rate of return:

$$\text{Accounting Rate of Return} = \frac{\text{Additional annual net income}}{\text{Average investment}}$$

where

$$\text{Average Investment} = \frac{\text{Initial investment} + \text{Estimated salvage}}{2}$$

To illustrate the application of the accounting rate of return, let's review the same case from Chapter 20 involving the purchase of a new machine (Figure 20–1, Chapter 20). The additional net income if the machine were bought was $10,000. The cost of the new machine was $40,000. Using the formula we compute:

$$\text{Accounting Rate of Return} = \frac{\$10,000}{\$20,000^*}$$

Accounting Rate of Return = 50%

$$\text{Average Investment} = \frac{\$40,000 + 0}{2}$$

*Average Investment = $20,000

Let's analyze another decision situation using the accounting rate of return. Assume Basinger Company is considering a capital investment that yields $6,000 in additional net income. The cost of the investment is $50,000 and is estimated to have a $4,000 salvage value at the end of six years. To compute the accounting rate of return on this capital investment:

$$\text{Accounting Rate of Return} = \frac{\$6,000}{\$27,000}$$

Accounting Rate of Return = 22.2%

where

$$\text{Average Investment} = \frac{\$50,000 + \$4,000}{2}$$

Average Investment = $27,000

As this example shows, the accounting rate of return on the average investment is 22.2%. If Basinger Company has a management guideline of accepting investments with an accounting rate of return exceeding 20%, then this capital investment would be acceptable.

NOTE The payback period and accounting rate of return ignores the time value of money. Both methods are easy to calculate but neither method considers the fact that money is worth more today than in the future.

SELF-STUDY QUIZ 21–2 Yohannes Company has a management guideline of accepting a capital project if it exceeds 25% on the average investment. The company is considering a capital investment that costs $80,000 and has a $10,000 estimated salvage value at the end of five years. The investment will increase net income by $15,000 a year.

1. Compute the accounting rate of return.
2. Should Yohannes Company accept this capital investment?

Answers at end of chapter.

NET PRESENT VALUE

LEARNING OBJECTIVE 3   The next evaluation method we will cover is more scientific than the previous two methods. The **net present value** method is based upon the time value of money. It factors in the concept that money is worth more if received today than if received sometime in the future. This is true for a couple of reasons. Money received today can be invested and earn interest. Compound interest can grow to a much larger dollar amount. Also, money received in the future has more risk attached to it. Predictions on cash flow become more uncertain the further one projects into the future. From a business standpoint, it is advisable to receive money earlier than later.

The concept of the time value of money is applied to capital budgeting decisions in the net present value method by discounting future cash flows to the present. As we have discussed earlier, money is not worth as much in the future as it is in the present. The interest rate or the discount rate decreases as we move to the future. Notice in the present value of a lump-sum table (Table 21–1) that the numbers get smaller as you move down the column from the top to the bottom.

To illustrate the usage of the present value of a lump-sum table (Table 21–1), assume we are to receive $10,000 in five years. The current interest rate is 5%. What is the present value of this $10,000? To answer this question, find

Periods	4%	5%	6%	8%	10%	12%	14%	16%	18%	20%	22%	24%	26%	28%	30%	40%
1	0.962	0.952	0.943	0.926	0.909	0.893	0.877	0.862	0.847	0.833	0.820	0.806	0.794	0.781	0.769	0.714
2	0.925	0.907	0.890	0.857	0.826	0.797	0.769	0.743	0.718	0.694	0.672	0.650	0.630	0.610	0.592	0.510
3	0.889	0.864	0.840	0.794	0.751	0.712	0.675	0.641	0.609	0.579	0.551	0.524	0.500	0.477	0.455	0.364
4	0.855	0.823	0.792	0.735	0.683	0.636	0.592	0.552	0.516	0.482	0.451	0.423	0.397	0.373	0.350	0.260
5	0.822	0.784	0.747	0.681	0.621	0.567	0.519	0.476	0.437	0.402	0.370	0.341	0.315	0.291	0.269	0.186
6	0.790	0.746	0.705	0.630	0.564	0.507	0.456	0.410	0.370	0.335	0.303	0.275	0.250	0.227	0.207	0.133
7	0.760	0.711	0.665	0.583	0.513	0.452	0.400	0.354	0.314	0.279	0.249	0.222	0.198	0.178	0.159	0.095
8	0.731	0.677	0.627	0.540	0.467	0.404	0.351	0.305	0.266	0.233	0.204	0.179	0.157	0.139	0.123	0.068
9	0.703	0.645	0.592	0.500	0.424	0.361	0.308	0.263	0.225	0.194	0.167	0.144	0.125	0.108	0.094	0.048
10	0.676	0.614	0.558	0.463	0.386	0.322	0.270	0.227	0.191	0.162	0.137	0.116	0.099	0.085	0.073	0.035
11	0.650	0.585	0.527	0.429	0.350	0.287	0.237	0.195	0.162	0.135	0.112	0.094	0.079	0.066	0.056	0.025
12	0.625	0.557	0.497	0.397	0.319	0.257	0.208	0.168	0.137	0.112	0.092	0.076	0.062	0.052	0.043	0.018
13	0.601	0.530	0.469	0.368	0.290	0.229	0.182	0.145	0.116	0.093	0.075	0.061	0.050	0.040	0.033	0.013
14	0.577	0.505	0.442	0.340	0.263	0.205	0.160	0.125	0.099	0.078	0.062	0.049	0.039	0.032	0.025	0.009
15	0.555	0.481	0.417	0.315	0.239	0.183	0.140	0.108	0.084	0.065	0.051	0.040	0.031	0.025	0.020	0.006
16	0.534	0.458	0.394	0.292	0.218	0.163	0.123	0.093	0.071	0.054	0.042	0.032	0.025	0.019	0.015	0.005
17	0.513	0.436	0.371	0.270	0.198	0.146	0.108	0.080	0.060	0.045	0.034	0.026	0.020	0.015	0.012	0.003
18	0.494	0.416	0.350	0.250	0.180	0.130	0.095	0.069	0.051	0.038	0.028	0.021	0.016	0.012	0.009	0.002
19	0.475	0.396	0.331	0.232	0.164	0.116	0.083	0.060	0.043	0.031	0.023	0.017	0.012	0.009	0.007	0.002
20	0.456	0.377	0.312	0.215	0.149	0.104	0.073	0.051	0.037	0.026	0.019	0.014	0.010	0.007	0.005	0.001
21	0.439	0.359	0.294	0.199	0.135	0.093	0.064	0.044	0.031	0.022	0.015	0.011	0.008	0.006	0.004	0.001
22	0.422	0.342	0.278	0.184	0.123	0.083	0.056	0.038	0.026	0.018	0.013	0.009	0.006	0.004	0.003	0.001
23	0.406	0.326	0.262	0.170	0.112	0.074	0.049	0.033	0.022	0.015	0.010	0.007	0.005	0.003	0.002	
24	0.390	0.310	0.247	0.158	0.102	0.066	0.043	0.028	0.019	0.013	0.008	0.006	0.004	0.003	0.002	
25	0.375	0.295	0.233	0.146	0.092	0.059	0.038	0.024	0.016	0.010	0.007	0.005	0.003	0.002	0.001	
26	0.361	0.281	0.220	0.135	0.084	0.053	0.033	0.021	0.014	0.009	0.006	0.004	0.002	0.002	0.001	
27	0.347	0.268	0.207	0.125	0.076	0.047	0.029	0.018	0.011	0.007	0.005	0.003	0.002	0.001	0.001	
28	0.333	0.255	0.196	0.116	0.069	0.042	0.026	0.016	0.010	0.006	0.004	0.002	0.002	0.001	0.001	
29	0.321	0.243	0.185	0.107	0.063	0.037	0.022	0.014	0.008	0.005	0.003	0.002	0.001	0.001	0.001	
30	0.308	0.231	0.174	0.099	0.057	0.033	0.020	0.012	0.007	0.004	0.003	0.002	0.001	0.001	0.001	
40	0.208	0.142	0.097	0.046	0.022	0.011	0.005	0.003	0.001	0.001						

TABLE 21-1
Lump-Sum Table
Present Value of $1;

$$P = \frac{F_n}{(1 + r)^n}$$

Periods	4%	5%	6%	8%	10%	12%	14%	16%	18%	20%	22%	24%	26%	28%	30%	40%
1	0.962	0.952	0.943	0.926	0.909	0.893	0.877	0.862	0.847	0.833	0.820	0.806	0.794	0.781	0.769	0.714
2	1.886	1.859	1.833	1.783	1.736	1.690	1.647	1.605	1.566	1.528	1.492	1.457	1.424	1.392	1.361	1.224
3	2.775	2.723	2.673	2.577	2.487	2.402	2.322	2.246	2.174	2.106	2.042	1.981	1.923	1.868	1.816	1.589
4	3.630	3.546	3.465	3.312	3.170	3.037	2.914	2.798	2.690	2.589	2.494	2.404	2.320	2.241	2.166	1.879
5	4.452	4.330	4.212	3.993	3.791	3.605	3.433	3.274	3.127	2.991	2.864	2.745	2.635	2.532	2.436	2.035
6	5.242	5.076	4.917	4.623	4.355	4.111	3.889	3.685	3.498	3.326	3.167	3.020	2.885	2.759	2.643	2.168
7	6.002	5.786	5.582	5.206	4.868	4.564	4.288	4.039	3.812	3.605	3.416	3.242	3.083	2.937	2.802	2.263
8	6.733	6.463	6.210	5.747	5.335	4.968	4.639	4.344	4.078	3.837	3.619	3.421	3.241	3.076	2.925	2.331
9	7.435	7.108	6.802	6.247	5.759	5.328	4.946	4.607	4.303	4.031	3.786	3.566	3.366	3.184	3.019	2.379
10	8.111	7.722	7.360	6.710	6.145	5.650	5.216	4.833	4.494	4.192	3.923	3.682	3.465	3.269	3.092	2.414
11	8.760	8.306	7.887	7.139	6.495	5.988	5.453	5.029	4.656	4.327	4.035	3.776	3.544	3.335	3.147	2.438
12	9.385	8.863	8.384	7.536	6.814	6.194	5.660	5.197	4.793	4.439	4.127	3.851	3.606	3.387	3.190	2.456
13	9.986	9.394	8.853	7.904	7.103	6.424	5.842	5.342	4.910	4.533	4.203	3.912	3.656	3.427	3.223	2.468
14	10.563	9.899	9.295	8.244	7.367	6.628	6.002	5.468	5.008	4.611	4.265	3.962	3.695	3.459	3.249	2.477
15	11.118	10.380	9.712	8.559	7.606	6.811	6.142	5.575	5.092	4.675	4.315	4.001	3.726	3.483	3.268	2.484
16	11.652	10.838	10.106	8.851	7.824	6.974	6.265	5.669	5.162	4.730	4.357	4.033	3.751	3.503	3.283	2.489
17	12.166	11.274	10.477	9.122	8.022	7.120	6.373	5.749	5.222	4.775	4.391	4.059	3.771	3.518	3.295	2.492
18	12.659	11.690	10.828	9.372	8.201	7.250	6.467	5.818	5.273	4.812	4.419	4.080	3.786	3.529	3.304	2.494
19	13.134	12.085	11.158	9.604	8.365	7.366	6.550	5.877	5.316	4.844	4.442	4.097	3.799	3.539	3.311	2.496
20	13.590	12.462	11.470	9.818	8.514	7.469	6.623	5.929	5.353	4.870	4.460	4.110	3.808	3.546	3.316	2.497
21	14.029	12.821	11.764	10.017	8.649	7.562	6.687	5.973	5.384	4.891	4.476	4.121	3.816	3.551	3.320	2.498
22	14.451	13.163	12.042	10.201	8.772	7.645	6.743	6.011	5.410	4.909	4.488	4.130	3.822	3.556	3.323	2.498
23	14.857	13.489	12.303	10.371	8.883	7.718	6.792	6.044	5.432	4.925	4.499	4.137	3.827	3.559	3.325	2.499
24	15.247	13.799	12.550	10.529	8.985	7.784	6.835	6.073	5.451	4.937	4.507	4.143	3.831	3.562	3.327	2.499
25	15.622	14.094	12.783	10.675	9.077	7.843	6.873	6.097	5.467	4.948	4.514	4.147	3.834	3.564	3.329	2.499
26	15.983	14.375	13.003	10.810	9.161	7.896	6.906	6.118	5.480	4.956	4.520	4.151	3.837	3.566	3.330	2.500
27	16.330	14.643	13.211	10.935	9.237	7.943	6.935	6.136	5.492	4.964	4.525	4.154	3.839	3.567	3.331	2.500
28	16.663	14.898	13.406	11.051	9.307	7.984	6.961	6.152	5.502	4.970	4.528	4.157	3.840	3.568	3.331	2.500
29	16.984	15.141	13.591	11.158	9.370	8.022	6.983	6.166	5.510	4.975	4.531	4.159	3.841	3.569	3.332	2.500
30	17.292	15.373	13.765	11.258	9.427	8.055	7.003	6.177	5.517	4.979	4.534	4.160	3.842	3.569	3.332	2.500
40	19.793	17.159	15.046	11.925	9.779	8.244	7.105	6.234	5.548	4.997	4.544	4.166	3.846	3.571	3.333	2.500

TABLE 21-2
Annuity Table
Present Value of an
Annuity of $1
in Arrears;

$$P_n = \frac{1}{r}\left[1 - \frac{1}{(1+r)^n}\right]$$

the 5% interest rate column and go down the left of the column (Years) until you reach five years. The discount rate is .784. Multiply this discount rate times the $10,000 and it equals the present value of this cash flow to be received in five years, $7,840 ($10,000 × .784). Stated another way, $7,840 will grow to $10,000 in five years at interest compounded at 5%, annually.

Before we can apply the net present value method to a capital budgeting decision, we need to cover the concept of an annuity, and how to use the present value of an annuity table. An **annuity** means an equal dollar amount paid or received each year for a period of two or more years. Many investments involve a series of cash flows over several years rather than a single cash flow occurring at the end of one year. The present value of a lump-sum table could be used to discount a series of cash flows over several years, but it takes more time and calculations. For example, assume Edgerton Company is to receive $5,000 a year for five years. The discount rate to be used is 5%. Figure 21–2 shows the present value of this series of cash flows, using the present value of a lump-sum table (Table 21–1).

FIGURE 21–2
Present Value of a Series of Cash Flows

Year	Cash Flow	Discount Rate 5% (Table 21–1)	Present Value of Cash Flow
1	$5,000	.952	$ 4,760
2	5,000	.907	4,535
3	5,000	.864	4,320
4	5,000	.823	4,115
5	5,000	.784	3,920
		4.330	$21,650

As Figure 21–2 shows, the present value of $5,000 to be received each year for five years, discounted at 5% is $21,650. However, if you add the five discount rates together (4.330) and multiply this times $5,000, you will get the same amount, $21,650 (4.330 × $5,000 = $21,650). Compare this discount rate (4.330) to the discount rate you will receive using the present value of an annuity table (Table 21–2) for 5% and five years. Notice that it equals the same discount rate. The present value of an annuity table will save you time and many calculations when the capital budgeting problem involves an annuity.

Now that we have covered the present value of a lump-sum and the present value of an annuity, we are ready to apply the net present value method to a capital budgeting decision. Assume that Edgerton Company is considering a proposal to invest $100,000 in a new machine that will yield $17,000 a year for 10 years. The estimated salvage value of this machine is $15,000 at the end of its estimated life of 10 years. Also assume that Edgerton's cost of capital is 12%. The **cost of capital** is a term used to represent how much the company pays to finance its assets. In other words, the cost of current liabilities, long-term liabilities, common stock and preferred stock, averages about 12%. The calculation of the cost of capital will not be covered in this textbook. Another term for cost of capital is the *required rate of return* or the *hurdle rate.* Edgerton Company wants to invest in projects that will exceed the cost of providing the debt and equity capital to finance them. Figure 21–3 shows how to analyze this investment using the net present value method.

FIGURE 21–3
Net Present Value Method

Items	Year(s)	Dollar Cash Flow	Discount Rate 12%	Present Value
Annual cash flow	1–10	$17,000	5.650	$ 96,050
Salvage value	10	15,000	.322	4,830
Total present value				$100,880
Less: Cost of investment				100,000
Net Present Value				$ 880

In this example, the decision would be in favor of accepting this capital project because the net present value is positive, $880. Actually, even if the net present value were zero, the investment should still be accepted. A zero net present value indicates that the return on the investment must be exactly 12%. That is, the discounted cash flows at 12% are exactly the same amount as the cost of the investment. Therefore, the investment itself must be yielding a 12% return. As a general rule, whenever the net present value of any capital project equals zero or greater, the investment should be accepted.

Let's use another example to demonstrate the net present value method. Assume that Edgerton Company is considering the purchase of a new machine that would cost $200,000. The machine would increase the company's cash flows through reducing operating costs by $40,000 per year and would have an estimated salvage value of $20,000 at the end of the asset's useful life of six years. Edgerton has a cost of capital of 10%. Should the company invest in this project? Figure 21–4 shows the solution.

FIGURE 21–4
Net Present Value of Decision to Purchase a New Machine

Items	Year(s)	Dollar Cash Flow	Discount Rate 10%	Present Value
Annual cash flow	1–6	$40,000	4.355	$174,200
Salvage value	6	20,000	.564	11,280
Total present value				$185,480
Less: Cost of investment				200,000
Net Present Value				$ (14,520)

NOTE Deduct the cost of the investment from the total present value of the proposed investment to yield the net present value.

As Figure 21–4 shows, the net present value of this investment equals a negative $14,520. Therefore, the investment should not be accepted. The investment itself yields a rate of return that is *less* than the interest rate used to discount the cash flows.

SELF-STUDY QUIZ 21–3 Zwicker Company is reviewing a capital investment that would cost $70,000 and provide an increase in the company's cash flows of $20,000 a year for the next five years. The investment would have a $10,000 salvage value at the end of five years. Zwicker Company has a cost of capital of 14%.

1. Compute the total present value of the cash flows.
2. Compute the net present value of the investment.
3. Should Zwicker Company accept the investment?

Answers at end of chapter.

TIME ADJUSTED RATE OF RETURN

LEARNING OBJECTIVE 4

The last evaluation method we will cover is the time adjusted rate of return method. This method resembles the net present value method in that it also includes the time value of money concept. The **time adjusted rate of return** computes what the return on the investment itself will generate over the life of the project. Also called the *internal rate of return*, the time adjusted rate of return is the discount rate that causes the net present value of the investment project to be equal to zero.

To illustrate how to use the time adjusted rate of return, assume that Tran Company is considering a capital investment project that costs $107,360. It promises an annual cash inflow of $16,000 over the next ten years. The salvage value on the asset is negligible and can be ignored. The management of Tran Company will only accept capital investments that yield a 10% rate of return or greater.

In order to find the time adjusted rate of return on this investment we must first compute the discount rate that causes the net present value of this investment to be zero. The time adjusted rate of return involves two steps. The first step divides the cost of the investment by the annual cash flows. This will give us an interest factor from which the time adjusted return can be determined.

Step 1: $\dfrac{\text{Cost of investment}}{\text{Annual cash flows}}$ $\dfrac{\$107,360}{\$16,000} = 6.71$

Step 2:   Using the present value of an annuity table (Table 21–2), go down the left column (Years column) until you reach the 10th year. Move across the 10-year line (horizontally), until you find an interest factor that equals or is close to 6.71. In our example, the time adjusted rate of return is 8%.

Since Tran Company will accept only those capital investments that equal or exceed a 10% internal rate of return, this investment would not be acceptable.

It becomes more difficult to arrive at the time adjusted rate of return when uneven cash flows occur, or when a salvage value must be considered. A trial and error method applies several different discount rates until one is reached that causes the net present value of the total cash flows to be equal to zero.

NOTE The net present value method and the time adjusted rate of return method are considered to be more scientific methods to evaluate an investment. Both methods consider the time value of money.

When the time adjusted rate of return or the internal rate of return equals or exceeds the firm's cost of capital, the investment should be accepted. Thus, a time adjusted rate of return less than the firm's cost of capital should not be accepted.

When the time adjusted rate of return is less than the firm's cost of capital, the net present value will always be negative. On the other hand, when the time adjusted rate of return exceeds the firm's cost of capital, the net present value will always be positive.

SELF-STUDY QUIZ 21–4   Blair Company is considering a capital investment that costs $92,780. The investment is projected to earn $20,000 in additional cash flow over the life of the project. The asset will be depreciated by the straight line method over its estimated useful life of eight years and will have no salvage value. Blair Company's cost of capital is 12%.

1. Compute the time adjusted rate of return.
2. Is this an acceptable investment for Blair Company?

Answers at end of chapter.

SELF-STUDY PROBLEM

Hein Corporation budgeted $300,000 in their annual budget for capital expenditures. They are reviewing three projects labeled A, B, and C. The following data relate to these three capital projects.

	Project A	Project B	Project C
Estimated life of project	10 years	10 years	10 years
Estimated salvage value	$50,000	$60,000	$40,000
Annual cash flows	30,000	35,000	45,000
Additional annual net income	20,000	25,000	35,000

Hein Corporation's cost of capital is 8%.

Required:

1. Compute the payback period for each project and select the project with the shortest payback period.
2. Compute the accounting rate of return for each project and select the project with the highest accounting rate of return.
3. Compute the net present value for each project and select the project with the highest net present value.

SOLUTION TO SELF-STUDY PROBLEM

1. Payback period **Project A**

$$\frac{\$300,000}{\$30,000} = 10 \text{ years}$$

Project B

$$\frac{\$300,000}{\$35,000} = 8.57 \text{ years}$$

Project C

$$\frac{\$300,000}{\$45,000} = 6.67 \text{ years}$$

Project C has the shortest payback period of 6.67 years.

2. Accounting rate of return   **Project A**

$$\frac{\$20,000}{\$175,000} = 11.43\%$$

Project B

$$\frac{\$25,000}{\$180,000} = 13.89\%$$

Project C

$$\frac{\$35,000}{\$170,000} = 20.59\%$$

Project C has the highest accounting rate of return of 20.59%.

3.   Net present Value

Project A

Items	Year(s)	Dollar Cash Flow	Discount Rate 8%	Present Value
Annual cash flow	1–10	$30,000	6.710	$201,300
Salvage value	10	50,000	.463	23,150
Total present value				$224,450
Less: Cost of investment				300,000
Net Present Value				$ (75,550)

Project B

Items	Year(s)	Dollar Cash Flow	Discount Rate 8%	Present Value
Annual cash flow	1–10	$35,000	6.710	$234,850
Salvage value	10	60,000	.463	27,780
Total present value				$262,630
Less: Cost of investment				300,000
Net Present Value				$ (37,370)

Project C

Items	Year(s)	Dollar Cash Flow	Discount Rate 8%	Present Value
Annual cash flow	1–10	$45,000	6.710	$301,950
Salvage value	10	40,000	.463	18,520
Total present value				$320,470
Less: Cost of investment				300,000
Net Present Value				$ 20,470

Project C is the only investment that has a positive net present value of $20,470

SUMMARY

Capital budgeting is the process of identifying profitable investments or capital expenditures that require the use of long-term funds. Most companies have more investment opportunities than funds available. Management needs to set guidelines that help them in selecting the most profitable investments. In this chapter we covered four methods of evaluating capital expenditures.

The first evaluation method covered the payback period. The **payback period** is the number of years it takes for an investment project to repay the initial cost of the investment. The formula for this method divides the initial cost of investment by the net annual cash inflow. The advantage of this method is that it emphasizes the recapture of cash. For a company short on cash this may be an appropriate evaluation technique. The disadvantage of this method is that it ignores large cash flows that could occur several years into the future. Only those capital projects that provide a fast cash recovery will be accepted.

The second evaluation method covered the accounting rate of return. The **accounting rate of return** method is popular because traditional financial statements can be used to gather the information. The formula divides the additional net income from the project by the average dollar amount of the investment. The disadvantage of this method is that it ignores the time value of money.

The third evaluation technique covered the net present value method. The **net present value** method factors in the time value of money. Future cash flows are discounted at a lower rate which reflects the fact that money is not worth as much in the future as it is in the present. The disadvantage of this method is that predicting cash flows well into the future is very difficult. The present value of future cash flows, both lump-sum and annuities, are discounted to the present using a discount rate. The firm's cost of capital is a reliable discount rate. The company should accept those capital investments where the net present value is zero or greater. Those capital investments that yield a net present value below zero should be rejected.

The fourth evaluation technique covered the time adjusted rate of return. This **time adjusted rate of return** method, also called the *internal rate of return*, computes what the return on the investment itself generates over the life of the project. If the time adjusted rate of return exceeds the firm's cost of capital, the investment project should be accepted. If the time adjusted rate of return is less than the firm's cost of capital, the investment project should be rejected.

KEY TERMS

Accounting Rate of Return. An evaluation technique that focuses on accounting net income rather than on cash inflows.

Annuity. An equal dollar amount paid or received each year for a period of two or more years.

Capital Expenditure. A cost that involves the use of a large amount of cash that will be tied up for a long period of time.

Cost of Capital. A term used to represent how much the company pays to finance the cost of its current liabilities, long-term liabilities, common stock, and preferred stock.

Net Present Value. An evaluation technique that focuses on the time value of money. The cost of the investment is subtracted from the total present value of all cash flows to yield the net present value.

Payback Period. The number of years it takes for an investment project to repay the initial cost of the investment.

Time Adjusted Rate of Return. An evaluation technique that computes the return on the investment itself will generate over the life of the project.

Time Value of Money. A concept that states that money received today is worth more than the same amount of money received in the future.

QUESTIONS FOR REVIEW

1. What is a capital expenditure?
2. What is meant by payback period? Explain how the payback period is computed?
3. As a general rule, would management prefer a capital expenditure to have a longer payback period or a shorter one? Explain.
4. Why is the payback method and the accounting rate of return, as evaluation techniques, considered non-scientific?
5. How is the accounting rate of return calculated?
6. How does the calculation of the average investment treat estimated salvage value?
7. What is meant by the time value of money concept?
8. What is an annuity?
9. What is the firm's cost of capital and how is it used in the net present value method?
10. What are other terms for the cost of capital?
11. When the net present value is positive, how does the discount rate compare with the firm's cost of capital?
12. What are the two steps involved in calculating the time adjusted rate of return?
13. When the time adjusted rate of return is more than the firm's cost of capital, should the capital investment be accepted? Explain.
14. If the time adjusted rate of return is less than the firm's cost of capital, will the net present value be positive or negative? Explain.

EXERCISES

21–1. Learning Objective 1. Using the Payback Period to Evaluate a Capital Expenditure.
Sproul Company is considering an investment that would cost $130,000 and would produce annual cash inflows of $40,000 a year for the next six years. Sproul Company has a policy to accept capital investments that have a payback period of four years or less.

1. Compute the payback period.
2. Should Sproul Company accept this investment project?

21–2. Learning Objective 1. Using the Payback Period to Evaluate a Capital Expenditure.
Conlee Corporation is reviewing two capital expenditure proposals. Either project would require a capital investment of $200,000, which is the dollar amount that Conlee Corporation had set aside in their capital budget. The projects, labeled A and B, have uneven cash flows. Conlee Corporation has a policy of accepting capital investments that have a payback period of less than five years.

	PROJECTED CASH RECEIPTS	
Year	Project A	Project B
1	$30,000	$20,000
2	60,000	80,000
3	50,000	25,000
4	30,000	45,000
5	20,000	50,000
6	40,000	20,000
7	50,000	30,000

1. Compute the payback period for each investment.
2. Which project would Conlee Corporation accept?

21–3. Learning Objective 2. Using the Accounting Rate of Return to Evaluate a Capital Expenditure.

Nelson Company is evaluating a capital investment that involves the purchase of a new machine that costs $80,000 and is estimated to have a $10,000 salvage value at the end of its estimated useful life of 10 years. The machine will increase annual net income by $10,000. Nelson Company has a management policy of accepting only those capital projects that have a minimum 25% accounting rate of return.

1. Compute the accounting rate of return.
2. Assume no salvage value on the machine. Would Nelson Company accept this investment proposal?

21–4. Learning Objective 3. Using Net Present Value to Evaluate a Capital Expenditure.

Ishmael Company is evaluating a capital investment that involves the purchase of a new machine. The machine cost $100,000 and is estimated to have a $12,000 salvage value at the end of its estimated useful life of six years. The machine is expected to increase annual cash flows during each of the next six years by $24,000. Ishmael Company's cost of capital is 12%.

1. Compute the net present value.
2. Should Ishmael Company accept this proposal?
3. Assuming no salvage value on the new machine, should Ishmael Company accept this proposal?

21–5. Learning Objective 3. Using Net Present Value.

Your rich uncle just passed away and left you a large inheritance. Since your now deceased uncle had taught accounting classes for many years at a local community college, he stated in his will that you will receive your inheritance only if you correctly answer a question regarding net present value. You have three choices and you must pick the choice with the highest net present value before you will receive any inheritance.

Choice 1.   You can have $21,000 immediately, and you will receive $20,000 a year for the next 5 years. The desired rate of return is 8%.

Choice 2.   You will receive $25,000 a year for the next 5 years. The desired rate of return is 8%.

Choice 3.   You will receive $20,000 a year for the next 5 years and a lump sum payment of $31,000 at the end of five years. The desired rate of return is 8%.

Select the correct choice and you will receive your inheritance.

21–6. Learning Objective 3. Computing the Present Value of an Annuity.

Your father promises to buy you a new car when you graduate from school at the end of four years. The car will cost $15,000. What lump-sum amount must your father invest now in order to have the $15,000 at the end of four years if he can invest the money at six percent?

21–7. Learning Objective 3. Computing the Present Value of an Annuity.

Lisa Block has just won one million dollars in the state lottery. The state will pay her $50,000 a year for the next 20 years. If Lisa can earn a 10 percent return on her money, what is the present value of winning this million dollars? Did Lisa actually win a million dollars?

21–8. Learning Objective 3. Computing Net Present Value.

Shaw Corporation has $80,000 to invest in a capital project. The company is reviewing two potential investments called Project A and Project B. The data on these investments follows:

	Project A	Project B
Annual cash inflows	$20,000	$15,000
Lump-sum receipt at end of 5 years	15,000	40,000
Life of the project	5 years	5 years

Shaw Corporation's cost of capital is 12 percent.

1. Compute the net present value of each investment project.
2. Which project should Shaw Corporation accept?

21–9. Learning Objective 4. Computing Time Adjusted Rate of Return.

Sheree Smith, a financial analyst, is reviewing three investment opportunities. The company will accept only those investments that have a 12% or higher time adjusted rate of return. Data on the three investments follows:

Investment 1 will cost $96,030 and will return $18,000 each year for 8 years.
Investment 2 will cost $104,120 and will return $20,000 each year for 7 years.
Investment 3 will cost $92,780 and will return $20,000 each year for 8 years.

1. Compute the time adjusted rate of return for each investment.
2. Which investment should Sheree accept?

GROUP A PROBLEMS

21–1A. Learning Objectives 1, 2, 3. Applying the Payback Period, Accounting Rate of Return and the Net Present Value, to Evaluate a Capital Project.

Schaeffner Company has $200,000 in their capital budget and is evaluating three investment opportunities. The data on the three investments, labeled X, Y, and Z, appear below:

	Project X	Project Y	Project Z
Cost of investment	$200,000	$200,000	$200,000
Cash inflow:			
Year 1	40,000	80,000	150,000
Year 2	100,000	80,000	100,000
Year 3	125,000	80,000	60,000
Year 4	150,000	80,000	40,000
Salvage value at end of four years	10,000	10,000	10,000
Additional annual net income	20,000	25,000	30,000

Required:

1. Compute the payback period for each investment.
2. Compute the accounting rate of return for each investment.
3. Assume that Schaeffner Company's cost of capital is 10%. Compute the net present value on each investment.
4. Which of the investments should Schaeffner Company accept? Why?

21–2A. Learning Objectives 3, 4. Applying the Time Adjusted Rate of Return and Net Present Value to Evaluate a Capital Project.

Bushell Company is reviewing two capital investments. Data on these two investments follows:

	Project 1	Project 2
Cost of investment	$144,200	$110,550
Annual cash earnings	40,000	30,000
Estimated life of project	5 years	6 years

Required:

1. Compute the time adjusted rate of return on each project.
2. Compute the net present value on each project, assuming the required rate of return is 16%.
3. Which investment, if any, should Bushell Company accept?

21–3A. Learning Objective 3. Using Net Present Value.

Knobel Company is reviewing two capital investments. Data on the two investments follow:

	Investment A	Investment B
Cost of investment	$100,000	$100,000
Annual cash inflows	30,000	20,000
Single cash inflow at end of 5 years	10,000	60,000
Life of the project	5 years	5 years

Knobel Company uses a 16% discount rate on all investments.

Required:

1. Compute the net present value on each investment.
2. Which investment should Knobel Company accept?

21–4A. Learning Objectives 1, 3. Comparing Payback Period to Net Present Value in Evaluating a Capital Investment.

The treasurer of Masterman Company uses the payback period to evaluate capital investments. The policy is to accept only capital investments that have a payback period of 2 years or less. The controller of Masterman Company prefers the net present value method to evaluate capital investments. The cost of capital for Masterman Company is 10%. Masterman Company is reviewing two capital projects. The data on each investment follows:

	Project A	Project B
Cost of investment	$100,000	$100,000
Cash inflows:		
Year 1	40,000	20,000
Year 2	60,000	30,000
Year 3	60,000	50,000
Year 4	60,000	400,000

Required:

1. Compute the payback period on each project.
2. Compute the net present value on each project.
3. Identify the strengths and weaknesses of the treasurer's policy of using payback period to evaluate capital projects.
4. Identify the strengths and weaknesses of the controller's policy of using net present value to evaluate capital projects.

GROUP B PROBLEMS

21–1B. Learning Objectives 1, 2, 3. Applying the Payback Period, Accounting Rate of Return and the Net Present Value, to Evaluate a Capital Project.

Anderson Company has $300,000 in their capital budget and is evaluating three investment opportunities. The data on the three investments, labeled X, Y, and Z, appear below:

	Project X	Project Y	Project Z
Cost of investment	$400,000	$400,000	$400,000
Cash inflow:			
Year 1	200,000	100,000	50,000
Year 2	150,000	100,000	100,000
Year 3	100,000	100,000	150,000
Year 4	50,000	100,000	200,000
Salvage value at end of four years	40,000	40,000	40,000
Additional annual net income	80,000	75,000	70,000

Required:

1. Compute the payback period for each investment.
2. Compute the accounting rate of return for each investment.
3. Assume that Anderson Company's cost of capital is 12%. Compute the net present value on each investment.
4. Which of the investments should Anderson Company accept? Why?

21–2B. Learning Objectives 3, 4. Applying the Time Adjusted Rate of Return and Net Present Value to Evaluate a Capital Project.

Campbell Company is reviewing two capital investments. Data on these two investments follow:

	Project 1	Project 2
Cost of investment	$187,410	$141,250
Annual cash earnings	30,000	25,000
Estimated life of project	9 years	10 years

Required:

1. Compute the time adjusted rate of return on each project.
2. Compute the net present value on each project, assuming the required rate of return is 10%.
3. Which investment, if any, should Campbell Company accept?

21–3B. Learning Objective 3. Using Net Present Value.

Mills Company is reviewing two capital investments. Data on the two investments follow:

	Investment A	Investment B
Cost of investment	$200,000	$200,000
Annual cash inflows	50,000	30,000
Single cash inflow at end of		
6 years	20,000	150,000
Life of the project	6 years	6 years

Mills Company uses a 14% discount rate on all investments.

Required:

1. Compute the net present value on each investment.
2. Which investment should Mills Company accept?

21–4B. Learning Objectives 1, 3. Comparing Payback Period to Net Present Value in Evaluating a Capital Investment.

The treasurer of Nehring Company uses the payback period to evaluate capital investments. The policy is to accept only capital investments that have a payback period of three years or less. The controller of Nehring Company prefers the net present value method to evaluate capital investments. The cost of capital for Nehring Company is 12%. Nehring Company is reviewing two capital projects. The data on each project follow:

	Project A	Project B
Cost of investment	$80,000	$ 80,000
Cash inflows:		
Year 1	40,000	10,000
Year 2	30,000	20,000
Year 3	20,000	40,000
Year 4	5,000	100,000

Required:

1. Compute the payback period on each project.
2. Compute the net present value on each project.
3. Identify the strengths and weaknesses of the treasurer's policy of using payback period to evaluate capital projects.
4. Identify the strengths and weaknesses of the controller's policy of using net present value to evaluate capital projects.

CASE FOR CRITICAL THINKING

The finance department has always evaluated projects using the payback period method or the accounting rate of return method. You have proposed a project that fails the test of both payback period and accounting rate of return, because the project has significant cash flows many years into the future. Explain to the finance department why the net present value or time adjusted rate of return methods are superior to payback period and accounting rate of return methods to evaluating an investment.

ANSWERS TO SELF-STUDY QUIZ 21–1

1. Payback period $= \dfrac{\text{Initial cost of investment}}{\text{Net annual cash inflow}}$

    $= 3.5$ years
2. Yes, the investment is acceptable because it has a payback of less than four years.

ANSWERS TO SELF-STUDY QUIZ 21–2

1. Accounting Rate of Return $= \dfrac{\text{Additional annual net income}}{\text{Average Investment}}$

    Accounting Rate of Return $\dfrac{\$15,000}{\$45,000} = 33.3\%$
2. Yes, the investment should be considered because it has an accounting rate of return that exceeds 25%.

ANSWERS TO SELF-STUDY QUIZ 21–3

Items	Year(s)	Dollar Cash Flow	Discount Rate 14%	Present Value
Annual cash flow	1–5	$20,000	3.433	$68,660
Salvage value	5	10,000	.519	5,190
Total present value				$73,850
Less: Cost of investment				70,000
Net Present Value				$ 3,850

Zwicker Company should accept the investment because it has a positive net present value of $3,850.

ANSWERS TO SELF-STUDY QUIZ 21–4

$$\frac{\text{Cost of investment}}{\text{annual cash flows}} \quad \frac{\$92,780}{\$20,000} = 4.639$$

Yes, this is an acceptable investment for Blair Company because the time adjusted rate of return exceeds the cost of capital.

PROJECT 3—BUDGETS AND STANDARD COSTS

Use of Cost Accounting in Planning and Control

You have been hired by South Company to be the cost accountant. Your supervisor has assigned you a variety of tasks involving many areas of cost accounting. Your supervisor has indicated that if you do these tasks well you will be in line for a promotion and a substantial pay raise.

Task 1

South Company has noticed wide cost fluctuations when comparing its electric bill to the total number of machine hours during the past six months. The data from the past six utility bills appear below:

Month	Number of Machine Hours	Total Electric Bill
June	100	$1,000
July	130	1,100
August	180	1,600
September	300	2,500
October	170	1,500
November	140	1,200

Instructions:

a. Using the scattergraph method, separate the utility cost into its variable and fixed cost portions. Put the cost formula in the format of $Y = a + b(x)$. How much would the utility bill be if 200 machine hours were used during the month?

b. Using the high-low method, separate the utility cost into its variable and fixed cost portions. Put the cost formula in the format of $Y = a + b(x)$. How much would the utility bill be if 200 machine hours were used during the month?

c. Using the least-squares method, separate the utility cost into its variable and fixed cost portions. Round the variable rate to the nearest 1,000th of a decimal point, and the fixed cost to the 100th of a decimal point. Put the cost formula in the format $Y = a + b(x)$. How much would the utility bill be if 200 machine hours were used during the month?

Task 2

Your supervisor asked you to prepare and analyze financial statements under direct costing and absorption costing. The production and sales data for South Company for the year ending December 31, 19X5, are given on the following page:

	Per Unit	%
Sales price	$50	100%
Variable costs:		
Direct Materials	9	
Direct Labor	14	
Variable Factory Overhead	5	
Variable Selling and		
Administrative Expense	7	
Total variable costs	35	70%
Contribution Margin	$15	30%

Fixed costs:	
Fixed Factory Overhead	$125,000
Fixed Selling and	
Administrative Expense	85,000
Total fixed costs	$210,000

Units produced: 25,000
Units Sold: 22,000

Instructions:

a. Calculate the unit product cost under the direct costing method.
b. Calculate the unit product cost under the absorption costing method.
c. Prepare an income statement under the direct costing method.
d. Prepare an income statement under the absorption costing method.
e. Reconcile the difference between the net income under direct costing and the net income under absorption costing.
f. Calculate the break-even point in units and sales dollars.
g. Prepare a break-even chart for South Company.
h. Calculate the dollar amount of sales necessary to earn a profit of $150,000.

Task 3

Your next assignment is to prepare a sales budget, production budget, and direct materials budget. Your supervisor also wants a schedule of cash collections and a schedule of cash payments for inventory. Use the below information:

	19X5 Quarter					19X6
	1	2	3	4	Year	1
Budgeted sales in units	3,500	5,000	9,000	4,500	22,000	5,000

1. Sales price per unit is $50.
2. Beginning balance of Accounts Receivable is $30,000.
3. All sales are on credit.
4. Collection of Accounts Receivable is 70% in the quarter of sale, 30% in the following quarter.
5. Desired ending inventory of finished goods is 20% of the following quarter's sales in units.
6. The beginning inventory of finished goods is 900 units.
7. Budgeted production needs for quarter 1 of 19X6 is 6,000.
8. Direct materials per unit is 4 pounds.
9. Desired ending inventory of direct materials is 25% of the next quarter's production needs.

10. The beginning inventory of direct materials is 5,500 pounds.
11. Beginning balance of Accounts Payable is $32,500.
12. Cost of direct materials to be purchased is $5 per pound.
13. Cash payments for purchases are 60% in the quarter of purchase and the remaining 40% in the following quarter.

Instructions:
Prepare the following budgets:

a. Sales budget and a schedule of budgeted cash collections.
b. Production budget.
c. Direct materials budget and a schedule of budgeted cash payments for materials.

Task 4

Your next assignment as cost accountant for South Company is to analyze and record direct material and direct labor variances. South Company uses a standard cost system. The standard costs for direct materials and direct labor appear below:

	Standard Cost Or Standard Rate	Standard Quantity Or Standard Hours	Standard Cost Per Unit
Direct Material	$ 5.00 ×	4 pounds =	$20.00
Direct Labor	12.00	2 hours	24.00

During the month of January, South Company produced 1,500 units of product using the following amounts of materials and labor:

6,200 pounds of material were purchased at $4.70 per pound. 6,100 pounds of material were used to produce 1,500 units of product. 3,120 hours were worked at an average wage rate of $12.60 per hour.

Instructions:

1. Calculate the direct materials cost and quantity variances.
2. Prepare the general jounal entry to record the purchase of direct materials and the material price variance. Date the journal entry as of January 10, 19X5.
3. Prepare the general journal entry to record the use of direct materials and the material quantity variance. Date the jounal entry as of January 31, 19X5.
4. Calculate the direct labor efficiency and rate variances.
5. Prepare the general journal entry to record the payment of the direct labor and the amount charged to production, and to record the labor efficiency and rate variances. Date the journal entry January 31, 19X5.

Task 5

Your next assignment is to calculate variable and fixed overhead variances. The standard costs for variable and fixed overhead appear on the following page:

	Standard Rate Per Hour	Standard Hours Per Unit	Standard Cost Per Unit
Variable Overhead	$5.00	2 hours	$10
Fixed Overhead	9.00	2 hours	18

Budgeted Fixed Overhead = $28,800

During the month of January, South Company recorded 3,120 direct labor hours to manufacture 1,500 units of product. The actual variable and fixed overhead incurred were as follows:

Actual Variable Overhead: $14,800
Actual Fixed Overhead   28,000

Instructions:

1. Calculate the variable overhead efficiency and spending variances.
2. Calculate the fixed overhead volume and budget variances.

Task 6

Your supervisor asks you to analyze several decisions that South Company management is reviewing. The first involves a decision as to whether a new machine should be purchased to replace an older machine.

DECISION 1—PURCHASING A NEW MACHINE TO REPLACE AN OLD MACHINE

	If Machine Is Not Bought	If Machine Is Bought
Annual Sales	2,000 units	2,000 units
Sales price per unit	$ 50.00	$ 50.00
Variable costs per unit to operate		
Direct Materials	$ 5.00	$ 4.00
Direct Labor	12.00	10.00
Variable Overhead	5.00	5.00
Fixed costs per year to operate	$50,000	$ 65,000*
Original cost of machine	$20,000	$100,000
Remaining book value of old machine	$10,000	
Expected life	4 years	4 years
Salvage value at end of expected life	0	0

*Includes depreciation on new machine of $15,000 ($60,000/4 = $15,000)

Requirement: Prepare an analysis showing the net advantage or disadvantage in purchasing the new machine.

DECISION 2

South Company is considering adding a new product line called product M. You have the following information to analyze this decision.

	Product M
Estimated sales	$200,000
Cost of Goods Sold	150,000
Gross Profit	$ 50,000
Operating Expenses	70,000
Net Income (Loss)	$ (20,000)

Additional Data:

Estimated sales and production in units	10,000
Sales Price per Unit	$20
Variable Manufacturing	
Cost per Unit	11
Variable Operating	
Expenses per Unit	4
*Allocated Fixed Manufacturing Costs	$40,000
*Allocated Fixed Operating Expenses	30,000

*60% of all allocated fixed costs will continue whether product M is produced or not.

Required: Prepare an analysis using the direct costing format of an income statement that shows the advantage or disadvantage of adding this product line.

DECISION 3—MAKING OR BUYING A PART

South Company is considering an offer from an outside supplier to provide 10,000 parts for $18 per part. The space that is now being used to manufacture the part could be rented for $60,000. Use the below data to analyze this situation.

	Per Unit	10,000 Units
Direct materials	$ 5	$ 50,000
Direct labor	4	40,000
Variable overhead	2	20,000
Supervisor's salary	3	30,000
Allocated general overhead	6	60,000
	$20	$200,000

Requirement: Prepare an analysis showing the per unit and total net advantage or disadvantage of continuing to make this part.

DECISION 4—SPECIAL PRICING A PRODUCT

South Company has been offered a special sales price for one of its products. The customer, located overseas, has offered to purchase 5,000 units of this product for $19 per unit. Use the information on the following page in your analysis.

South Company
Standard Cost Sheet

Direct Materials		$ 5.00
Direct Labor		9.00
Manufacturing Overhead		
Variable overhead	$2.00	
Fixed overhead	6.00	8.00
Total standard cost per unit		$22.00

South Company is operating above the break-even point and has excess capacity.

Requirement: Prepare an analysis showing the net advantage or disadvantage of selling at this special price.

Task 7

You have been asked to review South Company's capital budget. $100,000 is set aside for capital expenditures. There are three projects labeled A, B, and C that are being considered. Each project will cost $100,000. The following data relate to these three capital projects.

	Project A	Project B	Project C
Estimated life of project	5 years	5 years	5 years
Estimated Salvage Value	$20,000	$30,000	$40,000
Net Annual cash inflows	40,000	35,000	30,000
Additional annual net income	15,000	20,000	30,000

South Company's cost of capital is 20%.

Required:

1. Calculate the payback period for each project and select the project with the shortest payback.
2. Calculate the accounting rate of return for each project and select the project with the highest accounting rate of return.
3. Calculate the net present value for each project and select the project with the highest net present value.

Index